Iran

Paul Greenway
David St Vincent

Iran

2nd edition

Published by

Lonely Planet Publications
Head Office: PO Box 617, Hawthorn, Vic 3122, Australia
Branches: 150 Linden St, Oakland, CA 94607, USA
                10a Spring Place, London NW5 3BH, UK
                1 rue du Dahomey, 75011 Paris, France

Printed by
Craft Print Pte Ltd, Singapore

Photographs by

Glenn Beanland	Richard Everist	Gadi Farfour
Paul Greenway	Andrew Humphreys	Scott Kamana Stewart
Richard Plunkett	David St Vincent	Phil Weymouth
Robert Van Driesum		

Front cover: Xerxes' Gateway, Persepolis (Gadi Farfour)

First Published
August 1992

This Edition
May 1998

Although the authors and publisher have tried to make the information as
accurate as possible, they accept no responsibility for any loss, injury or
inconvenience sustained by any person using this book.

National Library of Australia Cataloguing in Publication Data

Greenway, Paul 1960-.
    Iran.
    2nd ed.
    Includes index.
    ISBN 0 86442 455 8.

    1. Iran – Guidebooks. I. Title

915.50454

text & maps © Lonely Planet 1998
photos © photographers as indicated 1998

Paul Greenway

Plucked from the blandness and security of the Australian Public Service, Paul has worked on many Lonely Planet guidebooks including *Indonesia*, *Madagascar*, *Mongolia*, and *Indian Himalaya*. During the rare times that Paul is not travelling, or writing, reading or dreaming about it, he relaxes to tuneless heavy metal music, follows useless Australian Rules football teams, and will go to any lengths to avoid settling down.

David St Vincent

The author of the first edition of this guidebook, David was born in the late '60s and brought up in the south of England. He took a year off after leaving school and travelled to Australia via the (then) USSR, Eastern Europe, the Middle East and Central Asia. He made four lengthy visits to Iran, during which he was brought before a revolutionary court on the imaginative charge of plotting to import Salman Rushdie's Satanic Verses, and deported in retaliation for the expulsion of some Iranians from the UK. David was also a contributor to Lonely Planet's guides to *Pakistan* and *West Asia on a shoestring*.

From Paul

There are numerous people to thank, and I apologise if I have left someone out. Thanks must go to the staff of the Iran Touring & Tourism Organisation in Tehrān, led by the able Farrokh Karami; and especially to Amir Asghari Fard, who helped me enormously (especially through the bureaucratic nightmare of getting a visa extension in Tehrān) and became a good friend in the process. I am very grateful to the staff at the Neda Rayaneh Institute in Tehrān for allowing me to regularly interrupt their workday and make contact with the outside world by email. Also, thanks to Farhad Sadeghi, from the Iran Cultural & Information Center in Canada, for his help and ideas.

In Iran, thanks to Ramin Asgarian for showing me around Mashhad; the walking encyclopaedia of Australian, English and American colloquialisms, Komeil Noofeli – you may meet him yourself in Shīrāz;

Colonel Mansour Rasty for giving me the visa extension in Shīrāz; Mr Ahadzadeh, and the Russian and Armenian bears who shared their room and whisky in Andīmeshk; Alī Amiri, in Bam, for some true Iranian hospitality; Ahmed Bahrami, who helped me get out of Chābahār, and proved to me that some of Tehrān is quite nice. Lastly, plaudits to the hundreds of Iranians who gave me directions and a smile.

I would like to thank everyone who has written to Lonely Planet with some ideas, comments and criticisms, especially those whose first language is not English, and who bothered to type the letter and reference the comments to a page number. Your names are listed on the next page.

Back home in Adelaide, South Australia, I would like to thank my mother, Audrey, for allowing me to put a makeshift office in her home, and for being a great Mum; to the rest of my family, Dad, Judy, Gran, Gill, Graham and the kids, for worrying about me; and to Richard and Janet Allen for being such great friends.

At Lonely Planet, thanks to Sam Carew for sending me to these weird and wonderful places, and apologies to all of the long-suffering editors, designers and cartographers who had to battle with my manuscript and maps.

From the Publisher

This book was edited in Lonely Planet's Melbourne office by Richard Plunkett, with help from Justin Flynn, Joyce Connolly and Michelle Glynn. Isabelle Young checked the health section. Glenn van der Knijff co-ordinated the mapping and layout of the book, with assistance from Anna Judd and Verity Campbell. Verity did the layout for the special sections. Margie Jung designed the cover and the back-cover map. Illustrations were done by Trudi Canavan and Tamsin Wilson, and Glenn Beanland took some nice photos for this second edition. A big thanks to the guys at Persian Bazaar in Hawthorn and Golriss Persian Rugs Gallery in Brunswick for their help with the Persian Carpets section. Yavar Dehghani handled the Fārsī script. Special thanks to Andrew Humphreys for writing the Persian architecture section, to Kamin Mohammadi for her short pieces on Lida Fariman and women travellers in Iran, and to Zoka Negar for her insights into Iranian cinema. Richard Plunkett would like to thank all the people who helped to steer him through Iran, especially Alī Fa'al of Mashhad, the staff of the Akhavan Hotel in Kermān and the friendly folks of Rāmsar.

Warning & Request

Things change – prices go up, schedules change, good places go bad and bad places go bankrupt – nothing stays the same. So, if you find things better or worse, recently opened or long since closed, please tell us and help make the next edition even more accurate and useful.

We value all the feedback we receive from travellers. Julie Young coordinates a small team who read and acknowledge every letter, postcard and email, and ensure that every morsel of information finds its way to the appropriate authors, editors and publishers.

Everyone who writes to us will find their name in the next edition of the appropriate guide and will also receive a free subscription to our quarterly newsletter, *Planet Talk*. The very best contributions will be rewarded with a free Lonely Planet guide.

Excerpts from your correspondence may appear in new editions of this guide; in our newsletter, *Planet Talk*; or in the Postcards section of our Web site – so please let us know if you don't want your letter published or your name acknowledged.

Thanks

Thanks to the many travellers who wrote with comments about our last edition, and with tips and comments about Iran (apologies if we've misspelt your name). If you wish to contact us by email with responses to this edition, you can reach us on talk2us@lonelyplanet.com.au.

Ali Akbary, Josep Albeniz-Fornells, Ali Amiri, Ton Baars, Warwick Ball, Laura Bertolotto, Jan Beukema, Roland Beutler, Jonathan Bickley, Zabukovac Blaz, Jean-Jacques Braun, Saskia Brinks, David Brown, Bryan Buffham, A Capelle, Mogens Christoffersen, Raphäe¹ Clerici, Brian Daken, Pat Daniel, Leendert Develing, Matt Dickie, Mahyar Ebrahimi, Lindsay Eccles, Bernard Feilden, Thomas W Fina, Hanne Finholt, Dr Pierre Flener, Neil Flintham, James Gallantry, Ray George, Massimo Giannini, Richard Gilpin, Maria Gonzalez, Matthias Gutzeit, Maria Hager, Slim Hamdani, Nigel Harris, Mark Horobin, Doms Hussmann, Simon James, Evert Jan-Groeskamp, David Kucera, Dr Rolf Lacher, Chris Lane, Azar Marashian, Yann Martel, Andrew Matheson, Sarah McAlpine, E Parkse, Sigrid Pearson, H&R Pfeiffer, Gregor Preac, Margaret Rey, Espen Rikter-Svendsen, Setudah-Nejad Shahab, Philip Shulman, Dafydd Stephens, Romul Torrents, John VanderVeen, Jerry Vinal, Peter Ward, Alison Wearing, James Woods and Negar Zoka.

Contents

Map Legend

ROUTES

├─┼─┼─┼─┼─◉─┼─┼─┤ .... Train Route, with Station

---------------------- Ferry

---------------------- Walking Track

Regional Maps

━━━━━━━━━ .... Freeway

━━━━━━━━━ .... Highway

━━━━━━━━━ .... Primary Road

═══════════ .... Unsealed Road

━━━━━━━━━ .... Minor Road

City Maps

━━━━━━━━━ .... Highway

----------- .... Unsealed Highway

━━━━━━━━━ .... Primary Road

----------- .... Unsealed Road

━━━━━━━━━ .... Street

═══════════ .... Unsealed Street

━━━━━━━━━ .... Lane

AREA FEATURES

.... City Park, National Park

.... Building

.... Pedestrian Mall, Plaza

.... Market

+ + + + + ... Cemetery

.... Built-Up Area

....

BOUNDARIES

━━━━━━━━━ .... International Boundary

━━━━ ━━━ .... Provincial Boundary

─ ─ ─ ─ ─ .... Disputed Boundary

HYDROGRAPHIC FEATURES

.... River, Creek

.... Intermittent River or Creek

>>> → ← .... Rapids, Waterfalls

.... Lake, Intermittent Lake

SYMBOLS

✪ **CAPITAL**	......National Capital	✈ .... Airport	▲ .... Mountain
◉ **Capital**	......Regional Capital	⸫ ..Archaeological Site	🏛 .... Museum
● **City**	.... City	🏦 .... Bank	)(............ Pass
● **Town**	.... Town	🏖 .... Beach	⛽ .... Petrol Station
● Village	.... Village	⊞ 🏧 ...Cathedral, Church	★ .... Police Station
		⌒ .... Cave	✉ .... Post Office
▪	.... Place to Stay	◐ .... Embassy	⚐ .... Ski Resort
▼	.... Place to Eat	🏰 .... Fort	🏛 .... Stately Home
☕	.... Café	✿ .... Garden	◉─╫─ .... Telecabin
		⊕ .... Hospital	☎ .... Telephone
		❶ .... Information	🏛 .... Temple
		☪ ...Islamic Monument	◘ .... Tomb
		⚑ .... Monument	🚶 .... Trail Head
		☾ .... Mosque	● .... Transport

Note: not all symbols displayed above appear in this book

Map Index

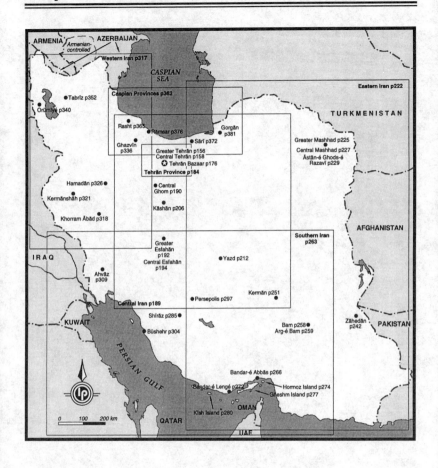

Introduction

Over the centuries, Persia has attracted some of the region's more gruesome invaders, and, later, some of the world's more eccentric explorers. Until the late 1970s, travellers happily rambled along the well-trodden trail between Europe and India; and all returned with stories of overwhelming hospitality from Iranians, and of a magnificent cultural legacy entirely unspoilt by tourism. But the Islamic Revolution in 1979, and the hideous Iran-Iraq War soon after, dissuaded all but the most adventurous to visit.

Only in the past few years has Iran started to recover from the excesses of the Revolution, and the aftermath of the War. The Iran government is now pensively starting to promote tourism (though conscious of the effect that hordes of rich non-Muslims may have on its religious and cultural values). Western travel agencies have started to send tour groups back to Iran, and the overland trail across Iran has truly reopened – especially as Afghanistan is sadly off limits to all but the truly fearless.

Iran has always had a vast amount to offer the traveller. For culture seekers, there are magnificent ruins of ancient cities, such as Persepolis, and others where you can roam around, often alone; glorious mosques and mausoleums, usually set in majestic gardens; and museums covering every conceivable matter of interest. The more adventurous can enjoy trekking among the surprisingly extensive mountain ranges, and budget-priced skiing with the *nouveaux riches* of Iran. Souvenir hunters will revel in limitless displays of ceramics, miniature paintings and, of course, the renowned Persian carpets.

Iran is easy to explore: it boasts an expansive network of buses, trains and planes, and there is a good range of accommodation in most places visitors will want to go. For some, the major attraction is that travel is cheap, and Iran represents extremely good value for your hard-earned dollar. However, if you are looking for buckets of fun and barrels of beer, as well as nightclubs and beach resorts, you may want to go elsewhere.

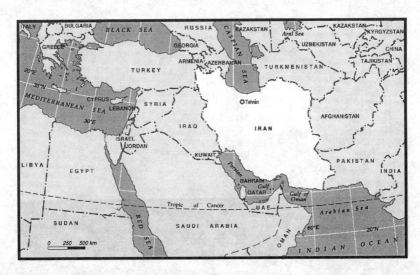

Forget the images of fervent anti-western marches and secret police: Iran is a remarkably safe country to travel around, and Iranians, including the police and military, are very friendly. Women should hold no fears: if you dress and act according to the admittedly strict local rules, you will be well treated (often better than foreign males), and you will suffer little, if any, of the hassles which women often endure in Pakistan and Turkey.

Iran will appeal to any genuine traveller – whether rich or poor, travelling independently or on an organised tour – who is prepared to respect the local people and their traditions, to be open-minded, and to adapt to unfamiliar circumstances. If you are one of these, post-revolutionary Iran is one of the most exciting, fascinating, welcoming, rewarding and, frankly, inexpensive countries yet to be 'discovered' by tourists. And *now* is the time to go.

Facts about Iran

HISTORY
Iranian history is a fascinating catalogue of disasters and short-lived triumphs, and of occasionally brilliant rulers succeeded by incompetents who failed to secure their inheritance.

Ancient History
The date of arrival of the first inhabitants on the Iranian plateau is not known, and still debated among historians. Continuing excavations, however, indicate that during the Neolithic times hunters lived in caves in the Zāgros and Alborz mountains, and in the south-east, but numbers were low until the improvement of agricultural methods.

The first distinct people to emerge on the plateau were probably the Elamites, who established a city at Shūsh in the far south-west. The Aryans came to the region in the second millennium BC, bringing with them some agricultural and domestic skills. From the mixture and migration of Elamites and Aryans, three main tribes were created: the Medes, who lived in the west (particularly around Hamadān); the Parthians, based in the far east; and the Persians, who lived in the south. Other tribes which invaded, and settled in, parts of the plateau included the Kasits, Assyrians, Urartians and Scythians, but none had much success or influence.

The Achaemenians (559-330 BC)
It is not until the middle of the 6th century, when the Achaemenian king, Cyrus II (also known as Cyrus the Great), ruled the region that Persian history can be properly documented. Cyrus II, who was the son of the Achaemenian king, Cambyses I, and the great-grandson of the great Median king, Cyaxerxes, was unusually benevolent compared to his successors and peers in the region. The Achaemenian dynasty is recognised as the founders of the Persian Empire, leading to the eventual creation of Iran.

Cyrus II ruled parts of what is now Turkey, Iraq, Greece, Syria and Israel, while Cyrus' son, Cambyses II, headed west to take most of Egypt. Subsequent Achaemenian rulers, Darius I (also known as Darius the Great) and Xerxes, expanded the empire all the way to India in the east, and the Aegean Sea in the west. The magnificent complex of Takht-é Jamshīd (better known to visitors as Persepolis) became the hub of the empire, while the Elamite city of Shūsh became the winter capital.

Darius' armies were defeated by Alexander the Great's army at Marathon, and the subsequent defeat of Darius' son, Xerxes, at Salamis, marked the end of the Achaemenian Empire.

Alexander the Great & the Seleucids (331-190 BC)
In the 4th century BC Alexander the Great invaded Persia, as the region had become known, after conquering most of Greece, Egypt, Turkey and Iraq. Despite three conciliatory offers from Darius I for a negotiated peace, Alexander entered Shūsh. From there, he took some time to cross the mountains to the east, but eventually entered Persepolis where he lived for several months. The great city was later burned down – historians are divided about whether it was accidental or in retaliation for the destruction of Athens by Xerxes.

Alexander spread his empire across to Afghanistan, Pakistan and India. After Alexander's death in 323 BC, the empire was divided into three squabbling dynasties, with Persia controlled by the Macedonian Seleucids. But the Seleucids had real problems controlling the numerous feisty ethnic minorities, in particular the nomadic Parthians.

The Parthians (190 BC-224 AD)
The Parthians had settled in eastern Persia, mainly along the Caspian coast, many

centuries before. Under the great king, Mithridates, the Parthians started to unite, and gradually controlled most of Persia. Their greatest achievement was probably the victory in 53 BC over the invading Romans, who were flushed by their success over the Britons a few years before. Yet the Parthians were surprisingly disinterested in expanding their empire beyond Persia. They were not nearly as despotic as later dynasties. Some of the greatest examples of early Persian architecture blossomed under the Parthians.

The Sassanians (224-637)
From the central regions of Persia not under direct control of the Parthians, came Ardeshir I, leader of the Sassanians, who defeated the Parthians in 224 AD. The dynasty was later taken over by Ardeshir's son, Shāpūr I, who also captured parts of the Roman empire. The Sassanians were unique in the region, and in Persian history, because they followed Zoroastrianism, though the Sassanian rulers were surprisingly indifferent about converting religious minorities. Some of the fire-temples built during this period still remain, as do the ruins of Firūz Ābād, Tāgh-é Bostān, and Neishābūr.

The Sassanians also developed small industries, promoted urban development in the villages, and encouraged regional trade through shipping across the Persian Gulf. Some of the great Sassanian kings were Firūz; the visionary and benevolent Khusro I; and Khusro II, who recaptured parts of Egypt and Turkey. However, fighting among factions within the empire, and wars against the Byzantine Empire, weakened the Sassanians, who eventually fell easily to the conquering Arabs.

The Arabs (637-1050)
A very important part of Persian history started when the Islamic Arabs conquered the Sassanians at Ghadisirya in 637 AD. The people of Persia generally found plenty to like about Islamic culture and religion, and happily forsook Zoroaster for the teachings of Mohammed with little need for force from the Arab conquerors – except for Yazd and

Kermān (both of which continued with Zoroastrianism for a few centuries more), and pockets of resistance from ethnic minorities in the mountains near the Caspian Sea.

During this period, the Arabic language and script were introduced, and a less despotic form of government was implemented. However, some Persian tribes – namely the Ziyarids and Buyids in the 9th century, and the Ghaznavids in the 11th century – refused to adopt the Arabic language, and fought for the re-emergence of the Persian language and culture. But it was the Turks to the west who brought about the downfall of the Arabs.

The Seljuq Dynasty (1051-1220)
The Turkish Seljuq dynasty controlled most of Persia following the capture in 1051 of Esfahān, which became the capital of the Seljuq dynasty under the leadership of Malik Shāh. Despite numerous rebellions throughout Persia, the Seljuqs managed to maintain control with a large, and well-paid, army.

The Seljuq dynasty heralded a new era of Persian art, literature and science, marked by people such as the mathematician and poet Omar Khayyām. The Seljuq period declined after the death of Malik Shāh, and in 1220, the empire suddenly collapsed when Chinggis Khaan (Genghis Khan) swept in and commenced a cold-blooded devastation.

The Mongols (1220-1380)
The rampaging Mongols came thundering across the Iranian plateau on their horses in the early 13th century. Initially under the leadership of Chinggis Khaan, and then his grandson, Hulagu Khaan, the Mongol rulers managed to control all of Persia, as well as an empire stretching from Beijing (China) to Istanbul (Turkey), despite tiny pockets of resistance in southern and northern Persia. Their Persian capital was at Tabrīz (which, they later found out, was too close to the Turks).

Tragically, the Mongols destroyed many of the Persian cities they conquered, thereby obliterating much of documented Persian history – and simply massacred anyone who had a problem with this. The Mongol empire came to an end when it simply ran out of effective rulers after the death of Sultan Abu Said in 1335.

The Timurid Dynasty (1380-1502)

The fragmented remnants of the Mongol empire were easy prey for the invading forces under the control of Timur (also known as Tamerlane). Timur came from a Turkified Mongol clan in what is now Uzbekistan. He also managed to defeat the Ottoman Turks in 1402. During his short reign, Timur managed to stop the constant warring, promoted cultural practices, and moved the capital from Tabrīz to Ghazvīn. He put down rebellions with brutal vigour. On his death in 1405, his empire came under the control of his squabbling and, at times, imbecilic, sons.

Western Persia was invaded by the Turkmen tribe in the mid-15th century. The Timurid dynasty eventually came to an end when the rest of Persia was taken by the Ottoman Turks, or came under the increasingly powerful and hostile influence of European colonialists such as Portugal, which had a foothold in the Persian Gulf.

The Safavid Dynasty (1502-1722)

Under the brilliant Shāh Abbās I, the Turkmen and Turks, as well as a few other invading armies, were eventually defeated, creating what is called the Third Great Empire in Persian history (after the Achaemenians and Sassanians). Abbās and his successors enshrined Shi'ism into the Persian religion and culture, and rebuilt Esfahān to a majesty that was the envy of regional empires, and of interest to visiting Europeans. Soon, English companies were given business concessions, but the Portuguese on Hormoz Island, in the Persian Gulf, were less welcome.

The death of Abbās in 1629, and the activities of his incompetent son, started the end of this great period in modern Persian history. Most of the subsequent rulers suffered – and often died – from drinking problems.

The Afghans (1722-1736)

The decline of the Safavid dynasty was hastened by an invasion of eastern Persia by the Ghilzais from Afghanistan in 1722. The Afghans placed the Persian capital, Esfahān, under siege, and eventually took control of the city, slaughtering thousands. The first ruler of the Ghilzais, Mahmud, eventually went absolutely bonkers, and was later murdered by a member of his army.

During this short period, pushes by the Russians, under Peter the Great, didn't go far, but the Turks again invaded western and northern Persia.

Nāder Shāh (1736-1747) & Karīm Khān Zand (1747-1779)

In 1736, Nāder Ghuli Beg, who later crowned himself Nāder Shāh, overthrew the Safavids (who had briefly replaced the Afghans again from 1729), and proceeded to scatter the Afghans, Russians and Turks to all directions. For an encore he rushed off to do a little conquering himself, returning from India loaded with goodies, but virtually exhausted the country with his warring. It was a relief to all, both inside and outside of Persia, when he was finally assassinated in 1747.

After Nāder Shāh's murder, Karīm Khān Zand eventually won power. A Lor, from what is now Lorestān, Karīm Khān Zand was almost unique in that he was benevolent, and wasn't too interested in war. He moved the Persian capital to Shīrāz, where he is still revered for building this great city. Sadly, nice guys don't last forever.

The Ghajars (1779-1921)

The bitter and twisted eunuch Agha Muhammed Khān, who had suffered from the excesses of Nāder Shāh, united the Turkish Ghajars. He created a capital in Tehrān, and eventually gained control of Persia from the ineffectual successors to Karīm Khān Zand in 1795. But Agha Muhammed Khān only ruled for two years before he was murdered. His successors were not memorable, and two even picked fights with Russia, which declined to be baited.

Within a few decades, however, the Russians, as well as the British, became more interested in Iran, and the money that could be made from growing tobacco, and, later, from drilling for oil. The 19th century was relatively peaceful after the British brokered a peace deal between Iran, Russia and Turkey.

One of the last Ghajar kings, Muzaffar al-Din (who reigned from 1896 until 1907), actually introduced the idea of elections, and a Legislative Assembly (which is still called the Majlis). But this didn't eventuate after al-Din died; instead, martial law and dictatorship was instigated by the ruthless Shāh Mohammed Alī in 1908. Shāh Ahmad later steered a neutral Iran through WWI, but Turkish alignment with Germany, and potential threats to British oil interests, resulted in British military occupation of parts of Iran during WWI, and for a few years after.

The Pahlavī Dynasty (1921-1979)

After the war, Britain's wish to remain in Iran, and to control the ruling Shāhs, was thwarted by a coup d'état in 1921. The charismatic and influential Persian, Rezā Khān, became prime minister in 1923, and the Ghajar empire was formally ended by the Majlis in December 1925.

During the first few years, Rezā Khān had to extinguish several rebellious groups, but agreed to respect the authority of the Majlis, though Rezā maintained almost complete control of Iran. He had the huge task of dragging the country into the 20th century: literacy was very poor; the transport infrastructure was rudimentary at best; the health system was virtually nonexistent; and industry and agriculture were stagnant. One of his more controversial decrees was to lift, literally, the Islamic veil worn by Iranian women; and to generally raise the status of women.

Iran (the new name was officially adopted in 1934) was again neutral during WWII, but Britain and Russia established spheres of influence over vast areas of Iran to ensure that Germany had no control of the country, or a corridor through Iran. In 1941, Rezā was forced into exile in South Africa because the Russians and British felt he was too friendly with the Axis powers. His 22-year-old son, Mohammed Rezā, succeeded him. After the war, the Russian forces were persuaded to depart (with difficulty and American connivance), and the young Shāh regained absolute power. Iran was now firmly aligned with the west.

The Shāh's government was repressive, but Iran again tried to rapidly modernise: illiteracy was reduced, women continued to be emancipated, land holdings were redistributed, health services improved and a major programme of industrialisation embarked upon, but the country experienced the inevitable conflicts resulting from a rapid 'westernisation' of a conservative, and mainly rural, Muslim population.

The last Shāh, Mohammed Rezā Pahlavī, fled Iran in 1979 and died in exile a year later.

PAUL GREENWAY

SCOTT KAMANA STEWART

DAVID ST VINCENT

PHIL WEYMOUTH

PHIL WEYMOUTH

DAVID ST VINCENT

FACES OF IRAN
Top: A Bandarī woman wears the *borqa* mask (left); a mullah or Muslim cleric of Esfahān.
Middle: Muslim girl (left); Kurdish family (right).
Bottom: Boys from the Caspian littoral (left); boys from the central plateau (right).

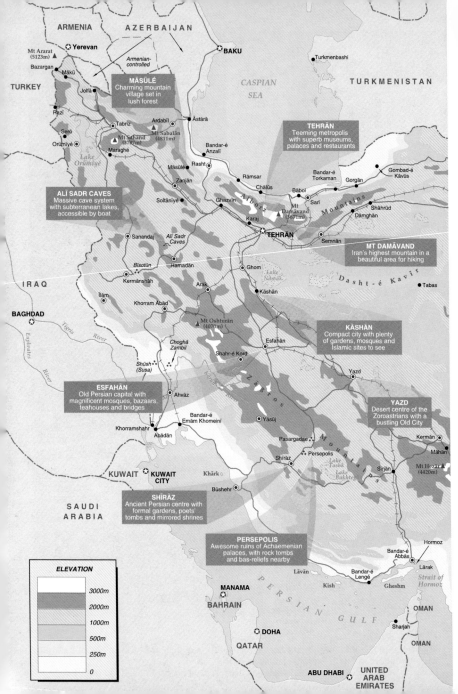

ARMENIA

AZERBAIJAN

BAKU

TURKMENISTAN

Turkmenbashi

CASPIAN
SEA

Mt Ararat
(5123m)
Yerevan

Bazargan

Mākū

Jolfā

TURKEY

Rezi

Serō

Orūmīyé

Lake
Orūmīyé

Tabriz

Maraghé

Mt Sahand
(3707m)

Ardabīl

Mt Sabalān
(4811m)

Āstārā

Bandar-é
Anzalī

Rasht

Āstārā

MĀSÜLÉ
Charming mountain
village set in
lush forest

Armenian-
controlled

TEHRĀN
Teeming metropolis
with superb museums,
palaces and restaurants

Rāmsar

Chālūs

Bandar-é
Torkaman

Gorgān

Gombad-é
Kāvūs

Māsülé

Zanjān

Soltānīyé

Ghazvin

Bābol

Sārī

Mt
Damāvand
(5671m)

Shāhrūd

Dāmghān

Albors

Mountains

ALĪ SADR CAVES
Massive cave system
with subterranean lakes,
accessible by boat

Sanandaj

Alī Sadr
Caves

Hamadān

Karaj

TEHRĀN

Semnān

MT DAMĀVAND
Iran's highest mountain in a
beautiful area for hiking

Dasht-é Kavīr

Bīsotūn

Ghom

Lake
Namak

Tabas

IRAQ

Kermānshāh

Arak

Kāshān

BAGHDAD

Īlām

Khorram Ābād

Euphrates

Tigris
River

Mt Oshturān
(4070m)

Choghā
Zambīl

Shahr-é Kord

Esfahān

KĀSHĀN
Compact city with plenty
of gardens, mosques and
Islamic sites to see

Yazd

Shūsh
(Susa)

ESFAHĀN
Old Persian capital with
magnificent mosques, bazaars,
teahouses and bridges

Ahvāz

Zagros

Kermān

YAZD
Desert centre of the
Zoroastrians with a
bustling Old City

Mountains

Bandar-é
Emām Khomeinī

Khorramshahr

Abādān

Yāsūj

Pasargadae

Persepolis

Shīrāz

Mt Hezār
(4420m)

Māhān

Lake
Tashk

Lake
Bakhteg

Sirjān

KUWAIT

KUWAIT
CITY

Khārk

Būshehr

SHĪRĀZ
Ancient Persian centre with
formal gardens, poets'
tombs and mirrored shrines

SAUDI

ARABIA

PERSEPOLIS
Awesome ruins of Achaemenian
palaces, with rock tombs
and bas-reliefs nearby

Lāvān

Kish

Bandar-é
Lengé

Gheshm

Hormoz

Bandar-é
Abbās

Lārak

Strait
of
Hormoz

OMAN

MANAMA

BAHRAIN

PERSIAN GULF

Sharjah

OMAN

DOHA

QATAR

ABU DHABI

UNITED
ARAB
EMIRATES

ELEVATION

3000m

2000m

1000m

500m

250m

0

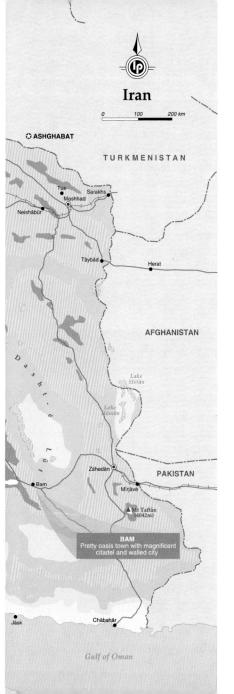

Iran

0   100   200 km

⬡ ASHGHABAT

TURKMENISTAN

Tus
Sarakhs
Mashhad
Neishābūr

Tāybād   Herat

AFGHANISTAN

Lake
Sīstān

Lake
Hāmūn

Zāhedān   PAKISTAN
Mirjāve

▲ Mt Taftān
(4042m)

● Bam

BAM
Pretty oasis town with magnificent
citadel and walled city

● Jāsk   Chābahār

Gulf of Oman

DAVID ST VINCENT

PHIL WEYMOUTH

DAVID ST VINCENT

Top: Shepherd and flock, Ghalé-yé Sāng.
Middle: Coppersmiths at work.
Bottom: Entrance to a medieval bazaar.

SCOTT KAMANA STEWART

SCOTT KAMANA STEWART

RICHARD PLUNKETT

STREET LIFE
Top: Pictures of leading religious and political figures on sale in Ghom.
Bottom Left: Grocery store open for business in Esfahān.
Bottom Right: Carrying water the old way into the upper citadel of the Arg-é Bam.

The 1974 oil price revolution turned out to be the Shāh's undoing. He allowed US arms merchants to persuade him to squander Iran's vast new wealth on huge arsenals of useless weapons. Fortunes were wasted on inappropriate development schemes. In the end, the flood of petro-dollars ended up lining the pockets of a select few while galloping inflation made the vast majority of the country worse off than before.

The Islamic Revolution

Since the beginning of the Pahlavī dynasty there had been smouldering resistance that occasionally flared into violence. Students wanted faster reform, devout Muslims wanted reforms rolled back, and everyone attacked the Pahlavīs' conspicuous consumption. As the economy went from bad to worse under the Shāh's post oil-boom mismanagement, the growing opposition made its presence felt with sabotage and massive street demonstrations. The Shāh responded with all the force available to the absolute ruler of an oil-rich country backed by the major western powers, and his security force, Savak, earned a horrific reputation.

In the late 1970s the Shāh's attempts to save his regime became increasingly desperate and brutal, and US support began to falter. In November 1978, he imposed martial law and hundreds of demonstrators were killed in street battles in Tehrān. He finally fled the country on 16 January 1979 (now a national holiday). In exile he was harried from country to country, and eventually died in Egypt in 1980.

His Holiness Grand Āyatollāh Hajjī Seyed Rūhollāh Mūsavī Khomeinī, the leading Shi'ite cleric, had been acknowledged as the leader of the Shāh's opponents – a group which covered every political shade from fundamentalist Muslims to Soviet-backed leftists. Many saw him as a figurehead, who, once the Shāh was ousted, would retire to a position akin to that of a constitutional monarch. They were very wrong. A charismatic figure commanding absolute loyalty in his followers, he is very little understood in the western world.

The Great Āyatollāh Khomeinī

Born in the small village of Khomein in central Iran, Seyed Rūhollāh Mūsavī Khomeinī followed in the family tradition by studying theology, philosophy and law in the holy city of Ghom. In the 1920s he earned the title of *āyatollāh* (the highest rank of Shi'ite cleric) and settled down to teach and write. He first came to public attention in 1962 when he opposed the Shāh's plans to reduce the clergy's property rights and emancipate' women.

In 1964 he was exiled to Turkey, then pushed on to Iraq where he remained until 1978 when he was shunted on to France. Here he found the eyes of the international press turned on him, and it is ironic that his cause was boosted by western media organisations, the BBC in particular, at a time when he was little known even in his home country. After the Shāh fled in 1979, Āyatollāh Khomeinī returned to a tumultuous welcome, and took control of the country. ■

Āyatollāh Khomeinī returned to Iran in triumph on 1 February 1979, greeted by adoring millions. His fiery brand of nationalism and Islamic fundamentalism had been at the forefront of the revolt, but few realised how much deep-rooted support he had and

The Confusion That is Iranian Politics

Politics is one of the more complex facets of the Islamic Republic, and figuring out exactly who is in charge of what isn't easy. One western diplomat described Iranian politics as being made up of a number of overlapping circles of power – whoever has their feet in the most circles concerned with a particular issue carries the day. Whether that's the Supreme Leader, the President, the ex-president or the *Majlis* (parliament) depends on the issue.

In a nutshell, these are the main institutions and figures in Tehrān's political circles. At the top is the Supreme Leader, Āyatollāh Alī Khameneī, the paramount political and religious authority. A former president, he was appointed after Emām Khomeinī died in 1989. The Supreme Leader is chosen by the Assembly of Experts for life, and has the final say in the country's policies. Having the knowledge to make decisions based on Islamic canon is a prime qualification.

President Mohammed Khatamī is responsible for the day-to-day running of the country. A president can only serve two four-year terms. Only four candidates were allowed to stand in the last election. The President appoints ministers, who must be individually approved by the Majlis.

The Majlis is not just a rubber-stamping body. Indeed it is one of the few parliaments in the region with real influence. The leading figure is the conservative Speaker, Alī Akbar Nateq Nouri. Besides his faction, the 270-member Majlis has groupings of left-wingers and pro-business types, plus a few token Christians, Jews and Zoroastrians. Tehrān province elects the most members to the Majlis, with 37 representatives, while Īlām sends only two.

Bills passed by the Majlis go to the 12-member Council of Guardians, a house of review similar to a Senate, and can halt a bill or send it back to the Majlis for amendment.

The President from 1989 to 1997, Hojjat-ol-Eslām Hashemi Rafsanjānī, is still on the scene. He is now head of the Expediency Council, once a largely honorary body which he has revamped. Essentially this body has the power to overturn the decisions of the Council of Guardians and approve bills passed by the Majlis. The Expediency Council has 25 members, mostly elder statesmen.

Richard Plunkett

how totally he reflected the beliefs, dreams and needs of millions of his people. Once in control, the Āyatollāh, soon to be known officially as Emām (Leader), proved the adage that 'after the revolution comes the revolution'. His intention was to set up a clergy-dominated Islamic Republic, and he achieved this with brutal efficiency.

Much of the credit for undermining the Shāh's regime lay with groups such as the People's Fedā'īyin and the Islamic People's Mojāhedīn, as well as the communists, but once the Shāh was gone they were swept aside. People disappeared from the streets, executions took place after brief and meaningless trials and minor officials took the law totally into their own hands. It looked as if the country might topple into civil war.

Almost immediately, the Islamic Republic found itself in a struggle against the rest of the world. As the sole custodian of 'true Islam', Iran has followed policies that are confrontationist and unashamedly designed to promote other Islamic revolutions.

The main opponent is the 'Great Satan' – the USA – as well as Israel. It is important to see this struggle from the Iranian point of view. Aside from its infidel (ie non-Muslim) culture, the US had supported the hated Pahlavīs, and Iraq during the Iran-Iraq War. To top it off, the Americans even shot down an unarmed Iran Air plane over the Persian Gulf in 1988. The Israelis are blamed for taking land from the Palestinians, and starting wars against Muslim states in the Middle East – all with the contrivance of the US.

Iran-Iraq War (1980-1988)

All this pales into insignificance, however, to the ghastly eight-year-long Iran-Iraq War that killed hundreds of thousands on both sides. In 1980, Iraq's president Saddam Hussein made an opportunistic land grab in Khūzestān province, taking advantage of Iran's domestic chaos, on the doubtful pretext that the oil-rich province was historically a part of Iraq. It was a disastrous miscalculation.

Saddam presented the shaky Iranian Revolution with an obvious and accessible enemy to rally against, and an opportunity to spread the Revolution by force of arms. Although the much smaller Iraq was better equipped, Iran drew on a larger population and a fanaticism fanned by the mullahs. For the first time since WWI the world witnessed the hideous reality of trench warfare and poison gas. (The Iranian government continues to claim that the poisonous gas was sold to Iraq by German companies.) The western powers and the USSR supported Iraq in the war, in the belief that Iraq was the 'lesser of two evils', and weapons were only sold to Iran at vastly inflated black-market prices. A cease-fire was finally negotiated in mid-1988, with neither side having achieved its objectives. This war is referred to by Iranians as the 'imposed war with Iraq'.

Iran Today

On 4 June 1989 Āyatollāh Khomeinī died, leaving an uncertain legacy to the country he had dominated for a decade. At his funeral an estimated crowd of 10 million, unprecedented in world history, came to pay their last respects, and the throng was so great that the car carrying the corpse had to be abandoned for a helicopter. After his death, the Muslim clergy and the Revolutionary Guards established their own, sometimes competing, bureaucracies and spheres of influence, and the parliament was also factionalised.

Two months later Hojjat-ol-Eslām Rafsanjānī was elected president, a post which had previously been largely ceremonial, and Khomeinī's position as Supreme Leader was taken by the former president, Āyatollāh Alī Khameneī. President Hashemi Rafsanjānī was re-elected in 1993, and he subsequently reconfirmed the *fatwa* (death sentence) issued against British author Salman Rushdie for blasphemy in his novel *The Satanic Verses*.

One major, recent development was the implementation of a trade embargo against Iran (see the Economy section later in this chapter) by the US, which alleges that Iran sponsors terrorist groups throughout the region, and destabilises the peace process in the Middle East. (At times, Iran has also been blamed for the unsolved bombing of US Marines in Saudi Arabia, and the downing of a TWA airliner, both in the early 1990s.) Relations between Iran and the US are still very poor, even if Iranian youth still clamber for news about US basketball and music. Since the election of a new Iranian president, however, the situation has shown signs of improvement.

In 1997, relations between Iran and Germany (Iran's major trading partner) also hit rock bottom following the ruling by a German court that the Iranian government was involved in the assassination of Iranian Kurdish dissidents in Germany several years ago. In protest, Germany (and most European countries, in support) withdrew their ambassadors. At the time of research, tensions between Iran and Germany remained high (though Germans can still safely travel to Iran).

In mid-1997, four presidential candidates were selected by the Council of the Guardians (see the Government & Politics section

Āyatollāh Alī Khameneī's black turban signifies that he is descended from the Prophet.

President Khatamī

Hojjat-ol-Eslām Seyed Mohammed Khatamī was born in 1943, the son of an āyatollāh from Yazd. Khatamī studied theology in Ghom, and then took degrees in philosophy at Esfahān and Tehrān. In 1978, he was sent to Hamburg to establish an Islamic Centre, but returned after the Islamic Revolution in 1979 to serve in the Majlis (parliament).

Khatamī was appointed Minister of Culture & Islamic Guidance from 1982 but was forced to resign in 1992 because of his perceived acceptance of the 'decadence' of the western world, including support for the controversial director, Mohsen Makhmalbaf (see the boxed text on him later in this chapter). Later, Khatamī became a presidential adviser, then head of the National Library in Tehrān, and was surprisingly elected President by a landslide in 1997. He has published three books, and speaks German, English and Arabic. ∎

later in this chapter) from 238 hopefuls. One of these, parliamentary speaker Alī Akbar Nateq Nouri, was backed by the Iranian parliament (Majlis). Much to the surprise of international monitors, the moderate, and potentially more visionary, Hojjat-ol-Eslām Seyed Mohammed Khatamī easily beat Nateq Nouri. To the credit of Nateq Nouri and the Majlis, there was very little (public) display of rejection of the wishes of the people, and Khatamī was approved as President. It seems that a number of women voters, as well as young people who remember little, if anything, about the coming of the Islamic Revolution and the excesses of the Pahlavī dynasty, are hoping Khatamī will change many of the more stern impositions of the Islamic Republic of Iran. Only time will tell, of course.

GEOGRAPHY

The Islamic Republic of Iran (Jomhūrī-yé Eslāmī-yé Īrān) is bordered to the north by the states of Armenia, Azerbaijan and Turkmenistan (all formerly of the USSR) and the Caspian Sea; to the east by Afghanistan and Pakistan; to the south by the Gulf of Oman and the Persian Gulf; and to the west by Iraq and Turkey. With an area of 1,648,000 sq km, Iran is more than three times larger than France; nearly one-fifth the size of the entire USA; and nearly as big as Queensland, Australia. About 14% of Iran is arable land; 8% is forest; 55% is natural (ie non-arable) pastures; and the remaining 23% is desert.

About half of the country is covered by mountains (see under Geology later). The two great Iranian deserts, the Dasht-é Kavīr (more than 200,000 sq km in size) and the Dasht-é Lūt (more than 166,000 sq km), occupy most of the north-east and east of the central plain. The central Iranian plateau is mostly desert of either sand or compacted silt and rock, and – except at its fringes where the tableland merges into the Zāgros and the Alborz mountains – most mountains in central Iran are unconnected and low. The settled areas are almost entirely confined to the foothills of mountains, though oasis towns, such as Kermān, are growing in size.

Most rivers in Iran drain into the Persian Gulf, the Caspian Sea, or one of a number of salty and marshy lakes such as the Orūmīyé and Namak lakes. The longest and sole navigable river is the Kārūn (890km long) in the south-west. The Caspian Sea (known in Fārsī as the Daryā-yé Khazar) is the world's largest lake, with an area of some 370,000 sq km. It is 'co-owned' by Azerbaijan, Russia, Kazakstan and Turkmenistan. (See the boxed text 'The Mighty Caspian Sea' in the Caspian Provinces chapter for more details.) The largest lake wholly within Iran is the 600-sq-km Orūmīyé Lake in the north-west.

The Persian Gulf is about 233,100 sq km, and becomes the Gulf of Oman east of the strategic Strait of Hormoz. Iran has dozens of tiny islands in the Gulf, most of which are uninhabited. Those that are – notably Gheshm and Kīsh – are being developed, attracting investors and tourists from the Gulf states; while other islands are used as bases for oil exploration.

GEOLOGY

Iran is dominated by three mountain ranges; the smaller, volcanic Sabalān and Tālesh ranges in the Āzarbāyjān provinces, which include Sabalān mountain (4811m), and provide fertile pastures for nomads; the very long, Jurassic-era Zāgros range, stretching from Kordestān province to Bandar-é Abbās, which is so vast that it makes road construction and habitation very difficult – although it contains a lot of oil; and to the north of Tehrān, stretching from the border of the independent republic of Azerbaijan towards Turkmenistan, is the dominant Alborz range, home of Iran's highest mountain, the permanently snowcapped Damāvand (5671m).

Iran is particularly susceptible to earthquakes, a result of monumental shifts in the mountain ranges during the Pliocene period. There have been 943 registered earthquakes in the last 20 years in Iran. The most devastating in recent times killed more than 45,000 people in northern Iran in 1990; and in the first half of 1997, there were three serious quakes: one measuring 5.5 on the Richter scale was centred around Ardabīl (see the boxed text 'The 1997 Earthquake' in the Western Iran chapter for details). Experts believe Iran will receive a 'Big One' (with the intensity of at least seven on the Richter

scale) every five years. A tragedy of epic proportions just waiting to happen is Tehrān; an uncontrolled urban mess of about 12 million people, mostly living in hastily-built high-rise apartments.

The other geological feature of interest to some visitors is the abundance of hot and cold water mineral springs. Most springs are located in the Caspian provinces, and around the volcanic areas in the north-western provinces. Water temperatures range from 19° C to 49°C, so be very careful before you jump into a spring – also, some springs contain chemicals which may do more harm than good. Locals (and hopeful tourist authorities) claim a soak in these springs can cure all sorts of illnesses, such as rheumatism, back pains and stomach ailments – but nothing has been proved.

CLIMATE

Because of its size, variety of topography and altitude, Iran experiences great extremes of climate. Winters (December to February) can be unpleasantly cold in most parts of the country, while in summer (June to August) temperatures as high as 40°C are nothing out of the ordinary. Regular rainfall is more or less restricted to the far north and west – generally also the coldest parts of Iran. Spring (March to May) and autumn (September to November) are the ideal times to tour Iran, but summer or winter can be OK, so long as you do a little planning, take a few precautions and avoid major religious holidays (see Public Holidays & Special Events in the Facts for the Visitor chapter).

Most of **western Iran** is generally the coldest and among the rainiest parts of the country. Temperatures well below zero are very common between December and February and sometimes fall as low as -20°C. Snow frequently remains until early spring, and later in the mountains. Summers are relatively mild, and spring and autumn are pleasant. Rainfall is heavy by Iranian standards: up to about 2000mm annually.

The **Caspian provinces**, and the area north of the Alborz range, is also fairly well-provided with rain, with an annual average of around 1300mm. The all-year cloud cover helps to keep summer temperatures a little more manageable than in places a short distance to the south, though humidity can be high in summer. Winter is milder here than elsewhere in the north of Iran. Spring and autumn are the best times to visit, but rainstorms at any time may thwart your plans.

In **eastern Iran** winters are cold, with temperatures hovering around or below zero, thanks to some icy air currents straight from Siberia. Summers are hot and dry. April to May and late September to early November are generally the most pleasant times to visit. Rainfall is about 250mm a year, highest around March and virtually nonexistent between June and September.

The Dasht-é Kavīr is harsh, inhospitable

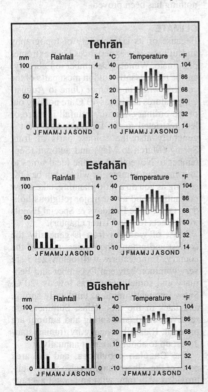

and very, very hot in summer. Winters are not much better, and at night the temperature can fall well below zero. If any time of year can be called 'pleasant' in this salty wasteland, it would have to be between October and December. The Dasht-é Lūt to the south is, if anything, even worse; almost completely devoid of water from any direction and the last word in extreme aridity.

In **Tehrān province** the climate can vary considerably from one end to the other. The central and southern parts of the province are hot, dry and stuffy in summer, but you only have to take a short bus ride up to the foothills of Damāvand mountain to cool down by several degrees. Winters in the capital can be very chilly, extremely so at night (frequently as low as -15°C), though any snow usually disappears by early March. Showers are frequent between November and mid-May, but rare in summer – the annual rainfall is about 240mm. May and autumn are generally the best times to visit.

Central Iran is very hot in summer, and it gets hotter the further south you go, though there is some relief at higher altitudes. Humidity is generally manageable. Winters are cold but not as severe as in the far west and north. Rainfall is erratic and varies from place to place; it rarely averages much more than about 250mm a year, however. Spring and autumn are generally very pleasant throughout central Iran, sunny but not oppressive in the day and cool at night.

In **southern Iran**, anywhere within about 200km of the Gulf is going to be frying-pan hot in summer (regularly up to 50°C), with very oppressive humidity; and there's little relief after dusk either. This part of Iran is to be avoided between early May and mid-October, if at all possible, but the winters are warm and highly agreeable: between late November and early March, Khūzestān province and the Persian Gulf are probably the most pleasant parts of Iran (and the most popular for northern Iranians). Rainfall is only about 150mm annually – mostly falling in winter.

Away from the Gulf proper, temperatures in southern Iran are a little lower. Summers are hot and dry, winters mild and dry. Up in Sīstān conditions are harsh: the hot season lasts from April to November with an average temperature of 50°C; winter is equally unpleasant with extreme cold until March. There is very little rain throughout south-eastern Iran and frost would be a great novelty. March to April and October to November are the best times to visit.

ECOLOGY & ENVIRONMENT

Massive, unrestrained urban and industrial development has caused irreparable environmental damage – and only recently has the government instigated some (limited) research to determine the extent of the ecological destruction within Iran.

Deforestation, erosion, and overgrazing are no more evident than on the southern slopes of the Alborz mountain range (and not far from the encroaching urban sprawl of northern Tehrān). The most potent example of urban sprawl can be seen along the main road along the Caspian Sea. Described in guidebooks only 20 years ago as a collection of quaint villages, the coastal road is now an unmitigated disaster of concrete homes and resorts, stretching nearly 400km from Rasht to Sārī. The worst instance of pollution is the ruinous contamination of the Persian Gulf by leaks from oil rigs and oil tankers; untreated sewage; and the unrestrained development on the islands of Kīsh and Gheshm. (Refer to the boxed text 'The Persian Gulf' in the Southern Iran chapter for more details.) Since the demise of the USSR, pollution in the Caspian Sea has increased as well.

The Iranian government has allocated some areas to help preserve the native flora and fauna, albeit rather perfunctorily (see under National Parks in the following Flora & Fauna section). In central Iran, and the north-western provinces, you may see some token efforts at reforestation. But it is frankly too little – but, hopefully, not too late.

FLORA & FAUNA
Flora

Despite expansive deserts, and unrestrained urban sprawl and development, Iran still hosts more than 10,000 species of flora – many of which are endemic. The northern slopes of the Alborz mountains (up to a height of about 2500m) are densely covered with a forest of broad-leaved deciduous trees which forms the largest area of vegetation in Iran. Here you will find the types of trees found in many European forests, such as the Caucasian wingnut *(Pterocarya fraxinifolia)*, as well as oak, maple, pine and elm. Extracts from some of these trees are used to produce glue, and various resins and dyes. The loveliest pockets of forest, which are bound to impress all nature lovers, are around Khalkhāl, south of Ardabīl; along the stunning road between Ardabīl and Āstārā; and at Nahar Khorān, just south of Gorgān.

In total contrast, the southern and eastern regions of Iran are almost bare, except for some scattered juniper trees; though there are smaller, less dense forests of oak and juniper on the higher slopes of the central and north-west Zāgros mountains, and in some of the southern parts of Khorāsān province. In the scrubland, you will find the prickly thrift *(Acantholimon)* and the camel's thorn *(Alhagi camelorum)*. Palm trees grow on the southern coastal lowland – especially near the Strait of Hormoz – and around the rare luxuriant oases which are dotted among the bone-dry nothingness.

One of the few places in Iran dedicated to the protection of local flora is the Iranian National Flora Research Garden, Iran's largest horticultural research station, and one of the biggest in the region. Located near the village of Paykanshahr, just off the highway between Tehrān and Karaj, the garden is open to the public every day, except Friday, from about 8 am to 3 pm. However, it is of more interest to 'budding' botanists.

Fauna
Mammals Of the 100 or more species of mammals found in Iran, about one-fifth are endemic. Most of the larger species are more common in the unexplored depths of the forest of Māzandarān province, such as wolf, jackal, wild boar, hyena, black bear and lynx. In the deserts and mountains, you are more

likely to come across the more sedate Persian squirrel and mongoose; galloping Persian gazelle; porcupine and badger; endemic Iranian wild ass; rabbit and hare; and the red, Jabir and Mesopotamian deer. Two of the more fascinating creatures are the huge ibex-like Alborz red sheep, with its black 'beard' and spiralling horns, found in the Alborz mountains; and the Oreal ram, the largest of its type in Iran, with a white 'beard' and enormous spiralling horns, found near the border with Turkmenistan.

One prize specimen that you are almost guaranteed not to find is the Persian lion, once the proud symbol of imperial Iran but generally believed to be extinct until an alleged sighting by a peasant in the Māzandarān forest a few years ago. You might still, however, with great patience or luck, manage to track down a leopard in south-eastern Iran, or even perhaps a tiger in the plains or forests of the Caspian provinces. There are wild Bactrian camels roaming the provinces of Kermān, Sīstān va Balūchestān and Khorāsān, but most are domesticated and belong to nomadic or semi-nomadic communities.

Birds Look up and you'll be able to enjoy a wide variety of birds, either indigenous to Iran or visitors from as far away as Europe. Among the more interesting, endemic and permanent feathered inhabitants are the golden eagle, found in the Caspian provinces; the tiny jiroft, common in Kermān province and along the Persian Gulf; the red-wattled lapwing; the yellow partridge; delijeh and balaban falcon, mainly in Hamadān province; and the unsavoury black vulture and black kite in the central plateau and deserts. Some migratory waterbirds include the greater flamingo, found in their thousands at Orūmīyé Lake, as well as the glossy ibis, and Smyrna kingfisher.

Fish The Persian Gulf hosts a wide range of tropical fish, as well as shark, swordfish and porpoise. The Caspian Sea has large shoals of sturgeon, which produces world-famous caviar; salmon and other fish; as well as the Caspian seal. Some of the more common fish found in the streams around the Alborz mountains include trout, chub and catfish.

Reptiles If you venture into the desert, you may stumble across a few snakes (of which only a couple are poisonous); and lizards, such as the metre-long waran, which abound in the truly desolate parts. In the mountains, the funny-looking Greek tortoise may waddle across your path.

National Parks

UNESCO has designated Orūmīyé Lake as an 'area of special interest' to protect the multitude of migratory birds, and the few animals which rely on the salty lake for their habitat. Anyone who does not live on the main island of Kabūdī, however, needs special permission from the Department of the Environment to visit the island, and to spend much time exploring the lake.

To its credit, the Iranian government has created a few national parks to protect its wildlife, but they are a far cry from the sort of national park you may see in western countries: the parks in Iran have no fenced areas or rangers, they are not mentioned on any maps, and few laws forbid hunting or development. Still, if you have a hankering for some wildlife, and access to a vehicle (no public transport or organised tours are available), the following national parks are large, and accessible:

Central Iran
> **Khabar va Rouchon,** where the Jabir deer roams, is about 200km south of Kermān city; **Mehrouyeh,** home of the black bear, is in the far south-east of Kermān province; and **Mooteh,** established to protect antelope, is about 50km south-west of Kāshān.

Eastern Iran
> **Tandoureh,** home to the Oreal ram, ibex and even a leopard, if you are lucky (or not), is near Darregaz (in Khorāsān province), on the border with Turkmenistan.

Southern Iran
> **Bakhtegān National Park,** established to protect migratory birds, is between Bakhtegān and Tashk lakes, about 80km east of Shīrāz.

Western Iran

Assād Ābād, home to various birds of prey such as the delijeh and balaban falcon, and ibex, is just off the road between Hamadān and Kermānshāh; and **Bījār,** home to hyena, jackal and fox, is about 15km north-west of Bījār town.

GOVERNMENT & POLITICS

After the Islamic Revolution, 98% of the population apparently voted to implement a unique form of Islamic government, with three levels of political power. A parliament called the *Majlis* comprises Islamic experts and revered Islamic leaders from around the country – including a representative from the Jewish and Zoroastrian communities, and two from the Armenian Christians. The Majlis has real power: it approves (but does not instigate, in theory) laws and economic decisions, but under the constitution it can 'investigate and examine all affairs of the country'. See the boxed text 'The Confusion That is Iranian Politics' earlier in this chapter.

The Majlis is dominated by the *velayat-é faqih,* or Supreme Leader. The first Supreme Leader was the revered Āyatollāh Khomeinī, who formed this position in accordance with his interpretation of the Quran. The current Supreme Leader, Āyatollāh Alī Khameneī, has enormous power: among other things, he can select (and sack) the Commander of the Armed Forces; can declare war or peace; and can veto the election of (and dismiss) the President. The other powerful position in the Majlis is the Speaker, currently held by Hojjat-ol-Eslām Alī Akbar Nateq Nouri. The Majlis is elected by the Iranian people every four years, but the candidates are carefully vetted before the elections.

The Iranian Flag

The Iran national flag comprises three colours: from top to bottom, green, white and red. On the bottom of the green stripe, and the top of the red stripe, are the words *allah-o-akhbar* (Allah is the Greatest). In the middle of the white stripe, is the national symbol of Iran, based around the calligraphic word, 'Allah'. ■

The National Liberation Army

Across the border from Khūzestān Province in Iraq, there is a highly-organised, heavily-armed and fanatical group of Iranian dissidents: members of the 30,000-strong National Liberation Army (NLA). What makes the NLA even more extraordinary is that more than one-third of the troops are women, while more than two-thirds of the officers are female. Established in 1988, members of the NLA wear no uniforms and have vowed to be celibate. The Army includes Iranians who have suffered religious and political persecution, as well as those who fled Iran in 1979 because they openly defied the rulers of the new Islamic Republic.

The NLA hopes to change the current regulations set up by the Iranian regime about the role of women, and wants to install their own (female) president, Maryam Rajavī, wife of a former head of the Islamic People's Mojāhedīn. The Army plans to enter Iran once there is some serious sedition within the country, and continues to promote its cause through the use of sophisticated anti-regime television and radio broadcasts into Iran. The Iranian airforce occasionally launches strikes against NLA bases – in which case it might be wise to avoid Khūzestān's border region. ■

According to the Iranian Constitution, the second level of power, the Council of the Guardians, 'safeguards the Islamic Ordinances and Constitution'. It comprises 12 Islamic jurists and religious experts, all selected by the Supreme Leader. The Council's main purposes are to uphold Islamic values, ensure that the parliament remains free of corruption, and approve the handful of presidential candidates.

Thirdly, the president manages (and elects himself) a cabinet, though final control always rests with the Majlis. The president is elected every four years (he is only allowed two terms), but the Iranian people normally only have four candidates to choose from. The current president is Hojjat-ol-Eslām Seyed Mohammed Khatamī (refer to the boxed text 'President Khatamī' earlier in this chapter).

Very little political opposition is tolerated. Dissidents either live under harassment in

Iran (for example, the members of the primary 'legal' opposition party, the Freedom Movement of Iran); or they form armies in neighbouring countries such as Iraq (see the boxed text 'The National Liberation Army' on the previous page); or operate political groups, or terrorist organisations such as the Mojāhedīn Khalq Organisation (MKO), in Europe or North America.

Currently, Iran is divided into 26 provinces, but as the population continues to grow, more will be created – especially out of the large and/or heavily populated provinces of Khorāsān and Māzandarān. Each province is ruled by a governor-general *(ostāndār)*, based in the provincial capital. Places designated as towns are ruled by a *farmāndār*, and villages by a *kadkodār*.

ECONOMY

Iran is still recovering economically from the Iran-Iraq War, even though it ended almost 10 years ago. Iraq bombed 87 Iranian cities (and virtually obliterated Ābādān and Khorramshahr), and nearly 3000 villages. More than 400,000 homes were destroyed; about five million Iranians lost their homes and jobs; and about 1.2 million were forced to flee the area, many migrating to Mashhad (which is about as far as they could go from the Iraqi border without leaving Iran). The long-term damage to the soil (where many landmines are still hidden), environment, and flora and fauna, is incalculable. The total damage bill for the war is estimated at a staggering US$1000 billion.

Despite this, and the trade embargo imposed by the USA, a high inflation rate

---

Some Economic Statistics

GDP Growth Rate: 4.2%
Income per capita: 2.5 million rials per annum; or US$5570 by purchasing power parity
Inflation: 18.8%
Exports: US$18.3 billion
Imports: US$15.1 billion

(now under some control), and a slump in oil prices, the precarious Iranian economy is still managing to function. The major industries are all owned by the government, including the main airline (Iran Air); the majority share of the largest shipping company (Indo-Iranian Joint Shipping Company); the major export earner (oil); and all media. Private industry is nascent, but heavily regulated by the state.

Oil

Oil was first produced in Iran at Masjed-é Soleimān (near Dezfūl, in the south-west) in 1908, and initially exploited on a large scale by the Anglo-Iranian Oil Company after WWI. Ābādān proved early on to be the most prolific site, and it wasn't long before it became a virtual colony of the international oil companies. However, the oil companies were nationalised by the Iranian government in 1950 (an annual public holiday celebrates the fact). Oil is currently drilled in southwestern Iran, and in the Persian Gulf; and sent to refineries near Tehrān, Tabrīz, Arāk and Esfahān.

Iran is currently the world's third-largest exporter of oil (after Saudi Arabia and Norway). Despite the low-grade output, which is unsuitable for some countries, and the US embargo, oil is overwhelmingly Iran's major export earner – it accounts for more than 40% of *all* government income. In accordance with quotas set by the Organisation of Petroleum-Exporting Countries (OPEC), Iran produces 3.6 million barrels per day, of which about 2.5 million is exported for about US$17 per barrel. Iran has an estimated 90 billion barrels left (give or take a barrel or two) – about 10% of the world's reserves. At this rate, however, supplies will run out after 70 years.

Agriculture & Fisheries

Less than half the country is considered cultivable, and only a small proportion of that actually goes under the hoe or the goat's hoof at any one time. Agriculture, which employs nearly 30% of the work force, is hampered by extreme temperatures, lack of water, soil salinity, plant diseases and the combination of inefficiency, poor infrastructure and lack of technology.

Wheat and barley are overwhelmingly the most important cereal crops (grown mainly in the Āzarbāyjān provinces). Less important these days is rice (grown mainly in the Caspian provinces), supplanted by (subsidised) bread as the new staple. All manner of fruits are grown in the less arid parts of the country, including pomegranates, grapes, figs, dates and strawberries; oranges, peaches, melons, apples and lemons are particularly prevalent in the Āzarbāyjān provinces; and the watermelons are huge in Khūzestān province. Other important crops include sugar beet, potatoes, nuts, tea (along the Caspian coast), tobacco, saffron and henna – most of which are exported no further than the nearest bazaar. Cotton is an increasingly important crop, as is silk, with the help of silkworms, in the Caspian region.

You won't see a vast amount of livestock in Iran, except perhaps in the more nomadic areas of western Iran. Sheep (about 45 million) and goats (about 25 million) are the most reliable and durable animals, and used for milk, meat and wool to make clothes and carpets. Among the nomads of the eastern and southern regions, camels are used for transport, wool, and milk.

Due to a lack of reliable rain in many parts of Iran, and the needs of a huge population, farmers must rely on modern, and traditional, irrigation systems. These systems include the ghanāt (see the boxed text 'The Ghanāt' below); dams, eg the Karaj dam, which supplies water and hydroelectric power for Tehrān; wells, which are common in remote areas; and the diversion of water from major rivers. Despite these problems, more and more land is being cultivated: the government plans to irrigate several million hectares of crops within the next 20 years and increase the exploitation of the country's water resources from 30% to 55%.

The increasingly important fishing industry is mostly owned by the Iranian government, and operates in the Persian Gulf (mainly near Bandar-é Abbās and Kīsh Island), as well as the Caspian Sea. Caviar is a very lucrative export (not hard to believe if you consider what it sells for in the west), with about half being collected from the poor sturgeons near Bandar-é Torkamān, near Turkmenistan.

Tourism

In the mid-1970s, as many as 500,000 foreigners visited Iran each year, and hotel development was a priority of the Shāh's fifth (and final) five-year plan (1973 to 1978). But the excesses in the aftermath of the Islamic Revolution, immediately followed by the long and nasty Iran-Iraq War, understandably encouraged most potential tourists to detour around, or fly over, Iran.

The Ghanāt
The traditional Iranian method of water supply – first seen in the central plateau at least 2000 years ago and still in use – is the *ghanāt* or underground water channel. To build a ghanāt – which is a highly-skilled, dangerous and well-paid job in Iran – you need first to bore a well down to an underground water source, which may be more than 100m deep, but must be at a higher level than the point at which the water is to be collected. Then you dig a tunnel, just wide and tall enough to crawl along, to carry the water at a very low gradient to that point. Narrow wells are dug down to the tunnel at regular intervals for ventilation and to dispose of the excavated soil or rubble.

Because of the hazards and expense involved in constructing a ghanāt, complex laws govern every aspect of its use and maintenance. There are reckoned to be more than 50,000 ghanāts in Iran, the longest of which measures more than 40km. Although modern irrigation projects such as the hydroelectric dam at Karaj have been a priority since the 1960s, ghanāts and other traditional methods of supplying water are still of great importance, and the ghanāt builders of Yazd (which is where they traditionally come from) are not yet redundant. ■

Official figures put current foreign visitors at 350,000 per year, but these are mostly Pakistanis, Azerbaijanis, Russians, Turks and Arabs from neighbouring Gulf states. Very few westerners visit Iran (possibly as few as 5000 in 1996), and many of these are Japanese (who get visas easily). Only in the past couple of years have all foreigners (except, to a lesser degree, Americans) been welcome. Travel to, and around, Iran has become safe and easy, hassles with visas notwithstanding.

Tourist authorities hope to lure rich Arabs from the Gulf states to the duty-free zones of Chābahār, and Gheshm and Kīsh islands. (The latter has a permanent population of 9000, but a staggering 400,000 Iranian and foreign tourists visit Kīsh Island every year.) The tourist authorities in Iran, and in neighbouring countries, are also trying to revive the famous Silk Road, hoping that foreigners will travel through Iran and Central Asia, on the way between China and Europe.

The Economy Today

The official Iranian unemployment figures are misleading, but it's clear that the highest rates of unemployment (16% to 20%), and the lowest standards of living, are found among the Kurds and Lors of western Iran. Tehrān boasts the lowest level of unemployment (6%), below the national average of about 9%.

Iran is sensibly developing many other industries, because oil supplies are finite; non-oil exports quadrupled to US$4 billion per year between 1989 and 1995. The Persian carpet is also a vital industry: Iran produces nearly one-third of all traditional carpets and rugs made worldwide, currently earning more than US$2 billion per year. Iran also exports other handicrafts, including art and gemstones, worth about US$8 million per year.

Industries such as steel and copper mining, cement and petrochemicals have increased production markedly in recent years, and are now worth about US$1.5 billion in exports each year. Iran has an estimated 20 trillion cubic metres of natural gas reserves (which should last more than 200 years). This has been an economic saviour, and pipelines are being hurriedly built to export gas from Iran and the Central Asian republics. It comes as no surprise that one of the major manufacturing industries is the production of the Paykan, that family sedan seen all over Iran. Nearly 80,000 are produced every year, overwhelmingly for domestic consumption.

One major hurdle to an improved economy is the trade embargo imposed by the US. In 1995, US trade with Iran was outlawed; and a year later, sanctions were tightened further when the US Congress legislated to penalise all foreign firms which invest more than US$40 million per year in Iran's oil and gas industries. At the time of writing, this has been ignored by European and Asian companies keen to exploit the vast gas and oil reserves in Iran, and by governments in the region, such as Turkey, which recently agreed to buy more than US$20 billion of gas from Iran in the next 25 years.

Iran is slowly trying to lessen its dependence on Europe for imports and exports, and looking to help develop the nascent Central Asian republics, and attract investment from the Gulf states and Asia. But because of the US embargo, and a general distrust of the politically sensitive, and potentially volatile, Iranian government by foreign firms and governments, foreign investment continues to be far less than Iran hopes.

POPULATION & PEOPLE

In 1996, Iran's population was 69,975,000 – and it is rising fast. In 1956, the population was 19 million, but by 2015, Iranian authorities fear the population will surge to a staggering 110 million. There has been a dramatic demographic shift from the countryside to urban areas, worsened by the upheavals caused by the Iran-Iraq War, when millions of internal refugees headed for the large towns and stayed put. Many Iranian towns have at least doubled in population since the Islamic Revolution, without any corresponding increase in housing or other facilities. About 60% of the population now live in cities; and about 15% of Iran's population squeeze into Tehrān. More than 300,000 nomads still roam the plains and mountain pastures.

Iran is by no means a homogeneous nation. Its location at the crossroads of Arabia, Turkey and Central Asia, and the changing frontiers of the Persian Empire throughout the centuries, has ensured that a multitude of peoples make their home within Iranian borders. The sheer diversity of the Iranian population, combined with centuries of mixing and migration, have made it diffi-

cult to draw even the vaguest of boundaries for the various ethnic groups inhabiting present-day Iran.

Iran's Population at a Glance

Population Under 15 years: 46%
Population Growth Rate: 1.8%
Birth Rate: 2.5%
Death Rate: 0.7%
Life Expectancy: 68 years
Infant Mortality: 4.3%

On the whole, ethnic strife isn't too much of a problem in Iran; the government is a lot more tolerant of minorities than many in the region. There are a few problems between the Iranian government and Kurdish separatists in Kordestān province, but not nearly as much discrimination and persecution for which Turkey and Iraq are infamous. What little racial animosity the Persians have is largely reserved for the Afghan refugees, who are privately blamed for almost every unresolved murder case or suspicious going-on from Khorāsān to Khūzestān.

Persians More than 65% of the inhabitants of Iran can be called Persians, or Fārsīs. They are the descendants of the Elamite and Aryan races who first set up camp in the central plateau back in the 2nd millennium BC, and gave Persia its name.

Āzarīs Āzarīs form the largest minority in Iran, with about 25% of the population. They speak a Turkic language, and mainly live in small villages in the Āzarbāyjān provinces. Refer to the boxed text 'The Āzarīs' in the Western Iran chapter for more details.

Kurds Kurds are spread across a large area of the Middle East, including a good part of eastern Turkey (maybe 10 million), north-eastern Iraq and small pockets of Syria. Although they have been around longer than any other people in the region (at least since the 2nd millennium BC), Kurds have never enjoyed the status of nationhood. Refer to the boxed text 'The Kurds' in the Western Iran chapter for more details.

Lors Representing about 2% of the population, Lors are thought to be part Persian and part Arab in origin, though they are probably a mix of the Kasits, who came to Iran about a couple of thousand years ago, and the Medes. Refer to the boxed text 'The Lors' in the Western Iran chapter for more details.

Arabs About 4% of the population are Arabs (about 2.5 million people). Most live in Khūzestān province; on some of the smaller Iranian islands in the Persian Gulf; and along the southern coast, where they have become partly Persianised and are often known as Bandarīs, from the Persian word for 'port' (see the boxed text 'The Bandarīs' in the Southern Iran chapter for more details). Arab men usually the wear the traditional floor-length shirt-dress which is called a *thobe* or *dishdasha*, as well as the loose headscarf called a *gutra*. Most Arabs in Iran still speak a dialect of Arabic.

Turkmen Of Turkic origin, Turkmen (who make up about 2% of Iran's total population) mostly live in the Torkaman Sahrā, the plain occupying much of the east of Māzandarān

Refugees

Iran hosts more refugees than any other country in the world, but has only recently requested, and received, any substantial international aid to help cope. Iran is in an unfortunate geographical position, surrounded by ethnic and political strife in all directions. To the west, Kurds, who are persecuted in Turkey and Iraq, flock to Iran, where they are left alone. A total of 600,000 Kurds, Lors and other ethnic minorities have fled Iraq for Iran since the start of the brutal Iran-Iraq war in 1980. Civil strife in Armenia and Azerbaijan to the north is putting further strain on Iran's economy.

An estimated 1.4 million Afghan refugees live in Iran; they originally fled the Soviet invasion, but stayed in Iran because of the persistent civil war in Afghanistan. Male refugees often end up leading tough (and truncated) lives as labourers for the construction industry. Based mainly in Mashhad and Tehrān, the Afghan refugees are now viewed by many Iranians as parasites, and blamed for various social and economic woes. They are being encouraged to return to Afghanistan by the Iranian government and the United Nations High Commissioner for Refugees, with limited success. ■

province and the north of Khorāsān province; and next to the Central Asian republic of Turkmenistan. Refer to the boxed text 'The Turkmen' in the Eastern Iran chapter for more details.

Nomads There are many nomadic groups in Iran. The Bākhtiarīs (Bactrians) live in the more remote parts of the provinces of Chahārmahāl va Bakhteyārī and Khūzestān, though many of them have now settled in villages and towns.

The Baluchīs, whose name literally means 'the wanderers', are one of the few peoples who largely retain a semi-nomadic way of life, perhaps because the extremely arid region where they roam is hardly suited to the settled life. They occupy the very sparsely populated desert region covering the far south-east of Iran and the far west of Pakistan. Very able riders, they are famous for their camel races.

The Ghashghā'īs live mainly in Fārs province. Many are still nomadic. Like so many of the minority peoples of Iran, the Ghashghā'īs are of Turkic stock, and have always been hard to subjugate.

Others Armenians and Jews are scattered throughout Iran, mostly in the cities. Armenians are particularly prominent in Tehrān and Esfahān, and are renowned for their trading and business skills. Jews have lived in Iran for more than 2500 years, but only a few thousand remain in Tehrān, Shīrāz and Esfahān.

EDUCATION

Schooling is not compulsory, but by and large Iranian families understand the need to provide their children with at least a basic education, so an impressive 95% of Iranian children (ie more than 18 million) currently receive primary or secondary schooling. Government-run schools are free of charge for all Iranians, though an increasing number of private schools are being established, which do charge comparatively high fees.

At the level of higher education, demand outstrips supply and often only the cleverest

and most favoured students can get a place at one of the state universities. Though the Iranian government does claim that more than one million Iranians currently attend a university, about half of these study at one of the growing number of private universities. A large number of affluent Iranians send their children to study in Europe.

A great deal of publicity has been given to the so-called 'Literacy Movement', which aims to teach reading and writing, as well as 'the revolutionary culture of Islam and religious matters' to everyone. Literacy rates in Iran are impressively high: about 77% of the population have some skills at reading and writing in Fārsī, compared with a literacy rate of 25% in neighbouring Pakistan. The literacy rate in Iran is higher (about 85%) in the cities, and lower (70%) in the countryside; and, though no statistics prove it, literacy rates are likely to be lower for females. (The female literacy rate, for example, is about 15% in Pakistan.)

ARTS

In Iran, as in all Islamic societies, art favours the non-representational, the derivative and the stylised rather than the figurative, the innovative and the true-to-life. Accurate representation of the human form has never been a part of traditional Islamic art, and though portraiture is not forbidden by Shi'ite Islam, it never really caught on in Iran until the introduction of the camera.

Many Iranian art forms predate the Arab conquest, but since nearly all of them reached their peak within the Islamic era, religious influences are rarely completely absent. Favourite motifs in Iranian art are geometrical shapes and patterns such as medallions and meanders; grapevines and other floral patterns, often very complex; and highly stylised real or imaginary creatures such as lions, elephants, peacocks, phoenixes and griffins. Human figures do turn up, but they tend to be very formalised. Calligraphy is highly prized in Iran and often merges into pictorial art, though modern examples are works of art in their own right.

continued on page 36

Persian Carpets

The gol motif is a stylised flower thought to represent a rose, a Persian symbol of life.

The best known Iranian cultural export, the Persian carpet, is far more than just a floor-covering to an Iranian. A Persian carpet or rug is a display of wealth, an investment, an integral part of religious and cultural festivals, and used in everyday life, eg as a prayer mat. Carpets have long been used as a form of currency, and weaving new carpets is a kind of savings account, which can be sold off in times of need.

History

The earliest known Persian carpet, which probably dates back to the 5th century BC, was discovered in a remote part of Siberia, clearly indicating that carpets were made in Persia more than 2500 years ago.

Historians know that by the 7th century AD Persian carpets made of wool or silk had become famous in court circles throughout the region. Their quality and subtlety of design were renowned, and carpets were exported to places as far away as China, though for many centuries they must have remained a great luxury in their country of production, with the finest pieces being the preserve of royalty. The early patterns were usually symmetrical with geometric and floral motifs designed to evoke the beauty of the classical Persian garden. Towards the end of the pre-Islamic period, stylised animal and human figures (especially royalty) became a dominant design element.

After the Arab Conquest, Quranic verses were incorporated into some carpet designs, and prayer mats began to be produced on a grand scale; secular carpets also became a major industry and were highly prized in European courts. Very few examples remain from before the 16th century, however, and little is known of early methods of weaving and knotting, or of differences in regional styles. The classification of existing pieces is often arbitrary.

During the 16th and 17th centuries, carpet making was given a high level of royal patronage and a favoured designer or weaver could expect great privileges. Sheep were specifically bred to grow the finest possible wool for weaving, and vegetable plantations were tended with scientific precision to provide permanent dyes of just the right shade. The reign of Shāh Abbās I marks the peak of Persian carpet production, when the quality of the raw materials and all aspects of the design and weaving were brought to a level never seen before or since, perhaps anywhere.

Towards the end of the 17th century, as demand for Persian carpets grew, so standards of production began to fall and designs tended to lack inspiration. A long period of stagnation followed, but the fall in standards has to be seen in perspective, for the finest Persian carpets of the 18th century and later still often led the world in quality and design. The reputation of modern Persian carpets has still not entirely recovered from the near-sacrilegious introduction of artificial fibres and dyes earlier this century.

Persian Carpets Today

Persian carpets are a huge export earner for Iran (see the Economy section in Facts about Iran for more details), but there are problems: weaving by looms, which made Persian carpets so special, are being supplanted by modern factories; young Iranians are not interested in learning the traditional methods of weaving; and cheaper, often blatantly copied, versions of 'Persian' carpets are being produced in India and Pakistan (where child labour is sometimes used; but not in Iran).

Iran is heavily promoting the prestige that the term 'Persian carpets' still evokes, recently recapturing a large slice of the world's trade in carpets and rugs. While some authorities hope that the export of Persian carpets and rugs from Iran will top US$17 billion per year by 2020, pragmatists concede that the costs of making genuine hand-made Persian carpets and rugs will increase to a point where consumers (mainly westerners) will be more happy admiring them in a local museum than forking out good money to buy them.

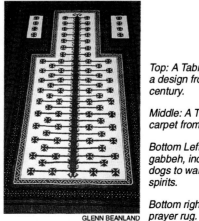

Top: A Tabrīzī carpet with a design from the 17th century.

Middle: A Turkmen carpet from Khorāsān.

Bottom Left: A tribal gabbeh, incorporating dogs to ward off evil spirits.

Bottom right: A Baluchī prayer rug.

Top: Hunters pursue deer on a carpet from Ghom, with a design from the Safavid era.

Middle: A finely woven Habibian carpet from Nā'īn, depicting mosiacs on the inside of a dome.

Bottom: A Toyserkan-design from western Iran.

Types of Carpets & Rugs

Persian carpets and rugs often come in three sizes: the *mian farsh* carpet is up to 3m long and up to 2.5m wide; the *kellegi* carpet is about 3.5m long and nearly 2m wide; and the *kenareh* carpet is up to 3m long and 1m wide. They are made from one of three basic materials. The best is wool (from sheep and goats, and occasionally camels), though the quality of wool does varies from one region to another. Cotton is cheaper and easy to use than wool; silk is mainly used for decorative rugs, as silk is not practical for everyday use.

Modern designs are either symbolic or religious (eg a lamp, indicating the sacred lamp in Mecca); reflections of the everyday life of the weaver; or inspired by whatever surrounds the weaver, eg trees, animals and flowers (particularly the lotus, rose and chrysanthemum). Common designs include *miri-bota*, the leaf pattern also found in rugs made in northern India, and probably a forerunner to the paisley patterns found in the west.

One different type of rug you may come across is the *kilim*, a double-sided flat-woven mat, without knots. These rugs are thinner and softer than other knotted carpets, and rarely used as floor coverings. They are popular as prayer mats (*kilim* is Turkish for 'prayer mat') and wall-hangings.

Making Carpets & Rugs

Most handmade carpets are made from wool. The wool is spun, usually by hand, and then rinsed, washed and dried. It is then lovingly dyed, making sure there's an even colour throughout the rug. In times gone past, dyes were extracted from natural sources such as herbs, skins of local fruit and vegetables and plants (eg indigo for blue, madder for red, and reseda for yellow). These days, however, chemical dyes are used, mainly aniline (which does sometimes fade) and chrome. After the rug has been made, it is then washed again to enhance the natural colours, though sometimes chemicals are used in the washing process.

ALL PHOTOS BY GLENN BEANLAND

Nomad carpet-weavers (usually women) use horizontal looms, which are lightweight and transportable. Carpets and rugs made by nomads are less detailed and refined because their equipment is not so sophisticated, but the quality of wool is often high, though sometimes a little uneven. Designs are usually unique, and conjured up by memory, or made up as they go along. These carpets and rugs are mainly weaved for domestic use, or for occasional trade, and are necessarily small because they must be carried by the nomads.

In the villages, small workshops (with men and women) have simple, upright looms, which create better designs, more variety, and extras such as fringes. Designs are usually standard, however, or copied from existing carpets or designs. In recent times, city factories have supplanted nomadic weavers and village workshops, producing carpets of monotonous design and variable quality – and most tourists won't know the difference.

Knots You may come across the terms 'Persian (or Senneh) Knot' (known in Fārsī as a *farsi-baf*) and 'Turkish (or Ghiordes) Knot' *(turki-baf)*. Both are used in Iran: the Turkish knot is common in the Āzarbāyjān provinces and western Iran. Without getting too technical, the Turkish knot is looped around two horizontal threads, with the yarn lifted between them, while the Persian knot loops around one horizontal thread, and under the next. The difference is not obvious to the layman.

As a rough guide, an everyday carpet or rug will have up to 30 knots per sq cm, a medium-grade piece 30 to 50 knots per sq cm, and a fine one 50 knots per sq cm or more. On a real prize piece you might have 500 or more knots per sq cm, but nowadays a museum is the only place you will find such an attempt at perfection. The higher number of knots per sq cm, the better the quality – and, of course, the higher the price.

A nomadic weaver can tie around 8000 knots each day; a weaver in a factory, about 12,000 knots per day. To find out how long the carpet or rug took to make (a big factor in the cost), determine the size of the rug; ask where it was made (by hand or in a factory); and use a calculator.

From Top to Bottom: The intricate flowers and tendrils of a Tabrīzī floral carpet; stylised flowers recall the Persian love of gardens in their largely arid country; gabbeh nomadic carpets feature animals scattered on large open fields of colour.

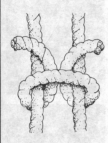

Top: The Turkish knot is invariably used by weavers in the Āzarbāyjān Provinces.

Bottom: The Persian knot is assymetrical; the geographical name has no significance.

Where to Find the Best

Experts happily argue about their favourites regions: some claim the carpets and rugs from Kermān province are the most colourful and soft; from Tabrīz, there is a great variety; Nā'īn boasts many with the highest number of knots; from Ghom, carpets and rugs are often more traditional; and from Kāshān, you may find some that are stronger and more dependable. The best range – but not the cheapest prices – can be found in the bazaars in the tourist centres, Tehrān, Esfahān and Shīrāz. In many cases the name of a carpet or rug indicates where it is made, or from where the design first originated.

If you have the time and interest, you may wish to hunt down something special in the following places:

- **Āzarbāyjān Provinces** The *heriz* and *mehriban* carpets found near the Azerbaijan border have bold designs: they often feature hunting scenes and tales from Ferdōsī's poem *Shah-nama*, usually on a mud-coloured background, with bizarre fringes.

- **Ghom** In the holy city of Ghom, you are more likely to see *gul-i-bulbul* carpets, made from goat's wool, and featuring a variety of designs with birds and flowers. The best are gorgeous, thin and strong, but these days many carpets for sale in Ghom are mass-produced for pilgrims.

- **Kermān** Kermān province is renowned for its soft and, often, very large carpets. They are very colourful, often containing shades of green (but not too much, as green is sacred to Islam), and usually made from locally-grown cotton. Designs feature local flowers, nuts and fruit, as well portraits of famous Iranians and foreigners.

- **Khorāsān** Carpets and rugs from this eastern province are influenced by the nomadic Turkmen, as well as the Arabs. They are often made of cotton, and feature designs in red.

- **Kordestān** Popular, but perhaps lacking the variety of those found in the villages of Lorestān, are the carpets and rugs made by the Kurds of western Iran. The centre for production, and sale, is the capital, Sanandaj, and Bījār where particularly hard-wearing rugs are made.

- **Lorestān** To help push-start the local economy, the Iranian government is actively promoting the ancient *gabbeh* carpets and rugs made by the Lors. Originally gabbehs featured plain patterns, but influences from India, and constant wars over the centuries, brought out harsh black and whites to symbolise bravery and victory. Lori carpets and rugs are normally made from wool, and dyes from fruit skins, such as pomegranates, and herbs (which are now hard to find). Designs may contain sporting and hunting scenes, local monuments or mosques.

For more information about Persian carpets and rugs, check out a few of the books listed in the Facts for the Visitor chapter; visit the annual Grand Persian Carpet Exhibition & Conference in Tehrān, usually held in August; visit the exquisite collection in the Carpet Museum in Tehrān; or contact the Export Promotion Center of Iran (PO Box 1148, Tajrīsh, Tehrān (☎ (21) 212 896; fax 2042 858), which organises the carpet fair. The *Iran Carpet* map produced by Ramezani Oriental Carpets, and available at the Gita Shenasi map shop in Tehrān, indicates the location of carpet weaving centres, but is of little additional use.

Some of the best and oldest examples of Persian carpets and rugs are found in museums outside of Iran: eg the national museums in Munich and Berlin; royal palaces in Denmark; and the Victoria & Albert Museum in London, which houses one of the world's oldest Persian rugs, made in 1529 for Sheikh Safī-od-Dīn from Ardabīl.

Buying Carpets & Rugs

Iranians have had more than a couple of thousand years to perfect the art of carpet-making – and just as long to master the art of carpet-selling. With hundreds of distinctive types of carpets around, it's going to take the western novice several years of study to be on equal terms with the shrewd Iranian carpet dealer (and Mercedes owner). If you don't know your warp from your weft, or your Turkish knot from your Persian knot, it might be worth reading up a little before visiting Iran, or taking a trustworthy Iranian friend with you when you look around the carpet shops.

If you know what you're doing, you might be able to pick up a bargain in Iran, but it's worth remembering that dealers in western countries often sell Persian carpets for little more than you'd pay in Iran (plus postage) – and carpet sellers in your home country know the market, bargain better, buy in bulk and save on transport costs. You are also much less likely to be ripped off by your local warehouse dealer than by a Persian bazaar merchant. Unless you're an expert, never buy a carpet or rug as an investment – buy it because you like it, and even then only if you have some idea of what sort of price you'd pay for a similar piece back home.

Before buying, lie the carpet or rug flat on the floor and check for any bumps or other imperfections. Small bumps will usually flatten out with wear, but if you find a big hump it is probably there to stay; if you're still sold on the carpet, look very disappointed and expect a generous price cut. To check if a carpet is handmade, turn it over. On a handmade piece the pattern will be distinct on the underside, the more distinct the better the quality. The commonest pile material is wool, which is tough and practical, and the best wool used is Iranian. Silk carpets are magnificent but they're largely for decoration and not very practical.

Taking Them Home

The whole business of clearing a carpet through customs and getting it to your doorstep takes one month (but allow two), and adds roughly about one-third to the cost – wrapping and posting a small carpet to Europe recently cost a traveller 50,000 rials. Some of the larger, older and more valuable carpets cannot be exported without special permission, so always check that yours doesn't belong to this category before paying for it. Also make sure whether you'll have to pay any transport costs or duties on delivery, and get everything down on paper. If in doubt, it's better to arrange to pay on delivery, so you don't risk being charged twice. The service is generally reliable, but it's up to you to work out a fail-safe agreement with the agent.

Regulations regarding the export of Persian carpets and rugs are a little confusing, so check the current situation with a reputable carpet dealer. Currently, each foreigner can take out of Iran (by air, overland transport, or by posting it back home), one Persian carpet, or two small Persian rugs, totalling 12 sq metres in size. If you want to buy anything larger, or buy more than two rugs, and take them out of Iran, the authorities deem that you are a carpet/rug trader, so you will need to complete the necessary paperwork, and pay the necessary duty, at the local customs office – all of which is designed to make sure that you do not bother breaking the 12 sq metre limit.

GLENN BEANLAND

A Shāh Abbās I hunting carpet, a design not made since the overthrow of the monarchy in 1979.

continued from page 31

Passion Plays

Almost all forms of theatre in Iran are based on Islam, and the most important is the *ta'ziyeh*, or passion play, which means Mourning for the Dead, and actually predates the introduction of Islam into Iran. The play is held in every city, town and village in Iran during the anniversary of Karbala, the battle in 680 in which Emām Hussein, the grandson of the Prophet, was murdered (refer to Public Holidays & Special Events in the Facts for the Visitor chapter for more details).

During the two days of mourning, groups of men and boys, dressed in black shirts, walk through the city streets, hitting their chest and back with a chain called a *shallāgh*. Others play drums and brass instruments, lead the chant (nowadays often with a loudspeaker), and carry flags and weapons symbolising the struggle against the infidels. The highlight for participants, and the hundreds of spectators, are the warriors dressed in traditional fighting outfits, and often on horses, who re-enact the martyrdom of Hussein.

The groups then go to a public place, sometimes a bazaar or town square, where a temporary platform or stage has been set up. Here actors in the appropriate garb, and carrying dangerous-looking weapons, continue to re-enact the martyrdom, often with too much passion. (The family of Hussein are usually dressed in green; while the 'baddies' are in red.) Traditional poems are also read out, and dramatic songs are played, accompanied by Iranian flutes and drums. It is a time where many mourners openly weep; others pray for health, wealth or a future family.

Music

You won't be able to hear, or buy, any western music in Iran, except perhaps for elevator muzak versions of pop tunes, or possibly Richard Clayderman (if you're really lucky). Most popular Iranian music is religious, while traditional music sometimes is not.

Traditional Traditional Persian songs are based on seven different types of melodies, so they can seem a bit monotonous. One popular type of song is termed the 'epic song', along the same lines as the 'epic poem' (see Poetry later in this section). Epic songs can be long – *very long* – and experts can spend most of their lives memorising verses.

The most appealing and melodious form of traditional music is found among the ethnic minorities: ie the Turkmen, in the remote regions of Khorāsān province; the Azārīs, whose unique style of music is often based around a love song; the Kurds, who have distinctive music based mainly around the lute, perform their version of the epic song, called a *bard*; the Lors often use an oboe-like instrument; and in the southern regions, along the Persian Gulf, the *demam*, a type of bagpipe, is popular. The music of Sīstān va Balūchestān is understandably similar to that found in Pakistan, and played on instruments such as the *tamboorak* (like the Pakistani *tambura*, a type of harmonium). Not surprisingly, the lyrics of most traditional music revolve around Islam, though some are based on love, and others celebrate victories over invading armies centuries before.

There are occasional music festivals, such as the annual Iranian Epic Music Festival (usually held in Tehrān in about April). However, you will have to seek out details, because these festivals are for the benefit of Iranians, not foreign tourists (although foreigners are welcome). One traditional group to look out for is Daryadelan. Originating from Būshehr province, this group tours internationally (but not often), and sings about the simple things in life, like God, family and fishing.

Modern Almost all modern music is religious, but slowly some form of Iranian pop music, under the watchful eye of Iranian authorities, is emerging. Many modern Iranian pop songs borrow rhythms and melodies from slightly out-of-date western dance music tunes. Some Iranian musicians fled the Islamic Revolution, and perform, unrestricted, outside of Iran, but within Iran, there is very little of interest for visitors. One popular singer is Shahram Nazerī, who combines traditional Iranian lyrics and poetry with traditional Iranian music. She has even recently toured the USA.

Pottery

Pottery is one of the oldest Persian art forms, and examples have been unearthed from burial mounds dating from the 5th millennium BC. Early pieces indicate they were for ornamental rather than domestic use, with detailed animals, such as boars and ibex, dominating the design. Persian pottery was initially unglazed, but glazed pottery dating back to the Elamite period has been unearthed from Choghā Zambīl. In the 1st millennium AD, pottery was painted with the simple geometric, floral and animal motifs that developed into the characteristic Persian style. The lotus flower (called a *niloofar* in Fārsī) has always been recognised as a symbol of life and of women. It features on a lot of Persian pottery, though the importance of the lotus predates the Arab (and Islamic) conquest of Iran.

15th century underglaze-painted blue and white dish from Mashhad

From the 9th century, Persia's detailed and colourful (mainly blue and green) glazed pottery became world famous; and the nomads of Khorāsān province had by then created their own style of glazing, adding early Islamic lettering styles such as Kufic to the design. Persian pottery reached its zenith in the 13th century, when a new type of clay was used to make the pottery more durable, and a number of new dazzling colours were introduced. Chinese influences became very strong during the Mongol period (1220-1380) and remained so until the mid-18th century. By then, the development of Persian pottery had suffered from incessant wars, and the increased number of imports from China.

The best examples of ancient Persian pottery were unearthed at Neishābūr, near Mashhad; Rey, near Tehrān; and near Gorgān. Many of these early finds can be seen at the Glass & Ceramics Museum and the National Museum of Iran in Tehrān, though some of the best examples are standing in the Louvre (Paris), and other museums outside of Iran.

1st millenium BC vessel from Tappé-yé Seyalk, near Kāshān

Poetry

While no-one knows the exact date of origin of the *Avesta*, the first example of Persian literature, it is known that Persian poetry first blossomed in the 9th century AD. With influences from nearby empires, various forms of Persian poetry developed, such as the *mathnavi*, with its unique rhyming couplets, and the *ruba'i*, similar to the quatrain (a stanza of four lines).

These styles later developed into the long and detailed 'epic poems', the first of which was Ferdōsī's *Shah-nama* finished in 1010 AD – with 50,000 couplets! Many epic poems regaled the glories of the old Persia before whichever foreigners had invaded and occupied the country at the time. The last truly great 'epic poem', *Zafar-nam*, covered the history of Islam from the birth of Mohammed to the early 14th century.

The next major form of Persian poetry to develop is known as *ghasidas*, poems of more than 100 couplets which do not rhyme. Famous exponents were Anvarī and Sanjar. Moral and religious poetry became famous following the success of Sa'dī's poems, such as *Bustan* and *Golestān*.

By the 14th century, smaller *ghazal* poems, which ran to about 10 non-rhyming couplets, were used for love stories. Ghazal poetry was made famous by Hāfez, and is still practised today. Persian poetry rarely produced anything exceptional after the Timurid dynasty (1380-1502).

Iranians still venerate their poets, often because the poets promoted Islam, and protected the Persian language and culture during times of occupation. Many poets have large mausoleums, and streets and squares named after them; eg Ferdōsī and Omar Khayyām are buried in huge (separate) gardens near Mashhad (see the boxed texts in the Eastern Iran chapter for more details about both poets); and the two famous poets from Shīrāz, Sa'dī and Hāfez (see the boxed texts in the Southern Iran chapter for more details).

Lesser known, and one of the few noted female poets, is Parvin E'tesami, renowned for her religious *Mecca of the Heart* and *Eye and Heart*. She died at the age of 35, and is now buried in Ghom – but without any memorials.

Film

Iran has had a long history of film-making, starting with *The Lor Girl* made in 1933. Since then, dozens of Iranian films have been produced each year (53 in 1996), and while most are the usual violent action flicks, with names like *Play with Death* and *Escape from Hell*, others have become remarkably successful overseas.

Films made in Iran must comply with Islamic and political directions set by the authorities, often leading to frustrated directors moving their productions outside of Iran. Iranian films rarely have a blatant Islamic message, however, though they invariably revolve around the theme of good over bad.

If you happen to be in Tehrān during the annual Fajr International Film Festival (in about late February), try to see a couple of new Iranian masterpieces (though they will be in Fārsī, and not subtitled in English). Otherwise, if you get a chance, check out some of these recent films (which should be subtitled into English, or your language, if released on video, or on screen, in the west):

Gabbeh – directed by Mohsen Makhmalbaf (see the boxed text on the next page), this film centers around a 'gabbeh', a type of Persian carpet made by the Ghashghā'ī nomads, and a nomad girl with the same name.

Leila – the final in a trilogy, directed by Dariush Mehrjoui, the film tells the story of a childless woman and her struggles with her husband and family.

Taste of Cherries – directed by Abbas Kiarostami, this film was co-winner of the prestigious Palme d'Or at the 1997 Cannes Film Festival. It was very controversial within Iran (where it still has not been shown at the time of research) because it deals with suicide, a taboo subject in Islam.

The White Balloon – this children's film, also directed by Abbas Kiarostami, won several international awards. It provides a fascinating look at the street life of Tehrān.

Zinat – directed by Ebrahim Mohktari, this simple story of a nurse at a health centre, also won plaudits at international film festivals.

Painting

The earliest known, distinctive style of Persian painting dates back to the Seljuq

Mohsen Makhmalbaf: Iran's Most Controversial Film Maker

Born in 1957 in Tehrān, Makhmalbaf first received infamy when he was imprisoned for four years after fighting with a policeman, but was released during the Islamic Revolution in 1979. He started to write books, but then turned to films, producing more than a dozen since 1982, including *Boycott*, *Time for Love*, and, more recently and provocatively, *Salaam Cinema* and *Gabbeh*. Many of these films are based on taboo subjects: *Time for Love* was filmed in Turkey because it broached the idea of adultery; and *Marriage of the Blessed* was a brutal film about casualties from the Iran-Iraq War.

Makhmalbaf refuses to follow the strict Islamic guidelines established by the Iranian authorities for local films, but does enjoy some comparative artistic freedom because he is so well-known. The support provided to Makhmalbaf by the then Minister of Culture, Seyed Mohammad Khatamī, during the early 1990s, was one of the reasons Khatamī was forced to resign. Ironically, Khatamī is now President of Iran, elected by a landslide partly because he is seen as a defender of artistic expression. ∎

period (1051-1200), which is often referred to by scholars as the 'Baghdad School'. Early painting was mainly used to decorate manuscripts and Qurans, though some 13th century pottery found near Tehrān indicates an early, unique Persian style of art. During the Mongol period (1220-1380), paintings were used to decorate all sorts of books.

Persian painting didn't come to notice again until the 16th century, with the development of a school of Persian art in Tabrīz, under the guidance of Sultan Mohammed. Many designs and patterns emanating from this school heavily influenced the design of carpets produced at this time. Persian art later flourished under the auspices of the great Shāh Abbās, who created an art centre in Esfahān. By the 18th century, distinctive Persian styles of art started to disappear when Indian and European influences inevitably spread into Persia. Interestingly, Persian artists did not sign their work during these early periods, so very few artists are known.

Calligraphy Not only was the Quran faithfully reproduced as a whole, but verses from it, and holy names such as Allāh and Mohammed, were used as decorations on religious buildings and elsewhere, as they are to this day. The formal, upright Kufic style of calligraphy was imported from the Arabian Peninsula, but several distinctly Persian calligraphic styles also emerged, some of them so elaborate as to verge on the illegible; eg *nashki*, which later developed into another renowned style known as *thuluth*.

By about the 16th century, Shīrāz was among the forerunners of calligraphy study and production in the Islamic world; followed by Esfahān. Some of the very best

Quranic calligraphy blends religious devotion with Iran's long-running artistic traditions.

examples of ancient and modern calligraphy can be seen at the Rezā Abbāsī Museum in Tehrān.

Miniatures Persian miniature painting first came to notice in the 15th century, and again re-emerged in the Safavid capital of Ghazvīn. Later miniature artists from eastern Iran, who had studied under the great Muhammedī in Herat (now in Afghanistan), started to influence this form of art.

Persian miniature paintings are now deservedly famous throughout the world. Although few are miniature portraits in the western sense of the word, the best examples do display great intricacy and attention to detail. Favourite themes include courting couples in traditional dress, polo matches and hunting scenes. Some of the best modern miniatures come from Esfahān. Not many great examples can be found in museums in Iran, and most early works are housed in museums and private collections in Britain.

Metalwork

Much of the early metalwork in Persia had military purposes, but during the Achaemenian (559-330 BC) and Sassanian (224-637 AD) periods, metalwork began to develop for domestic and ornamental purposes. With influences from Turkey and China, engraved Persian metal products, mainly made from copper and bronze, were soon sought by affluent Europeans and Chinese. Gold and silver have traditionally been an indulgence of royalty and the very rich; some beautiful works have been excavated around the former ancient capital of Hamadān.

Traditionally, trays, dishes, tea-services, bowls and jewellery are the most common items. The National Museum of Iran in Tehrān has the best collection of metalwork from Iran; the collection of silverware, some of which dates to the Sassanian period, is particularly stunning.

Glassware

Excavations in Rey, near Tehrān, and at Neishābūr, near Mashhad, reveal ancient

16th century cat-shaped Persian bottle

glassware, and evidence of unique, Persian glass-making traditions, dating back about 4000 years. The best places to see examples of Persian glassware is the Glass & Ceramics Museum in Tehrān, though many museums throughout Iran boast a few fine specimens of glassware, as well as ceramics and porcelain.

Woodwork

One of the most intricate styles of woodwork is *moarraq*, or marquetry. Initially influenced by artisans from India, a particular Persian style of marquetry developed through the centuries. A number of woods are often used, such as betel, walnut, cypress and pine, with the inlaid pieces made from animal bones, shells, bronze, silver and gold. Genuine Persian moarraq contains no paints; the colours come from the inlaid pieces.

Designs are often religious, but some simply show a number of animals or birds. The designs are traced on paper, and then pasted to a piece of plywood. The design is then completed with the particular wood; the inlaid bits and pieces are included; and the final product is then coated with varnish. Moarraq can be made into furniture, bookcases, wall-hangings and, often, boxes for ornamental or domestic purposes.

SOCIETY & CONDUCT

If you observe the same simple courtesies as you would in western societies, and keep within Iranian law and customs, you will be doing more than many modern-day foreign travellers in Islamic countries, and be respected by the vast majority of Iranians with whom you come into contact. At the same time, there are inevitably different ways of doing things in a country with such an ancient civilisation as Iran's. Iranian etiquette is complex and Iranians are usually very forgiving of innocent gaffes by foreigners, but the rewards for learning the rules will more than repay the initial investment in time and effort.

Iranians are, generally, highly hospitable to foreigners – almost embarrassingly so sometimes – but you do have to do your bit. The theory is that anyone for whom you do a favour has a duty to do another for you at some later date. Of course in practical terms there is no way that foreigners can repay in kind all the Iranians who give them a meal, hospitality or accommodation, but the principle remains. One simple way of showing gratitude is to respect the Iranian social code in your dealings with Iranians.

It is always important to travel responsibly anywhere, including Iran; ie travellers should minimise their impact on the environment, respect the people, and make every effort to understand their culture, traditions and religion. You can easily do your bit by disposing of rubbish properly, especially in the countryside; asking permission before pushing your way into any particularly holy mosques, for example; choosing products made by, and tours run by, Iranians, rather than foreigners; and showing an interest in the Iranian way of life.

Dos & Don'ts

The following is only a short selection of tips.

- Always be punctual for appointments, but don't expect Iranians to turn up on time – rules are different for foreigners and Iranians. Adjust yourself to the Iranian sense of time and expect the occasional delay: be patient and build them into your itinerary.
- Never get straight to the point when dealing with Iranians. Accept or offer up to three cups of tea before getting down to serious business of any kind. Expect any preliminary conversation to be confined to inquiries after each other's health and other small talk.
- It is the Iranian custom for friends to exchange presents when arriving or leaving. Bringing a few, cheap souvenirs from home is a great idea. If you have no suitable present to offer, a dinner invitation won't cost you much but it will mean a lot to your hosts.
- Never accept a present or service of any kind without first politely refusing twice. The same applies in reverse if you are offering something to an Iranian.
- Be extremely wary of making comments to strangers that may incriminate yourself or another person, even if innocuously intended or made in a joking way. Never underestimate the ruthlessness or strength of the Komīté (religious police) and its network of informers. Don't be the first to open a discussion of politics with a stranger. Remember that your views may appear to be just as extremist to some Iranians as theirs do to you.
- Never sit next to a member of the opposite sex who is not your spouse or a close relative, unless specifically invited to do so, even if there is no other spare seat (except in a shared taxi or on an aeroplane).
- Respect the Iranian dress code rigorously at all times.
- Always remove your shoes when visiting a mosque or other Islamic religious building, or on entering a private house, unless you're specifically invited to keep them on. You may be offered indoor slippers.
- Most private houses have a pair of sandals by the entrance to the lavatory, which should be exchanged for any indoor slippers on entering and leaving and not taken into the rest of the house.
- Never turn your back on anyone; point the sole of your shoe or foot at anyone; or walk in front of someone praying to Mecca. If you do so inadvertently or unavoidably, excuse yourself by saying *bebakhshīd*.

- Rather than say 'no' outright and risk causing offence, Iranians will use any number of circumlocutions and diplomatic half-promises. These can easily be misunderstood by a foreigner. Frankness and conciseness are not attributes very highly regarded by most Iranians.
- Don't shake hands or make any physical contact in public with a member of the opposite sex. Kissing or holding hands in public are only acceptable between members of the same sex, and are not signs of homosexuality (which is highly illegal in Iran, anyway).
- When making a personal compliment to or about someone, eg when telling a mother how handsome her child is, always say *māshallāh* (God has willed it) for fear of invoking divine nemesis. The idea is that all beauty and goodness are the gifts of God and can be taken away by Him at any time.
- Don't be afraid to accept invitations from Iranians (except from any Iranian male to any foreign woman; unless the woman understands the probable implications of the acceptance). Iranians have always entertained predominantly at home and you will never understand Iran if you don't make an effort to meet Iranians on their own terms.
- Finally, don't expect to be told when you have broken one of the many unwritten laws of Iranian etiquette. It is worth explaining to friends that you are a novice in Iranian ways and would appreciate guidance.

There are some taboo subjects for conversation: crusading attempts on behalf of feminism, atheism, Zionism or free love will usually prove spectacularly unsuccessful. It is an offence to criticise any of the āyatollāhs, or especially to defame any of the prophets of Islam. In Iran you have to be more careful than in most countries about what you say and in whose company you say it. On the other hand, money, religion (but nothing anti-Islam) and even sex (but nothing pornographic) are all favourite subjects at the dinner table and elsewhere. In Iran, it is not generally considered rude to ask questions about a person's salary, standard of living or marital status. 'Are you married?' and 'How many children do you have?' are standard ice-breakers. 'Where are you from?' is the standard opening for almost every conversation initiated by an Iranian; you will hear the question (in English or Fārsī) so often, it will send you batty after a few weeks.

Dress

The Iranian dress code is not only inspired by Quranic commands and reinforced by social custom, but also rigidly reinforced by law, so flouting the rules is more than just bad manners. Men must wear full, loose trousers; never shorts (except when swimming at a segregated beach, or playing official sports). These days, loose short-sleeve shirts, or T-shirts (but never singlets), are quite acceptable, but long-sleeved shirts are better when visiting homes, mosques or government offices.

Refer to the Women Travellers section in the Facts for the Visitor chapter for vital information about what women must wear in Iran.

Laws on dress are more strictly enforced during Ramazān when Iranians, never the most colourful of dressers at the best of times, avoid reds and any other bright colours. Colours are also subdued during Moharram, the month of mourning. (Refer to Public Holidays & Special Events in the Facts for the Visitor chapter for more details.) Be particularly careful about what you wear when dealing with officialdom, eg crossing borders and applying for visa

The *chādor*, which literally means 'tent', upholds the Islamic code of decency.

extensions; entering a mosque or anywhere religious; and visiting a home of an Iranian.

Iran must have one of the highest proportions of men with beards or moustaches of any country in the world, though it is often difficult to distinguish between an attempt at a full beard and what is merely a bad shave. Beards or moustaches are the height of respectability in Iran, so foreign men need not bother packing any shaving gear (or they can get an occasional shave in a local barber). For some reason, ties are seen as an unwelcome symbol of western cultural imperialism (but you are unlikely to be packing one of these anyway).

Visiting Mosques

Only at the Hazrat-é Masumeh, the shrine of Fātemé at Ghom, is entry by non-Muslims completely forbidden, but otherwise most mosques will allow infidels (nonbelievers) to visit – except during services on Friday, and any time on mourning days. Some mosques have restrictions about photography anywhere near or outside the mosque; and you can *never* take photos inside a functioning mosque. Only at the Āstān-é Ghods-é Razavī, a very holy shrine in Mashhad, will a non-Muslim probably need a Muslim guide.

Always take your shoes off at the doorstep of a mosque (and make sure your feet and/or socks are clean). At larger mosques, there is often an attendant or someone who looks after the shoes of visitors, and you could ask him for permission to enter, making it clear that you are not a Muslim. Some historic mosques, and other Islamic buildings, no longer ordinarily function as such, but have been made into museums or simply abandoned. At a few there is a nominal entrance fee, though some have now become blatant tourist attractions which charge foreigners a blatant tourist price.

RELIGION

The Islamic Republic of Iran is, of course, overwhelmingly Muslim, and Islam is the state religion. Iran follows the Shi'ite sect of Islam rather than the more common Sunni

sect followed in other Islamic countries. According to official statistics, 98.8% of the population follow Islam, of which 91% follow the Shi'ite sect. The figures for the minorities – Christians (0.7%), Jews (0.3%), Zoroastrians (0.1%), with another 0.1% comprising of religions such as Sikhism and Buddhism – are probably underestimated as many call themselves Muslims in official documents. You should never tell an Iranian that you do not have a religion; if you are an atheist, or agnostic, temporarily accept a religion for the length of your trip to Iran. Muslim Iranians are happy to accept that you are a Christian, but avoid telling anyone the truth if you follow Judaism or are Jewish (though there are a handful of Jews in Iran). If you are a religious convert, be discreet about it; people who have changed their religion to anything other than Islam are viewed with suspicion.

The recognised non-Muslim minorities pose little threat to the Iranian government. In return for their acquiescence they are granted certain concessions, and in matters of moral laws they are allowed to be tried by their own religious leaders, who have absolute discretion over any decision. Religions or churches that seek to convert Muslims are not tolerated. The 250,000-odd Baha'is (a religion founded last century in Iran, which sees itself as a purified Islam) have not had their faith recognised by the authorities and keep a very low profile. Many Baha'is have emigrated since the Revolution.

Islam

Muslims believe the religion preached by the Prophet Mohammed to be God's final revelation to humanity. For them, the Quran, God's Word revealed through the Prophet, supplements and completes the earlier revelations around which the Christian and Jewish faiths were built, and corrects human misinterpretations of those earlier revelations. For example, Muslims believe that Jesus was a prophet second only to Mohammed in importance, but that his followers later introduced into Christianity the heretical idea that Jesus was the son of God. Adam,

Abraham, Moses and a number of other Christian and Jewish holy men are regarded as prophets by Muslims. Mohammed, however, was the 'Seal of the Prophets' – the last who has, or will, come.

The Faith The essence of Islam is the belief that there is only one God, and that it is the people's duty to believe in, and serve, Him in the manner which He has laid out in the Quran. In Arabic, *islam* means submission and a *muslim* is one who submits to God's will.

In the first instance, one does this by observing the five pillars of the faith:

1. **The profession of faith (shahadah).** To become a Muslim one need only state the Islamic creed: 'There is no God but God, and Mohammed is the messenger of God' – but with conviction.

2. **Prayer (salat).** Muslims are required to pray five times every day: at dawn, noon, mid-afternoon, sunset and about 90 minutes after sunset. Prayers follow a set ritual pattern which varies slightly depending on the time of the day. During prayers, a Muslim must perform a series of prostrations while facing in the direction of the Kaaba – the ancient shrine at the centre of the Grand Mosque in Mecca. Before a Muslim can pray, however, they must perform a series of ritual ablutions, and if no water is available for this purpose, sand or dirt may be substituted.

3. **Charity or Alms (zakat).** Muslims must give a portion of their income to help those poorer than themselves. How this has operated in practice has varied over the centuries; either it was seen as an individual duty or the state collected zakat as a form of income tax to be redistributed through mosques or religious charities.

4. **Fasting (sawm).** It was during the month of Ramazān that Mohammed received his first revelation in 610 AD. Muslims mark this event by fasting from sunrise until sunset through Ramazān each year. (See Public Holidays & Special Events in the Facts for the Visitor chapter for more details.)

5. **Pilgrimage (hajj).** All Muslims who are able to do so are required to make the pilgrimage to Mecca at least once during their lifetime. However, the pilgrimage must be performed during a specific few days in the first and second weeks of the Muslim month of Zū-l-Hejjé. Visiting Mecca and performing the prescribed rituals at any other time of the year is considered spiritually desirable, but it is not hajj. Such visits are referred to as *umrah* or 'little pilgrimage'.

Beyond the five pillars of Islam, there are many other duties incumbent on Muslims. In the west, the best known, and least understood, of these is *jihad*. This word is usually translated into English as 'holy war', but it literally means 'striving in the way of the faith'. Exactly what this means has been subject of keen debate among Muslim scholars for the last 1400 years. Some scholars have tended to see jihad in spiritual, as opposed to martial, terms.

Muslims are forbidden to eat or drink anything containing pork, alcohol, blood or the meat of any animal which died of natural causes (as opposed to being slaughtered in the prescribed manner). Muslim women may not marry non-Muslim men, though Muslim men are permitted to marry Christian or Jewish women (but not, for example, Hindus or Buddhists).

The Law The Arabic word *shari'a* is usually translated as 'Islamic Law'. This is misleading. The sharia is not a legal code in the western sense of the term. It refers to the general body of Islamic legal thought. At the base of this lies the Quran itself, which Muslims believe to be the actual speech of God, revealed to humankind through Mohammed. Where the Quran does not provide guidance on a particular subject, Muslim scholars turn to the *Sunnah*, a body of works recording the sayings and doings of the Prophet and, to a lesser extent, his companions as reported by a string of scholarly authorities. There are many Sunnah authorities and their reliability is determined by the school of Islamic jurisprudence to which one subscribes. There are four main Sunni, and two principal Shi'ite, schools of Islamic jurisprudence.

The Quran and Sunnah together make up the sharia. In some instances, the sharia is quite specific, such as in the areas of inheritance law and the punishments for certain offences. In many other cases it acts as a series of guidelines. Islam does not recognise a distinction between the secular and religious lives of believers. Thus, a learned scholar or judge can with enough research and if necessary, through use of analogy, determine the proper 'Islamic' position on, or approach to, any problem.

Sunnis & Shi'ites The schism that divided the Muslim world into two broad camps took place only a few years after the death of the Prophet. When Mohammed died, in 632 AD, he left no clear instructions either designating a successor as leader of the Muslim community or setting up a system by which subsequent leaders could be chosen. Some felt that leadership of the community should remain with the Prophet's family, and supported the claim of Ali Bin Abi Taleb, Mohammed's cousin and son-in-law and one of the first converts to Islam, to become the *khalif* (caliph), or leader. But the community initially chose Abu Bakr, the Prophet's closest companion, as leader, and Ali was also passed over in two subsequent leadership contests.

Those who took Ali's side in these disputes became known as the 'Shi'a', or 'Partisans (of Ali)'. Ali eventually became caliph, the fourth of Mohammed's successors, in 656, but was assassinated five years later by troops loyal to the Governor of Syria, Mu'awiyah Bin Abu Sufyan, a distant relative of the Prophet who subsequently set himself up as caliph.

This split the Muslim community into two competing factions. The Sunnis favoured the Umayyads, the dynasty which was established by Mu'awiyah. As it developed over the succeeding generations, Sunni doctrine emphasises the position of the caliph as both the spiritual head of the Muslim community, and the temporal ruler of the state in which that community existed. Sunni belief essentially holds that any Muslim who rules with justice, and according to the sharia, deserves the support of the Muslim community as a whole.

Shi'ites, on the other hand, believed that the descendant of the Prophet through Ali's line should lead the Muslims. Because Shi'ites have rarely held temporal power their doctrine came to emphasise the spiritual position of their leaders, the *emāms*.

The split widened and became permanent when Ali's son Hussein was killed in brutal circumstances at Karbala (now in southern Iraq) in 680. Over the centuries, Sunnism has developed into the 'orthodox' strain of Islam; and most of the Muslims in the world are Sunnis – except in Iran, where the overwhelming majority are Shi'ite.

Christianity

Christianity thrived in Iran long before the introduction of Islam, and some of its first saints were martyred in Persia. The majority of Christians in Iran are Armenians, who first settled at Jolfā on Iran's northern border, then were moved on to 'New Jolfā' in Esfahān by Shāh Abbās I. They are respected for their business skills and powers of organisation.

There are smaller communities of Protestants, Roman Catholics, Chaldeans (Catholic Rite), Orthodox, Adventists, Nestorians and others. The Episcopal Church of Iran (part of the Anglican Communion) has churches in Tehrān, Esfahān, Shīrāz and Kermān, all of which welcome fellow Christians. The largest communities are in Orūmīyé, Tabrīz, Tehrān (in particular the neigh-bourhood around Nejātollāhī Ave), Esfahān (especially in the suburb of Jolfā), Shīrāz and the Āzarbāyjān provinces.

There are churches in almost every large Iranian town, but they are often rather difficult to find. Many are not marked on maps, even in Fārsī, and most are hidden behind high walls and are almost unidentifiable from the street.

As a general rule, Muslims do not visit non-Islamic religious buildings and their

The Persian cross is an ancient Christian symbol often seen in Iranian churches.

knowledge of other religions is as scant as most westerners' knowledge of Islam.

Zoroastrianism

Zoroastrianism is an ancient religion which was once the state creed, but faded away after the Arab Conquest (from 637). At one stage Zoroastrianism stretched all the way to the Mediterranean, only to be pushed back by Christianity from the west and Buddhism from the east, before Islam flooded all three. Today, Zoroastrians are found mainly in Yazd (their traditional centre), Shīrāz, Kermān, Tehrān and Esfahān.

Though Zoroastrians are now very few in number in their place of origin, some of their customs and beliefs are firmly entrenched in Iranian life. Their symbolism is an important part of Iranian art, and many aspects of their faith have a certain appeal to Iranian Muslims. Many of the most famous pre-Islamic monuments in Iran have clear Zoroastrian symbols. Refer to the boxed text 'Zoroastrianism' in the Central Iran chapter for more details.

Judaism

The Jewish population has fallen sharply since the Islamic Revolution, though there are still some significant communities in Hamadān, Tehrān, Shīrāz and Esfahān, where they are active in the bazaar and the jewellery trade. There is even a synagogue in Hamadān, and a mosque dedicated to a Jewish prophet in Shūsh.

LANGUAGE

The national language of Iran is Persian, also known as Fārsī, an Indo-European language. The other main regional languages are Turkish, Āzarī, Kurdish, Arabic and Lorī (spoken by the Lors); and there are dozens of other tongues throughout the 26 provinces, such as Gīlākī (spoken in Gīlān), Balūchī (in Sīstān va Balūchestān) and Turkmen (in Khorāsān).

The Arabic script was adapted to Persian after the introduction of Islam, but there is no standard method of transliterating Persian into English so that English speakers can pronounce it. The transliteration system used in this book (and explained in the Persian Language Guide at the end of this book) is designed to give a good indication of how colloquial Persian is pronounced. Classical Persian, which an Iranian would use for reading a speech or writing a book, is not the language of everyday speech.

English is understood by some educated middle-class men and women in the major cities, most employees of middle and top-end restaurants and hotels, and just about everyone working at a travel agency and airline office. Thankfully, just about every village, town and city, and most streets and squares within the towns and cities (but not the smaller villages), are named, and signed, in English. However, if you are travelling independently, and using budget accommodation and restaurants, you cannot rely entirely on English, so you should learn a few basic phrases and sentences in Fārsī. At the very least try to recognise the Arabic numerals used in Iran (and, if possible, say them in Fārsī), to help you identify prices, bus and train numbers, and addresses. Almost every Iranian with whom you will do business will know the 'English' numerals, so a pocket calculator is very handy for 'discussing' prices.

Refer to the Persian Language Guide at the back of this guidebook for an overview of important Fārsī words and phrases, transliterated into English, and written in the Persian script.

Persian Architecture

Persian architecture has a very long and complex history, and is often regarded as the field in which Persia made its greatest contribution to the world's culture. Although Persian styles differ sharply from any other Islamic architectural tradition, they have strongly influenced building throughout much of the Islamic world, especially in Central Asia, Afghanistan, Pakistan and India.

The two important religious influences are Zoroastrianism, dominant before the Arab Conquest of 637 AD, and the subsequent introduction of Islam. Most of the greatest buildings were built with a religious purpose, and even in secular buildings religious influences are rarely entirely absent – even Persian churches often incorporate Islamic features.

What makes Persian architecture different?

If there is one defining aspect of Persian architecture, it's a monumental simplicity combined with lavish use of surface ornamentation and colour. The ground plans of Persian buildings are typically very simple affairs mixing only a few standard elements – usually a courtyard and arcades, rectangular entrance porticoes and *eivāns* (rectangular, barrel-vaulted halls opening onto the courtyard).

The typical Persian mosque design evolved from a standard model based on the design of the Prophet Mohammed's house in Medina. It comprises an entrance eivān which leads into a large courtyard surrounded by arched cloisters. Behind these are inner eivāns, one of them featuring a *mehrāb*, a decorated niche indicating the direction of Mecca, the focal point of the interior of the mosque.

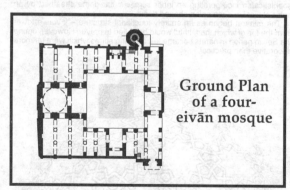

Ground Plan of a four-eivān mosque

These basic building blocks are then covered with an amazing density of decoration which leads the observor to imagine that the architecture is far more complex than it actually is. Since the depiction of religious figures is not part of the Islamic artistic tradition, the decorations are geometric, floral or calligraphic. Mosaics forming the single word 'Allāh', repeated hundreds of times in a highly stylised script, may alone make up the decoration of a wall. Often they are so closely moulded into the design that they appear to be an intrinsic part of the structure. The colours need to be bright and bold because the sunlight is often extremely harsh.

Top Left: Colourful patterns of mosiacs are a theme of Persian decoration (photograph by Gadi Farfour).

Above: Every mosque has a mehrāb – a niche in the wall facing Mecca.

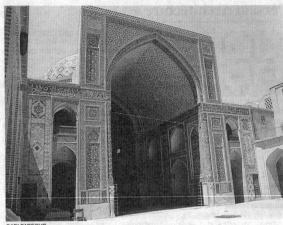

GADI FARFOUR

Domes & Minarets

The development of the dome is one of the greatest achievements of Persian architects. The Sassanians (224-637) were the first to discover a satisfactory way of building a dome on top of a square chamber by using two intermediate levels, the lower octagonal and the higher 16-sided, on which the dome could rest – known as a squinch. Later domes became progressively more sophisticated incorporating an inner semi-circular dome sheathed by an outer conical or even onion-shaped dome.

The minaret began as an entirely functional structure – it was a tower from the top of which the faithful would be called to prayer. However, during the Seljuq period minarets became tall, tapering spires which were far more decorative than practical.

Top: The vaulted eivān or hall of this mosque recalls the Prophet Mohammed's house in Medina.

Bottom: While the Sassanians pioneered dome-building in Persia, the Islamic era up until the 15th century saw the artistic apogee of the dome, covering them in bright geometric patterns and Quranic calligraphy.

*Top: Intricate mould-
ings in the eivān of
Esfahān's Masjed-é
Emām.*

*Bottom: A striking
bulbous dome adorns
the shrine of Alī Ebn-é
Hamzé, Shīrāz.*

DAVID ST VINCENT

Top: Iran's holiest shrine,
the Astan-é Ghods-é
Razavī in Mashhad.

Bottom: Detail of the
eivān mouldings from
the Masjed-é Jame'-yé
Atīgh, Shīrāz.

GADI FARFOUR

ANDREW HUMPHREYS

ANDREW HUMPHREYS

Historical Summary

Before the 7th Century BC The only substantial remains are those of the remarkable Elamite ziggurat (a tiered temple) at Choghā Zambīl. The earliest building material was sun-dried mud brick. Baked brick was used for outer surfaces by the 12th century BC. The ancient inhabitants of Persia imbued the mountains with great religious symbolism, and structures were built in imitation of mountains, giving rise to the characteristic pyramidal ziggurats – particularly in remote and flat regions, like Choghā Zambīl.

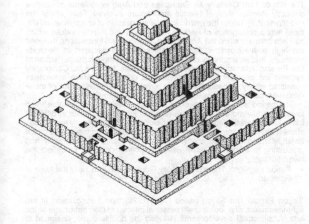

Top Left: The startling shape of the Shīrāz shrine shows the Persian mastery of dome construction.

Top Right: The great portal of the Masjed-é Jāme' in Yazd.

Left: The Choghā Zambīl ziggurat functioned as a temple in the form of a sacred mountain, towering over the flat Mesopotamian plain.

Until the Arab Conquest The surviving sites from the Achaemenian Period (559-330 BC) include the magnificent ceremonial palace complexes and royal tombs at Pasargadae, Shūsh, Persepolis and Naghsh-é Rostam. They are decorated with bas-relief figures of kings, soldiers, supplicants, animals and the winged figure of the Zoroastrian deity, Ahura Mazda.

Remains from the Achaemenian Period show links with the earlier ziggurat in both shape and decoration. The Achaemenian style also incorporated features based on Egyptian or Greek models. Colossal halls were supported by stone and wooden columns with typically Persian bull's-head capitals. Materials were imported from throughout Persia and beyond, but the usual building materials were sun-dried brick and stone.

Alexander the Great's conquest (in 331 BC) brought a virtual end to the Achaemenian style in Persia. The following relatively dormant period under the Seleucids (until 190 BC) marked the introduction of Hellenism to Persia. No great examples remain today, though the Temple of Artemis at Kangāvar (near Kermānshāh), with Greek capitals and built to honour a Greek goddess, is the best preserved. Under the Parthians (190 BC-224 AD), Hellenism and indigenous styles merged, along with some Roman and Byzantine influences, and several characteristically Persian features arose, including the eivān.

In the Sassanian period, buildings became larger, heavier and more complex. The four-eivān plan with domed square chambers became increasingly common. Decoration became more adventurous and more use was made of colour, especially in frescoes and mosaics. The Sassanians built fire-temples throughout their empire, and the simple plan of the earliest examples was retained throughout the pre-Islamic era, even in the design of churches.

Arab Period The Arab Conquest did not supplant the well-developed Sassanian style, but it did introduce the Islamic element which had such a pervasive impact on the Persian arts. Not only did the Arab Period (637-1050) shape the nature and basic architectural plan of religious buildings but it also defined the type of decoration – no human representation, however stylised, was permitted, and ceremonial tombs or monuments to individuals were also out of favour. Instead of grand palace complexes built as symbols of royal majesty, there came mosques designed as focal points for the social life of ordinary people.

The 9th to 11th Century As Sassanian and Arab ingredients merged, a distinctly Persian style of Islamic architecture evolved. From about the mid-9th century, under the patronage of a succession of enlightened rulers, there was a resurgence of Persian nationalism and Persian values which had lain dormant since the Arab Period. Architectural innovations included the high pointed arch, stalactites (rib-like mouldings used to decorate recesses) and an emphasis on balance and scale, though the perfection of the Persian Islamic style took many centuries to achieve. Calligraphy became the principal form of architectural decoration, which sometimes consisted wholly of inscriptions. Little remains of the architecture of these dynasties, but one good example is the Masjed-é Jāme' at Nā'īn.

The period also marks the emergence of a series of remarkable tomb towers, usually more secular than religious in purpose, which in different forms lasted until the late 15th century. Built of brick and usually round, they show a development of ornamentation progressing from the simple to the lavish, starting with little more than a single garter of calligraphy and graduating to elaborate basket-weave brickwork designed to deflect the harsh sunlight.

- Period Highlight: The extraordinary Gombad-é Kāvūs near the town of Gombad.

Seljuq Period The Seljuq period (1051-1220) saw a succession of enlightened rulers who took a great personal interest in their patronage of the arts. Architectural developments included the double dome, designed to achieve the best visual impact from both interior and exterior, a widening of vaults, improvement of the squinch and refinement of glazed tilework,

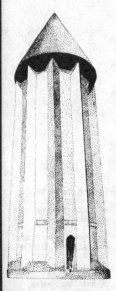

The Gomad-é Kāvūs tomb tower, 55m-high and built entirely of brick.

especially in mehrābs. A meticulous unity of structure and decoration was attempted for the first time, based on rigorous mathematical principles. Stucco, incorporating arabesques and Persian styles of calligraphy, was increasingly used to enhance brick surfaces.

- Period Highlight: The original part of the Masjed-é Jāme' in Esfahān.

Mongol Period Although traditionally seen by Iranians as a dark age in their history, the Mongol period (1220-1380) did add much to the development of Persian architecture. The conquest of Persia by Chinggis Khaan, and his rampaging hordes, was at first purely destructive, and many Persian architects fled the country. The Mongol style, designed to overawe the viewer, was marked by towering entrance portals, colossal domes, and vaults reaching into the skies. It also saw a refinement of tiling, often based on geometric and floral lines, and calligraphy, often in the formal angular Kufic script imported from Arabia. Increasing attention was paid to the interior decoration of domes, which were more closely moulded into the whole design.

- Period Highlight: The most magnificent surviving Mongol structure is the tower at Soltānīyé, near Zanjān.

Timurid Period The Timurid period (1380-1502) marks a refinement of Seljuq and Mongol styles. The period features an exuberance of colour and a greater harmony of structure and decoration. Even in buildings of colossal scale, the monotony of large empty surfaces was avoided by the use of translucent tiling. Arcaded cloisters around inner courtyards, open galleries, and arches within arches were notable developments.

- Period Highlight: The best surviving examples of Timurid architecture inside Iran are the remarkable Masjed-é Azīm-é Gōhar Shād in Mashhad, and the Masjed-é Kabūd in Tabrīz.

Safavid Period This period (1502-1722) was a comparatively stable and prosperous time, and a succession of enlightened and cultivated rulers, most notably Shāh Abbās I, saw the final refinement of styles which marks the culmination of the Persian Islamic style of architecture. Its greatest expression is Shāh Abbās I's royal capital of Esfahān, a supreme example of town planning, with one of the most magnificent collections of buildings from one period anywhere in the Islamic world. At its centre is the vast Meidūn-é Emām Khomeinī, still one of the world's largest squares, with the superb Masjed-é Emām as its focal point. There are other fine examples of Safavid architecture at Ghazvīn, while the Holy Shrine of Emām Rezā at Mashhad gained much of its present magnificence in Safavid times.

The death of Shāh Abbās I in 1629 marked the beginning of the end for the golden age of Persian architecture. The Madrasé-yé Chahār Bāgh, in Esfahān, is an outstanding architectural work for its period, but it and other buildings of the late Safavid period are really little more than a swan song.

- Period Highlight: Esfahān's Masjed-é Emām.

Andrew Humphreys

Facts for the Visitor

PLANNING
When to Go
Generally the best times to visit are mid-April to early June, and late September to early November – this avoids the long, cold winter (except in the south, where there is no winter to speak of), the Iranian New Year or Nō Rūz (on about 21 March) and the summer, which can be unpleasant in much of the country. The school holidays run for about two weeks after the Iranian New Year; and from about 20 May (in the south) or, elsewhere, from about 5 June, and finish on about 6 September. However, even in the popular Caspian provinces, the school holidays will have little effect on your travel plans.

The most agreeable time to visit the southern coast is in winter, and the north-west and north-east are at their best between late spring and early summer, and between late summer and early autumn. The Gulf coast is horrible in summer. For more specific information, see the Climate section in the Facts about Iran chapter.

Many people prefer not to visit Iran (or any Islamic country) during Ramazān, the Muslim month of fasting, but other than most restaurants closing between dawn and dusk, Ramazān is not that bad for travelling. (Refer to Public Holidays & Special Events later in this chapter for more details.)

What Kind of Trip?
Most people have little more than two weeks at their disposal. If time is short, but the pockets are deep, consider taking advantage of the extensive network of very cheap and frequent flights, so you won't waste precious daylight hours looking out the window of a bus driving across boring empty desert. Alternatively, you could base yourself somewhere like Tehrān, Rasht, Shīrāz or Esfahān, from where you can take short trips, without the drawbacks of long-distance travelling.

Travelling independently anywhere around Iran is perfectly feasible for anyone who accepts that travel can be long and boring at times (unless you fly); the food is occasionally monotonous; the evenings can really drag for lack of entertainment; and communication with locals is often limited because of the language barrier. Being part of an organised tour will alleviate most of these frustrations, but it is, of course, less flexible, and far more expensive. One disadvantage to travelling alone is that single rooms are rare, so you will often have to fork out for a twin or double room. Females may feel more comfortable travelling in a group or with a male, but no foreign female should have any problems as long as they are dressed appropriately (see Women Travellers later in this chapter).

Maps
The maps of the provinces and cities in this guidebook should satisfy most travellers, though a more detailed map of Iran (in English) is a good idea. If you are planning a lot of travelling, you can complement an English-language map of Iran with another in Fārsī and English.

A city map or two, especially somewhere chaotic like Tehrān (refer to Maps in the Tehrān chapter for details), is a good idea if you are spending a while in one particular city, or driving.

The undisputed king of map-making in Iran is Gita Shenasi. This company publishes an impressive array of maps covering all major cities in Iran, the whole country and individual neighbouring countries. The older city maps with the red frames list the names of the streets, suburbs and squares in English, but everything else, including text and indexes, are in Fārsī.

You can buy Gita Shenasi maps at a few bookshops and bookstalls throughout the country, but often supplies are limited. In

Rasht, for example, no maps of Rasht are available, but you will find lots of maps of Mashhad and Shīrāz. If you going to be staying for some time in one particular city or province, and the maps in this guidebook aren't sufficient, visit the office of Gita Shenasi (which has one of those typically confusing Iranian addresses): 15 Ostad Shahrīvar St, Razī St, Valī-yé Asr Crossroads, Enghelāb Ave; PO Box 14155/3441 (☎ (21) 679 335; fax 675 782).

The Ministry of Culture & Islamic Guidance also publishes maps of some provinces, but these are not much good because a lot of the text is in Fārsī, and the detail is only useful if you are trekking in the countryside.

The *General Map of Iran* (1:1,000,000), published in English by Gita Shenasi and available in Iran, is probably the best of the lot, and will satisfy most visitors. Anyone interested in carpets, may want to pick up the *Iran Carpet* map (10,000 rials) from Gita Shenasi, though it's of little general use. Train buffs will want to buy Gita Shenasi's *General Map of Railways: Islamic Republic of Iran & Its Corridors* (10,000 rials), which shows the rail system in Iran and neighbouring countries, and includes a history and table of distances in English and Fārsī. The excellent map put out by the upmarket AITO company (refer to Organised Tours in the Getting Around chapter) is pretty, details all major attractions in the country and includes a kilometre chart.

The best dual-language map (in Fārsī and English) is the *Tourist Map of the Islamic Republic of Iran* (1:2,500,000), published by the Ministry of Culture & Islamic Guidance. Available in some tourist offices and bookshops in Iran, this map clearly marks all the main and secondary roads, railway lines, distances between main towns, and petrol stations; the only disadvantage is that it doesn't show provincial boundaries.

The Bartholomew map (1:2,500,000) of Iran is still available in some countries, but the best English-language map available outside the country is *Iran* (1:2,000,000), part of the GeoCenter's World Country Map series. It is a little dated (eg it does not show

new provincial boundaries) but otherwise it's excellent, and certainly worth buying before you leave home. Serious trekkers and mountain climbers should pick up the relevant TPC or ONC topographical maps published by the Defense Mapping Agency Aerospace Center in the USA.

What to Bring

In the past, the backpack has had bad connotations in Iran, but these days you are more likely to be the object of giggling from school kids (who think backpacks are ungainly) than anything else. Hotels are usually happy to hold luggage for guests, even for several weeks, and some train stations have luggage lockers. Surplus gear, and souvenirs bought along the way, can always be posted safely and cheaply out of Iran.

Here are a few things to consider taking:

A universal sink plug; favourite cosmetic or personal items (basic things like soap and toothpaste are cheap and easy to find); lip balm (the very dry weather can wreck your kissing gear); shaving kit (though you can get a shave at any barber, and beards are fashionable anyway); camera and film (print film is widely available, though), with a robust carrying case including a bag of silica gel to protect the camera from changes in temperature and humidity; tubes of detergent and a scrubbing brush, together with a length of cord or string for a makeshift washing-line; at least six colour passport photos; photocopies of the first few pages of your passport (keep another copy at home); address and telephone number of your embassy in Tehrān (try to memorise the telephone number); address book; notebook; short-wave radio; Swiss Army knife; compass; toilet paper, if you can't adjust to local customs; torch (flashlight); longlife candles and matches for occasional power cuts; water container; small presents from home for Iranian friends (chosen more for novelty than monetary value); money belt; sewing kit with spare shoelaces and buttons; a medical kit (see the Health section); and several large and interesting books, as an alternative to the less than frenzied Iranian nightlife.

Clothing The following is only a rough guide; read the Climate section in the Facts about Iran chapter before considering what clothes to bring. For essential advice on what is considered acceptable clothing in Iran, refer to the Society & Conduct section in the Facts about Iran chapter, and the Women Travellers section later in this chapter.

In summer, take lightweight and easily washable clothes of natural fabrics, a cardigan or pullover for the cooler nights, a pair of sunglasses and a hat which will protect your face from the sun. (Women can wear a hat over their headscarf or chādor – it may look unfashionable, but it beats the hell out of being burnt to a crisp.)

In winter, take mostly warm clothing, including a coat, scarf and hat, and two or three thin sweaters rather than one thick one and, if you're likely to need them, boots or shoes equipped to cope with heavy snow and slippery pavements. In spring and autumn you should aim for a sensible compromise, according to the conditions in the places you are going to visit. An umbrella is useful at any time.

Iranians of both sexes often wear sandals or flip-flops (thongs) around their home or hotel room, but foreigners should not wear uncovered shoes outside of their rooms. Good walking shoes are best.

SUGGESTED ITINERARIES

What kind of trip you take obviously depends on the amount of time you have (or been given on your visa); your budget; your particular interests; how you travel; and how you enter and exit Iran. Many visitors travel overland between Turkey and Pakistan (or Turkmenistan), and luckily a lot of what you should see is along the main road between Pakistan and Tehrān, with a detour to Shīrāz.

One Week

It is best to restrict yourself to two or three main towns; and you don't want to spend precious time on a bus or train, so fly. Base yourself in and around Tehrān (two days), Esfahān (two) and Shīrāz and surrounds (three). While you could travel across Iran by bus and train between Pakistan and Turkey in one week, you will spend almost all of your time travelling, and seeing nothing of the country. If you have a transit visa for seven days or less, get an extension as soon as you can.

Two Weeks

Most travellers can get a visa (and an extension) totalling two weeks (or longer). If you have the funds you can see more, or stay longer at some places, by flying. (The number of days listed below include travelling time by bus or train.)

The best itinerary should be based along the lines of Bam (one day), Kermān (two), Yazd (two), Esfahān (two) and Shīrāz and surrounds (three). If you are flying in or out of Tehrān, you can then spend the remaining few days in Kāshān (two days), and in and around Tehrān (two). If you are travelling overland towards the Turkish border, you could then go quickly via Kāshān (one), Hamadān (one), Takht-é Soleimān (one) and Orūmīyé or Tabrīz (one).

In winter, avoid the cold weather and fly to the Persian Gulf area, though many Iranians will be doing the same: therefore, accommodation and transport can be hard to arrange.

One Month

This is the best length of time for most travellers. For the first half, travel along the road between Bam and Esfahān, with a detour to Shīrāz, as described above, with an additional day or two at Kāshān, or, perhaps, a detour from Shīrāz for a few days along the Persian Gulf, based at Bandar-é Abbās or Būshehr.

For the second half of the month, start from Tehrān (two-three days), and visit the Caspian region: Shāhrūd (one day); Gorgān and around (two-three), and then off to Mashhad if you wish for a few days, and fly back to Tehrān; Rasht and around (two-three days); Ghazvīn and around (two days); and then back to Tehrān, or head north via Ardabīl (two days) or Zanjān (one day).

Alternatively, if you are going to or coming from Turkey by land (or can fly between Tehrān and Orūmīyé or Tabrīz), you may wish to spend the final two weeks in the north and west: ie Tehrān (two-three days); Rasht and around (two-three days); Ghazvīn and around (two days); Hamadān and around (two days); Takht-é Soleimān (one-two days); Orūmīyé or Tabrīz (two days); and Mākū (one day).

Two Months

You may get a visa and a couple of extensions for as long as two months, but don't count on it (and you will probably waste a few days getting extensions anyway). If you have two months at your disposal, spend longer in each of the places described under One Month above, and consider flying to more remote regions for a few days: ie Mashhad, Bandar-é Abbās, Būshehr and Ahvāz. If you have time left over, and feeling a bit adventurous, do some skiing, hiking or some other activity, depending on the season.

TOURIST OFFICES
Local Tourist Offices
The ominous-sounding Ministry of Culture & Islamic Guidance is responsible for 'cultural affairs, propaganda, literature and arts, audio-visual production, archaeology, preservation of the cultural heritage, tourism, press and libraries'. You may have noticed that the word 'tourism' was squeezed in there, giving you a fair indication of how unimportant tourism is to the Iranian government. However, there is a chance that the new president will create a separate tourist department.

The ministry has an office in every provincial capital, but only a handful cater for tourists and can provide any helpful information for foreigners. Some other mildly useful tourist offices are run by local government authorities. Most tourist offices have someone who can speak English, but maps and glossy brochures are very rare. In fact, the only tourist office in the whole country worth visiting is in Esfahãn. The address and phone number of the useful tourist offices are listed in the relevant sections.

If you can find one, the tourist offices are generally open from 8 am to 2 pm, Saturday to Wednesday, and on Thursday between about 8 am and noon. There are also small information booths at the main bus terminals, train station and international airport terminal in Tehrãn, and at two bus terminals in Shīrãz, but these are of limited value for foreigners because staff speak little, if any, English.

Tourist Offices Abroad
Sorry, but there are none. You could try to prise some information from your local embassy or consulate, but don't hold your breath. The best source of information about anything to do with Iran (besides this guidebook, of course) is on the Internet. Refer to the Online Services section later in this chapter.

VISAS & DOCUMENTS
How ready the Iranians are to let you into their country depends very much on the state of their relations with your government at the time. Citizens of small inoffensive countries like Ireland, New Zealand and San Marino are the greatest beneficiaries of this policy. Israelis are not allowed in under any circumstances, nor are any women who refuse to wear the appropriate clothing. US citizens are more welcome than before, but until recently only those with a cogent reason for visiting, or travelling with an organised tour, have been given a visa.

Passport
Make sure your passport has several spare pages for visa extensions and stamp-happy immigration officials. By Iranian law, your passport must be valid for more than six months after your intended departure.

Most hotels want to look after your passport while you stay there because a member of the local police/security force will almost certainly visit your hotel, and take details from your passport. If you don't leave your passport at the hotel reception, you may be asked to supply your passport in person to the police/security officer (even in the middle of the night), and dealing with these people is best avoided. The best compromise is to leave your passport at the hotel reception during the night, but ask for it back during the day, in case you need to show it to the police when you are out, or change money at the bank. If you don't want to leave your passport at a hotel at any time, providing the receptionist with a photocopy of the relevant pages of your passport (ie with your photo, personal details and visa) may be allowed after some argument.

Visas
Every traveller to Iran needs a visa. Anyone from a handful of countries, such as Slovenia (apparently because Iran owes Slovenia heaps of money), Macedonia (ie the Former Yugoslav Republic of ...) and Turkey, can get a three-month tourist visa on arrival, or at a diplomatic mission beforehand, without problems. Japanese travellers can get a three-month tourist visa at an Iranian consulate or
continued on page 58

Highlights of Iran

Don't miss the ancient, fabulous city of Shīrāz and the magnificent ruins at nearby Persepolis. Esfahān is the most architecturally stunning city in Iran. Yazd city is the Zoroastrian centre of Iran and has the fascinating inhabited Old City. Kāshān has preserved much of its cultural distinctiveness; and the old city of Bam is a genuine highlight for most visitors.

Tehrān, the overcrowded and polluted capital, is architecturally a tragedy and sociologically a mess, but it does have a number of museums to see and many of the best restaurants, shops and hotels.

Many travellers bypass western Iran, which is a shame, because the Alī Sadr caves, near Hamadān, are fantastic. The Caspian region deserves a look, especially the mountain village of Māsūlé. If the weather is right, go down to the shores of the Persian Gulf and visit some of the islands.

	Location	Comments
Mosques & Shrines		
Holy Shrine of Emām Rezā The foremost Shi'ite shrine in Iran.	Mashhad	Non-Muslims will probably need a guide. Dress correctly. Security is tight.
Masjed-é Emām Probably the most magnificent mosque in Iran.	Esfahān	The entrance fee is 15,000 rials. Visit a couple of times if you can afford it.
Masjed-é Jāme' It dominates the old city of Yazd, and is strikingly beautiful.	Yazd	Easy to find.
Palaces, Gardens & Mausoleums		
Ārāmgāh-é Hāfez The tomb for the renowned poet, Hāfez, is set in a lovely garden.	Shīrāz	The bookshop is worth a browse. The teahouse is wonderful.
Bāgh-é Eram Not as visited as other places in Shīrāz, these gardens are the best in the city, and the palace is pretty.	Shīrāz	The palace is not open. The entrance fee is reasonable.
Bāgh-é Tārīkhī-yé Fīn A garden and pool in a beautiful setting.	Near Kāshān	Easy to reach.
Bogh'-é-yé Sheikh Safī-od-Dīn A marvellous collection of ancient mausoleums, gardens and museums.	Ardabīl	Not on the usual route for travellers, but worth visiting.
Chehel Sotūn A charming palace with 20 columns.	Esfahān	It has an excellent bookshop. Offers great photo opportunities.
Gombad-é Soltānīyé A huge 14th century mausoleum. One of the few legacies of the Mongols.	Near Zanjān	It will be under restoration for years to come, but is still worth visiting.
Bazaars		
Bāzār-é Esfahān Vast and fascinating; great for souvenir-hunters.	Esfahān	Can be combined with a walking tour of the city.
Bāzār-é Vakīl More sedate than most bazaars, it has several attractions inside.	Kermān	Try to go a couple of times. Visit the authentic teahouse inside.
Museums		
Carpet Museum The best place to go if you are interested in looking at, or thinking of buying, Persian carpets or rugs.	Tehrān	Easy to combine with other museums or restaurants nearby.

National Jewels Museum
Though obscenely ostentatious, this   Tehrān   Only open for six hours a week.
small collection is still fascinating.

Glass & Ceramics Museum
The best place in Iran to admire old   Tehrān   Easy to reach from Ferdōsī Square.
and new glassware and pottery.   Set in a charming garden.

National Museum of Iran
The most-visited museum in Iran. It   Tehrān   Not signed in English, but easy to find.
contains a vast collection from the
main ancient cities in Iran.

Ancient Cities

Arg-é Bam
This abandoned, but partially restored,   Bam   Try to visit twice: in the early morning
ancient city and citadel is a highlight of Iran.   and late afternoon.

Persepolis
The most famous, and visited, ancient city   Near Shīrāz   Entrance costs 15,000 rials. Need to
in Iran; the ruins of a vast Achaemenian   arrange transport. Some imagination
capital.   is required to conceive the majesty of
                                                         the former city.

Takht-é Soleimān
An appealing, and remote, ancient city,   Western Iran   It is not easy to reach, but possible on
overlooking a natural pool.   public transport. Great hiking in the area.

Yazd
The largest inhabited old city in Iran, right   Yazd   Don't be afraid of getting hopelessly lost.
in the middle of bustling Yazd. It is
fascinating to wander around.

Landscapes

Alī Sadr Caves
If you are sick of mosques, ancient cities   Near Hamadān   You can take a paddle boat around the
and bazaars, head to these fantastic caves.   lake inside the cave. Hotels and
                                                            restaurants are available at the caves.

Darband & Tōchāl
These walking trails and chair lifts in   Tehrān   There are places to eat along the trails.
northern Tehrān are easy to follow.

Nahar Khorān
A pretty pocket of forest with walking trails.   Near Gorgān   Hotels and restaurants are in the area.

Other

Bridges
In the middle of the city, there are several   Esfahān   Go on a 'teahouse crawl' from one
charming ancient bridges, complete with   bridge to another.
teahouses underneath.

Towers of Silence
The absorbing ruins of a Zoroastrian fire   Yazd   Easy to reach from downtown Yazd.
temple and ancient village.   Great views from the top of the hill.

Falak-ol-Aflak
A fantastic old fortress which dominates   Khorram Ābād   Still under restoration, so is partially
the city.   closed, but worth a look anyway.

Ghara Kelīsā
This remote Armenian 'Black Church' is   Western Iran   It is almost impossible to reach by
truly ancient and historic.   public transport, so charter a taxi.

Māsūlé
This gorgeous village, perched in the   Near Rasht   One hotel is available (and more being
Alborz mountains, is a highlight for many.   built). Great hiking everywhere nearby.

continued from page 55

embassy without a problem. However, for everyone else, getting a visa is a hassle, but don't let this put you off – just allow enough time to get the visa.

The information in this section can be confusing, so the best general advice is: apply for a tourist visa (extendable) for two weeks or one month in your home country if flying into Iran; or a transit visa (extendable) along the way if you are travelling overland to Iran, as long as you have plenty of time to wait for the visa.

Visa regulations between Iranian embassies and consulates differ: some only issue transit visas to travellers, a few are happy to give one-month tourist visas, and others try very hard to put you off the idea of applying in the first place. Sometimes it is next to impossible to get a visa in your home country, while the Iranian consulate in another country will issue you a tourist visa in 48 hours. In general, consulates in countries that attract few applicants are the most likely to oblige with visas. But not always.

If you can't get a visa in time, or at all, in your home country, don't give up. Either telephone the Iranian consulate in a neighbouring country (see the list later in this section) or make a point of dropping in at every Iranian mission on your way to Iran. If you can only get a short transit visa, don't worry – getting an extension inside Iran is often far easier than obtaining any sort of visa in the first place. Visa costs are as impossible to understand as the visa process itself, but the cost for most travellers seems to be the equivalent of about US$50: eg for Brits in London, the visa cost is UK£30, Canadians in Canada pay C$65 and Germans in Germany are slugged DM80 – yet Australians in Australia pay nothing. Work that out.

When applying, you will need to complete two or three application forms (in English; Iranian embassies or consulates in western countries should be able to translate the forms into Fārsī); provide up to four passport size photos (complete with the hejāb for women); and pay the visa fee. You may (or may not) be asked to provide: photocopies of your airline tickets in and out of Iran (tell them that you're going in or out by bus if you haven't got any); letters from employers (rarely asked); letters of recommendation from your embassy (a diplomatic nonsense, but often requested if you do not apply in your home country); proof of funds (rarely asked); and any student or press cards, if applicable. You may also have the visa marked with intended points, or means, of entry and exit, car registration numbers, if applicable, and the names of any travelling companions in Iran – but these stipulations are rarely requested these days. While foreign women do not have to wear a headscarf, or chādor, on their passport photos, you *must* wear something dark to cover your hair and neck on any photos used for visa applications and visa extensions.

If you are arranging your tourist or business visa through a relative, travel agency or business contact in Iran, they will need (preferably by fax, to expedite things): your full personal details; complete passport information; your general itinerary, in brief; your arrival and departure times, and flights; and anything else which may help your cause. A few weeks later, your sponsor will send you back an authorisation number from the Ministry of Foreign Affairs in Tehrān, which you then use to collect your visa from the relevant embassy. Alternatively, you can ask that the authorisation number be faxed from Iran to the relevant Iranian embassy, and then your passport will (hopefully) be sent to you by mail (preferably certified) from the embassy.

While it may take two or three weeks for authorisation to come through for a visa, even a short transit visa, you do not normally have to leave your passport at the embassy while you wait. So if, for example, you are applying in New Delhi, India, you can apply for the visa (but not leave your passport), travel around India for a few weeks, and then pick up your Iranian visa later (you hope).

While we don't advocate that you lie on your visa form, don't complicate matters by providing peculiar occupations: a 'teacher', 'student', 'nurse' or 'businessman' (but only on a business visa) are more acceptable than something unloved like a 'journalist' or vaguely suspicious like a 'manager' (or distinctly unsavoury like a 'distributor of Salman Rushdie books'.)

Never be put off if the Iranian embassy or consulate refuses to issue you a visa the first time you apply; just try again. One traveller said of his initial refusal for an Iranian visa in Istanbul: 'I got the strong impression that this was fairly normal procedure, and a note of a previous refusal on your application can actually count in your favour'.

If you have any queries about visas, and have access to the Internet, it is definitely worth checking out the excellent web site created by the Iranian Embassy in Ottawa, Canada: http://www.salamiran.org. This site lists the telephone and fax numbers of major Iranian embassies; it provides advice on visas; and there's even a visa application form which you can download or print.

Finally, something else to remember: every part of every day counts towards the length of your visa; eg if you arrive at the airport, or cross the border, at five minutes before midnight, one day of your precious visa has already been used.

Transit Visa A transit visa is valid for a stay of (usually) seven or 10 days, and is extendable. It is mainly requested by, and given to, foreigners who are travelling overland into and out of Iran; eg anyone travelling through Iran between Turkey and Pakistan. Travellers often get them along the way, for instance in Istanbul or Ankara (Turkey), New Delhi (India) or Karachi (Pakistan). The main advantage of a transit visa is that you normally do not need a sponsor in Iran.

Multiple entry transit visas are not normally issued, and it is not possible to apply for a second visa on the same passport while a previous one is still valid (though you can extend the original transit visa). In theory, transit visas should be issued within a few days – but it often takes two or three weeks – and you may still need a letter of recommendation from your embassy if you apply from outside your home country. Transit visas are normally valid for three months, ie

you must enter Iran within three months of the date of visa issue – but make sure of this when you apply.

Tourist Visa Tourist visas are mainly for people flying in and out of Iran for business, to visit family or on part of an organised tour group. These visas are for two weeks or one month, and can be extended. If you ask for a one-month tourist visa, you may also need to provide a brief itinerary of your trip. Tourist visas are generally valid for three months; ie you must enter Iran within three months of the date of visa issue.

Regulations about whether you need a sponsor in Iran for a tourist visa differs from one embassy or consulate to another. If you do not have a sponsor, ask another Iranian embassy or consulate in a neighbouring country about their stipulations for a tourist visa; or ask for a transit visa instead and get it extended in Iran.

If you still need to provide a sponsor in Iran, and you don't have one, contact (by fax) a travel agency in Iran. Some agencies which have assisted foreign travellers include Sogol Tour & Travel, and Caravan Sahra – refer to the Travel Agencies section in the Tehrān chapter for contact details. Alternatively, contact a foreign specialist travel agency or visa service (eg those listed under Embassies later in this chapter, or under Organised Tours in the Getting There & Away chapter). These Iranian and foreign agencies may charge up to US$50 for their services (on top of the visa fee), but you are usually under no obligation to take any of their tours.

Business Visa Before a two-week or one-month (extendable) business visa is issued you must have a genuine business contact in Iran who can sponsor your visit through the Ministry of Foreign Affairs in Tehrān. Business visas are generally valid for three months; ie you must enter Iran within three months of the date of visa issue.

Visa Extensions The general rule with any Iranian visa is that you can get one (and sometimes two) extensions of up to two weeks each without too much hassle. If you are lucky, an extension of one month once is possible, but your chances of getting more than two extensions range from negligible to nil. (I was interviewed by the secret police for an hour while they tried to fathom why I wanted three extensions, despite all sorts of nice paperwork from embassies and various ministries.)

You can normally only apply for an extension a few days before the visa is due to expire. If you have a five or seven-day transit visa, get it extended as soon as you can in a city where you are more likely to be successful (see below) – and always bear in mind that on Thursday afternoon, Friday, and public holidays, nothing will get done. Visa extensions are normally handled at the provincial police headquarters (*shahrbānī*) or a provincial government office (*shahrdārī*), though sometimes you must go to a special Foreign Affairs office, or some place with an unpleasant name like the Aliens Bureau. These are located in every provincial capital (the addresses are listed under Information in the relevant sections). However, while the relevant offices in every provincial capital can, in theory, extend your visa, those in some cities (eg Semnān and Rasht) are very reluctant; it's all too hard, you see.

The visa extension office in Tehrān is the worst place to go, because there are so many other non-Iranians hoping for extensions on their work visas. The best places to try are Tabrīz, Esfahān, Shīrāz, Kermān, Mashhad and Zāhedān, which is just as well because these are pleasant places to hang around for a while and wait (with the notable exception of Zāhedān). The officer in charge of visa extensions in Shīrāz is particularly helpful, as one traveller confirmed:

It took only 90 minutes to get a 10-day extension on our transit visas. I am sure we would have got longer easily if we had asked: the officer apparently didn't understand why embassies are so reluctant to allow more time into Iran and when translating my application into Fārsī, he wrote 'tourism' under 'reason for which extension is required'.

Raphaël Clerici, Switzerland

The procedure for applying for a visa extension goes something like this:

Step 1: Find the correct office, and go there when it is open.

Step 2: Present yourself neatly, and be polite and well-dressed. Women must wear a headscarf, or chādor, on any photo they submit with their application, and when they visit the visa extension office. It will probably be easier if foreign women travelling on their own visit the visa extension office with a foreign male friend.

Step 3: Obtain and fill out the visa application form (in duplicate) in English and Fārsī. If the visa officer does not speak English, and you don't know Fārsī, find someone who can help. You can take the application form from the office, and return it later.

Step 4: Buy a 1000-rial stamp from any Bank Melli branch; and present the bank teller with your application forms, which must also be stamped.

Step 5: Provide necessary documentation: two photocopies of whatever relevant documents you may have, including two of the front pages of your passport (ie with photos and personal details) and your original Iranian visa; and two passport-sized colour photos (with the proper hejāb for women). One traveller did not have any passport photos, so she successfully used two photocopies of her photo from her passport. However, this should not be relied on.

Step 6: Possibly buy a cardboard file. In Tehrān, you even have to provide two paper clips. Ask someone where you can buy these.

You may get your visa extension on the spot, a few hours later or sometimes the next day – but if you ask nicely, and make some excuse about being a hurry to see 'your lovely country', the visa officer may hurry it up for you. However, this will not work at all in Tehrān.

Photocopies

We suggest that you keep a photocopy of your vital documents at home and in a safe place in your baggage: ie passport details, credit card number(s), airline tickets, other important travel documents, and a list of travellers cheques. Although travellers cheques are next to worthless in Iran, you'll need the details of them if you are travelling in other regional countries.

Travel Insurance

A travel insurance policy to cover theft, loss and medical problems is a wise idea. There are a wide variety of policies available and your travel agent will be able to make recommendations. The international student travel policies handled by STA Travel, or other student travel organisations, are usually good value. Check the small print:

- Some policies specifically exclude 'dangerous activities' which can include scuba diving, motor cycling, and even trekking. If such activities are on your agenda you don't want that sort of policy.
- You may prefer a policy which pays doctors or hospitals direct rather than you having to pay on the spot and claim later. If you have to claim later make sure you keep all documentation. Some policies ask you to call back (reverse charges) to a centre in your home country where an immediate assessment of your problem is made.
- Check if the policy covers ambulances or an emergency flight home. If you have to stretch out you will need two seats and somebody has to pay for them.
- Make sure that the policy covers Iran, and the general region. Some insurers, particularly in the US, still consider the region a 'danger zone' and either do not cover there, or will insist on exorbitant premiums.

Driving Licence & Permits

Refer to the Land section in the Getting There & Away chapter for information about what is needed if you are bringing your own car into Iran.

Student Cards

One *very* annoying aspect of travelling around Iran is the ridiculous 'foreigners' price' of between 10,000 and 15,000 rials which anyone who does not look Iranian must pay to visit almost every tourist attraction. With a current International Student Card (or anything of any date, which looks like one), and a smattering of relevant words in Fārsī, you can often get a 50% discount at some tourist sites, including the National Museum of Iran, Carpet Museum and Glass & Ceramics Museum – all in Tehrān; the Masjed-é Emām mosque in Esfahān; Persepolis; and the old city of Bam.

EMBASSIES

Iranian Embassies Abroad

Iran is very well represented overseas, and even if a country is not listed here, there is a good chance that it does have Iranian diplomatic representation. The embassies or consulates may be able to provide some useful, but limited, information about Iran, but do not always take everything that a member of staff says at face value; some travellers have received some bad advice in the past.

Most of the following information comes from the same little green booklet published by the Ministry of Foreign Affairs that every Iranian embassy, consulate and MFA official uses, and the list provided by the Iranian Embassy in Ottawa. Some details are possibly out of date, so always check locally.

Afghanistan
    There used to be Iranian representatives in Herat and Kabul, but these buildings are unlikely to be still standing. In any case, they were certainly not operating at the time of research because of the 'difference in opinion' between the dominant Taliban militia in Afghanistan and the Iranian government.

Australia
    25 Culgoa Crt, O'Malley, ACT 2606 (☎ (02) 6290 2421; fax 6290 2431). They will issue transit visas, and a two-week tourist visa, to Australians without problems. A one-month tourist visa can be issued with an itinerary. Sponsors are not normally needed.

Austria
    Jaures Gasse 9-1030, Vienna (☎ (1) 712 2650; fax 713 5733)

Azerbaijan
    4 Bouniat Sardaroff St, Baku (☎ (12) 926 177; fax 926 453)

Bahrain
    Villa 1 & 2, Road 3221, Manama (☎ 722 400; fax 722 101)

Canada
    245 Metcalfe St, Ottawa, Ontario, K2P 2K2 (☎ (613) 235 4726; fax 232 5712; email iranemb @salamiran.org)

China
    San Li Tun Don Liu Jie, Beijing (☎ (10) 532 2040; fax 532 1403)

Denmark
    Gronningen 5, 1270 Copenhagen (☎ 141 269; fax 149 894)

France
    4 Ave d'Iena, 75016, Paris (☎ 01 47 20 30 95; fax
    40 70 01 57)
Germany
    Embassy: Godesberger Allee 133-137, 5300,
    Bonn (☎ (228) 816 110; fax 376 154)
    Consulate-General: Guiollettstrasse 56, 6000
    Frankfurt (☎ (69) 560 0070; fax 560 0071)
    Consulate-General: Bebelalle 18, 2000 Hamburg
    (☎ (40) 514 4060; fax 511 3511)
    Consulate-General: Mauerkircherstrasse 59,
    8000 Munich (☎ (89) 927 9060; fax 981 0105)
    The cost for Germans is a high DM80, but a
    transit or tourist visa can be issued within two
    weeks, and no sponsor is apparently needed.
    (Despite tensions between Iran and Germany at
    the time of research, Germans have no problems
    getting visas.)
Greece
    16 Stratigou Kalari St, Paleo Psychico, Athens
    (☎ (1) 647 1436; fax 647 9930)
India
    Embassy: 5 Barakhamba Rs, New Delhi (☎ (11)
    332 9600; fax 332 5493).
    This is one of the easier places to get a five-day
    transit visa, though you will need a letter of
    introduction from your embassy, and it will take
    two to three weeks to issue.
    Consulate-General: 1st floor, 47 Laxibai,
    Jagmohandad Rd, Mumbai (Bombay) (☎ (22)
    822 0073; fax 811 8948)
    Consulate-General: 8-2-502/1 Banjara Hills Rd,
    No 7, Hyderabad (☎ (40) 357 22; fax 225 061)
Iraq
    Saalehhiyeh-Karaadeh, Maryam, Baghdad
    (☎ (1) 538 3595; fax 537 5636)
    This is probably not the best place to apply for an
    Iranian visa.
Ireland
    72 Mount Merrion Ave, Blackrock, Dublin
    (☎ (1) 885 881; fax 834 246)
Italy
    Embassy: Via Della Camilluccia 651/657, Rome
    (☎ (6) 329 4294; fax 327 3757)
    Consulate-General: Piazza Diaz 6, 20123 Milan
    (☎ (2) 805 2615; fax 7200 1189).
    According to one Italian traveller, Milan is not a
    good place to try.
Japan
    10-32-3 Chome Minami Aazabu, Minato-ku,
    Tokyo (☎ (3) 3446 8011; fax 3446 2383)
Jordan
    Vasser Ben Jomayel Shaare, Omar Ben
    Abdolaziz, Shaare Abdolaahe Be Rabie, Amman
    (☎ (6) 962 560; fax 695 544)
Kuwait
    Esteghlal St, Bomeidelghar, Kuwait (☎ 256
    1084; fax 529 868)

Lebanon
    Bear Hassan, Beirut (☎ (1) 300 007; fax 321 229)
Netherlands
    Javadtraat-54, 2585, The Hague (☎ (70) 346
    9353; fax 392 4921)
New Zealand
    151 Te Anau Rd, Roseheath, Wellington (☎ (4)
    862 976; fax 863 065)
Oman
    Jameat A'Duwal Al-Arabiya St, Medinat
    Qaboos, Muscat (☎ 699 626; fax 696 888)
Pakistan
    Embassy: House 222-238, St 2, G-5/1, Islamabad
    (☎ (51) 822 694; fax 824 839)
    Consulate-General: 81 Shahrah-i-Iran, Clifton
    Beach, Karachi (☎ (21) 530 638; fax 530 594)
    Consulate-General: 82-E-1, Gulberg III, Lahore
    (☎ (42) 870 274; fax 870 661)
    Consulate: corner of Park and University Rds,
    Peshawar (☎ (521) 412 59)
    Consulate: 2/33 Hali Rd, Quetta (☎ (81) 737 25;
    fax 752 55)
    In Pakistan, foreigners can currently only apply
    for Iranian visas in Islamabad, Lahore or
    Karachi; but not at the consulates in Quetta or
    Peshawar. Also, we continue to get reports that
    getting a visa of any sort anywhere in Pakistan is
    not easy.
Qatar
    West Bay, Diplomatic Area, Doha (☎ 835 300;
    fax 439 550)
Russia
    Pokrovsky Blvd 7, Moscow (☎ (095) 917 7282;
    fax 230 2897)
Saudi Arabia
    Diplomatic Quarter, Riyadh (☎ (1) 488 1916; fax
    488 1890)
Spain
    28016 Calle Jeres 5, Madrid (☎ (1) 345 0112; fax
    457 8103)
Sweden
    Vastra Yttringe Gard Elfviksvagen, Stockholm
    (☎ (8) 765 0819; fax 765 3119)
Switzerland
    Embassy: Thunstrasse 68, 3006, Berne (☎ (31)
    351 0801; fax 351 5652)
    Consulate: 28A, Chemin du Pt-Saconnex,
    Geneva (☎ (22) 347 4171; fax 789 1485)
Syria
    Autostrad Al-Mazzeh, Damascus (☎ (11) 222
    6459; fax 222 0997)
Thailand
    602 Sukhumvit Rd, Bangkok (☎ (2) 259 0611;
    fax 259 9111)
    Travellers report getting a transit or tourist visa
    without a sponsor within three weeks.
Turkey
    Embassy: Tahran Cadessi 10, Kavaklidere,
    Ankara (☎ (312) 438 2195; fax 440 3429)

Consulate-General: Ankara Caddesi 1/2, Cagaloglu, Istanbul (☎ (212) 513 8230; fax 511 5219) – but apply at the Commercial Office in the same building, not the Consulate.

Consulate: just off Alivari Caddesi (across from the Education Faculty), Erzurum (☎ (442) 218 3876)

Consulate: Esentepe Mah, Iran Caddesi, Kiziltoprak, Trabzon (☎ (462) 248 52; fax 248 54)

If you are heading across Turkey from Europe, try in Istanbul and, if unsuccessful, in Ankara. The consulates at Erzurum and Trabzon should only be used as an absolute last resort – they will probably send you back to Ankara or Istanbul anyway. Normally, the missions at Ankara and Istanbul can issue a five or seven-day transit visa within three weeks; and anyone with a smattering of Fārsī, and a nice smile, may get a two-week transit visa in Istanbul within a few days.

United Arab Emirates (UAE)
Embassy: Karama St, Diplomatic Area, Abu Dhabi (☎ (2) 447 618; fax 448 714)

Consulate-General: Diplomatic Area, Dubai (☎ (4) 521 150; fax 526 739)

UK
Embassy: 27 Princes Gate, London SW7 1PX (☎ (171) 584 8101; fax 589 4440)

Non-British travellers can usually get a one-week transit visa within two weeks, but a letter of recommendation from your embassy in London is required. British citizens can get a 10-day transit visa in London for UK£30 within a week; longer for a tourist visa.

Action Visa (☎ (0171) 388 4498) charges UK£25 (plus visa fee) to arrange an Iranian business visa, within two weeks and without invitations or sponsors. For tourist visas contact Magic Carpet Travel – see page 137 for contact details.

USA
The Iranian Interests Section is in the Embassy of Pakistan, 2209 Wisconsin Ave, NW, Washington, 20007 (☎ (202) 965 4990).

Until recently you were unlikely to get a visa here unless you were an Iranian expatriate visiting family or on business; had a genuine business reason (not likely given the US trade embargo); or on an organised tour. Independent travellers can try here, but be prepared to try in Europe or Canada, or along the way. Latest reports are that visas are more readily available.

Travel to Iran is *not* illegal (in US or Iranian law) for Americans, but the problems are a general distrust of Americans by the Iranian government; hindrances to visa issue caused by retaliation by Iran for the trade embargoes; and the trade embargoes themselves. Despite US State Department warnings, Americans should not be afraid to travel independently to Iran, but they may need to be a little circumspect while there, particularly

when discussing politics and telling people where they are from.

Yemen
Corner of Hadded and Zobiary Sts, San'a (☎ (1) 243 439; fax 268 115).

Foreign Embassies in Iran

Most countries have embassies in Tehrān. It is a very good idea to register (a telephone call will do) with your embassy if you plan to be in Iran for, say, more than 10 days, or you're going to any remote regions of Iran. Your embassy may also have a reading room, where you can catch up with news (and football scores) from home. They are also the best source of advice if anything goes wrong, eg if you want any medical attention.

All foreign embassies are in Tehrān, and listed under Information in the Tehrān chapter. There are also consulates for: the UAE in Bandar-é Abbās; India in Shīrāz and Zāhedān; Turkey in Orūmīyé and Tabrīz; Pakistan in Mashhad and Zāhedān; and Afghanistan in Mashhad (though for how much longer, no-one is sure). Though I never found it, there is apparently a Turkmenistan consulate in Mashhad. Refer to the relevant sections for the addresses and telephone numbers of these consulates.

CUSTOMS

You may bring into Iran duty-free: 200 cigarettes, 50 cigars or 250g of tobacco; and a 'reasonable quantity' of perfume. But no alcohol, of course.

According to the customs declaration, which you must fill in when you enter Iran, you are not allowed to bring in:

'Firearms and ammunition; records (and compact disc), cassettes (both audio and video) which are undesirable and books and any magazines which have pictures of women showing any hair or flesh; publications and films which are in violation of public order and decency and the national and religious values of the country (and you don't decide what is decent, of course); transmission apparatuses such as walkie-talkie type devices, mobile telephones (this restriction may become obsolete when these become more widely available in Iran); seeds, flower bulbs and other parts of plants; alcoholic beverages and narcotic drugs.'

To this list, you can add: any pork product, and anything written by Salman Rushdie. Always be careful about which books you bring in – anything, however harmless, with a picture of a women showing flesh (except for the face and hands) or hair will get confiscated. It is best to avoid bringing in any foreign magazines because there is bound to be a picture in it which, according to customs regulations, will 'promote moral and ideological perversion'.

On Arrival
Whether arriving by air, or travelling overland, you must fill out a customs declaration, written in English (which you can complete in English). The form seeks normal personal and passport details, and asks whether you have anything illegal to declare. Once you have completed the form (carry a pen handy), show it to the customs officer, who stamps it. You must keep this form for the length of your trip and show it to another customs officer on departure. Or so the theory goes. Most airports have a red channel to go through if you have anything to declare; the green channel, if you don't. At the border, just tell the customs office that you have nothing to declare (unless you do, of course).

At the international airports, your cabin luggage – but rarely your hand luggage – may be inspected, but foreigners are often whisked through customs quickly (though less commonly at the airport in Tehrān). At the Iranian borders, you will probably be shown through customs, and your bags won't be inspected. Some things that customs officers are always interested in are foreign magazines (which they often confiscate anyway); audio cassettes (five of my cassettes were listened to by someone from a special department at the airport in Tehrān, and then stamped individually as 'OK'); and any video cassette (blank or not).

On Departure
You may take out anything you legally imported into Iran, together with anything you legally obtained in the country – this includes Iranian handicrafts (but not carpets or rugs) up to the value of 150,000 rials (so keep a receipt handy), as long as they are not for the 'purpose of trade'; one or two Persian carpets or rugs (see the Persian Carpets section in the Facts about Iran chapter for details); and 150g of gold and 3kg of silver – but neither with gemstones. If you exceed the stated values, or quantities, you will need an export permit from the local customs office.

On departure, you must fill out another customs declaration (and also show the customs form which you filled out on arrival, and should have kept during your trip). The form which you fill out on departure asks you to list: your 'personal effects' (this is not explained, so just list a few uninteresting items); 'carpet/rug' (see the special Persian Carpets section in the Facts about Iran chapter); and 'gold ornaments', 'silverware' and 'musical instruments' (see General Export Restrictions under Things to Buy at the end of this chapter).

The form also asks you to list 'other goods' you are taking out of Iran, but there is no explanation about what these may be. If you have some cheap (ie under the value of 150,000 rials), non-antique stuff, such as a couple of miniature paintings, write them down on the form in case your luggage is checked – but there is a very good chance that the form won't be looked out at anywhere, or, if it is, by anyone who understands English. Finally, you must list the amount of foreign currency you have (a bit pointless, because there is currently no currency declaration); and the number of Iranian rials you have (200,000 rials is the maximum you can take out).

Currency Declaration
In the not too distant past, foreigners had to complete a detailed list of all currency they planned to bring into Iran. This meant that you could not change any money at the very favourable 'street rate' (unless you 'forgot' to declare some cash) – though the currency declaration was almost never checked on

departure. Thankfully, this currency declaration is no longer required, so you can change money however you wish. But always be mindful that the authorities could always reintroduce the currency declaration at some stage in the future.

Duty-Free Zones

The islands of Kīsh and Gheshm, and the port of Chābahār, are duty-free zones. Before you buy any souvenir or electronic good at these places, make local inquiries about customs regulations for bringing them back to 'mainland' Iran. The customs rules are complicated, and the procedures are an absolute nightmare, so avoid buying anything duty-free while at these places, if possible.

MONEY
Costs

For most travel necessities, and even luxuries, Iran is inexpensive by international standards. A bare minimum budget, for budget hotels, Iranian food and overland transport, is 30,000/40,000 rials per day, travelling as a single/double. Unless you thrive on discomfort, however, you should double this to 60,000/80,000 rials per day for a single/double. This will provide you with decent budget accommodation (and, occasionally, a splurge on a decent middle-range place); one decent western meal every day; first-class transport by bus and shared taxi; chartered taxis around town (and sometimes in the countryside); and visits to all the important tourist attractions. Add to this the cost of internal flights. You will need plenty more rials, as well as US dollars, if you are staying at top-end hotels. Costs for most things are higher in Tehrān, but easily the most expensive place in Iran is Kīsh Island, a luxury, duty-free port and holiday centre in the Persian Gulf.

There is really no need to be too stingy or frugal in such a cheap country. If you are travelling as a single, finding someone to share a double room will save some money, as single rooms are rare. Naturally, looking for cheap accommodation is a way of saving

money, but paying an extra 10,000/15,000 rials for a single/double, if you bargain well, will add considerably to your comfort level. Sleeping on buses is not a recommended way of saving money, but taking a sleeper on an overnight train is worth considering, especially through boring scenery. The cost of entering most tourist attractions will eat into your budget, so you may want to rationalise these visits, or get a student card (see Visas & Documents earlier in this chapter).

Dual Pricing

One unfortunate part of travelling in Iran is the dual-pricing for foreigners. Before you get too angry, however, remember that most Iranians receive a pitiful wage, and the official exchange rate (currently 3000 rials for US$1) is high, while the unofficial 'street rate' (currently 4800 rials for US$1) is extremely advantageous.

Thankfully, these 'foreigners' prices' are only used in three areas. Firstly, all tickets on international flights (and ferries) bought by foreigners in Iran must be paid for in US dollars (whether cash or credit cards). Secondly, foreigners are often charged 10,000 to 15,000 rials to enter a tourist attraction, while Iranians (and anyone who looks and speaks like an Iranian) pay as little as 1000 rials for the same thing. Unless you are a good debater, and speak Fārsī, the only way to get around this is to produce a student card (see Visas & Documents earlier in this chapter), or ask an Iranian friend to buy your ticket.

Lastly, hotels at the top of the budget range, most middle-range hotels, and all top-end hotels, are allowed to charge foreigners in US dollars, at a high rate set by the government. But only the top-end hotels will *always* charge foreigners in US dollars, and rarely negotiate. As one traveller put it: 'If you are paying dollars, you are paying too much.' Unlike entrance fees to tourist attractions and international airline tickets, you can usually get a decent reduction in the room rate if the price is originally quoted in US dollars – and then ask to pay in rials, which you changed at the favourable 'street rate'. (See the Accommodation section later in this chapter for tips about negotiating the price of a hotel room.)

Cash

Given the government's distaste of all things American, it is ironic that the major currency for foreign tourism and trade is the mighty US greenback. Bring nothing else but US dollars in cash, unless you absolutely must: UK pounds and Deutschmarks are accepted at some banks (but at unfavourable official rates), or can sometimes be changed with a moneychanger, or in a bazaar shop. Travellers using budget hotels, or those who bargain successfully with managers of middle-range hotels, will never need to pay for anything with US dollars, but will carry US dollars in cash to change at the 'street rate' in exchange for wads of rials.

When changing US$100, for example, at the 'street rate' you will receive almost 500,000 rials – often in grubby 2000 rial-notes. This adds considerable bulk to your money belt. In this case change money frequently, or securely spread the load among your baggage, or travelling companions.

Travellers Cheques

Don't bother taking travellers cheques of any denomination or currency to Iran unless you absolutely, positively, must. The only banks in the whole country where you can be sure they will be changed is the Bank Melli branch at the international airport in Tehrān, and the Bank Melli central branch on Ferdōsī St in Tehrān. If you have travellers cheques, you will have to keep coming back to Tehrān to change them, or change heaps of travellers cheques at one time while in Tehrān. You may have problems changing American Express travellers cheques because US embargo restricts (or forbids) US firms trading with Iran. You will also have to wait for a few hours for the paperwork to be completed, and you will, of course, only get the official rate, not the more favourable 'street rate'. If that isn't bad enough, you will be charged up to 10% commission. Take US dollars instead.

Credit Cards

An increasing number of middle-range hotels (and all top-end places) accept Visa or MasterCard – but certainly not anything from that US icon, American Express. However, if your Visa or MasterCard has been issued in the US, it may be useless because of the US trade embargo.

You can also buy a place on an organised tour, souvenirs at expensive gift shops, and internal and international flights, with Visa or MasterCard, but very little else. The significant disadvantages of buying something with a credit card, as opposed to using rials are: getting authority from the relevant credit card office may take up to 30 minutes; you may be charged an extra 5% commission; and prices will be converted using the official (unfavourable) exchange rate.

You can also use Visa or MasterCard for cash advances at the central branches of Bank Melli at many provincial capitals. Again, this should be used as a last resort: the banks usually charge a commission of up to 5%; you may have to wait one or two hours for any cash advance to be authorised; and you will only receive rials at the official rate. One stunned traveller, however, did write to say that he was able to obtain US dollars (or UK pounds) with his Visa card at the Bank Melli central branch in Tabrīz – he then changed the US dollars into rials at the 'street rate' right outside the bank. Another traveller wrote to us later to say that he had similar success (with US dollars) at the Bank Melli central branch on Ferdōsī St in Tehrān. This may be worth a try.

International Transfers

It is possible to have money transferred from overseas into a bank in Iran, and to collect it in Iranian currency. In theory, however, the process takes between three days and a week by telex. Most of the major Iranian banks have branches in Europe, mainly UK, France and Germany, but not in the US. If possible, have the money sent through a branch of an Iranian bank; otherwise you could discuss the options with a friendly bank manager in

Tehrān. All sorts of arrangements are possible with private moneychangers.

Currency

The official unit of currency in Iran is the rial. In conversation Iranians usually refer to the *tōmān*, a unit of 10 rials, though in writing, prices are mostly expressed in rials. Since the unit of currency is often omitted, you have to make absolutely sure whether you are talking about rials or tōmāns before settling on a price. After a while, however, you will soon get to know the approximate price for most things, and whether you and the buyer are talking about rials or tōmāns. The exceptions are the few goods or services where the price can vary enormously, eg handicrafts and souvenirs; or an empty taxi, where a '200' fare in rials means it's a shared taxi, while '200 tōmāns' means you have probably chartered it.

Rials are sometimes written in English as Rls or IR, but neither is a standard abbreviation. There are coins for 250, 100 and 50 rials, but you rarely see the 20, 10, five and two rial coins in circulation. One rial coins (no longer minted) are considered lucky despite being utterly worthless. There are notes for 10,000, 5000, 2000, 1000, 500, 200 and 100 rials. Most notes in the last three denominations are usually filthy, but worth keeping to pay for fares in shared taxis.

Banknotes are easy to read: the numbers and names are printed in Fārsī and English. However, coins are only marked in Fārsī script and Arabic numerals.

Currency Exchange

At the time of writing, the *official* exchange rates, set by the Central Bank of Iran, was:

Australia	A$1	=	2249 rials
Canada	C$1	=	2172 rials
France	FFr10	=	5150 rials
Germany	DM1	=	1734 rials
Japan	¥100	=	2647 rials
UK	UK£1	=	5004 rials
US	US$1	=	3000 rials

(the 'street rate' is US$1 = 4800 rials)

Surplus rials can be changed back into foreign currency at a major bank, but only if you show them the original exchange receipt (which is no good, of course, if you've changed it at the 'street rate'). You are not allowed to take more than 200,000 rials out of the country if you leave Tehrān. A list of current official exchange rates is printed every day in the *Tehrān Times*.

Changing Money

There are three ways to change money (preferably US dollars): at the official, and unfavourable, exchange rate at a bank; at the favourable 'street rate' at a legal, though uncommon, money exchange office; and on the illegal black market, anywhere.

Banks It seems that about every fourth building in Iran is a bank. All have the word 'Bank' boldly written across the building in English, but only a very, *very* few will change money. Almost all will only change US dollars in cash, but, often, UK pounds or Deutschmarks in cash, also. All banks use the unfavourable, official exchange rate set by the government. One traveller reported that when he went to change US$40 at a bank, the staff told him the amount was too small and directed him to the black market moneychangers just outside the front door. The only time I changed money at a bank, other than a small amount at the airport when I arrived, was at the Bank Melli at Būshehr. The teller asked what exchange rate I wanted. He gave me the official exchange rate but provided no receipt, so he probably later changed my US dollars at the 'street rate'.

In every provincial capital, you can change money at the central branch of the Bank Melli, and in larger cities you can usually change money at the central branches of the other major banks: Bank Mellat, Bank Tejarat, Bank Sepah and Bank Saderat. Banks which offer foreign exchange facilities nearly always have the sign 'Exchange' or 'Foreign Exchange' in English displayed at the entrance or somewhere else visible from the street. At all these banks there should be at least one person who speaks competent English. You will need to take your passport with you when changing money.

Most of the top hotels have moneychanging facilities, but mainly for guests.

Although hours do vary a little, most banks, including their foreign exchange counters, are open from Saturday to Wednesday, between 8 am and 4 pm, and between 8 am and noon on Thursday. Banks along the Gulf coast usually close for the afternoon and reopen in the early evening, all year round. Branches inside hotels keep their own peculiar hours, and airports have a bank open whenever international flights arrive or depart. Any bank on the Iranian side of a main border should be open 24 hours, or at least for as long as the border is open.

Money Exchange Offices Easily the safest, and most advantageous, way of changing cash is with an official, and legal, money exchange office. These can be found in several major cities, but not, however, in Tehrān. Look for a small shop, with the words 'currency' or 'exchange' in English. (The offices I found are mentioned under Money in the relevant chapters.) These offices mainly want US dollars, but major European currencies are often accepted.

These exchange offices list (in Fārsī) the official government exchange rate on their window, or somewhere in the shop, yet without asking (but you should always confirm anyway) they will happily give you the unofficial, 'street rate' of exchange – currently 4800 rials for US$1, and rising. Changing money in an exchange shop, rather than out in the street, gives you far more security from the prying eyes of potential robbers and police (or informers). You are also less likely to get ripped off because they do not want to be visited by the police if you complain, and you know where to find them again.

If you can carry around a fair wad of rials, change enough at one money exchange office to last a few weeks, or until you know

you will come across another, because these exchange offices are not at all common.

If you can't find an official money exchange office, ask discreetly at a souvenir or carpet shop in a bazaar; they may be able to help you, or find someone who will. Otherwise, talk to someone trustworthy who works at your hotel, and for a negotiable commission of about 5%, they can usually find someone and even make the transaction, a good way of minimising any risk.

Black Market In some parts of Tehrān, and outside main banks in some cities, it is common to see black market traders flashing wads of banknotes at passing traffic and pedestrians. They offer the same unofficial 'street rate' as the money exchange offices mentioned above, but changing on the street is illegal, and there is an increased chance of being arrested, robbed or ripped off. However, at the Iranian side of a border, the black market or 'free market' (*bāzār-é āzād*) is the only way of changing money at the 'street rate'. Just be careful.

The US dollar is the major currency required, but Deutschmarks, especially closer to Turkey, are popular and fetch a good exchange rate. Along the Gulf there is a thriving business in UAE dirhams, and in the north there is a small trade in Russian roubles. Turkish lira is treated with utmost scorn everywhere except in small places close to the Turkish border. Afghan and Pakistani currencies are bought and sold near the respective borders. There is a small trade in Iranian currency in most of the neighbouring countries, especially in Istanbul.

Tipping
In most cases, tipping is no more and no less than it should be – an optional reward for good service. Although there are many circumstances where a small tip is expected, you are extremely unlikely to have a waiter hovering expectantly near your table after delivering the bill. If too many foreigners allow themselves to be overcharged and tip excessively, however, they will make life difficult for future travellers. On the other

hand, it's worth remembering that many Iranians in a service capacity do make a special effort to help foreigners, and probably deserve some extra appreciation to supplement their meagre wages.

It is usually correct to offer a small amount of money or a small present to anyone who acts as a guide for you or opens a building which is normally closed, but this may be refused, even if you insist twice, as custom demands.

Bargaining

As a rough guide, you can tell whether the price of an item is negotiable by the presence or absence of a price label. In the bazaar, virtually all prices are negotiable, whereas in shops bargaining is often a complete waste of time. Even where there is no listed price, you may find that everywhere in town charges almost exactly the same for an identical article anyway. If you always assume that you are being cheated, you will offend people who would never try to take advantage of a foreigner, and if you always accept the first price you are offered you will surely be taken for a ride more than once. It is impossible to give any hard-and-fast rules about bargaining; in one place the first price you are offered may be 50% above the going rate, in another 500%, and in a third it may be exactly the same as the locals pay.

The fares in private taxis are always negotiable, but not in any other form of transport – including a shared taxi – because these prices are set by the government. Rates in all hotels and mosāferkhūnés are open to negotiation, except top-end places. Prices in restaurants are set; food in bazaars (but not in shops) is sometimes negotiable, but probably not worth the effort. Everything else is negotiable, particularly handicrafts.

Once you have agreed on a price, you can't change it later. If you don't fix a price at the outset (eg chartering a private taxi), it is too late to complain about it later. The only sure way to avoid being cheated is to know the correct price, and for this knowledge you have to spend some time in Iran, or rely on the advice of locals. And even then, the correct price can vary significantly from place to place. And finally, don't get too perturbed about constantly bargaining (unless you have been fully and unethically ripped off); remember you may be arguing frantically about the rial equivalent of US$0.20.

POST & COMMUNICATIONS

The post and telephone offices are often combined in smaller towns, while in larger cities, the post and telephone/telegraph offices are separated. These offices are rarely signed in English, but fairly obvious from the post boxes or telephone booths outside or nearby. The post and telephone/telegraph offices are also included on all maps of provincial capitals in this guidebook.

Postal Rates

Postage is very cheap, and the service is generally reliable. Travellers in Europe constantly report receiving mail, and even carpets, by air from Iran within four or five days; within four weeks by sea mail. The cost for a postcard by air mail is 350 rials to Europe, North America and Australasia (though I was once charged 300 rials to Australia, and the postcard got there). The cost for a normal-sized letter by air mail to anywhere outside Iran is 800 rials.

Sending Mail

The Iranian international postal service is reliable and reasonably swift; the domestic service is reliable, but slow. In fact, sending a letter from Iran to the other side of the world often takes no longer than getting it from one part of Iran to another. It is not safe to send cash through the post. If you are sending mail to a complicated address or to somewhere remote, try to get someone to write the address in Fārsī on the envelope.

Some of the Iranian stamps are very colourful, and you may want to leave space on your envelope or postcard for as many as possible. Post office clerks are usually happy to let foreigners rummage through the latest issues, or else you can buy some of the collectors' items, at upwards of twice the face value. Postal boxes are few and far between, except outside post offices.

Parcel Post Sending parcels out of Iran is a major exercise in form shuffling, guaranteed to take at least twice as long as it should. You have to take your package – unwrapped – to the parcel post counter *(daftar-é amānāt-é postī)* at the head post office *(postkhūné-yé markazī)* in any provincial capital. The package will be checked, packaged and signed for in triplicate. You may need to show your passport. The sections on Customs (earlier) and Things to Buy (later) list the current export and customs regulations for some handicrafts and carpets/rugs, though what is allowed to be posted out of Iran is sometimes up to the customs officer on duty.

Receiving Mail

You can have mail, including parcels, sent to you care of the local head post office anywhere in Iran, though the service is very little used, even in Tehrān. Instruct all correspondents to write your name very clearly and to underline your surname. Since most people fronting up at the poste restante counter *(daftar-é post restānt)* are foreigners, mail is filed according to the Latin alphabet. Always ask for a check on every conceivable initial of your first name, surname or title; bearers of multi-barrelled surnames are in for fun. Poste restante mail appears to be held almost indefinitely, even in spite of requests for it to be forwarded. There is a purely nominal collection fee. Take your passport with you.

Telephone

Except for remote parts of the country, and some less developed villages, making telephone calls within Iran, and overseas, is easy: from most hotels or private homes, as well as telephone or post offices, in any major city or town, you can get a line through to your home country in less than 30 minutes, and often within a few seconds. Costs are not cheap for international calls and always be careful what you say: never underestimate the resources of the security/police forces.

One new innovation, which is only available in Tehrān at the moment, is the *kard telefon*, the sort of telephone card now used in many countries for local or international calls. This card makes it much easier than finding the appropriately-sized coins for local calls. There are not a lot of telephones which take these cards at the moment, but there is bound to be more in the future. These cards can be bought at some bookstalls (but not all), or sellers, along Ferdōsī St and around Emām Khomeinī Square, in Tehrān, for 9000 rials each.

Local Calls Most public telephone boxes are only good for local calls. They were built aeons ago, and still only take five rial or 10 rial coins (for one or three minutes, depending on the sort of phone). But these coins are almost impossible to find because they are too small to include in your change, and locals won't swap them if they can possibly help it. Local calls are so cheap, however, that your hotel will probably allow you to make a few local calls for nothing. Airports and major bus stations usually have a public telephone providing free local calls.

You can use the private pay phones at most hotels and at some shops. These cost 50 rials (for reasons unknown, the 50 rial coin must be the copper variety, not the silver one); and last three minutes for a local call. Place the 50 rial coin in the slot, and push it into the phone; when the call is answered, push the button, and your coin will disappear.

Calls Within Iran Calls to other places within Iran can be made from private homes; hotels (for an extra charge); certain telephones at airports and main bus stations; or outside most post or telephone offices. Although charges are low, a large pocketful of 50 or 100 rial coins, or a telephone card, is required if you're talking for more than a minute or two. It is also possible to book internal calls at any telephone office, but this may involve a wait of 15 to 30 minutes. From smaller villages, it's often difficult to make an internal call anywhere at busy times.

The telephone area codes in this book are

listed under Information in the relevant section, or included as a prefix to other numbers.

International Calls You can make international calls at a telephone office (*markaz-é telefon* or *edāre-yé koll-yé mokhābarāt*) in any city or town, though it is quicker and easier from major centres, such as Tehrān, Esfahān or Shīrāz. Long-distance calls can also be made from most hotels, and even mosāferkhūnés. The commission charged by a hotel is often not unreasonable (except in up-market places), and it's often easier than finding, and waiting at, the main telephone office.

For each international call, you are charged for a minimum period of three minutes, plus each subsequent minute (or part thereof). If there is no connection there is no charge. Reverse-charge calls cannot be made to or from Iran. The cost per minute (with a minimum of three minutes) is 7810 rials to Europe; 9600 rials to Australia; and as much as 13,500 rials to the USA.

Calling London from Iran
London telephone numbers currently have two codes (☎ 0171 or ☎ 0181) before a seven-digit number, but as of Easter Saturday 2000, the area code will change to 020. Subscribers will also have to put a 7 in front of numbers that used to have an 0171 code and an 8 in front of those with an old 0181 code. Please modify the London numbers given throughout this book accordingly.

Fax, Telegraph & Email
Fax You can often send faxes from the main post and telephone office in any provincial capital, many middle-range and top-end hotels, and some budget hotels.

From the (budget) Amir Kabir Hotel in Esfahān, for example, the cost per A4 page is 15,000 rials to the UK and Europe, and 20,000 rials to Australia or North America. From the post office at Emām Khomeinī Square in Tehrān, for example, it is a fair bit cheaper: 10,000 rials per A4 page to UK and Europe, 11,000 rials to Australia and 15,000 rials to North America. Sending a fax from

Iran isn't cheap. If you want to send a few words this may be cheaper (but not as quick).

Telegraph From just about every main telephone office, or the occasional special telegraph office (*telegrāfkhūné*), you can send telegrams out of Iran in English, or within Iran in Fārsī. This ends up being far cheaper than sending a fax if you don't need to fill up a full A4 page. Charges to most western countries are around 150 rials a word with a minimum of seven words. International telegrams out of Iran rarely take more than a couple of working days to get through, and staff seem to try hard: one Swiss traveller reported that the telegraph office at Emām Khomeinī Square in Tehrān 'even called my hotel because they were not sure of the French spelling'.

Some top hotels run a telex machine for the use of guests, but at about double the rate charged by the telephone or telegraph office.

Email Though there are a few Internet service providers in Iran (see Online Services later in this chapter), they cater exclusively for private users. There are no Internet cafés, or drop-in email centres, but if you find one please send us an email and let us know!

BOOKS
Most books are published in different editions by different publishers in different countries. As a result, a book might be a hardcover rarity in one country but readily available in paperback in another. Fortunately, bookshops and libraries search by title or author, so your local bookshop or library is best placed to advise you on the availability of the following recommended reading.

You should be particularly careful about carrying any books with you into Iran: anything with a hint of immorality on the cover or in the title, anything disrespectful to the government, or, of course, anything written by Mr Rushdie, is likely to get confiscated. You can pick up some novels in French, English and German from a few bookstalls in Tehrān, but generally speaking you should bring all your own reading material. Bring lots of books: the social scene in Iran is not exactly riveting.

Lonely Planet

Lonely Planet covers the region extensively. Among our travel survival kits are *Turkey*, *Pakistan*, *Central Asia* (Turkmenistan and so on) and the *Arab Gulf States* (Bahrain, Kuwait, Oman, Qatar, United Arab Emirates and Saudi Arabia). For broader coverage of the region, pick up *Middle East on a shoestring*, which covers the Arab Gulf states, plus Afghanistan, Egypt, Iran, Iraq, Israel and the Palestinian territories, Jordan, Lebanon, Syria, Turkey and Yemen.

Guidebooks

There is very little in the way of modern guidebooks about Iran (and you are holding the best anyway!). If you browse through some of the bookshops listed in the relevant sections, you will often be able pick up a few very outdated, but fascinating, guidebooks, written before the Islamic Revolution (in 1979).

Gita Shenasi, *Iran Today*. This guidebook, published in 1995, is mildly useful, but provides little extra to supplement the Lonely Planet guidebook, and omits everything about the Caspian provinces. *Iran Today* is widely available in Iran, and costs 30,000 rials – but don't bother buying the sister guide to Tehrān, which is very dated (1991).

Golshani, MMA, *A New Guide to Iran (Persia)*. Printed in 1971, and certainly no longer 'new', this is a gem, and worth picking up anywhere you can in Iran. The chapter about 'Cabarets & Nightclubs' is a classic, and the prices for the Hilton Hotel in Tehrān (US$9/12 for a single/double) should not be taken literally, but there are some handy insights into pre-Revolutionary tourism in Iran.

Ministry of Foreign Affairs, *A Glance at the Islamic Republic of Iran*. Available at the bookshop in the MFA, near Emām Khomeinī Square in Tehrān, this is an interesting, pocket-sized guide, including all sorts of details about Iran, though it naturally toes the government line.

Tagg, Roger, *Travels with a Peykan* (sic). This is another pre-Revolutionary gem, detailing trips by the day, and the weekend, for expats based in Tehrān. The road instructions are obsolete, and don't rely on the maps, but there are some handy hints.

Tourism Development & Promotion Department, *Welcome to Iran*. This pre-Revolutionary booklet concentrates on the 'Asian Highway' between Turkey and Afghanistan (when it was safe to drive there). You can ignore the section entitled 'Night Owl's Tehran' but there is some useful advice.

Travel

Azadi, Sousan, *Out of Iran*. This a revealing, though one-sided, autobiography of a member of the westernised Iranian élite who stayed on after 1979, resolutely refusing to give up the pleasures of life proscribed under the Islamic Republic. The story closes with her harrowing escape from Iran in 1982, in the untrustworthy hands of Kurdish smugglers.

Byron, Robert, *The Road to Oxiana*. Widely acknowledged as one of the great travel books of its era, this is a vividly observed and often hilarious diary of a slow passage from England to the River Oxus (the Amu Darya) in north-west Afghanistan, with lengthy jaunts through Iran en route. Although Byron has a scholarly preoccupation with Islamic architecture, the book remains a classic travel book more for its lively descriptive prose and for its often biting sketches of contacts with local people and encounters with disobliging officials.

Curzon, GN, *Persia and the Persian Question*. This two-volume opus is characteristically scathing about all things Persian. (Curzon is probably more famous for saying: 'My name is George Nathaniel Curzon. I am a most superior person.') An historical work, as well as a travel book, the original is now very hard to come by, but an abridged reprint, *Curzon's Persia*, skips the heavier historical chapters.

Danziger, Nick, *Danziger's Travels: Beyond Forbidden Frontiers*. A true modern adventurer, Danziger travelled through Turkey, Iran, Afghanistan, Pakistan and China to Hong Kong, without much regard for tiresome formalities like visas, entry and exit stamps, or travel permits. It is loaded with enough hair-raising adventures to make all but the most seasoned traveller feel inadequate.

Newby, Eric, *A Short Walk in the Hindu Kush*. One of those gloriously eccentric travel books that could only have been written by an Englishman, it covers a haphazard 1950s jaunt by the author and friend from England to the Hindu Kush by way of Turkey and Iran.

Sackville-West, Vita, *Passenger to Teheran*. This thin volume details the exploits of an Englishwoman travelling by car across Europe, Turkey and Iran. The memoirs are often amusing, though not always politically correct.

Stark, Freya, *Beyond Euphrates*. This classic is packed with affectionate reminiscences from a fearless lone woman's travels through Luristan (roughly the present-day province of Lorestān) and other remote parts of Iran in the 1930s.

Stark, Freya, *Valleys of the Assassins*. The redoubtable Miss Stark describes a similarly uncompromising journey through the mountainous Caspian region of that name.

History & Politics

Ghirshman, R, *Iran: From the Earliest Times to the Islamic Conquest*. Though written in 1954, this history is still the easiest to read (and carry), and includes plenty of sketches and photos to help you make some sense out of the various dynasties and archaeological sites. It is available from a few bookshops around Iran.

Rahnema, Saeed & Behdad, Sohrab, *Iran After the Revolution: Crisis of an Islamic State*. This book outlines, through a number of essays by prominent Muslims and Islamists, the achievements (or lack of them) of the Iranian governments since the Islamic Revolution.

Simpson, John, *Behind Iranian Lines*. This is one of the best accounts of life after the Islamic Revolution; Simpson shared Khomeinī's fateful Paris to Tehrān flight in 1979, and took full advantage of an unexpected invitation to return in 1987.

Poetry

All three of these books are available at the bookshop at Hāfez's tomb in Shīrāz.

Hāfez, *Fifty Poems of Chemsed Din Mohammed Hafiz* (sic). This definitive work of the renowned Shīrāzī poet, commonly known as Hāfez, includes poems in Fārsī, and translated into English, German and French (50,000 rials).

Khayyām, Omar, *Rubaïyat of Omar Khayyam*. This very famous work of Khayyām now includes poems translated into English, French and Arabic (30,000 rials).

Ross, James, *Sadi's Gulistan or Flower Garden*. This is the most renowned collection of translated poems by the other famous Shīrāzī poet, Sa'dī. It is in English and costs a reasonable 18,000 rials.

Handicrafts

Fokker, N, *Persian & Other Oriental Carpets for Today*. This is a detailed and concise history of carpets, and an explanation about carpet-making, in the region, including Iran and Turkey.

Fukai, Shinji, *Persian Glass*. Everything you need to know about the intricate glasswares of Iran is included in this fine book.

Hull A & Barnard N, *Persian Kilims*. This new and impressive volume covers a lot of what most visitors need to know about Persian carpets and rugs, and includes heaps of helpful photos.

Liebetrau, Preben, *Oriental Rugs in Colour*. Probably the most useful guide to take around with you, this pocket-sized book includes a history and explanation of carpets and rugs in the region, including Iran and Turkey.

Sakhai, Essie, *Oriental Carpets: A Buyer's Guide*. This is very useful for anyone contemplating buying a carpet who doesn't know the *ghiordes* knot from the *senneh* knot.

Souvenir Books

Most cities have a few bookshops which sell a range of books about Iran, in English or a combination of English and Fārsī. Those with glossy photos often make excellent souvenirs, and though expensive by Iranian standards, they are usually a bargain compared with what they would cost you at home.

The Cultural Heritage of the Isfahan (sic) Province Organisation puts out a marvellous range of booklets about each attraction in Esfahān. They are cheap, and easy to carry, but only available at the Chehel Sotūn palace in Esfahān. Also, the Office of Exhibitions and Promotions Affairs publishes an excellent range of booklets about most provinces (but not all, yet). These are hard to find, but make excellent souvenirs.

Isfahan: The Living Museum. This is an impressive souvenir of Esfahān, but expensive at US$20.

Tehran at a Glance. Though the text (in English and Fārsī) is limited, it overflows with excellent photos of the city and province of Tehrān, including many fascinating old black and white shots of what the city used to look like (55,000 rials).

Dutz, Werner Felix & Matheson, Sylvia, *Parsa Persepolis*. This is one of the best books about Persepolis available in Iran.

Kasraian, N, *Isfahan*. With captions in English, and a number of outstanding photos of Esfahān, this makes a great souvenir of a great city.

Kasraian, N, *Persepolis*. Though the photos are excellent, most of the text and captions are in Fārsī, so it's more useful as a souvenir than a guide for traipsing around Persepolis.

Salar-Behzadi, Abdolreza, *Arg-e-Bam*. Though most of the text is in Fārsī, the photos (with captions in English) make this a worthwhile souvenir of your visit to the magnificent old city of Bam. It is available at the gate to the old city for a reasonable 18,000 rials.

Waite, James & Heydari, Jamieh, *Earth, Wind & Water*. Mr Waite produces a range of impressive books about Iran, all with magnificent photos.

Waite, James, *Iran: A Visual Journey*. This is another excellent publication by Mr Waite, jam-packed with outstanding photos.

Yassavoli, Javad, *The Fabulous Land of Iran*. One of the best, this is a marvellous collection of photographs about Iran – by Iranian photographers.

General

Boyle, J, *Persia: History and Heritage*. This is the best book to buy for an overview of all that is worth knowing about Iranian history, carpets, literature, painting, architecture, pottery and so on. Published in the UK, it's also available in Iran (59,000 rials).

Clavell, James, *Whirlwind*. This novel includes some historical information, and though an exciting read, the mood is gloomy at times.

Frye, Richard, *Persia* and *A Heritage of Persia*. These volumes are among the best books published prior to the Revolution on the history and culture of Iran.

Hekmat, Forough-es-Saltaneh, *The Art of Persian Cooking*. The definitive book about Iranian cuisine (including how to make your own kebabs when you get home – if you can ever face another one!). It is available in many shops in Iran.

Hobson, Sarah, *Through Persia in Disguise*. Published in 1973, this intriguing book is the forerunner to a number of biographies of women who have travelled through Islamic countries – but in this case, the author disguised herself as a boy.

Matheson, Sylvia, *Persia: An Archaeological Guide*. Most of the information in this scholarly but very readable companion to almost every significant historical or ancient ruin in Iran is still valid, though some of the travel details have inevitably become outdated, and the book only covers sites up to the Seljuq era (1051-1220).

Meshkati, Nosratollah, *A List of the Historical Sites and Ancient Monuments of Iran*. Though as dry as it sounds, this exhaustive work summarises every place worth visiting (and many more that are not), and includes some history, descriptions and, often, photos. Available in some bookshops in Iran, it is for the archaeological enthusiast, rather than the average tourist.

Pope, Arthur Upham, *Introducing Persian Architecture*. This short illustrated book, which is sadly almost unobtainable in western countries is a concise introduction to the marvels of Iranian building styles through the ages.

Rahman, Afzalur, *Islam: Ideology and the Way of Life*. Easy to read and well set out, this is a very useful guide for any non-Muslim wanting to learn more about Islam. Published in the UK, it should be available in other western countries.

Sami, Ali, *Persepolis*. Though it has not been reprinted since 1975, this is still probably the best and most useful of the locally-produced guides to Persepolis.

Saremi, Katayun et al, *Iranian Museums*. Though hardly riveting reading, this is the best (and probably the only) list of all the numerous museums throughout Iran. Written in English and Fārsī, it is available in Iran (69,000 rials).

Language

There are literally dozens of Fārsī-English (and vice versa) dictionaries for sale in Iran. Almost without exception, however, they cater for Iranian students learning English, so they translate every English word directly into Fārsī – useless for foreigners who don't read Fārsī script. Most of the phrasebooks listed below are only available at the Bouali Hotel bookshop in Hamādān.

Persian Language Guide. This thin volume (thankfully) ignores grammar, and provides many useful words and sentences. You can buy it in English or German.

Elwell-Sutton, LP, *Colloquial Persian*. This pocket-sized phrasebook is very handy, and includes some lessons on grammar and a very extensive dictionary.

Hawker, CL, *Simple Colloquial Persian*. This pocket-sized yellow and green booklet was printed before the Islamic Revolution, and covers most grammar and vocabulary.

Miandji, AM, *Modern Farsi*. This concentrates more on grammar than most users would prefer, but it's useful enough.

Nejad, H Hozhabr, *How to Learn Farsi in 29 Days?* Apparently more of a question than a statement, the author claims you can learn Fārsī in exactly 29 days. This small book is easy to use, though the grammar section is tough going. It is only available at the bookshop inside the Ministry of Foreign Affairs complex, in southern Tehrān.

ONLINE SERVICES

Iran is slowly joining the rest of the world through its own Internet service providers, though, of course, the requisite technology is only available to a tiny fraction of the population. The two main Internet service

Iran on the Internet

Online Service	Information	Address
Lonely Planet	Updated information from other travellers; worthwhile links	http://www.lonelyplanet.com/letters/meast/ira_pc.html
Iran Culture & Information Centre (Canada)	Excellent history and culture; and many links	http://www.IranVision.com
	Excellent links to permanent sites on Iran; travel section is also helpful	http://www.payvand.com
Neda Reyaneh	A well-organised site from Iran; lists many helpful addresses	http://www.neda.net
Iranian Embassy, Ottawa	Useful for visas (there's even a visa application form on the site); and other stuff of interest to all travellers	http://www.salamiran.org
Iranian Government	Colourful, and informative; lists embassy contact details, customs rules, and so on	http://www.netiran.com
University of Texas	Maps and geographical information	http://www.lib.utexas.edu/Libs/PCL/Map_collection/Atlas_middle_east
Bilkent University, (Turkey)	General travel advice	http://www.bilkent.edu.tr/pf/travel/iran.guide.html
	A useful site for culture, history and so on	http://www.iranonline.com
	One of the best for culture and history	http://www.knight3.cit.ics.saitama-u.ac.jp/hobbies/iran
	Photos of major sites of interest	http://www.mcrweb.com/iran
Export Promotion Center of Iran	All the business advice you may need	http://www.iranexport.com

providers are Irnet (support@Irnet.ir) and the Neda Rayaneh Institute (support@neda.net).

NEWSPAPERS & MAGAZINES
Newspapers
Of the 70 newspapers published every day in Iran, four are in English. If you ignore the extreme bias against the US and Israel, these English-language newspapers do include a number of interesting articles (bought or copied from reputable journalism agencies) about many places in the world, including photos of TV images from CNN. Some travellers may want to buy a newspaper for its

excellent coverage of European football (soccer) and basketball from the US (of all places).

The newspapers are all based in Tehrān, though you can usually pick up a current issue (or, maybe one a few days late) at bookstalls in most major cities in the country. The four newspapers are:

Iran Daily – this paper plans to devote a few pages each Thursday to local tourism. Many photos are in colour, and the newspaper is easy to read.

Iran News – this really toes the official line, but has a good world news section and some handy classifieds. (Its web site is http://netiran.com/news/IranNews/current/html)

Kayhan International – a fairly boring translation of the uninteresting government mouthpiece, and includes lots of riveting articles about meetings between the Iranian and Yemeni ministers of education.

Tehran Times – it publishes special liftouts at auspicious times, such as Nō Rūz, which are definitely worth picking up. It also has the best cartoons (from the US), and a good classifieds section.

Magazines

Local In recent times, a number of excellent English-language magazines about tourism in Iran have been produced, but they have all folded; look out for any new publications about tourism. An impressive range of locally-produced (mostly business) magazines in English are still produced and available at bookstalls in Tehrān. They are published every (Muslim) month, and include:

Envoy – a new glossy investment magazine published in Canada, but no other details were available at the time of writing.

Iran Exports & Imports – glossy but full of ads (5000 rials); PO Box 14335/746, Tehrān (☎ (21) 8801 800; fax 890 547).

Iran Today – another glossy business magazine, full of ads (10,000 rials); PO Box 19395/4363, Tehrān; (☎ (21) 8085 215; fax 8084 030).

Mahjubah – subtitled 'The Islamic Magazine for Women', it is exactly that, but interesting enough for foreign (male and female) readers; PO Box 14155/3899, Tehrān (☎ (21) 8897 662; fax 892 725).

Foreign In Tehrān, and a few other major cities in Iran, you may be able to pick up a copy of the latest issue of an international magazine, but prices (set by the magazines themselves, not by the shopkeepers) are quite high: eg *Time* (13,000 rials), *Newsweek* (11,000 rials) or *National Geographic* (31,000 rials). All pictures of women showing any flesh whatsoever will be blacked out by the censors, though articles criticising the Iranian government remain curiously untouched. You can even pick up some magazines published before the Islamic Revolution: I was desperate enough to buy a 1967 copy of *Reader's Digest*!

RADIO & TV

All Iranian radio and television stations are very heavily controlled by the state, and will be for a long time yet.

Radio

Most of the numerous radio stations are based in Tehrān and relayed to each province, though many provinces also have their own stations. As well as programs in minority languages such as Kurdish, Lors and Āzarī, there are programs in English, Spanish, French and Arabic, though don't rely on them for impartial news coverage. In 1997, former President Rafsanjānī inaugurated a Youth Radio Network to 'help strengthen the educational infrastructure of Iran's youth', so you can be sure that heavy metal and rap music won't feature too much.

The BBC World Service, most European international radio services and Voice of America can be picked up clearly in most parts of the country. The BBC is listened to by millions of Iranians, rightly distrustful of the state media network. Short-wave radios can be found in the most unlikely places, from the lowliest Afghan refugee's hovel to the bedside of the late Āyatollāh Khomeinī, who reportedly was an avid follower, if not supporter, of the BBC Persian Service.

Television

There are five television channels in Iran – imaginatively known as Channels 1, 2, 3, 4 and 5. They are all based in Tehrān, though a few programs emanate from some of the provinces. The few foreign programs are wholesome and not even remotely offensive, such as the adventures of *Skippy: The Bush Kangaroo*, or *The Little House on the Prairie*, and all badly dubbed into Fārsī. During religious holidays, all channels will show nothing but religious programs (replacing any normal international televised event such as the FA Cup final from London).

At around 11 pm, on Channel 4, there is a 15 minute bulletin of news in English. If you crave after some serious international news, however, take a short-wave radio, or buy an issue of *Time* or *Newsweek*.

Only at the upmarket hotels will you be able to see any satellite TV, such as CNN. In fact, any Iranian who wants a satellite dish must make a special application to the relevant ministry; permits are usually only granted to foreigners or Iranians who have already lived in the west, experienced the 'decadence' there, and unlikely to be 'corrupted' further by satellite TV. Confiscating illegal satellite dishes in Tehrān is big business.

PHOTOGRAPHY & VIDEO
Film & Equipment
Most towns in Iran have at least one photographic shop for film and/or development, though the range of film and camera equipment available is limited (except in Tehrān and Mashhad). Try to bring as much equipment or film as you are likely to need with you. Kodak, Agfa and Fuji are the most commonly available film brands. Average prices are 9000 to 10,000 rials for a roll of 24 exposures (print films); Kodak slide film, including processing, costs 26,000 rials. Always check the 'best before' date on the side of the box, as it may have been stored for ages in less than ideal conditions.

All over Iran there are small backroom photographers specialising in portraits, recognisable by the faded samples displayed at the entrance. Many of them do passport photos very cheaply, about 8000 rials for four colour shots ready to be collected the next day.

Photography
In most places at most times of the year lighting conditions during the day are good, so you can usually afford to use very slow-speed film. In fact one of the main problems is that the strong sunlight throws reflections on the lens (preventable with a lens hood) and casts very noticeable shadows which can spoil an otherwise good photograph. For this reason, buildings are often best photographed with the light directly overhead. For panoramic shots, however, the very bright light around noon can make photos looked washed out and lacking in depth, and often you'll find better lighting conditions shortly after sunrise or just before dusk. Timing is critical, for the light can change completely in a few minutes at the start and end of the day.

Many mosques and other buildings are poorly lit inside, so you'll need long exposures (several seconds), a powerful flash or faster film. A portable tripod can be very useful.

Video
Properly used, a video camera can give a fascinating record of your holiday. As well as videoing the obvious things – sunsets, spectacular views – remember to record some of the ordinary everyday details of life in the country. Often the most interesting things occur when you're actually intent on filming something else. Remember too that, unlike still photography, video 'flows', so, for example, you can shoot scenes of countryside rolling past the train window, to give an overall impression that isn't possible with ordinary photos.

Video cameras these days have amazingly sensitive microphones, and you might be surprised how much sound will be picked up. This can also be a problem if there is a lot of ambient noise – filming by the side of a busy road might seem OK when you do it, but viewing it back home might simply give you a deafening cacophony of traffic noise. One good rule to follow for beginners is to try to film in long takes, and don't move the camera around too much. Otherwise, your video could well make your viewers seasick! If your camera has a stabiliser, you can use it to obtain good footage while travelling on various means of transport, even on bumpy roads. And remember, you're on holiday – don't let the video take over your life, and turn your trip into an epic Cecil B De Mille production.

Make sure you keep the batteries charged, and have the necessary charger, plugs and transformer for the country you are visiting. Bring your own video cassettes, but remember that customs officials are eager to confiscate blank or used video cassettes on arrival if they believe there is any likelihood of something 'immoral' being on the tape.

Finally, remember to follow the same rules regarding peoples' sensitivities as for still photography – having a video camera shoved in their face is probably even more annoying and offensive for locals than a still camera. Always ask permission first.

Restrictions

You shouldn't have any problems photographing most of the things that tourists are expected to photograph, but elsewhere be prepared for a lot of stares if you stroll around with a suspicious-looking camera slung over your shoulder; a mile-long telephoto lenses is also bound to arouse curiosity. One traveller was told not to photograph anything outside the window on an Iran Air flight 20,000 feet in the air, but this seems a little paranoid, even in Iran.

Photography inside a mosque is generally never allowed, but outside or in the grounds of the mosque, photography is usually allowed – but always be respectful. Some mosques and museums do not permit still or video cameras at all (or charge you for using them), but there is always a sign indicating any restrictions (which are mentioned in the relevant text throughout the book anyway.)

At some government buildings, look out for (and observe) any 'No Photography' sign, or symbol of a camera with a cross through it. Don't take photos within range of any airport, naval dockyard, military installation, embassy/consulate, prison, train station, telephone office or anywhere else with security implications, or anything within several kilometres of any land border. If in doubt, ask first.

Photographing & Filming People

Most Iranians are happy to have their picture taken by camera or video if you ask them, and quite often it's hard to get children away from the front of your lens. Never point the lens at women without permission, and respect any refusal. Always be respectful

about photographing or filming anyone in a mosque.

Airport Security

In some airports, particularly in the southeast of the country, customs officials may take batteries out of all electrical equipment, including cameras and camera flashes, and put them in a security box together with guns and other 'dangerous' items. When you arrive at the other end you may have a long wait for your package to emerge.

Almost all airports have x-ray machines for checking luggage, but the customs guards are usually (but not always) happy to inspect camera bags separately.

TIME

Iranians place little value on time. You will see very few public clocks, even in Tehrān (and most are wrong, anyway, so beware); and many Iranians do not possess such a thing as a watch. Promises like 'I'll see you at seven' should never be taken literally, especially when the meeting is at your place. The Iranians' flexible sense of time does not always work both ways, however, as Iranians generally expect foreigners to be punctual.

Time throughout Iran is 3½ hours ahead of Greenwich Mean Time (GMT). Clocks go forward one hour between mid-March and mid-September. When it's noon in Tehrān (during normal, non-summer time), it is:

San Francisco	12.30 am
New York and Toronto	3.30 am
London	8.30 am
Ankara (and all of Turkey)	11.00 am
Baku (and all of Azerbaijan)	11.30 am
Moscow	11.30 am
Kabul	1 pm
Islamabad, Quetta and Karachi	1.30 pm
Ashghabat (and all of Turkmenistan)	1.30 pm
Tokyo	5.30 pm
Sydney	6.30 pm
Auckland	8.30 pm

ELECTRICITY

The electricity system is on 220V, 50 cycles AC. The sockets have two circular holes. Since few hotels have a backup generator powerful enough to provide emergency lighting in guests' rooms, keep a torch or at least some candles in an easily accessible part of your luggage – though electricity supplies have improved markedly since the 'black' days after the Iran-Iraq War.

WEIGHTS & MEASURES

Various parts of the Persian Empire used to have their own system of weights and measures, but nowadays the metric system has permeated to almost every part of Iran. There is a standard conversion table at the back of this book.

You may still come across the *sīr* (about 75g) and the *chārak* (10 sīr) in some remote places. Gold and other precious metals are still often measured by the *mesghāl*, equal to 4.7g. The *farsang* is an old Persian measure of distance which used to differ from place to place but is about 6km. Feet and nautical miles continue to be used in aeronautical and naval circles.

LAUNDRY

There are reliable laundries, and dry cleaning services, in most Iranian cities (but no laundrettes), and many hotels will have a laundry service for guests. Invariably, your clothes will be scrubbed thoroughly to remove all the sand, mud and muck (and the odd button) you've accumulated on your trip, and then lovingly ironed, and finally wrapped in a newspaper to take away. 'Where is a laundry?' translates in Fārsī as *Rakhtshūkhūné kojāst?*

Prices are cheap, and slightly negotiable: a grimy shirt and trousers in Bandar-é Abbās cost me 3500 rials in total; a huge bundle of filthy stuff costs 8500 rials in Shīrāz. Most laundries will not accept underclothes, and laundry workers (who are mostly male) will not accept female underclothes. Generally, you can, and should, wash your 'smalls' in the hotel sink; hot water is plentiful and washing detergent and soaps are widely available. If you're doing your own washing, a universal bath plug is indispensable.

HEALTH

Travel health depends on your predeparture preparations, your daily health care while travelling and how you handle any medical problem that does develop. While the potential dangers can seem quite frightening, in reality few travellers experience anything more than upset stomachs.

Iran is not an unhealthy country by the standards of West Asia. Your chances of falling prey to some tropical disease are generally a lot lower than in places further east, though if you do want to come back with an interesting oriental malady to liven up your dinner-table conversation, the opportunities are there. Malaria is very infrequent, but there have been some rare cases of cholera.

Predeparture Planning

Immunisations For some countries (including Iran) no immunisations are necessary, but, like many countries, if you are coming from infected areas of Africa or South America, proof of vaccination against yellow fever is usually required before entry into Iran. Be aware that there is often a greater risk of disease with children and during pregnancy.

Everyday Health
Normal body temperature is 37°C or 98.6°F; more than 2°C (4°F) higher indicates a high fever. The normal adult pulse rate is 60 to 100 per minute (children 80 to 100, babies 100 to 140). As a general rule the pulse increases about 20 beats per minute for each °C (2°F) rise in fever.

The respiration (breathing) rate is also an indicator of illness. Count the number of breaths per minute: between 12 and 20 is normal for adults and older children (up to 30 for younger children, 40 for babies). People with a high fever or serious respiratory illness breathe more quickly than normal. More than 40 shallow breaths a minute could indicate pneumonia. ■

Plan ahead for getting your vaccinations: some of them require more than one injection, while some vaccinations should not be given together. It is recommended you seek medical advice at least six weeks before travel.

Record all vaccinations on an International Health Certificate, available from your doctor or government health department.

Discuss your requirements with your doctor, but vaccinations you should consider for this trip (and for the general region) include:

- *Hepatitis A* The most common travel-acquired illness after diarrhoea, and it can put you out of action for weeks. Havrix 1440 is a vaccination which provides long term immunity (possibly more than 10 years) after an initial injection and a booster at six to 12 months. Gamma globulin is not a vaccination but a ready-made antibody collected from blood donations. It should be given close to departure because, depending on the dose, it only protects for two to six months.

  Twinrix, a combined hepatitis A and hepatitis B vaccination, is also available. This combined vaccination is recommended for people wanting protection against both types of viral hepatitis. Three injections over a six-month period are required.
- *Typhoid* This is an important vaccination to have where hygiene is a problem. Available either as an injection or oral capsules.
- *Diphtheria & Tetanus* Diphtheria can be a fatal throat infection and tetanus can be a fatal wound infection. Everyone should have these vaccinations. After an initial course of three injections, boosters are necessary every 10 years.
- *Meninogococcal Meningitis* Healthy people carry this disease; it is transmitted like a cold and you can die from it within a few hours. There are many carriers and vaccination is recommended for travellers to certain parts of Asia, India, Africa and South America. A single injection will give good protection for three years. The vaccine is not recommended for children under two years because they do not develop satisfactory immunity from it.
- *Hepatitis B* This disease is spread by blood and by sexual activity. Travellers who should consider a hepatitis B vaccination include those visiting countries where there are known to be many carriers, where blood transfusions may not be adequately screened or where sexual contact is a possibility. It involves three injections, the quickest course being over three weeks with a booster at 12 months.

- *Polio* Polio is a serious, easily transmitted disease, still prevalent in many developing countries. Everyone should keep up to date with this vaccination. A booster every 10 years maintains immunity.
- *Rabies* Vaccination should be considered by those who will spend a month or longer in a country where rabies is common, especially if they are cycling, handling animals, caving, travelling to remote areas, or for children (who may not report a bite). Predepature rabies vaccination involves having three injections over 21 to 28 days. If someone who has been vaccinated is bitten or scratched by an animal they will require two booster injections of vaccine, those not vaccinated require more.
- *Tuberculosis* TB risk to travellers is usually very low. For those who will be living with or closely associated with local people in high risk areas such as Asia, Africa and some parts of the Americas and Pacific, there may be some risk. As most healthy adults do not develop symptoms, a skin test before and after travel to determine whether exposure has occurred may be considered. A vaccination is recommended for children living in these areas for three months or more.

Malaria Medication Malaria is one of the world's greatest killer diseases in tropical and subtropical countries. In Iran the risk is not very great, but there is a slight danger between March and October, mainly in the Persian Gulf region. The malaria parasite is spread by certain species of mosquito, and quickly goes on to infect its new host's liver and bloodstream.

- Antimalarial drugs do not prevent you from being infected but they kill the malaria parasites during a stage in their development and significantly reduce the risk of becoming very ill or dying. Expert advice on medication should be sought, as there are many factors to consider including the area to be visited, the risk of exposure to malaria-carrying mosquitoes, the side effects of medication, your medical history and whether you are a child or adult or pregnant. Travellers to isolated areas in high risk countries may like to carry a treatment dose of medication for use if symptoms occur.

Health Insurance Make sure that you have adequate health insurance. See Travel Insurance under Visas & Documents earlier in this chapter.

Travel Health Guides If you are planning to be away or travelling in remote areas for a long period of time, you may like to consider taking a more detailed health guide.

Staying Healthy in Asia, Africa & Latin America, Dirk Schroeder, Moon Publications, 1994. Probably the best all-round guide to carry; it's compact, detailed and well organised.

Travellers' Health, Dr Richard Dawood, Oxford University Press, 1995. Comprehensive, easy to read, authoritative and highly recommended, though it's rather large to lug around.

Where There is No Doctor, David Werner, Macmillan, 1994. A very detailed guide intended for someone, such as a Peace Corps worker, going to work in an underdeveloped country.

Travel with Children, Maureen Wheeler, Lonely Planet Publications, 1995. Includes advice on travel health for young children.

There are also a number of excellent travel health sites on the Internet. From the Lonely Planet home page there are links at http://www.lonelyplanet.com/weblinks/weblinks.htm to the WHO and the US Centers for Disease Control & Prevention.

Other Preparations Make sure you're healthy before you start travelling. If you are going on a long trip, make sure your teeth are OK. If you wear glasses take a spare pair and your prescription.

Basic Rules

Food There is an old colonial adage which says: 'If you can cook it, boil it or peel it you can eat it, otherwise forget it', but in Iran, a salad served in any decent restaurant is generally safe. Vegetables and fruit which cannot be peeled should be washed with purified water. Beware of ice cream which might have been melted and refrozen; if there's any doubt (eg a power cut in the last day or two) steer well clear. Shellfish such as mussels, oysters and clams should be avoided as well as undercooked meat, particularly in the form of mince. Steaming does not make shellfish safe for eating.

The general rule is: if a place looks clean and well run and the vendor also looks clean and healthy, then the food is probably safe. In general, places that are packed with travellers or locals will be fine, while empty restaurants are questionable. The food in busy restaurants is cooked and eaten quite quickly with little standing around and is probably not reheated.

Medical Kit Check List

Consider taking a basic medical kit including:

☐ **Aspirin** or paracetamol (acetaminophen in the USA) – for pain or fever.

☐ **Antihistamine** (such as Benadryl) – useful as a decongestant for colds and allergies, to ease the itch from insect bites or stings, and to help prevent motion sickness. Antihistamines may cause sedation and interact with alcohol (not a problem in Iran) so care should be taken when using them; take one you know and have used before, if possible.

☐ **Antibiotics** – useful if you're travelling well off the beaten track, but they must be prescribed; carry the prescription with you.

☐ **Loperamide** (eg Imodium) or Lomotil for diarrhoea; prochlorperazine (eg Stemetil) or metaclopramide (eg Maxalon) for nausea and vomiting.

☐ **Rehydration mixture** – for treatment of severe diarrhoea; particularly important for travelling with children.

☐ **Antiseptic** such as povidone-iodine (eg Betadine) – for cuts and grazes.

☐ **Multivitamins** – especially for long trips when dietary vitamin intake may be inadequate.

☐ **Calamine lotion** or **aluminium sulphate spray** (eg Stingose) – to ease irritation from bites or stings.

☐ **Bandages** and Band-Aids.

☐ **Scissors, tweezers** and a **thermometer** (note that mercury thermometers are prohibited by airlines).

☐ **Cold and flu tablets** and **throat lozenges** – pseudoephedrine hydrochloride (Sudafed) may be useful if flying with a cold to avoid ear damage.

☐ **Insect repellent, sunscreen, lip balm, chap stick** and **water purification tablets**.

☐ **A couple of syringes** – in case you need injections in a country with medical hygiene problems. Ask your doctor to write a note explaining why they have been prescribed.

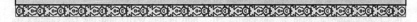

Nutrition

If your food is poor or limited in availability, if you're travelling hard and fast and therefore missing meals, or if you simply lose your appetite, you can soon start to lose weight and place your health at risk.

Make sure your diet is well balanced. Cooked eggs, beans, lentils and nuts are all safe ways to get protein. Fruit you can peel (bananas, oranges or mandarins for example) is usually safe (melons can harbour bacteria in their flesh and are best avoided) and a good source of vitamins. Try to eat plenty of grains (including rice) and bread. Remember that although food is generally safer if it is cooked well, overcooked food loses much of its nutritional value. If your diet isn't well balanced or if your food intake is insufficient, it's a good idea to take vitamin and iron pills.

In hot climates make sure you drink enough – don't rely on feeling thirsty to indicate when you should drink. Not needing to urinate or passing small amounts of very dark yellow urine are danger signs. Always carry a water bottle with you on long trips. Excessive sweating can lead to loss of salt and therefore muscle cramping. Salt tablets are not a good idea as a preventative, but in places where salt is not used much adding salt to food can help. ■

Water Water is safe to drink in Tehrān, and in just about everywhere else in the country. (I drank several litres of water every day, and had no problems.) Unless you can live on tea, soft drinks, or milkshakes (made with unboiled local water anyway), you will probably end up drinking tap water anyway. Bottled mineral water is very hard to find, and probably not much better than the stuff coming out of the tap. It is easy enough to bring a water container (or reuse a plastic mineral water bottle), and refill it with tap water constantly, with a purification tablet or two for good measure.

Water Purification The simplest way of purifying water is to boil it thoroughly. Vigorously boiling for five minutes should be satisfactory; however, at high altitude water boils at a lower temperature, so germs are less likely to be killed. Boil it for longer in these environments.

Consider purchasing a water filter for a long trip. There are two main kinds of filters. Total filters take out all parasites, bacteria and viruses, and make water safe to drink. They are often expensive, but they can be more cost effective than buying bottled water. Simple filters (which can even be a nylon mesh bag) take out dirt and larger foreign bodies from the water so that chemical solutions work much more effectively;

if water is dirty, chemical solutions may not work at all. It's very important when buying a filter to read the specifications, so that you know exactly what it removes from the water and what it doesn't.

Simple filtering will not remove all dangerous organisms, so if you cannot boil water it should be treated chemically. Chlorine tablets (Puritabs, Steritabs or other brand names) will kill many pathogens, but not some parasites like giardia and amoebic cysts. Iodine is more effective in purifying water and is available in tablet form (such as Potable Aqua). Follow the directions carefully and remember that too much iodine can be harmful.

Medical Problems & Treatment

Self-diagnosis and treatment can be risky, so you should always seek medical help. Although we do give drug dosages in this section, they are for emergency use only. Correct diagnosis is vital.

Antibiotics should ideally be administered only under medical supervision. Take only the recommended dose at the prescribed intervals and use the whole course, even if the illness seems to be cured earlier. Stop immediately if there are any serious reactions and don't use the antibiotic at all if you are unsure that you have the correct one. Some people are allergic to some commonly prescribed antibiotics such as penicillin or sulpha drugs; carry this information when travelling, eg on a bracelet.

Medications If you require a particular medication take an adequate supply, as it may not be available locally. There is a minimal charge for medicines on prescription, more than 90% of which are made in Iran, but few are labelled in English. You should be careful when buying drugs as the expiry date may have passed, or correct storage conditions may not have been followed.

If you're looking for a particular medicine over the counter, try to find out its generic name rather than its western trademark, which may not be used or understood in Iran. Take the prescription with you wherever you travel, to show that you are legally using the medication – it's surprising how often over-the-counter drugs from one place are illegal without a prescription or even banned in another. Pharmacies are easy to spot in Iran, and often have the word 'drug' in English on the shop window. Pharmacists are well-trained, and usually speak enough English to make sure you get the right medication.

Medical Facilities If you are mildly sick, you should seek advice from someone at your hotel, or an Iranian friend. They should be able to find a reputable doctor who speaks English, and hopefully one who will come to your hotel. If your situation is more serious, contact your embassy, which should be able to recommend a reputable doctor and/or hospital – and arrange everything, if they feel inclined.

If the illness or injury is life-threatening, contact your embassy immediately and consider flying home (assuming you have medical insurance to cover the costs).

The standard of medical facilities varies greatly throughout Iran. The best place to fall ill is Tehrān – a disproportionate number of doctors and medical establishments are in the capital. Many of the doctors in Tehrān, and the major provincial cities, received their training in the west and in most large places

you shouldn't have much problem finding one who speaks English. Conversely, in less developed areas medical facilities are often far from adequate.

Doctors' surgeries often concentrate around the major hospitals, and along main roads in the centre of town. More often than not, the doctors' signposts, usually hanging off the side of an office block, are standard and easy to recognise: they are square with black or blue edges, surrounding the name and specialty of the doctor (mostly in English).

Consultations are very cheap (about 8000 rials), but if you want a reputable doctor, who has been trained in a foreign country and speaks English, the doctor will probably charge more – about 30,000 rials (and this is no time to be stingy).

There are ambulances in most major cities, but it's not unusual for the ambulance services to spend more time arguing between each other about who will transport the victim than taking them to hospital.

Environmental Hazards

Altitude Sickness Lack of oxygen at high altitudes (more than 2500m) affects most people to some extent. The effect may be mild or severe and occurs because less oxygen reaches the muscles and the brain at high altitude, requiring the heart and lungs to compensate by working harder. Symptoms of Acute Mountain Sickness (AMS) usually develop during the first 24 hours at altitude but may be delayed up to three weeks. Mild symptoms include headache, lethargy, dizziness, difficulty sleeping and loss of appetite. AMS may become more severe without warning and can be fatal. Severe symptoms include breathlessness, a dry, irritative cough (which may progress to the production of pink, frothy sputum), severe headache, lack of coordination and balance, confusion, irrational behaviour, vomiting, drowsiness and unconsciousness. There is no hard-and-fast rule as to what is too high: AMS has been fatal at 3000m, though 3500m to 4500m is the usual range.

Treat mild symptoms by resting at the same altitude until recovery, usually a day or two. Paracetamol or aspirin can be taken for headaches. If symptoms persist or become worse, however, *immediate descent is necessary*; even 500m can help. Drug treatments should never be used to avoid descent or to enable further ascent.

The drugs acetazolamide (Diamox) and dexamethasone are recommended by some doctors for the prevention of AMS, however their use is controversial. They can reduce the symptoms, but they may also mask warning signs; severe and fatal AMS has occurred in people taking these drugs. In general, we do not recommend them for travellers.

To prevent acute mountain sickness:

- Ascend slowly – have frequent rest days, spending two to three nights at each rise of 1000m. If you reach a high altitude by trekking, acclimatisation takes place gradually and you are less likely to be affected than if you fly directly to high altitude.
- It is always wise to sleep at a lower altitude than the greatest height reached during the day if possible. Also, once above 3000m, care should be taken not to increase the sleeping altitude by more than 300m per day.
- Drink extra fluids. The mountain air is dry and cold and moisture is lost as you breathe. Evaporation of sweat may occur unnoticed and could result in dehydration.
- Eat light, high-carbohydrate meals for more energy.
- Avoid alcohol as it may increase the risk of dehydration (not a problem in Iran).
- Avoid sedatives.

Fungal Infections Fungal infections occur more commonly in hot weather and are usually found on the scalp, between the toes or fingers, in the groin and on the body (ringworm). You get ringworm (which is a fungal infection, not a worm) from infected animals or other people. Moisture encourages these infections.

To prevent fungal infections wear loose, comfortable clothes, avoid artificial fibres, wash frequently and dry carefully. If you do get an infection, wash the infected area at least daily with a disinfectant or medicated soap and water, and rinse and dry well. Apply an antifungal cream or powder like tolnaftate (Tinaderm). Try to expose the infected area to air or sunlight as much as possible and wash all towels and underwear in hot water, change them often and let them dry in the sun.

Heat Exhaustion Dehydration and salt deficiency can cause heat exhaustion. Take time to acclimatise to high temperatures, drink sufficient liquids and do not do anything too physically demanding.

Salt deficiency is characterised by fatigue, lethargy, headaches, giddiness and muscle cramps; salt tablets may help, but adding extra salt to your food is better.

Anhydrotic heat exhaustion, caused by an inability to sweat, is quite rare. It is likely to strike people who have been in a hot climate for some time, rather than newcomers.

Heatstroke This serious, occasionally fatal, condition can occur if the body's heat-regulating mechanism breaks down and the body temperature rises to dangerous levels. Long, continuous periods of exposure to high temperatures and insufficient fluids can leave you vulnerable to heatstroke.

The symptoms are feeling unwell, not sweating very much (or at all) and a high body temperature (39°C to 41°C or 102°F to 106°F). Where sweating has ceased the skin becomes flushed and red. Severe, throbbing headaches and lack of coordination will also occur, and the sufferer may be confused or aggressive. Eventually the victim will become delirious or convulse. Hospitalisation is essential, but in the interim get victims out of the sun, remove their clothing, cover them with a wet sheet or towel and then fan continually. Give them fluids if they are still conscious.

Hypothermia Too much cold can be just as dangerous as too much heat. If you are trekking at high altitudes or simply taking a long bus trip over mountains, particularly at night, be prepared. In northern Iran and the Caspian provinces, always be prepared for cold, wet or windy conditions at any time of the year, even if you're just out walking or hitching.

Hypothermia occurs when the body loses heat faster than it can produce it and the core temperature of the body falls. It is surprisingly easy to progress from very cold to dangerously cold due to a combination of wind, wet clothing, fatigue and hunger, even if the air temperature is above freezing. It is best to dress in layers; silk, wool and some of the new artificial fibres are all good insulating materials. A hat is important, as a lot of heat is lost through the head. A strong, waterproof outer layer (and a 'space' blanket for emergencies) are essential. Carry basic supplies, including food containing simple sugars to generate heat quickly and fluid to drink.

Symptoms of hypothermia are exhaustion, numb skin (particularly toes and fingers), shivering, slurred speech, irrational or violent behaviour, lethargy, stumbling, dizzy spells, muscle cramps and violent bursts of energy. Irrationality may take the form of sufferers claiming they are warm and trying to take off their clothes.

To treat mild hypothermia, first get the person out of the wind and/or rain, remove their clothing if it's wet and replace it with dry, warm clothing. Give them hot liquids – no alcohol (not a problem in Iran) – and some high-kilojoule, easily digestible food. Do not rub victims, instead allow them to slowly warm themselves. This should be enough to treat the early stages of hypothermia. The early recognition and treatment of mild hypothermia is the only way to prevent severe hypothermia, which can be a life-threatening condition.

Jet Lag Jet lag is experienced when a person travels by air across more than three time zones (each time zone usually represents a one-hour time difference). It occurs because many of the functions of the human body (such as temperature, pulse rate and emptying of the bladder and bowels) are regulated by internal 24-hour cycles. When we travel long distances rapidly, our bodies take time to adjust to the 'new time' of our destination,

and we may experience fatigue, insomnia, disorientation, impaired concentration, anxiety and loss of appetite. These effects will usually be gone within three days of arrival, but to minimise the impact of jet lag:

- Rest for a couple of days prior to departure.
- Try to select flight schedules that minimise sleep deprivation; arriving late in the day means you can go to sleep soon after you arrive. For very long flights, try to organise a stopover.
- Avoid excessive eating (which bloats the stomach) and alcohol (which causes dehydration) during the flight. Instead, drink plenty of uncarbonated, non-alcoholic drinks such as fruit juice or water.
- Avoid smoking.
- Make yourself comfortable by wearing loose-fitting clothes and perhaps bringing an eye mask and ear plugs to help you sleep.
- Try to sleep at the appropriate time for the time zone you are travelling to.

Motion Sickness Eating lightly before and during a trip will reduce the chances of motion sickness. If you are prone to motion sickness try to find a place that minimises movement – near the wing on aircraft, close to midships on boats, near the centre on buses. Fresh air usually helps; reading and cigarette smoke don't. Commercial motion-sickness preparations, which can cause drowsiness, have to be taken before the trip commences. Ginger (available in capsule form) and peppermint (including mint-flavoured sweets) are natural preventatives.

Prickly Heat Prickly heat is an itchy rash caused by excessive perspiration trapped under the skin. It usually strikes people who have just arrived in a hot climate. Keeping cool, bathing often, drying the skin and using a mild talcum or prickly heat powder or resorting to air-conditioning may help.

Sunburn In the deserts of Iran or at high altitude you can get sunburnt surprisingly quickly, even through cloud. Use a sunscreen, hat, and barrier cream for your nose and lips. Calamine lotion or Stingose are good for mild sunburn. Protect your eyes with good quality sunglasses, particularly if you will be near water, sand or snow.

Pollution Air pollution is a major problem in Tehrān, most of all in summer. Tehrānīs tell the visitor, almost with pride, that they live in one of the most polluted cities in the world. If you suddenly start spluttering and coughing, and develop headaches and stomach pains, after a day or two in the capital, or suffer from bad asthma, you're probably just reacting very naturally to the unhealthy air. Escape from Smog City, or head up the hills in northern Tehrān – you'll stage a miraculous recovery.

Infectious Diseases

Diarrhoea Simple things like a change of water, food or climate can all cause a mild bout of diarrhoea, but a few rushed toilet trips with no other symptoms is not indicative of a major problem.

Dehydration is the main danger with any diarrhoea, particularly in children or the elderly as dehydration can occur quite quickly. Under all circumstances *fluid replacement* (at least equal to the volume being lost) is the most important thing to remember. Weak black tea with a little sugar, soda water, or soft drinks allowed to go flat and diluted 50% with clean water are all good. With severe diarrhoea a rehydrating solution is preferable to replace minerals and salts lost. Commercially available oral rehydration salts (ORS) are very useful; add them to boiled or bottled water. In an emergency you can make up a solution of six teaspoons of sugar and a half teaspoon of salt to a litre of boiled or bottled water. You need to drink at least the same volume of fluid that you are losing in bowel movements and vomiting. Urine is the best guide to the adequacy of replacement – if you have small amounts of concentrated urine, you need to drink more. Keep drinking small amounts often. Stick to a bland diet as you recover.

Lomotil or Imodium can be used to bring relief from the symptoms, though they do not actually cure the problem. Only use these drugs if you do not have access to toilets, eg

if you *must* travel. For children under 12 years Lomotil and Imodium are not recommended. Do not use these drugs if the person has a high fever or is severely dehydrated.

In certain situations antibiotics may be required: diarrhoea with blood or mucous (dysentery), any fever, watery diarrhoea with fever and lethargy, persistent diarrhoea not improving after 48 hours and severe diarrhoea. In these situations gut-paralysing drugs like Imodium or Lomotil should be avoided.

A stool test is necessary to diagnose which kind of dysentery you have, so you should seek medical help urgently. Where this is not possible the recommended drugs for dysentery are norfloxacin 400mg twice daily for three days or ciprofloxacin 500mg twice daily for five days. These are not recommended for children or pregnant women. The drug of choice for children would be co-trimoxazole (Bactrim, Septrin, Resprim) with dosage dependent on weight. A five-day course is given. Ampicillin or amoxycillin may be given in pregnancy, but medical care is necessary.

Amoebic dysentery is gradual in the onset; fever may not be present. It will persist until treated and can recur and cause other health problems.

Giardiasis is another type of diarrhoea. The parasite causing this intestinal disorder is present in contaminated water. The symptoms are stomach cramps, nausea, a bloated stomach, watery, foul-smelling diarrhoea and frequent gas. Giardiasis can appear several weeks after you have been exposed to the parasite. The symptoms may disappear for a few days and then return; this can go on for several weeks. Tinidazole, known as Fasigyn, or metronidazole (Flagyl) are the recommended drugs. Treatment is a 2mg single dose of Fasigyn or 250mg of Flagyl three times daily for five to 10 days.

Hepatitis Hepatitis is a general term for inflammation of the liver. It is a common disease worldwide. The symptoms are fever, chills, headache, fatigue, feelings of weakness and aches and pains, followed by loss of appetite, nausea, vomiting, abdominal pain, dark urine, light-coloured faeces, jaundiced (yellow) skin and the whites of the eyes may turn yellow. **Hepatitis A** is transmitted by contaminated food and drinking water. The disease poses a real threat to the western traveller. You should seek medical advice, but there is not much you can do apart from resting, drinking lots of fluids, eating lightly and avoiding fatty foods. People who have had hepatitis should avoid alcohol for some time after the illness, as the liver needs time to recover.

Hepatitis E is transmitted in the same way. It can be very serious in pregnant women.

There are almost 300 million chronic carriers of **Hepatitis B** in the world. It is spread through contact with infected blood, blood products or body fluids, for example through sexual contact, unsterilised needles and blood transfusions, or contact with blood via small breaks in the skin. Other risk situations include having a shave, tattoo, or having your body pierced with contaminated equipment. The symptoms of type B may be more severe and may lead to long term problems. **Hepatitis D** is spread in the same way, but the risk is mainly in shared needles.

Hepatitis C can lead to chronic liver disease. The virus is spread by contact with blood usually via contaminated transfusions or shared needles. Avoiding these is the only means of prevention.

HIV & AIDS HIV, the Human Immunodeficiency Virus, develops into AIDS, Acquired Immune Deficiency Syndrome, which is a fatal disease. HIV is a major problem in many countries. Any exposure to blood, blood products or body fluids may put the individual at risk. The disease is often transmitted through sexual contact or dirty needles – vaccinations, acupuncture, tattooing and body piercing can be potentially as dangerous as intravenous drug use. HIV/AIDS can also be spread through infected blood transfusions; some developing countries cannot afford to screen blood used for transfusions.

If you do need an injection, ask to see the syringe unwrapped in front of you, or take a needle and syringe pack with you.

Fear of HIV infection should never preclude seeking treatment for serious medical conditions.

Intestinal Worms These parasites are most common in rural, tropical areas. The different worms have different ways of infecting people. Some may be ingested on food including undercooked meat and some enter through your skin. Infestations may not show up for some time, and although they are generally not serious, if left untreated some can cause severe health problems later. Consider having a stool test when you return home to check for these and determine the appropriate treatment.

Schistosomiasis Also known as **bilharzia**, this disease is carried in water by minute worms. However, the threat in Iran is negligible. They infect certain varieties of freshwater snails found in rivers, streams, lakes and particularly behind dams. The worms multiply and are eventually discharged into the water.

The worm enters through the skin and attaches itself to your intestines or bladder. The first symptom may be a tingling and sometimes a light rash around the area where it entered. Weeks later a high fever may develop. A general feeling of being unwell may be the first symptom, or there may be no symptoms. Once the disease is established abdominal pain and blood in the urine are other signs. The infection often causes no symptoms until the disease is well established (several months to years after exposure) and damage to internal organs irreversible.

Avoiding swimming or bathing in fresh water where bilharzia is present is the main method of preventing the disease. Even deep water can be infected. If you do get wet, dry off quickly and dry your clothes as well.

A blood test is the most reliable test, but the test will not show positive in results until a number of weeks after exposure.

Sexually Transmitted Diseases Gonorrhoea, herpes and syphilis are among these diseases; sores, blisters or rashes around the genitals, discharges or pain when urinating are common symptoms. In some STDs, such as wart virus or chlamydia, symptoms may be less pronounced or not observed at all, especially in women. Syphilis symptoms eventually disappear completely but the disease continues and can cause severe problems in later years. While abstinence from sexual contact is the only 100% effective prevention, using condoms is also effective. The treatment of gonorrhoea and syphilis is with antibiotics. The different sexually transmitted diseases each require specific antibiotics. There is no cure for herpes or AIDS.

Typhoid Typhoid fever is a dangerous gut infection caused by contaminated water and food. Medical help must be sought.

In its early stages sufferers may feel they have a bad cold or flu on the way, as early symptoms are a headache, body aches and a fever which rises a little each day until it is around 40°C (104°F) or more. The victim's pulse is often slow relative to the degree of fever present – unlike a normal fever where the pulse increases. There may also be vomiting, constipation, diarrhoea and abdominal pain.

In the second week the high fever and slow pulse continue and a few pink spots may appear on the body; trembling, delirium, weakness, weight loss and dehydration may occur. Complications such as pneumonia, perforated bowel or meningitis may occur.

The fever should be treated by keeping the victim cool and giving them fluids as dehydration should be watched for. Ciprofloxacin 750mg twice a day for 10 days is good for adults.

Chloramphenicol is recommended in many countries. The adult dosage is two 250mg capsules, four times a day. Children aged between eight and 12 years should have half the adult dose; and younger children one-third the adult dose.

Insect-Borne Diseases
Filariasis, dengue fever, leishmaniasis and typhus are insect-borne diseases, but they do not pose a great risk to travellers to Iran. For more information on them see Less Common Diseases at the end of the Health section.

Malaria This serious and potentially fatal disease is spread by mosquito bites. If you are travelling in endemic areas it is extremely important to avoid mosquito bites and to take tablets to prevent this disease. Symptoms range from fever, chills and sweating, headache, diarrhoea and abdominal pains to a vague feeling of ill-health. Seek medical help immediately if malaria is suspected. Without treatment malaria can rapidly become extremely serious and can even be fatal.

If medical care is not available, malaria tablets can be used for treatment. You need to use a malaria tablet which is different to the one you were taking when you contracted malaria. The treatment dosages are mefloquine (two 250mg tablets and a further two six hours later) and fansidar (single dose of three tablets). If you were previously taking mefloquine then other alternatives are halofantrine (three doses of two 250mg tablets every six hours) or quinine sulphate (600mg every six hours). There is a greater risk of side effects with these dosages than in normal use.

Travellers are advised to prevent mosquito bites at all times. The main messages are:

* wear light coloured clothing
* wear long pants (necessary in Iran anyway) and long-sleeved shirts
* use mosquito repellents containing the compound DEET on exposed areas (available in most grocery shops in Iran)
  Prolonged overuse of DEET may be harmful, especially to children, but its use is considered preferable to being bitten by disease-transmitting mosquitoes.
* avoid wearing perfumes or aftershave
* use a mosquito net impregnated with mosquito repellent (permethrin) – it may be worth taking your own
* impregnating clothes with permethrin effectively deters mosquitoes and other insects

Cuts, Bites & Stings

Rabies is passed through animal bites. See Less Common Diseases at the end of this section for details of this disease.

Bedbugs & Lice Bedbugs live in various places, but particularly in dirty mattresses and bedding, shown by spots of blood on bedclothes or on the wall. Bedbugs leave itchy bites in neat rows. Calamine lotion or Stingose spray may help.

All lice cause itching and discomfort. They make themselves at home in your hair (head lice), your clothing (body lice) or in your pubic hair (crabs). You catch lice through direct contact with infected people or by sharing combs, clothing and the like. Powder or shampoo treatment will kill the lice and infected clothing should then be washed in very hot, soapy water and left in the sun to dry.

Insect Bites & Stings Bee and wasp stings are usually painful rather than dangerous. However in people who are allergic to them severe breathing difficulties may occur and require urgent medical care. Calamine lotion or Stingose spray will give relief and ice packs will reduce the pain and swelling. There are some spiders with dangerous bites but antivenenes are usually available. Scorpion stings are notoriously painful and in some parts of Asia, the Middle East and Central America can actually be fatal. Scorpions often shelter in shoes or clothing.

Cuts & Scratches Wash well and treat any cut with an antiseptic such as povidone-iodine. Where possible avoid bandages and Band-Aids, which can keep wounds wet. Coral cuts are notoriously slow to heal and if they are not adequately cleaned, small pieces of coral can become embedded in the wound.

Leeches & Ticks Leeches may be present in damp rainforest conditions (not common in Iran); they attach themselves to your skin to suck your blood. Trekkers often get them on their legs or in their boots. Salt or a lighted cigarette end will make them fall off. Do not pull them off, as the bite is then more likely to become infected. Clean and apply pressure if the point of attachment is bleeding. An insect repellent may keep them away.

You should always check all over your body if you have been walking through a potentially tick-infested area as ticks can cause skin infections and other more serious diseases. If a tick is found attached, press down around the tick's head with tweezers, grab the head and gently pull upwards. Avoid pulling the rear of the body as this may squeeze the tick's gut contents through the attached mouth parts into the skin, increasing the risk of infection and disease. Smearing chemicals on the tick will not make it let go and is not recommended.

Snakes To minimise your chances of being bitten always wear boots, socks and long trousers when walking through undergrowth where snakes may be present. Don't put your hands into holes and crevices, and be careful when collecting firewood.

Snake bites do not cause instantaneous death and antivenenes are usually available. Immediately wrap the bitten limb tightly, as you would for a sprained ankle, and then attach a splint to immobilise it. Keep the victim still and seek medical help, if possible with the dead snake for identification. Don't attempt to catch the snake if there is a possibility of being bitten again. Tourniquets and sucking out the poison are now comprehensively discredited.

Women's Health

Gynaecological Problems Sexually transmitted diseases are a major cause of vaginal problems. Symptoms include a smelly discharge, painful intercourse and sometimes a burning sensation when urinating. Male sexual partners must also be treated. Medical attention should be sought and remember in addition to these diseases HIV or hepatitis B may also be acquired during exposure. Besides abstinence, the best thing is to practise safe sex using condoms.

Antibiotic use, contraceptive pills, sweat

and synthetic underwear can lead to fungal vaginal infections when travelling in hot climates. Maintaining a high level of personal hygiene, and wearing loose-fitting clothes and cotton underwear will help to prevent these infections.

Fungal infections, characterised by a rash, itch and discharge, can be treated with a vinegar or lemon-juice douche, or with yoghurt. Clotrimazole pessaries, nystatin, miconazole or vaginal cream are the usual treatment.

Pregnancy It is not advisable to travel to some places while pregnant as some vaccinations normally used to prevent serious diseases are not advisable in pregnancy, eg yellow fever. In addition, some diseases are much more serious for the mother (and may increase the risk of a stillborn child) in pregnancy, eg malaria.

Most miscarriages occur during the first three months of pregnancy. Miscarriage is not uncommon, and can occasionally lead to severe bleeding. The last three months should also be spent within reasonable distance of good medical care. A baby born as early as 24 weeks stands a chance of survival, but only in a good modern hospital. Pregnant women should avoid all unnecessary medication, vaccinations and malarial prophylactics should still be taken where needed. Additional care should be taken to prevent illness and particular attention should be paid to diet and nutrition. Alcohol and nicotine, for example, should be avoided.

Less Common Diseases
The following diseases pose a small risk to travellers, and so are only mentioned in passing. Seek medical advice if you think you may have any of these diseases.

Cholera This is the worst of the watery diarrhoeas and medical help should be sought. Outbreaks of cholera are generally widely reported, so you can avoid such problem areas. *Fluid replacement is the most vital treatment* – the risk of dehydration is

severe as you may lose up to 20 litres a day. If there is a delay in getting to hospital then begin taking tetracycline. The adult dose is 250mg four times daily. It is not recommended for children under nine years nor for pregnant women. Tetracycline may help shorten the illness, but adequate fluids are required to save lives.

Dengue Fever There is no preventative drug available for this mosquito-spread disease which can be fatal in children. A sudden onset of fever, headaches and severe joint and muscle pains are the first signs before a rash develops. Recovery may be prolonged.

Filariasis This is a mosquito-transmitted parasitic infection found in many parts of Africa, Asia, Central and South America and the Pacific. Possible symptoms include fever, pain and swelling of the lymph glands; inflammation of lymph drainage areas; swelling of a limb or the scrotum; skin rashes and blindness. Treatment is available to eliminate the parasites from the body, but some of the damage already caused may not be reversible. Medical advice should be promptly sought if the filariasis infection is suspected.

Leishmaniasis A group of parasitic diseases transmitted by sandfly bites, found in many parts of the Middle East, Africa, India, Central and South America and the Mediterranean. Cutaneous leishmaniasis affects the skin tissue causing ulceration and disfigurement and visceral leishmaniasis affects the internal organs. Seek medical advice as laboratory testing is required for diagnosis and correct treatment. Avoiding sandfly bites is the best precaution. Bites are usually painless, itchy and are yet another reason to cover up and apply repellent.

Rabies Rabies is a fatal viral infection found in many countries. Many animals can be infected (such as dogs, cats, bats and monkeys) and it is their saliva which is infectious. Any bite, scratch or even lick from a warm-blooded, furry animal should be cleaned immediately and thoroughly. Scrub with soap and running water, and then apply alcohol or iodine solution. Medical help should be sought promptly to receive a course of injections to prevent the onset of symptoms and death.

Tetanus Tetanus occurs when a wound becomes infected by a germ which lives in soil and in the faeces of horses and other animals. It enters the body via breaks in the skin. All wounds should be cleaned promptly and adequately and an antiseptic cream or solution applied. Use antibiotics if the wound becomes hot, throbs or pus is seen. The first symptom may be discomfort in swallowing, or stiffening of the jaw and neck; this is followed by painful convulsions of the jaw and whole body. The disease can be fatal.

Tuberculosis (TB) TB is a bacterial infection usually transmitted from person to person by coughing but may be transmitted through consumption of unpasteurised milk. Milk that has been boiled is safe to drink, and the souring of milk to make yoghurt or cheese also kills the bacilli. Travellers are usually not at great risk as close household contact with the infected person is usually required before the disease is passed on.

Typhus Typhus is spread by ticks, mites or lice. It begins with fever, chills, headache and muscle pains followed a few days later by a body rash. There is often a large and painful sore at the site of the bite and nearby lymph nodes are swollen and painful. Typhus can be treated under medical supervision. Seek local advice on areas where ticks pose a danger and always check your skin (including hair) carefully for ticks after walking in a danger area such as a tropical forest.

A strong insect repellent can help, and serious walkers in tick areas should consider having their boots and trousers impregnated with benzyl benzoate and dibutylphthalate.

TOILETS

The toilets in Iran are either the European sit-down type, or the Asian squat kind, but even if you pay US$40 for a hotel room, you may still have to squat over a hole in the ground, so be prepared for this at any place. Public toilets, which may not always be that clean, are few and far between – a main park in the centre of town is a good place to start looking. There are always toilets at bus or train stations, or airport terminals. Doing your 'business' in a clean, modern and often European-style toilet while visiting a museum, or other tourist attraction, is a great idea.

Toilet paper is only reliably provided in top-end hotels, so always bring your own if you don't want to do it the local way (ie the left hand and an urn of water). Some grocery shops in major cities sell toilet paper, but it may take some time to hunt down the right shop. Next to the toilet there is often a bucket full of used toilet paper. Please dispose of your toilet paper in the bucket; many toilets are not designed for paper. Every toilet you are likely to use is connected to sewers, and most have flushes, though sometimes you have to pour water (there is always a tap in the toilet) down the hole.

WOMEN TRAVELLERS
Attitudes to Women

Islam, and in particular the Iranian interpretation of Islam, does impose a number of constraints on women, and no foreign woman should visit Iran unless she is prepared to fit in with the social code. You may not agree with all or any of it, but if you are not prepared to observe the rules you will simply be refused entry into Iran, or have an extremely unpleasant time; Iran is not the place to make a feminist statement. But in general, the only hassle for foreign women is wearing the appropriate type of clothing (see later on); and the good news is that foreign women who have travelled – or struggled – through Pakistan and/or Turkey will feel far more comfortable in Iran.

The downside is that you may feel isolated because of difficulties in making contact

Women Travellers in Iran

Courtesy and charm are embedded in the Iranian character, social laws of hospitality and welcome being particularly strong. The attitude to women in Iran is in keeping with these customs, and with an extra layer of respect. Women travellers should experience nothing but a friendly reception wherever they go, as long as they respect the laws of the country.

Iran has been much maligned, especially for its attitude to women. However, Iranian fundamentalism is considered liberal in its treatment of women in the Middle East: in Iran, they have access to education and careers. There is not what people from western countries would call equality, but when you glance at Iran's eastern neighbour, Afghanistan, where women are barely let out of the house, Iran seems positively progressive. There is a branch of Islamic feminism now recognised, influenced mainly by ex-President Rafsanjānī's daughter, a member of Parliament who is responsible for advances such as women being permitted to ride bicycles and hop on the back of their men's moped. (This is a particularly enchanting contradiction: it would be considered immodest for a woman to drive her own moped, but hitching up a chādor to clamber on behind your man is fine.)

Hejāb ('modest dress') laws are usually enforced at airports and other borders. Some airports are stricter than others: Shīrāz, Esfahān and Bandar-é Abbās airports are three to watch out for. Men and women enter by different doors. Once through the door bearing the sign 'sisters', body searches are carried out by serious-looking female security. These can feel curiously intrusive and the best way to avoid this is to make sure that you are wearing no jewellery or carrying anything that creates a bump under the layers of clothes.

Kamin Mohammadi

with local people, not because they don't want to be friendly but because they are afraid to make the first move. Even when travelling with a man, Iranian men and women (in company of an Iranian man) will almost constantly talk to the foreign man. This can often be unsettling, especially if the conversation lasts several hours over dinner, and you, as a woman, are rarely spoken to, or even acknowledged.

If you want to make contact with people, you are going to need self-confidence. You may find it easier to stick to making friends with Iranian women, but not many female Iranians speak English (except some middle or upper class Tehrānīs), so you should try to learn some Fārsī. If you aren't prepared to make an extra effort, you may find yourself marginalised and you may miss out on the best that Iran has to offer.

As a foreign woman, I was the subject of constant (and unbelievable!) curiosity. Local women would stare at me all the time. The first who spotted me would advise her friends or relatives, and they would all stare, pointing at me and laughing behind their veils (chādors). I was totally covered in black (apart from my face and hands) but they would recognise me as a foreigner from miles away ... very few women dared to talk to me. The two who did were very nice and hospitable, and we ended up having dinner in the house of one of them.

Laura Bertolotto, Italy

On the plus side, a foreign woman will sometimes be considered as an honorary male, and accepted into all-male preserves, such as the teahouse, in a way that no Iranian woman could ever be. Of course, you can also enter female society far more than any man (Iranian or foreign) could ever do. Unaccompanied foreign women are often treated with extra courtesy and indulgence because of their perceived vulnerability. When it comes to finding scarce hotel accommodation or plane tickets, or lining up at places like the visa extension office, an unaccompanied woman is almost certainly at an advantage over a man in the same position.

Although the girls in our group were obliged to wear a headscarf (the penalty for not doing so is 74 lashes), they were treated with friendliness, courtesy and respect by most Iranian men. That was not the case in Pakistan. A female would certainly get more harassment walking past a building site in England than in Iran.

Pat Daniel, UK

Safety Precautions

Many Iranian men are sexually repressed, and some do have distorted ideas about western women, but it is very wrong to think that every male has sexually-motivated ulterior motives. If you keep strictly to the dress and social codes, you will earn the respect of local people and you are unlikely to suffer any serious harassment. Never lead men on; they don't need much encouragement here. In Iran, the man does the wooing.

Always lock the door of your hotel room, and reinforce your security with something solid like a chair under the door handle. Some male (and even female) hotel staff and guests will try to open the door to your room using the 'I've gone in the wrong room' excuse. Most do not have bad intentions: they just want to see what you look like without a scarf and coat. Women can normally stay in cheap hotels, and can often share rooms with a foreign male companion, even if he is not your husband. Refer to Dangers & Annoyances later in this chapter for more details on sharing rooms with men.

If you do become a victim of harassment, tell your persecutor firmly but politely to desist (English will do), and try to enlist the sympathy of other Iranians around you. If they think that someone is behaving badly towards you, they are very likely to stop him out of shame. If you scream blue murder you won't gain anyone's sympathy and the situation may even get worse. If the problem persists, a mere mention of the word 'Komīté' (religious police) can have an instantly sobering effect, though if you really do want to complain to the authorities, the local police are the first people to go to. Thanks to social constraints, you will rarely be alone with an Iranian male unless you want to be (and perhaps not even then), but if a situation is likely to turn out that way, it is wise to exercise caution.

Some foreign women may feel happier about going to Iran in a group or with a male companion, but neither is by any means necessary. It might be a good idea to wear a wedding ring, whether you are married or not, to ward off any unwelcome attention, and at times it may be sensible to say that your husband is travelling with you or about to join you – but in general, Iranians will respect your status because they know that foreigners have different rules. Iranian women can, and do, travel unaccompanied in their own country, though to a far lesser extent than western women.

What to Wear

By law, all females over the age of seven must wear the *hejāb* – the general term to describe the type of Islamic dress required for females in Iran. Foreign women do not have to wear the chādor, that all-encompassing, head-to-toe black 'tent' (which is what

---

Khatamī & womens' rights

Since coming to office in 1997 President Khatamī has put a new emphasis on the status of women, stating that discrimination between men and women was an oppression of men, women and a humane society. Khatamī has appointed a woman as one of his vice-presidents as well as two female cabinet ministers, the first since the 1979 revolution. One is a minister without portfolio with a special advisory role on women, the other is the environment minister. Both are former academics.

When he was Minister for Culture under President Rafsanjānī, Khatamī allowed a female pop singer to hold a concert in Tehrān (to a female audience). He lost his cabinet post in 1992 for doing so.

In 1997 four women were named as family court judges, while the previous year the first female prosecutor was appointed. Accounts of crimes against women now feature in Iran's media, when not so long ago they were largely kept secret.

Iran opposes Afghanistan's Taliban militia, who have practically banned women from leaving their homes. Iran has refused to recognise the Taliban as the Afghan government, and it has been a strong critic of the Taliban's ideas on the role of women, which it describes as a 'headache'.

Richard Plunkett

'chādor' means in Fārsī) which most Iranian women wear, unless you visit a particularly holy place on a mourning day. However, if you wear a chādor you are more likely to be respected.

The second evening in the bazaar in Rasht, I was approached by a group of men. The leader said politely in good English that my wife was not dressed properly. My wife asked: 'Why? What is wrong with my dress?' As a good Muslim, he continued to talk to me ... the same evening my wife bought a modern chādor and felt more at ease (though too hot). Our Iranian female friends also felt more at ease with my wife's chādor.

Jan Beukema & Saskia Brinks, Netherlands

Cover up properly in black or dark colours. Cover your hair better than the locals do. You'll be amazed by the result. Nasty comments will turn into big smiles and freebies.

Hanne Finholt, Norway

The most common mode of dress for middle and upper class Iranian women, and one that foreign women can easily buy and use, is the *roupush*, a sort of baggy trench coat – though you will have to bring something like this with you to get past the immigration officials at the border or airport. The coat must be below the knee; for comfort, a light fabric is recommended if travelling in the summer; a dark, plain colour is preferable (black is not necessary); the coat must not show any shape of the body; the coat has to be buttoned to the neck; and trousers (jeans are OK) must be worn underneath. Alternatively, wear a longer coat which reaches the ankles, so you don't have to wear trousers. In this case, thick, dark socks or tights will complete the ensemble.

To top it off, women who do not wear a chādor, must wear a scarf. This should be in a plain colour (though some Iranian women are starting to wear bright patterns); and it must cover the neck, throat and all hair, allowing a fringe of a couple of centimetres. Women must wear covered shoes: sneakers are OK, but sandals or flip-flops are not acceptable outside of your hotel room. Try to wear very little make-up, or better, none at all; and keep jewellery to a minimum.

Don't underestimate the possibility of gaining the attention of the ubiquitous Komīté, who are often on the lookout for foreign women who are dressed improperly:

I travelled around a bit with a Dutch woman ... she wore flower-patterned trousers, a normal shirt, and a headscarf. No coat of dark colours. People in the street went mad at seeing her – the traffic stopped ... on two occasions, a soldier bitterly argued with her, but she just ignored him. A few times, male teenagers sought some physical contact.

Laura Bertolotto, Italy

GAY & LESBIAN TRAVELLERS

Homosexuality is illegal in Iran, and punishable by hundreds of lashes or even worse (though foreigners are more likely to get deported). But this should not deter gay and lesbian travellers from visiting Iran (questions about sexuality are not asked on visa applications, or at immigration). All gays and lesbians must simply refrain from all overt signs of affection in public, and even abstain from homosexual activity in the privacy of their own hotel room (which could be under some sort of surveillance by the police).

DISABLED TRAVELLERS

As long as you are healthy, and come with the right frame of mind, there is no reason why a disabled traveller cannot enjoy much of what Iran has to offer. Depending on the nature of your disability, you may wish to fly rather than take long-distance (but still reasonably comfortable) buses or trains, and stay at upmarket hotels which should have elevators and European-style, sit-down toilets. The downside is that Iran is not set up for wheelchairs, so ramps are virtually non-existent.

SENIOR TRAVELLERS

Senior travellers can enjoy most of Iran's attractions, as long as they are fit and healthy, and come with the right attitude. You may want to fly rather than take long-distance buses or trains, and stay at up-market hotels which have elevators, English-speaking staff, decent beds and a restaurant downstairs, as well as European-style, sit-down toilets. You should bring your own medications, and prescriptions, though medical facilities in the major cities are quite good.

TRAVEL WITH CHILDREN

In Iran, foreign children will be the source of much amusement and curiosity (which may, however, drive the children to despair after a while). Most simple medications, as well as powders, nappies (diapers) and so on, are available in major cities, though you may want to bring your own. Travel is easy, and middle-range hotels are mostly comfortable, so the hardest part will be trying to keep them entertained. Remember that all females over the age of seven, must wear the hejāb (see the Women Travellers section).

Anyone contemplating taking children to Iran should read *Travel with Children* by Lonely Planet's Maureen Wheeler. She has travelled all around the world with her kids, and lived to tell the tale.

DANGERS & ANNOYANCES

Although the Islamic Republic has been notorious for certain sorts of excitement involving foreigners, it has settled down considerably since the fanatical excesses after the Islamic Revolution. Incidents such as embassy sieges, the arrest and imprisonment of westerners without good reason, and protests by using incendiary devices are things of the past, though there are dissident groups operating in Iran, and the political situation can get volatile at times.

While foreigners do still suffer very occasional harassment from rogue elements of the security forces or, much more rarely, from individual Iranians, there are certain precautions that every visitor can take to significantly minimise the risk.

Crime

The pervasive influence of Islam, with its duties of courtesy and hospitality towards guests, reinforced by the vigilance of the law in tracking down and punishing offenders, makes Iran one of the safest countries in Asia for the foreign visitor.

Of course crime does exist in Iran, in spite of some of the world's severest penalties, so it pays to take the usual precautions. When travelling long distances by public transport, especially on international services, take your passport, money and camera as hand luggage and guard them at all stops – there is always a very slight possibility of theft by other passengers or at the frequent checkpoints en route, but mugging is extremely unlikely. A small number of pickpockets operate in some crowded bazaars.

Theft of luggage from a room in a hotel or mosāferkhūné (budget guesthouse) isn't very likely, since the staff keep a careful watch over visitors and residents. Nonresidents often have to leave their identity cards at reception if they want to go upstairs, and in many places they're strictly forbidden from any part of the hotel except the ground floor and restaurant. Hotels are securely locked or guarded at night. Most places also have a safe for guests' valuables. But don't be lulled into a false sense of security; practise normal security precautions.

The theft of motorcycles has become common recently, particularly in Tehrān. And even locals worry about parking their cars in the streets of Zāhedān, and anywhere near the Afghan and Pakistani borders (see under Car & Motorcycle in the Getting Around chapter).

In most cases the most valuable possession which westerners bring to Iran – and the hardest to replace – is a foreign passport. Largely because of the difficulties Iranians face in travelling legally to western countries, but also partly because of certain underworld operations, there is a booming black market in forged, stolen or illegally issued foreign passports, visas and work permits.

Precautions

Before entering Iran, memorise the address and telephone number of your diplomatic mission in Tehrān. (See the list in the Tehrān chapter for details. If yours isn't listed, check with your foreign ministry. If your country doesn't have a mission in Iran, find out which embassy, if any, looks after your country's interests in Iran.) Many western consulates advise their nationals to register with them on arrival in Iran (in person or by telephone); a good idea if you are in Iran for 10 days or more, or planning on going to remote places.

Traffic

Whenever the English-language newspapers print another story of another horrific car accident, they include (almost with pride) the claim that Iran has 'the highest rate of traffic accidents in the world' – presumably per person. More than 200,000 road accidents are *reported* every year (and how many more are not reported?), ie one accident per year for every 15 vehicles on the road. More than 5000 people die every year on the roads in Iran.

If you have travelled elsewhere in the region, you may be used to the traffic chaos throughout Iran; if you have arrived from the west, you will be horrified. Theoretically, there are road rules, but no-one pays a blind bit of notice to them. The willingness of a car to stop at a red light at a busy intersection is directly proportional to the number of armed traffic police the driver can see within rifle range. Some cars and all motorbikes (and sometimes even buses), use the designated bus lanes – which usually go in the *opposite* direction to the rest of the traffic. Motorbikes, with four children and three chickens on board, go through red lights, drive on footpaths and speed through crowded bazaars for one simple reason: they *can*. All this would be funny if it wasn't so damn dangerous.

While traffic in major cities rarely goes fast enough for your taxi or bus to have a serious accident, never underestimate the possibility of dying a horrible death under the wheels of any sort of vehicle while crossing the road. No vehicle whatsoever will stop at any pedestrian crossing at *any* time. Resist the temptation to amble across an eight-lane roundabout at peak time in downtown Tehrān with your back to the traffic like many Tehrānīs do. Always, look for the occasional walkway above or under the road, mainly used by crippled old Iranian ladies and terrified foreigners of all ages. The best idea is safety in numbers: shuffle across the road in a tightly-huddled group of locals. Drivers are less likely to run over a group of people because of the paperwork at the police station, and the potential damage to their precious Paykan.

Unmarried Foreign Couples

In the past, foreign unmarried couples have found it very difficult to share a room while travelling around Iran. Recently, however, hotel staff are starting to understand the weird and 'immoral' wishes of foreigners, and will often allow an unmarried couple to share a room. One easy way out is to take with you, or buy along the way, a wedding ring for the female (and, if possible, one for the male; this works even better); hotel receptionists often now accept that 'strange young foreign females' do not accept their husbands' family name.

I had planned to go to Iran by myself, but eventually a (male) friend of mine joined me. In the visa application we wrote we were married (he is Dutch, I am Italian, and we applied in Switzerland). Nobody ever doubted it, apart from a hotel owner who did not believe that people of different nationalities can be married. We just said it is possible, and that was it.

Security

Iran once had a reputation as a dangerous country for westerners to visit, but this is largely undeserved, especially now that things have settled down considerably. Open hostility towards western visitors (including Americans) is very, very rare in Iran and has declined in recent years. We continue to receive dozens of letters from foreigners who have been constantly surprised at the kindness and generosity shown to them during their visit to Iran, regardless of their own nationality. If you make an effort to fit in with local customs, you are very unlikely to be treated with anything but extreme courtesy and friendliness.

Police & Security Forces The Iranian police have a far better reputation for probity and efficiency than their counterparts in other countries in the region. There is a number of police forces (the exact name of the forces, and their uniforms, even confuse locals), but as long as you behave yourself, and dress appropriately, you will normally receive nothing but a smile, and a helping hand if you need it.

There is a traffic police force, but they long ago gave up policing the traffic. The highway police patrol the main intercity roads, attend to traffic accidents and man checkpoints. The ones to watch out for are the dreaded Komīté (Komīté-yé Enghelāb-é Eslāmī), literally the Islamic Revolutionary Committee or 'religious police'. Their primary roles are the monitoring of internal security and the enforcement of Islamic law, but they have also helped the army, navy, air force, border guards, regular police and highway police. They are recognisable by short stubbly beards, black collarless shirts and green fatigues; their symbol is an arm with a bandaged hand clutching a rifle. Be particularly obsequious if any of them cross your path – though this is unlikely if you behave yourself.

Bogus Police A few embassies in Iran have warned travellers about the possibility of being stopped by bogus policemen, as one recent traveller reported:

I was walking along the Chamrān Highway in Tehrān when a white Paykan stopped alongside me. There were two men in the car. One of them shouted 'Police: Stop', and showed me what he said was a police ID. He said he was searching for hashish, cocaine and heroin. I showed him the contents of my pockets. He asked to see my money and asked if I had 'papers' for it. I showed him my cash which he grabbed from me. I tried to get it back but he pushed me violently in the chest and I fell backwards. By the time I got to my feet, they were gone. I reported the matter to the real police who were most sympathetic. They told me they *never* stop foreigners, especially in plain clothes.

Peter Ward, UK

Another traveller also wrote to us with a very similar story; this time he was robbed just

north of Ferdōsī Square in Tehrān. We have never heard of any unpleasant behaviour from any *real* police or military officials against foreigners, so if you are forced to show passports and/or money by nasty men claiming to be police expect the worse. Refuse to cooperate unless you, and some local Iranians you must reel in for support, are satisfied that they are genuine. Never hand over anything vital like your passport or money while in the street; demand to visit the police station.

Security Checks Gun-toting Komīté, soldiers and regular policemen roam the streets and patrol the highways, checking on the movements of pedestrians and road users, but they very rarely trouble foreigners. Passport and baggage inspections and body frisks are routine (for everyone) on entry to some train stations and ports, at all airports, at some public gatherings and sometimes outside post and telephone offices, museums and other public buildings. After a fatal bomb blast a few years ago, security at public places in Mashhad is tighter than anywhere else in the country.

Foreigners are expected – though not legally compelled – to carry their passports with them at all times. If your visa is in order and nothing on your person is likely to inflict grievous bodily harm, have no fear. Sometimes cameras arouse suspicion (but the only time I thought I was in trouble for taking a photo near a police/security building. I found out the guards only wanted me to take a picture of themselves, and to deliver a copy to them the next day).

Checkpoints Refer to the Getting Around chapter for information about the frequent roadblocks-cum-checkpoints around the countryside.

Political Crises
The fundamentalists you may see on TV chanting 'Death to America! Death to Israel! Death to Britain!' (or whatever country is out

of favour at the time) are declaring their sincere hatred of the governments of those countries, and not of their private citizens. The late Āyatollāh Khomeinī is on record as saying that he had nothing against westerners as individuals, but only against their political leaders.

Iran is no stranger to political crises, and the situation is so liable to sudden change that it's hard to know what is going on. While the US and Israeli governments get most of the abuse thrown at them all the time, Germany suddenly became unpopular during the time of research. (A German court had alleged that the Iranian government was involved in the murder of some Iranian Kurdish dissidents in Germany.) This culminated in mammoth, and at times frightening, government-organised marches in every major city, and rallies outside the German embassy in Tehrān. Regardless of your nationality, stay well clear of all political marches and gatherings; don't take photos, don't discuss current politics with anyone you don't know well, and keep a low profile. It is also a very good idea to bring a short-wave radio with you to Iran, so you know what is going on.

LEGAL MATTERS

Like most things in Iran, the legal system is based on the principles of Islam, but it is not as extreme as some countries like the Sudan or Iraq where various parts of one's anatomy can be lopped off for any of a number of minor crimes. Refer to the Religion section in the Facts about Iran chapter for a rundown on Islamic *sharia* law.

Generally, the same activities which are illegal in your home country are illegal in Iran, but they usually attract harsher penalties. For Iranians, this may mean a public flogging for minor crimes, while more than 100 serious crimes, including adultery, homosexuality, and extreme blasphemy, carry the death sentence. For most minor crimes, foreigners will probably just get deported.

Drugs carry *extremely* harsh punishments, and the Iranian government takes its war against drug use (and drug smuggling from Pakistan and Afghanistan) very seriously. The smallest amount of hashish can carry a minimum six-month jail sentence, and don't expect any successful assistance from your embassy, a fair trial or a comfortable cell. We very strongly urge you to avoid using, carrying or selling any type of drugs (or alcohol). As one western diplomat put it, if you want to smuggle drugs you'd be better off doing it in Thailand – if you get caught there, at least you'll go to jail and live.

There are two crimes which foreigners may need to be aware of: homosexual activity is highly illegal, and for some Iranians has resulted in the death penalty; and the deliberate refusal to comply with the hejāb (the Islamic law regarding a woman's dress) may result in a public flogging. There are a few other odd crimes: in late 1995, the sale of seedless watermelons was banned because it apparently 'promotes homosexuality and asexuality'. (I did not find any seedless watermelons, so I cannot comment whether this is true or not!)

Getting Arrested

In the past, a few foreigners were subjected to arrest by the Komīté, but we have heard of no examples in the past few years. Nearly always the arrest is arbitrary, and simply because you are a foreigner, so you should be released after answering a few innocent questions.

In the very unlikely event that you get arrested, do not reply to, or appear to understand, any questions in any language but English (unless you speak Fārsī); and answer all questions politely, openly and diplomatically. Since the primary motives for arresting a foreigner without charge are usually curiosity, mild suspicion and the desire to appear powerful, answer your interrogators in such a way that their curiosity is satisfied, their suspicion allayed and their self-importance flattered. Take special care not to incriminate yourself or anyone else, Iranian or foreign, with a careless statement. Mention the name of your ambassador as often as possible, and try to get in contact with your embassy in Tehrān *immediately*.

BUSINESS HOURS

Knowing what is open, and when, is virtually a full-time occupation in itself. Few places have set opening and closing times, but you can rely on the fact that most places will close on Friday. Many shops and businesses all over Iran close during the afternoon for a siesta (from about 1 pm to 3 or 4 pm), and along the hot Persian Gulf, the siesta understandably stretches until about 5 pm. The only thing that does not stop during the afternoon throughout Iran is public transport.

The most likely time you will find anything open is between 9 am and noon, from Saturday to Wednesday. The following is a list of general opening times, but don't blame us if it still isn't open when you get there!

CALENDAR

Three calendars are in common use in Iran. The Persian solar calendar is the one in official and everyday use; the Muslim lunar calendar is used for Islamic religious matters; and the western (Gregorian) calendar is used in dealing with foreigners and in some history books. The Zoroastrians also have their own calendar (see the boxed text on the next page).

Traditionally both the Persian and Muslim days are reckoned as starting at sunset, but nowadays midnight is, for most practical purposes, regarded as the start of the Persian day. There is no easy way of converting a date from one system to another except by referring to an Iranian diary or calendar.

Persian Calendar

The modern Persian solar calendar, a direct

General Business Hours

Type of Business	Usual Days of Opening	Approximate Opening Times
Banks	Saturday to Wednesday, and Thursday morning	About 8 am to 4 pm; and 8 am to 12 pm (Thursday)
Government Offices	Saturday to Wednesday, and Thursday morning	8 am to 2 pm; and 8 am to 12 pm (Thursday)
Hotels	Every day	About 7 am to 11 pm (guards usually on duty at night)
Iran Air	Every day but Friday afternoon	7.30 am to 6 pm; and 7.30 am to 12 pm (Friday)
Mosques	Every day (but generally closed to foreigners on Friday mornings and mourning days)	Daylight hours
Museums	Six days a week, with a rostered day off (which can be any day of the week)	Generally 8.30 am to 5 pm
Post & Telephone Offices	Every day	8 am to 7 pm (closed earlier in smaller towns)
Private Businesses	Every day but Thursday afternoon and Friday	8 am or 9 am to 5 pm; and 8 am or 9 am to 12 pm (Thursday) – but closing for a siesta is not uncommon
Restaurants	Every day, but most are closed on religious holidays	12 to 2 pm; and 7 pm to 10.30 pm (often 8 pm to 10 pm in hotel restaurants)
Shops	Every day but Friday	8 or 9 am to about 1 pm; and 3 or 4 pm to 8 or 9 pm

descendant of the ancient Zoroastrian calendar, is calculated from the first day of spring in the year of the Hegira *(hejrat)* – the flight of the Prophet Mohammed from Mecca to Medina in 622 AD. It has 365 days (366 every leap year), with its New Year *(Nō Rūz)* usually falling on 21 March according to the western calendar. Dates given by the Persian calendar sometimes have AHS added after the year, when written in English. The names of the Persian months are as follows:

	Persian Month	Approximate Equivalent
SPRING (Bahār)	Farvardīn	21 Mar-20 Apr
	Ordībehesht	21 Apr-21 May
	Khordād	22 May-21 Jun
SUMMER (Tābestān)	Tīr	22 Jun-22 Jul
	Mordād	23 Jul-22 Aug
	Shahrīvar	23 Aug-22 Sep
AUTUMN (Pā'īz)	Mehr	23 Sep-22 Oct
	Ābān	23 Oct-21 Nov
	Āzar	22 Nov-21 Dec
WINTER (Zamestān)	Dei	22 Dec-20 Jan
	Bahman	21 Jan-19 Feb
	Esfand	20 Feb-20 Mar

The Zoroastrian Calendar

The Zoroastrian calendar has a solar year of 12 months of 30 days each, and five additional days. The week has no place in this system, and each of the 30 days of the month is named after and presided over by its own angel or archangel. The 1st, 8th, 15th and 23rd of each month are holy days. As in the Persian calendar, the Zoroastrian year begins in March at the vernal equinox. The months of the Zoroastrian calendar (most of which have the same names as the Persian calendar) run as follows:

SPRING (Bahār)	Farvardīn
	Ordībehesht
	Khordād
SUMMER (Tābestān)	Tīr
	Amordād
	Shahrīvar
AUTUMN (Pā'īz)	Mehr
	Ābān
	Āzar
WINTER (Zāmestān)	Dei
	Bahman
	Andarmaz

Muslim Calendar

The Muslim calendar, which is in official or unofficial use in all Islamic countries, starts from the month before the Hegira but, since it is based on the lunar year of 354 or 355 days, it is currently out of step with the Persian solar calendar by some 40 years. The names of the 12 months of the Muslim calendar in Fārsī are, in order: Moharram, Safar, Rabī'-ol-Avval, Rabī'-ol-Osānī (or Rabī'-ol-Ākhar), Jamādī-l-Ūlā, Jamādī-l-Okhrā, Rajab, Sha'bān, Ramazān, Shavvāl, Zū-l-Gha'dé and Zū-l-Hejjé.

PUBLIC HOLIDAYS & SPECIAL EVENTS

It is very important to take note of the public holidays, especially if you are travelling with a short visa which you hope to extend at a government office. Just about everything that can open will close on a religious holiday, but not necessarily so on a national holiday. But during public holidays, all forms of transport will still function normally, and all hotels will remain open (though understaffed), but only restaurants in a few upmarket hotels will usually be operating. During special mourning days, such as the anniversary of the martyrdom of Emām Hussein, thousands of men march around the streets, halting traffic in most cities.

Religious Holidays

The religious holidays listed on the next page follow the Muslim lunar calendar, so the dates according to the western calendar vary considerably every year. They are normally celebrated or commemorated with a public holiday, extended by government decree for a day or more if it falls near the Iranian weekend – but you probably won't know this unless you ask (or read Fārsī). The dates of religious holidays can change suddenly, however; in 1997 the Supreme Leader moved the anniversary of the death of the

Prophet's daughter Fatima forward by three weeks. Check the newspapers for upcoming holidays.

1 to 3 Shavvāl *Eid-é Fetr* is the Festival of the Breaking of the Fast that marks the end of Ramazān (see below). After sunset on the last day of Ramazān, Muslims spill out onto the streets, drivers honk their horns in celebration (which they do during the rest of the year anyway), and virtually everyone indulges in some serious overeating.

18 Zū-l-Hejjé *Ghadir-é Khom* commemorates the day that the Prophet Mohammed appointed Emām Alī as his successor, while returning to Mecca.

9 & 10 Moharram is the anniversary of the martyrdom of Hussein, the third emām of the Shi'ites, in battle at Karbala in October 680 AD. This is celebrated by religious dramas and sombre parades of devout Shi'ite men in black shirts. (See Passion Plays in the Arts section of the Facts about Iran chapter for further details.)

20 & 21 Safar or *arbaeen* is the 40th day after 9 & 10 Moharram, ie the commemoration of the assassination of Emām Hussein.

17 Rabī'-ol-Avval is the birthday of the Prophet Mohammed.

Ramazān Many Muslims do not regard the dawn to dusk month of fasting, known in Iran as Ramazān, as an unpleasant ordeal, but as a chance to perform a sort of ritual cleansing of body and mind. Some people, especially in urban centres, don't fully observe the fast, but most will fast for at least part of it. Ramazān is imposed on everyone in Iran, but foreigners and non-Muslims can still eat, drink (but not alcohol) and smoke behind closed doors, or in public with everybody else when night falls. Some Muslims are exempted from the fast (eg pregnant women, travellers, the elderly, and those who are sick and do not feel that they are able to keep to the fast), but they cannot eat or drink in front of others who are fasting.

Ramazān can be a trying period for non-Muslims, particularly when it coincides with a spell of hot weather. It is considered a very great sin to drink alcohol during Ramazān, and the penalties are much stiffer than at other times of year. The Komīté is at its most active at this time, and are often on the lookout for Iranians, and foreigners, who do not dress respectfully: long-sleeve shirts are preferable for men, and women must, of course, obey the hejāb.

Internal airlines still serve food to passengers in the daytime during Ramazān, and roadside cafés cater for travellers (and anyone else, for that matter). Many hotels in all categories keep their restaurants open in the daytime during Ramazān, or at least allow foreigners to order food in their rooms, since guests (Muslim or not) can consider themselves to be travelling and hence free from the obligation to fast. Other restaurants either close altogether or else only open for dinner after dark. Many shops selling food remain open throughout Ramazān, and you can buy food to take away and eat in your room.

During Ramazān, you shouldn't have too many problems in the larger cities, but you may not find any source of food at all during the daytime in rural areas and small towns. For this reason, Ramazān is probably not the best time of year to travel adventurously. Also, businesses and shops keep odd hours, tempers can flare and very little serious business gets done. Public transport continues to function, but schedules are often reduced. Not surprisingly, Eid-é Fetr, the day after Ramazān is finished, is celebrated in grand style.

National Holidays

To confuse matters, national holidays follow the Persian solar calendar, but they usually fall on the same day each year according to the western calendar. If they fall near the Iranian weekend, an extra holiday is sometimes declared. Like religious holidays (see above), most government offices are closed, easily disrupting your travel plans.

11 February (22 Bahman)
    is known as the Magnificent Victory of the Islamic Revolution of Iran, ie the anniversary of Khomeinī's coming to power in 1979.

20 March (29 Esfand)
    is Oil Nationalisation Day.

21 to 24 March (1 to 4 Farvardīn)
    is the *Eid-é Nō Rūz* or Iranian New Year (see the 'Traditions at Nō Rūz' boxed text on next page).

1 April (12 Farvardīn)
is Islamic Republic Day, marking the anniversary of the establishment of the Islamic Republic of Iran in 1979.

2 April (13 Farvardīn)
is the 13th day of the Iranian New Year. It is an ancient holiday when Iranians traditionally leave their houses for the day (see below).

4 June (14 Khordād)
is known as the Heart-Rending Departure of the Great Leader of the Islamic Republic of Iran, commemorating the death of Emām Khomeinī in 1989. About 500,000 Iranians flock to Tehrān, Ghom (where he trained and lived) and the village of Khomein (where he was born). Try not to be in Tehrān a few days before or after this event; if you are, don't expect to find anything open, or get on any transport.

5 June (15 Khordād)
is the anniversary of the arrest of Emām Khomeinī in 1963, following his speech urging the Muslims of the world to rise up against the superpowers.

28 June (7 Tīr)
is the anniversary of the bomb blast in 1980 at a meeting of the Islamic Republic Party which killed the revered Dr Seyed Beheshtī and several others.

8 September (17 Shahrīvar)
is known as the Day of the Martyrs of the Revolution.

Nō Rūz Even before the Achaemenian period (559-330 BC), the coming of spring was celebrated on a large scale throughout Persia, and today the Iranian New Year, or Nō Rūz, is a huge family celebration. Starting on the spring equinox (around 21 March), Iranians traditionally return to their home villages and towns to celebrate the New Year with their friends and relatives.

On *Sīzdah Bedar*, the 13th day of the Persian New Year, Iranians avoid the bad luck associated with the number 13, and go to the countryside for a picnic with plenty of friends and relatives. At this time, some unmarried women pray for a perfect husband during the coming year, plates are sometimes smashed, traditional food is cooked, and children play games.

It is exceptionally difficult to find hotel accommodation throughout the Iranian New Year period (about 10 days before and after 21 March), and all forms of public transport are also very heavily booked. Most businesses (but not hotels), including many restaurants (except those in decent hotels), will close for about five days after the start of the New Year period, ie about 21 to 25 March inclusive. Although Nō Rūz is great fun if you are staying with, or visiting, Iranian friends, it is not a very sensible time to travel to Iran, as one expatriate Iranian returning home confirmed:

As I was visiting family, I specifically visited during the Iranian New Year. This is a great time to get everyone together but definitely the wrong time to visit Iran and its many attractions ... This is the only time Iranians have off and whilst this time of year is very festive (very much like Christmas) ... most, if not all, Iranians are on vacation at this time, and everyone will be visiting the sites you want to visit!

Azar Marashian, Australia

Special Events
The national holidays listed above are not celebrated as much as you might expect; and there are very few public events of interest

---

Traditions at Nō Rūz
The lead-up to the Iranian New Year is traditionally a time to spring-clean the home and plant seeds. Closer to Nō Rūz, tables are specially laid, a tradition called *haft seen*. The table must contain seven articles, symbolising good triumphing over evil, including apples, garlic, vinegar and olives (the names of which, in Fārsī, all start with a specific sound similar to an English 's'). Eggs are also symbolic: often a mother has to eat one cooked egg for every child she has.

At the stroke of midnight at Nō Rūz, the family recites a special prayer seeking happiness, good health and prosperity. And then the serious eating and partying begins: a special Nō Rūz rice dish is passed around, and presents, known as *eidi*, are distributed by the older folk among the young. For the next two weeks, most families visit relatives and friends all over the country. ■

to non-Muslims. The religious holidays are generally sombre times when Iranians visit a mosque, though some occasions, such as the anniversary of the martyrdom of Hussein (see page 101), when thousands of men in black shirts march in the streets for hours flagellating themselves with steel chains, can be an incredible sight.

For most Iranians, the main nonreligious cultural event of the year is the extended period of celebrations marking the Persian New Year. Other than this, there are very few great cultural events of particular appeal to visitors, except perhaps for market day in the provinces, and it is difficult to find information about these except locally.

ACTIVITIES

Travelling around Iran shouldn't be limited to visiting mosques, traipsing around archaeological sites, and poking around bazaars. If you love the outdoors, there is plenty of space and scenery, and away from the big cities you will certainly appreciate the serenity and clean air. See the Trekking in Iran section at the end of this chapter for trekking information.

Skiing

Skiing is becoming popular among middle and upper class Iranians, and foreigners who appreciate that Iran is one of the least expensive skiing destinations in the world. The season is long, the snow is often like powder, and there are several downhill skiing areas, with resorts, within an hour or two by road from Tehrān.

Prices & Etiquette Thankfully, there is no discrimination against foreigners (except for the hotels), so the use of a ski lift costs as little as 15,000 rials a day – though there are occasional restrictions because the equipment is often so antiquated. You can hire full equipment (ie skis, poles and boots; but not clothes) at the resorts for about 20,000 rials a day, or from a couple of camping shops along the walking trail starting at Darband in northern Tehrān (see the Trekking in Iran section at the end of this chapter).

Men and women have to ski on different slopes (the women's slopes are apparently easier), and both sexes have separate ski lifts. Women must still wear appropriate clothing, which can be as daring as a baggy coat (below the knee), jeans and a woollen hat, but don't take too many risks because the Komīté often checks female attire at the resorts.

When to Go The season in the Alborz mountains (where most of the slopes are located) gets going in about the middle of January and lasts until a little after the Iranian New Year (about 21 March) though in some parts of the country, particularly near Tabrīz, the season can last as late as mid-May. The slopes and resorts are particularly busy around the Iranian New Year period, and popular with Iranians on Thursday and Friday, and with diplomats and expats on Saturday, but on other days you may have some parts of the slopes to yourself. Lifts normally operate between 9 am and 4 pm every day.

Where to Go Of the dozen or more skiing areas in the Alborz mountains, not far from Tehrān, only three are easily accessible, and have reliable facilities and equipment for hire. Based near the village of Shemshak, Darbansar Resort is the best for those who are still learning, while many experienced skiers base themselves at the Shemshak Resort nearby. The largest and most popular resort (which is overcrowded at times) is Dīzīn (☎ (21) 5607 814), the place to be seen by the in crowd. Based at the village of Shaleh, Dīzīn also boasts tennis courts, children's playground and summer activities such as grass skiing (what else?), hiking and horse-riding. For cross-country skiing, you can try the Kalardasht region in Māzandarān province, and anywhere you fancy around Mt Damāvand.

Places to Stay & Eat All resorts have upmarket hotels, which normally charge foreigners in US dollars: ranging from about US$25/35 per single/double to US$100 for a room in the main resort at Dīzīn. A few restaurants serve western and Iranian food at reasonable prices, though bringing a picnic from Tehrān, if you are just coming for the day, is a great idea.

Getting There & Away If you have access to a vehicle, you can pick and choose any of the resorts along the main road north of Tehrān, and stay wherever you want (or just take a day trip from Tehrān). If you are relying on public transport (ie shared taxis or minibuses from the Eastern Terminal in Tehrān), you will be limited to the three major resorts listed earlier. You will also need to do a bit of hitching to get from the main road to the slopes (which is very hard if you are carrying equipment), but hitching a ride between resorts with some fellow skiers is easy if you have the cheek to ask.

An alternative is to take an all-inclusive accommodation and ski package, regularly advertised during winter in the English-language newspapers, or arranged by a few upmarket hotels or the skiing agency (see the following Agencies section) in Tehrān. Though you will probably be charged 'foreigners' prices' in US dollars (unless you are good at bargaining), prices are low compared with what you probably pay at home. Taking a skiing package also takes the hassle out of organising everything, so you can concentrate on skiing.

Agencies One of the very few recognised ski agencies in Iran is Iran Khudro, 33 Sadābād St, Tajrīsh Square, Tehrān; PO Box 19615/519 (☎ (21) 276 701; fax 265 555). The office is closed in summer (when I visited). There is an Iranian Skiing Federation somewhere in Tehrān, but at the time of research the exact location and details were unknown. The Mountaineering Federation of Iran (see the Trekking in Iran section later) will know the current contact details of the Skiing Federation.

Beaches
There are a few sandy beaches open to the public along the Persian Gulf and the Caspian Sea, but Iranians are not beach-

combers or sun-worshippers, so beach activities are very, *very* low-key. The coast along the Caspian has a few expensive hotels with private beaches, but it sure isn't the Costa del Sol or French Riviera.

Swimming and sunbathing is segregated – ie separate public beaches for men and women – and not much fun for women because they must still keep to the full hejāb at all times. Even if you think you've found a secluded beach for some non-segregated swimming, or sunbathing for the ladies, there is a good chance you will be found by some locals, who may report your 'immoral' activities to the local authorities, and/or spend several hours looking at you.

Do not swim anywhere in the Persian Gulf unless there are locals paddling around in the water; one reason for the decline in pearl fishing in recent years is the increase in the shark population.

Other Activities
If your aim in life is to go fishing, hunting, shooting or canoeing in Iran, or if you want to do something unusual like track down tigers, have a word with someone at an Iranian embassy before making any plans. These are things very rarely done by foreigners, and you can do with all the official support you can get.

Cycling
> There is only one bicycle track (with bicycle hire) in the whole country: on Kīsh Island. Iran is not well-suited for leisurely bike riding: 30 seconds in city traffic is enough to make you wish you hadn't bothered.

Diving
> The only place in Iran with a recognised site for scuba diving and snorkelling is Kīsh Island, and this is a very expensive place. Refer to the Kīsh Island section in the Southern Iran chapter for more information.

Fishing
> If you can get on a boat, the best place to head for is the Caspian Sea where salmon, bream, mullet and sturgeon are found in large quantities. You can also find trout in the Sefīd River, in the Caspian region; as well as fish in the Karaj River and Karaj Dam; several streams around Mt Damāvand; the Zāyandé River, not far from Esfahān; and the Kārūn River in the south-west.

The only places to buy or rent fishing equipment are the couple of shops at the southern end of Ferdōsī St in Tehrān.

Hang-gliding

The cliffs near the village of Lārijān, about halfway between Tehrān and Āmol, is where intrepid (mainly expat) hang-gliders practise their stuff on weekends, much to the amazement of hundreds of awe-struck Iranian picnickers.

Watersports

Water-skiing, and other watersports, is theoretically possible in many of the rivers and lakes, but the main place for rich Tehrānīs, and expats, is the Karaj Dam, north of Karaj. It is also possible, if you have your equipment, on Vahdat Dam, near Sanandaj, and Anzalī Lagoon, near Bandar-é Anzalī. Women, of course, must wear the full hejāb, which may not help with the aerodynamics of water-skiing.

COURSES

There are very few courses you can sign up for, and the main problem is that you probably won't get a visa long enough to learn anything anyway. The English-language newspapers from Tehrān sometime advertise courses in Fārsī, but these are predominantly for diplomats who have a visa which is long enough to learn the language.

Traditional Iranian music classes are sometimes organised by the Arghanoun Cultural & Musical Association in Tehrān (☎ (21) 8262 584). These courses (in English) show foreigners and Iranians how to play traditional instruments, and explain some of the musical history of Iran. Check out the classifieds in the English-language dailies for details of this course, and any others which may pop up.

WORK

Unless you have some skill which is in particular demand in Iran (such as engineering or medicine), are married to an Iranian or are a Shi'ite Muslim, your chances of finding legal paid work in Iran range from negligible to nil. Some Iranian companies, mostly government enterprises, take foreigners on short-term contracts, but they do not recruit expatriates inside Iran. Even if you did get a job offer, the work permit is not a mere formality: westerners are only likely to get one if a government department or semi-government organisation is prepared to push the Ministry of Labour very hard on their behalf.

The many English-language schools throughout the country do not need casual labour, and even if you found one that did, you wouldn't get a work permit unless you had family ties in Iran. In any case wages in Iran are lamentable by western standards, and only a limited amount can be repatriated at the official rate. For foreigners who are already established in Iran, (eg spouses of diplomats), some jobs are advertised in the English-language newspapers from Tehrān.

ACCOMMODATION

Generally, Iran has an excellent range of accommodation, from the cheap and cheerful (though some cheap places are grubby and noisy) to the opulent and luxurious. Between the two there's usually something to suit everyone. If you turn up late at night in certain places at certain times of the year you will have trouble, but even if you front up in Mashhad at midnight at the peak of the pilgrimage season, someone will almost certainly take pity on you before you have to start looking for a park bench.

All hotels, and some *mosāferkhūnés* (lodging houses), are categorised, regulated and inspected by the Ministry of Culture & Islamic Guidance. Hotels are classified according to a star system, with five stars for a luxury establishment with private bathrooms in every room, and one star for a place offering only simple accommodation, but with at least some bathroom or shower facilities and usually a few rooms with private bathrooms. There is also a grading system for mosāferkhūnés which classes them as 'superior', '1st class' or '2nd class'. In the last of these categories you can expect almost unimaginable deprivations.

In general, places listed under 'budget' include mosāferkhūnés, a few backpacker lodges, one-star hotels and two-star places which offer a reasonable price for foreigners; 'middle' are two and three-star hotels; and 'top end' are four and five-star hotels. As an alternative, there are 'homestays' (a room in someone's home) and 'suites' (usually fully-equipped apartments) along the coast of the Caspian. Prices are generally lowest in the east and south-east of the country, and highest in Tehrān and along the Caspian Sea. In small towns or villages with no hotels, some mosāferkhūnés charge everyone more because of the lack of competition.

There are no set rules about whether breakfast is included in the room charge: upmarket places often do not, but some cheap places may. It seems the further away from Tehrān you go, the less likely breakfast is included. In any case, many places will supply a cooked breakfast, with plenty of tea, for about 3000 rials, and tea is available (and often free) all day at just about every hotel and mosāferkhūné in the country. Almost all hotels, and most mosāferkhūnés, can provide a business card, with the name, address and telephone of the hotel in Fārsī and English. Use this to ask directions to your hotel if you get lost, to show to a taxi driver for a ride home, or pass it on to fellow travellers if you have found anywhere particularly good (but please tell us too!).

Payment

Most middle-range places, and all top-end hotels, can – and will – charge foreigners much more than Iranians, and charge in US dollars (see Dual-Pricing in the earlier Money section). Never be put off checking out a room in the middle range, because almost all hotel rates in this price bracket are negotiable (the notable exception is the large number of places run by the government agency, ITTO). Always try to negotiate with the hotel manager: he invariably understands the advantages of filling beds with paying (foreign) customers more than other hotel staff.

If, for example, you are offered the ridiculous 'foreigners' price' of US$25/40 for a single/double in a middle-range hotel, argue immediately for the 'Iranian price'. This rarely works, however, unless you are particularly assertive and speak Fārsī. So, ask for a reduction to, say, US$15/25, using the reasonable argument that the 'foreigners' price'

is way too high, or that you may stay there more than one night. Once he agrees, tell them that you have no US dollars, and you want to pay in rials. He must by law charge you at the official rate (currently, 3000 rials = US$1), so in this example the hotel rate is 45,000/75,000 rials. If you have changed your money at the 'street rate' (4800 rials = US$1), then you will only pay the rial equivalent of US$9/16 for a classy room in a middle-range hotel.

Booking & Registration

If you want to stay at a certain hotel, or you are arriving late, it is worth booking by telephone a day ahead, or from the airport or bus/train terminal (where a free telephone is often available) as soon as you arrive. If you turn up at an airport or bus/train terminal in a large and unfamiliar city, it is often worthwhile telephoning around to see which places have rooms in your price range, though some hotels are wary about agreeing to take strangers before they turn up in person. If you plan to return on a particular date to the town where you're staying, it's a good idea to book a hotel room in person before you leave.

In any case, you will very rarely have problems finding a room in your budget range – but not always in the place you prefer – except during the Iranian New Year (see under Public Holidays & Special Events earlier in this chapter) and in Mashhad during pilgrimage season. If you can't find anywhere at all you can ask the tourist office (if there is one), or at the local police headquarters, though you won't have much say over what sort of accommodation you get.

Most hotels have a shortage of single rooms, so if you are travelling on your own, you will often have to fork out for a double or twin room, or find a travelling companion to share a room with. Refer to the earlier Dangers & Annoyances section about finding accommodation as an unmarried foreign couple.

At every hotel and mosāferkhūné all guests (Iranian or foreign) must fill out a registration form on arrival. An official from the local police/security force will come to the hotel to inspect the registration form, and, often, your passport. The official also has the right (which is rarely enforced) to make further inquiries about any particular guest. Usually, the hotel management wants to hold on to your passport for your entire stay on the grounds that the police/security officer may come at any time and ask to see it (which is true). Refer to Passports in the earlier Visas & Documents section for advice about leaving your passport at hotels.

Camping

Camping on a regular basis is not really a viable accommodation option in Iran. Because of fears about security, the authorities don't like anyone pitching tents at unofficial sites except nomads, and least of all foreigners. Except for the very few government camp sites, or private land which the owner has given you permission to use, almost everywhere in Iran counts as an unofficial camp site.

Since many parts of the country are military or restricted zones, and it is not always immediately obvious when you are in or near one, there is a risk of unknowingly camping in an area where your mere presence would attract a great deal of suspicion. Naturally, camping anywhere within binocular (or machine-gun) range of a border area is most inadvisable, and avoid camping anywhere near the borders of Afghanistan or Pakistan, or near the Kurdish parts of northern Iraq and south-eastern Turkey.

If you are planning a long trek, or some mountaineering, you will have to camp, of course, but it's still sensible to discuss your plans with the provincial tourist office first (if there is one). They may be able to write a letter of introduction on your behalf, arrange a guide if you need one or help you in some other way. They can also warn you of any dangers such as wild animals or security problems. Bring all the camping and cooking equipment you may need with you, though a few shops do rent and sell gear in Tehrān (see the later Trekking in Iran section for details).

Budget

Mosāferkhūnés At the lowest end of the market is the mosāferkhūné, literally a 'traveller's house'. This term covers anything from a bed in a noisy, grotty, male-only dormitory (for about 5000 rials per person per night) to a simple, small, private room, often with just a sink, though sometimes it does include a private (hot) shower and/or toilet. Prices for this range from about 8000/12,000 rials for a single/double to about 15,000/25,000 rials.

Sadly, some mosāferkhūnés will not accept foreigners, primarily due to some opposition from the police. Even if the mosāferkhūné has a sign above the door in English, and the manager speaks English, no amount of pleading will make him risk incurring the wrath of the local police. However, if you go to an identical place across the road, the manager may risk it, or have the necessary documents. Finding a mosāferkhūné that will accept foreigners is particularly hard in Būshehr, Bandar-é Abbās, Hamadān, Tabrīz, Kermānshāh, Esfahān, Mashhad, Kāshān and Rasht.

If you are fed up with this restriction, or really desperate to find a mosāferkhūné that will accept you, go to the local police headquarters. If you plead and speak some Fārsī (or you're good at explaining things by gesticulation), ask for an official permit allowing you to stay at any mosāferkhūné in the town or city. Many mosāferkhūnés do not have signs in English, so you should learn to recognise the Arabic script for the word 'mosāferkhūné' or suitable phrases asking for directions in Fārsī.

Hotels The correct word for hotel in Fārsī is *mehmūnkhūné*, but these days the word 'hotel' (from the French) is commonly used in signs (in English) and understood by locals. The word *mehmūnpazīr* is also sometimes used to describe a basic one-star hotel which is still one step above a mosāferkhūné.

A room in a one-star hotel is often similar in standard to a private room in a no-star mosāferkhūné, though some in the former category are far better and surprisingly good value. A room in a decent one-star hotel should have a private bathroom, with a shower (usually hot) and toilet (often a squat toilet). There is often some added gimmick like a telephone, which you won't use (even if it does work). Don't pay extra for a room with a television which will only show incomprehensible local programs; though a fridge to keep your drinks and food cold is a good idea. In some one-star hotels, at least one member of staff can make a stab at conversation in English. Prices in this range start at about 15,000/25,000 rials and go up to about 25,000/40,000 rials, depending on your negotiating skills.

Homestays The other budget alternative, which is only available in a few towns along the Caspian Sea, is the 'homestay' (the word is part of the local vernacular in the relevant towns). These are simply a spare room, with or without private facilities, in the home of a local, costing from 10,000 to 15,000 rials for a double room (singles are rarely available). At a homestay, the rooms are invariably clean, the prices are usually negotiable, and it's a good way to meet a local family.

Middle
Hotels In a two or three-star hotel you should be able to have a reasonable conversation in English with the manager or receptionist; enjoy a private bathroom with a hot shower, and toilet (often the sit-down style); relax on the chairs provided in the room; eat at the hotel restaurant; and use the functioning private telephone by the bed (though it probably won't have direct dialling facilities). The room also often contains a TV and fridge.

Prices for foreigners will often be quoted in US dollars, and whether you pay the full price in US dollars, or get a heavy reduction and pay in rials, is dependent on your negotiation skills (see Payment earlier). Prices for hotels in this range start at about US$10/15 for a single/double and go up to as much as US$25/40. If you normally stay at places

listed in the 'budget' range in this guidebook, don't be afraid of checking out a place in the middle-range. If you bargain hard and well, you can get some middle-range luxury and comfort for a budget price.

Suites One pleasant alternative, currently only found in Rāmsar on the Caspian Sea, is the 'suite' (the word is understood by locals). A suite is actually a fully-equipped apartment, with two bedrooms, a sitting room (with TV), bathroom and kitchen (with fridge and stove). Depending on your negotiating skills, and the seasonal demand, this luxury can cost as little as 50,000 rials per suite – an absolute bargain and worth a splurge.

Top End
Most four and five-star hotels will have all sorts of modern gimmicks like boutiques in the lobby, a restaurant serving western food, a traditional teahouse or coffee-room, room service most hours of the day, and an overnight laundry service. A few also have bookshops, private taxi services, hairdressers, swimming pools and, of course, shops selling Persian carpets. Rooms are luxurious, but prices are very high: they start from US$25/40 for a single/double, and finish at something like US$75/120. Prices are almost never negotiable, payment is only is US dollars, and watch out for additional taxes as high as 17%.

FOOD
At its best, Iranian cuisine is very good indeed. With its emphasis on the freshest ingredients, especially vegetables and fruit, and its relatively low levels of red meat and fat, it is also remarkably healthy. The problem is that to enjoy the full range of Iranian cooking you need to be invited to a number of Iranian houses, or stick to the restaurants in the up-market hotels which serve good Iranian food for tourists. Sadly, for the budget-minded traveller, there is little more to tempt the tastebuds than two or three

standard dishes of kebabs or chicken, with rice, vegetables and bread.

Generally, the Iranian diet is heavily based on rice, bread, fresh vegetables, herbs and fruit. Meat, usually minced or cut into small chunks, is used to add flavour but is rarely the dominant ingredient, except in kebabs. The standard meat is lamb or mutton, though beef and veal also turn up from time to time; for religious reasons, pork never does. The most expensive meat is chicken, which is often spit-roasted and served whole or by the half. Duck is sometimes used and goose, pigeon, pheasant, grouse and all manner of game are also available but rarely standard fare. Goat, camel and buffalo meat are eaten in rural areas, but are only sold in small quantities in the towns. Sadly, fish can be hard to find even on the Persian or Caspian coasts.

A large number of fresh herbs and spices is used in Iranian cooking, often with great subtlety. Very few settlements in Iran are without their spice market; some mainstays are turmeric and saffron, nutmeg and cardamon. Nuts, and fresh or dried fruit, are commonly included in meat and poultry dishes to create a peculiarly Iranian blend of the sweet and the savoury.

It is not the custom for Iranians to talk much at meals. Cutlery is normally a fork and spoon rather than a knife and fork, except in the better class of restaurants and westernised households. Other than snacks and kebabs served with bread, eating with the hands is less common than in Arab countries or Pakistan, but where eating with your hands is customary you should never put your left hand into a communal food dish; the left hand is used for something else.

For a list of items which may (but often may not) be on offer for meals and snacks, also in the Fārsī script, see the Persian Language Guide at the back of this guidebook.

Rice

Rice is often served in vast helpings with many Iranian dishes, though due to an agricultural policy promoted by the Iranian government, rice is being slowly supplanted by bread as a major element of some dishes. Iranian rice from the rainy plains of Māzandarān province is considered by many – not only Iranians – to be some of the world's best. However, the best stuff is often sold to Russia, and what you eat in Iran has probably been imported from Thailand or elsewhere.

Rice in general is called *berenj*. *Chelō* is boiled and steamed rice, often the base for meals such as *chelō morgh* (chicken and rice). Rice cooked with other ingredients, such as nuts and spices, is called *polō*. Rice served in Iran is always fluffy and tender, and never sticky or soggy. Often the cook will steam rice with yoghurt or an egg yolk to make a crunchy golden crust at the bottom of the pan, which is broken up and served on top of the rest of the rice. Saffron is also frequently used to flavour and colour the rice. If the rice is served with a slab of butter on top, lovingly blend the butter into the rice for a few minutes as the Iranians do; it really livens up the rice if it's a bit bland or dry.

Bread & Cake

Iranian bread, known generally as *nūn*, is always fresh, and you can always buy it in a bakery for a few hundred rials. There are four main varieties of Iranian bread, which are either baked in cavernous clay furnaces, or briefly plunged into the flames of a pit-oven.

Lavāsh is a flat and very thin type of bread which is folded twice into a square. It keeps for months. *Sangak* is a thicker bread, oval-shaped and pulpy, which is baked on a bed of stones to give it its characteristic dimpled look. (Make sure all the stones are removed before putting your teeth into it.) *Taftūn* is crisp, about 1cm thick and oval-shaped, with a characteristic ribbed surface. *Barbarī* is the elite of Iranian breads: crisp and salty, with a glazed and finely latticed crust. It is best when hot from the oven.

One of the many joys of travelling around Iran, even in more remote places, is the variety of cakes. These are sold in cake shops in the bazaar, or along the main streets in the centre of town. The shortbreads can get a bit stale after a few days, and the cakes with cream (not the real stuff) may not be exactly what you are used to at home, but they liven up a bland meal of kebabs, and are great for scoffing down on lengthy bus or train rides. Some cake shops have chairs and tables where you can enjoy some cakes with a cold drink, but for a tasty combination of tea and cakes eat them in a teahouse. My favourite bakeries are in western Iran, especially Hamadān city, where you can pig out on a plate of delectable little treats for as little as 1000 rials.

Yoghurt & Ice Cream

Another great Iranian staple is yoghurt, called *māst*, similar to Greek or Turkish yoghurt. It's sometimes served on its own with lavāsh bread, commonly used as a cooking ingredient, and often mixed into rice, with diced cucumber or other vegetables, fresh herbs and spices. It is also automatically served as a side-dish in many restaurants – if you don't want it, let the waiter know because you will pay for it otherwise.

After a meal, try to find somewhere which serves delicious ice cream, especially the soft-serve stuff in a crunchy cone. This is not so easy to find in Tehrān, but in most hot or touristy places, there are usually a few ice

cream stalls along the main roads. If the shop and vendor look clean there is a very good chance the ice cream is safe.

Soup & Stew

Iranian soup *(sūp)* is thick and filling. Even thicker is *āsh*, more of a pottage or broth; thicker still is *ābgūsht*, almost a stew, which is served as a first course or more commonly as a main dish. Ābgūsht is the only dish at many of the cheaper restaurants and teahouses, where it is also known as *dīzī*. A thick brew of potato chunks, fatty meat and lentils, ābgūsht is mashed in a bowl and served with sangak bread: it makes a filling and inexpensive meal. The best ābgūsht is served in Tabrīz (see the boxed text in the Western Iran chapter), and along the walking trail north of Darband, near Tehrān. The dividing lines between sūp, āsh and ābgūsht can be hazy, however.

Khōresht is a blanket term for any kind of thick meaty stew with vegetables and chopped nuts. It's a more sophisticated version of ābgūsht, and usually more delicious. Often mixed with rice, khōresht is a safe and tasty alternative to boring, ubiquitous kebabs. One of the prizes of Iranian cooking is *fesenjān* (refer to the boxed text below). It's quite an honour to be served this

---

The Recipe for Fesenjān

This is a traditional *khōresht*, an Iranian stew which has been made for centuries, and is particularly popular during festivals and at mourning times. In addition to 2.2kg (one pound) of meat, which can be duck, chicken, lamb or even ground meat, you need:

½ tablespoon of cardamom powder; a little salt (optional); ½ teaspoon of turmeric;
  ½ teaspoon of pepper; one tablespoon of flour
⅓ cup of hot water
½ cup of finely chopped walnuts
one eggplant (or pumpkin, if you prefer); one finely diced onion
1½ cups of pomegranate juice (or use half lemon and half tomato juice)

Fry the onion, with the pepper and turmeric. Fry the lamb or ground meat in the remaining oil; or cook the duck or chicken until brown. Douse the meat in flour and walnuts; fry for a few minutes more. Add water, pomegranate (or lemon) juice, and salt (if required). Cover the pot, and simmer for 30 minutes.
  Chop the eggplant (or pumpkin) into small pieces; fry for a few minutes; then place on top of the meat. Cook for another 15 minutes longer – but add the cardamom powder after the first five minutes. Naturally, this should be served with your best Iranian rice (or whatever you have at home). ■

at an Iranian home; some restaurants serve it too, but the quality just isn't the same.

Kebabs

The main dish served in eating houses throughout Iran is the *kabāb*, a long thin strip of meat or mince served with a mound of rice (known as *chelō kabāb*) or, more often these days, with bread and grilled tomatoes. The kebabs are usually sprinkled liberally with sumac (*somāgh*) and sometimes accompanied by a raw onion, a pat of butter and a bowl of yoghurt to stir into the rice.

When made with lamb fillet, it's known as *fillé kabāb* and is invariably delicious. *Kabāb-é makhsūs* (special kebab) is a larger strip of meat than average and is also made of good quality lamb; *kabāb-é barg* (leaf kebab) is thinner and varies in quality, but is usually good. The more common and cheaper version is the *kabāb-é kūbīdé* (ground kebab), made of minced meat of some description with bone and heaven knows what else. If you ever watch this being made (the 'meat' is kneaded hurriedly, and placed on the skewers by hand, the fingers forming the corrugations), you may never have one again. Another Iranian favourite is the *jūjé kabāb*, marinated chicken kebabs served in the same way as normal kebabs. These are more expensive than normal kebabs, and the quality does vary.

Kebabs are either grilled for a few minutes over charcoal (which is far better) or over a gas-heated flame (avoid these). If you order tomatoes as well, they are always burnt on the outside, and raw in the middle – but it doesn't really matter. If you are travelling as a twosome, and you're not particularly big eaters or lovers of kebabs, you can usually share a plate of kebabs between two people, and supplement it with tomatoes, bread, rice, soup and salad.

Other Dishes

Kūkū is a very thick Iranian omelette cut into wedges and served hot or cold. Spinach kūkū is a regular feature of Iranian home cooking. *Dolmé*, like Turkish *dolma*, is a stuffed vegetable, fruit or vine leaf, with a mixture of rice and vegetables or meat (or both) as the filling. *Ghormé-yé sabzī* is an occasionally rather bitter stew of lamb, spinach and dried lime. *Kofté* are meatballs, similar to Turkish *köfte*.

Vegetarians

Unless you are cooking for yourself, it would be hard to maintain a healthy diet in Iran without eating some animal products. As one traveller wrote: 'three of the four vegetarians in my group succumbed, and the fourth looked pretty ropy.' The Fārsī phrase for 'I am a vegetarian' is *geyāh khār hastam*.

Most restaurants offer at least one vegetable dish, but sometimes small pieces of meat will be used in them for flavouring. The main vegetarian alternative is a salad, pretty much a part of a meal in any decent restaurant anyway. At some snack bars, the Lebanese-style *falafel* is always good with fresh bread and vegetables. A meat-free khōresht is also sometimes available in a snack bar; just look in the glass freezer and choose whatever looks edible – though the khōresht may have included meat at some stage. A few stalls in some towns sell boiled eggs or roasted potatoes in their jackets; otherwise they have skewered tomatoes or onions, kebab-style with bread, rice and salad, without the kebabs.

The best idea is to buy your own food at the markets, and create your own meals (supplemented by vitamin tablets, if you can). Nuts and fruits, as well as vegetables such as cucumbers, tomatoes and pickles, are excellent, commonly available and very cheap. There is also plenty of fresh bread, as well as cheese and eggs for non-vegans.

Western Food

Western-inspired dishes, particularly steaks and schnitzels, are available at some of the better restaurants, particularly in the up-market hotels. These may not be perfect, or cheap (7000-10,000 rials a dish) compared to Iranian food, but they are worth an occasional splurge to boost morale and satisfy whingeing tastebuds. Brightly decorated restaurants selling 'fast' food such as pizzas, hamburgers and fried chicken are popular with trendy young locals of either sex, and are often surprisingly good – though service is often not 'fast'.

Breakfast

Breakfast is usually *lavāsh* bread with goat's milk cheese (often bitter), yoghurt, jam (often made from carrots) or honey (rare). This is often accompanied by a fried or boiled egg or two, and always washed down with gallons of tea. There seems to be no set rules about which sort of hotels include breakfast in their tariffs; it's best to ask. If breakfast is not included, it shouldn't set you back more than about 3000 rials (except in top-end hotels).

Nuts, Fruits & Sweets

Nuts and fruit are passed around Iranian houses all day long, and eaten in copious quantities. Most Iranian fruit is good, some of it among the best in the world. There are very few fruits which will not grow in Iran; even pineapples, mangoes and bananas can be found in southern Balūchestān. Particularly recommended are pomegranates, peaches and watermelons, and rosy-fleshed grapefruit which are perfect to eat without sugar. Iranian almonds and hazelnuts are highly edible, and the pistachios are really excellent.

Iranian confectionery tends to err on the sickly side of sweet, but if you have a sweet tooth, try the delicious and refreshing *pālūdé*, the tooth-breaking *gaz* or delicious products made from honey, particularly in north-western Iran.

Restaurants

The standard of restaurants varies considerably throughout Iran. You can eat at a *kabābī* (kebab shop), Iranian-style hamburger joint or Iranian restaurant (the best are often in hotels), or enjoy a drink or snack in a cake shop or teahouse. There are even a few decent western-style hamburger joints, and a couple of excellent pizza places (a lot of research was done on the latter). However, if you are travelling in a group and you want,

for example, a cup of tea, a cola and a cake, you may have to go to three different places.

It is important to note that most restaurants (but not those in hotels) close by 7 pm on Friday; after this you may struggle to find somewhere to eat. On religious holidays, almost every place selling food will be shut, markets and bazaars included, so be prepared. There is a restaurant of some description in almost every airport; somewhere to eat at most bus or train stations in major towns; and roadside cafés along all intercity highways.

Many restaurants (ie those not in a hotel) are invisible from the main road, often in basements or upper storeys with only a sign in Fārsī at street level. The fact that a restaurant has a sign in English doesn't necessarily mean that there will be a menu in English, or that anyone working there will understand English. Conversely, the lack of a sign in English doesn't mean that foreigners are not welcome. Try to learn the Arabic script – or some appropriate phrases to ask directions in Fārsī – for *restōrān*, *kabābī* or *salon-é ghezā* (food hall). The easiest eating places to spot are the hamburger joints and kabābīs which tend to congregate around main squares in the towns.

Many restaurants don't have even a menu in Fārsī, let alone English, and even if there is one in Fārsī, the waiter may not bring it to you because he will assume that you won't understand it. To order, learn a few important words, point at the appropriate phrases in the Persian Language Guide at the back of this guidebook, or indicate something edible from the display window or on someone else's table. Try to learn the Arabic numerals so you know the prices.

At restaurants where there is a man sitting at a desk by the entrance, you often give him your order and pay at the same time. Alternatively, the waiter takes your order and brings the bill to your table and you pay the man at the desk. If no-one brings you a bill, you pay at the desk before leaving. At roadside cafés you usually pay in advance and are given some tokens to take to the serving area in exchange for your meal. At restaurants where there is no-one at the front desk, you sit down at an empty table and the waiter will serve you and bring you the bill – and you pay the waiter. (If that all seems a bit confusing, don't despair: after three months of research, I never completely understood the system. If in doubt, follow the lead of the waiter.) If you don't have the exact change and you offer an amount not very much higher than the bill, the waiter may assume that the change is a tip.

Hamburger Joints Stretched along many main streets in town, you will see dozens of modern and clean hamburger joints. Here you can have reheated sausage or hamburger meat ('sausage' and 'hamburger' are always understood by the men behind the counter), placed between a fresh roll and topped with tomato and pickles (I *hate* pickles). These are Iranian-style hamburgers, as opposed to the more expensive but tastier western-style hamburgers, served in more upmarket places. Iranian-style hamburgers are always cheap: about 2000 rials with a soft drink (soda).

Kabābīs All over the major cities, and in every small town in the countryside, there are dozens, if not hundreds, of kabābīs. These sell, you guessed it, kebabs (with meat, but rarely chicken), often accompanied by grilled tomatoes, onions and bread. Cold drinks (but rarely tea) are also sold. Search for a kabābī that looks clean: sometimes skewers are not properly cleaned between use; cutlery is washed with little effort; and leftover bread is reused. This is rare though; most kabābīs are fairly hygienic. The price of a plate of kebabs, with the accompaniments, depends on the type of kebabs you choose (see the earlier Kebabs section).

Hotel Restaurants Some budget hotels, and just about every middle-range and top-end hotel, has a restaurant, often unsigned and located on the top floor or in the basement. At the very least, there is always some place

in the hotel where tea is always on the boil (and very cheap, or even free, for guests).

Hotel restaurants are often the best place to enjoy a decent meal, and they are open to anyone, whether you are a guest or not. The range of meals, type of food, and prices, are often a reflection of the standard of the hotel – but not always. Never be put off at least checking out the menu in a restaurant in a middle or top-end hotel. A number of up-market hotel restaurants offer excellent meals for about 10,000 rials (about US$2 at the 'street rate'), terrific morale boosters after days and days of boring kebabs. Hotel restaurants are usually open at breakfast for guests, and to the public and guests for lunch between noon and 2 pm, but often later than normal restaurants for dinner, ie from about 8 pm.

DRINKS
Tea
The national drink of Iran is undoubtedly *chāy*. It's always served scalding-hot, black and strong, traditionally in a small glass cup without a handle (so it's very hard to pick up). By the stringent laws of Iranian hospitality, any host is honour-bound to offer a guest at least one cup of tea before even considering any sort of business, and the guest is expected to drink it. To the outsider it may seem that the greatest decision most Iranians make all day long is how many lumps of sugar to have with their tea.

The tea is not usually made from the choicest of leaves, and those that do reach the pot tend to be stewed rather than merely scalded; it's perfect for anyone suffering from a tannin deficiency but hard to enjoy without sugar. Only in the most up-market hotel restaurants will you ever be offered milk with your tea.

Within reach, there is always a bowl of sugar cubes or *ghand*, often crudely hacked from huge rocks of sugar. It is customary to dip the sugar cube into the glass of tea to 'clean' it, then try to place the cube between the front teeth before pouring the brew through it. It's quite a feat to pick up this trick, and in the mouth of a novice the ghand lasts a matter of seconds; an Iranian can keep it going for a whole cup or more. If you are more inclined to place the sugar cube in your glass, bring your own teaspoon; these are almost never supplied anywhere in Iran.

If the tea is too hot and you can't pick up the glass, if you are in a hurry, or you want to do what the Iranians often do, pour your tea into the saucer (always provided) and slurp it loudly. Sometimes a bowl of mints is also placed on the table. These are for sucking, and not for putting in your glass.

The Teahouse The *chāykhūné*, or teahouse, is a great Iranian institution. It's normally an all-male retreat, though foreign women are often allowed in by becoming a temporary honorary male. In the teahouse, regulars sit all day drinking pot after pot of chāy, pausing only to chat or smoke the hubble-bubble (see the boxed text below) – and order more tea. The chāykhūné used to be, and still is in some places, a centre for social life and also for the exchange of news, information and gossip – perhaps, like a bar or pub in western countries. Until the 1979 Revolution, many chāykhūnés regularly offered poetry recitals, story telling, animal shows and other cultural performances to pull in the crowds, but nowadays only very few places cling to the old traditions.

It is fascinating to watch the manager of the teahouse do his stuff. Very strong tea is usually made in a kettle and placed on top of an urn called a *samovar*, full of piping hot water. (Interestingly, 'samovar' is a Russian word, indicating from where tea was first introduced into Iran. Refer to the boxed text in the Caspian Provinces chapter for more details.) The tea is a combination of the concentrate in the kettle, and hot water from the samovar, and served in tiny glasses (or pots in posh places) for about 200 rials a glass.

Coffee

Iranian coffee *(ghahvé)* is the same as Turkish coffee. Remember to let the brew settle and then only drink three-quarters of it (unless you enjoy coffee grit). Iranian coffee is served strong, black and sweet, with a spoon to stir the sugar. Nescafé has made its impact on Iran, and because it is very expensive you'd better look jolly pleased if anyone offers you a cup. Instant coffee is often served with milk, or sometimes made into a rather good milkshake.

Coffee is quite rare, however; only up-market restaurants and airlines will offer you any. If you can't live without your coffee fix, bring your own jar from home, or the good stuff from Turkey, and learn how to ask for a glass of hot water in Fārsī (and be prepared for some quizzical looks in reply).

Other Drinks

All sorts of delicious fresh fruit juices and milkshakes are served at ice cream parlours, cafés and street stalls throughout Iran. The latter are often semi-prepared in electric

---

Smoking the Hubble-Bubble

While in Iran, do what the Iranians do: pop into a teahouse and try a drag or two on the hubble-bubble (known as a *nārgīlé* or *ghalyān*). Sitting and puffing on the pipe, oblivious to the outside world, will acclimatise you to the normal Iranian state of mind. It is a very social, traditional custom that all foreigners, including women, can enjoy; and perhaps the greatest act of cultural integration that a foreigner can make in Iran, short of converting to Shi'ite Islam. You'll also get a mild buzz as you draw in the tobacco smoke and make that satisfying bubbling noise in the water pipe.

Smoking the hubble-bubble is taken very seriously, and you are bound to get it wrong the first few times, but not for lack of friendly advice. At only about 500 rials for 10 to 20 minutes worth of tobacco, it has to be worth a try. If you are a little self-conscious at first, try the hubble-bubble at one of the teahouses set up for Iranian and foreign tourists, before you venture into an authentic Iranian teahouse and show the locals how it's done. ∎

milkshake makers, and then pepped up with some ice cream or milk, and ice. As a general rule, if the juice is orange in colour, it's made from rock melon (cantaloupe) or carrot; light yellow is banana; anything else, you better ask! While these fruit drinks are considerably more expensive (800 to 1000 rials) than a soft drink, the reduction in the damage to your teeth often outweighs the damage to your wallet. For some reason, the fruit shakes at Ahvāz are fantastic, and probably the best thing about that hot and unexciting city.

Tehrān boasts some of the purest tap water in the world – it comes straight from springs in the Alborz mountains and is clean and tasty. Outside Tehrān, the tap water varies widely in quality, though it's generally safe to drink everywhere. It is very hard to buy bottles of mineral water, so one excellent way of replenishing the internal liquid supply is to slurp on a cold water fountain, often found at airline offices, banks and museums.

Dūgh is made of churned sour milk or yoghurt, mixed with either sparkling or still water and often flavoured with mint and other ground herbs. It is a popular Iranian cold drink (but I found it completely undrinkable).

All sorts of colas are available, including the US icons Pepsi and Coke, and the locally-produced Parsi Cola and Coolack Cola (with familiar looking bottles); as well as delicious orange and lemon soft drinks (sodas). Some of my favourites are Shad Noosh lemonade; Fana orange (without the 't'); the unfortunately-named Arso orange; and Coffy Cola in the uniquely-shaped bottle. Avoid buying any soft drink in a can: you end up paying maybe 10 times more because the can is expensive and not reusable. A bottle of cola or orange fizzy stuff costs about 250 rials.

'Iranian beer' *(mā'-osh-sha'īr)*, often labelled as 'nonalcoholic malt beverage', tastes like, well, nonalcoholic beer. One of the better local brands is Delster, but international brands such as Oranjeboom and Bavaria also offer nonalcoholic beer. Prices range from about 600 rials for a bottle of locally-brewed stuff to a comparatively pricey 2400 rials for an imported brand in a decent restaurant. Some desperates (not me, I might add) mix their nonalcoholic beer with rotgut (illegal) vodka.

Alcohol

Alcohol is strictly forbidden to Iranians who are Muslim, though alcohol is permitted for religious purposes, such as communion wine in churches, and to non-Muslims with special permission. There is a black market in alcohol, and staff of an unnamed airline do sell duty-free western-made liquor in special shops in northern Tehrān.

The Komīté sometimes roam through towns, acting on tip-offs or looking out for flats and houses where parties are in progress. The best organised parties always have a relay of lookouts; whenever the red alert is raised, the music is turned off, all females present make sure they are dressed properly, while the men head off for another room or a neighbour's flat. The host makes sure that anything incriminating is either extremely well hidden or flushed down the lavatory. This frequently rehearsed routine could be performed in less than two minutes.

ENTERTAINMENT

Iran offers very little in the way of organised entertainment or nightlife. Bring a book. Bring lots of them. Iranian television is so uninteresting that a lot of Iranians don't bother watching it; they spend their leisure time visiting family and friends, playing with their children and going to the mosque.

Other favourite activities for young Iranians at a loose end include eating out, drifting between the homes of friends and relatives, window-shopping, playing street-football, and walking, motorcycling or driving in no particular direction for no particular reason (and, of course, in the fastest possible time). These activities are usually carried out in groups, for most Iranians feel lonely in a party of fewer than three. On Friday, many Iranians visit or entertain friends and relatives, or go into the countryside for a picnic. Many Tehrānīs flock to the lower slopes of the Alborz mountains for a spot of hiking.

Quran Recital Contests

This is about the only cultural activity to have flourished since the Islamic Revolution. These recitals can be quite interesting for the sheer range of contestants, from haggard old men and mullahs to boys of about seven, and for the amazing powers of memory they demonstrate. However, you will have to be invited, and you must dress and act appropriately.

Cinemas

Each city has a few cinemas along the main street, showing Iranian-made films, mostly violent, and all in Fārsī. Go to a cinema to witness a slice of Iranian social life, not to see, or understand, a decent film. (See Films under Arts in the Facts about Iran chapter for more information about Iranian films.)

Only as recently as 1997 have a few foreign films officially been allowed into Iran, and shown at selected (and often remote) cinemas in northern Tehrān. These films are usually heavily censored, deleting all 'immoral' scenes or sexual references (while happily leaving in all the gory violence), and badly dubbed into Fārsī. While some films, such as *Malcolm X* and *Dances With Wolves*, are American, they are chosen because they often denigrate the American way of life, and the politics of Uncle Sam.

Discos & Nightclubs

Dream on.

Music

Western pop music is basically unavailable to most Iranians, although nonthreatening artists such as Mariah Carey and Michael Jackson are (barely) tolerated. Just about the only western artist openly on sale, besides classical music, is the muzak pianist Richard Clayderman.

Many Iranian pop singers and musicians moved to the west after the Islamic Revolution, and most of the commercially available modern music now has a religious theme, and is not particularly memorable. (See Music under Arts in the Facts about Iran chapter for more information about traditional and modern Iranian music.) Many young Iranians are hungry for recordings of the latest western pop groups, so they will gratefully welcome a gift of a cassette.

SPECTATOR SPORT

Football (soccer) is the major sport in Iran. The national championship (which was won in 1997 by the Pirouzi club of Tehrān) lasts from about October to June; and games are played throughout the country on Thursday and Friday. Iran has a fine international side which qualified for the 1998 World Cup, and several Iranians play in major European football leagues, particularly in Germany.

Second in popularity is wrestling, which you can sometimes witness (if you ask around) at a *zurkané* which literally means 'house of strength'. Iranian wrestlers often perform admirably at international competitions: the three Iranian wrestlers who won medals at the Olympic Games in Atlanta in 1996 were hailed as heroes when they returned to Iran. Other popular sports are volleyball, swimming, karate, fencing and horse-riding.

One of the more peculiar sports played in Iran would have to be that legacy of English colonialism known as cricket. This is played at Chābahār, of all places, as well as Tehrān. If cricket is a little too sedate for you, go to the auto drag races held at the Āzādī Stadium in Tehrān. If you've spent a long time travelling around Iran, you will appreciate the extreme irony of paying money to witness hundreds of Paykans scream around in a circle. In Sīstān va Balūchestān province, you may come across some traditional camel racing.

Polo is probably a Persian invention, and was certainly played here in the reign of Darius the Great. Some 2000 years later, Shāh Abbās I used to enjoy watching his courtiers play the odd chukka in the main square in Esfahān. However, the game seems

Lida Fariman – Sportswoman

One of the most enduring scenes of the 1996 Atlanta Olympic Games was the sight of Lida Fariman leading the Iranian team around the stadium. Cloaked in her white hejāb, she proudly brandished her country's flag as she strode out ahead of the 25 men that made up the rest of Iran's Olympic team. A striking moment in Olympic history, and a vital signal that attitudes in the Islamic Republic of Iran are changing.

Lida Fariman shoots. She was quickly out of the competition; her score of 379 out of 400 was highly respectable for someone so young and inexperienced, but not enough to qualify for the finals. Fariman was disadvantaged by her heavy black head-dress in a stifling indoor arena: she was constantly wiping away beads of sweat from her brow. She bore her failure with dignity, saying it was what she had expected.

Fariman's significance goes way beyond the competition itself. Quite apart from the honour of bearing the flag bestowed on her by the rest of the team, she is the only Iranian woman to have made it to the Olympics since the Islamic Revolution in 1979, and her presence highlights the difficulties that Iranian sportswomen face. Fariman herself acknowledged that her prominence in the Games could only encourage others.

Islamic law in Iran makes public competition difficult for women. Since they are only allowed to show their faces and hands in public, there are few sports which women can partake in. Shooting is easy: it only presents problems of discomfort for the competitor, but a case in point is the Iranian women's canoeing team who qualified for the Games but were unable to go because of the possibility of violating hejāb laws if they competed without their veils. The Islamic Women's Games, and other women's sports in Iran, can only be attended by women spectators and television coverage is banned.

During the Olympics, Lida Fariman was kept separate from the other competitors. She was driven to the shooting complex every day, and was always escorted around the Olympic village. She was unable to enjoy most of the social activities that are part of the community of the Games, and her contact with other athletes was closely monitored.

However, the fact that she was allowed to appear at all shows a willingness in the Islamic Republic to allow women more equality and, though a small step, it is a start. With the election of a new president, Hojjat-ol-Eslām Seyed Mohammed Khatamī, whose principal votes appear to have come from women and young people hoping for more moderate laws, we can only watch further developments with interest. Many Iranian women will be looking to Lida Fariman as an example of exemplary and liberated Islamic achievement.

Kamin Mohammadi

to have died out completely in Iran since the Revolution.

Though widely played in Iran for at least 1500 years, chess became illegal shortly after the Revolution on the grounds that it encourages the *harām* (forbidden by Muslim law) practice of betting. Chess sets were traded on the black market until early 1989, when the game became legal again by a final goodwill edict of Āyatollāh Khomeinī. Possession of playing-cards, banned for the same reason, is still a criminal offence.

Iran, and in particularly Tehrān, has excellent sporting facilities and there is always some international sporting carnival going on somewhere. Foreigners are normally welcome to attend; check out the sports sections in the English-language newspapers. At the time of research, the Sixth International Women's Games were being held in Tehrān, in a bid to boost the profile of female sports in Iran. Lida Fariman is the only Iranian women to have excelled on the international sporting arena in recent times (see the boxed text above).

THINGS TO BUY

Iran is a buyers' market for souvenirs, and you will find it hard not to pick up a thing or two (or more). Thanks largely to the shortage of tourists, mass production is not common, prices are low and the quality is generally high, even at the budget end of the market. Naturally, the bazaar is the best place to start looking, but in places like Esfahān and Shīrāz, where foreign tourists are more common, it is harder to get a good price. If you don't care much for haggling, and don't have much time to look around, the government-run Iran Handicrafts Organisation has stores in most provincial capitals.

Various places in Iran specialise in certain products. Often knowing the best place to buy your souvenir is as important as getting a good price.

Art

Probably the best place to buy miniatures (mīnyātūrhā) is Esfahān, but watch out for overpricing at the more tourist-orientated shops. Tehrān bazaar and Khorram Ābād are also good; and miniatures, and picture-frames (ghābhā-yé aks), are good in Orūmīyé.

Books

The Cultural Heritage of the Isfahan (sic) Province Organisation puts out a marvellous range of booklets about each attraction in Esfahān. Refer to the Books section earlier in this chapter for some ideas about souvenir books to take home.

Carpets

Refer to the special Persian Carpets section in the Facts about Iran chapter for full details.

Ceramics & Pottery

There are dozens of shops and factories selling ceramics (sefālgarī) and mosaic tiles (mōzā'ī-hā) at Lālejīn, near Hamadān; Marāghé, near Tabrīz; Mīnāb, near Bandar-é Abbās; and around Rasht and Māsūlé.

Clothes

Lightweight shoes, known as giveh and abas (traditional coats without sleeves) are available in Kermānshāh and Khūzestān provinces. All sorts of beautiful stuff made from a silk called tirma is found in Yazd province. Traditional woollen Kurdish coats and hats from Kordestān and Īlām provinces are popular. Uniquely embroidered abas from villages near Bandar-é Abbās and Būshehr make great souvenirs.

Electronic Goods

Nothing traditional about these, but Iranians love stocking up on the latest electronic must-haves. You should avoid buying any electronic goods at any duty-free zone (see Customs earlier) because of the mind-boggling bureaucracy and two-day wait for customs clearances.

As Iran hasn't signed any international copyright agreements, computer software is very cheap (50,000 rials for MS Office 97). Check the computer shops around Jomhūrī-yé Eslāmī St in Tehrān.

Glassware

Intricate glassware (shīshé ālāt), the product of centuries of Persian glass-blowing tradition, can be bought at Yazd city, Tehrān and Meimand, near Kermān city.

Jewellery

Be wary when buying jewellery (javāher ālāt), though there is plenty of gorgeous stuff to choose from: traditional jewellery from Kordestān; turquoise from Mashhad; and necklaces and earrings, made from threads of silver called a filigree, from villages in Zanjān province. Export restrictions apply (see the following section).

Leather & Silk

Bags made from leather (charmīné) from Hamadān and Yazd city are popular; and Tabrīz is renowned for its silk (abrīshom).

Metalwork

Some souvenirs to pick up include: ornamental and functional knives from Zanjān; anything made of silver and gold from Khūzestān province, Kermān city and Shīrāz; and tea-sets (servīs-hā-yé chāy) and hubble-bubble pipes (nārgīlehā) made from copper (mes) and bronze (beronz). Export restrictions apply (see below).

Spices

The main spices to pick up are henna (hannā) from many places, particularly Tabrīz; and saffron (za'farān) in Mashhad.

Stamps

The handful of street traders, near the post office at Emām Khomeinī Square in southern Tehrān, are the best people to visit to buy new or old stamps (tambrhā) for souvenirs. Some old commemorative issues can also be bought at the main post office in Yazd.

Woodwork

For carvings and inlaid boxes (ja'behā), it's hard to go past Orūmīyé and Esfahān. For baskets and knick-knacks made from bamboo, look around Rasht and nearby villages. For moarraq (marquetry) try Esfahān.

General Export Restrictions

Refer to the Customs section earlier in this chapter for details about what you can take out of the country. Many traders, aware of the rather low cost restriction of 150,000 rials, offer to undervalue the price of goods on a receipt issued to foreigners.

Officially you will need permission to export anything 'antique' (ie more than 50 years old), including handicrafts, gemstones, coins and manuscripts. (The authorities are particularly sensitive about the export of old or valuable Qurans.) There is also some sort of prohibition on the export of large quantities of saffron for trade purposes, but details were unclear at the time of research.

If you want to export, by mail, a few books

(whether old or new; Islamic or not), you should get permission from the Ministry of Culture & Islamic Guidance in Tehrān. (I managed to take out dozens of books in my normal luggage without a problem though.)

Another export item for which you may need a permit from the Ministry of Culture & Islamic Guidance is a *tombak* drum, though it seems that the export of smaller musical instruments, such as an Iranian flute, do not need a permit. If you are worried whether an expensive item will be confiscated, have a word with the local customs office *(edāré-yé gomrok)* before you buy anything, or place it carefully in your hand luggage, which is almost never searched, or x-rayed, on departure.

Trekking in Iran

Vast distances, some boring countryside, changeable weather and short visas are not conducive to long-distance trekking, but Iran does offer many excellent one-day walks, several five to seven-day hikes across mountains and through forests, a few challenging mountain climbs, and a couple of full-scale expeditions for the more adventurous.

In remote regions, especially near any border, you may accidentally stumble across a military/police/security area. A few phrases of Fārsī, or an Iranian guide, will help smooth any misconceptions. Drinking water is often scarce, so take your own supplies in the desert regions, and purification tablets or water filters in other places. For treks of more than a couple of days in remote areas, you should take (or rent) camping equipment, including a good sleeping bag.

Though some mountains have huts for climbers, the huts may be closed, full or inadequate, so a tent is an important alternative. Take your own food from a major town before you start, or buy food at villages along the way; alternatively, bring from home (or rent in Tehrān) any cooking equipment you may need.

HIKING

For day hikes, as opposed to trekking for a few days, head out to one of the places listed below. In most cases what little detail you need is provided in the relevant sections; otherwise, just head out in any direction you fancy. Take food and water; a jumper and wet weather gear in case of a change in the weather; a compass; and, if possible, a map. If you can, let someone know where you are going.

Hormoz Island
    Easily accessible from Bandar-é Abbās, this island in the Persian Gulf is sparsely populated, and begging to be explored. (Go there before it becomes another duty-free-port-cum-industrial zone!)
Kalardasht
    Not really accessible unless you have your own vehicle, this depression, south of Chālūs, and based around Hasan Keif village, is a marvellous place to wander around. To fully explore the region, you will need a few days, so take camping and cooking equipment.
Kermān
    Only a short taxi ride from Kermān city you can hike in the Pāye mountains, soak up some fresh air, and admire some rare forest.
Māsūlé
    This gorgeous village, near Rasht, is the perfect place to base yourself while you explore the valley. There's a hotel in the village, and good camping nearby.
Nahar Khorān
    Just south of Gorgān, this is a picturesque pocket of forest. You can stay in a hotel in Nahar Khorān, or camp nearby, and go for several day hikes.
Northern Tehrān
    Many Tehrānīs love to hike up the trails heading north of Tehrān, especially Darband and Tōchāl.
Orūmīyé
    From the Park-é Shahr (City Park), in Orūmīyé, just head south-west along the river, and keep going – plenty of charming countryside awaits.
Takht-é Soleimān
    A short stroll from the majestic ruins of Takht-é Soleimān is a small volcanic mountain called Solomon's Prison. It dominates a wonderful area for hiking.

ROCK CLIMBING

If clambering up rocks, and rocky hills, is more your thing, there are several excellent, and accessible, places to try. The rocks which surround Bījār in Kordestān province are begging to be explored; the rocky hills which line the main road through Khorram Ābād are easy to reach and extensive; the road between Kermānshāh and Bīsotūn is lined with awesome rocks and cliffs (some have ancient statues and inscriptions carved in them); and anywhere around Mākū, there are plenty of rocky hills – but stay within eyesight of the town, if possible, or take a guide, because this is close to the Turkish border.

DESERTS
Dasht-é Kavīr
With the right preparation and attitude, and an experienced guide, there is no reason why you cannot trek across some, or most, of this vast desert. Alternatively, go on an organised trek with one of the agencies listed below.

One main trekking route takes at least eight days (about 300km), from Vārāmīn to Kāshān, via the eastern side of Namak Lake. You can save three days' trek by renting a car as far as Mobarakiye. If you have a 4WD, and get permission from the relevant authorities (best to ask at the Mountaineering Federation first; see page 123), you can drive the whole way in two to three days.

Dasht-é Lūt
One awesome trek, which is possible with a lot of preparation, and an experienced guide or two, is dubbed the 'Silk Road': a 20 to 30-day trek (about 700km) from Vārāmīn to Tabas in the middle of the massive and desolate Lūt desert.

From Vārāmīn, head to the eastern side of Namak Lake via Mobarakiye, and then trek south-east to Bayāzīye, and on to Tabas. An experienced guide will find water along the way, and avoid drug smugglers (who cross the Lūt between Afghanistan or Pakistan, and Turkey), as well police looking for drug smugglers. You can arrange this trek for a negotiable, and all-inclusive, US$1000 per person at the Mountaineering Federation.

CASPIAN PROVINCES
One of the best regions to trek is from Tehrān, across or through the Alborz moun-

tains, to the Caspian Sea (or vice versa). The advantages are: accessibility by local public transport, as well as privately-chartered taxi; a heavily populated region with many villages along the way where you can find food, water, shelter (if necessary), and directions; and it's an easy route, basically heading north (or south from the Caspian). Allow about five to seven days for the following trails, depending on how much mountain climbing you do; and whether you use public transport some of the way.

Ābyek to Abbās Ābād, via Mt Alam
From somewhere near Ābyek, about halfway between Karaj and Ghazvīn, head north-east towards Mt Alam (4850m). After Alam, you go through *birun bashm* country (which means 'the country where it does not freeze'); along the depression of Kalardasht; and finish at Abbās Ābād, just west of Chālūs. A guide is not needed.

Garmabdar to Nōshahr
This is an easy three or four days, though you will need a guide to steer you through some of the dense forest. Take a minibus or charter a private taxi to Garmabdar, head north but detour around Mt Darband Sar (4542m).

Karaj to Chālūs
This trek has been destroyed by the ugly urban sprawl of Karaj. From Karaj, head north to the picturesque Karaj Dam; bypass the road between Āsārā to Gachsar; and then head towards the Caspian Sea, via the Kandovān tunnel, north of Gachsar. A guide is not needed, as a lot of the trek is along established roads.

Shāhrūd to Gorgān
You don't need a guide, though he will be able to point out some ancient monuments along the way, and steer you through some pockets of dense forest. From Shāhrūd, just head north-north-west towards Nahar Khorān, just south of Gorgān. This trek will take about four days. Alternatively, walk along the main road between Shāhrūd and Gorgān, via Āzād Shahr; but catch some public transport along part of the road.

MOUNTAINS
It may come as a surprise to some that Iran boasts a number of high mountains, many permanently snowcapped. With the appropriate preparation, most mountains can be climbed by a fit person, without special equipment, experience or a guide – but always check the situation before embarking on a mountain trek.

The range which most visitors will see from Tehrān are the magnificent Alborz mountains, which has about 70 peaks more than 4000m high. In addition to the mountains listed below, you can try the snow-capped volcano Mt Taftān (4042m), near the Pakistani border; and the Hezār (4420m) and Lālezār (4374m) peaks in the Pāye mountains, south of Kermān.

Mt Damāvand

The most popular, and accessible, mountain is Mt Damāvand (5671m), a volcano with sulphuric fumes at the top (which are strong enough to kill stray sheep). It was first climbed by a westerner in 1837. The normal starting point is Reine (see the Around Tehrān section of the Tehrān chapter for more details about Reine), where there is (or rather was) a mountaineering club at the junction where the main road enters the village. Tragically, the manager of the club, an expert local mountaineer, and his sons, died a few years ago while trying to climb the mountain. This gives you some idea of the potential dangers.

From Reine, you can take an ordinary vehicle as far as Gusfan Sarah (at about

Trekking Locations in Iran

Trek/walk location

ARMENIA
Armenian-controlled
AZERBAIJAN

CASPIAN SEA

TURKMENISTAN

Mākū

Mt Sabalān (4811m)
Tabrīz
Ardabīl
Orūmīye
Mt Sahand (3707m)
Rasht
Māsūlé
Kalardasht
Zanjān
ALBORZ
Sārī
Nahar Khorān
Mashhad
Takht-é Soleimān
Mt Alam (4850m)
MOUNTAINS
Bījār
Northern Tehrān
Sanandaj
TEHRĀN
Mt Damāvand (5671m)
Hamadān
Kermānshāh
Bīsotūn
Ghom
Dasht-é Kavīr
Arāk
Īlām
Khorram Ābād
Mt Oshturān (4070m)
AFGHANISTAN
Esfahān
Dasht-é Lūt
Shahr-é Kord
IRAQ
Yazd
Ahvāz
Yāsūj
Kermān
Shīrāz
Mt Lālezār (4374m)
Mt Hezār (4420m)
Zāhedān
KUWAIT
Būshehr
PAKISTAN
Mt Taftān (4042m)
PERSIAN GULF
Bandar-é Abbās
Hormoz Island
0   100   200 km
OMAN
Strait of Hormoz
QATAR
UAE
Gulf of Oman

3000m), where there is a small room for guests at the mosque. From here, walk, or ride a donkey, for about four hours to a hut (at 4100m), where you can stay overnight. The hut may be full, so bringing a tent (and leaving it at the hut for the final assault) is a good idea. Next morning get up at about 3 am for a tough seven-hour climb to the summit to enjoy the views before the clouds cover the peak, and the sulphur fumes become overpowering. It's another four to five hours back to the hut from the peak. There is drinkable water until about 3200m, but watch out for urinating goats – though some locals claim there is a natural spring at 4400m.

Mt Alam

The best place to start an exploration of Mt Alam (4850m), and the dozens of peaks higher than 4000m in this part of the Alborz, is Rudbarak, about 20km north-east of Alam mountain. At Rudbarak, you can find somewhere to stay if you ask around, and organise a guide if you need one. You can also hire donkeys and porters, if you want some luxury.

It generally takes two days to trek from Rudbarak, via Vanderaban village, to the first hut at Sarchal (at 3900m), where you can stay and cook meals (there is even a kitchen). Another hut at 4200m was recently destroyed, and may not be rebuilt by the time you get there. From Sarchal, the climb to the peak and back, along the easiest route (ask local directions if you have no guide), can be done in one day. You can walk from Alam to another peak, called Mt Takht-é Soleiman (4490m), in one day, along a thin ridge, but this is one for the experts. Seek local advice before attempting this.

Mt Sabalān

Visible from most parts of Ardabīl province, the peak of Sabalān (4811m) is not a difficult climb, as long you have brought camping and cooking equipment. The best starting point is Sareiyn (where there is accommodation), a short trip by taxi or minibus from the provincial capital of Ardabīl. A guide is not needed, but ask around Sareiyn if you want one (though you probably won't find anyone with experience or knowledge).

Mt Sahand

The beautiful Sahand volcano (3707m) is smaller than the others, so it's an easier climb. Despite the proximity to Tabrīz, very few people seem to climb Mt Sahand, so it's not easy to arrange guides (which are not needed anyway), or transport. The best idea is to visit the friendly people at the tourist office in Tabrīz first, then ask around Aziz Ābād for guides, donkeys or porters. This village, about halfway up the mountain, is the starting point for treks in the area, and is accessible by minibus from Marāghé.

Mt Oshturān

Part of the mighty Zāgros mountain range, Mt Oshturān (4070m) is the highest of many peaks taller than 3500m. You can just trek around the region, and admire luscious waterfalls, two very pretty volcanic lakes called Upper and Lower Gahar, and thousands of hectares of forests and wildflowers (including bright red tulips) – or climb Oshturān mountain.

Mt Oshturān is in Lorestān province, a few kilometres south of Aznā, and about 80km east of Khorram Ābād. In fact, if you take the train between Arāk and Dezfūl, the first tunnel south of Aznā goes under part of Oshturān. To start a trek, charter a taxi to Aznā from Khorram Ābād.

GUIDES & PORTERS

The best time to climb any mountain in Iran is between June and the end of August (or even up to the end of September if the weather holds out). The cost of a guide depends on your bargaining skills, the number of climbers in the group, the equipment needed, the length of the trip and the difficulty of the route you want to take. A figure of about 55,000 rials per day for a guide is not bad; porters will cost about 30,000 rials per day; and donkeys, including a donkey guide, about 25,000 rials per day. On an organised trek arranged in Iran, expect to pay US$25 to US$35 (or the rial equivalent) per person per day, which should include food, all equipment, porters (and/or donkeys) and a guide.

Before you attempt any serious mountain climbing, you are well advised to contact the helpful guys at the Mountaineering Federation of Iran (details below).

EQUIPMENT RENTAL

Trekking is one of those indulgent sports enjoyed by crazy foreigners, so very few shops in Iran rent equipment, and/or provide advice. The best place to start asking around for equipment and, especially, advice, is the Mountaineering Federation, though three camping shops do rent and sell camping and cooking equipment, as well trekking clothes and boots. All three are about 200m along the walking trail which starts at the end of the ski lift at Darband, in northern Tehrān (see the Around Tehrān section of the Tehrān chapter for details). Staff at these shops speak little, or no, English, so advice is limited.

MAPS

There is very little in the way of specialised trekking or mountain climbing maps. If you are thinking of climbing any mountain described here, you probably won't need a map – either take a guide, or if you have some experience, just head on up. If trekking, rather than just hiking for the day (when you can rely on a compass, or asking directions), bring from home the relevant TPC or ONC

series of topographical maps published by the Defense Mapping Agency Aerospace Center in the USA. In Iran, you can contact one of the agencies listed below; or check out what the Gita Shenasi map shop in Tehrān has in stock – they may have a map of the Alborz mountain range in English.

TREKKING & MOUNTAINEERING AGENCIES

For organised trekking and mountain climbing, contact one of these agencies:

Azadi International Tourism Organisation (AITO)
This upmarket agency offers an impressive Desert Trek, by jeep and on foot, across parts of Dasht-é Kavīr: AITO building; 37 Eight St, Ahmad Ghassir Ave, Tehrān; PO Box 1585/1756 (☎ (21) 8732 191; fax 8732 195).

Caravan Sahra
This recommended agency specialises in all sorts of trips, including trekking, mountain climbing and, according to its brochure, other 'adventure tours': Javaherī building, 125/4 Shariatī Ave, Tehrān; PO Box 14875/153 (☎ (21) 7502 229; fax 767 184; email caravan@neda.net).

Kasar Trekking Agency
This private trekking agency is run by one of the guys at the Mountaineering Federation; contact details are the same (see below).

Mountaineering Federation of Iran
The undisputed experts in anything relating to mountain climbing, and trekking, in Iran, the Federation is an absolute mine of information and advice (and some staff speak good English): 15 Varzandeh St, Motaffeh Ave, Tehrān (about 200m up from the former US Embassy); PO Box 15815/1881 (☎ (21) 8839 928; fax 836 641).

Getting There & Away

You can enter or leave Iran by air, road or sea – but for reasons only known to the relevant authorities, foreigners cannot currently cross the border between Turkey and Iran by train. Most business visitors, and foreigners on package tours, come and go by air, while most independent travellers do so by road. Sea routes across the Persian Gulf or Caspian Sea are rarely used by foreigners, as they are slow and infrequent, but there is no reason why you cannot enter or leave Iran this way.

AIR

There is an impressive, but complicated, array of flights into and out of Iran. Most land at Mehrābād international airport in Tehrān, but some regional airlines use the 11 other international airports dotted around the country. The mammoth Emām Khomeinī international airport, currently under construction to the south of Tehrān, will replace Mehrābād airport, but won't be ready for many years (and certainly not within the life of this edition).

Buying Tickets

Your plane ticket will probably be the single most expensive item in your budget, and buying it can be an intimidating business. There is likely to be a multitude of airlines and travel agents hoping to separate you from your money, and it is always worth putting aside a few hours to research the current state of the market.

Types of Tickets There are plenty of discount tickets which are valid for 12 months, allowing multiple stopovers with open dates. These tickets allow for a great deal of flexibility. APEX (Advance Purchase Excursion) tickets are sold at a discount but will lock you into a rigid schedule. Such tickets must be purchased two or three weeks ahead of departure, do not permit stopovers and may have minimum and maximum stays as well as fixed departure and return dates. Unless

you really have to return at a certain time, it's best to purchase APEX tickets on a one-way basis only. There are stiff cancellation fees if you decide not to use your APEX ticket.

'Round-the-World' (RTW) tickets are usually offered by an airline or combination of airlines, and let you take your time (six months to a year) moving from point to point on their routes for the price of one ticket. The main restriction is that you have to keep moving in the same direction. One of the drawbacks is that because you are usually booking individual flights as you go, and can't switch carriers, you can get caught out by flight availabilities, and have to spend less or more time in a place than you want.

Refer to the 'Air Travel Glossary' boxed text on pages 126 and 127 for explanations of the terms used by travel agencies.

Shopping Around Start early: some of the cheapest tickets have to be bought months in advance, and some popular flights sell out early. Talk to other recent travellers – they may help you to avoid some of the same old mistakes. Look at the advertisements in newspapers and magazines (not forgetting the press of the community whose country you plan to visit), consult reference books and watch for special offers.

An increasingly popular and useful way to get information about current flights and fares, and to even book tickets directly with the airlines or travel agencies, is to access the relevant World Wide Web sites. The award-winning site run by Lonely Planet (http://www.lonelyplanet.com.au), is the best place to look for some useful hints from other travellers, as well find links to sites which provide travel details and costs. Refer to the Online Services section in the Facts for the Visitor chapter for some ideas about where to start surfing the Internet.

Once you have done this, phone (or email) a few travel agents. (While airlines can supply information on routes and timetables;

except in times of inter-airline war they do not supply the cheapest tickets.) Find out the fare, the route, the duration of the journey and any restrictions on the ticket. Then sit back and decide which is the best option to suit you.

You may discover that those impossibly cheap flights are 'fully booked, but we have another one that costs a bit more ... ' or the flight is on an airline notorious for its poor safety standards and leaves you in the world's least favourite airport in the middle of the journey for 14 hours. Or they claim to have only two seats left for that country for the whole of July, which 'we will hold for you for a maximum of two hours ... '. Don't panic – keep ringing around.

Please use the fares quoted in this book as a guide only. They are the official fares provided by the airlines at the time of writing (unless stated otherwise), but you can often find a travel agency which will discount the official fare. Quoted airfares do not necessarily constitute a recommendation for the carrier.

Bucket Shops If you are travelling from the UK or the USA, you will probably find that the cheapest flights are being advertised by obscure bucket shops whose names haven't yet reached the telephone directory. Many such firms are honest and solvent, but there are a few rogues who will take your money and disappear, to reopen elsewhere sometime later under a new name.

If you are suspicious about a firm, don't give them all the money at once – leave a deposit of 20% or so and pay the balance when you get the ticket. If they insist on cash in advance, go somewhere else. And once you have the ticket, ring the airline to confirm that you are actually booked on the flight.

Travel Agencies You may decide to pay more than the rock-bottom fare by opting for the safety of a better known travel agent. Firms such as STA, which has offices worldwide, Council Travel in the USA, or Travel CUTS in Canada, are not going to disappear

overnight, leaving you clutching a receipt for a nonexistent ticket; they all offer good prices to most destinations.

For further ideas about where to start looking for fares to or from Iran, contact the travel agencies and tour companies listed under Organised Tours in the Getting Around and Getting There & Away chapters, the Iranian travel agencies listed in the Tehrān chapter, and check out the Online Services section in the Facts for the Visitor chapter.

Precautions Once you have your ticket, write the ticket number down, together with the flight number and other details, and keep the information somewhere separate. If the ticket is lost or stolen, this will help you to obtain a replacement.

It's sensible to buy travel insurance as early as possible. If you buy it the week before you fly, you may find, for example, that you're not covered for delays to your flight caused by industrial action, or cancellation costs should you unexpectedly become sick. Refer to Travel Insurance in the Visas & Documents section of the Facts for the Visitor chapter for further information.

Discounts Some airlines offer discounts of up to 25% to student card holders. Besides having an International Student Identity Card (ISIC), an official-looking letter from your university (college) is also required by some airlines. Many airlines also require you to be aged 26 or under to qualify for a discount. These discounts are generally only available on ordinary economy-class fares. You wouldn't get one, for instance, on an APEX or a RTW ticket since these are already discounted.

Frequent flyer deals are available on many airlines flying to Iran or the general region. If you fly frequently with one airline, eventually you may accumulate enough points to qualify for a free ticket or other goodies. If you fly often, contact the airlines for information before buying your ticket.

Airlines usually carry babies up to two years of age at 10% of the relevant adult fare, and a few may carry them free of charge. For

Air Travel Glossary

Apex Apex, or 'advance purchase excursion' is a discounted ticket which must be paid for in advance. There are penalties if you wish to change it.

Baggage Allowance This will be written on your ticket: usually one 20kg item to go in the hold, plus one item of hand luggage.

Bucket Shop An unbonded travel agency specialising in discounted airline tickets.

Bumped Just because you have a confirmed seat doesn't mean you're going to get on the plane – see Overbooking.

Cancellation Penalties If you have to cancel or change an Apex ticket there are often heavy penalties involved, insurance can sometimes be taken out against these penalties. Some airlines impose penalties on regular tickets as well, particularly against 'no show' passengers.

Check-In Airlines ask you to check in a certain time ahead of the flight departure (usually 1½ hours on international flights). If you fail to check in on time and the flight is overbooked the airline can cancel your booking and give your seat to somebody else.

Confirmation Having a ticket written out with the flight and date you want doesn't mean you have a seat until the agent has checked with the airline that your status is 'OK' or confirmed. Meanwhile you could just be 'on request'.

Discounted Tickets There are two types of discounted fares – officially discounted (see Promotional Fares) and unofficially discounted. The lowest prices often impose drawbacks like flying with unpopular airlines, inconvenient schedules, or unpleasant routes and connections. A discounted ticket can save you other things than money – you may be able to pay Apex prices without the associated Apex advance booking and other requirements. Discounted tickets only exist where there is fierce competition.

Full Fares Airlines traditionally offer 1st class (coded F), business class (coded J) and economy class (coded Y) tickets. These days there are so many promotional and discounted fares available from the regular economy class that few passengers pay full economy fare.

Lost Tickets If you lose your airline ticket an airline will usually treat it like a travellers cheque and, after inquiries, issue you with another one. Legally, however, an airline is entitled to treat it like cash and if you lose it then it's gone forever. Take good care of your tickets.

No-Shows No-shows are passengers who fail to show up for their flight, sometimes due to unexpected delays or disasters, sometimes due to simply forgetting, sometimes because they made more than one booking and didn't bother to cancel the one they didn't want. Full-fare passengers who fail to turn up are sometimes entitled to travel on a later flight. The rest of us are penalised (see Cancellation Penalties).

On Request An unconfirmed booking for a flight, see Confirmation.

children between the ages of four and 12, the fare on international flights is usually 50% of the regular fare or 67% of a discounted fare (these days most fares are likely to be discounted).

Travellers with Special Needs

If you have special needs of any sort – you've broken a leg, you're vegetarian, travelling in a wheelchair, taking a baby or terrified of flying – you should let the airline know as soon as possible so they can make arrangements accordingly. You should remind them when you reconfirm your booking (at least 72 hours before departure) and again when you check in at the airport. It may also be worth ringing round the airlines before you make your booking to find out how they can handle your particular needs.

Airports and airlines can be surprisingly helpful, but they do need advance warning. Most international airports will provide escorts from check-in desk to plane where needed, and there should be ramps, lifts, accessible toilets and reachable phones for wheelchair-bound travellers. Aircraft toilets, on the other hand, are likely to present a problem; travellers should discuss this with

Open Jaws A return ticket where you fly out to one place but return from another. If available this can save you backtracking to your arrival point.

Overbooking Airlines hate to fly empty seats and since every flight has some passengers who fail to show up (see No-Shows) airlines often book more passengers than they have seats. Usually the excess passengers balance those who fail to show up but occasionally somebody gets bumped. If this happens, guess who it is most likely to be? The passengers who check in late.

Promotional Fares Officially discounted fares like Apex fares which are available from travel agents or direct from the airline.

Reconfirmation At least 72 hours prior to departure time of an onward or return flight you must contact the airline and 'reconfirm' that you intend to be on the flight. If you don't do this the airline can delete your name from the passenger list and you could lose your seat. You don't have to reconfirm if your stopover is less than 72 hours. It doesn't hurt to reconfirm more than once. A few airlines don't require reconfirmation, others absolutely insist on it.

Restrictions Discounted tickets often have various restrictions on them – advance purchase is the most usual one (see Apex). Others are restrictions on the minimum and maximum period you must be away, such as a minimum of 14 days or a maximum of one year. See Cancellation Penalties.

Standby A discounted ticket where you only fly if there is a seat free at the last moment. Standby fares are usually only available on domestic routes.

Tickets Out An entry requirement for many countries is that you have an onward or return ticket, in other words, a ticket out of the country. If you're not sure what you intend to do next, the easiest solution is to buy the cheapest onward ticket to a neighbouring country or a ticket from a reliable airline which can later be refunded if you do not use it.

Transferred Tickets Airline tickets cannot be transferred from one person to another. Travellers sometimes try to sell the return half of their ticket, but officials can ask you to prove that you are the person named on the ticket. This is unlikely to happen on domestic flights, on an international flight tickets may be compared with passports.

Travel Agencies Travel agencies vary widely and you should ensure you use one that suits your needs. Some simply handle tours while full-service agencies handle everything from tours and tickets to car rental and hotel bookings. A good one will do all these things and can save you a lot of money but if all you want is a ticket at the lowest possible price, then you really need an agency specialising in discounted tickets. A discount ticket agency, however, may not be useful for other things, like hotel bookings.

Travel Periods Some officially discounted fares, Apex fares in particular, vary with the time of year. There is often a low (off-peak) season and a high (peak) season. Sometimes there's an intermediate or shoulder season as well. At peak times, when everyone wants to fly, not only will the officially discounted fares be higher but so will unofficially discounted fares or there may simply be no discounted tickets available. Usually the fare depends on your outward flight – if you depart in the high season and return in the low season, you pay the high-season fare. ■

the airline at an early stage and, if necessary, with their doctor.

Buying International Tickets in Iran

Foreigners can use rials to buy tickets on internal flights within Iran (and no proof of official exchange is required), but *all* tickets on all international flights on all airlines flying out of Iran must be bought with US dollars cash (or with major credit cards; but not American Express). Iranian and foreign airlines operating out of Iran have little problem filling seats, so there are very few discounted fares. For a list of the head offices

for the major airlines which fly to and from Tehrān, refer to the Getting There & Away section in the Tehrān chapter.

Iran Air

The main international airline in Iran is the government-run Iran Air, though a couple of smaller private Iranian airlines do operate a handful of international flights. Iran Air is not a bad airline, though it doesn't serve alcohol, female passengers have to wear the hejāb, and service could be better. (I may have been unlucky: there were no pillows or blankets for any passengers on the overnight flight from Kuala Lumpur.) Iran Air has a vast network of flights to Asia, the Middle East and Europe, but nothing directly to North America or Australia. Before you board Iran Air, your Iranian visa will be thoroughly scrutinised several times.

It is often hard to confirm, change or buy an Iran Air ticket on an international flight at any ordinary Iran Air office in Iran which normally only handles domestic flights; you will have to go to an Iran Air office in a city which has international flights on Iran Air. The schedules and prices listed in this book for Iran Air are based on flights during summer (April to October); in winter, there is sometimes a reduction in prices, and in the frequency of flights. Iran Air often throws in an internal flight (return) with any international ticket, but this is not as generous as it sounds: the most expensive return ticket on any internal airline within Iran costs as little as US$50 (in rials, at the 'street rate').

Iran Air has sales offices in the following major cities. (The addresses for the offices in Copenhagen and Stockholm were not known at the time of writing.)

Almaty (Kazakstan)
    Hotel Aksundar, Room 115 (☎ (3272) 344 949)
Amsterdam
    Stahouderskade 2, 1054 ES (☎ (20) 683 7744)
Baku (Azerbaijan)
    28 May St (next to Aeroflot) (☎ (12) 987 259)
Damascus (Syria)
    11 Engineers building, Maysaloun Ave (☎ (11) 221 7911)
Doha (Qatar)
    PO Box 6740 (opposite Diwan Amiri) (☎ 323 666)
Dubai (UAE)
    2nd floor, DNATA Amiri Center, Al Maktoum St (☎ (4) 226 733)
Frankfurt
    Am Hauptbahnhof 10 (☎ (69) 2560 0613)
Geneva
    9 Rue Chantepoulet 1201 (☎ (22) 731 0130)
Hamburg
    Ernst-Merck Strasse 12/14 (☎ (40) 245 500)
Istanbul
    17 Valikonaği Cadd, Harbiye (☎ (216) 225 0255)
Karachi
    Room 10, Hotel Mehran (☎ (21) 528 274)
Kuala Lumpur
    Wisma Equity, 150 Jalan Ampang, 50450 (☎ (3) 261 1351)

Kuwait
    8 Al Kazemi building, Khalid Bin Walid St (☎ 245 1180)
London
    73 Picadilly St (☎ (171) 491 3656)
Manama (Bahrain)
    Chamber of Commerce building; PO Box 1044 (☎ 210 414)
Milan
    10 Via Albircci (☎ (2) 878 793)
Moscow
    9 Maly Gnezd, Nikovsky Tverskaya St (☎ (095) 229 9182)
Mumbai (Bombay)
    Sander Mahal Marine Drive, 400020 (☎ (22) 364 0732)
Paris
    33 Ave des Champs Elysees (☎ 01 42 25 99 06)
Rome
    55 Via Bissolati, 55-00187 (☎ (6) 474 1141)
Sharjah (UAE)
    Arabian Travel Agency, PO Box 1477, Port Rd (☎ (6) 350 000)
Singapore
    115 Airport Cargo Rd, Changi airport (☎ 542 7666)
Tokyo
    1-3-5 Akasaka building, Asakasa 1-Chome, Minato-ku (☎ (3) 3586 2101)
Vienna
    Opernring 1, 1010 (☎ (1) 586 5601)

The USA & Canada

Despite the very limited tourism between the US and Iran, it's not too hard or expensive to find a flight from the US to Tehrān, usually via Europe or the Middle East as there are no direct flights between Iran and the US.

There are masses of combinations of flights and fares; the best seem to be via Europe on British Airways or KLM, or via the Middle East on Emirates (from the United Arab Emirates), Pakistan International Airlines (PIA) or Kuwait Airways. Good places to look for bargains are the classifieds in the *Iran Times*, a newspaper published (in English) in Washington; Explorer Travel Consultants in New York (☎ (212) 239 1012) and Travelure in California (☎ (818) 247 6960; fax 244 3882).

If you check round a few travel agents, or better, surf the Net, you could pick up a return ticket to Tehrān from Los Angeles, via Europe, for as little as US$1150. From the east coast (New York) return flights to Tehrān, via Europe, are comparatively better value at about US$850. Most travel agencies recommend the better airlines, such as Lufthansa (via Frankfurt), but you may be looking at US$2200 return from the west coast, or US$1800 return from the east coast, to Tehrān.

Likewise, no airline flies directly between Iran and Canada. Like their southern neighbours, Canadians will have to fly to Iran via Europe or the Middle East on the airlines listed above.

Australia & New Zealand

There are no direct flights between Australia or New Zealand and Iran, but there are a few good options: Malaysia's MAS airline flies from most Australian cities to Kuala Lumpur, with connections to Tehrān on Iran Air, for A$2100 return in high season and A$2000 in low season; Emirates flies from Australia via Dubai (UAE) for A$1840 return in high season and A$1540 in low season; Kuwait Airlines combines with a number of Asian and Australian carriers via Asia and Kuwait to Tehrān for A$1890 return in high season and A$1765 in low season; and Gulf Air offers return flights from Australia via Bahrain for A$2100 in high season and A$1830 in low season.

One of the best places to check out flights to Iran is Homa Travel, Chatswood Central, 1-5 Railway St, Chatswood, NSW 2067 (☎ (02) 9413 3655; fax 9413 3677). The company is run by an expatriate Iranian who knows what it's all about.

New Zealanders will have to take similar connections in Asia, for a little more than Australians have to pay.

The UK

One of the cheapest flights from London to Tehrān, via Damascus, is with Syrian Arab Airlines for UK£341 return, plus UK£25 in taxes. If you don't mind dismal service, and probably spending a night in Moscow at your own expense, Aeroflot is about the same price. Other cheap, but indirect, flights between London and Tehrān include Turkish Airlines, via Istanbul, and PIA, via Karachi. You could also travel to mainland Europe and look for something cheap from there.

The full fare on Iran Air from London (leaving on Tuesday, Thursday and Sunday) to Tehrān is UK£428/857 one way/return, but you can get this fare discounted to about UK£550 return at a travel agency. British Airways, Austrian Airlines and Lufthansa also fly between London and Tehrān for similar prices as Iran Air.

Continental Europe

Iran Air, and several major European carriers, fly directly between most west European cities and Tehrān. The following table provides an overview of the full economy (ie nondiscounted) fares for Iran Air flights to Tehrān.

From	Cost: One Way/Return	Days
Amsterdam	US$645/1290	Thurs and Sun
Copenhagen	US$850/1700	Sun
Frankfurt	US$645/1290	Mon, Wed, Fri and Sat
Geneva	US$633/1265	Tues and Fri
Hamburg	US$700/1400	Thurs and Sun
Moscow	US$367/734	Fri
Paris	US$645/1290	Tues and Fri
Rome	US$550/1100	Tues
Stockholm	US$850/1700	Thurs and Sun
Vienna	US$633/1265	Sat

The same sort of full economy fares to Tehrān – but always open to discounts from travel agencies – are offered by the following European airlines: Lufthansa; Air France; Aeroflot; Alitalia; Austrian Airlines; JAT (from Yugoslavia); KLM, often with an interesting stopover in Baku (Azerbaijan), for about US$850 return from Amsterdam or Milan; SAS; and Swiss Air. For something a little different, try the twice-weekly flight between Tehrān and Varna (on the Bulgarian coast of the Black Sea) on Balkan Airlines.

Frankfurt and Amsterdam are normally good places to look for discounted flights from bucket shops.

Turkey

Because the two countries are neighbours, and road transport is regular and cheap, there are few flights between Iran and Turkey. Currently, Iran Air flies between Tehrān and Istanbul for US$350/700 (one way/return) on Monday and Friday. Turkish Airlines returns the compliment, and flies between Istanbul and Tehrān, for about the same price.

Middle East

Not surprisingly, most countries in the Middle East and the Persian Gulf region are connected by regular air transport to Iran. These flights are almost exclusively used by businessmen, tourists and pilgrims from the region, but foreigners can use them, and it's an interesting way of entering or leaving Iran.

Besides the places listed below, the new

Middle East to Iran Air Routes

From	To	Cost: One Way/Return	Days	Airline(s)
Abu Dhabi (UAE)	Shīrāz	US$124/248	Thurs	Iran Air and Gulf Air
Bahrain	Shīrāz	US$94/188	Thurs and Sun	Gulf Air
	Shīrāz	US$94/188	Thurs	Iran Air
	Tehrān	US$120/240	Sat	Gulf Air
Damascas (Syria)	Tabrīz	Unavailable	Tues	Bon Air
	Tehrān	US$227/454	Mon and Fri	Iran Air
Doha (Qatar)	Būshehr	US$103/206	Sun	Iran Air
	Shīrāz	US$104/208	Sat	Gulf Air
	Shīrāz	US$103/206	Fri	Iran Air
	Tehrān	US$104/209	Tues	Gulf Air
	Tehrān	US$104/208	Fri	Iran Air
Dubai (UAE)	Ābādān	US$105/210	Sun	Iran Asseman
	Bandar-é Abbās	US$62/124	Tues and Sun	Iran Air and Iran Asseman
	Būshehr	US$116/232	Thurs	Iran Air
	Esfahān	US$120/240	Wed and Sun	Kish Airlines
	Kīsh Island	US$120/240	Wed	Kish Airlines
	Mashhad	US$180/360	Mon	Iran Asseman
	Shīrāz	US$105/210	Every day but Fri	Iran Asseman
	Shīrāz	US$124/248	Mon, Wed and Sat	Iran Air
	Tehrān	US$113/226	Mon, Wed and Sat	Iran Air
Kuwait	Ahvāz	US$145/290	Fri	Iran Asseman
	Esfahān	US$122/244	Sat	Iran Air
	Mashhad	US$144/288	Fri (June to Oct only)	Iran Asseman
	Mashhad	US$162/324	Wed	Iran Air
	Shīrāz	US$118/236	Mon	Iran Asseman
	Tehrān	US$145/290	Thurs	Iran Asseman
	Tehrān	US$122/244	Wed and Sun	Iran Air
Manama (Bahrain)	Shīrāz	US$95/180	Thurs	Iran Air
Sharjah (UAE)	Bandar-é Abbās	US$62/124	Thurs and Sat	Iran Air

Central Asia to Iran Air Routes

From	To	Cost: One Way/Return	Days	Airline
Almaty (Kazakstan)	Tehrān	US$275/550	Thurs	Iran Air
Ashghabat (Turkmenistan)	Mashhad	US$115/230	Mon and Fri	Iran Asseman
	Tehrān	US$167/234	Wed	Iran Air
Baku (Azerbaijan)	Tabrīz	US$210/420	Fri	Iran Air
	Tehrān	US$186/372	Mon	Iran Air
Bishkek (Kyrgyzstan)	Mashhad	US$225/450	Sat	Iran Asseman
	Tehrān	US$225/450	Tues	Iran Asseman
Dushanbe (Tajikistan)	Mashhad	US$165/330	Tues and Fri	Iran Asseman
Tashkent (Uzbekistan)	Tehrān	US$223/446	Wed	Iran Air

international airports on Gheshm and Kīsh islands will also have future flights with Iran Air and other regional airlines.

Central Asia
Flying via one of the former Soviet states in Central Asia is a fascinating way to enter or leave Iran, though flights are not frequent, and they are prone to change and cancellation. See the table above.

Rest of Asia
To avoid some long and boring overland trips from the subcontinent you may consider flying, though this means you may have to backtrack if you wish to visit eastern Iran, because flights go straight to/from Tehrān. One traveller took the Karachi-Tehrān flight (full fare: US$252/504 one way/return) because, as he wrote, 'I did not have time to travel *overland* for 36 hours to Quetta, then another 24 to Taftan', and another 24 hours or more to Tehrān. Iran Air also flies between Tehrān and Karachi on Wednesday for the same price.

Between Iran and India, Iran Air flies from

Tehrān to Mumbai (Bombay) on Friday for US$307/614; Air India offers the same flight for the same price. Elsewhere in Asia, JAL and Iran Air fly between Tehrān and Tokyo (US$860/1720) twice a week; and Iran Air goes to Kuala Lumpur for US$613/1226.

LAND
For decades, the traditional overland passage (sometimes known as the Hippie Trail) between Europe and Kathmandu or anywhere in India, has been difficult, but never impossible. While excitements in Iran frightened off many overlanders in the 1980s, and problems in Afghanistan still deter all but the truly fearless, the 1990s have seen the opening of several new overland routes through this part of the world.

Currently, it is safe and easy to travel overland into Iran from Turkey and Pakistan, and the more adventurous are successfully crossing into Iran from the newly-opened borders with the former Soviet states of Azerbaijan and Turkmenistan. However, the situation with the Iran-Armenian border is not clear; the border with Afghanistan is

The Silk Road

No one knows for sure when the miraculously fine, soft, strong, shimmering and sensuous fabric spun from the cocoon of the *Bombyx* caterpillar first reached Europe from China. The Parthians, one of the first peoples to settle on the Iranian plateau, were the most voracious foreign consumers of Chinese silk by the close of the 2nd century BC. In about 105 BC, the Parthians and China had exchanged embassies and inaugurated official bilateral trade along the caravan route that lay between them. With this, the Silk Road was born – in fact, if not in name.

It took up to 200 days to traverse the 8000km route, though geographically the Silk Road was a complex and shifting proposition. It was no single road, but rather a web of caravan tracks that thread through some of the highest mountains and bleakest deserts on earth. Though the road map expanded over the centuries, the network had its main eastern terminus at the Chinese capital Ch'ang-an (now Xian); west of there, the route divided at Dunhuang, one branch skirting the dreaded Taklamakan desert to the north, while the other headed south. The two forks met again in Kashgar, where the trail headed up to any of a series of mountain passes.

The Silk Road entered Iran anywhere between Mary (now in Turkmenistan) and Herāt (now in Afghanistan), and passed through Mashhad, Neishābūr, Dāmghān, Semnān, Rey, Ghazvīn, Tabrīz and Mākū, before finishing at Constantinople (now Istanbul). In the winter, the trail often diverted in a more westerly direction from Rey, and passed through Hamadān to Baghdad.

Goods heading west and goods heading east did not fall into discrete bundles. In fact, there was no 'through traffic'; caravanners were mostly short and medium-distance haulers who marketed and took on freight along a given beat according to their needs and inclinations. At any given time any portion of the network might be beset by war, robbers or natural disaster. In general, the eastern end was enriched by the importation of gold, silver, ivory, jade and other precious stones, wool, Mediterranean coloured glass, grapes and wine, spices and – an early Parthian craze – acrobats and ostriches. Goods enriching the western end were silk, porcelain, spices, gems and perfumes. And in the middle lay Central Asia and Iran, great clearinghouses which provided its native beasts – horses and two-humped Bactrian camels – to keep the goods flowing in both directions.

The Silk Road gave rise to unprecedented trade, but its true glory and unique status in human history were the result of the interchange of ideas, technologies and religions that occurred among the very different cultures that traded along it. Religion alone presents an astounding picture of diversity and tolerance that would be the envy of any modern democratic state. Manichaeism, Zoroastrianism, Buddhism, Nestorian Christianity, Judaism, Confucianism, Taoism and the shamanism of grassland nomads coexisted and in the some cases mingled – until the coming of Islam.

Eventually the Silk Road was abandoned when sailors from the new European colonial powers discovered alternative sea routes in the 15th century. It is only in last few years that the Silk Road has attracted interest again: this time, for trade between Iran and the newly-opened Central Asian republics, and as a tourist attraction. ■

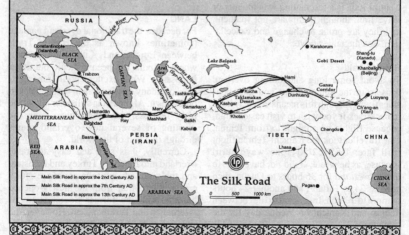

The Silk Road

Main Silk Road in approx the 2nd Century AD
Main Silk Road in approx the 7th Century AD
Main Silk Road in approx the 13th Century AD

0   500   1000 km

currently closed; and independent travellers are not allowed to cross into Iraq from Iran.

Bringing Your Own Vehicle

Immediately following the 1979 Islamic Revolution, driving across Iran was unwise – now it's relatively easy and a popular way to get around, as long as you can handle Iranian driving habits. As long as you are prepared, and have the right attitude and documents, there is nothing stopping you driving to, and around, Iran.

To bring your own vehicle into Iran, you have to satisfy the sort of requirements sought in most other countries in the region. For a start, you must be more than 18 years old and have a current International Driving Permit. For the vehicle, you'll need a *carnet de passage* and a *diptyque* or a *triptyque*, which can be obtained from the relevant international automobile organisation in your country. If you have any queries, or want further information about driving to and around Iran, contact the Touring & Automobile Club of the Islamic Republic of Iran (☎ (21) 8740 411; fax 8740 410), PO Box 15875/5617, 12 Nobakht St, Khorramshahr Ave, Tehrān.

Iranian customs will probably note the vehicle details in your passport to make sure you don't leave the country without your car. Crashing a vehicle in Iran, or having it stolen, is not recommended. Third party insurance is compulsory for foreign drivers, and you can obtain this outside Iran (but make sure the policy is valid for Iran and accredited with Iran Bimeh, the Iranian Green Card Bureau), or at a major border.

Most motorists will travel via Turkey, crossing the Turkey/Iran border at Gürbulak/ Bāzargān (which is easier) or Yüksekova/ Serō (which is not as safe because you must travel through Kurdish parts of Turkey). Be prepared for a long wait and a thorough vehicle search at either border, especially at Bāzargān where the line of waiting vehicles can stretch to the horizon.

The only crossing in the east is the Iran/Pakistan border at Mīrjāvé/Taftan. If you have time to line up for ages, and possess

the appropriate documents, you can also take your vehicle across the border between Iran and Azerbaijan at Āstārā. In the future, you may also be able to cross the Iran/ Turkmenistan border in your own vehicle at Sarakhs/ Saraghs. No border-post is open at all into Afghanistan, and foreigners cannot cross the Iran/Iraq border by vehicle.

One final option is to book you and your vehicle on a ferry across the Persian Gulf (refer to the Sea section later for details); or, possibly, across the Caspian Sea between Baku (Azerbaijan) and Bandar-é Anzalī.

For more information about driving around Iran, refer to the Car & Motorcycle section in the Getting Around chapter.

Turkey

There are two main crossings along the 1270km border with Turkey. The main one is at Gürbulak (Turkey) and Bāzargān (Iran). While this is certainly the busiest, it is also the best for overland travellers because of the hotels, moneychanging facilities and regular transport on either side of the border. For further details, refer to the Bāzargān section in the Western Iran chapter.

It is also possible for foreigners to travel through the border at Yüksekova (Turkey) and Serō (Iran), but some travellers have had difficulties at this border in recent times – refer to the Serō section in the Western Iran chapter for more details. This route is rarely used by foreigners because much of east and especially south-east Turkey is unsafe due to conflict. In particular, certain splinter groups of the rebellious PKK (Kurdish Worker's Party) have taken to kidnapping foreigners travelling in Turkish-controlled Kurdish areas without PKK permission.

Bus The Bāzargān border crossing is one of the most congested bottlenecks in West Asia, and the delay at the border can be very wearisome. There are two options by bus. The easier is to take a direct long-distance bus to, say Tehrān or Tabrīz, from Istanbul, Ankara or Erzurum, but this involves lengthy delays while you wait hours for everyone else on your bus to be cleared through customs and immigration (which may take you, as a foreigner, less than an hour to clear).

Every week, several long-distance buses travel between Istanbul and Ankara, and Tabrīz, Esfahān or Shīrāz; and several every day between Istanbul, via Ankara, and Tehrān (refer to Getting There & Away in the individual sections for details). From Tehrān, the cost to Istanbul and Ankara (which is the same fare) is 69,000/81,000/115,000 rials for buses with 32/29/22 seats. If you are going on a long-distance haul, it's certainly worth paying extra for some comfort.

However, it is far better to travel between Turkey and Iran in stages, and enjoy some of eastern Turkey and northern and/or western Iran along the way. Taking a bus to – but not across – either border will also do away with waiting – for up to 50 fellow-passengers to clear customs. You can cross the border in one day using public transport between Dogubeyazit (Turkey) and Mākū (Iran), or even as far as Erzurum (Turkey) and Tabrīz (Iran) if you start early and you are lucky enough to cross the border with minimum fuss.

Expect considerable delays in winter as the high mountain passes near both borders are frequently snowbound. For about 10 days either side of the Iranian New Year, or Nō Rūz (21 March), when the domestic demand for transport becomes very heavy, Iranian buses are normally not allowed to operate international services, but Turkish buses continue to service this route.

Train Once upon a time, there was a weekly train between Istanbul and Tehrān, via Ankara, Van and Tabrīz, but because Van and surrounds are not safe from PKK attacks, foreigners are currently not able to travel between either country by train. The direct bus, or better, a combination of several buses, is far quicker anyway – but not as interesting.

Pakistan
Along the 830km border with Pakistan, the only recognised crossing for foreigners, and

the only one you should use unless you have permission from immigration officials from both countries, is at Mīrjāvé (Iran) and Taftan (Pakistan). Refer to the Mīrjāvé section in the Eastern Iran chapter for details about using public transport across this border.

Bus There is no direct bus across the Mīrjāvé-Taftan border from either side. This is not a problem, because using a combination of any conceivable road transport, or the train, is very easy.

Train There are *still* plans to lay the 600km or so track between Kermān and Zāhedān, but for many years to come travellers will have to take a bus west from Zāhedān.

Twice a week, a Pakistani train putters along the track between Quetta and Zāhedān in both directions. Though the train saves you changing transport midstream, and it is quaint (well, for the first few hours at least), taking a combination of bus, minibus and shared taxi to either side of the border, and crossing the border on foot, is far, far quicker.

Azerbaijan
The two recognised crossings along the 768km border with Azerbaijan which foreigners can use are at Jolfā (Iran) and Julfā (Azerbaijan); and Āstārā (Iran) and Astara (Azerbaijan). Because of fighting and blockades between Armenians and Azerbaijanis, foreigners should cross at Āstārā where transport is more regular, and the border is closer to the Azerbaijan capital, Baku. Refer to the Āstārā section in the Caspian Provinces chapter for more details.

Bus Every day a bus goes from Tehrān to Baku, via Āstārā. Taking the bus, which is certainly cheaper than by plane, is probably better than doing it yourself because of the uncertainties of travelling independently in rural Azerbaijan. The only drawback is the inordinate delays crossing the border at Āstārā in any sort of vehicle – it may end up being quicker to cross the border yourself, and hitching a ride on any public transport heading north or south.

Train There is a train line between Tabrīz and Jolfā, and on to Julfā (on the Azerbaijan side of the border) but it's currently only used for cargo. No-one is permitted to cross this border by train.

Armenia

The border between Iran and Armenia is only 35km long. With the simmering conflict between Armenia and Azerbaijan, foreigners are not apparently allowed to cross the border between Armenia and Iran in either direction – but the situation was not entirely clear at the time of writing. In any case, you should not attempt this crossing by any mode of transport without proper advice and authority from relevant Armenian officials.

Turkmenistan

Though the border is long (1206km), the only recognised border crossing for Iranians, Turkmen and foreigners, is at Sarakhs (Iran) and Saraghs (Turkmenistan). Refer to the Sarakhs section in the Eastern Iran chapter for more details.

Bus No direct bus travels through the border from either side, but you can easily take buses or shared taxis to Sarakhs from Mashhad, cross the border yourself, and then take further transport into Turkmenistan (or vice versa).

Train The modern train station at Sarakhs, on the Iranian side of the border, and the brand spanking new railway line (costing more than US$200 million), lay virtually idle at the time of research, because of different railway gauges. With the aid of some bogie-changing equipment, this problem should be sorted out by the time you read this, allowing you to cross the border by train.

Afghanistan

Until recently, foreigners could cross the border between Afghanistan and Iran at Tāybād (Iran) and Eslām Ghalé (Afghanistan), which is connected by bus to the regional centre of Herat. However, travel to Afghanistan during the perpetual and bloody civil war is certainly not recommended; in any case, the Taliban forces in Afghanistan closed the border at the time of research because of the Iranian government's refusal to recognise them as Afghanistan's new rulers.

Iraq

The only crossing into Iraq at Khosravī in Kermānshāh Province is used by Kurdish refugees coming from Iraq, and by the very, very occasional organised tour group. It is not open to independent foreign travellers.

Syria

Though Iran and Syria do not share a common border, each week several buses take the *very* long trip (about four days) between Tehrān or Tabrīz and Damascus. The bus is far cheaper than flying, of course, and foreigners can pay in rials in Iran – whereas international flights must be bought in US dollars.

SEA

Iran has 2410km of coastal boundaries along the Persian Gulf, Gulf of Oman and Caspian Sea, but there are only a few ways to enter or leave Iran by sea.

Persian Gulf

The main shipping agency in Iran for trips across the Persian Gulf is Valfajre-8 Shipping Company, a subsidiary of the Islamic Republic of Iran Shipping Line (IRISL). At the time of research, Valfajre-8 had ferries from Bandar-é Abbās to the United Arab Emirates: ie to Sharjah (US$38/46/49 for 3rd/2nd/1st class, and US$300 for a car) on Monday, Wednesday and Saturday; and to Dubai (US$45/52/55; no cars) on Thursday. Schedules change regularly, so always make local inquiries or check with the Valfajre-8 office in Tehrān (see under Boat in the Getting There & Away section in the Tehrān Province chapter for details). Fares must be paid in US dollars.

There are also occasional passenger ferries (but not for cars) between Bandar-é Abbās and Manama (Bahrain) with a Bahrain-based ferry service for US$85/150 one way/return. Tickets are available at International Travel on Al-Khalifa Ave, in Manama, or ask at any travel agency in Bandar-é Abbās.

For further details about ferries across the Persian Gulf, see under Getting There & Away in the Bandar-é Abbās section in the Southern Iran chapter.

Caspian Sea

Currently, there is only one way for foreigners to enter Iran from any country with a Caspian Sea coast – though this may well change. At the time of research, the Blue Ocean Shipping Company (☎ (21) 8744 051; fax 8743 364) in Tehrān planned to offer passenger ferry services between Bandar-é Anzalī and Nōshahr, and various unnamed foreign ports along the Caspian Sea.

At the moment, a passenger-cum-cargo boat leaves Bandar-é Anzalī every alternate Monday for the Azerbaijan capital of Baku. The fare is 198,000 rials, plus some unspecified, and possibly unauthorised, 'fee' of 120,000 rials. The 16-hour trip is not too uncomfortable, but you will need to bring plenty of food, water and patience. For current information, ask at the customs office in Bandar-é Anzalī.

DEPARTURE TAXES

The situation regarding departure taxes on international flights was, at the time of research, as clear as mud. It seems that all tickets on Iran Air bought overseas include the Iranian departure tax (but double check this when you confirm your outward flight from Iran). Some foreign airlines flying from Tehrān (but not from other international airports in Iran) include the Iranian departure tax in the fare, but others don't: eg on Air France, the departure tax is included, but not on Lufthansa. There is nothing to do but check, and double-check, with your airline, and the relevant airline office in Tehrān, and

if you have to pay the departure tax, make sure you have enough rials with you.

From Tehrān, the tax (if you have to pay it) is currently 70,000 rials. From other cities in Iran, the departure tax for all international flights (except Iran Air) is *not* included in your fare: you must pay anything between 70,000 and 92,500 rials when you book at the airline office, or pay at the airport when you depart.

ORGANISED TOURS

Many travellers visit Iran on an organised tour, and this trend is likely to continue as long as visas for independent travellers are difficult to obtain and extend. Other good reasons to consider an organised tour is that few Iranians outside the tourist industry speak English, and a tour guide should be able to provide you with loads of information about the places you are visiting (though we hope this guidebook will be sufficient for most travellers). Naturally, these tours are expensive, and you often sacrifice a lot of flexibility and independence.

Because Iran has yet to become a significant tourist destination, and it remains difficult for Americans to visit Iran, not many reputable foreign travel agencies bother organising tours to Iran on a regular basis. You can ask your travel agent about organised tours to Iran, but by far the best way is to contact the following agencies directly, or use the Internet, if you can. Some travel agencies these days deal exclusively over the Net, and don't even have a recognised office as such. Costs of organised tours naturally depend on the length of the tour, mode of transport, type of accommodation and current exchange rate.

Here are a few experienced and reputable agencies which offer organised tours to Iran.

The USA & Canada

Americans may feel more comfortable going on an organised tour – and it may be the only way they can get a visa anyway. If you have access to the Internet, the online services listed in the Facts for the Visitor chapter have good links to web sites in the US and Canada which provide information about travel and organised tours to Iran.

Bestway Tours & Safaris
3526 West 41st Ave, Vancouver, BC, V6N 3E6 (☎ (604) 264 73 78; fax 264 7774; email bestway@bestway.com) – it runs several more adventurous trips.

Citad
(☎ (800) 876 2704; fax (212) 768 3898) – based in New York, this consultancy firm, run by an Iranian, runs a few tours each year.

Distant Horizons
350 Elm Ave, Long Beach, CA 90802 (☎ (800) 333 1240; fax (562) 983 8833; email disthoriz@aol.com) – this is an impressive outfit which focuses on the more senior travellers among us.

Geographic Expeditions
2627 Lombard St, San Francisco, CA 94123 (☎ (415) 922 0448; fax 346 5535; email info@geoex.com) – it describes its tours as 'strenuous', probably another term for 'busy'.

Iran Tours Corporation
PO Box 10660, Kansas, MO 6418-0660 (☎ (816) 436 7791; fax 436 2875; email info@irantours.com) – it offers an excellent range of tours, and has an office in Tehrān.

Johan Tours
928 Park St East, Vienna, VA 22180 (☎ (703) 281 0809; fax 281 5520) – run by expatriate Iranians, this agency is recommended by the Iranian Interests Section at the Pakistani Embassy in Washington, for what it's worth.

Silk Road Tours
(☎ (604) 925 3831; fax 925 6269; email silkroad@smart.com).

Sunship International Inc
28E Jackson Blvd, Suite 1306, Chicago, Ill (☎ (312) 427 4774; fax 427 5455) – they offer upmarket tours.

Voyage Afrolympic
(☎ (514) 274 0000; fax 270 5457) – based in Montreal.

Australia & New Zealand

Purely Persian Rugs
198-200 Through Rd, Burwood, Victoria 3125 (☎ (03) 9882 7541; fax 9836 4849) – though primarily a Persian carpet importer, the Iranian owner also runs three-week tours to Iran.

Russian Passport/Red Bear Tours
Suite 11a, 401 St. Kilda Rd, Melbourne, Victoria 3004 (☎ (03) 9867 3888; fax 9867 1055; email passport@werple.net.au; web site http://www.travelcentre.com.au).

Steppes West
2a/197 Military Rd, Neutral Bay, NSW 2089 (☎ (02) 9904 4166; fax 9909 3771; email westpty@intercoast.com.au) – ties in visits to Iran with other countries in Central Asia.

Sundowner Adventure Travel
600 Lonsdale St, Melbourne, Victoria 3004 (☎ (03) 9600 1934; fax 9642 5838) – this company runs trips through Iran, often combined with Pakistan and/or Turkey.

The UK

Ace Study Tours
Babraham, Cambridge CB2 4AP (☎ (0123) 835 055; fax 837 394) – the best place to ask about study and Fārsī language tours.

Classic Tours
148 Curtain Rd, London EC2A 3AR (☎ (0171) 613 4441)

Exodus
9 Weir Rd, London SW12 OLT (☎ (0181) 673 0859) – one of the many tours they run all over the world is to Iran.

Hinterland Travel
2 Ivy Mill Lane, Godstone, Surrey RH9 8NH (☎ (01883) 743584) – they claim to be able to show you the 'real Iran', tied in with trips to Turkmenistan and Uzbekistan.

Magic Carpet Travel
125 Rylston Rd, London SW6 7HP (☎ (0171) 385 9975) – they can tailor organised tours to specific needs, and also arrange visas for independent travellers.

McCabe Travel
53/55 Balham Hill, London, SW12 9DR (☎ (0181) 675 8886; fax 673 1204).

Continental Europe

Association Culturel de Voyages
39 rue des Favorites, 75738, Paris Cedex, France (☎ 01 40 43 20 21; fax 01 40 43 20 29)

Catai Tours
(web site http://www.catai.es/eafrica.html; email catai@catai.es) – based in Spain, it is ideal for Spanish-speaking travellers.

Clio
34 rue du Hameau, 75015, Paris, France (☎ 01 53 68 82 82; fax 01 53 68 82 60) – it also has offices in Lyon and Marseille.

Clio
11 rue du Mont-Blanc CH1201, Geneva, Switzerland (☎ (22) 731 70 26).

Malibu Travel Inc
Damrak 30, NL-102 LJ, Amsterdam, the Netherlands (☎ (20) 623 4912; fax 638 2271; email malibu@euronet.nl) – well set up with an informative web site.

Orients
    29 rue des Boulangers, 75005, Paris, France
    (☎ 01 46 34 29 00; fax 01 40 46 84 48).
VS Studienreisen GmbH
    Augsburgerstrasse 31, D-10789, Berlin,
    Germany (☎ (030) 213 8832; fax 213 8842).

WARNING

The information in this chapter is particularly vulnerable to change: prices for international travel are volatile, routes are introduced and cancelled, schedules change, special deals come and go, and rules and visa requirements are amended. Airlines and governments seem to take a perverse pleasure in making price structures and regulations as complicated as possible. You should check directly with the airline or travel agent to make sure you understand how a fare (and ticket you may buy) works. In addition, the travel industry is highly competitive and there are many lurks and perks.

The upshot of this is that you should get opinions, quotes and advice from as many airlines and travel agents as possible before you part with your hard-earned cash. The details given in this chapter should be regarded as pointers and are not a substitute for your own careful, up-to-date research.

Getting Around

Although Iran's transport system isn't as developed as western countries, it's considerably better than most countries in the region. Importantly, all public transport is frequent, reliable, relatively safe and very cheap. Iran has more than 155,000km of roads (about 25,000km is paved), 39 airports (a dozen can be used for international flights), and 7740km of railways (but not all are used for passenger services), so finding something going your way is easy.

Whichever form of public transport you take, try to book tickets as early as you can; even if you have a change of plans, and must forfeit your bus or train ticket, or pay a (small) surcharge for changing a plane ticket, there is a certain security in having confirmed tickets at times that suit you.

Nō Rūz & Ramazān

While school holidays do not generally cause a problem when you want to find or book public transport, you should seriously consider avoiding Iran altogether for about 10 days before and after Nō Rūz, the chaotic Iranian New Year which starts on or about 21 March.

Transport can also sometimes be a bit of a problem during the Muslim month of dawn-to-dusk fasting, known as Ramazān: Iranian bus companies are often not allowed to operate international services at this time and have to divert spare buses to supplement domestic services (though Turkish buses still run in and out of Iran). Travellers, both foreign and Muslim, are excused from normal requirements during Ramazān, and are allowed to eat and drink during the day. Finding or booking seats during the post-Ramazān celebrations, known as Eid-é Fetr, can be difficult because many Iranians visit their relatives at this time.

For more information about both events, refer to the Public Holidays & Special Events section in the Facts for the Visitor chapter.

Roadblocks

One annoying aspect of travelling by bus, minibus, shared taxi or private vehicle is the number of roadblocks throughout the country. These are usually located at a major road junction, or a few kilometres either side of a main city; a few are also dotted around remote areas for no particular reason. The roadblocks are more frequent, and thorough, anywhere near a border, particularly near Pakistan and Afghanistan (from where drugs are smuggled west towards Europe), and on roads heading north from the major ports along the Persian Gulf.

On Public Transport Unless you are smuggling something illegal (and for heaven's sake don't!), you don't need to be concerned about these roadblocks. At most of them, you just have to wait while the driver of whatever vehicle you are in stops, and shuffles across to the guard to get some sort of stamp of approval. In these cases, the process is all over in a few minutes. Sometimes a customs official, or someone from the secret police, may walk up and down the aisle in the bus, or look through the taxi window, presumably searching for obvious smugglers or dissidents. The officials may ask to see your passport, more out of curiosity than anything else. Just do what they say, and answer any questions politely and briefly. Don't worry: neither I, nor any other traveller I have met, or anyone who has written to us, has had any trouble; the officials seem to be under instructions to be nice to foreigners, which is very reassuring.

In places near the borders, or Persian Gulf, customs searches are more thorough. The official will often look more closely at the passengers, and search hand luggage. Often, all passengers have to get out of the minibus, bus or shared taxi, identify their luggage, carry it a few metres up the road, and wait while the vehicle is searched. Very rarely will your main luggage be searched individually.

Again, foreigners are often given special consideration, and rarely have to suffer the indignation of the nosy questions and intrusive baggage searches which Iranians often must endure.

Driving Your Own Vehicle If you are driving your own vehicle, the hardest part is knowing which roadblocks to stop at. I could never work it out: trucks stop at all of them; buses and minibuses stop at some (the driver seems to know which); shared taxis are often waved through, especially if the driver knows one of the guards; and private vehicles rarely bother stopping at all.

As a rule of thumb, any foreigner driving their own vehicle near any border should stop and go through the motions of checking in with the police-cum-customs. If you wind down your window, smile nicely, and give them your best 'I don't know what to do and I don't speak Fārsī' look, you will often be waved through. If that doesn't work, get out of the vehicle and walk towards the guard – you may then be told to get back in the car and not bother. The worst that can happen is that you have to show your passport, licence and vehicle documents. Very rarely will you have any hassles as long your documentation is in order.

In other parts of the country, generally stop if other private vehicles do, but always look out for any official waving at you. After a while you will get to know which roadblocks to bother with, but if in doubt, it doesn't hurt to stop and ask the police/customs officer what to do. The roadblocks are well marked in English, and are virtually a regional social centre: you can often pick up some food and water; useful instructions or advice on road conditions from the guards (if you speak Fārsī); go to the toilet; or pick up some hitchers, if you want (or ask about a lift yourself).

AIR

Iran must be one of the cheapest countries in the world for domestic flights, especially if you have changed your money at the unoffi-

cial 'street rate'; eg a 90-minute flight right across the country costs as little as 105,000 rials (US$22 at the 'street rate'; US$35 at the 'official rate'). Even if you are the sort of traveller who prefers to experience the country by using public transport on terra firma, you should still consider taking a few flights for some obvious reasons: your time is probably limited; your visa will probably not be long enough for you to use public transport to remote cities; all fares are very cheap; the country is vast, and the scenery is often boring; and, finally, flights (particularly on Iran Air) are reliable, frequent, and safe (especially compared with other airlines in the region). Think about it.

Bookings

Thankfully, foreigners do not have to pay for domestic flights in hard currency, so you pay in rials and no proof of 'official' exchange (ie at the bank) is required. Tickets are not transferable, and when you check in, the name on your passport is checked with the name on your ticket. There are children's fares (the discount varies), but there is no student discount. Return tickets cost exactly twice the single fare, and the price for a ticket on, say, a flight from Tehrān to Mashhad is virtually the same for all airlines operating on this route.

The two major internal airlines – Iran Air and Iran Asseman – are well set up, and all offices are computerised, so you can book and/or confirm any domestic flight from any office in the country. But only at Iran Air and Iran Asseman offices in the larger cities with international flights on these two airlines can you confirm, change or book a ticket on an international flight.

When you book a domestic ticket on any airline, don't always accept on face value any comment that the 'flights are full'. It may appear that way on the computer a week before the flight, but four days before departure additional seats often mysteriously appear. If still unsuccessful, try again the day before departure, when even more spare seats sometimes materialise. As a last resort, you can always try to get a ticket at the airport; there can be a few cancellations at the last minute. In most cases, if you can book ahead, you will have few problems getting on a flight when you want – unless you are there around Nō Rūz.

If you give the airline plenty of notice, they will only rarely charge you an extra fee if you change departure dates. There may be a 1000 rial charge if you change the point of origin or destination within a few days of the departure date, and there can sometimes be a cancellation fee of up to 40% of the ticket price if you cancel within 24 hours of the departure time. You have little chance of getting a full refund for cancelled tickets. The departure tax is included in the fares on domestic flights.

Iran Air

Subtitled the Airline of the Islamic Republic of Iran, with the symbol of Homa, the mythical bird, Iran Air is the government-owned national carrier. It boasts an extensive network of flights to most provincial capitals, as well as places of interest to travellers. This airline is worth using almost exclusively because it's far more reliable than the others. Flight details are included in the relevant Getting There & Away sections throughout this guidebook.

Iran Air has at least one sales office in each of the places it serves, as well as one in Rāmsar. The airline has very little in the way of in-flight service: there are no magazines or videos, and there is nothing to read except the sick bag (in English), but often the steward can rustle up an issue of the *Tehran Times* on more popular flights. A carton of fruit juice, a cup of tea or coffee or a sandwich, all wrapped in excessive amounts of plastic, will be plonked on your table on longer flights.

Iran Air sometimes uses planes with the words in English on the side, 'Iran Air Tours', and the prefix TX rather than IR for the flight number. I never quite worked out why (TX often indicates that the plane is an old Russian Tupolev, but not always). If in doubt, go by the flight number rather than the two-letter prefix before it.

Iran Asseman

Described in the previous edition of this book as 'one of the world's more hopeless airlines', Iran Asseman has certainly lifted its game in recent years – though some wags still call the airline 'the Flying Mausoleum'. Asseman is now a viable alternative to Iran Air on major routes where Iran Air flights may be full, or to more remote places which Iran Air does not bother with. However, Iran Asseman schedules are often a complete mystery (even to Iran Asseman staff) and timetables do change regularly, so be wary. Asseman sometimes does not have an office in a town to which it flies, or the offices are hard to find (eg in Tehrān), so book at the airport or, better, with a reputable travel agency in town.

Other Airlines

Just about everywhere you want to go is covered by Iran Air and/or Iran Asseman, but on more popular routes, and to some remote destinations, there are five other quirky domestic airlines to choose from: Bon Air; Caspian Air; Kīsh Airlines; Mahan Air; and Saha Air.

The schedules for these airlines are virtually impossible to find (even for Lonely Planet authors), flights are infrequent and unreliable, and the cancellation of flights, and even bankruptcy of the airline itself, is not uncommon.

With the occasional exception of Caspian Air and Mahan Air, offices for these airlines either don't exist, they are hard to find, or if you do find them, they're closed. If you still want to use one of these airlines, book at an authorised travel agent or find their ticket booth at the relevant airport.

At the Airport

One pleasant aspect about flying in Iran is the surprising orderliness of the airports and, generally, the passengers. At the terminals in most major cities, there is a large noticeboard with the departure and arrival times, as well as the airline name and number, in English and Fārsī. Often, a departure or arrival will be preceded by an announcement in English and Fārsī; if there isn't, someone will always help you out. Larger terminals have information booths, often with English-speaking staff, but almost every tourist information counter at every airport is closed or not staffed.

It is a good idea to check in for all domestic flights about one hour before departure. This allows you enough time to sort yourself out at the terminal, check in your luggage; get the seat you prefer; struggle through the two or three x-ray machines, and personal checks of hand baggage and frisks; and enjoy a cup of tea or a meal before you leave. Seats are allocated on the more popular flights; but on some of the smaller flights, you find your own seat once you are on the plane.

One annoying security precaution, which only seems to take place on flights in the south and south-east, is the removal of batteries from anything in your hand luggage. If the customs officer finds any batteries in your camera, camera flash, Walkman or whatever, while searching your hand luggage, the batteries must be carried on the flight by the captain. And then you have to wait for the batteries after you arrive. (In my case, this wait meant that I missed the only passenger bus from the airport to Chābahār, more than 40km away.)

BUS

If you can't go to somewhere in Iran by bus (or minibus), the chances are that *no-one* wants to go there. More than 20 bus companies offer hundreds of services all over the country, so business is highly competitive, the fares are very cheap and, generally, there are regular departures. Most buses are comfortable, with your own cushioned seat; and standing is not normally allowed.

Don't be confused by the names of the destinations on a bus – it is quite common for a bus travelling between, for example, Khorram Ābād and Ahvāz, to have 'Tehrān-Istanbul' written on the front or side in English. Other English words written on the bus indicating good luck and their love of God do not always translate particularly

well, such as my favourite, 'We Go To Trip Good By'.

Bus Companies

Since the Islamic Revolution (in 1979), bus companies have been organised into cooperatives, and they are usually referred to simply as Cooperative Bus Company No X *(Sherkat-é Ta'āvonī Shomāré X)*, or whatever number it is. The best companies, with the most extensive network of services, are TBT (also known as Cooperative Bus Company No 15); and Cooperative Bus Company No 1 (often with the words in English 'Taavoni' or 'Bus No One').

Recently a few private bus companies have sprung up, such as Sayro Safar (or other similar transliterations into English). These companies offer slightly more luxury, for a little more (and it's worth paying the extra). It can be confusing when one company buys a bus from another without changing the name in English on the side. In most cases, the differences between bus companies are only slight; it is not worth seeking out a specific company, just take any bus which is going your way when you want.

Classes & Seats

From most cities and provincial centres there are usually two classes of long-distance bus: 'lux' which is the regular (2nd) class, and 'super', or 1st class. (Sometimes there is 'super lux' which is not that much more super or luxurious than the other two.) 'Lux' buses have a few more seats than 'super', so it's slightly less comfortable, but it is cheaper than super – but generally the price difference is not worth quibbling about. For long trips, ask for a ticket for 'super' class, and a single seat (if you want one), or find a bus company that will. If it's a short trip, you are not fussy, or seats are at a premium, just take whatever you can.

In theory, most seats recline; in reality they often don't. If you are travelling alone, you will often be given a single seat in super class. The seats at the back are the ones to avoid if you pre-book a ticket; they are on top of the back wheels and the engine, and passengers picked up along the way tend to congregate at the back. Seating is generally arranged so that women sit next to women, and men next to men, except for married couples. If in doubt, ask at the time of booking. It is not acceptable for a man to sit next to an unrelated woman, even if there's only one spare seat on the bus. There may be a last minute rearrangement of seats if the gender mix is unacceptable.

The Journey

Don't count on averaging more than 60km/h on most routes. Although many journeys run overnight, it's difficult to sleep well on buses, and they are not a recommended way of cutting down on accommodation costs. Some of the longer journeys, eg Mashhad to Ahvāz, take more than 24 hours. It can get very cold at night, even in spring and autumn, so make sure you have warm clothes with you in the bus. Try to get a seat at the front in winter, because the heater is usually only powerful enough to keep the driver and the front row or two of passengers happy.

The drivers are generally safe and polite, and the crew and other passengers try to make travelling by bus a civilised affair. Smoking on board is permitted in moderation, but, thankfully, Iranian buses are never the nicotine-filled chambers endured by bus passengers in Turkey. There is usually a bucket at the end of every row of seats, so you shouldn't finish the journey with other people's spat-out nutshells all over your clothes and fag ends all over the floor.

If you go to a few remote places, or somewhere like Zanjān which is a junction town, you may need to hail down a passing bus (or minibus or shared taxi, if you prefer). Position yourself close enough to the window to shout out your destination, but close enough to the kerb to avoid getting run over – a combination which is not as simple as it sounds. Roadblocks, roundabouts, cafés where buses stop for refreshments and junctions are always the best places to hail down passing buses.

Whether the bus stops for food and drink along the way seems to depend on the whim of the driver – and perhaps, sometimes, even the wishes of the passengers. Any trip of more than six hours will almost certainly stop every five or six hours at a roadside café. These serve reasonably sanitary food, but the choice is often limited to kebabs, kebabs or kebabs, as well as tea and cold drinks. Taking your own food, especially munchies like pistachios, tasty cakes and fresh fruit, is a great idea. Safe, free and, often, ice-cold, water is normally available on the bus, but bring your own cup if you don't want to share the communal glass with other passengers. If you sit right at the front, you may even be offered a glass of tea when the driver and his assistant eventually open up the thermos.

Tickets

You can buy tickets up to one week in advance at the bus station, though a few bus companies have ticket offices in some larger cities. (Travel agencies never handle bus tickets.) If you have set plans, it is a good idea to buy a ticket one or two days before you want to go. This allows you to plan your time in the particular city accordingly. Booking an advance onward ticket as soon as you arrive saves you making a special trip to the station (if there is no ticket office in the city).

However, some travellers do not bother pre-booking seats. From one major city to another, eg Shīrāz to Esfahān, a bus from one company or another leaves every 10 to 15 minutes, so you may get on one as soon as you arrive at the terminal, but then again you may have to wait 30 to 40 minutes if the other buses are full. From mid-sized cities, such as Hamadān or Kermān, a bus going in your direction will leave about every hour; from smaller places, there may only be one or two buses a day to your destination, so in this case it pays to book ahead.

Even if the bus you *must* travel on is 'full' according to the bus company, never give up. Still go there at the time of departure, and let the driver, ticket collector and man at the bus company office know that you want a seat on that bus. There is a good chance that someone with a pre-booked ticket will not turn up, or, lo and behold, they can find you a seat at the back. Looking desperate, helpless and lost always helps.

The tickets themselves are incomprehensible, even for most locals. If you don't speak Fārsī, you won't know if the scrawled (Arabic) numbers indicates the day of departure, time of departure, bus number, seat number, platform number, bus company number or fare. Before handing over your money to the ticket office, always triplecheck these details. And at the time of departure, always check with the driver, his assistant or other passengers to make sure you get on the right bus. Making yourself known, and waiting in the bus company office, is a good idea – the staff invariably take the trouble to look after you. You will be shown to your seat by someone from the bus company if you are unsure.

Schedules

Each bus company has a schedule of sorts, but unless you speak Fārsī, or you find someone who speaks English (which is rare), there's not much point bothering to find out anything more than if there is a bus heading your way on the day you want. At the bus terminals in Tehrān, Esfahān, Tabrīz and Shīrāz (but nowhere else in the country) there are information booths where someone may conjure up a few words of English.

Details of bus services, journey times and fares mentioned in this book were correct at the time of research, but should only be taken as a guide – these things change regularly in Iran. Allow for considerable delays in winter, or if the police/customs officials at the roadblocks are being more vigilant than usual.

Bus Terminals

With a few notable exceptions, bus terminals are way out in the suburbs of every major town, but easy enough to reach by shared taxi, less so by local bus. In some cities, there's more than one bus terminal; if in doubt, ask someone at your hotel, or charter a taxi to the relevant terminal.

Bus terminals are invariably well set up,

and easy to use once you get the hang of it. The bus companies which operate to and from the terminal will have an individual office inside a building, or huddled around the bus departure area. Some companies have signs indicating the name or number of the company in English, but very rarely will destinations be listed in English. So, unless you speak Fārsī, or recognise the destination in the Arabic script, keep asking for the location of the correct bus company office. If you ask 'Shīrāz?', 'Esfahān?' (or wherever) enough times someone will soon help you.

Often it's easy enough to listen for a tout, who is busy drumming up business, to shout out the name of the destination(s) of the services run by his company – or the destination of a bus about to leave shortly. In larger terminals, touts working for the bus companies will probably approach you and (often annoyingly) guide you to the relevant ticket office or bus. Remember that claims by the touts that their bus 'is leaving now' may not always be true.

Bus terminals always have somewhere to eat – usually kebabs or Iranian-style hamburgers, as well as cold drinks and, of course, tea. Bigger terminals may have an information booth, a post office, police station and even a hotel in the complex – but generally there are very few cities with hotels near the bus terminals.

MINIBUS

As an alternative to the bus, or to complement busy bus routes, minibuses are often used for shorter distances to and from less populated and important towns and villages. Sometimes there is no choice between the minibus or bus; just take whichever is going your way. One area where you will use a lot of minibuses is along the coast of the Caspian Sea, and between towns in the Caspian provinces and Tehrān.

For some reason, minibuses generally cost a little bit more than buses, but not enough to worry about. The advantages of minibuses are that they often travel faster than the larger buses, and they carry fewer passengers, so they spend less time dropping off and picking up passengers along the way, or filling up with passengers in the first place. On the downside, minibuses are not as comfortable; you can never pre-book a ticket; they almost always leave *only* when full, so waiting can take time; on popular routes, as many passengers as possible will be squeezed in; and no water is served.

You pay for minibus tickets either before you get on, during the trip or when you get off – every journey is different, so just follow everyone else. Minibuses either leave from special minibus terminals or from a main bus terminal. If you are confused, just charter a private taxi and tell him you want to go to the *termīnāl-é Rasht*, Tehrān or wherever. For hints about the protocol of minibuses, eg sitting next to an unrelated member of the opposite sex, and hailing down passing minibuses, refer to the Bus section earlier.

TRAIN

The Islamic Republic of Iran Railways is impressive if you consider the mountainous terrain that many of the tracks must pass through: the great Trans-Iranian Railway built in the 1930s to connect the Caspian Sea at Bandar-é Torkamān with the Persian Gulf at Bandar-é Emām Khomeinī is one of the great engineering achievements of the 20th century.

Trains can be described as comfortable (in 1st class), fairly efficient, reasonably fast and certainly cheap. However, the railway system is a disappointment, and don't be surprised if you never get around to using it for the following reasons: trains are far less frequent than buses, minibuses and shared taxis; flights are cheap and quick; to some popular places, like Esfahān and Kermān, trains only leave a few days a week; trains do not go everywhere, and miss popular destinations such as Shīrāz; buying a ticket can be difficult, especially at any place along a route; departure and arrival times for most places along the route are often lousy – they are designed for the comfort of passengers going the whole way; train stations are often remote, and you usually have to pre-book at

---

For Train Buffs

Most travellers end up using buses, minibuses and shared taxis to travel around Iran, but for anyone who is interested in trains, there is much to like about Islamic Republic of Iran Railways. Here are a few facts and figures for the train buffs:

Track Length: 7740km
Gauge: 1.435m
No. of Locomotives: 566
No. of Passenger Coaches: 1066
Annual Passengers: 9.7 million
No. Train Stations: 299
Longest Train Line: Tehrān to Bandar-é Abbās (1483km) ∎

---

the station, then wait hours for the train to arrive; and the scenery along some of the routes is fairly boring.

There *are* some advantages, however: for longer, and overnight, trips the train is a far more comfortable alternative (in 1st class sleeper) than the bus – sleeping on a bus is not restful, nor a good way to save time or money on accommodation. Also some trains do go through pleasant scenery while buses speed through one dreary town after another. Trains are also safer than buses. The most exciting trips are between Tehrān and Tabrīz (or return) for the scenery and excellent service on that particular train; and between Tehrān and Mashhad (or return) for the number of tunnels and the scenery, and as a better alternative to the bus (but not the flight).

Classes

All trains have two classes; some have three. You can buy tickets for any class at the place where the train is leaving from. But if you want to buy a ticket from anywhere along a route, you may only be able to buy 2nd class tickets, and then you'll have to squeeze in with the rest of humanity. If 2nd class is all too much, you can often upgrade to 1st class along the way, if there is room. On trains which travel overnight, ie usually to or from Tehrān, the 1st class has sleepers – four or six bunks in a small carriage, like in India, Pakistan and Turkey.

As a rough guide, a seat in 2nd class costs about the same as 'lux' class on the bus, and a 1st class train seat about twice as much as the 'super' class on the bus. Train services called 'express' are a little faster than the 'regular' because they stop at fewer stations in between.

The Journey

A guard will often come round and take orders for tea and meals – reasonably good and inexpensive – to be served some time later in your compartment, or you can eat in the restaurant car. Many passengers prefer to bring their own food. Iced water is also available. (If you object to sharing glasses, bring one of your own.) The trains are fairly safe, more so than in India or Russia, but chain your luggage to something solid if you leave your compartment, or ask someone you trust to look after it. There are, at least in theory, smoking and nonsmoking compartments, but the latter are rarely respected even by the guards.

Schedules

All trains originate from Tehrān; there are no through services. To get from Tabrīz to Kermān, for example, you would have to buy a second ticket and change trains in Tehrān. Travellers heading to Pakistan can only get as far as Kermān by train, and have to continue by bus to the Pakistani border, though there have been plans to extend this line for years. Currently, passengers cannot use trains to travel to some ports on the Persian Gulf (not that you would want to anyway); nor all the way to the Turkish or Azerbaijan borders.

There is apparently an official train timetable; none were available in Tehrān. (I did see one at the ticket office in Sārī, but the station master wasn't about to let me have it.) In any case, the timetable is in Fārsī, and of little use to travellers. More details can be found in the relevant, individual Getting There & Away sections.

Tickets

Buying tickets is a hassle. In most cases, you can only buy tickets at the train station itself, though Esfahān does have a booking office in the city, and in Yazd, a travel agency sells tickets. Like most things in Tehrān, buying a ticket is a trauma; anyone with limited time and patience is bound to take another form of transport. Buying a ticket at any station along a route is a matter of pot luck, and waiting. In this case, take a bus.

It's not possible to book a return ticket; you will have to do that when you arrive at your destination. If you can, book tickets as early as possible. In Tehrān, and other major places such as Esfahān, Tabrīz and Mashhad (ie where trains originate), you can buy tickets in advance – 15 days seems the normal period. Advance bookings cost an extra 20%, and it's worth paying considering how cheap tickets are anyway.

If getting a ticket is dragging you down to the depths of despair, but you are still determined to use the train, ask around for someone at the station to help you. You may find someone willing to do the queuing, arguing and negotiating for an extra fee – again, this is well worth paying extra for.

TAXI

Unlike some other countries in the region, taxis – whether shared or privately chartered – are a worthy option. The vehicles are fairly new, rarely break down and passengers are normally not squeezed in like sardines.

Shared Taxi

Between any major town with a sizeable population, less than three hours away by car, you can be sure a shared taxi is available. Speed is the main advantage because shared taxis are generally more uncomfortable than the bus (but better than the minibus). Two people are squeezed into the front passenger seat, so never sit there unless you have no choice (or you have a good friend to share the seat with). Three people will sit in the back of the shared taxi, which is not uncomfortable – unless you are built like an NBA basketballer or a sumo wrestler.

Shared taxis need less people to fill it up, so they depart fairly quickly and reasonably often. Though some buses leave half-empty, knowing they will pick up passengers along the way, a shared taxi will *never* leave with an empty seat (unless a passenger pays for it). Drivers can sometimes stop the vehicle for toilet breaks and photo opportunities, and they have been known to take foreigners to their hotel – but not that often.

These vehicles are sometimes referred to as a *savari* in the local vernacular. The word 'taxi', often transliterated into English and written on top of the vehicles as 'taksi', is the only word you need to know; if you want to clearly identify a shared taxi from a private, chartered taxi, use the word 'savari'. Most of the time, shared taxis are the ubiquitous Iranian-made Paykans, but for some reason taxi drivers around the Caspian provinces use huge, old battered (but sometimes lovingly restored) Mercedes Benz.

As a general rule, a shared taxi costs three times more than the 'lux' price of a bus. This may seem a lot more in rials, but if you work it out in your own currency using the unofficial 'street' exchange rate, shared taxis are still cheap, and worth using for a quick trip, especially through a dull stretch of countryside. If you wish to hurry up a departure, or crave a little extra comfort, you can always pay for an empty seat, and if your understanding of Fārsī is good enough, you can agree to pay the difference between the full fare and any fare the driver may pick up along the way.

Taxi drivers are generally honest and considerate, with the notable exception of a few operating out of Esfahān (see Local Transport later in this chapter). Men and women, whether foreign or Iranian, married or not, can sit next to each other in the back of a shared taxi, but only married Iranians, or foreign couples (married or not), can share the 'cosy' passenger seat.

Most of the time shared taxis leave from inside, or just outside, the relevant bus terminal, though occasionally there are special terminals or junctions for shared taxis heading in particular directions. If you are confused, charter a private taxi and ask the driver to take you to the relevant terminal/junction for a shared taxi going your way. You cannot pre-book a seat in a shared taxi; they leave when they are full.

Private Taxi

Almost every single taxi (with a driver) in the country is available for hire. If you have heaps of cash, or you're travelling in a group, chartering a private taxi, or hiring your own shared taxi, is worth considering: it allows you to stop for photos; you can often make detours to visit places along the way (for a little extra); you can leave when you want to; and there is more space in the vehicle.

Needless to say, the price of a private taxi is open to negotiation. One excellent way of not getting ripped off is to ask the driver of a shared taxi for the price per person for a certain trip. For example, from Tehrān to Ghom, the price per person in a shared taxi is 5000 rials. Multiply this figure by five (the number of passengers in a shared taxi); therefore 25,000 rials (or about US$5 at the 'street rate') is all you need to pay for this trip in a private taxi, unless you want to make a detour, or pay for some waiting time.

PICK-UP

Very, very occasionally, you may come across a utility with a canvas cover, called a *pik-up* . These are mainly found in the southern region, eg around Bandar-é Abbās. If you are tall, or want a bit of extra comfort, try to get to the pick-up early and negotiate the price for the front seat, which will be far more comfortable than being squeezed into the back. Prices are very cheap, but the comfort level is also very low.

CAR & MOTORCYCLE

A few travellers take a vehicle across Iran, as part of a trip between Europe and the subcontinent. This naturally gives you a lot more flexibility, but the distances are great, the countryside is often boring, and the traffic is truly horrendous.

Taking Your Own Vehicle

The first hassle which can drive you to despair (or to the nearest border out of Iran) is the border check. The customs officials are often under instructions to assume that foreigners driving a foreign vehicle have the opportunity to carry drugs – and the Iranian authorities take their fight against drug trafficking seriously. While it may take an hour to walk through the Iranian border, taking a vehicle across takes five hours or more. Plan ahead and bring loads of patience. Once past the border, the second hassle is the number of roadblocks (see under Roadblocks earlier).

Many people driving across Iran complain about the long distances and the boring scenery. There are large towns at least every 100km throughout the country, except in the remote deserts of eastern Iran, where you should carry extra food and water. Never drive off the main road near the Pakistan, Iraq or, especially, the Afghan border: if you don't come across some suspicious drug smugglers, you will probably come across some very suspicious customs and police officials. The major concern for anyone who has not driven in this part of the world is the appalling traffic – especially worrying for anyone on a motorbike. See under Road Rules later in this chapter and the Dangers & Annoyances section in the Facts for the Visitor chapter for more details.

Now the good news. The road surfaces are generally excellent, and you will only come across poor or unpaved roads if you are keen enough to head into the desert, or remote mountain regions. Just about every road sign you will ever need is in English, including directions to almost every city, town and village, the names of main roads and squares in most towns, and general safety instructions (which you are advised to take notice of, though Iranians, of course, ignore them). If there are no signs in English along the road, you are probably somewhere you shouldn't be (near the border, in a military area, and so on); or somewhere you don't want to be (a boring stretch of nothingness).

Any foreigner driving any vehicle in Iran will need an international driving licence, and if you are bringing a car into Iran, a *carnet de passage* is necessary (refer to Car & Motorcycle in the Getting There & Away chapter for more information). If, heaven forbid, you should have any sort of accident in Tehrān, ring the Road Accident Department (☎ 197). Elsewhere ring the local police headquarters; most have individual traffic accident departments.

When visiting major cities, look for a hotel with secure, off-street parking – not always easy to find because hotels are often in the centre of town, and every square metre is used for something more important. In some cities, however (even Tehrān), there are parking lots. You'll often find one just off a busy road; look for a sign with a big letter 'P' in blue, or a picture of car and an arrow. Try to leave your car at, or near, your hotel, and use public transport in the city – unless you have some exceptional driving skills, and an excellent insurance policy. Be especially careful about leaving your car unattended anywhere in eastern Iran – it may be stolen, stripped, driven across the border of Afghanistan or Pakistan, and bought by a drug smuggler before you've finished your plate of kebabs.

Road Rules

There are none. In theory, however, the rule of the road is to drive on the right. Driving your own vehicle across Iran is not a task to be taken lightly: take 10 Iranian car drivers and an otherwise deserted open road and you can be sure that all 10 will form a convoy so tightly packed that each of the rear nine can read the speedometer of the car in front. The phrase 'optimum braking distance' has no meaning in Iran. Any vehicle going less than 100km/h is probably driven by a petrified foreigner; and only foreigners wear motorcycle helmets or use seat belts. Vehicle insurance is a must, and not just for legal reasons.

I saw a dead body for the first time while in Iran. In fact, I saw three, from three separate car accidents. In each case, a sheet had been perfunctorily placed across the body, while a policeman, covering his nose because of the stench of burnt human flesh, waved our vehicle past. Refer to the Dangers & Annoyances section in the Facts for the Visitor chapter for some tips about how to avoid being one of the alarming statistics.

Petrol & Repairs

As you would expect, petrol is ridiculously cheap – 160 rials per litre for unleaded petrol, and 220 rials per litre for super – and Iranians will stare in disbelief if you tell them how much you pay for petrol at home. There are petrol stations (open every day) in, or just outside of, every major town. These stations are often full of impatient shared taxis, trucks, buses, minibuses and private vehicles, so fill up completely whenever you can, but always carry extra supplies, just in case.

So many Iranians drive their own vehicle that even the tiniest village has some filthy shop where you can arrange repairs for your car. These places are always spread around the ugly outskirts of town, along the main arterial roads. Of course, the price for any repair work is open to negotiation, and you should always be careful of inferior spare parts, or unscrupulous mechanics (or anyone else) taking an undue interest in your car.

Rental

Because there is a lack of foreign tourists (and very few willing to risk life and limb), as well as cheap, reliable and frequent public transport, renting your own car or motorbike is almost impossible to arrange. During three month's research, only one car rental agency came to my notice – in Tehrān (refer to the Tehrān Province chapter for details). A few minutes in Iran traffic should convince you that renting a car is not a great idea anyway.

Books & Maps

If you are *still* serious about driving around Iran, look out for a couple of pre-Islamic Revolution guidebooks. (I only found them at the Bouali Hotel bookshop in Hamadān.) The first is *Travels with a Peykan* (sic) by Roger Tagg. You can safely ignore a lot of outdated descriptions, such as 'little villages'

along the Caspian coast, which are now part of an ugly urban sprawl, but it does offer a lot of information on places to visit within one or two days by car from Tehrān.

The second is *Welcome to Iran*, published by the former Tourism Development and Promotion Department. It gives useful details – though outdated in parts – of places to see along the road from Bāzargān (at the Turkish border) to Tāybād (at the Afghan border), via Tabrīz, Zanjān, Ghazvīn, Tehrān, Gorgān and Mashhad.

If you are doing some extensive driving in the countryside you will need a map with the names of all important towns in English and Fārsī. This is not hard to find in Iran (refer to Maps in the Planning section of the Facts for the Visitor chapter for details). The town maps in this guidebook are more relevant for people using their feet and/or public transport, so if you are driving into, and around, places like Shīrāz, Esfahān, Mashhad or Tehrān (try not to!), a larger, city map will help you get around and find your way out of the cities.

BICYCLE

There is no reason why you cannot take your own bike into Iran, and travel around the country. (We even got a nice letter from a German woman who travelled for two months around Iran on her own.) But anyone contemplating this should be aware of the vast distances, the hot and boring stretches of road with few villages and tough mountainous stretches, and the appalling traffic. If you get tired, fed up, scared of the traffic or your visa is running out, you can usually put your bike in the luggage section of a bus, or better, on a train.

The advantages are the excellent quality of roads and the friendly people, as one cyclist wrote:

The drivers in Iran are more polite than their colleagues in Pakistan or India. In many cases, they wave and blow their horn, as if you are of the same breed. And they really are considerate while driving (but not always). They often offer you a ride, food, drinks, or just a conversation. Sometimes even hashish!
Ton Baars, the Netherlands

Naturally you should carry loads of water; enough food to last for long stretches between villages (where there is always something to eat); camping equipment if you are not sticking to major towns; a decent map of Iran; and a phrasebook. There is nowhere to rent bicycles for long distances, so bring your own.

Although it may be very tempting, you should *never* wear shorts, and women must wear the hejāb, which does not include the sort of tight-fitting trousers suitable for cycling. Crossing the border at Bāzargān (to Turkey) and Mīrjāvé (to Pakistan) on a bicycle is hassle-free. Unlike other people in the Middle East and subcontinent, Iranians very rarely use bikes, so finding repairers and spare parts can be a problem.

HITCHING

Hitching is never entirely safe in any country in the world, and we don't recommend it. Travellers who decide to hitch should understand that they are taking a small but potentially serious risk. However, many people do choose to hitch, and the advice that follows should help to make their journeys as fast and safe as possible.

Hitching, as commonly understood in the west, rarely exists in Iran. Although you will often see people standing along roads looking for a lift, they are actually waiting for a seat on a bus, minibus or shared taxi – for which they are charged the normal fare. Occasionally foreigners will be given lifts free of charge by private drivers, in return for English practice or simply out of hospitality, but you won't get very far (nor will your visa be long enough), if you hang around waiting for free rides. Except when visiting remote archaeological sites, you should always use the cheap and reliable public transport.

HIKING

As a way of seeing the country, saving money and meeting people, hiking around Iran is not worth considering for a few obvious reasons: roads and trails are long, hot and often boring, or mountainous; you will have to carry all your own gear; in some

places you may arouse the suspicions of local security forces; and, more importantly, you are unlikely to get a visa which will allow you much time to enjoy a lot of hiking.

But there are certainly a few recognised short treks through picturesque scenery, and plenty of great spots for day hikes. Refer to the Trekking in Iran section in the Facts for the Visitor chapter for more details.

BOAT

Despite the lengthy stretches of coast along the Caspian Sea and the Persian Gulf, very few domestic passenger services operate. Ferries travel between the mainland and some islands in the Persian Gulf: eg to Kīsh Island, regular boats leave from Bandar-é Lengé, Bandar-é Abbās and Bandar-é Chārak; less often to more remote and less interesting islands in the Gulf. Numerous speedboats also travel between Bandar-é Abbās and Hormoz and Gheshm islands.

There are currently no passenger services between towns along the Persian Gulf, nor along the Iranian coast of the Caspian Sea. Very occasionally, passenger boats putter along the Kārūn river, the only navigable river in Iran; and ferries across Iran's largest lake, Orūmīyé, supplement the unfinished causeway.

LOCAL TRANSPORT
To/From the Airport

Only at a few international and domestic airports is there a special bus service, or a public bus, so in most cases transport to and from an airport is by private or shared taxi. At some, a combination of public buses and shared taxis are possible, but this is generally more trouble then it's worth, especially if you are arriving in a strange town for the first time, and have some luggage (which covers most visitors).

At most airports, you will be met by a gaggle of taxi drivers foaming at the mouth in anticipation of overcharging a naive foreigner. If you have doubts about the price of a private taxi, ask a local; or look for some fellow passengers to share the cost of a private taxi. Some cities have official airport taxis, marked as such in English. These are invariably more expensive than normal private taxis, so avoid them if you can.

Refer to the Getting Around section in the Tehrān Province chapter for information about how to deal with taxi drivers to and from the airport in Tehrān.

Bus

Most Iranian towns and cities have a local bus service. These buses are often new and Iranian-made, though in the outer suburbs of Tehrān you may be astounded to see a converted old double-decker bus, imported from England a few decades ago. Because local buses are often crowded, and shared and private taxis are always available and cheap, only the more adventurous or frugal bother using them.

Buses are also difficult to use unless you know exactly where you and the bus are going, or you can speak and read Fārsī. Bus numbers and destinations are marked only in Fārsī (though sometimes in English in Tehrān and Shīrāz). The only service with an available timetable is in Tehrān, and it's printed in Fārsī, of course. If you have any doubt whatsoever, ask someone – locals are normally more than happy to help (even if you may not entirely understand their reply).

Bus stops are clearly marked, often with a circle in red and blue. Buses do not always set out and return by the same route, and services change frequently without notice. You buy your tickets in obvious little booths, located along the main streets of the cities or at the bus stations. They all seemed to be staffed by grumpy old men who speak no English. Tickets normally cost 50 rials each, though depending on the distance and the city, a trip costs 100 to 200 rials (ie two or four tickets). Sometimes your change from a taxi or bus driver will include a 50 rial bus ticket – it is almost a second currency in Iran.

In local buses (but not the intercity, long-distance ones), all women (including the foreign variety), and small children of either gender, have to sit at the back of the bus. Because so few women travel by bus, women often get a seat, while men usually have to stand, squashed like sardines, at the front. This segregation can be complicated if you are travelling as a mixed couple, and need to communicate about when to get off. Bus travellers either give their tickets to the driver before they get on, or after they get off, depending on the local system – but women must pass their tickets to the driver while leaning through the front door of the bus, without using the steps into the front of the bus.

Minibus

If you thought using local buses was a hassle, don't even bother working out the infrequent and desperately crowded minibuses. Quite often they are so crammed with passengers that you can hardly see out of the window to tell where you are going. You normally pay in cash when you get on – about 100 rials a ticket. Men and women get a seat anywhere they can; there is no room for segregation. Minibuses stop at normal bus stops.

Trolleybus

Iran boasts exactly one environmentally-friendly electric trolleybus line (in Tehrān), even if the dedicated lane for the trolleybuses is more often used by buses belching carbon monoxide and recalcitrant motorcyclists. The same system of paying and segregation applies as for local buses.

Taxi

For many Iranians, and just about every foreign traveller, a shared or private taxi is the quickest, and most hassle-free, way of getting around a town or city.

Shared Taxi In most towns and cities shared taxis often duplicate, and even replace, local bus services. They usually take up to five passengers, two in the front passenger seat; three in the back – but rarely more. A shared taxi, whether official or unofficial, will nearly always be a Paykan sedan, usually coloured orange, or with a dash of orange somewhere. After a while you will get used to them.

Shared taxis usually travel every few seconds between major squares, and along major roads, in every town and city. They will often make slight detours for passengers at no extra charge, or for a longer detour, you may be charged 200 rials or so extra. Shared taxis will either hang around places where they are more likely to get fares – eg bus, train stations or airports; at major town squares; or you can just hail one on the road.

Normally getting a shared taxi goes something like this. Lean out a few metres from the kerb: close enough for the driver to hear you shout your destination, but close enough to make a mad dash to the relative safety of the footpath if you have to. If the driver has a spare seat, he will slow down for a nanosecond while you shout your destination. Don't bother with anything in any language along the lines of 'Iran Hotel, on the corner of ... ': the driver will have lost interest after the word 'hotel', picked up someone else and be halfway there before you know it. Use a major landmark or a town square as a destination, even if you are getting off before then. Shout it quickly and loud: '... *DŌS* ...!' will do for Ferdōsī St or square; similarly, '... *HESHT* ...!' for Beheshtī St or square; and so on. The driver will either completely ignore you (and don't get angry if he does; time is money), or give you a quick beep on the horn and pull over for half a second while you leap in.

When you want the driver to stop you simply say *kheilī mamnūn* (thank you very much) or any other obvious noise. Drivers will appreciate exact change (so always have plenty of coins and those filthy 200 and 500 rial notes handy); you normally pay after the car has stopped. Fares, which are fixed by the government, currently range from about 150 to 1500 rials, depending on the distance and the city (Tehrān is naturally the most expensive; while Yazd is cheap). Always check out what other passengers pay.

If you get into an empty shared taxi in some places, particularly Esfahān and Tehrān, there is often an expectation that you want to charter it privately. Be careful if you don't.

Private Taxi Any taxi without passengers – whether an obvious shared taxi, or a more expensive private taxi – can be chartered to go anywhere in town, or outside the town if you wish. Simply hail the vehicle down, give the driver a brief indication of where you want to go – unless it's a complicated deal, including waiting time – and ask the price. Immediately offer about half what he suggests. You shouldn't be too upset if you end up paying about 70% of the originally quoted price; it is up to you whether you want to spend a lot of time haggling over one thousand rials (about US$0.20 at the 'street rate').

Agency Taxi These are also agency or 'telephone' taxis. These normally don't stop to pick up other passengers, so you have to order them by telephone or at an agency office. There are taxi agency offices in even the smallest of towns, and hundreds in Tehrān. Some of the top hotels run their own taxi services, and any hotel or mosāferkhūné can order a taxi for a guest. Naturally, this is the most expensive way of travelling by taxi, but you get a better car, peace of mind if anything goes wrong, and, possibly, a driver who speaks English.

ORGANISED TOURS

Few travel agencies in Iran organise trips for foreigners within Iran: they mainly sell airline tickets, act as local operators for foreign travel companies, or offer the sort of trips for Iranian tourists where no English is spoken, attractions are often Islamic in nature, and the standard of food and accommodation may not suit. Most organised tours around Iran start and finish in Tehrān, with a quick look around the capital, before concentrating on the must-sees: Shīrāz and Esfahān, with either Tabrīz or Kermān, and possibly Bam, thrown in. For a list of reputable travel agencies in Tehrān, refer to the Travel Agencies section in the Tehrān Province chapter.

The handful of Iranian travel companies listed below offer something different, and they are well established and used to catering for foreigners. However, you cannot just ring the agency, or turn up at their office, and expect to go on an organised tour within a day or two – but with prior notice, they can let you know in advance what is happening. Though based in Tehrān, these agencies have offices, or representatives, in the major cities in Iran, and can provide guides who speak English, French, German and Japanese, and sometimes Spanish and Italian. Costs depend on the length of the tour, mode of transport, type of accommodation and the current exchange rate. Foreigners will be expected to pay in foreign currency, mainly US dollars.

Azadi International Tourism Organisation
AITO offers a fascinating, though upmarket and expensive, range of tours. These include 'Cultural' (ie the major archaeological sites); 'Nomads' (with trips around Ardabīl and Hamadān); 'Trekking' (across the desert, as well as mountaineering); and 'Carpets' for anyone interested in Persian carpets. Their contact details are: 8th St, Ahmād Gassir Ave; PO Box 15875-1765 (☎ 8732 191; fax 8732 195).

Caravan Sahra Co
One of the most impressive agencies, which doesn't mind handling tours for more down-to-earth, smaller-spending travellers, this agency organises trips for cultural and archaeological buffs; trekking and mountain climbing; and study and language courses. Their address is 125/4 Sharī'atī Ave; PO Box 14875-153 (☎ 7502 229; fax 7671 840; email: caravan@neda.net).

Iran Air Tours
With more than 25 years experience in catering for foreigners, this agency handles middle-priced tours, and is affiliated with Iran Air. Besides the usual places, it arranges tours of the Caspian provinces and western Iran. The address is 191 Motahharī Ave, Mofatteh Crossroads (☎ 8758 390; fax 8755 884).

Iran Touring & Tourism Organisation
The ITTO is the quasi-government tourist bureau run by the Ministry of Culture & Islamic Guidance, though it's really a travel agent. It runs a heap of tours, using a vast range of two and three-star hotels, concentrating on the usual places, as well as western Iran and pilgrimage sites. The address is 154 Keshavarz Blvd (☎ 656 715; fax 656 800).

Persepolis Tour & Travel Agency
This impressive company offers a range of tours under the headings of 'Pilgrimage' (visiting the major mosques, naturally); '30 Day Tour' (covering the major cities, plus the Caspian region, Mashhad, northern and western Iran); and 'Tehrān Highlights', as well as skiing trips at Dīzīn. The address is 100 Nejātollahī St (☎ 8810 526; fax 8808 534).

Tehrān Province

استان تهران

Tehrān province, which holds more than one-sixth of the country's population, most of them in the sprawling, chaotic capital city, is at the southern edge of the Alborz mountains and the northern edge of the Kavīr desert. Most travellers end up spending several days in Tehrān city, whether they want to or not, but if you can escape the capital, there are barren hills to scramble around, lush valleys to explore and even a majestic mountain to climb.

Tehrān

تهران

Iran is not blessed with one of the world's loveliest capitals. Pollution, chronic over-crowding and a lack of any responsible planning have all helped to make Tehrān a metropolis which even the most effusive travel agents would have difficulty praising. If you're expecting an exotic crossroads steeped in oriental splendour, you'll be sadly disappointed. The distances are vast, the traffic is appalling and the main sights are spread out. You'll need a week to make a start, but by then you begin to appreciate the city's better points.

However, the hotels are good, the variety of restaurants is impressive, the facilities are far ahead of those anywhere in the provinces, and the Tehrānīs are friendly. There are a fair number of things to do and see, which you won't find elsewhere, including several excellent museums. Despite its drawbacks, spending time in Tehrān is worthwhile.

One drawback is the heavy smog which permanently hovers over the city. At some times of the year, especially in summer, it descends with unbearable effect and drives people out of Tehrān in coughing wheezing droves, while the radio warns those with a heart condition not to leave their houses. Head to the northern hills.

TEHRĀN PROVINCE AT A GLANCE

- **Capital:** Tehrān
- **Area:** 28,198 sq km
- **Population:** approximately 12 million
- **When to Go:** Any time is bearable; April to October is best, though summer can be hot, and spring is often wet.
- **Highlights:** National Museum of Iran; Glass & Ceramics Museum; National Jewels Museum; Sa'd Ābād Garden Museum; Rezā Abbāsī Museum; Reine & Mt Damāvand.

HISTORY

Human settlement of the region dates from Neolithic times, but the development of Tehrān, which started as a small village in the foothills of the Alborz mountains, was very slow and its rise to prominence largely accidental. A succession of visitors to Tehrān from the 10th to 13th centuries described it as a village of half-savages who lived in underground dwellings and practised highway robbery. In 1197, after the Mongols sacked the nearby town of Rey (at that time the major urban centre in central Persia), Tehrān began to develop in its place as a small, moderately prosperous trading centre.

In the mid-16th century, Tehrān's attractive natural setting, many trees, clear rivers and good hunting brought it into the favour of the early Safavid king, Tahmāsb I. Under his patronage, gardens were laid out, brick houses and caravanserais were built and heavily fortified walls were erected to protect the town and its steadily increasing population of merchants. It continued to grow under the later Safavid kings, and European visitors wrote of its many enchanting vineyards and gardens.

As a result of the Ghajar threat to his throne, in 1758 Karīm Khān Zand transferred his army here from his capital at Shīrāz, with the intention of moving in on his enemy. At the same time he refortified Tehrān and began the construction of a royal residence. Perhaps he had intended to move his capital here, but when his army killed the Ghajar chieftain, Muhammed Hasan Khān,

and took his young son Agha Muhammed Khān hostage, Karīm Khān abandoned the unfinished palace and returned to Shīrāz.

In 1789, Agha Muhammed Khān declared Tehrān his capital, and six years later he had himself crowned as shāh of all Persia. He destroyed the city walls of Shīrāz, disinterred the corpse of Karīm Khān and carried it back to Tehrān in a final act of revenge. At this time, Tehrān was no more than a dusty town of around 15,000 souls. The town continued to grow slowly under later Ghajar rulers.

From the early 1920s, the city was extensively modernised on a grid system, and this period marked the start of the phenomenal population growth and uncontrolled urban development that continues to this day. In 1887, the population was 250,000, and by 1930 had only increased to 300,000. By 1939, it had rocketed to half a million, with the city's rapid expansion only slowing during WWII. In 1956, however, the population was 1.8 million; by 1976, it had risen to 4.5 million; and by the time of the 1986 census, Tehrān's population had soared to more than 8.7 million. Exact figures of the current population are unavailable, and the government possibly underestimates the figure anyway, but it is probably more than 10 million.

ORIENTATION

Tehrān is so vast that getting hopelessly lost at least once is a near certainty, no matter what form of transport you take. Thankfully, about 90% of the streets that you are likely to visit are marked in English, but there are areas with no signs in any language, for example around the Tehrān Bazaar, south of Shahr Park, around the Iranshahr Hotel, and in the ugly and appallingly crowded suburbs of southern Tehrān.

If you need landmarks, the Alborz mountains, known as the 'North Star' of Tehrān, are to the north; and the huge telephone office at Emām Khomeinī Square dominates inner southern Tehrān. It is worth noting that many roads which run north to south slope down as they head south.

Around Emām Khomeinī Square, there

Construction – The Only Game in Town

It doesn't take visitors to Tehrān long to realise that the capital's sprawl and congestion is being driven by the booming building industry. This is partly due to the difficulties private enterprise finds in investing in areas outside the construction industry.

Iran's banks usually don't pay interest on deposits for several years. The country's stockmarket is tightly held and regulated and doesn't offer attractive rates of return. Investing in new businesses is not easy, due to the informal but powerful protectionist guilds in each industry. Going into exporting or importing means negotiating the bewildering bureaucracy which oversees Iran's semi-controlled economy.

Construction and real estate speculation, on the other hand, offers a solid hedge against the rather hefty inflation rate. It is said that construction companies invariably make a loss or just break even with some imaginative accounting – like many developing countries, government employees shoulder much of the tax burden. The industry is also fortunate to have a favourable labour market. Many construction workers are Afghan refugees, forced to find work wherever they can.

Richard Plunkett

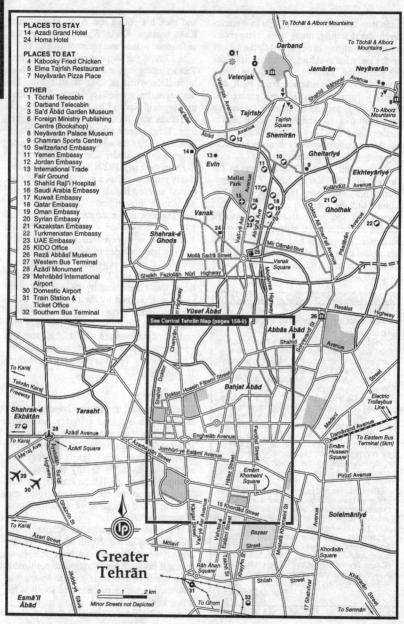

PLACES TO STAY
14 Azadi Grand Hotel
24 Homa Hotel

PLACES TO EAT
4 Kabooky Fried Chicken
5 Elma Tajrīsh Restaurant
7 Neyāvarān Pizza Place

OTHER
1 Tōchāl Telecabin
2 Darband Telecabin
3 Sa'd Ābād Garden Museum
6 Foreign Ministry Publishing
   Centre (Bookshop)
8 Neyāvarān Palace Museum
9 Chamran Sports Centre
10 Switzerland Embassy
11 Yemen Embassy
12 Jordan Embassy
13 International Trade
    Fair Ground
15 Shahīd Rajī'ī Hospital
16 Saudi Arabia Embassy
17 Kuwait Embassy
18 Qatar Embassy
19 Oman Embassy
20 Syrian Embassy
21 Kazakstan Embassy
22 Turkmenistan Embassy
23 UAE Embassy
25 KIDO Office
26 Rezā Abbāsī Museum
27 Western Bus Terminal
28 Āzādī Monument
29 Mehrābād International
    Airport
30 Domestic Airport
31 Train Station &
    Ticket Office
32 Southern Bus Terminal

To Tōchāl & Alborz Mountains
To Tōchāl & Alborz Mountains
Darband
Jamārān
Neyāvarān Avenue
Velenjak
Velenjak Avenue
Tajrīsh
Ābād
Avenue
Tajrīsh Square
Shemīrān
Shahīd Bāhonar Avenue
To Alborz Mountains
Gheitārīyé
Evin
Ekhteyārīyé
Kolāhdūz Avenue
Mellat Park
Vanak
Afrīghā Ave
Gholhak
Doktor Alī Sharī'atī Avenue
Pāsdārān Avenue
Shahrak-é Ghods
Vali-yé Asr Avenue
Mollā Sadrā Street
Vanak Square
Mīr Dāmād Blvd
Modarres Highway
Sheikh Fazlollāh Nūrī Highway
Yūsef Ābād
Highway
See Central Tehrān Map (pages 158-9)
Abbās Ābād
Shahīd Sadrevard St
Avenue
Resālat Highway
To Karaj
Tehrān Karaj Freeway
Chamrān
Doktor
Doktor Hosein Fātemī Street
Bahjat Ābād
Ferdosī Street
Madanī
Electric Trolleybus Line
To Eastern Bus Terminal (5km)
Shahrak-é Ekbātān
Tarasht
Āzādī Avenue
Āzādī Square
Ayatollah Sa'īdī
Engheläb Avenue
Āzarbāyjān Street
Hāfez Street
Jomhūrī-yé Eslāmī Avenue
Vahdat-é Eslāmī Street
Emām Khomeinī Square
Emām Hussein Square
Damāvand Avenue
To Karaj
Me'rāj Ave
Qazvīn St
15 Khordād Street
Sh Mostafā Khomeinī St
Pīrūzī Avenue
Soleimānīyé
To Karaj
Āzarī Street
Jāddé-yé Sāvé
Mōlavī
Karīm Khān Zand Avenue
Vali-yé Asr Avenue
Rey Street
Bazaar
Street
Khorāsān Square
Greater Tehrān
Rāh Āhan Square
Shūsh Street
17 Shahrīvar Street
Khāvarān Street
Esmā'īl Ābād
0   1   2 km
Minor Streets not Depicted
To Ghom
To Semnān

are a few government offices, some good transport and plenty of cheap hotels, so most travellers base themselves there. This part of town has changed over the past few decades and is now fairly dirty, run-down and unfashionable, but it's still safe and cheap. The smarter residential and business areas have gradually shifted northwards, so in practical terms there is no centre to speak of.

Tehrān is bisected by Valī-yé Asr Ave, which runs north-south for more than 20km, from Tajrīsh to the train station. One of the main streets running from east to west is Āzādī Ave which starts at the Āzādī Monument, near the airports, and turns into Enghelāb Ave west of Enghelāb Square. If you are using public transport, try to get to know the names and locations of the main squares as soon you can.

Maps

If you are only stopping in Tehrān a few days, seeing the major sights, and staying at a hotel listed in this guidebook, the maps of Greater Tehrān and Central Tehrān in this guidebook will be enough. If want to explore the city in depth, walk a lot or visit friends or places in remote suburbs, you will definitely need a more detailed map.

Make sure you get one of the following large and new maps, printed in English:

New Map of Tehran – this is an excellent map published by Gita Shenasi. It is brightly coloured, easy to use and has a separate 'annexed' directory, but it's large and expensive at 20,000 rials. It is available at the National Museum of Iran, the Gita Shenasi map shop (see Maps in the Planning section of the Facts for the Visitor chapter for the address), and some of the top-end hotels.

Metropolitan Map – though old (it still lists the East German embassy), it has been well designed and is easy to carry. Published by the Sahab Geographic & Drafting Institute, the map costs 15,000 rials, but I could only find it at the bookshop at the Laleh International Hotel.

Tourist Map of Iran & Tehran – this map is small, cheap (4500 rials) and the easiest to use and to find. Published by Gita Shenasi, the map covers the same area as the maps in this guidebook, but in more detail. The map of Iran on the other side is fairly useless.

Addresses

Despite what may be written on many maps, the name of a suburb is almost never used in an address. An address may contain as many as three street names, starting from the most important highway or square nearby, then a smaller avenue which runs off it, and then the street where you'll eventually find (you hope) the building you want. The word *kheyābūn* (street or avenue) is often omitted from addresses. Somehow local taxi drivers can work it all out.

INFORMATION
Visa Extensions

Unfortunately, Tehrān is probably the worst place in the country to get your visa extended. The location of the visa office regularly moves; you have to compete with hundreds of Afghans and Pakistanis, among others, also seeking visa extensions; the office is hopelessly understaffed; and you may have to spend up to five days of your precious time waiting for the damn extension. (Refer to the Visas & Documents section of the Facts for the Visitor chapter for suggestions of where you should extend your visa, and how to do it.)

Currently, visa extensions are possible at the Department of Foreign Affairs (☎ 894 761) *(not* the Ministry of Foreign Affairs near Emām Khomeinī Square) at the building occupied by the ominous-sounding Disciplinary Force of the Islamic Republic of Iran. The building, on Khalantarī St, just off Nejātollāhī St, is signed in English. Look for the long line (or huddle) of bearded Afghans, but remember to check the current location first.

The office is open every day but Friday and public holidays, from 8 am to 1.30 pm. Start lining up well before 8 am to apply for the extension, and to later collect your passport (hopefully with an extended visa), queue up with your receipt before 11 am. Foreigners with a bit of cheek can usually get away with looking helpless and jumping the queue. There is usually a separate line for ladies, so foreign women may be able to

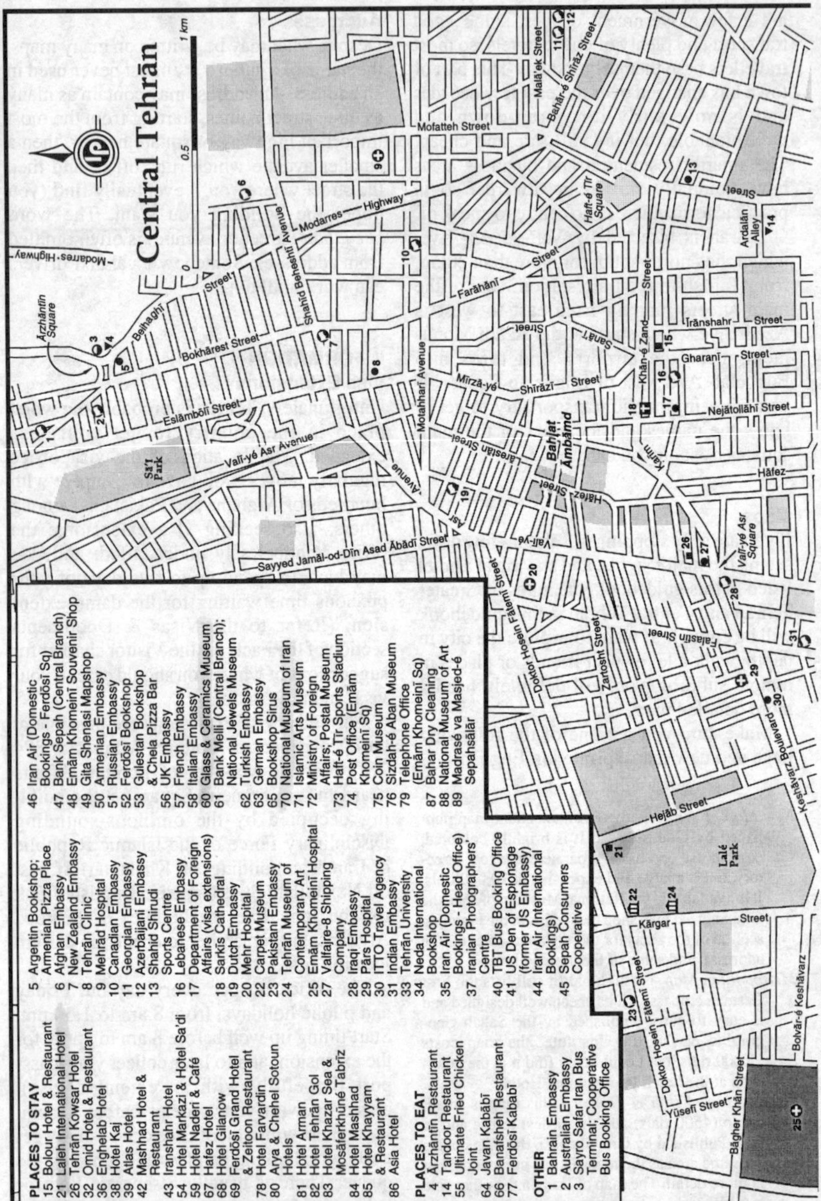

Central Tehrān
0
0.5
1 km
PLACES TO STAY
15 Bolour Hotel & Restaurant
21 Laleh International Hotel
26 Tehrān Kowsar Hotel
32 Omid Hotel & Restaurant
36 Enghelab Hotel
38 Hotel Kaj
39 Atlas Hotel
42 Mashhad Hotel & Restaurant
43 Iranshahr Hotel
54 Hotel Markazi & Hotel Sa'di
59 Hotel Naderi & Café
67 Hafez Hotel
68 Hotel Gilanow
69 Ferdōsī Grand Hotel & Zeitoon Restaurant
78 Hotel Farvardin
80 Arya & Chehel Sotoun Hotels
81 Hotel Arman
82 Hotel Tehrān Gol
83 Hotel Khazar Sea & Mosāferkhūné Tabrīz
84 Hotel Mashhad
85 Hotel Khayyam & Restaurant
86 Asia Hotel
PLACES TO EAT
4 Ārzhāntīn Restaurant
14 Tandoor Restaurant
55 Ultimate Fried Chicken Joint
64 Javan Kabābī
66 Banafsheh Restaurant
77 Ferdōsī Kabābī
OTHER
1 Bahrain Embassy
2 Australian Embassy
3 Sayro Safar Iran Bus Terminal; Cooperative Bus Booking Office
5 Argentin Bookshop; Armenian Pizza Place
6 Afghan Embassy
7 New Zealand Embassy
8 Tehrān Clinic
9 Mehrād Hospital
10 Canadian Embassy
11 Georgian Embassy
12 Azerbaijani Embassy
13 Shahid Shirudi Sports Centre
16 Lebanese Embassy
17 Department of Foreign Affairs (visa extensions)
18 Sarkis Cathedral
19 Dutch Embassy
20 Mehr Hospital
22 Carpet Museum
23 Pakistani Embassy
24 Tehrān Museum of Contemporary Art
25 Emām Khomeinī Hospital
27 Valfajre-8 Shipping Company
28 Iraqi Embassy
29 Pārs Hospital
30 ITTO Travel Agency
31 Indian Embassy
33 Tehrān University
34 Neda International Bookshop
35 Iran Air (Domestic Bookings - Head Office)
37 Iranian Photographers' Centre
40 TBT Bus Booking Office
41 US Den of Espionage (former US Embassy)
44 Iran Air (International Bookings)
45 Sepah Consumers Cooperative
46 Iran Air (Domestic Bookings - Ferdōsī Sq)
47 Bank Sepah (Central Branch)
48 Emām Khomeinī Souvenir Shop
49 Gita Shenasi Mapshop
50 Armenian Embassy
51 Russian Embassy
52 Ferdōsī Bookshop
53 Gulestan Bookshop & Chela Pizza Bar
56 UK Embassy
57 French Embassy
58 Italian Embassy
60 Glass & Ceramics Museum
61 Bank Melli (Central Branch); National Jewels Museum
62 Turkish Embassy
63 German Embassy
65 Bookshop Sirus
70 National Museum of Iran
71 Islamic Arts Museum
72 Ministry of Foreign Affairs; Postal Museum
73 Haft-é Tīr Sports Stadium
74 Post Office (Emām Khomeinī Sq)
75 Coin Museum
76 Sizdah-é Aban Museum
79 Telephone Office (Emām Khomeinī Sq)
87 Bahar Dry Cleaning
88 National Museum of Art
89 Madrasé va Masjed-é Sepahsālār
Ārzhāntīn Square
Modarres Highway
Beihaghī Street
Bokhārest Street
Eslāmbōlī Street
Valī-yé Asr Avenue
Sa'ī Park
Shahid Beheshtī Avenue
Mofatteh Street
Malā'ek Street
Bahār-é Shīrāz Street
Farāhānī Street
Haft-é Tīr Square
Motahharī Avenue
Mīrzā-yé Shīrāzī Street
Sanā'ī Street
Khān-é Zand Street
Īrānshahr Street
Gharanī Street
Ardalān Alley
Nejātollāhī Street
Karīm
Hāfez
Lārestān Street
Bahjat Ābād
Asr Avenue
Sayyed Jamāl-od-Dīn Asad Ābādī Street
Doktor Hosein Fātemī Street
Zartosht Street
Falastīn Street
Valī-yé Asr Square
Keshāvarz Boulevard
Hejāb Street
Lalé Park
Kārgar Street
Bolvār-é Keshāvarz
Yūsefī Street
Bāgher Khān Street

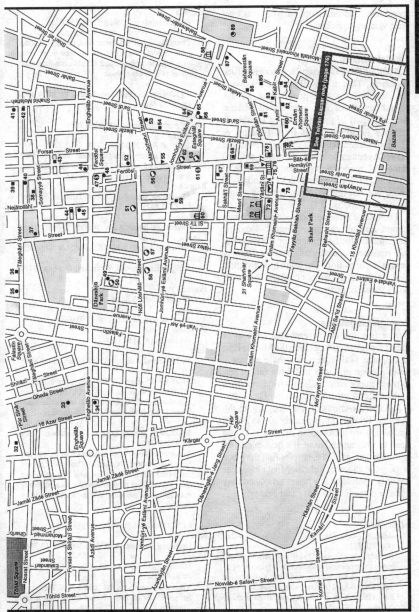

spend less time lining up, but you won't get your visa any quicker.

Tourist Offices

Incredibly, there is currently no tourist office in Tehrān. This may well change following the election of a new government, so ask your hotel about any new tourist offices. Although part of the Ministry of Culture & Islamic Guidance, the Iran Touring & Tourism Organisation (ITTO) (refer to the Travel Agencies section later in this chapter) is a travel agency and not a tourist office. It is excellent for booking tickets and local tours, but not really set up for advice and recommendations.

The tourist information booths at the train station and airport have English-speaking staff, and are the best places for advice about rail transport and flights, but not for any general information. The main bus terminals also have information counters, but staff don't speak English.

Foreign Embassies

Below is a list of the embassies for most major western countries, and the Middle East and Persian Gulf states – but there are many more foreign missions in Tehrān (and a few in other major cities in Iran – see Embassies in the Facts for the Visitor chapter).

We are conscious of not clogging up the maps of Tehrān in this guidebook, so not all embassies are included on our maps. If you need to visit an embassy, it's best to charter a private taxi, and let the driver find the place among the chaos of Tehrān. Most embassies are only open for a few hours a day, and they usually close on Thursday and Friday.

Afghanistan
> Beheshtī Ave, Pakistan St, next to 4th Alley (☎ 8738 703)
> At the moment visas (US$30) can still be issued but as the embassy represents the Afghan government, which has been ousted from Kabul by the Taliban, it is hard to give much credence to what they claim. It is open every day from 9 am to 2 pm.

Armenia
> Ostad Shahrivar St, Razī St (☎ 674 833)
> It is open between 9 and 10 am from Monday to Thursday – but get there well before opening time to avoid the crush. For a three-week visa, you need two photos and US$50, but they take about two weeks to issue.

Australia
> 13 Khaled Islambuli Ave, 23rd St (☎ 8724 456; fax 8720 484)

Austria
> 78 Ārzhāntīn Square (☎ 8710 753)

Azerbaijan
> Sharī'atī Ave, 10 Malak St (☎ 7502 724)
> The visa situation for foreigners was in turmoil at the time of writing. The embassy is open from 9 am to noon, every day but Friday.

Bahrain
> 31 Khaled Islambuli Ave (Ārzhāntīn Square) (☎ 8772 847)

Belgium
> Shabdiz St, Babak Alley (☎ 2009 554)

Canada
> Motahharī Ave, 57 Shahid Sarafraz St (☎ 8732 623)

Egypt
> Afrīghā Expressway, 70 Esfandiar St (☎ 8711 286)

France
> 85 Nōfl-Lōshātō St (☎ 767 005)

Georgia
> Sharī'atī Ave, Malak St (☎ 7500 073)

Germany
> Ferdōsī St (☎ 3114 111)

India
> 46 Mir-emad Ave, corner of Ninth St (☎ 8755 103)
> Visas for 15 days (30,000 rials), three months (120,000 rials), or six months (240,000 rials) are issued within a couple of days. It is open between 9 and 11 am from Saturday to Wednesday.

Iraq
> Sharī'atī St, Roomi Bridge, 17 Karamian Alley (☎ 221 067)
> You are unlikely to get a visa to Iraq unless you have been invited. Independent travellers cannot cross the border between Iran and Iraq, and there are no direct flights. A visit to the Iraqi embassy may also spark the interest of the Iranian security forces.

Italy
> 81 Nōfl Lōshātō St (☎ 6496 955)

Japan
> Corner of Bucharest and Fifth Sts (☎ 8713 396)

Jordan
> Mahmodieh St, Shadavar St 6, 2nd Alley (☎ 8090 734)
> Visas are easy to get, but costs vary. It is open between 9.30 am and 2.30 pm from Saturday to Thursday.

Kazakstan

Sharī'atī Ave, Shahīd Kolāhduz Ave, Behyār St (☎ 8908 723)

Kuwait

Afrīghā Expressway, 39 Babak Bahramī St (☎ 2255 997)

Lebanon

Just off Gharanī St (☎ 8984 501)

Visas are relatively easy to obtain, but costs vary. It is open between 8.30 am and noon from Monday to Wednesday.

Netherlands

Motahharī Ave, Sarbedaran St, 36 Jahansouz Alley (☎ 896 011)

New Zealand

Shīrāzī Ave, 29 Mirza Hassani Alley (☎ 8715 061)

Norway

Pāsdārān Ave, 412 Kohestān St (☎ 2589 379)

Oman

Afrīghā Expressway, Golshahr St (☎ 2250 807)

Pakistan

Fātemī Ave, Jamshid Ābād Shomalī St (☎ 934 332)

A one-month visa costs about 70,000 rials (but varies from one nationality to another), and takes one or two days to obtain. The embassy is only open on Monday and Saturday from 9 to 11 am, though you can ring them during normal business hours.

Qatar

Afrīghā Expressway, Golafshān St (☎ 2259 978)

Russia

Nōfl Lōshātō St (☎ 671 161)

Saudi Arabia

Afrīghā Expressway, 10 Sabah Blvd (☎ 2050 081)

Only expat workers and pilgrims are likely to get a visa; you need a genuine sponsor.

Sweden

Pāsdārān Ave, 2 Nastaraan St (☎ 2296 802)

Switzerland

5 17th St, Khaled Islamboli Ave (☎ 268 226)

Syria

Afrīghā Expressway, 19 Iraq St (☎ 205 9031)

Requirements and costs for visas vary from one nationality to another. It is open every day from 9 to 11 am.

Tajikistan

Pāsdārān Ave, Purebtehāj St, Zayn'alīi Alley

Turkey

Ferdōsī St (☎ 3115 299)

Most westerners can get a visa on entry to Turkey, but you can check here beforehand. Staff speak English. It is open between 9 and 11 am from Sunday to Thursday.

Turkmenistan

Pāsdārān Ave, 39 Gholestan St (☎ 2542 178)

Five-day transit visas cost US$10, take a few days to issue and you'll need a letter of introduc-

tion from your embassy in Tehrān. The embassy is open between 9 and 11 am on Monday, Thursday and Saturday, but only between 2 and 4 pm, on the same days, for visa collection.

UK

Ferdōsī St (☎ 675 018)

United Arab Emirates (UAE)

355 Vahid Dastjerdi Ave (☎ 2221 333)

A one-month visa costs 18,000 rials and takes two or three days to issue. You'll need three photos and a sponsor in the UAE. The embassy is open between 8.30 am and noon from Saturday to Wednesday.

USA

Currently, the Interests Section of the USA (☎ 8715 223) is located in the Swiss embassy (see details earlier in this section), but this does change from time to time. It is important to note that the Swiss are not allowed to offer some normal consular services for US citizens, such as replacing passports, or issuing visas to the US.

Uzbekistan

Pāsdārān Ave, Famanieh St, Boostan St, 6 Nastaran Alley (☎ 2299 158)

Yemen

Afrīghā Expressway, Ofoq Mahmaz Alavī Giti St

Money

If you arrive by air, you will have to change some money at the airport to pay for a taxi, at least. The Bank Melli branch, just after the immigration counter at the international airport in Tehrān, will change most major currencies in cash and travellers cheques, and provide cash advances (in rials) on Visa or MasterCard.

It seems that every other building in Tehrān is a bank, but only a handful of the larger branches change money – and all at the official and unfavourable exchange rate. Most banks located along Ferdōsī St and around Ferdōsī Square have foreign exchange facilities. The best place to go is Bank Melli (central branch), on Ferdōsī St, which changes travellers cheques (but not American Express); counter 12 provides cash advances in rials (and sometimes, incredibly, in US dollars) on Visa and MasterCard. Almost no bank in northern Tehrān will change money – the upmarket hotels will, both for guests and the public, but at the official rate.

Unlike most other cities in Iran, Tehrān has no official money exchange office. The best place to change money at the unofficial 'street rate' (on the black market) is along northern Ferdōsī St (on the eastern side) and around Ferdōsī Square. Just go for a short stroll and you will be approached several times by greedy black marketeers blatantly waving bundles of rials. If at all possible, change money at a shop or at your hotel, rather than with anyone who guides you into a laneway where you could be spotted by the police, or robbed by the black marketeer. It is worth spending a few minutes finding someone in a souvenir or carpet shop who will change money.

Post & Communications

The post and telephone offices, which most travellers will use, are around Emām Khomeinī Square. Although not marked in English, the post office is obvious by the post boxes outside. It is open from 8 am to 7 pm every day, but stamps (from counters 31 and 32) are only available until 5 pm on Friday. You can send faxes from counter 29. This post office has a poste restante, but it is unclear which post office in Tehrān has the main poste restante. The best idea to clearly label letters: 'Poste Restante, Post Office, Emām Khomeinī Square, South Tehrān'.

The main telephone office, for telegrams, faxes and telephone calls, is on the south side of Emām Khomeinī Square. The Telephone Booking Office inside is quite well-organised: there is even a sign in English, 'Please Do Keep Silence and Calm' (which is, of course, totally ignored). Staff, who speak English, can connect your call in a few minutes. The office is open 24 hours every day, and the entrance is to the side, off Nāser Khosrō St. The telephone area code is 021.

There are hundreds of other post and telephone offices all over town, often based around a main square. Most of the larger and better hotels can also arrange international calls for you, though you obviously pay more for this service.

To make your own calls, ring one of the following numbers (staff should speak some English): Telephone Information Center (☎ 118) for a directory of numbers within

Tehrān and the rest of Iran; International Telephone Information (☎ 195) for a list of international area codes, but not telephone numbers; and Reservation of International Telephone Calls (☎ 199) for arranging a call if you do not have access to direct dialling.

Travel Agencies

Tehrān is dotted with travel agencies, but the better ones are along, or near, Nejātollāhī St. Most do little more than sell airline tickets, and a few work as local operators for overseas tour companies. Some of the few agencies which run local tours, have English-speaking staff and are reliable for buying airline tickets are listed below.

Azadi International Tourism Organisation
    37 8th St, Ahmād Gassir Ave; PO Box 15875/1765 (☎ 8732 191; fax 8732 195) – for more details, refer to the Organised Tours section in the Getting Around chapter.
Caravan Sahra Co
    125/4 Sharī'atī Ave; PO Box 14875/153 (☎ 7502 229; fax 7671 840; email caravan@neda.net) – for more details, refer to the Organised Tours section in the Getting Around chapter.
Gardesh Travel Agency
    56 Gharanī St (☎ 8898 130; fax 8172 729)
Iran Air Tours
    191 Motahharī Ave, Dr Mofatteh crossroads (☎ 8758 390; fax 8755 884) – for more details, refer to the Organised Tours section in the Getting Around chapter.
Iran Aviation Travel Agency
    18 Gharanī St (☎ 8897 836; fax 8897 840)
Iran Touring & Tourism Organisation
    154 Keshāvarz Blvd (☎ 656 715; fax 656 800) – for more details, refer to the Organised Tours section in the Getting Around chapter.
Persepolis Tour & Travel Agency
    100 Nejātollāhī St (☎ 8810 526; fax 8808 534) – for more details, refer to the Organised Tours section in the Getting Around chapter.
Sogol Tour & Travel Agency
    65 Zohreh St, Modarres Expressway; PO Box 16315/439 (☎ 8849 082; fax 8849 086; email sogol@neda.net.ir) – they can organise local tours in English, French or German, and handle visas for independent travellers.
Tavakoli International Travel & Tour
    25 Fallahpour St, Nejātollāhī St (☎ 8810 905; fax 657 262)

Touring & Automobile Club
  12 Nobakht St, Khorramshahr Ave (☎ 8740 411;
  fax 8740 410) – the best place to get information
  about driving around Iran. There is a travel
  agency downstairs, but it's not very convenient.

Bookshops

Enghelāb Ave, south of the Tehrān University, boasts one of the longest stretches of bookshops in the world; mainly wall-to-wall shops selling books in Fārsī about medicine and architecture, among other scholastic pursuits. Among these you may find a few books in English, but these shops cater exclusively for students from the university. The best in this area is Neda Interntional (sic) Bookshop.

Of the masses of other bookshops (most signed in English) elsewhere in the city, the following are worth a browse: Bookshop Sirus; Gulestan Bookshop; Argentin Bookshop; and the Foreign Ministry Publishing Centre (not signed in English). One of my favourites is the Ferdōsī Bookshop, where you can buy pre-Revolution guidebooks in English, sci-fi novels in German, and Persian cookbooks in French, as well as old and new magazines in English.

There are bookshops inside most top-end hotels. Prices for books are very high by Iranian standards, but they're well below what you'd pay in western countries. The National Museum of Iran has a very good bookshop, with many books and maps in English – but at tourist prices. The bookshop at the Sa'd Ābād Garden Museum boasts one of the best range of tourist-oriented books in English about Iran. The bookshop, grandly named the Center for the Publication of the US Espionage Den's Documents, next to the US Den of Espionage (once known as the US embassy), looked like it was closing down at the time of research – possibly through lack of interest these days.

Laundry

For some reason, Tehrān is not overrun with laundries and dry cleaning services. Your hotel can usually arrange something. If not, and you are in the south of the city, the best is Bahar Dry Cleaning.

Medical Services

Tehrān has by far the largest concentration of doctors and hospitals in Iran, and the quality of medical care is reasonably high by international standards. Your embassy in Tehrān should be able to recommend a doctor or hospital. Most doctors in Tehrān received training in the west, and you should have few problems finding one who speaks English (or even French or German).

The best place to find the surgery of a reputable doctor is along the more upmarket streets, such as Valī-yé Asr, Keshāvarz and Tāleghānī, and near major hospitals. One private ambulance service is Iran Emdad (☎ 6436 662); otherwise ring the telephone inquiries number (☎ 115) and ask for an ambulance.

If you have no luck getting a recommendation from your embassy, the following hospitals are accessible, clean and reputable:

- Emām Khomeinī Hospital (☎ 930 040)
- Mehr Hospital (☎ 656 130)
- Mehrād Hospital (☎ 8590 004)
- Pārs Hospital (☎ 650 051)
- Shahīd Rajā'i Hospital (☎ 291 001)
- Tehrān Clinic (☎ 8728 113)

Emergency

If any emergency is not immediately life-threatening, and it happens to take place during normal business hours, it's worth contacting your local embassy immediately. They should be able to provide the current emergency numbers, and possibly some translation assistance, if needed. There are police stations all over the city. If you need to find one, contact your embassy first, or talk to someone at your hotel about getting some help with translating.

Otherwise, you can contact the telephone numbers listed below, but don't expect anyone to understand English. (The local English-language newspaper *Tehran Times* sometimes publishes an updated list of these numbers.)

- Accidents (☎ 197)
- Customs (Airport) (☎ 91 021)
- Emergency Assistance (☎ 198)
- Fire Brigade (☎ 125)
- Mehrābād (Tehrān) international airport (☎ 91 021)
- Ministry of Foreign Affairs (☎ 3 211)
- Pharmacy (☎ 191)
- Police (☎ 129)
- Red Crescent (Islamic Red Cross) (☎ 890 111)
- Traffic Accidents (☎ 197 or 342 443)

Dangers & Annoyances

One step and one breath is all it takes to realise that the traffic and pollution in Tehrān is indescribably appalling. Nearly 40% of all transport is in small cars, mainly Paykans, pumping out more than 50 million tonnes of carbonated gases in the air every year, including 1.3 million tonnes of carbon monoxide. Vehicles in Tehrān alone use 10 million tonnes of fossil fuels each year. And it is getting worse. Finding the right mixture of nitrogen, oxygen and carbon dioxide can be a problem. If the pollution starts to hurt your throat, or you have asthma, head for the hills – Darband, Tajrīsh or around Mt Damāvand (see the Around Tehrān section later in this chapter).

Though crime is negligible in Iran, it is probably most prevalent in the capital, Tehrān. Simply do not walk around with flashy jewellery, money belts outside your clothes or bags and cameras just hanging off your shoulder. Be careful, but don't be paranoid.

Many of the main streets are lined with canals or *jubs*, which originally served to distribute drinking water down through the city. They can quickly turn into raging torrents after rain, so watch out.

Refer to the Dangers & Annoyances section in the Facts for the Visitor chapter for tips on how to avoid getting run over in Tehrān.

MUSEUMS
Glass & Ceramics Museum

The Glass & Ceramics Museum (☎ 675 614) is one of the most impressive in Tehrān, not only for its exhibits but the building itself is one of the most interesting examples from the Ghajar period (1779-1921). Built as a private residence for a prominent Persian family, it later housed the Egyptian Embassy and was converted into a museum in 1976.

The building marks a move away from purely Persian traditions and exhibits a wide range of eastern and western styles, but in this case in a successful blend. The graceful wooden staircase and the classical stucco mouldings on the walls and ceilings are particularly delightful, and there are many delicate carvings and other decorations. Surrounding it is a small but lovely garden, which is worth a visit in itself.

Unlike most museums in Iran, this is professionally organised; each piece is labelled in English, and there are long explanations in English about, for example, Persian traditions of glass blowing. The museum has hundreds of exhibits dating from the 2nd millennium BC, organised chronologically into galleries. Generally, pottery is on the 1st floor, and glass and ceramics, on the 2nd

---

Museums, Museums, Museums

One thing going for Tehrān is the number of good museums – even if they are relatively expensive to enter, a hassle to find and get to, and only a few have captions in English.

The first thought about building a museum in Iran came after Nader Shāh came back with so many treasures from a rampage in India that he needed somewhere to store it all. One of the first modern museums, the Emarat-é Masudieh Museum in Tehrān, was built during the Ghajar period, and is now part of the Ministry of Education. As excavations revealed more and more ancient treasures, and Persian armies continue to loot a few neighbouring empires, the need for a national museum grew. The National (or Archaeological) Museum of Iran, sometimes called the Mūzé-yé Īrān-é Bāstān (Museum of Ancient Iran), was eventually built between 1932 and 1937.

There are now dozens of museums in Tehrān, and dozens more throughout Iran. More than 40 are owned by the Iranian Cultural Heritage Organisation, while many others are affiliated with the Organisation, but run by the Ministry of Culture & Islamic Guidance and the Ministry of Agriculture, among others. ■

floor. There is a library with more than 4000 books, including some art books in English. A small shop sells a guidebook in English about the museum, as well as some replicas of the items on display.

The museum is open from about 9 am to 5 pm every day, except Monday and public holidays. It is easy to find, and the entrance fee is 10,000 rials.

Sizdah-é Aban Museum

This small museum (☎ 671 915), once actually used as a stable for the Shāh, is crammed solid with various bronze figures by the famous modern Iranian sculptor Seyed Alī Akbar San'atī. This very muddled exhibition also has some Mexican carvings, a couple of martyrs' tombs from the Iran-Iraq War, a group sculpture of a human sea of prisoners in chains, and watercolours by San'atī.

Nothing is labelled in English (and neither is the museum), but it doesn't really matter. It's open daily, except public holidays, from 8 am to 7 pm. Entrance is often free, but the man at the entrance may want a small fee. Don't hand over more than 5000 rials – it's not worth any more than that.

National Museum of Iran

Also known as the Archaeological Museum of Iran (☎ 672 061), this may be one of the highlights of your visit to Tehrān. All captions are now in English, and as no guides or guidebooks are available, just wander around. The items in the museum will probably mean more to you if you come here after you've visited the archaeological sites – particularly Persepolis – in the countryside.

This marvellous collection includes ceramics, pottery, stone figures and carvings, among other things, dating from around the 5th and 4th millennium BC. They are mostly taken from excavations at Persepolis, Esmā'īl Ābād (125km west of Tehrān), Shūsh, Rey and Tūrang Tappé. From Shūsh, there is a stone capital of a winged lion, some delightful pitchers and vessels in animal shapes, and glazed bricks decorated with double-winged mythical creatures.

From Persepolis, you can see a 6th century BC audience hall relief of Darius I from the Treasury, a frieze of glazed tiles from the Central Hall of the Apadana Palace, a famous trilingual Darius I inscription, a human-headed capital and a carved staircase, four foundation tablets inscribed in cuneiform, a stone capital and the base of a column, a marble statue of Penelope from the Treasury, and the paw of a stone lion.

The museum has a very good bookshop, with many titles in English – but at tourist prices. Postcards (including excellent photos of the displays in the Islamic Arts Museum next door), videos, maps and dictionaries are also on sale. Photos are allowed, but you will need a strong flash, and many exhibits are behind glass display cabinets anyway.

The museum is not signposted in English, but it's easy to spot. The entrance (modelled on a Sassanian palace) is directly opposite a small park along Emām Khomeinī Ave. It is open from 9 am to 1 pm, and 2 to 5 pm, every day but Tuesday. The bad news is that foreigners must pay a ridiculous 15,000 rials entrance fee.

Islamic Arts Museum

Next door to the National Museum is the Islamic Arts Museum. The name is a misnomer actually; it is sometimes, and more appropriately, called the Museum of the Islamic Period. Unless you are particularly interested in Islamic art and history (and rolling in rials), you may find the displays here a bit similar to those in the National Museum. If you have limited time and money, you may wish to visit one or the other.

The Islamic Arts Museum has displays containing various carpets, textiles, ceramics and pottery, as well as silks from Rey; portraits from the Mongol period (1220-1380); an impressive collection of coins dating from the Sassanian period (224-637); and excellent examples of stucco work from various mosques throughout the country. In the middle of the ground floor is a shrine surrounded by Qurans, written in diverse scripts from different centuries.

Photos are allowed but, again, many exhibits are in glass displays. There is another bookshop, but little is available in English. Captions are in English, and English-speaking guides are available at the reception desk (though no-one understood me when I inquired about their rates). The opening hours are the same as the National Museum next door; ie 9 am to 1 pm, and 2 to 5 pm, every day but Tuesday. Entrance costs another whopping 15,000 rials.

Rezā Abbāsī Museum

Named after one of the great artists of the Safavid period (1502-1722), this museum is one of the best in Tehrān, but sadly ignored by most visitors. The ground floor contains stunning examples of Islamic painting, the earliest dating to the 14th century, as well as a special section displaying calligraphy from ancient Qurans. Upstairs, the galleries contain delicate pottery and exquisite jewellery from several dynasties. Further up again is a library with more than 6000 books, mostly in Fārsī, for students.

The museum (☎ 863 001) is open from 9 am to 1 pm, and 2 to 6 pm, every day but Tuesday. It is not signed in English, so, if in doubt, ask. Entrance is 10,000 rials. Postcards and books (a few in English) are on sale at reception.

Tehrān Museum of Contemporary Art

This museum contains interesting (and sometimes a little weird) paintings from modern Iranian artists, as well as regular, temporary exhibitions featuring Iranian and foreign photographers and calligraphers. There is a café inside which ought to be a popular hangout for arty types, but isn't. The museum is popular with locals, not least because of the cheap entrance fee and the wonderfully comfortable seats around the corridors. Captions are in English.

This museum is open from 9 am to 6 pm every day but Friday, when it's only open from 2 to 6 pm. Foreigners pay the same as Iranians (500 rials), which is a rather rare, but welcome, occurrence. You can easily combine this with a visit to the Carpet Museum (see next page), just up the road.

Sa'd Ābād Garden Museum

In the grounds of what used to be the Shāh's summer residence (with 18 or so palaces) is the Sa'd Ābād Garden Museum (☎ 2282 031). There are now many museums to choose from within the complex, and all are expensive to enter, so you may wish to visit only one or two, depending on your interests. While this museum is presumably meant to malign the opulence of the shāhs of the Pahlavī dynasty (1921-1979), it paradoxically seems to glorify the fineries of royalty, like a British royal palace.

Museums What is now called the **National Palace (White) Museum** (☎ 282 077) was the last Shāh's palace (with 54 rooms). The two bronze boots outside are all that remains of a giant statue of Rezā Shāh Pahlavī. Upstairs in the Ceremonial Dining Room, the 145 sq metre carpet is said to be one of the largest ever made in Iran, but it's not as large as the monster weaving downstairs in the Ceremonial Hall, which measures an incredible 243 sq metres.

The palace belonging to the Shāh's nephew Shahrām, who was only 16 at the time of the Islamic Revolution (in 1979), houses the interesting **Military Museum** (☎ 283 013). This has a collection of armoury, including a 1979 present from President Saddam Hussein of Iraq to the Shāh. Nearby is the enormous **Green (Shahvand) Palace** (☎ 287 067), the former office of the Shāh. It now contains a collection of carpets, furniture and other oddments, not dissimilar to the furniture in the National Palace Museum.

No prizes for guessing who lived in the **Mother's Palace** (☎ 282 063), but the new name – the Reversion & Admonition Museum – may have some reaching for their dictionaries. The building has been partially used for film archives; the rest contains more glorious antique furniture. The **Museum of Fine Arts** (☎ 285 021) has some charming Persian oil paintings dating back to the 18th century, including several portraits (a rare form in Islamic art), and some very beautiful inlaid furniture.

Also in the complex, you may wish to visit: the small **Natural History Museum** (☎ 283 057), once belonging to the Shāh's daughter, Shāhnāz, which contains various stuffed animals and hunting trophies; the **Museum of Athnological Research** (sic) with a few waxworks; and the **Akhbar Miniatur Museum** (sic).

Entrance The entire complex is open every day from about 8 am to 6 pm, but each museum has different opening hours. Sadly, you must leave your camera, and all bags, at the counter near the entrance (though I saw a busload of foreigners happily snapping away at the great views of Tehrān and the Alborz mountains from one palace). Make sure you visit the bookshop, which boasts one of the best ranges of tourist-oriented and English-language books about Iran.

The grounds are quite extensive, so allow plenty of time; you could also spend a pleasant couple of hours just wandering around the gardens. Because the museums have different opening hours (which also change regularly), you may miss out on what you want to see. It's best to come in the morning when most museums are more likely to be open. All captions in every museum are in English.

It costs 15,000 rials to visit *each* museum, and you can't just go in and look at the gardens, unless you pay at least 15,000 rials. If you are dead keen, a ticket for all the museums will cost you a exorbitant 60,000 rials. You must get your ticket stamped at the office marked in English: 'Public Relations'. Near the entrance, there is a teahouse, where you can smoke the hubble-bubble. (For some reason, my ticket entitled me to a free cup of tea. Try it yourself.) It is not a bad idea to combine a visit to the garden museum with lunch at a nice restaurant at Tajrīsh or Neyāvaran.

Getting There & Away To get there, take a shared (or private) taxi from Tajrīsh Square,

or walk about 1.5km from Tajrīsh Square, along Shahīd Ja'afarī St.

Carpet Museum

The two floors of the Carpet Museum (☎ 653 200) house more than 100 pieces from all over Iran, dating from the 18th century to the present day. Although the exhibition is not particularly vast it more than makes up in quality what it lacks in quantity. If you have any interest in carpets, or want to check out the sort of rugs you can't afford, this should be one stop on your busy itinerary.

The museum is open every day except Tuesday from 9 am to 6 pm. Entrance costs 10,000 rials. Inside, a shop sells postcards and books (but only a few in English); a library (most books are in Fārsī, also) is available for students; and a decent café sells drinks and snacks. To ensure the preservation of the carpets from damage inflicted by flashes, cameras are not allowed.

Āzādī Monument

Built in 1971 to commemorate the 2500th anniversary of the Persian Empire, this inverted Y-shaped 45m-high 'Freedom Monument' is close to the airports and the Western bus terminal – if you arrive at either place you can't help but notice it. Upstairs, the **Āzādī Museum** (☎ 6058 191) contains a small collection of art and archaeological finds. You can take a lift to the top for a lofty view of Tehrān, smog permitting.

The museum is open from 10 am to noon, and from 3 to 6 pm, every day but Saturday. There's a pleasant park with a lake nearby, but the appalling noise of the surrounding traffic will ruin all pretences of serenity.

Golestān Palace & Gardens

The Golestān Gardens complex comprises several buildings, most of which are not currently open to the public. One that is, the White Palace, houses the **Ethnographical Museum** (☎ 3110 653), a colourful exhibition of wax dummies wearing ethnic costumes and holding traditional cooking and musical implements. While mildly interesting, only a few of the exhibits have captions in English. The museum is open from 8 am to 3 pm from Saturday to Wednesday. Cameras are not allowed, and the entrance fee is 10,000 rials.

Not long after my visit, the **Golestān Palace** (☎ 3113 335) itself was reopened to the public as a museum. Built during the Ghajar period (1779-1921), this magnificent former royal palace will contain displays of diamonds and photography, among other things, and should be definitely worth visiting. No other details were available at the time of writing.

National Jewels Museum

This museum (☎ 3110 101) has a stunning display of jewels; so many it is overwhelming, even vulgar. You can see the Daryā-yé Nūr (Sea of Light) diamond weighing 182 carats and said to be the largest uncut diamond in the world; the Peacock (or Naderī) Throne, made in 1798 and encrusted with 26,733 gems; and the jewelled globe, made in 1869, using 51,363 precious stones. (I pity the royal jewel counter.)

This museum is only open for a few hours each week (currently on Sunday, Monday and Tuesday, from 2 to 4 pm), so it's worth ringing ahead if you are coming a long way. Entrance is 10,000 rials; and the ticket specifically reminds patrons, in English, that 'no arms' are allowed. This presumably refers to weapons, not limbs. All captions are in English.

The museum is located in a vault in the basement of the central branch of Bank Melli; look for the huge black gates, and a couple of machine-gun toting guards. The small bookshop sells a guidebook in Fārsī, but the 300 rial postcards of the extravagant items contain explanations, and are worthy souvenirs. Not surprisingly, cameras and bags must be left at reception, and be careful not to set off any alarms, and thus attract the attention of those burly armed guards.

Neyāvarān Palace Museum

If you are visiting the Sa'd Ābād Garden Museum, you may also want to see the last Shāh's second palace, now converted into the Neyāvarān Palace Museum (☎ 2282 012). There is nothing particularly stunning inside this museum, but the five hectares of gardens are lovely. (No sitting on the grass, please.) All captions in the museum are in Fārsī.

Entrance is a hefty 15,000 rials; and another 3000 rials is demanded if you want any photos of the grounds – but photos inside the museum itself is not allowed. Take a shared taxi east of Tajrīsh Square, and ask to be dropped off at the end of Bāhonar Ave, about 100m from the entrance of the museum.

Other Museums

If you have certain interests, and loads of time, there are plenty of other museums to visit. The **Postal Museum** (☎ 671 028) is on your right after you enter the Bāgh-é Melli arch (which is worth admiring in itself), leading to the Ministry of Foreign Affairs complex. The **Coin Museum** (☎ 3111 271) is right behind the Bank Sepah branch, just west of Emām Khomeinī Square, but I went there five times, and it was closed each time. (No-one could tell me when it *is* open.) The **Iranian Photographers' Center** has displays from local photographers, and is open from 9 am to 7 pm, except Fridays (3 to 7 pm). Entrance is free. And the **National Museum of Art** (☎ 3116 329) contains another collection of fine ceramics and handicrafts. It is open from 7.30 am to 2.30 pm every day but Friday. Entrance costs 10,000 rials.

MOSQUES

There are surprisingly few mosques and mausoleums worth visiting in Tehrān. Visit a few museums in Tehrān, and allocate your time and money for the magnificent mosques in Kermān city, Yazd city, Shīrāz and Esfahān, or in nearby Kāshān and Ghom.

Masjed-é Emām Khomeinī

The mosque (sometimes still known as the Masjed-é Shāh) is very much a working mosque, one of the largest and busiest in Tehrān. The building itself, though dating from the very early 18th century, is not the attraction: you go there to see Islam in action. Since the courtyard is not cut off from the surrounding area and hundreds of people hourly pass through on their way to and from the bazaar, it's no problem at all for non-Muslims to stand and watch the faithful performing their ablutions and praying. Entrance is free, but taking photos is strictly prohibited.

Madrasé va Masjed-é Sepahsālār

Built between 1878 and 1890, the Commander-in-Chief's Theological College and Mosque is one of the most noteworthy examples of Persian architecture of its period, as well as among the largest. The poetry, inscribed in several ancient scripts in the tiling, is famous. If you ask politely you might be allowed to climb its minarets, cool down in its shaded courtyard, or shout and wait for the echo in the marble pillared room.

CHURCHES

Although most of the Christians in Iran are Armenians, there is also a sprinkling of Protestants, Assyrians, Catholics and Orthodox Christians, and all have churches in Tehrān, mostly in the same district as the Sarkīs Cathedral.

Sarkīs Cathedral

In case you think that Islam has a monopoly on Iranian life, go to the north end of Nejātollāhī St and visit this impressive Armenian cathedral. Built between 1964 and 1970, it is wondrous not so much for any great beauty but because of what it is and where it is: this is by far the most visible and important non-Islamic religious building in Tehrān.

It's open free of charge to visitors daily except Sunday, and you can often find an Armenian who speaks English willing to show you around. The area immediately to the south is the Armenian quarter of Tehrān, the centre of a thriving community.

PARKS & GARDENS

To escape the noise and pollution, or to do some people-watching for a few hours (especially on the busy Friday holiday), look for one of the many parks or gardens in the city – but try to avoid anywhere which plays tinny music and speeches over the loudspeakers. Besides the lovely gardens in the Glass & Ceramics Museum, the Sa'd Ābād Garden Museum and the Neyāvarān Palace Museum (all mentioned earlier), Tehrān boasts many other patches of adorable greenery, but here are two of my favourites.

You can enjoy **Lalé Park** before or after visiting the nearby Carpet Museum and Tehrān Museum of Contemporary Art. Or perhaps have some tea or lunch at the pricey Laleh International Hotel just around the corner, or at one of the cafés and kabābīs in the south-west corner of the park. Near the cafés, there are a few good souvenir shops, all with Iranian (ie not tourist) prices.

If you are staying in southern Tehrān, try to spend some time in **Shahr Park**. You can go ice skating (in winter), take a boat trip on the tiny lake (in summer) and enjoy tea or a hubble-bubble at the fantastic Sofre Khane Sonnati Sangalag teahouse (refer to Places to Eat later in this chapter).

US DEN OF ESPIONAGE

The only indication that this vast complex used to be the US embassy (but now predictably called the US Den of Espionage) is a single faded symbol of the Bald Eagle on one of the entrances. The shop on the corner, called the Center for the Publication of the US Espionage Den's Documents, used to sell anti-American propaganda in English, including copies of secret incriminating documents painstakingly pieced together from the shredder after the Islamic Revolution, but sadly it seems the shop will close in the future.

TEHRĀN UNIVERSITY

There is nothing stopping you strolling around the grounds of the impressive Tehrān University, though none of the buildings are old or particularly interesting. The prayers held here every Friday morning are especially fascinating to watch. It won't take more than a few minutes to meet someone willing to practise their English who can show you around. The main entrance is along Enghelāb Ave.

PLACES TO STAY

Decent accommodation can be hard to find sometimes, so if you have not arranged accommodation beforehand, try telephoning your chosen hotel from the airport or bus/train station on arrival. It's hopeless to arrive in Tehrān without a reservation within 10 days either side of the Iranian New Year or Nō Rūz (about 21 March). In view of the distance between hotels, and the possible problems finding a decent room in your price range, it is worth hiring a taxi when you first arrive in Tehrān.

Unless stated otherwise, all places listed here have their names in English near the door. Finding a place with, or near, a decent restaurant is a good idea, especially if you're staying in a seedy area.

Places to Stay – budget

Camping After finishing the research trip for this book, we received a letter to say that a new *tourist camp site* (☎ 8028 625) has been established at Jadde-yé Saveh, Kasemabad, near the construction site that will eventually become the Emām Khomeinī international airport (28km south of Tehrān). Guides are available at the site, and there is a restaurant, but no other details are available.

Hotels Just about every cheap place is in the southern part of the city, within about a 1km radius of Emām Khomeinī Square, though this area is noisy, grubby and there are only a few decent restaurants. There are about a dozen cheap places to stay near the corner of Amīr Kabīr and Mellat Sts. More atmospheric – but also noisy – is the Tehrān bazaar area. Remember: in Tehrān you certainly get what you pay for. It is worth paying more in Tehrān for comfort, peace and safety.

The cheapest place in town has to be the *Hotel Shams* (☎ 390 446) in the bazaar dis-

trict. The staff are friendly, but the rooms are very basic, as you'd expect, for 8000 rials a double. Also in the bazaar area are the cheap, friendly and rudimentary *Hotel Piroz* and *Misagh Hotel* for about the same price. Don't expect a lot of sleep anywhere in the bazaar, however, except on Friday.

Arya Hotel (☎ 3113 011) is located behind a mosque (so it's noisy). Rooms are tiny but reasonably clean for 15,000 rials a double. In the same laneway is the *Chehel Sotoun Hotel* (☎ 312 248) (unsigned in English). Clean but basic doubles cost 15,000 rials, while a dorm costs as little as 5000 rials. There are a couple of other places a few metres away. Someone working at one of these hotels will probably find you and guide you along.

Often recommended by budget travellers is the friendly *Hotel Khazar Sea* (☎ 3113 760) – look for the small sign in English at the second lane on the left heading east of the intersection of Amīr Kabīr and Mellat Sts. Basic rooms cost about 12,000 rials. A few metres away, the *Mosāferkhūné Tabrīz*, not signed in English, is also a good option at 12,000/15,000 rials for a single/double.

Along the southern end of Mellat, and in laneways off Amīr Kabīr, there are a couple of other nondescript places in the 10,000/15,000 rials range. They are often quieter, but they may not always take foreigners. Look for a sign with the word 'Hotel' in English hanging off any part of any building.

Hotel Khayyam (☎ 3112 757) is off the main road and is therefore wonderfully quiet. The rooms are small, but nicely furnished, and cost a negotiable 55,000/60,000 rials a double without/with a bathroom. The restaurant is also a bonus. *Hotel Mashhad* (☎ 3113 062) (not to be confused with the Mashhad Hotel, near the former US embassy) has tiny doubles, like cells, with grimy toilets. But for 10,000 rials a double, it's a real bargain for Tehrān.

In the same area, the *Hotel Tehrān Gol* (☎ 3113 477) has been a long-term favourite, so it's often full. These days, however, it's overpriced and extremely noisy. The rooms, with a bathroom, cost US$10 (and payment in rials is not always possible). It also has a handy restaurant.

Hotel Farvardin (☎ 302 777) is just back from the main road – look for the words in English 'Hotel Hotel' above a bright doorway. The staff can speak a modicum of English, but it's a noisy spot. A decent single/double/triple, with a fan and a shared bathroom (I couldn't find the shower), costs 15,000/25,000/33,000 rials. You may get a bed in a dorm for as little as 11,000 rials per person. It also has a small restaurant.

Hotel Gilanow (☎ 3118 264) is almost permanently full of traders from Russia and other former Soviet states. The rooms overlooking an internal courtyard are nice and quiet, and cost a reasonable 18,000 rials per person, but I found the staff very unfriendly. Maybe I was just unlucky.

One of my favourites in this range is the homely *Hotel Arman* (☎ 3112 323). A pleasant, clean room, in a fairly quiet area, with a private bathroom and air-con, cost a reasonable US$10/12. To get this price, you will have to bargain with the manager, who speaks some English (none of the staff do), and he'll want US dollars. The restaurant downstairs is very good. It's just a few metres down a laneway off the southern side of Ekbātān St.

Another good and central option is the *Hafez Hotel* (☎ 679 063), just down the appropriately-named Bank Alley. The large and modern rooms are quiet and have a fridge, but the shared toilets are a bit grubby. Rooms cost 40,000/60,000 rials, but if you talk to the manager, he is happy to negotiate.

There are a couple of other places to try in southern Tehrān as a last resort, or if you are only staying for one or two nights. *Hotel Markazi* (also known as *Hotel Central Iran*) (☎ 3115 764) charges a reasonable 30,000 rials per (small) room with bathroom. Next door, the *Hotel Sa'di* costs a little less, but was being renovated at the time of research, so it may now cost more.

One of the very few places in this range in the northern parts of the city is the rather dingy *Hotel Kaj* (☎ 8808 195) – look for the sign in English from Tāleghānī St. It's in a quiet backstreet, almost next to the Tehran Times office, but the rooms are dirty. Rooms cost US$8/20, but it's not hard to get a double for US$12.

Places to Stay – middle

For about twice the price of the cheaper places you can find somewhere with five times the comfort level. This is well worth considering: Tehrān is exhausting enough without having to deal with a ratty hotel. Just about every middle-range hotel will have a restaurant, and rooms will have a private bathroom. Payment is usually required in US dollars, but if you can negotiate a lower price, and pay in rials, you can often get a bargain.

One of the better places in southern Tehrān is the *Ferdōsī Grand Hotel* (☎ 6459 991) (formerly known as the *Hotel Bozorg*). It is stylish, central and the service is good, though it is often packed with traders from Russia and other former Soviet countries – but don't be put off by this. A single/double costs US$36/53 with colour TV (which is no great advantage). More rooms were being built at the time of research.

Rooms at the *Atlas Hotel* (☎ 896 058) cost a negotiable US$20/30. The rooms are quiet and have huge baths, and some have views over a courtyard. This is a good option. Also very good, and central to the northern part of the city, is the *Bolour Hotel* (☎ 8829 881). The rooms are cosy, the staff friendly and it has a good restaurant – no wonder it's often full. They charge US$24/31, but get a room away from the main road.

Another good choice is the *Mashhad Hotel* (☎ 8825 145) (not to be confused with the grotty Hotel Mashhad) – look for the huge word 'Restaurant' in English on the roof. The rooms are large, beautifully furnished and have B&W TVs and lovely bathrooms. Rooms start at US$25/40, but can be negotiated down to a bargain 40,000 rials per person when business is quiet. If it's busy, try a couple of others a few hundred metres further down Mofatteh, such as the *Hotel Marlik* and *Hotel Mina* for the same price.

Another excellent choice in the inner west of the city is the *Omid Hotel* (☎ 6414 564). The friendly staff speak English; it's in a quiet location; and the large modern rooms, with kitchen, fridge, TV, video and stove, cost US$35/40, including breakfast. It is highly recommended.

There are a few other decent places. The rooms at the *Iranshahr Hotel* (☎ 8834 976) have a kitchen and TV. They cost US$30/40, including breakfast, which is a little over-priced, but the staff are open to negotiation. It is recognisable by the bright red and yellow canopy, and the huge letters in English spelling out the name of the hotel. *Hotel Naderi* (☎ 674 872) for US$20/30/37 a single/double/triple, plus 17% tax, is too much. However, one pair of travellers got a double for 90,000 rials plus tax. It's on a noisy street so try to get a room facing the garden. The staff don't speak much English, but it is central, and the café and cake shop downstairs are excellent. As a last resort for about US$25/35, try the *Enghelab Hotel* (☎ 6463 293), and the *Asia Hotel* (☎ 3118 551), which is currently being renovated.

Places to Stay – top end

There are quite a few four and five-star hotels in Tehrān, most of them hopelessly inconvenient to the rest of the city, and pointless for anyone wanting to use public transport. All demand US dollars, and plenty of them. Below is a selection of places which are comparatively central and reasonable value.

Azadi Grand Hotel (☎ 2073 021) is close to the International Trade Fair Ground, but nothing else. It charges US$65/75 for a single/double.
Homa Hotel (☎ 8773 021) also charges US$65/75.
Laleh International Hotel (☎ 656 021) costs US$75/110 plus tax. It was undergoing extensive renovations at the time of research, so it should be better.
Shahr Hotel (☎ 770 041) is the extraordinary green place opposite the Eastern bus terminal, with what looks like a UFO on the roof. Elegant rooms cost US$80 a double, plus 19% tax.
Tehrān Kowsar Hotel (☎ 89 121) is where the owners claim that 'Our Honour is our Hospitality'. Rooms are quiet and cost US$42/47; it's good value and central.

PLACES TO EAT

While most hotels have signs in English, most restaurants which are not part of a hotel or serve western-style fast food do not. A lot of places are not open on Friday evenings, and just about *everything* in the whole city will close on a public holiday, so eating at a hotel restaurant is probably your only option.

Kabābīs

Kebabs are the standard ration at most of the cheaper restaurants in Iran, and Tehrān is no exception. If you're staying in central or southern Tehrān you won't have to look far; even richer Tehrānīs head south if they're looking for a good kebab. There are dozens of almost identical restaurants in and around Emām Khomeinī Square, along Ferdōsī St, and around the corner of Jomhūrī-yé Eslāmī and Mellat Sts.

One of the old favourites is *Javan Kabābī*, next to Alipour Karam Alley (signed in English) – look for the dangling ice cream cones outside. Another good one is the downstairs *Ferdōsī Kabābī*. Some staff speak English, and they can order you a full chicken kebab meal, including salad, rice, drinks and bread, for less than 10,000 rials.

Fast Food

There are thousands of places around Tehrān selling Iranian-style hamburgers, but not many offer decent western-style hamburgers, pizzas or fried chicken. The best western-style fast food restaurants can be found along the upper reaches of Valī-yé Asr Ave, on Tajrīsh Square and around the corner of Valī-yé Asr and Enghelāb Aves.

If you have been travelling around the countryside for a while (and love pizzas as much as I do), you'll be glad to know there are a few decent pizza joints in Tehrān. Probably the best in town (and a lot of research was done on this topic) is the *Neyāvarān Pizza Place*, not far from the Neyāvarān Palace Museum. Excellent pizzas for one cost about 7500 rials.

Another favourite is the *Elma Tajrīsh Restaurant*. It serves scrumptious pizzas for one hungry person, salad and a drink for 7800 rials. Other tasty treats include real hamburgers, half-decent lasagne and deep-fried chicken, all at reasonable prices. Next door, another popular place, unnamed in English, serves cheap western fare, mainly western-style hamburgers.

Armenian Pizza Place, next door to the Argentin Bookshop, is also worth a visit if you are in that part of town. *Chela Pizza Bar* has a menu in English (a rarity). It offers fried chicken and chips (French fries) for 4250 rials, and Iranian-style hamburgers for 2000 rials. Sadly, pizzas were not available when I visited.

Handy to those staying in southern Tehrān is the *Banafsheh Restaurant*. It is not marked in English, but obvious by the bright red furniture and pictures of huge hamburgers on the window. The friendly manager speaks excellent English. Large pizzas, enough for one, are a little overpriced, but worth a splurge, at 9000 rials – even if the mushrooms tasted a little odd. The chips (1500 rials per plate) alone are worth a visit.

To try some finger lickin' chicken go to the *Ultimate Fried Chicken Joint*. (Well, that's the moniker I gave it based on the scrappy sign in English outside.) The food is excellent, but a little pricey at 9500 rials for fried chicken, chips, salad, bun and cola. The *Kabooky Fried Chicken* may have a funny name, and look suspiciously like something from a famous US fried chicken company, but the food is tasty and reasonably priced.

Restaurants

Most of the places classed as 'restaurants' serve western food, at tourist prices, but they are worth an occasional splurge: remember, the choice of food in the countryside is significantly worse than in Tehrān. *Tandoor Restaurant* in the Hotel Tehrān Sara is generally regarded as the best place in town for a curry. A two-course meal, with the trimmings, costs about 20,000 rials, and what may have once been a 'beer garden' is pleasant in summer.

If you are near Ārzhāntīn Square, call in to the *Ārzhāntīn Restaurant*. Unsigned in English, it's the green place next to the huge

supermarket. It offers one of the best western-style hamburgers in town, even if there is too much sauce (ketchup), for 4500 rials. Tasty Chinese food, and steak with vegetables, costs about 9500 rials. It is deservedly popular with locals, as well as diplomats working in the area.

Hotel Restaurants

Anyone can eat at the hotel restaurants listed in this book, whether you are a guest or not. One of the best in southern Tehrān is the *Zeitoon Restaurant* in the ground floor of the Ferdōsī Grand Hotel. The menu is in English, though the staff don't speak anything but Fārsī. Meals range from 9000 to 15,000 rials, which seems a lot, but the meals are large and tasty, and worth paying a few extra rials. One of the very few decent places to eat around Amīr Kabīr St is the *Hotel Khayyam* with Iranian dishes priced at about 6500 rials.

In the northern parts of the city, check out the *Bolour Hotel*. The restaurant on the 6th floor has excellent service plus a menu in English. Meals, such as chicken and rice, cost a surprisingly reasonable 5800 rials. Also very good, with dishes from 9000 to 14,000 rials, as well as excellent service and a menu in English, is the *Omid Hotel*.

There are a couple more to consider. The restaurant on the 6th floor of the *Mashhad Hotel* is classy, but overpriced at 12,000 to 16,000 rials per course plus 15% tax. What should be superb views are blocked by an annoying row of shrubs. The Laleh International Hotel has several restaurants with prices which are not unaffordable if you order wisely: the *Tiare* serves Polynesian food, the *Namakdoon* has Iranian dishes, and the *Rotisseri* offers French cuisine.

Bakeries, Cafés & Teahouses

Tehrān has some excellent cake shops and confectioneries (and a lot of research was done on this topic too). Many of the best are owned by Armenians, and the greatest concentration is along Nejātollāhī St, and around the corner of Jomhūri-yé Eslāmī and Sa'dī Sts.

One of the best is the café and patisserie under (and belonging to) the *Hotel Naderi*. You can enjoy small but delectable pastries for about 500 rials each with great coffee and Iranian nonalcoholic beer, among an intellectual set who seem to eat, drink and chat there for hours. One particularly good place for tasty ice cream (1000 rials), in a crunchy cone, is the *Ārzhāntīn Restaurant*.

There are surprisingly few traditional teahouses; you'll have to go to the countryside for these. *Sofre Khane Sonnati Sangalag* teahouse in the southern end of Shahr Park is a marvellous place to unwind, enjoy traditional Iranian hospitality and admire the locally-made carpets and gold products around the room. Though it often caters for tour groups, the public is always welcome if no group is there.

ENTERTAINMENT

Although the rigid social constraints of the Khomeinī brand of Islam have undoubtedly loosened recently, there is still very little to do in the evenings in Tehrān. There certainly aren't any nightclubs, bars or discos (except perhaps very, very deep underground). The Miami and Baccara nightclubs, and The Underground and La Bohème discos, described in guidebooks published before the Islamic Revolution (in 1979) have long since gone, and unlikely to reappear in the foreseeable future. Bring a big book with lots of words.

Cinemas

A few carefully chosen foreign films are occasionally shown in cinemas in remote parts of northern Tehrān, but they will all be censored and badly translated into Fārsī. If you want to see an action flick, Iranian-style, head to the number of cinemas along southern Lālezār St and eastern Jomhūrī-yé Eslāmī St. Every day films are shown about every two hours between 10 am and 8 pm, and cost about 1200 rials to enter.

Theatre

Foreign language students at the universities occasionally perform plays in the original script, such as Shakespeare, and in period dress. If you're interested you will have to ask one of the English-language students who are bound to approach you if you spend much time in Tehrān, particularly around Tehrān University. Other plays and theatre productions (in Fārsī) are held for upper-class Iranians, and rarely advertised in local English-language newspapers. You will have to ask Iranian friends or your hotel what is going on and where.

Music

Organised public performances of Iranian music are rare. Again, your best bet is to rely on the guidance of an Iranian friend, or talk to the staff at your hotel to find out what is going on. Special festivals, such as the Iranian Epic Music Festival held in April, may be advertised in the English-language press, but don't count on it. Until Iran is ready for something different, most concerts will be extremely traditional, such as a solo male performer plucking at a *tar*, with or without singing.

SPECTATOR SPORT

The main sport is football (soccer). It's played at 10 major stadiums around the city; the biggest games are played at the Azadi Sports Stadium (way out in the western suburbs), which can hold up to 100,000 screaming fans. Local English-language newspapers rarely have information about local games, so you will have to make inquiries. Matches are usually played on Thursday and Friday.

In the Azadi Sports Stadium complex (☎ 942 014) you may also be able to see some wrestling at the Azadi Hall; and motor racing with six categories of cars – all Paykans with different-sized engines. Save yourself time and money, and just sit in the middle of any main square in Tehrān. More sedate is the occasional game of cricket, also played at the Azadi Sports Stadium – though not in front of 100,000 screaming fans.

Other places where different sports are regularly held are the Haft-é-Tīr Sports Stadium (☎ 673 365); Chamrān Sports

Centre (☎ 263 031); and Shahid Shirudi Sports Centre (☎ 8822 110) where many sporting clubs have their headquarters.

THINGS TO BUY

Locals claim that Valī-yé Asr Ave is the longest thoroughfare in the world (so don't try walking from one end to the other). It's one of the major shopping districts of Tehrān. To many Tehrānīs the idea of a perfect night out is to go window-shopping, and the northern part of Valī-yé Asr Ave is one of their favourite places to do it.

Bazaar

Far more than just a market place, the **Tehrān Bazaar** is traditionally the Wall St of Tehrān and hence Iran, where the prices of staple commodities are fixed. Sadly, the bazaar is now gradually declining in size, importance and the quality of decent shops, and many merchants have recently moved their businesses north of the bazaar. Tehrān's bazaar, never much of an architectural jewel, has grown haphazardly and is nowadays rather sleazy, but it's worth spending one or two hours (longer if you can't find your way out).

The bazaar is a city in a city, encompassing

Grumblings from the Bazaar

All is not well among the carpet sellers of the main bazaar in Tehrān. Their main cause for concern is the iniquitous tax system, which sellers claim is too high. At the time of research, this lead to the ultimate sacrificial protest by normally avaricious carpet sellers: closure of their shops for half a day. This tax hike has been exacerbated by a worrying decline in the number of carpets and rugs bought in the bazaar, especially by tourists. Many countries now import cheaper 'Persian carpets' from India, China and other Asian countries, and as manufacturing costs rise, the profit margin decreases – but the taxes continue to increase, much to the chagrin of carpet sellers from the bazaars around Iran. ■

---

more than a dozen mosques, several guest-houses (see Places to Stay earlier), a handful of banks (not for changing money), one church and even a fire station. Each corridor specialises in a particular trade: copper, paper, gold, spice and carpets, among others. In the last of these expect to be pounced on and whisked off on a tour that inevitably ends with a highly professional demonstration of hard-sell carpet marketeering.

Where To Shop 'Til You Drop

Shopping is great in Tehrān, but you just have to know where everything is. Besides looking around the Tehrān Bazaar, the following list may help:

Goods	Location
Carpets and Souvenirs	Ferdōsī St
Clothes	Valī-yé Asr St
Electronics	northern Emām Khomeinī Square
Fish (and chessboards, would you believe?)	Jomhūrī-yé Eslāmī St, east of Ferdōsī St
Greeting Cards	just west of Bahārestān Square
Grocery Shops	Ārzhāntīn Square; Nōfl Lōshātō St
Jewellery	Jomhūrī-yé Eslāmī St, east of Ferdōsī St; Valī-yé Asr Square
Nuts and Ice creams	northern Mostafā Khomeinī St
Postcards	Hotel bookshops (best are in Hotel Laleh)
Photographic	Sūr-é Esrāfīl St; north of Falastīn Square
Travel Agencies and Airline Offices	Nejātollāhī St
Vehicle Spare Parts	Ekhbātān St; Amīr Kabīr St

The main entrance to the bazaar is along 15 Khordād Ave. Don't bother going during late afternoon on Thursday, or any time on Friday, when the place resembles a ghost town.

Souvenirs

Besides the hundreds of places in the Tehrān bazaar, there are a few souvenir shops around town which have an excellent selection, and reasonable prices. Prices are generally fixed, but if you buy a couple of things, or are good at bargaining, you can get a discounts without too much of a problem.

The dozen or more places along Ferdōsī St are a good place to start looking. Otherwise, check out the Sepah Consumers Cooperative; the various branches all over town of the Iran Handicrafts Organisation; the shops in the south-west corner of Lalé Park; or the place with the snappy title of the Fair and Store of Self Sustain Productions of Komité Emdad Emām Khomeini.

Stamp collectors may want to look at what a few sellers along Post Alley, next to the post office at Emām Khomeinī Square, have to offer. Around the Coin Museum, there are often a few old coins for sale.

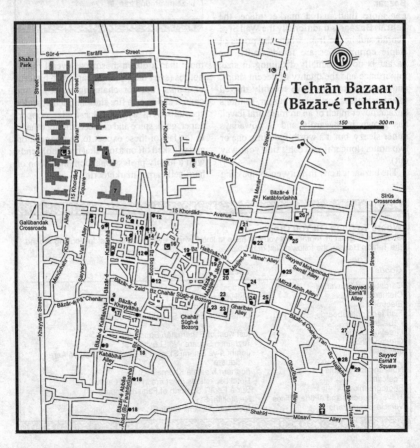

Tehrān Bazaar
(Bāzār-é Tehrān)

GETTING THERE & AWAY

The problem with travel in Iran is not how to get to Tehrān, but how to avoid it. Tehrān is the hub of almost all bus, train and air services. Every town and city of any size in Iran has a direct link to Tehrān by bus, usually by air and sometimes by train. Generally it's easier to get a ticket into Tehrān than out, and it's always a good idea to book a ticket out of Tehrān as soon as you arrive, if possible.

Air

Every day there are flights between Tehrān and most provincial capitals, and every major city you are likely to want to visit, on one of the two main domestic airlines – Iran Air and Iran Asseman. Less often there are flights to and from Tehrān on one of the smaller airlines: Mahan Air, Bon Air, Saha Air, Caspian Air and Kīsh Airlines.

1	Pā Manār
2	General Office of Customs (Edāré-yé Koll-é Gomrokāt)
3	Masjed-é Ark
4	Golestān Palace & Gardens
5	Hotel Shams
6	House of Strength (Zurkhané-yé Nejāt)
7	Bank Melli Iran (Bazaar Branch)
8	Tobacconists
9	Shoemakers
10	Bookbinders
11	Haberdashers
12	Great Bazaar
13	Goldsmiths & Silversmiths
14	Saddlers
15	Broadcloth sellers
16	Masjed-é Emām Khomeinī
17	Tailors
18	Carpetsellers
19	Tinsmiths
20	Masjed-é Jāme'
21	Plastic Goods Merchants
22	Booksellers
23	Coppersmiths
24	Boxmakers
25	Blacksmiths
26	Piroz & Misagh Hotels
27	Emāmzādé-yé Sayyed Esmā'īl
28	Carpenters
29	Knifemakers
30	Armenian Church of St Thaddeus (Kelīsā-yé Hazrat-é Tātāvūs)

For an overview of domestic flights to and from Tehrān, refer to the Domestic Air Routes chart in the Getting Around chapter. Refer to the relevant Getting There & Away sections throughout this guidebook for details on the schedules and costs of internal flights to and from Tehrān. For information on international flights in and out of Tehrān, refer to the main Getting There & Away chapter.

If you need to know anything about any domestic or international flight to or from Tehrān, contact the relevant airline offices listed below, or try ringing the Mehrābād international airport in Tehrān (☎ 91 021), or the special Domestic & Foreign Flights Information number (☎ 91 028).

Airline Offices Most airline offices in Tehrān are along, or very near, Nejātollāhī St. They are well-signed in English and easy to find (so they are not listed on the maps in this guidebook). Staff normally speak good English. Airline offices are generally open from about 9 am to 4 pm, Saturday to Thursday.

It is often just as easy to buy a ticket at a reputable travel agency (refer to the Travel Agencies section earlier in this chapter), though you will be better off confirming an onward booking in person at the relevant airline office. For the smaller internal airlines, ie Kīsh, Saha, Mahan, Caspian and Iran Asseman airlines, it's easier to buy a ticket at a travel agency, or at the crowded counters in the domestic airport.

Aeroflot
    23 Nejātollāhī St (☎ 8829 118)
Air France
    882 Enghelāb Ave (☎ 674 110), near Ferdōsī Square
Air India
    Motahharī Ave, 32 Sarafraz St (☎ 629 892)
Alitalia
    Ārzhāntīn Square (☎ 621 889)
Austrian Airlines
    Motahharī Ave, 32 Sarafraz St (☎ 627 821)
British Airways
    Sayeh St, Valī-yéAsr Ave (☎ 2014 552)
Caspian Airlines
    3 Karīm-Khān-é Zand (☎ 8807 633)

Emirates
Ārzhāntīn Square (☎ 835 057)
Gulf Air
63 Nejātollāhī St (☎ 8820 840)
Iran Air – there are three Iran Air offices:
The small office (☎ 8826 532) on Ferdōsī Square handles domestic flights only. It is open every day from about 8 am to 5 pm; closed on Friday and public holidays. The main office for domestic flights (☎ 91 111; ☎ 9112 650 for reservations) is along Tāleghānī St. It is open from 7.30 am to 5.30 pm every day, and 7.30 am to noon on Friday. This is a good place to book and confirm tickets. The head office for international flights (☎ 9112 591; ☎ 6001 191 for reservations) is along Nejātollāhī St. It is open from 7.30 am to 6 pm every day but is closed on Friday and public holidays. Get there early in summer.
Iran Asseman
Terminal 4, Mehrābād international airport (☎ 6459 445); or 1km from Makhsoms Karaj Rd (☎ 6400 257)
JAL
Nejātollāhī St (☎ 8823 186)
JAT
310 Mirdamad St (☎ 2269 915)
Kīsh Airlines
Mirdamad St (☎ 8776 184)
KLM
Motahharī Ave, 2 Sarafraz St (☎ 627 562)
Kuwait Airways
86 Nejātollāhī St (☎ 838 997)
Lufthansa
31 Khāled Eslāmbōlī St (☎ 623 382)
Mahan Air
31 East Jahan-é Koodak, Vanak Square (☎ 8772 605)
PIA
66 Nejātollāhī St (☎ 8824 195)
Saha Air
Terminal 4, Mehrābād international airport (☎ 6994 450)
SAS
Bank Sepah building, 3 Gharanī St (☎ 892 227)
Saudi Airlines
Nejātollāhī St (☎ 8828 133)
Swissair
Ārzhāntīn Square, 69 Bucharest St (☎ 8748 332)
Syrian Arab Airlines
Fallāh Pūr St, Nejātollāhī St (☎ 835 057)
Turkish Airlines
219 Motahharī Ave (☎ 627 464)

International Arrivals Though the crowds and noise may be intimidating to anyone who has not travelled in this part of the world before, customs and immigration procedures at the Mehrābād international airport in Tehrān are not that much of a hassle. But they do take a long time. Immigration is painless, as long as your visa is in order. (You probably won't be allowed on the plane to Iran in the first place if it isn't.) The log jam is at customs; you may have to wait two hours to get processed. Try to find the small customs declaration form (See Customs in the Facts for the Visitor chapter for more information), and have a pen ready to fill it out.

The tourist information counter will probably be closed, though you may be able to pick up a map there. The tourist information booth at the domestic airport, nearby, is very helpful, and worth using. See the Getting Around section later in this chapter for tips on dealing with those damn taxi drivers.

Despite the sign in English at the Bank Melli office immediately after immigration, you do not have to fill out a currency declaration. This small bank will change major foreign currencies in cash, and, usually, travellers cheques; cash advances (in rials) on Visa and MasterCard are also possible. Change enough money to get transport to your hotel, then change more at a money exchange office or with a black marketeer to get the 'street rate'. Avoid any monetary dealings with taxi drivers who will invariably offer you far less than the current 'street rate' of exchange; the police keep a close eye on black marketeers at the airport as well.

International Departures Leaving Tehrān on an international flight is not nearly as traumatic as arriving, though you will have to make sure that you allow plenty of time to get to the airport and clear customs. If you leave your hotel about 3½ hours before departure, you will be fine. Also make sure you go to the correct airport: ie international or domestic (about 1km apart).

If you have changed some money legally at a bank, and have a receipt to prove it, you can convert unused rials into US dollars cash at the bank in the international departure lounge. There are a couple of reasonable, but pricey, souvenir shops in the international departure lounge to spend your remaining rials.

Bus

There are four bus terminals in Tehrān, but surprisingly there is only one specific bus ticket office in the city: the TBT bus booking office. One excellent place to check out bus schedules, and to buy an advance ticket for any of seven major bus companies, is at the office marked in English 'The Union of Countrys (sic) Travelling Companies' at the Sayro Safar Iran bus terminal at Ārzhāntīn Square. But please note: while you can buy tickets at this private terminal, all buses not run by Sayro Safar will leave from one of the three normal terminals.

Terminals The busiest terminal in Tehrān is the Western bus terminal (☎ 6062 854) *(termīnāl-é gharb)*. It naturally caters for places to the west of Tehrān, as well as a few other destinations, including Ankara and Istanbul in Turkey, and Baku (Azerbaijan). It's well set up with dozens of bus company offices, and a restaurant, post office, police station and information booth. To get there, take a shared taxi heading west from Emām Khomeinī Square, or catch anything going to Āzādī Square, and walk to the huge terminal.

The Southern bus terminal (☎ 555 175) *(termīnāl-é jonūb)* has buses to the south and south-east of Tehrān, as well as Damascus (Syria). This terminal is a huge circular building, also well set up with a restaurant and information booth. To get there, take a shared taxi heading south from Emām Khomeinī Square. Try to avoid the expensive taxi agency which operates from this terminal. (I had to pay 7000 rials to reach Emām Khomeinī Square, and three freeloaders also piled in. I argued heavily, and much to my amazement, got a refund of 3000 rials from the taxi driver.)

The Eastern bus terminal (☎ 7860 151) *(termīnāl-é shargh)* has buses to Khorāsān province and the Caspian region. This is a small and easy terminal to use. Take a shared taxi to Emām Hussein Square, and then another shared taxi, or try the trolleybus, directly to the terminal.

Finally, there is a private terminal run by Sayro Safar Iran bus company at Ārzhāntīn

Square, accessible by shared taxis and local buses from most places in the south. This station is easier to reach than the others, and you can book tickets with Sayro Safar Iran, or with other bus companies at the nearby booking office.

Schedules Masses of buses leave Tehrān every few minutes to just about every city, town and village throughout the country – but you will need to know which terminal the buses leave from. To add to the confusion, some buses leave from two or more terminals.

The following list includes services to all major destinations with direct buses from Tehrān. Refer to the Bus section in the Getting There & Away chapter for details about international bus services.

Destination	Terminal	Price in Rials for Lux/Super
Ahvāz	Southern	8500/9500
Ardabīl	Western and Sayro Safar	7800/8500
Āstārā	Western	5500/6000
Bandar-é Abbās	Southern	13,700/14,500
Būshehr	Southern	11,200/12,900
Chālūs	Western	4200/4700
Esfahān	Southern and Sayro Safar	4300/4900
Ghazvīn	Western and Southern	1600/200
Ghom	Southern	2000 (one class only)
Gorgān	Eastern	4700/5000
Hamadān	Western	4100/4400
Īlām	Western	8500/10,300
Kermān	Southern and Sayro Safar	9500/10,700
Kermānshāh	Western	6300/6900
Mākū	Western	9600/10,500
Mashhad	Eastern, Southern and Sayro Safar	9200/10,000
Orūmīyé	Western	9800/10,700
Rāmsar	Western	5700/6100
Rasht	Eastern and Sayro Safar	4900/5600
Sārī	Eastern	3800/4200
Semnān	Southern	4500/5000
Shīrāz	Southern and Sayro Safar	8800/9700
Tabrīz	Western	7700/8500
Yazd	Southern and Sayro Safar	6300/7400
Zāhedān	Southern	15,300/16,900

Train

All train services around the country start and finish at the impressive train station in southern Tehrān. The destination and times of arrivals and departures are helpfully listed in English on a huge board at the entrance. The staff at the tourist information booth (☎ 556 114) speak English, and are walking timetables, which is just as well as the only timetables they have are in Fārsī. If you ask nicely they may help you buy a ticket at an office upstairs in the main building, otherwise you'll have to suffer the torment of the main ticket office (see Tickets following).

Schedules The prices and days of departure in the timetable listed below are liable to change, but it does give you some idea of the frequency of direct trains to major destinations. Remember that while there are no trains directly to Semnān, for example, the very frequent trains to Mashhad also stop at Semnān.

Destination	Days	Price in Rials for 2nd/1st class
Ahvāz	Three every day	8300/19,150
Bandar-é Abbās	Tues, Thurs and Sun	33,250 (1st class only)
Esfahān	Mon, Wed and Sat	5420/13,150
Ghazvīn	One every day	8200/15,250
Ghom	One 'regular' and one 'express' every day	2000/4000
Gorgān	Mon, Wed and Sat	4900/12,150
Kermān	Mon, Wed and Fri	14,200/25,200
Mashhad	Up to seven per day, depending on demand	9250/21,200
Sārī	One every day	3950/11,500
Tabrīz	Two 'express' and one 'regular' every day	12,650/17,150
Yazd	Mon, Wed and Fri	7800/18,150

Tickets Buying a ticket is such a hassle in Tehrān that you will probably give up and head to the nearest bus terminal. The place to buy train tickets is unmarked in English; it's a small building behind a blue gate, 200m east of the train station. Go through the gates, and turn immediately to your left – just look for the chaos. Nothing is signed in English, so you will have to ask someone which line to join for a ticket to your destination. Avoid the first line as you come in the main entrance, unless you want a job on the railways. Surprisingly, no travel agency or ticket office in town sells train tickets; hopefully, this will change in the future.

You can buy tickets a week or more in advance. The 20% surcharge for advance tickets is worth paying to ensure a seat on a train you want – and the tickets are very cheap anyway. The ticket office is open from 7 am to 7 pm every day. The train station and ticket office is easy to reach on any shared taxi heading south from the south-west corner of Emām Khomeinī Square.

Minibus

A few towns in central Iran and nearby parts of the Caspian provinces are linked to Tehrān by minibus. They are generally a little more expensive than buses, but leave more regularly because they have fewer seats to fill. They leave from specially designated sections within the Eastern, Southern and Western bus terminals, depending on the destination – refer to the Bus section earlier.

Shared Taxi

Most towns within about three hours by car from Tehrān are linked by shared taxi, eg Āmol, Sārī, Semnān, Kāshān, Ghom, Zanjān and Rasht – and anywhere along the way. Prices are two to three times the price of the 'lux' class in the bus, but are worth paying for to enjoy some comfort and speed. For day trips from Tehrān (see Around Tehrān later in this chapter), use a shared taxi, if possible. Shared taxis leave from specially designated sections inside, or from just outside, the appropriate bus terminals, depending on the destination – refer to the Bus section earlier.

Boat

Naturally, you can't get to Tehrān by boat, but the Valfajre-8 Shipping Company (☎ 8722 975), hidden behind Valī-yé Asr Square, is the place to ask about current schedules of ferries from southern Iran across the Persian Gulf.

GETTING AROUND
To/From the Airport

Taxi If you are arriving in Tehrān for the first time, and have some luggage, it's wise to bite the bullet and pay for a private taxi to your hotel, especially as you may be doing a bit of looking around to find a suitable hotel. The taxi drivers who speak a bit of English are becoming a bit of a rip-off, so ignore comments like 'I know a cheap hotel' (unlikely); or 'Want to change money?' (The rate will be marginally more than the bank rate, but far below the 'street rate'.)

Avoid the drivers working for the official Airport Taxi Service who loiter around waiting for naive foreigners. They want at least 30,000 rials from either airport to the city centre. Find a normal private taxi, and don't pay more than 15,000 rials. (Ask the tourist information booth at the domestic airport about current taxi fares into the city.) To either airport (which costs 10,000 to 15,000 rials from southern Tehrān), the driver will avoid paying the car park entrance fee and drop you off about 200m from the international airport, or about 50m from the domestic airport.

If you want a shared taxi (about 3000 rials from the airport to the city centre), ask around or tell a taxi driver you want to share, and he will look for other passengers going the same way. Alternatively, get a lift by taxi or bus to Āzādī Square, and then catch another shared taxi to your destination.

Bus If you are confident, and have little luggage, public buses (200 rials) leave every 15 to 20 minutes from immediately outside the domestic airport – but not from the international airport, about 1km away. Ask the friendly ladies at the tourist information booth at the domestic airport about the current bus timetable. Bus No 511 and bus No 518 travel between the domestic airport and Enghelāb and Vanak Squares.

Bus

Extensive bus services cover virtually all of Tehrān, but they are often crowded and slow, so most travellers use shared taxis. Bus tickets cost 100 or 200 rials; as a guide, pay 100 rials for any trip covered by the Central Tehrān map in this guidebook; 200 rials for anywhere further. Buses run roughly from 6 am until 10 or 11 pm, earlier on Friday and public holidays. You must buy tickets from designated ticket booths along the main streets, and at the bus terminals, and give the driver your ticket when you get on the bus.

Buses normally travel from one local bus station to another, so you may need to take more than one. Bus stations you are likely to use are at: Emām Khomeinī Square, for the inner south of the city; the station on the opposite side of Emām Khomeinī Ave from the National Museum of Iran, for the inner west; Ārzhāntīn, Vanak and Valī-yé Asr Squares, for the inner north; Āzādī Square, for the outer west; and Rāh Āhan Square, for the far south.

The buses often have numbers – but never the destinations – in English. If you read Fārsī you can buy a local bus timetable (800 rials), but the only place I could find this was, paradoxically, the tourist information booth at the train station. The buses listed below should suit most travellers. Each number refers to buses going in both directions, eg bus No 219 travels from Enghelāb Square to Ferdōsī Square and vice versa.

Bus No	From	To
126	Ārzhāntīn Square	Tajrīsh Square
127	Valī-yé Asr Square	Tajrīsh Square
128 and 144	Valī-yé Asr Square	Emām Khomeinī Square
219	Enghelāb Square	Ferdōsī Square
511 and 518	Domestic Airport	Enghelāb and Vanak Square

Minibus

There are a few very crowded public minibuses in the suburbs, but most travellers are not likely to use them. If you do, finding the right minibus going your way is not easy, so ask, ask and ask. A few private minibuses have irregular schedules: one, for instance, travels between Enghelāb and Tajrīsh Squares. Tickets cost from 200 to 500 rials, depending on the distance.

Trolleybus

One excellent – but, sadly, unique – innovation is the electric trolleybus. Currently, there is only one line, running between the Eastern bus terminal and Emām Hussein Square. It is useful for getting to or from that terminal, but for nothing else.

Underground

Tehrān *desperately* needs an underground (subway), and Tehrānīs have been told it will be completed 'in about 10 years' for the past 30 years. There is little sign of it being completed in the next 10 years, though the construction further disrupting the normally chaotic traffic around Emām Khomeinī and Haft-é Tīr Squares will result in at least two underground stations (in about 10 years).

Taxi

Shared Taxi Taxi fares in Tehrān are higher than in the rest of Iran; they appear to be rising faster than the rate of inflation too, and the minimum fare of 500 rials will not get you very far. For longer distances, expect to pay between 1000 and 2000 rials. Always watch what other passengers are paying: you'll soon have a good idea of what the current rates are.

Like most cities, shared taxis usually travel along the main roads between the following main squares: Emām Khomeinī, Vanak, Valī-yé Asr, Tajrīsh, Ārzhāntīn, Āzādī, Ferdōsī, Enghelāb, Haft-é Tīr, Rāh Āhan and Emām Hussein. These squares may have up to six mini-terminals for shared taxis heading in every conceivable direction, so you have to ask around. You may get a shared taxi all the way from, say, Emām Khomeinī Square to Tajrīsh Square (2000 rials), but you will probably have to get a connection at Valī-yé Asr or Vanak Squares.

Private Taxi Taking a private taxi is worthwhile if you are in a group, in a hurry or just don't like squeezing into a shared taxi. Any shared taxi can be hired for a private trip; look for an empty taxi – which is not always easy – and negotiate a price. For any distance, say from Emām Khomeinī Square to

Valī-yé Asr Square, the fare will be about 7000 rials. In the northern suburbs, and at the airport and Southern bus terminal, avoid any smart-looking taxis with the words in English 'Taxi Service' on top. They cost far more than normal private taxis, and prices are often not negotiable. If you are going to visit a few places in a hurry, you can always hire a normal taxi for a negotiable 10,000 to 12,000 rials per hour. Blue Agency taxis operate in the northern suburbs, but are more expensive than the normal orange ones.

Car & Motorcycle

The traffic in Tehrān is homicidal and no rules are observed. Traffic lights, indicators, footpaths and the like are totally ignored. Of all the cars in Iran, almost half are registered in Tehrān, and at times it seems like all of these are on the road (or footpath) at the same time. Most foreign drivers give up soon after arriving and quickly assimilate the lawless aggression of the natives. Drive with 100% attention at all times – or, better still, don't drive at all. Refer to the Dangers & Annoyances section in the Facts for the Visitor chapter for more information about how to avoid an ugly death in Tehrān traffic.

Rental We could only find *one* company silly enough to rent cars around Tehrān. (They would never answer their telephone, so no prices are available.) If you are keen (or stupid) enough to drive in Tehrān, try 24 Hours Rent Cars (sic) (☎ 834 490). The classifieds in any of the local English-language newspapers sometimes list car rental agencies, or ask at a travel agency (though they may strongly advise against it).

Around Tehrān

If you plan well and start early, the following places are possible as day trips from Tehrān: Ghom, Kāshān and Ghazvīn in central Iran; anywhere along the road to Chālūs in the Caspian provinces; and anywhere towards Āmol, especially for views of Damāvand along the way. Refer to the relevant sections for more details.

For information about skiing and hiking near Tehrān, refer to the Activities section in the Facts for the Visitor chapter.

NORTHERN TEHRĀN

If Tehrān is getting you down (and it will if you stay too long), head for the hills around northern Tehrān. There are three particularly pleasant areas to spend a few hours, and to enjoy a meal or drink. Tajrīsh is a charming area, populated by upper-class Tehrānīs. The pace is more relaxed and there's a good choice of restaurants (see Places to Eat earlier for a few recommendations). It is well-connected with the rest of Tehrān by bus and shared taxi. Nearby, Neyāvarān has some lovely gardens and also a few decent places to eat. Take a shared taxi from Tajrīsh Square. Thirdly, there's Darband (see under Darband in the Telecabins section below).

TELECABINS

Tehrān boasts not one, but two, telecabins (chair lifts). The one to Tōchāl is longer, but the one from Darband offers much prettier scenery, more places to eat and drink along the way, and it's cheaper. And if you want to walk some of the way, the trail from Darband is far easier than to Tōchāl. Both telecabins are only open a couple of days a week.

Tōchāl توچال

Iran claims to have the world's longest (unlikely) and highest (possibly) telecabin, the Telé Kābīn-é Tōchāl. It runs from a station at the far north of Velenjak Ave up part of Tōchāl mountain, 7.5km away, stopping at two stations. Some local optimists (maybe the same ones who think the underground in Tehrān will be finished in 'about 10 years') plan to link this telecabin with the one near Chālūs (see the Caspian Provinces chapter), somehow linking Tehrān with the Caspian Sea by telecabin.

You can walk some or all of the way up the mountain (plenty of masochistic locals walk it on Friday), and use the telecabin when your legs have given up. A *teahouse* at

both stations, and at the start, will help to ease your recovery; and a short walk from the last stop leads to a *restaurant*. The views of smog-laden Tehrān are superb, though the mountains are astoundingly barren and quite ugly. The forests start near Mt Damāvand (see Mt Damāvand later in this chapter) and head further north towards the Caspian Sea. Views are often disrupted by large posters of Emām Khomeinī on the windows of the telecabins. Honest.

This telecabin only operates from 8 am to 3 pm on Tuesday, Thursday and Friday, but you can walk along the trails up the mountain any time you want. From the northern end of Tajrīsh Square, take a shared taxi to 'Valenjak Telecabin'. From where the taxi drops you off, a short walk leads to a stop where you catch a minibus (500 rials) to the start of the telecabin. A return trip on the telecabin for both stations costs 9500 rials; you can get on and off as you like – part of your ticket is ripped off each time. Tickets to one or two stations, or just one way up or down, cost less.

Darband دربند

Darband is one of the nicest parts of Tehrān, and definitely worth a visit. A telecabin takes you some of the way up the hill, or you can walk as long as your legs will take you. (It's far easier than going up Tōchāl mountain.) There is really only one trail, and it gets mighty crowded on Thursday afternoon and Friday, so if you can live without a ride on the telecabin, go to Darband on another day.

The trail goes on and on, past some waterfalls and over a few streams, and is lined with *cafés*, *kabābīs* and *drink stalls*. They are normally open when the telecabin is operating, but a few will open the rest of the week in summer. A dish of ābgūsht, a kebab or two, a cold drink or a huff and a puff on the hubble-bubble, at a café by the stream, is delightful, and you can easily forget about being in Tehrān for a while.

This telecabin is open from 5.30 am to 7.30 pm on Thursday and Friday only. Tickets cost a reasonable 1000 rials one way, and 1500 rials return, to the only station. To

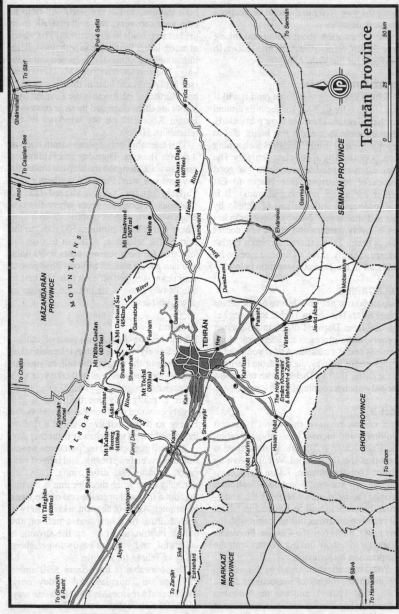

Tehrān Province

get there, take a shared taxi heading north from Tajrīsh Square, or it's an easy walk up Darband St from the Sa'd Ābād Garden Museum. The shared taxi will take you to Darband Square from where it's another 1.5km walk to Sarband Square, and the start of the telecabin ride and the walking trail.

REY رى

One of the most historical places in Tehrān province is Rey, now sadly swallowed up by the urban sprawl of Tehrān. In the 11th and 12th century, Rey was the regional capital, and larger than Tehrān, but was later destroyed by rampaging Mongols, who left very few ruins of buildings from the Sassanian (224-637 AD) and Achaemenian (559-330 BC) periods.

The main reason to visit Rey is to see the lovely **Emāmzadé Shah-é Abdal-Azim**, built for a descendant of Emām Hussein. This mausoleum has detailed tilework, a golden dome, a pool in the courtyard, and a 14th century box, with intricate carvings, constructed from betel wood. In the same complex, is another shrine for Emāmzadé Hamzē (brother of Emām Rezā).

Other attractions include the Sassanian remains of the **Ghal'-é Tabarak** fortress, on a nearby hill; the 12th century **Gombad-é Toghral**, the 20m tomb tower of a Seljuq king in the town centre; and the **Cheshmeh Ali** mineral springs with some **carvings** nearby from the Ghajar period (1779-1921).

However, finding these without a guide and a vehicle can be frustrating. You can hire a taxi from Rey for a negotiable 10,000 rials per hour. From Tehrān, catch a minibus or shared taxi from the Southern bus terminal, or charter your own vehicle.

VĀRĀMĪN ورامين

More interesting, and easier to get around, than Rey, Vārāmīn is still designated as a village, though it will soon become part of southern Tehrān. Many of the historical buildings have been destroyed by earthquakes, but it's important as much of what remains was built by the Mongols (who destroyed much of Rey).

Worth a look is the **Borj-é Aladdin** tomb, next to the main roundabout. It is more than 17m tall, and has been dated back to the 13th century. Nearby (ask for directions) is the famous **Masjed-é Jāme'** mosque, built during the 13th century. The dome, tiling, inscriptions and symmetrical eivāns are renowned.

You can catch one of the trains heading towards Gorgān, or, better, take a minibus or shared taxi from the Southern bus terminal in Tehrān.

MT DAMĀVAND کوه دماوند

The magnificent conical volcano of Mt Damāvand (5671m) is the highest in the country. You can see it on the 10,000 rial note, on bottles of Damarvand Spring water and from the air as you fly into Tehrān – smog permitting. Shaped like Mt Fuji, the mountain is worth a closer look, even if you have no intention of climbing it. The mountain of Damāvand should not be confused with the village of Damāvand to the south of the mountain. The mountain is actually just in Māzandarān province, but is more easily accessible from Tehrān.

See the Trekking in Iran section in the Facts for the Visitor chapter for details about climbing Mt Damāvand.

Reine رينه

From Tehrān, the natural starting point for exploring the mountain and the nearby countryside is the pretty village of Reine. From Reine, there are gorgeous views of other picturesque villages nestled over the other side of the valley. Even if you are not climbing the mountain, there are plenty of trails around the place to enjoy. There is no hotel, but if you ask around, especially if you want to climb the mountain, someone will put you up in their home for about 10,000 rials per person. There are a couple of shops and *kababīs* in the village.

Getting There & Away Reine is not particularly easy to reach. Take a shared taxi or minibus from Tehrān's Eastern bus terminal towards Āmol and get off at the junction to

Reine, which is unsigned in any language but not long after the 'Amol 75' sign. (You will have to pay the full Tehrān-Āmol fare.) At the junction, where there is a decent *restaurant*, a shared taxi should be waiting for passengers going to Reine. Either wait for it to fill up, or charter the taxi up the hill to the village. You may want to walk back from Reine to the highway, but the road *up* is very steep. Getting back to Tehrān from the highway, especially on a public holiday, may take some time. (I had to wait for more than three hours before gratefully squeezing into a minibus going back to the Eastern bus terminal.)

One excellent option if you have a few rials up your sleeve, or if you are travelling in a group, is to charter a taxi from Tehrān there and back for about 50,000 rials, plus a negotiable extra payment for waiting. This allows you to stop along the way for a picnic, or for lunch at one of the many restaurants along the road; take photos of the majestic mountains; explore streams and caves along the way; and to drive further past Reine, on the road up the mountain.

THE HOLY SHRINE OF EMĀM KHOMEINĪ
The Resting-Place of His Holiness Emām Khomeinī, when completed, will be one of the greatest Islamic buildings in modern history, though currently it is quite unimpressive and the crowds behave in a surprisingly irreverent manner.

Non-Muslims can enter the shrine itself. Shoes should be removed, naturally; men enter to the right, ladies to the left. You will be frisked, and no cameras are allowed (but outside the shrine, photos are OK). The room (which reminds me of a ice-skating rink, minus the ice) is full of families having picnics, kids rolling coins along the floor and homeless men sleeping. Apparently, the Āyatollāh asked that his shrine become a public place where people can enjoy themselves, rather than a mosque – and he got his wish.

The complex contains several shops, where you can pick up various tacky souvenirs; a post office; a bank (not for foreign

> **Mourning Days at the Holy Shrine**
> The Islamic Republic's final send off to its founder and inspiration – Āyatollāh Khomeinī – in 1989 culminated in the largest funeral ever held in the world, a crush of 10 million inconsolable mourners. Twice the crowd made it physically impossible for the hearse to reach the cemetery. Even when a helicopter hastily brought into service the next day landed, no amount of armed Komité guards could prevent the crowd from pushing forward to rip pieces off the shroud as holy relics.
>
> Even 10 years later, hundreds of thousands of mourners visit his shrine on and around 4 June, the anniversary of his death. Unless you thrive in chaos, you are advised to avoid this place a few days before and after this date. ■

exchange); and, incongruously, a branch of the nationwide Refah department store. There are also several decent *restaurants* and *snack bars*, so you can stay for lunch. It is open every day, and entrance is free.

Avoid *at all costs* any official mourning day (refer to the Public Holidays & Special Events section in the Facts for the Visitor chapter) when the place can be a seething mass of humanity (see the 'Mourning Days at the Holy Shrine' boxed text above).

The shrine complex is appropriately on the road between Tehrān, the town that launched the Islamic Revolution, and Ghom, where the great man underwent his theological training. It is not far from the southern edge of Tehrān, near the Behesht-é Zahra, and a trip to both is easily combined. The authorities plan to build an underground line to the shrine from southern Tehrān ('in about 10 years').

Don't take the bus to Ghom, as it often takes forever to fill up, and the shrine complex is only a few kilometres south of Tehrān. You could charter a taxi there from Tehrān for about 10,000 rials per hour. If you don't mind a squeeze, take the bus from Emām Khomeinī Square. Getting from the complex to Tehrān is easier – just look around for a minibus, bus or shared taxi from around the main car park.

BEHESHT-É ZAHRĀ

This is the main military cemetery for those who died in the Iran-Iraq War (1980-1988). It will be familiar to many from the moving TV and newspaper pictures taken of hysterical mourners during the height of the conflict. The cemetery tragically contains thousands and thousands of graves, most with a tall gravestone with a picture of their bereaved son, father, brother, husband and so

on. You can easily combine it with a trip to the Holy Shrine of Emām Khomeinī (see previous page).

The cemetery is behind the shrine complex. Walk east from the back of the shrine complex for 500m, past a huge civilian cemetery, and over the main road. The Behesht-é Zahrā is packed on mourning days, but it's eerily empty and moving on other days.

Central Iran

ایران مرکزی

The dry and dusty plain of central Iran is relatively sparsely populated, with a few large towns and little in between. The two great deserts of Iran occupy the east of the region, and even in the more hospitable parts to the west most of the settlements began as oases and largely remain so today. If you travel by land across this mostly barren heartland you can begin to appreciate the appeal to ancient travellers of these settled oases with their caravanserais. Their inhabitants have sought throughout history to give them an air of security and stability, echoed in the many sturdy monuments that survive as a testament to their builders.

For most visitors the main draw is Esfahān, but the towns of Yazd and Kāshān also have many worthwhile attractions. There are also quite a few interesting monuments scattered around the region which are easily accessible from the main transit routes, though few are prehistoric sites. The culture and language is almost entirely Persian, but several local dialects are spoken.

Markazī Province

استان مرکزی

- **Capital:** Arāk
- **Area:** 29,530 sq km
- **Population:** approx 1.4 million

Markazī (Central) province isn't actually the central province of Iran – that position goes irrefutably to Esfahān province – but evidently no-one could think of anything better to call it. A few years ago, the province was subdivided into Markazī and Ghom provinces, and now there is very little in Markazī to justify much time.

It's not that the province, or the capital and only city, Arāk, are ugly or boring, it's that there is not even a museum or mosque worth visiting, and only one archaeological site of

CENTRAL IRAN AT A GLANCE

- **Provinces:** Markazī, Ghom, Esfahān, Chahārmahāl va Bakhteyārī, Yazd and Semnān.
- **When to Go:** Spring (March to May) is ideal. Summer can be very hot, though bearable in the north, and around the hills. Winter is cold, but not too bad.
- **Highlights:** Bridges, palaces, mosques and bazaar in Esfahān; Old City of Yazd; ancient village of Abyaneh; and the gardens at Fīn, near Kāshān.

any interest: the ruins of the 12th-century **Astan-é Haftādo-o-Do-Tan**, or Mausoleum of the 72 Martyrs. The two domes contain some very old wooden boxes, and there's a cemetery in the courtyard. The mausoleum is in Sārūq, accessible by minibus from Arāk.

ARĀK

اراك

Arāk is not a city known for its great cultural or historical legacy, and there's nothing to justify a stopover, so continue on to Ghom, Khorram Ābād or Hamadān. At an altitude of 1759m above sea level, Arāk is a little cooler than other places in the region, which is one advantage in summer.

If you do get stuck in Arāk, try the *Hotel*

Kheibar, on Khordād St, near the entrance to Arāk from Tehrān. It charges about 40,000 rials a double. The rooms are pleasant at the *Hotel Lādan*, on Shahīd Ghods St, but its not easy to negotiate a reduction from the asking price of US$15/25 a single/double.

Among other destinations, there are direct daily buses to Shīrāz, Esfahān and Tehrān. Several trains pass every day to Ghom, Tehrān and Ahvāz.

SĀVÉ

Another important transit centre, Sāvé, on one of the two main roads between Tehrān and Hamadān, was an important regional centre before its destruction by the marauding Mongols in the 13th century.

These days the town is of interest to travellers principally for its two extremely fine minarets. The one belonging to the **Masjed-é Jāme'** dates from 1110 and has a well-preserved series of girders with intricate, raised geometric brickwork patterns and inscriptions, and is widely acknowledged as the finest minaret of its type in Iran. The minaret of the **Masjed-é Meidūn**, on the main square a few hundred metres to the north of the first, is less well-preserved and much simpler in

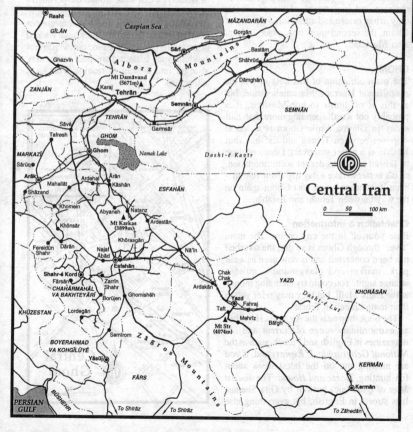

Central Iran

0   50   100 km

design, but it dates from 1061 and is also of some interest.

There is nowhere to stay in Sāvé, so you must take a day trip by minibus, shared taxi or private taxi from Tehrān, Ghom or Arāk.

Ghom Province   استان قم

- **Capital:** Ghom
- **Area:** 10,930 sq km
- **Population:** approx 910,000

Ghom province separated from Markazī province a few years ago in recognition of the size and importance of the province's only urban centre and attraction – the city of Ghom, the second most holy place in Iran, after Mashhad.

GHOM   قم

The main attraction of this holy city is the magnificent Hazrat-é Masumeh shrine, but as this is off-limits to non-Muslims, it is probably not worth spending more than half a day in Ghom. While Ghom is a decent stopover between Tehrān and Esfahān (but Kāshān is a better stopover), Ghom is close to Tehrān and lacks decent accommodation, so it's better to take a day trip from Tehrān – even if it means going past Ghom again on the way between Tehrān and Esfahān.

Orientation & Information

Base yourself in the city centre. The main 'river' through Ghom is so dry, the riverbed has been concreted and is now used as a car park, market and playground – quite a strange sight. You could try changing money at the Bank Melli, but they may refer you to their main branch in Tehrān.

The bookshop near the Al-Zahra Hotel has an extraordinary range of current and old magazines in English and French, such as the *National Geographic*, *L'Express* and, if you are missing out on the latest news about fox-hunting, *Horse and Hound*. The *Tourist Map of Qom* (sic) put out by Gita Shenasi lists streets in English, but everything else

you want to know is in Fārsī. The telephone area code for Ghom is 0251.

Hazrat-é Masumeh

The town owes its development and eminence as the burial place of Fātemé (sister of Emām Rezā), who died and was interred here in the 9th century. This extensive complex was built under Shāh Abbās I and the other Safavid kings, anxious to establish their Shi'ite credentials and to provide a counterweight to the sect's shrines at Najaf and Karbala, then under Ottoman occupation. The magnificent golden cupola of the shrine was an embellishment built by Fath Alī Shāh.

While you can walk around the perimeter of the complex, and soak up the atmosphere and admire its majesty, non-Muslims are not allowed inside. Some travellers have walked in pretending to be Muslim, but we do not condone such blatant disrespect – you may also get into a heap of trouble with local authorities.

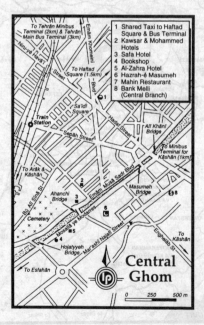

Places to Stay

Ghom lacks any decent budget hotels, which is a good reason to take a day trip from Tehrān. Many cheap places will not accept foreigners – and most places will be full during any religious holiday commemorating Emām Khomeinī.

The best place to start looking is the huddle of mosāferkhūnés directly opposite the 'river' from the shrine complex. Among some others, the *Safa Hotel* (☎ 58 457) (signposted in English) costs a reasonable 12,000/15,000 rials for a single/double. The *Mohammed Hotel* costs 20,000 rials per room. I was taken to an unsigned (in any language) mosāferkhūné at the end of a laneway behind the Safa, and charged 10,000 rials for a simple room with shared facilities.

Many mosāferkhūnés will direct you to the *Al-Zahra Hotel* (☎ 744 004), which charges foreigners a crazy, non-negotiable US$25/35. Most of the other expensive places are between the Al-Zahra and the shrine complex. The *Kawsar Hotel* (☎ 49 571) costs US$18/24/29 plus 17% tax, and the staff can't be bothered negotiating a sensible price.

Places to Eat

Don't get too excited about fine dining in Ghom. A few *kabābīs* are located along the main street between the cemetery and the Kawsar Hotel, but none are anything special. For something decent, you will have to go to one of the restaurants in the pricey hotels on the southern side of the river, such as the *Al-Zahra Hotel*, or try the *Mahin Restaurant* for decent Iranian food at decent Iranian prices.

Things to Buy

One thing you must try is the sinfully delicious pistachio brittle known as *sōhūn*, produced locally and available in almost every main street of Ghom. Not sickly sweet like so much Iranian confectionery, sōhūn becomes an obsession once you've tasted it. Gaz (Iranian nougat) is also widely stocked here.

Stalls around the shrine complex sell prayer rugs, small tablets of compressed earth used in Muslim prayers, inscriptions from the Quran, pictures of Mecca and many other religious items. Flails wielded by the devout during processions in Moharram are also on offer, if not always on display. The Persian carpets made in Ghom are particularly good, though much of what is on sale has been mass-produced and lacks detail and elegance.

Getting There & Away

Try to avoid travelling to or from Ghom on Friday, and certainly on any holy day, because a lot of transport will be packed to the hilt. If you must go on a holy day, you may be forced to charter your own taxi from Tehrān.

Bus & Minibus The main bus terminal in Ghom has buses to Rasht, Kermānshāh and Shīrāz, but nowhere else. To destinations like Esfahān and Tehrān, and most places to the south and west, you'll have to hail one of the many passing buses at Haftad Square in the northern part of the city. Some buses are full, however, so you'll have to compete with other frustrated passengers for a seat.

From Tehrān, buses leave from the Khavarpayme Travelling Company station inside the Southern bus terminal; or from the same terminal, take any bus (2000 rials) heading down the main southern road. (Get on one that is almost full; the bus I took to Ghom from Tehrān took nearly two hours to fill before it departed.)

Minibuses regularly leave Ghom for Kāshān and Tehrān from the special terminals located in the outer suburbs. Charter a private taxi to take you there.

Shared Taxi It's easier and quicker, but more expensive, to take a shared taxi to major places like Esfahān and Tehrān (5000 rials) from Haftad Square, or from the main bus terminal. From Tehrān, regular shared taxis leave from outside the Southern bus terminal.

CENTRAL IRAN

CENTRAL IRAN

Train The train station is conveniently located in central Ghom, but departure times for Tehrān are not kind: the two direct daily trains to Tehrān (2000/4000 rials for the regular/express service, 2nd class only) leave at night. There's also daily trains to Arāk (1500 rials, 2nd class); Kermān (2500 rials, 2nd class) on Monday, Wednesday and Friday; and Esfahān (1400 rials, 2nd class) on Monday, Wednesday and Saturday. These trains also arrive and depart at inconvenient times, so take a bus or shared taxi.

Esfahān Province

استان اصفهان

- **Capital:** Esfahān
- **Area:** 104,650 sq km
- **Population:** approx 4.4 million

This vast province is the geographical centre of Iran, stretching from the Dasht-é Kavīr desert in the north-east to within 150km of the Persian Gulf in the south-west, and is crisscrossed with many of the most important ancient and modern trade routes in Iran. Though mostly arid, several high mountains, such as Mt Karkas (3899m), and rivers, such as the mighty Zāyandé, dominate the landscape. The province has many attractions, and is also renowned for its fruit, particularly quinces and apples.

ESFAHĀN

اصفهان

The cool blue tiles of Esfahān's Islamic buildings, and the city's majestic bridges, contrast perfectly with the hot, dry Iranian countryside around it: Esfahān is a sight you won't forget. Not only is the architecture superb and the climate pleasant, but there's a fairly relaxed atmosphere here compared with many other Iranian towns. It's a city for walking, getting lost in the bazaar, dozing in beautiful gardens, and meeting people (population: approximately 1.3 million). The more time you have the better, because here it's easy to appreciate many of the finest aspects of Persian culture.

The reputation of Esfahānīs amongst other Persians is not altogether enviable; avarice and niggardliness being accounted their chief characteristics. Thus it is commonly said of anyone who is very careful of his expenditure that he is 'as mean as the merchants of Esfahān, who put their cheese in a bottle, and rub their bread on the outside to give it a flavour'. Another illustration of this alleged stinginess is afforded by the story of an Esfahānī merchant, who one day caught his apprentice eating lunch of dry bread and gazing wistfully at the bottle containing the precious cheese; whereupon the merchant proceeded to scold the unfortunate youth roundly for his greediness, asking him if he 'couldn't eat plain bread for one day?'

Edward Browne
A Year Amongst the Persians (1893)

The famous half-rhyme *Esfahān nesf-é jahān* (Esfahān is half the world) was coined in the 16th century to express the city's grandeur; you may well agree it has a ring of truth even today. There is so much to see that you will probably end up rationing your time and money, and concentrating on the must-sees such as the Emām Mosque, Emām Khomeinī

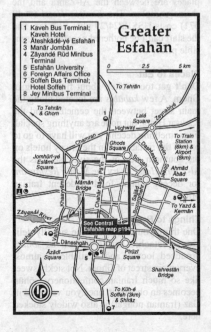

1 Kaveh Bus Terminal; Kaveh Hotel
2 Āteshkādé-yé Esfahān
3 Manār Jombān
4 Zāyandé Rūd Minibus Terminal
5 Esfahān University
6 Foreign Affairs Office
7 Softeh Bus Terminal; Hotel Softeh
8 Jey Minibus Terminal

Greater Esfahān

0   2.5   5 km

TEHRĀN

Top: A view over the Tehrān metropolis towards the snowcapped Alborz Mountains.
Middle Left: Looking back on Tehrān's smog from the Tōchāl Telé Kābīn (chair lift).
Middle Right: The Āzādī monument, built by the last Shāh in 1971.
Bottom Right: Bustling street scene in the leafy suburbs of northern Tehrān.

SCOTT KAMANA STEWART

SCOTT KAMANA STEWART

DAVID ST VINCENT

DAVID ST VINCENT

CENTRAL IRAN
Top: The doors of the Zoroastrian temple in Chak Chak, Yazd province (left); the formal gardens of the Bāgh-é Tārīkhī-yé Fīn outside Kāshān (right).
Bottom: Esfahān's Shahrestān bridge at sunset (left); the ornate minarets over the portal of the Masjed-é Emām, Esfahān (right).

Square, the fire-temple, Chehel Sotūn Palace, Vānk Cathedral, a stroll through the bazaar, and tea in one of the teahouses under one of the bridges. A lot of attractions have an annoying habit of closing for a few hours in the middle of the day (and Islamic places are usually closed on Friday mornings), so plan your days accordingly, and enjoy a long lunch and/or siesta like the Esfahānīs.

Try not to visit around Nō Rūz, when finding accommodation in Esfahān can be a hellish ordeal. And, by the way, Esfahānīs, with the notable exception of a few taxi drivers, are not nearly as unpleasant as Mr Browne contends.

History

Iran had been in a period of decline until the early 1500s when the first rulers of the Safavid dynasty (1502-1722) chucked the Mongols out of the country. Shāh Abbās I (also revered as Shāh Abbās the Great) came to power in 1587, extended his influence over rivals within the country, and then pushed out the Ottoman Turks, who had occupied a large part of Persia. With his country once more united and free of foreign influence Shāh Abbās I set out to make Esfahān a great and beautiful city. Its period of glory lasted for little more than 100 years, however: an invasion from Afghanistan hastened the decline and the capital was subsequently transferred to Shīrāz and then to Tehrān.

The power and breadth of Shāh Abbās' vision is still very much in evidence, though what remains is just a small taste of what the city looked like at its height. During his rule Esfahān produced some of the most beautiful and inspiring architecture, art and carpets seen anywhere in the Islamic world.

Orientation

The main street, Chahār Bāgh (Four Gardens), was built in 1597, and was once lined with many palaces. Although about 5km long, most travellers will base themselves along the middle section of the street, called Chahār Bāgh Abbāsī St, between Sī-o-Sé bridge and Shohadā Square. Most of the sights, shops, offices and hotels are within easy walking distance of this part of Esfahān, and it's a pleasure to wander along the tree-lined avenues. The few outlying attractions are easily visited by shared or private taxi.

The Zāyandé river starts in the Zāgros mountains, flows from west to east through the heart of Esfahān, and then peters out into the Kavīr desert. It separates the northern part of the city from the Armenian quarter in Jolfā.

Maps If you need a map to complement the two in this guidebook, pick up the free *Tourism Map & Guide of Isfahan* (sic), published by the Ministry of Culture & Islamic Guidance, and available from the helpful tourist office in Esfahān. The red Gita Shenasi map *Isfahan* (sic) (1500 rials) is now out of date, and of little value. Gita Shenasi will probably release a new map of Esfahān in the future.

Information

Visa Extensions Esfahān is a great place to get a 10 or 14-day extension, not least because the city is such a wonderful place to hang around while you wait – even though most travellers seem to have been able to get their visa extended within a couple of hours. However, one traveller later reported seeing a sign in English: 'No extensions granted for transit visas. Please do not ask questions'. Even so, travellers were still successful in getting their transit visas extended. Go to the 2nd floor of the Foreign Affairs Office (☎ 688 644), opposite Esfahān University. Take a shared taxi from the southern end of Sī-o-Sé bridge.

Tourist Offices Esfahān boasts the best tourist office (☎ 228 491) in the country, and we can only hope that other cities in Iran will take note. The office is centrally located (on the ground floor of the Alī Ghāpū Palace); staffed by friendly English-speaking personnel, who have nothing to do but advise tourists; and they can provide an excellent (free) map. It is only open from 8 am to 1 pm, every day, but the management plans to increase opening hours in the future.

Money The central branches of the big three banks – Bank Melli, Bank Tejarat and Bank Mellat – have foreign exchange facilities. It is quicker (not to mention far more financially advantageous) to change money with an official moneychanger. Surprisingly, we only found one (as shown on the map) where the manager happily changed US dollars at the 'street rate'. A few souvenir shops along Chahār Bāgh Abbāsī may also change US dollars at the 'street rate', but ask discreetly.

Post & Communications The head post office is along Neshāt St, but there are more convenient offices on Enghelāb-é Eslāmī Square, and the western side of the mammoth Emām Khomeinī Square. The central telephone office is easy to find along Beheshtī St. The useful *Amir Kabir Hotel* (see Places to Stay below) also has an international fax and telephone service. The telephone area code for Esfahān is 031.

Travel Agencies For a town with a large influx of foreign and Iranian tourists, there are surprisingly only a few decent travel

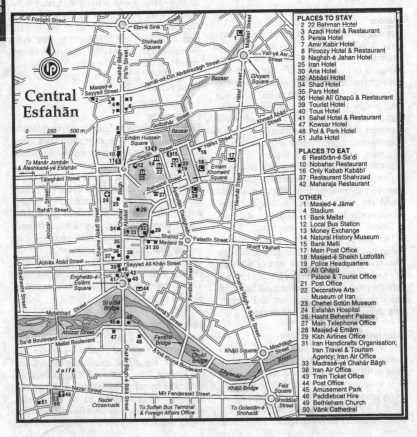

PLACES TO STAY
2 22 Bahman Hotel
3 Azadi Hotel & Restaurant
5 Persia Hotel
7 Amir Kabir Hotel
8 Piroozy Hotel & Restaurant
9 Naghsh-é Jahan Hotel
25 Iran Hotel
30 Aria Hotel
32 Abbāsī Hotel
34 Shad Hotel
35 Pars Hotel
36 Hotel Alī Ghapū & Restaurant
39 Tourist Hotel
40 Tous Hotel
41 Sahel Hotel & Restaurant
47 Kowsar Hotel
48 Pol & Park Hotel
51 Julfa Hotel

PLACES TO EAT
6 Restōrān-é Sa'di
10 Nobahar Restaurant
16 Only Kabab Kabābī
37 Restaurant Shahrzad
42 Maharaja Restaurant

OTHER
1 Masjed-é Jāme'
4 Stadium
11 Bank Mellat
12 Local Bus Station
13 Money Exchange
14 Natural History Museum
15 Bank Melli
17 Main Post Office
18 Masjed-é Sheikh Lotfollāh
19 Police Headquarters
20 Alī Ghapū
     Palace & Tourist Office
21 Post Office
22 Decorative Arts
     Museum of Iran
23 Chehel Sotūn Museum
24 Esfahān Hospital
26 Hasht Behesht Palace
27 Main Telephone Office
28 Masjed-é Emām
29 Kish Airlines Office
31 Iran Handicrafts Organisation;
     Iran Travel & Tourism
     Agency; Iran Air Office
33 Madrasé-yé Chahār Bāgh
43 Iran Air Office
43 Train Ticket Office
44 Post Office
45 Amusement Park
46 Paddleboat Hire
49 Bethlehem Church
50 Vānk Cathedral

agencies. The best and most central is Iran Travel & Tourism Agency (☎ 223 010). It can handle bookings for international and domestic, and arrange sightseeing tours around Esfahān.

Bookshops Esfahān is one of the better places in Iran for browsing around bookshops; and most sell books in English about Esfahān. (Refer to Books in the Facts for the Visitor chapter for some recommendations.) The bookshop at the Kowsar Hotel is expensive, but has a good range of books in several languages. The tiny stall in the gardens of the Chehel Sotūn Palace has an excellent selection of books. It also sells a magnificent collection of booklets (3000 rials each) with glossy photos of local attractions, as well as some postcard-sized prints of watercolours showing Esfahān's majestic buildings (1500 rials each).

One of the best bookshops in the country is the Farhangsara-yé Esfahān Bookshop. The manager speaks English, and sells current editions of *Newsweek*, *Time* and *National Geographic*. The shop is not marked in English, so look for the *Time* sticker on the door. Also worth checking out is the Bastan Bookshop. Most newspaper stalls along Chahār Bāgh Abbāsī St sell current issues of the daily English-language newspapers from Tehrān.

Emergency There are several hospitals in Esfahān. The best, and most central, are probably Dr Shāri'atī Hospital (☎ 272 001), Esfahān Hospital (☎ 268 011) and Eisā Ebn-é Maryam Hospital (☎ 239 012). For medical emergencies, telephone the general inquiries number (☎ 118 or 275 555). Most doctors have offices along Shahīd Madanī St. The main police office (☎ 247 921) is behind the Alī Ghāpū Palace.

Emām Khomeinī Square

Still sometimes known as Naghsh-é Jahān Square, this huge, open square is one of the largest in the world (500m by 160m), and a majestic example of town planning. Built in 1612, many of the most interesting sights in

Esfahān are clustered around the square, and it's a place you just keep coming back to again and again. The original goal posts from Shāh Abbās' polo ground are still in place at the far ends of the square.

Shops line the square: many specialise in brassware and there is some interesting stuff among the tacky souvenirs and postcards. You'll still need all your bargaining skills, and watch out for the hard sell from the carpet showrooms. The open-air prayer services held here every Friday always attract a large number of Muslim worshippers, and are well worth watching. One charming but certainly touristy thing to do is to take a ride on a horse and buggy around the square.

Also try to visit the square in the evening, at about 8 pm, when it's (usually) beautifully illuminated; you get a different perspective, with local families replacing Iranian and foreign tourists. But some travellers have reported going there in the evening, and the square hasn't been lit up, so you may be unlucky.

Mosques

If there is one mosque you should see in Iran, the Masjed-é Emām is it. Every other building in Esfahān pales into insignificance.

Masjed-é Emām Previously known as the Masjed-é Shāh, this magnificent mosque is one of the most stunning buildings in Iran. It's completely covered, inside and out, with the pale blue tiles that have become an Esfahānī trademark.

The main dome (54m high) is double-layered, and though the entrance, flanked with its twin minarets (both 42m high), faces squarely out onto the square, the mosque itself is at an angle to face towards Mecca. It was built over a period of 26 years by an increasingly impatient Shāh Abbās I, and eventually completed in 1638.

The tiles of the mosque take on a different hue according to the light conditions, and every hour brings a new face to this wonder of the Islamic world. The magnificent entrance portal, some 30m tall, is a supreme example of architectural styles from the

Safavid dynasty, combining sumptuous tilework and calligraphy, complex stalactite mouldings and a consummate use of colour and scale, setting the scene for the interior and dwarfing the visitor who passes through its doorway, which is tiny in comparison to the portal.

Going through a short corridor, you then enter a hallway leading into the inner courtyard which is surrounded by four *eivāns* (halls). Three lead into vaulted sanctuaries, the largest to the south. In the east sanctuary, look out for a few black paving stones underneath the dome, which when stamped upon create seven clear echoes. Try it for yourself; everyone else does. To the east and west of the mosque there are two *madrasés* (theological schools).

The whole mosque complex is lavishly decorated with tiles, and the design of the building gives the place a refreshing air of tranquillity that could never be found in the Holy Shrine in Mashhad, on which this complex was originally modelled. The best time to take photographs is around 11 am, when the sun is overhead.

This is one of the few mosques in Iran to charge entry (to foreigners), and while it sticks in the throat to pay 15,000 rials, fork out the money because this is a very special place. You could always have a whinge about the price to the ticket-seller for what it's worth (probably nothing). The mosque is open from about 7 am to 7 pm every day, except on Friday mornings. Photos are allowed.

Masjed-é Sheikh Lotfollāh This small mosque was built during Shāh Abbas' time, and dedicated to his father-in-law, Sheikh Lotfollāh, a holy preacher. This beautifully proportioned and decorated 17th-century mosque, with some of the best mosaics from that era, took nearly 20 years to complete. The pale tiles of the dome change colour, from cream through to pink, depending on the light conditions; and the mosque is unusual because it has no minaret or courtyard.

The figure painted in the middle of the floor under the dome is a peacock; at certain times of the day, the sunlight enhances the peacock's tail. The mosque was once called the Women's Mosque, because there is apparently a tunnel between this mosque and the Alī Ghāpū Palace, allowing women from the old dynasties to attend prayers without being seen in public.

However, after the majesty of the Emām Mosque not far away, many may find this mosque a disappointment. Photos are allowed, but you will need a powerful flash inside the poorly lit chamber of the dome. Entrance costs 5000 rials, and it's open every day from 7 am to noon, and 3 to 7 pm.

Madrasé-yé Chahār Bāgh Previously known as the Madrasé-yé Mādar-é Shāh (Theological School of the Shāh's Mother), you will probably pass the school many times while walking along Chahār Bāgh Abbāsī St. The courtyard is extraordinarily beautiful and restful, but unfortunately the complex is currently closed to the public.

Masjed-é Jāme' This mosque is a museum of Islamic architecture: it displays styles from the 11th century to the 18th century, from the stylish simplicity of the Seljuq period (1051-1220), through the Mongol period (1220-1380) and on to the more baroque, Safavid period. Parts of the mosque have even been dated back to the Buyid dynasty which ruled part of Persia for a few years in the 10th century. A history of the mosque is written on a notice board at the entrance of the mosque, but it's rather hard to decipher.

Entrance costs 5000 rials. (The ticket-seller speaks fluent French, and is keen to *parle français* with any foreigner, whether you speak French or not.) The mosque is open from 7 am to 7 pm every day, and is worth visiting in conjunction with a walk along the amazing bazaar. However, you will probably be disappointed with this mosque after seeing the Masjed-é Emām.

Palaces
Alī Ghāpū Palace This six storey palace was built in the 18th century on a square plan as

a functioning seat of government, and included a huge pavilion from where Safavid rulers could watch the activities in the square below. Many of the valuable murals and mosaics which once decorated the many small rooms, corridors and stairways have been destroyed, partly in the Ghajar period (1779-1921), and since the Islamic Revolution (in 1979).

Unfortunately, the palace is currently completely devoid of any furniture, so there is nothing to see inside except the beautiful fretwork stalactites on the top floor, chiselled out in the shapes of musical instruments and vases. The only reason to fork out another 15,000 rials is to enjoy the same magnificent views of the square that Alī Ghāpū enjoyed from the top of the palace. If you can live without the views, save your money for something else.

Chehel Sotūn Museum & Park This marvellous pavilion was built as a reception hall by Shāh Abbās I in the 17th century. The name means 'The Forty Columns', and though there are only 20 columns, a reflecting pool is provided to see the other 20. A more mundane explanation is that 40 was once used synonymously with 'many' in the ancient Persian language, and still is in some quarters. The palace is a marvellous sight when lit up at night, but you will have to make do with a postcard, because the gardens are usually closed after dark.

The small **museum** (☎ 226 86) inside the building contains a collection of ceramics, old coins, pottery, and several Qurans – though unfortunately many exhibits are not labelled in English. Six friezes were painted on the inside walls, depicting such scenes as the battle between Shāh Abbās and the Uzbeks, and Shāh Tahmāsb entertaining a king from Turkmenistan. One of the interior domes is in a fairly good state of repair, but the other two have only a few traces of gold and other colours.

The 67,000 sq metre gardens, with its large pool (110m by 16m), are also superb, and worth a wander around. Bring your own food and drink, and have a picnic; and don't

forget to check out the tiny bookstall (see Bookshops earlier) in the grounds.

Entrance costs the normal 10,000 rials, but at least you get a pretty ticket. Get there early in the morning for the best photos. The park and museum are open every day from about 8 am to noon, and 2.30 to 7 pm, but the exact times depend on the season. If it's open, try to visit (or visit again) after dark, when the palace is majestically reflected in the pool.

Hasht Behesht Palace This small Safavid garden palace, called Hasht Behesht (Eight Paradises), was built in the 11th century. It has some charming and impressive mosaics and stalactite mouldings, but has been slowly (very slowly) undergoing renovation for at least 20 years. Entrance costs the requisite 10,000 rials, which is too much. You can easily just admire the palace from the outside, and enjoy the surrounding Shahīd Raja'ī park (no entrance fee).

Museums
Natural History Museum The building which houses this museum (☎ 297 00) was built during the Timurid period (1380-1502), and is quite interesting in itself. Inside there's a haphazard display of molluscs, stones and stuffed animals, some of them labelled with their Latin names – but few explanations are in English. The museum is open from 9 am to 1 pm, and 3.30 to 7 pm every day, and costs a reasonable 1000 rials, which is just as well because it is not worth paying much more.

Decorative Arts Museum of Iran This new museum was temporarily closed when I tried to visit it, and no amount of shameless begging, and showing of letters of introduction from important (or so I thought) people, could persuade the guards to let me in. It does look inviting, but we can't tell you much more than the museum was built in 1996; it is open every day but Tuesday and public holidays, from 9 am to 1 pm, and 2 to 4 pm; entrance costs 10,000 rials; and no cameras are allowed inside. Please write to us, and let us know what's inside.

Bridges

One of your lasting impressions of Esfahān will undoubtedly be the old bridges which cross the Zāyandé River. Try to spend as much time as you can exploring the bridges, enjoying the teahouses underneath (refer to Places to Eat later), and strolling between them along the river banks, especially at sunset.

Sī o Sé Bridge The Pol-é Sī o Sé (Bridge of 33 Arches) links the upper and lower halves of Chahār Bāgh St. It was built in 1602 and is attractive, though not of any outstanding architectural merit. At more than 300m long, it's a great place to walk – there's no vehicles, mercifully, except recalcitrant motorcyclists of course. The *teahouses* are marvellous.

Khājū Bridge This bridge is shorter (132m long), but more attractive. Built by Shāh Abbās I from about 1650, it doubles as a dam, and has always been as much a meeting place as a functioning bearer of traffic.

It has two levels of terraces overlooking the river; the lower contain locks regulating the flow of the river. If you look hard, you can still see original paintings and tiles (though no-one is sure when these were created), and the remains of some stone seats built for Shāh Abbās I and his cronies to sit and admire the views. In the centre, a pavilion was built exclusively for the pleasure of Shāh Abbās I. This is one of the best places in Iran to enjoy a chāy.

Mārnān Bridge Located in the western part of the city, this bridge is not of much interest in itself, but serves as a finishing point for a stroll along the banks of the river. It was built in the Safavid period, and is not nearly as long as the others.

Shahrestān Bridge Also known as the Jey bridge, this is the oldest of the bridges spanning the river. Though about 3km east of the Khājū bridge, it's worth visiting, and the walk there is very pleasant. Most of its present stone and brick structure (100m long with eleven arches) is believed to date from the 12th century, though it stands on the foundations of a much earlier bridge built during the Sassanian period (224-637).

Chubī Bridge Nearly 150m long, with 21 arches, this bridge was built by Shāh Abbās II, primarily to help irrigate palace gardens in the area. This bridge is often ignored, which is a shame because it houses one of the best *teahouses* in the city.

Jolfā   جلفا

Jolfā is the Armenian quarter of Esfahān. It dates from the time of Shāh Abbās I, who set up this colony of Christians from the town of Jolfā (now on Iran's northern border), and named the village 'New Jolfā'. The skills of these industrious merchants and entrepreneurs were coveted, but the Armenians were kept in one area and away from the Islamic centres. As Esfahān expanded, Jolfā became another suburb, but the inhabitants have always been predominantly Christian.

Vānk Cathedral Built between 1655 and 1664 with the encouragement of the Safavid rulers, this is the historic focal point of the Armenian church in Iran. The exterior of the church is unexciting, but the interior is richly decorated, and shows a mixture of styles – mainly, Islamic Persian and Christian European – that characterises most churches in Iran.

The attached **museum** (☎ 434 71) contains more than 700 handwritten books, including what is apparently the first book printed in Iran, and other ethnological displays relating to Armenian culture and religion. There's even a small drawing by Rembrandt. The church and museum are open to visitors from 8 am to noon, and 2 to 5 pm, Monday to Saturday. Entrance is free.

Golestān-é Shohadā

The Rose Garden of Martyrs is a cemetery for those who died in the Iran-Iraq War. The rows and rows of photographs on the tombstones are an unforgettable sight. By the entrance there is also a modern, domed **mausoleum** to Āyatollāh Shams Ābādī, who is said to have been assassinated by the last Shāh's secret police shortly before the Islamic Revolution.

The cemetery is about 1.5km south of the Khājū bridge. To get there take a shared taxi from the southern side of the bridge to Pīrūzī Square, and then walk east for about 400m. Otherwise, it's an easy walk from Khājū bridge.

Manār Jombān

In Kaladyn, about 7km west of the city centre, is the tomb of Abu Abdollah. The tomb is normally known as Manār Jombān (Shaking Minarets) because, in theory, if you lean hard against one minaret it will start to sway back and forth; and so will its twin. Although by no means unique in this respect, the Shaking Minarets are probably the most famous of their kind. The minarets probably date from the Safavid period, though the tomb underneath was built in the 14th century.

The minarets were closed at the time of research for, of all things, renovations. Once restored, they may not sway any more. In any case, if you have limited time, give them a miss.

You can take a local bus (100 rials) from the bus station near Emām Hussein Square, or charter a private taxi for about 5000 rials return, including a side-trip to the fire-temple (see below).

Āteshkādé-yé Esfahān

This disused fire-temple, perched on top of a small hill, is another 1.5km further west from the Manār Jombān, along the same road. Dating from Sassanian times, these ancient mud-brick ruins give you a good view back to the city, and of the Zāyandé river.

The area is mostly fenced off, but there are gaping holes in the wire, so it's easy to get in and climb to the top of the hill. Entrance is free. It's impossible to miss from the main road.

Places to Stay

Because of a local police regulation, some cheap mosāferkhūnés will not accept foreigners, even if they have signs in English above the door. Just about every budget place, and many in the middle range, have shared bathroom facilities. Prices are often negotiable, but less so in the busy season (July-September). If you normally look for somewhere in the budget range, you can always try to negotiate a reduced rate at a place in the middle range.

It's best to find somewhere central – within walking distance of Chahār Bāgh Abbāsī St, though most places directly on the main road will be very noisy. Unless stated otherwise, every mosāferkhūné and hotel has a sign in English

Places to Stay – budget

Deservedly the most popular place in this range is the *Amir Kabir Hotel* (☎ /fax 236 813). The rooms could be a bit cleaner, and some of them are noisy, but it's friendly and central, and the brothers who manage the place speak good English. It also has an international fax and telephone service, a laundry, a traveller's information board and a fascinating guest book, with hints and comments from other travellers. Twin rooms cost 16,000 rials.

The *Shad Hotel* (☎ 236 883) is very friendly and a good, central option. Small, clean twin rooms cost 20,000 rials. This is probably your best option if the Amir Kabir is full, or their rooms aren't suitable. A little quieter than most, because it's just off the main road, is the *Tourist Hotel* (☎ 263 094). They charge 35,000/50,000 rials for a single/double, which is not great value, but prices are negotiable.

In a noisy (but very handy) part of town is the Sahel Hotel. They currently charge 20,000/35,000 rials; renovations currently under way will improve the standard of the rooms, but the price is also likely to rise. The *22 Bahman Hotel* (☎ 203 953) is also noisy, but large clean rooms with a fridge cost a negotiable 30,000/60,000 rials. As a last resort, the *Tous Hotel* (☎ 260 068) has noisy doubles for 40,000 rials.

Places to Stay – middle
The places listed below which charge in rials will normally negotiate in the quiet season, but you will have less success with anywhere that wants the US greenback.

The *Naghsh-é Jahan Hotel* (☎ 232 352) charges 45,000/60,000/72,000 for a single/double/triple, with shared bathroom, but discounts down to as little as 30,000 rials per triple are possible, making this a real bargain. The rooms at the *Iran Hotel* (☎ 262 010) are OK for 40,000/60,000 rials, but the staff are not particularly friendly and it's noisy. The entrance is about 20m down a laneway off Chahār Bāgh Abbāsī St.

Better than most others in this price range is the friendly *Pars Hotel* (☎ 261 018). The staff speak some English. Rooms with a fridge and TV, but a shared bathroom, cost 40,000/60,000 rials for a twin/triple.

My favourite in this range is the *Aria Hotel* (☎ 227 224). It's in a good, quiet location and the manager speaks English. Rooms, with a private bathroom and maybe a balcony as well, are good value for US$15/20/24 – and payment is possible in rials. The pleasant communal sitting area is great for meeting other travellers.

Another excellent choice is the *Hotel Soffeh* (☎ 686 462), at the Soffeh bus terminal. Though hopelessly inconvenient to the city, it is excellent for late night arrivals and early morning departures by bus. The rooms are clean and quiet (courtesy of double-glazing), and come with a TV and bathroom. They cost US$20/30, but the friendly, English-speaking manager can be persuaded to offer a 50% discount. At the northern Kaveh bus terminal, the *Kaveh Hotel* (☎ 415 055) is also good value. Large rooms with a TV and bathroom, cost 40,000/50,000 rials, and it's reasonably convenient.

On the southern side of the river is the quiet, spacious and well-named *Pol & Park Hotel* (☎ 612 785). They want US$20/30 plus 17% tax, but it's obviously better value if you can bargain them down a bit. The *Persia Hotel* (☎ 204 062) is friendly, the manager speaks English and the rooms are large, clean and have a bathroom. They cost 45,000/60,000/72,000 rials. As a last resort, try the *Julfa Hotel* (☎ 244 442) in the Armenian part of town, where a simple room with air-con costs 60,000 rials; or the *Azadi Hotel* (☎ 204 011) which charges 62,400/93,600 rials, but is only worthwhile if you can get a discount.

Places to Stay – top end
With its glorious air of faded elegance, the *Abbāsī Hotel* (☎ 226 009), luxuriously created in the shell of an old caravanserai, is undoubtedly the most romantic place to stay in Esfahān, if not Iran. Some rooms are surprisingly ordinary (but apparently they will be better furnished in the future), but the setting is superb. If you are contemplating a splurge somewhere during your trip, seriously consider this place. Rooms cost 195,000/285,000 rials, plus a small tax, but foreigners can pay in rials, which is unusual for an upmarket place. The hotel is certainly worth visiting to see the extravagance of the decorations, the magnificence of the courtyard, or just to linger over a pot of tea in its chāykhūné.

The *Kowsar Hotel* (☎ 402 36) is Esfahān's other five-star place with a five-star price: US$74/115, plus tax (but they do take rials). It's comfortable, most of the modern fittings work, and it has a fine view of Sī o Sé Bridge and the river, but it lacks the character of some other luxury hotels in Iran.

Other flashy, pricey and non-negotiable places, are the central *Piroozy Hotel* (☎ 236 586) for US$45/65; and the *Hotel Alī Ghāpū* (☎ 231 282) for US$41/75 plus 17% tax.

Places to Eat
There's a good selection of eateries in Esfahān, from the cheap and cheerful to the sophisticated and expensive, so if you've been in the countryside eating little else but kebabs, enjoy. Many of the restaurants along Chahār Bāgh Abbāsī St are downstairs, and

many have no signs in English. And don't forget to visit a teahouse (or two) under one of the bridges.

Kabābīs & Snack Bars If you must have another kebab, or Iranian-style hamburger, there are plenty of places along most of Chahār Bāgh Abbāsī St and Hāfez St, heading east of Emām Khomeinī Square, and near many of the hotels.

One of the best Iranian restaurants in town is the *Nobahar Restaurant*, signed in English and next to the Naghsh-é Jahan Hotel. A plate of fish without rice, a crisp salad (a rarity), fresh bread, soup and cola costs 9000 rials. This is probably priced a little more than it should be for tourists, but the food is tasty, and the menu is in English.

Another good place for an Iranian feed is the *Restōrān-é Sa'di*, not marked in English, but downstairs and immediately opposite the Amir Kabir Hotel. It has a menu in English, with helpful explanations of the dishes, but no prices are listed. A plate of chelō kabāb costs 4500 rials. Another good one is the *Only Kabab Kabābī*; well that's the name on the window.

My favourite for Iranian food, tea, a hubble-bubble and some of the best views in town, is the restaurant on the top floor of the *Sahel Hotel*. The outdoor but undercover setting is superb, with traditional seats and rugs, and sketches along the wall. A plate of decent kebabs cost 5500 rials. This place should not be confused with the more up-market Sahel Restaurant, next to the cinema, around the corner.

Fast Food One of the best places for some western-style fast food is the unnamed place a few doors south of the Amir Kabır Hotel. They serve tasty chips (French fries), hot dogs, pizza (for 6000 rials) and scrumptious western-style hamburgers for a reasonable 1500 rials.

Restaurants The *Maharaja Restaurant* continues to get mixed reviews. The menu (in English) offers tasty Iranian food for 7500 to 10,000 rials and western dishes like steak or schnitzel for about 10,000 rials. The curries are spicy – and pricey – at 11,000 rials.

One place heartily recommended for a bit of a splurge is the spacious and classy *Restaurant Shahrzad*. Western meals, such as schnitzel with the trimmings, cost a reasonable 9200 rials; fish dishes, 11,000 rials; and kebab-oriented meals are about 10,000 rials. The waiter will unload a salad, soup, bread and cola onto your table almost as soon as you sit down. You will pay for all of this, so if you don't want it, stop him quickly. This place is so popular in the peak season, you may have to get there early, or line up outside the door.

Hotel Restaurants Unlike other cities, the choice of restaurants is good, so there's no need to eat at your hotel unless you want to. The public is always welcome at hotel restaurants. At the *Chehelsotoun Restaurant*, in the glorious Abbāsī Hotel, you are paying more for the elegance of the decor than the quality of food, but prices are not unreasonable considering the decor and service. Western meals, such as steaks, are about 12,000 rials, which is not too bad if you've changed money at the 'street rate'.

Surprisingly reasonable value can also be found at the classy restaurant at the *Piroozy Hotel*; and the restaurant at the *Hotel Alī Ghāpū* offers French cuisine (more like 'Fārsench' cooking actually). Good value is also available at the strange restaurant at the *Azadi Hotel*. The menu in English (actually, in 'Fārsglish') offers decent chelō kabāb for 6500 rials; something called a 'chenitzel' (I think I know what they mean) for 8500 rials; and daily specials (listed as 'day food') for 5500 rials.

Teahouses One thing you must do in Esfahān is take a pot of tea, for about 1000 rials, at one of the many teahouses under the bridges. If you are staying in Esfahān for a few days, try each of them, and let us know your favourite.

The Sī o Sé bridge has several *teahouses* at either end where you can enjoy a pot of tea, or a cooked breakfast for about 4500 rials. My favourite is the gorgeous little *teahouse* in the middle of the Chubī bridge, with its traditional settings and views of the raging torrent. One English traveller wrote to say that the '*teahouse* under the Khājū bridge is worth the round-trip to Iran'. While this teahouse may seem a long way to come for a cuppa, the setting is superb, and the tea is delicious.

An attraction in itself is the majestic Abbāsī Hotel. If your budget doesn't stretch to a night in the hotel, have a pot of tea or coffee at the *Naghsh-é Jahan Restaurant* for about 2000 rials. Dress reasonably nicely, otherwise the doorman may not be keen to let you in. There are also *teahouses* in the bazaar (see Things to Buy on this page).

Tasty Treats Esfahān gets my vote as one of the best places in the country for ice cream. Soft-serve ice cream in a crunchy cone, from *stalls* on, or just off, Chahār Bāgh Abbāsī St, cost only 300 to 500 rials; and many places also serve delicious fruit shakes for about 1200 rials.

The most famous speciality of the town is *gaz,* a delicious kind of nougat usually mixed with chopped pistachios or other nuts. It isn't generally served in restaurants, but you can easily pick it up in the *confectionery shops* along Chahār Bāgh Abbāsī St.

Entertainment

Besides eating, and enjoying a tea at a marvellous teahouse, there isn't much to do in the evenings. The cinema (marked in English) on the western side of Enghelāb-é Eslāmī Square shows reasonable Iranian films in Fārsī throughout the day for about 1200 rials a ticket. Those with children, or anyone young at heart, may want to see what the amusement park has to offer.

You can also hire a paddleboat from the spot indicated on the map for about 3500 rials per hour – a great way to visit the bridges, especially late in the afternoon. If you really want to keep fit, visit all the attractions in Esfahān on foot.

Things to Buy

There are plenty of handicrafts shops in the bazaar and around Emām Khomeinī Square, mostly deserted and pining for the good old days of busloads of free-spending foreign tourists. Even so, many of the salesmen speak good English and haven't forgotten their sales patter, and foreign customers still need all their wits about them to drive a hard bargain. The shops directly facing Emām Khomeinī Square almost always have higher prices than those a few metres down a laneway further into the bazaar. Prices are often marked – but they are certainly always negotiable.

Locally produced, hand-printed table-cloths and bedspreads, marquetry, miniatures, metalwork (brass, copper and silver), and Persian carpets are the main items. Remember that Esfahān isn't the only place in Iran to buy handicrafts; almost everything for sale here can also be found in other large cities at similar, and often lower, prices. If the salesmen at the bazaar or around Emām Khomeinī Square are getting you down, try the Iran Handicrafts Organisation shop.

Bazaar The Royal Bazaar, Great Bazaar or Bazar-é Esfahān, is one of the highlights of Esfahān, linking Emām Khomeinī Square with the Masjed-é Jamē, several kilometres away. The bazaar was mostly built during the early 16th century, though some of it dates back almost 1300 years. It has made excellent use of light by placing large windows in the high domed ceilings.

The bazaar covers an enormous area. As you wander you will find shops that sell almost every imaginable item, as well as mosques, teahouses, banks, bath houses and even gardens. Like most Iranian bazaars, part of this one is loosely divided into several interconnecting corridors, each specialising in a particular trade or product, with makers of samovars (tea urns), shoemakers, dyers, carpet dealers and goldsmiths all having their own quarters.

You will also probably meet some interesting characters, as one reader reported:

As I was inspecting some strange-looking seeds at a spice stall in part of the bazaar, the English-speaking owner gave me a recipe for making a delicious drink which is also apparently good for stomach complaints and fatigue. There are two types of seeds: one blue, called *tokh-mé sharbatī*; and another orange one called *khakishir*. Soak 50g of the blue seed in water for a few minutes, drain and then add it with 50g of the orange seed in a litre of ice cold water. Add sugar to taste in the mixture, and stir continuously for 15 minutes, so that all the sugar is dissolved and the seeds are swollen. Shake and serve immediately.

Getting There & Away

Air It is not unusual for the Esfahān airport to be covered with sand; and it was closed for four days during the time of research because of sandstorms.

There are two offices for Iran Air, about 400m apart. The office (☎ 228 999) on Chahār Bāgh Abbāsī St only handles domestic bookings; the office (☎ 228 200) in the shopping complex along Shahīd Madanī St handles domestic and international bookings and confirmations. Both offices are open from 7 am to 6.30 every day but Friday.

Iran Air flies from Esfahān to the following places in Iran:

Destination	Days	Cost (rials)
Ahvāz	Daily	40,000
Bandar-é Abbās	Monday, Thursday and Saturday	70,000
Būshehr	Wednesday	51,500
Kermān	Friday	52,500
Kīsh Island	Daily (by Kīsh Airlines only)	160,000
Mashhad	Daily	74,500
Shīrāz	Daily	40,000
Tehrān	Several daily	40,000
Zāhedān	Friday	78,000

International Services Kīsh Airlines (☎ 211 906) has flights to Dubai for US$120/ 240 one way/return on Wednesday and Sunday. Iran Air has flights every Saturday between Esfahān and Kuwait City for US$122/244.

Bus Most of the long-distance buses travel overnight, which isn't a recommended way of saving on accommodation costs. Book seats as soon as you can, although you can usually get a bus from either terminal to a major destination within an hour or so. Surprisingly enough, none of the bus companies have booking offices in the city, so you'll have to buy your ticket at either of the main bus terminals.

There are two bus terminals – the Soffeh bus terminal (☎ 688 341) in the far south, and the Kaveh bus terminal (☎ 415 051) in the inner north. Both of the terminals are clean and well-organised: some bus companies have a computerised advance-booking system, and a few even list their destinations in English. The location of the terminals has nothing to do with the destinations of the buses; the terminals are located in the south and north for the convenience of folk living at either end of this sprawling city. All buses you will want leave from the more convenient Kaveh bus terminal in northern Esfahān.

From both terminals, buses leave several times a day to the places listed below – and to major destinations like Tehrān and Shīrāz, buses depart every few minutes. There are also buses to Istanbul – though exact costs and schedules were not available at the time of research. Among other places, buses leave Esfahān for the following cities (prices listed below are in rials, for lux/super class).

Destination	Distance	Time	Cost (rials)
Ahvāz	765km	14 hours	12,500/15,000
Bandar-é Abbās	1082km	18 hours	8900/11,600
Hamadān	492km	7 hours	5700/7200
Kāshān	209km	4 hours	2300/3300
Kermān	703km	12 hours	6600/7200
Kermānshāh	665km	9 hours	7800/8500
Rasht	737km	12 hours	7900/9500
Sanandaj	672km	10 hours	9400/10,300
Shīrāz	481km	8 hours	5500/6000
Sirjān	657km	11 hours	7300/8400
Tabrīz	1038km	16 hours	12,000/12,800
Tehrān	414km	7 hours	4300/4900
Yazd	316km	6 hours	3500/4000
(from Jey and Kaveh terminals)			
Zāhedān	1244km	21 hours	12,900/15,300

Minibus To add to the confusion, there are also two separate minibus terminals. From the Zāyandé Rūd minibus terminal (☎ 759 182), minibuses leave for regional towns to the west of Esfahān which travellers are unlikely to want to visit. To Shahr-é Kord (107km, 1¾ hours, 1200 rials), minibuses leave the Zāyandé Rūd terminal about every hour, as well as from the Kaveh bus terminal – (it *is* confusing). To get to the Zāyandé Rud minibus terminal, catch a shared taxi from Āzādī Square.

From the tiny Jey minibus terminal (☎ 510 003), minibuses go to Nā'īn and Ardestān (both for 1000 rials), and for some reason, some buses going to Yazd also leave from here. To get to this terminal, take a shared taxi from Ahmād Ābād Square.

Train Express trains leave Esfahān at 8 pm on Tuesday, Friday and Sunday for Tehrān (5420/13,150 rials, 2nd/1st class), via Kāshān and Ghom, but most people choose to travel to or from Esfahān by bus or by plane. It is important to note that from Esfahān, *all* trains go north towards Tehrān, and not to anywhere further south than Ardakān. You cannot travel by train between Esfahān and Kermān, for example, without changing trains at somewhere like Kāshān or Ardakān.

Thankfully, you don't have to go all the way to the train station to book a seat. Unsigned in English, the tiny ticket office (☎ 224 425) is wedged between the Bank Mellat and Bank Tejarat buildings on Enghelāb-é Eslāmī Square. The staff member speaks enough English to ensure that you get on the right train, and tickets can be bought up to one week in advance. The office is open from 8 am to 4 pm every day, but is closed on Thursday.

The train station (☎ 450 02) is way out to the east of the city, close to the airport. Passengers with prebooked train tickets can catch a special bus from outside the Kowsar Hotel an hour before the train leaves – tee this up with the ticket office. Or you can take a shared taxi from Ghods or Lalé squares.

Shared Taxi While buses to all destinations leave from either bus terminal, shared taxis leave from outside the four terminals, depending on the location of the destination: ie from the Soffeh bus terminal, shared taxis head to places to the south; Kaveh bus terminal (to the north); Zāyandé Rūd minibus terminal (to the west); and the Jey minibus terminal (to the east).

If there are enough passengers, shared taxis all the way to Tehrān or Shīrāz are possible, but generally the only provincial cities, or places of interest to travellers, with regular shared taxis from Esfahān are Shahr-é Kord, Natanz, Ardestān and Nā'īn.

Getting Around
Esfahān has long had the justifiable reputation as home to some of the most annoying taxi drivers in the country. Just about all of them have no compunction about overcharging any foreigner silly enough to pay too much.

If you want a shared taxi, never get into an *empty* shared taxi, because unless you can speak Fārsī, the driver will assume you want to charter the whole taxi and you will be charged accordingly. And if you have agreed to charter the entire taxi to the Kaveh bus terminal, for example, don't be surprised if the driver picks up a few other paying passengers along the way anyway.

To/From the Airport The airport is way out of town. There is currently no airport bus service, so to get *to* the airport look for a shared taxi (about 4000 rials) from Ghods or Lalé squares. From the airport, ask around for any shared taxi heading into the city, from where you may need another to get to your hotel.

Chartering a taxi is a good idea, and not bad value at 10,000 rials *to* the airport – though the scoundrels working for the Airport Taxi Service at the airport will naturally want more for a private taxi.

Bus & Minibus There is no need to allocate precious time getting the hang of local buses and minibuses – there are shared taxis everywhere, and they are normally cheap. If you want to give it a try, buses and minibuses leave the local bus station, near the Chehel Sotūn Palace, to every direction every few minutes. Just ask, and keep asking. Tickets costs 50 or 100 rials, depending on the distance, and are available at the local bus station, and at special booths along Chahār Bāgh Abbāsī St.

Shared Taxi The long Chahār Bāgh is the main thoroughfare through the city, and every couple of seconds a shared taxi goes *mostaghīm* (straight ahead) for about 250 rials – but don't be surprised if you have to argue to get 100 rials change from a 500-rial note for a 250 rial ride. To outlying destinations, such as the transport terminals, look for taxis heading in the right direction from the following places: Lalé, Ghods and Ahmād Ābād squares (for anywhere to the east); Emām Hussein and Shohadā squares (to the north); and the southern side of Sī o Sé bridge and Āzādī Square (to the south and west).

Private Taxi Depending on the distance – and, more importantly, your negotiating skills – a fare in a private taxi around town costs from 2000 to 4000 rials. Luckily there are so many taxis, that it's easy to negotiate by threatening to find another one. Avoid the annoying taxi drivers who hang around the eastern entrance to Emām Khomeinī Square – they are like vultures the way they wait for gullible tourists.

You can always hire a private taxi for 10,000 rials an hour within the city limits (and as far west as the Āteshkādé-yé Esfahān), but bargain hard.

AROUND ESFAHĀN

There is not a heap of things to do in the vicinity of Esfahān, which is just as well because you'll need all your spare time to explore the attractions in Esfahān itself. For other ideas, also refer to the Around Kāshān section later in this chapter, because Esfahān is just within a day trip of Kāshān and its nearby attractions.

Kūh-é Soffeh

This small hill is in the extreme southern end of town – you will probably need to charter a taxi to get there. You can walk around the hill at any time, but the best time is from 7.30 am on Friday, when hundreds of Esfahānīs gather there for a short hike, and crowds of segregated men, and women, meet each other (often for the first time) and chatter away while hiking. It is a great way to meet some Iranians, but you will feel more comfortable, and be more accepted, if you are accompanied by an Iranian friend.

Ardestān اردستان

Ardestān is an ancient city dating to the Parthian period (190 BC-224 AD), but also the birthplace of a Sassanian king, Khosro Anushirvan. The town is worth visiting for the 10th-century **Masjed-é Jāme'**, with its brick dome, beautifully ornamented prayer-hall, mehrāb and simple brick minaret. The **Masjed-é Pamenar** from the Seljuq period (1051-1220) is nearby. It has what is believed to be the second oldest minaret in Iran (dated to 1068).

The only hotel which will take foreigners is the *Jahāngardī Inn* (☎ (03242) 3501) which is run by the ITTO, and costs a non-negotiable US$25/35 for a single/double. It is best to take a day trip from Esfahān (ie by minibus from the Jey minibus terminal); or on a minibus, or any bus heading south, from Kāshān.

Nā'īn نائين

Slumbering Nā'īn, an important transit centre at the geographical centre of Iran, is a good stop off between Yazd and Kāshān or Esfahān. It is also known for its carpets, and the 10th-century **Masjed-é Jāme'**. This rambling mosque from the early Islamic period still has some features from the 10th century, and is especially notable for its fine mehrāb, and its innovative, yet simple, use of stucco decoration.

Places to stay include the *Nā'īn Hotel* (☎ (03267) 3081) for 40,000 rials a double; or the ITTO's *Jahāngardī Inn* (☎ (03267) 3665) for US$15/25 a single/double. Or alternatively, take a day trip from Yazd on any bus heading north; from Esfahān by minibus from the Jey minibus terminal, or any bus heading towards Yazd; or, at a pinch, from Kāshān on any bus heading south towards Yazd.

KĀSHĀN   كاشان

Renowned over the centuries for its ceramic tiles, pottery, textiles, carpets and silk, Kāshān is an attractive oasis town, and also the birthplace of the famous poet Sohrab and the artist Sepehria. Kāshān is also of interest for its connections with Shāh Abbās I; it was a favourite town of his, and he beautified it and asked to be buried here. There are a surprising number of things to see in, and around, Kāshān, so it's an ideal place to stop for a day or two between Tehrān and Esfahān, though the choice of hotels is limited.

History
Recent excavations date the original inhabitants of the area to the Achaemenian period (559-330 BC), while some buildings have been dated as early as the Sassanian period (224-637 AD). Kāshān was all but destroyed during the Arab invasion (637), and by various earthquakes, though, thankfully a few ancient relics and buildings survived. Kāshān once again prospered during the Seljuq dynasty (1051-1220), and became famous for its textiles and pottery. The rampaging Mongols came next, and Kāshān was devastated again. It regained some former glory during the Safavid dynasty (1502-1722), some rulers and kings preferring to live in Kāshān than the capital, Esfahān. These days, Kāshān is overshadowed by Esfahān, but it retains some real charm and history.

Orientation & Information
Most streets, and all squares, are signed in English, and it's easy enough to see the sights on foot from the city centre of Kamāl-ol-Molk Square. The red Gita Shenasi map is dated, and only lists the main streets in English; the map in this book is all you need.

Zeyārat-é Habīb Ibn-é Mūsā
While the complex looks impressive from the outside, the revered Shāh Abbās I would be disappointed with the comparative size of his unimpressive tomb. The whole place was undergoing extensions at the time of research, so it may become larger and more interesting in the future. Entrance is free.

Masjed-é Soltaniye
Lost in the midst of the labyrinthine bazaar is the Soltaniye Mosque, dating back to the Seljuq period. Surprisingly little is known about the history of this mosque, but if you

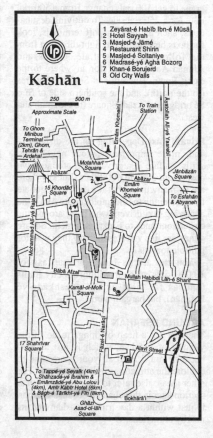

Kāshān

1 Zeyārat-é Habīb Ibn-é Mūsā
2 Hotel Sayyah
3 Masjed-é Jāmé
4 Restaurant Shirin
5 Masjed-é Soltaniye
6 Madrasé-yé Agha Bozorg
7 Khan-é Borujerd
8 Old City Walls

Kāshān
The origins of the name of the ancient city of Kāshān are unknown, but still heartily debated among experts. Some state that the name comes from the type of glazed tiles produced in the area, called *kashi*; others argue that the city was named after the *Kashou* tribe which originally inhabited the area. Poets claim that Kāshān is based on the ancient word for 'temple'; and one Iranian lexicographer said that 'kāshān' is a type of home made from bamboo. If that isn't enough to confuse everyone, a famous local historian has written that the name of the city comes from *key ashian*, which means 'Place of Rulers'. ■

are traipsing through the bazaar, make sure you have a look.

Madrasé-yé Agha Bozorg

This mosque and theological school is famous for its lovely portal and minarets. You'll have to wake up the gatekeeper, probably dozing at the entrance. He will gleefully take 10,000 rials for a ticket, and provide a guided tour in Fārsī. This place is not as worthwhile as other attractions, so you may want to give it a miss.

Khan-é Borujerdī

Originally built as a private residence in the early 19th century, this **museum** contains charming wall paintings and a lovely courtyard, and if you ask, you can climb to the top of a building next door to enjoy some great views. The house is most famous for its odd, complicated series of wind tunnels which manage to capture the occasional breath of wind.

The museum can be a little hard to find. From Alavī St, turn right opposite another old house and pool currently being restored, then walk about 80m along a tiny lane. If in doubt, ask; locals will know where it is. Entrance costs another 10,000 rials, and is worth it for the serenity, and fascinating design. The gatekeeper sells postcards, and a few books (mostly in Fārsī).

Shāhzadé-yé Ibrahim

This delightful shrine was built in the Ghajar period (1779-1921), and boasts beautiful tilework, two colourful minarets and a pretty courtyard. It is located just off the main road to the gardens at Fīn; turn right before the Amīr Kabīr Hotel, and follow the lane for a few hundred metres. You'll probably have to charter a private taxi in combination with a visit to the gardens at Fīn. Entrance is free.

Emāmzade-yé Abu Lolou

On the road from Kāshān to Fīn, and virtually opposite the Shāhzadé-yé Ibrahim, Emāmzade-yé Abu Lolou probably dates back to the Mongol period (1220-1380), though it has been heavily renovated and extended many times since. The shrine is not as interesting as other sites, but worth a look if you have a vehicle, especially when you visit the gardens at Fīn.

Masjed-é Jāme'

This much-restored mosque is relatively unimpressive. It dates from the Seljuq and Timurid (1380-1502) periods, and has a mehrāb from the 11th century, and a minaret with some ancient inscriptions.

Old City Walls

One of the few remnants of the ancient city of Kāshān, these walls are more impressive after dark, when they are spectacularly illuminated.

Bāgh-é Tārīkhī-yé Fīn

This famous and very beautiful garden, with its pools and orchards, is a highlight of Kāshān. Designed for Shāh Abbās I, this classical Persian vision of paradise has always been prized for its natural springs and still contains the remains of his two storey palace. The garden has other Safavid royal buildings, though they have been substantially rebuilt, and others were added in the Ghajar period. The palace is also infamous as the sight of the murder in 1852 of the revered Mirza Taghī Khān, commonly known as Amīr Kabīr.

Inside the grounds, a mildly interesting **museum** (☎ 4477) contains archaeological items from Tappé-yé Seyalk and Choghā Zambīl, among other sites. Foreigners are charged another 10,000 rials to the museum, and it's not worth it. A picturesque *teahouse* is located at the back of the gardens (and a few others are outside, near the entrance); and a shop in the grounds sells some postcards of the gardens and other attractions in and around Kāshān.

The gardens are open from about 8 am to about 6 pm every day except Friday – but double-check because the allocated day off changes from time to time. Entrance to the gardens costs 10,000 rials. The gardens are in the village of Fīn, about 8km south-west of central Kāshān. You can get there by shared taxi from central Kāshān, but it's better to charter a taxi for about 6000 rials return, including waiting time, and see a few others sights nearby.

Tappé-yé Seyalk
تپه سیلک

This is probably the richest archaeological site so far uncovered in central Iran, though the most interesting finds have been moved to various institutes and museums, including the National Museum of Iran in Tehrān, and the Louvre in Paris. A large number and variety of pottery and domestic implements, made from stone, clay and bone from as early as the 4th millennium BC, have been discovered at the site but there is nothing much of interest to the average visitor.

Seyalk is 4km to the north-east of Fīn, on the right of the road from Kāshān. You will need to charter a taxi to get there, and to find the site.

Places to Stay & Eat
Most of the handful of mosāferkhūnés in Kāshān refuse to take foreigners, and they will direct you to the Hotel Sayyah. Save your leg muscles, and go straight to the *Hotel Sayyah* (☎ (0361) 445 35). The official price is US$15/20 for a small, pleasant single/double, with a spotless shared bathroom, but it isn't too hard to negotiate this down to a reasonable 30,000/40,000 rials.

On the main road, about 2km before the gardens at Fīn, the *Amīr Kabīr Hotel* (☎ (0361) 300 091) is the only option in the middle range. Rooms are overpriced at US$25/40, so try to bargain. It is in a lovely spot, close to the Fīn gardens, but a fair way from town.

Nothing will excite the taste buds in Kāshān. The *Amīr Kabīr* has a restaurant for guests and the public, but the Sayyah doesn't. Your best bet is the *Restaurant Shirin*, on the steps leading up into the bazaar. Decent Iranian dishes cost about 5500 rials, and the staff are friendly. The streets around the Sayyah have a few decent *kabābīs*.

Getting There & Away
Bus & Minibus Buses and minibuses leave for Esfahān and Tehrān every 10 to 15 minutes from the main bus and minibus terminal near Emām Khomeinī Square. The makeshift terminal at 15 Khordād Square caters for buses passing through Kāshān on the way to Tehrān, Yazd and Esfahān, and is a good place to pick up a bus to these places. If you start really early you could even take a day trip to Kāshān from Tehrān.

The terminal for minibuses to Ghom is about 2km west of 15 Khordād Square – take a private taxi out there. At Valī-yé Asr Square, a few metres from the Ghom minibus terminal, check out what gets my vote as the most amazing modern sculpture of any square in Iran: a Mayan pyramid with a gushing waterfall.

Shared Taxis There are not many shared taxis going to anywhere of interest from Kāshān. You may be able to get to Esfahān or Ghom by shared taxi, but minibuses leave far more regularly. Shared taxis leave from outside the relevant minibus terminal; or check out what is leaving from around 15 Khordād Square.

Train There are three express trains a week (Tuesday, Thursday and Saturday) to Tehrān (5400/13,150 rials for 2nd/1st class), via Ghom. To Kermān, via Yazd, trains come by on Monday, Wednesday and Saturday (14,200/25,200 rials). Unfortunately, arrival and departure times are so haphazard (and usually in the middle of the night), that most travellers are forced to take a bus or minibus. The train station is in the inner north of Kāshān, within walking distance of the city centre.

Getting Around

Kāshān is small enough to walk around, but if you are feeling a little lazy, or you're in a hurry, you can hire a taxi for a reasonable 8000 rials per hour. This is especially useful for visiting the gardens at Fīn, and other attractions nearby.

AROUND KĀSHĀN
Ardehal
اردهال

About 40km west of Kāshān, there is a magnificent **Seljuq tomb** built for Alī Ibn Mohammed Baqar, on the slope of a hill with two courtyards and two balconies. The village of Ardehal is more famous for its annual carpet washing ceremony (see 'The Ceremony at Ardehal' boxed text below.)

Abyaneh
ابیانه

One of the more fascinating villages in the country has to be Abyaneh. Most of what remained intact from the ravages of time and invading armies dates to the Safavid period (1502-1722), and most of the inhabitants were Zoroastrians, but later converted to Islam. Although recognised for its antiquity and uniqueness by UNESCO, some travellers find this village less interesting than the magnificent old city of Yazd: Abyaneh is almost deserted because most inhabitants have gone to the big towns to look for work, so the village does lack character.

Serenely situated at the foot of Mt Karkas (3899m), Abyaneh is cool in summer, and frightfully cold for the rest of the year. The location of Abyaneh is fascinating in itself: the village faces the east for maximum sun and was built high to minimise the effects of floods and howling gales in winter; and the houses were built in a huddle to increase their security against frequent raids by marauders

and on the rocks rather than on valuable farm land. Most of the homes were built from mud-brick and clay; and like Māsūlé, near Rasht, many laneways, and the front yards of some homes, were built on top on the roofs of homes below.

As you wander around the village, try to look for the 14th-century **Emāmzādé-yé Yahya**, and the **Zeyaratgah shrine** with its tiny pool, and views of the village. Probably the most beautiful building is the 14th-century **Masjed-é Jāme'** with its mehrāb (made from walnut wood), and ancient carvings. On the top of the rocky hills are the remains of a couple of **castles**, known locally as *haman*.

You may need to ask directions to find the places listed above, but if you have time just wander around and you will stumble across most of them anyway. In the future, English-speaking guides may approach you – and using a guide is not a bad idea (for a tip of about 2000-3000 rials).

Getting There & Away There is nowhere to stay in Abyaneh, and nowhere to buy food or drink, so come prepared.

Abyanch is 71km from Kāshān, and not easy to reach. The cheapest way is to take a

---

The Ceremony at Ardehal

On 6 October every year, a bizarre carpet-washing ceremony *(ghali shuran)* is held at Ardehal. Started more than 1200 years ago, the ceremony commemorates the legend of a son of an Emām from Medina who lived in Ardehal. The Emām's son had a premonition in his sleep that a local governor planned to assassinate him. He and his supporters thwarted the initial assassination attempt, but the son was later killed while praying on a mat. His followers later placed his body on the carpet, and washed his body, in accordance with traditions at the time, before burying him.

On the anniversary of his murder, thousands of locals, joined by visitors from Kāshān, Ghom and as far away as Yazd, carry the same carpet (or rather what is left of it) from the shrine, beat the carpet to symbolise their hatred of the murderers, and then wash it in a local stream. ■

regular minibus from Kāshān towards Natanz (or any bus heading south from Kāshān), get off at the signed turn-off and then wait for another lift – you may even need to walk the 12km to Abyaneh from the turn-off.

Alternatively, chartering a taxi for a half-day from Kāshān should cost about 30,000 rials after some bargaining. Try to find a taxi driver who knows the village, and can help you find its main attractions. Chartering also allows you to stop along the way and admire the magnificent scenery.

Chahārmahāl va Bakhteyārī Province

استان چهارمحال وبختیاری

- **Capital:** Shahr-é Kord
- **Area:** 14,820 sq km
- **Population:** approx 900,000

This mountainous, and comparatively tiny, province was previously part of an even larger Esfahān province. When Isabella Bird travelled here in 1890, she described much of her route as previously unexplored (see *Journeys in Persia and Kurdistan*). She gave the picture of a wild and inhospitable terrain inhabited by fiercely independent and warlike tribespeople (principally Lors and Bakhteyārīs) governed by feudal chieftains.

There is very little reason for any modern-day traveller to visit this province, or even go through it. The province is only regularly linked by public transport with Esfahān.

SHAHR-É KORD
شهرکرد

Nestled in the mountains, this sleepy provincial capital has little to offer the tourist, or justify a detour. The major sight of interest is the **Masjed-é Atabakan**, which was undergoing extensive renovations at the time of research. And if you are really stuck for something to do, visit the **Natural History Museum** (☎ (0381) 235 72). It apparently contains plenty of stuffed animals and is

open from about 7 am to 2 pm every day (but I couldn't find it, and none of the locals knew much about it).

Places to Stay & Eat

The *Hotel Enghelab* is the cheapest option at about 25,000 rials a double, but it's sometimes reluctant to accept foreigners. The recognised tourist hotel is the ITTO's *Shahr-é Kord Inn* (☎ (0381) 248 92). They charge foreigners US$30 for a double, so try to get the Iranian rate of 25,000 rials. For those who want a little more comfort, for about US$25/45 a single/double, try the *Shahr-é Kord Azadi Hotel* (☎ (0381) 300 20). There are plenty of *kabābīs* and *hamburger joints* along the main street, but you are better off eating at a hotel.

Getting There & Away

Shahr-é Kord is really only linked by public transport with nearby Esfahān. About every hour, minibuses (1200 rials) and shared taxis (5000 rials) travel between the Zāyandé Rūd minibus terminal in Esfahān and the terminal in Shahr-é Kord, about 3km out on the Esfahān side of the town centre. Shahr-é Kord is close enough to be a day trip from Esfahān, but there is more enough in Esfahān itself to keep you busy.

Yazd Province
استان یزد

- **Capital:** Yazd
- **Area:** 72,342 sq km
- **Population:** approx 830,000

Bordered by the great landmasses of Khorāsān, Kermān, Fārs and Esfahān provinces, Yazd province is almost unrelieved desert except for the provincial centre of Yazd city, and a few other towns nearby. To relieve the monotony, there are a few mountains in the south, such as Mt Sīr (4074m), which is covered with snow all year. Water flowing from these mountains, and vast irrigation schemes involving more than 2500

CENTRAL IRAN

ghanāts which draw water from underground springs (see the boxed text 'The Ghanāt' in the Facts about Iran chapter), have brought some of the desert to life, so fruits and cotton can be grown.

To make the most of the occasional floating breeze in summer, Yazd province is famous for its *bādgīrs*, or wind-towers. The province and city of Yazd, which means 'to feast and worship' in ancient Persian, is also the centre for the Zoroastrian faith (see the boxed text 'Zoroastrianism' on page 214).

YAZD یزد

Midway between Esfahān and Kermān, Yazd is a particularly relaxed, tree-lined town (population: 320,000), with enough sights to justify at least a couple of days – the town is also surprisingly good value. Wedged between the northern Dasht-é Kavīr desert, and the southern Dasht-é Lūt, Yazd boasts the best old – and inhabited – city in Iran.

At an altitude of 1230m, Yazd can be quite cold in winter, but very hot in summer. Yazd was an important centre for pre-Islamic Zoroastrianism, and there is still a substantial minority of Zoroastrians today. The city has always been a great weaving centre, known for its silks and other fabrics even before Marco Polo passed through along one of the Silk Roads in the late 13th century.

History

Although Yazd dates from Sassanian times (224-637), its history is fairly undistinguished. It was conquered by the Arabs in about 642, and subsequently became an important station on the caravan routes to Central Asia and India, exporting its silks, textiles and carpets far and wide. It was spared destruction by Chinggis Khaan (Genghis Khan) and Timur (during the Timurid dynasty from 1380 to 1502), and flourished in the 14th and 15th centuries, yet its commercial success and stability were never translated into political status. Like most of Iran, the town fell into decline after the end of the Safavid era (1502-1722), and remained little more than a provincial outpost until the extension of the railway line to Yazd under the last shāh.

Orientation

The centre of Yazd is Beheshtī Square (sometimes still known by its old name of Mojāhedīn Square). If you stay within walking distance of this square, most sights and restaurants can be visited on foot. When walking around the old city, expect to get hopelessly lost – just ask for directions when you want to get out.

Maps The free *Tourist Map of Yazd Province*, published by the Ministry of Culture & Islamic Guidance, should be available from the tourist office in Yazd (if or when it is open), but it's fairly useless for anyone who doesn't understand Fārsī. The familiar red map (1500 rials) produced by Gita Shenasi is dated, and everything you need to know (except the street names) is in Fārsī. The map in this guidebook is all you need anyway.

Information

Visa Extensions For visa extensions, visit the large, unsigned and heavily guarded building directly opposite the entrance to the bus terminal. It is open from 8 am to 2 pm, Saturday to Wednesday. If you have any problems, ask for assistance from your hotel – the Aria Hotel claims to be able to help its guests. Otherwise, it's easier to get an extension in Kermān or Esfahān.

Tourist Office The new tourist office (☎ 350 77) is in the middle of the old city, a few metres from Alexander's Prison. Unfortunately, I can't tell you much about the office: I visited it three times, and rang it several more times, but no-one was there. If you think a visit there is worthwhile, head up Sayyed Gol-é Sorkh St, turn east (right) down a lane which starts opposite a telephone booth (the only one on the street), and keep walking.

Money You can change money upstairs at the central branch of Bank Melli. To change money at the favourable 'street rate', and in a safe location, change your US dollars at Amin Money Exchange.

Post & Communications The main post office is right next to the Bank Melli, and sells a fascinating selection of commemorative stamps which may interest philatelists. The main telephone office on Motahharī St is a little inconvenient, but there's a handy telephone office just north of Āzādī Square. The telephone area code for Yazd is 0351.

Travel Agencies The Yazd Gasht Travel Agency can organise English-speaking

guides to show you around town for a very reasonable US$2/3 (or the rial equivalent) for a half-day/full-day tour. Inquire at the Aria Hotel (see Places to Stay later).

One of the best agencies in the country is the Saadat Seyr Travel Agency (☎ 660 693; fax 666 599). The staff speak English, and can organise train tickets from Yazd up to one month in advance.

Bookshops The Jahaferī Bookshop offers an amazing range of maps for most major cities in the country, including Yazd. The shop in the foyer of the Hotel Safā'iyé has a

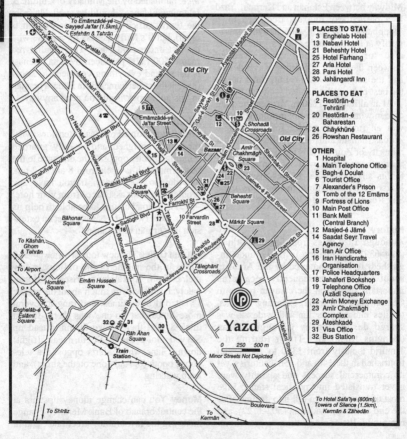

PLACES TO STAY
3 Enghelab Hotel
13 Nabavi Hotel
21 Beheshty Hotel
25 Hotel Farhang
27 Aria Hotel
28 Pars Hotel
30 Jahāngardī Inn

PLACES TO EAT
2 Restōrān-e Tehrānī
20 Restōrān-e Baharestan
24 Chāykhūné
26 Rowshan Restaurant

OTHER
1 Hospital
4 Main Telephone Office
5 Bagh-é Doulat
6 Tourist Office
7 Alexander's Prison
8 Tomb of the 12 Emāms
9 Fortress of Lions
10 Main Post Office
11 Bank Melli (Central Branch)
12 Masjed-é Jāmé
14 Saadat Seyr Travel Agency
15 Iran Air Office
16 Iran Handicrafts Organisation
17 Police Headquarters
18 Jahaferī Bookshop
19 Telephone Office (Āzādī Square)
22 Amin Money Exchange
23 Amīr Chakmāgh Complex
29 Āteshkadé
31 Visa Office
32 Bus Station

Yazd

0   250   500 m

Minor Streets Not Depicted

To Hotel Safa'iyé (800m),
Towers of Silence (1.5km),
Kermān & Zāhedān

small, but pricey, collection of interesting English-language books, maps and handicrafts.

Emergency For general emergencies dial the directories number (☎ 118), or for anything medical (☎ 495 50). The main hospital (☎ 431 35) is in the far north-western part of the city; and the police headquarters (☎ 402 20) is on Āzādī Square.

Old City
According to UNESCO, Yazd is one of the oldest towns in the world – every visitor should spend a few hours getting completely lost in this living museum. Look out for the tall wind-towers, or *bādgīrs*, on rooftops, designed to catch even the lightest breeze and direct them to underground living rooms. In the hot summers they are very necessary, and more healthy than modern air-conditioning.

The adobe architecture here is of great interest, though it takes some time to explore and appreciate it. The building styles are simple, traditional and quite exotic compared with the uniformity of most of the other large towns of Iran. The town is the colour of clay, from the sun-dried bricks. The residential quarters appear almost deserted (but they aren't) because of the high walls, protecting the houses from the very narrow and labyrinthine *kūchés* (alleys) crisscrossing the town.

Towers of Silence
If you are hankering after a bit of fresh air, and enjoy a short climb, head out to these Zoroastrian sites, built on two small hills. Among these Towers of Silence, you may see the odd broken human bone, where in the past the dead were exposed to the attentions of vultures.

At the foot of the hills there are several other disused Zoroastrian buildings including a defunct well, two small *bādgīrs*, an *ashpāzkhūné* (kitchen) and a lavatory. Some surveying at the time of research indicates either the construction of a hamburger stall, or some renovations (hopefully the latter). It

is quite likely that the area will be eventually fenced off, and an entrance fee will be requested.

To get there, take a shared taxi to Abazar Square, about 3km south of Mārkār Square, and then another shared taxi, or bus, past two more squares along the road to the south. Then you will have to walk about 2.5km – the towers are easy to spot from the main road. Alternatively, charter a private taxi for about 5000 rials return, including waiting time.

Āteshkadé
This small Zoroastrian temple attracts followers from around the world. The sacred flame behind a glass case visible from the small **museum** inside has apparently been burning since about 470 AD, and was transferred from its original site in 1940. If you ask nicely, there may be someone who speaks English and can explain things to you, otherwise it's all a bit incomprehensible to most visitors. There is a small garden, and a couple of paintings, including one of Zoroaster, but nothing much else to see.

Enter from a small gate along an alleyway to the west. The Āteshkadé is opposite what is currently a huge hole in the ground, but what promises to be the upmarket *Isatis Hotel* in a few years. Entrance is free, but a donation (say, about 1000 rials) is welcome. It is open every day from 7 am to noon, and 4 to 7 pm.

Fortress of Lions
In the north-east of Yazd, another Zoroastrian building, the **Ghal'é-yé Asadān**, (Fortress of Lions) houses a Zoroastrian eternal flame moved there some 20 years ago. It is often closed, however, but if you are interested, ask someone at the Āteshkadé to let you in, or ask when the fortress is open to the public.

Alexander's Prison
Allegedly built by Alexander the Great, this prison was renowned throughout the region; even the poet Hāfez wrote from Shīrāz about the prison's less than salubrious conditions.

Now renovated, the prison is mildly interesting, but not a must. The small **display** of the old city of Yazd is probably just as interesting as the prison itself.

Entrance costs 5000 rials. It is signed in English, next to a garden in the old city, and a few metres from the tourist office. Refer to the Tourist Office section earlier for tips about how to find the prison.

Tomb of the 12 Emāms

This early 11th century tomb is almost next door to Alexander's Prison. It has fine inscriptions inside, with the names of each of the Shi'ite emāms, none of whom is buried here. Although the mausoleum is small, dusty and almost forgotten, it is nonetheless a well preserved building from the Seljuq period (1051-1220).

The mausoleum is often closed, so ask around or at the tourist office nearby (if the tourist office itself is open, of course). Refer to the Tourist Office section earlier for tips on how to find the mausoleum.

Masjed-é Jāme'

Even if you are all 'mosqued out', have a look at this magnificent building, constructed under the direction of Bibi Fatema Khatoun, the redoubtable wife of a former governor of Yazd, Amīr Chakhmāgh. This well preserved 14th-century mosque was built on the site of a 12th-century building (which was converted from an earlier fire-temple, no doubt without the Zoroastrians' permission).

This mosque dominates the old city, with its remarkably high, tiled entrance portal, flanked with two magnificent minarets and adorned with an inscription from the 15th century. The beautiful mosaics on the dome and on the mehrāb are also superb. The interior of the mosque is cleverly ventilated and well lit. In the courtyard of the mosque there is a narrow stairwell leading down to a disused ghanāt.

If you slip the caretaker about 1000 rials (like other Iranians do), he will allow you to climb the stairs above the entrance for great views of the old city. Otherwise, entrance is free.

Amīr Chakhmāgh Complex

Also designed by the wife of Amīr Chakhmāgh, this small set of buildings contains a small, decaying **bazaar** and the crumbling **Masjed-é Takyeh**. At the entrance from Amīr Chakhmāgh Square, look out for the huge, round and wooden *palm nakhl*, an important piece of stage

---

Zoroastrianism

Zoroastrianism was the main religion across the Iranian plateau until the Arab Conquest brought Islam to the people. Zoroastrians are followers of Zoroaster (Zartosht), who was probably born about 550 BC at Mazar-é Sharif in what is now Afghanistan (though several places in present day Iran also claim the honour). Zoroastrianism was one of the first religions to postulate an omnipotent, invisible god. They worship fire as a symbol of God, and keep 'eternally' burning flames at their temples.

Since Zoroastrians believe in the purity of the elements, they refused to bury their dead (because it pollutes the earth) or cremate them (because it pollutes the atmosphere). Instead the dead were exposed on 'towers of silence', where they were soon cleaned off by the vultures – but this practice is rarely undertaken these days. Instead, deceased Zoroastrians are nowadays often buried in graves lined with concrete, to prevent 'contamination' of the earth.

The Zoroastrian men aren't easily distinguished from Muslims, though they tend to be close-shaven, but the Zoroastrian women can be recognised by their patterned headscarves and embroidered dresses with white, cream or red as the predominant colours. They never wear chādors, but they must follow the strict hejāb laws, nevertheless.

Of the 150,000 or more Zoroastrians in the world, an estimated 30,000 still live in, and around, Yazd city. Today the religion is going through a period of updating and readjustment as strict regulations on marriage have resulted in a great decline in the numbers of adherents. ■

equipment in the nighbourhood productions of the traditional passion play. (See under Arts in the Facts about Iran chapter for more details.)

Bāgh-é Doulat

This mildly interesting residence of the former ruler, Karīm Khān Zand, was built in about 1750. It is renowned for having the highest bādgīr in the old city, standing more than 33m high. The stained glass windows are also a delight.

Entrance is 3000 rials, though it's not clear if entrance is normally free and the 3000 rials goes into the pocket of the gatekeeper. The building and gardens were undergoing renovation at the time of research. You are not allowed to walk among the orchards, though you many not know because the warning signs are in Fārsī. It is open every day from about 8 am to 5 pm, though it may be closed in the middle of the day if the gatekeeper fancies a siesta.

Emāmzādé-yé Sayyed Ja'far

This shrine is decorated inside with tens of thousands of modern mirror tiles of various colours illuminating the whole mosque. It is still undergoing extensive renovations, but worth a visit for the lovely gardens and the exquisite mosaics. The shrine is on the left-hand side of the road, about 1.5km further on from the hospital. Entrance is free, and it's open every day, during daylight hours.

Places to Stay

Should you find that all the hotels and mosāferkhūnés in town are full, there is a heated waiting-room at the bus terminal where you can attempt to sleep the night in the company of dozens of poor Iranians. Most hotels are signed in English, unless stated otherwise. Try to get a room away from a busy road, at one of the hotels in the centre of town.

Places to Stay – budget

There are a couple of real dives for about 6000/8000 rials a single/double around the southern part of Mārkār Square, but it's worth paying a little extra for some security, cleanliness and a peaceful night.

The place which most budget-minded travellers head to is the *Aria Hotel* (☎ 304 11), a few metres back from the main road (and easy to miss). Simple rooms (and some are a bit grubby), with a private shower but a shared toilet, cost 15,000 rials per person. (One traveller I met later wasn't complimentary about the Aria: the roof of his room crashed in on him during the night.)

Nearby, the *Beheshty Hotel* (☎ 247 17) continues to get mixed reviews. One traveller wrote to say that she only got 'a mattress on a concrete floor', though the rooms (for a negotiable 20,000/30,000 rials for a double/triple) that I saw were quite reasonable. Staff speak some English. It's a few metres from the main road, so it's also easy to miss. Another good cheap hotel is the *Pars Hotel* (☎ 627 24), as long as you can stand endless traffic noise. A bright, airy and clean single/double/triple costs 14,000/17,000/21,000 rials.

Places to Stay – middle & top end

The *Hotel Farhang* (☎ 665 012) used to be a favourite among travellers, but is now overpriced at 60,000 rials, though the reasonable rooms, with a private bathroom, do include three single beds. It is not signed in English, and is on a busy road. The entrance is just along a laneway off Emām Khomeinī St.

The *Nabavi Hotel* (☎ 612 89) is central, and charges US$25 per double, but the manager does accept rials. The rooms are huge, and contain three beds, a fridge, sitting room and dining table – it's ideal for a small group or family. Other places to try are the excellent *Hotel Safā'iyé* (☎ 498 11), great value at the Iranian price of 52,000 rials per double, but overpriced for foreigners at about US$40; the inconvenient, but comfortable and popular *Jahāngardī Inn* (☎ 324 39), run by the ITTO for US$25/35 a single/double; and the inconvenient *Enghelab Hotel* (☎ 561 11), for US$35/45, and not quite as luxurious as it appears from the outside.

Places to Eat

Yazd is not blessed with a great choice of places for a feed. If you are staying at a hotel in the suburbs, you will probably be obliged to eat dinner at the hotel restaurant to avoid going out far in the evening. If you have a sweet tooth, try some of the *pashmak* sweets, renowned in Yazd and available in many shops around Beheshtī Square.

Beheshtī Square is crowded with dozens of places selling Iranian-style hamburgers, and kebabs (of course). If you are staying around here, try the *Rowshan Resturent* (sic), which can dish up a half-decent jūjé kabāb, a limp salad and a cold drink for 8000 rials. Better is the *Restōrān-é Baharestan*. Though not marked in English, the friendly manager speaks good English, and the kabāb-é kūbīdé, plus tomatoes, bread and cola for 3500 rials is excellent value.

For a tasty cooked breakfast, a pot of tea and an inhalation or two on the hubble-bubble, head straight for the unnamed *chāykhūné*, near the Hotel Farhang. It's not signed in English, but it is recognisable by, of all things, a picture of Donald Duck enjoying the hubble-bubble.

For something a bit better, the bright and large *Restōrān-é Tehrānī* is recommended. It is a little pricey, and not particularly convenient, but one reader did claim it as the 'best restaurant in Iran'. The restaurant is unsigned in English, but the menu is in 'Fārsglish', with such delights as 'specific fiah' (fish with rice) for 9500 rials. I was not game to try the unimaginable 'stoe and rice' or the 'lowl and rice'.

Lastly, the topnotch place in town is the restaurant at the *Hotel Safā'iyé*, where one reader stated that the 'māst with garlic was a dream'. Prices are not as high as you may expect – about 12,000 rials for a two-course meal, including drinks – and the service and setting is excellent.

Things to Buy

The many bazaars in the old city, and the Iran Handicrafts Organisation, are probably the best places in Iran to buy silk, known locally as *tirma*, brocades, glassware and cloth –

products which brought the town its prosperity in centuries gone by. Finding the best places to buy these goods in the old city is a nightmare, so keep walking until you find a decent shop, or take an Iranian friend with you. Almost everything in Yazd is cheaper than elsewhere is Iran, so you may want to stock up on a few souvenirs.

Getting There & Away

Air Yazd is only linked with a few places. Iran Air (☎ 283 79) flies to Bandar-é Abbās on Thursday and Sunday (57,500 rials); to Mashhad, also on Thursday and Sunday (61,000 rials); to Tehrān, several times a day (49,000 rials); and, finally, to Shīrāz (49,000 rials) on Saturday.

Flights on Iran Asseman seem to have been postponed indefinitely, but daily flights to Tehrān on Asseman may recommence sometime in the future for the same prices as Iran Air.

Bus & Minibus Many bus companies have offices along Emām Khomeinī St; most do not have signs in English, so look for an office with one man, one desk and one phone, and, maybe, a few customers. All buses leave from the main bus terminal, accessible by shared taxi from Beheshtī and Āzādī squares, or by bus No 27 from Beheshtī Square.

Among other places, buses leave Yazd for these cities at least several times a day (prices are in rials for lux/super):

Destination	Distance	Time	Cost (rials)
Ahvāz	1008km	20 hours	11,500/16,700
Bam	581km	9 hours	6900/7800
(or catch anything going to Zāhedān)			
Bandar-é Abbās	671km	11 hours	6950/10,750
Esfahān	316km	6 hours	3500/4000
Kermān	387km	6 hours	3800/4200
Kermānshāh	1081km	16 hours	13,100/14,500
Mashhad	939km	16 hours	11,100/13,250
Sanandaj	968km	16 hours	14,270/15,590
Shīrāz	440km	7 hours	5300/5800
Tabas	419km	8 hours	7000 (lux only)
Tehrān	677km	10 hours	6300/7400
Zāhedān	928km	14 hours	10,500/11,000

Train Like most places in central Iran, the trains to and from Yazd are so infrequent (compared to buses), and the departure times are so lousy, that they're only of interest to train buffs. There are two trains from Yazd to Tehrān (7800/18,150 rials for 2nd/1st class) on each of three different days: Tuesday, Thursday and Saturday. (A short-cut, built at a staggering 235 billion rials, will shorten the trip between Yazd and Tehrān by about 100km.) To Kermān, (5000/10,000 rials) one train comes by from Tehrān, also on Tuesday, Thursday and Saturday. There are no direct trains from Yazd to Esfahān.

The train station (☎ 559 50) is next to the main bus terminal. Get there by a shared taxi from Beheshtī or Āzādī squares, or on bus No 27 from Beheshtī Square. Easily the best place to purchase your train ticket, up to one month in advance, is the Saadat Seyr Travel Agency (see under Travel Agencies earlier).

Shared Taxi Yazd is so remote, that shared taxis are rarely used as a means of getting to Yazd, though you can always hire one to take you to places of interest nearby (see Around Yazd below).

Getting Around

To/From the Airport There is no airport bus service, so you must take a shared taxi from Enghelāb-é Eslāmī Square for about 1000 rials, or a private taxi to/from your hotel for about 5000 rials.

Bus Yazd is small enough to walk around, and shared taxis are cheap, so local buses are not really worth considering. There is one useful bus – No 27 – between Beheshtī Square, and the bus and train terminals, and the visa office.

Taxi Taxi fares, like most things in Yazd, are cheap; probably the cheapest in Iran, so save your leg muscles, and catch a cab. The standard fare in a shared taxi anywhere around town is currently 250 rials (but check the current price when you get to Yazd). Even for private taxis, the fare is between 1000 and

2000 rials around town, and as far as the bus and train terminals.

AROUND YAZD

Taft تفت

Only 18km south-west of Yazd, and under the looming Mt Sīr, Taft is cooler than Yazd, and worth a quick look around, if you have time. Huge pomegranates are the staple agricultural product. The ghanāts provide water for some pretty gardens, and there's also a few **mosques** of interest to those who can't get enough of them. Take a minibus or shared taxi from inside the main bus terminal in Yazd.

Ardakān اردکان

In the middle of the desert, about 60km north-west of Yazd, Ardakān is a regional agricultural centre, courtesy of the amazing ghanāt irrigation system, and famous for its camels. Ardakān's desert setting, rather than any buildings, is worth a half-day trip from Yazd, but the town does have the requisite **Masjed-é Jāme'**, as well as a few Zoroastrian sites, but nothing as grand as those in Yazd.

You could stay at the overpriced ITTO *Jahāngardī Inn* (☎ (03542) 6969) for about US$25/35, but it's better to make a day trip from Yazd. To get there, take a minibus, or any bus heading north-west along the main highway, from the main bus terminal in Yazd.

Chak Chak چك چك

This important Zoroastrian fire-temple is on a hill about 50km to the north-west of Yazd. It attracts thousands of pilgrims for an annual festival which lasts for 10 days from the beginning of the third month after the Iranian New Year, Nō Rūz (about 21 March).

If you want to visit the temple, it's best to get the permission of the authorities at the Āteshkadé in Yazd city first. The return trip by private taxi, along a difficult stretch of road off the main route to Tabas, will cost around 25,000 rials, including waiting time. There is no public transport.

Semnān Province

استان سمنان

- **Capital:** Semnān
- **Area:** 91,538 sq km
- **Population:** approx 550,000

This large province, once known as Kūmesh, forms part of the commercially vital link between the central plateau and Khorāsān province, and then to Central Asia. Most of it is rendered almost entirely uninhabitable by the encroaching Dasht-é Kavīr desert, except for the settlements lying along the Tehrān to Mashhad road, to the south of the Alborz Mountains. The climate is hot and dry in the south, while milder and cooler in the north and east.

The province is famous for growing some of the best pistachios in Iran, as well producing pottery, carpets, and other textiles. Many Semnānīs speak one of a variety of dialects, such as Semnānī, Sorkheī and Sharmirzadī.

SEMNĀN   سمنان

An ancient town probably dating back to the Sassanian period (224-637), Semnān lies on the northern edge of the Dasht-é Kavīr, and owes its origins and mixed fortunes to its place on the historic trading route between Tehrān and Mashhad. The town has been occupied by a long succession of invaders, including the Mongols and the Timurids, neither of whom did anything to enhance it. The attractive older part of Semnān city hasn't been modernised too much and there are still a few interesting historic buildings.

Orientation & Information

Most points of interest are in, or near, the central bazaar. The main east-west street, Emām St, is an extension of the road from Tehrān and goes past the bazaar, while the north-south Ghods St joins the road to Mashhad.

The police headquarters, where you could try for a visa extension (but they will probably tell you to go to Tehrān), is on the corner of Tāleghānī and Shohadā Sts; the Bank Melli is along Emām St, just east of the bazaar; and the telephone and post offices are north of the bazaar, along Tāleghānī St. The telephone area code for Semnān is 02231.

Masjed-é Jāme'

The present structure of the Friday Mosque (which was closed at the time of research) dates from 1424, and has an impressive entrance portal and some interesting stucco around its mehrāb. The magnificent 21m brick minaret dominates the town. It probably dates from the 11th century, and has a charming octagonal balcony with a inscription slightly below it. The mosque is in the bazaar.

Masjed-é Emām Khomeinī

Founded under Fath Alī Shāh in the 1820s, this mosque (also undergoing renovations at the time of research) is one of the best surviving buildings in Iran from this period (see the boxed text on the next page). It has a very fine tiled mehrāb with stalactites. The high entrance portal is also very attractive; in the same clay colour as the whole of the old city, it has the ribs of its stalactites delicately picked out in contrasting colour, while there are some understated geometric motifs and inscriptions on the façade. It is about 200m east of the Masjed-é Jāme'.

Places to Stay & Eat

Easily the best place to head for is the friendly and central *Hotel Kormesh*, next to the park on Emām Square. Rooms without/with a bathroom cost a bargain 10,000/15,000 rials. Other alternatives are inconvenient and costly: the *Hotel Ghods* (☎ 22 177), on the road to Dāmghān, costs US$20/30 for a single/double; and the ITTO-run *Jahāngardī Inn* (☎ 27028), which is on Shāhmirzād St, costs the same.

Besides the usual *kabābīs* and uninspiring hamburger joints, the best restaurant in town is the *Mohel Restaurant* – but it doesn't open for dinner until 8.30 pm. There is a small sign in English above the door – or look for the

The Ghajar Period of Architecture
The style from the Ghajar period (1779-1921) marks the rather unhappy transition between the golden age of Persian architecture (culminating under the Safavid dynasty, 1502-1722), and the creeping introduction of western-inspired uniformity from the mid-19th century onwards. Now widely regarded as tasteless, flimsy and uninspired, the equivalent of icing-sugar sculptures on a wedding cake, the Ghajar style did nevertheless produce a few fine buildings, including the Emām Khomeinī mosque in Semnān, and the Eram Palace in Shīrāz. Almost no structures of great beauty were built in Iran after this period. ■

picture of a steaming chelō kebāb – at the entrance to the Emām Khomeinī mosque.

Getting There & Away
Bus Buses go every day to Tehrān (4500/5000 rials for lux/super class) from the main bus terminal, about 3km west of the bazaar; take a shared taxi from Motahharī Square. To Mashhad, and anywhere east of Semnān, it's best to hail down any bus heading your way along the main road outside the terminal.

Minibuses are the normal form of regional transport. They go to Dāmghān about every hour (1200 rials) and to Shāhrūd (2000 rials) every one to two hours. The minibus terminal is on the corner of Ghods and Haft-é Tīr streets, about 1.5km north of the bazaar.

Train Semnān is on the line between Tehrān (2000/4000 rials for 2nd/1st class) and Mashhad (7500/15,500 rials). However, most trains leave in the middle of the night, and tickets are very hard to buy, so take the bus or minibus. The train station is 1.5km south of Emām Square.

DĀMGHĀN دامغان
This sleepy (almost comatose) and historic town, settled at least since the 8th century, contains what may be the oldest surviving mosque in Iran. There are also several interesting and ancient minarets and tomb-towers

in Dāmghān, similar to those built in Māzandarān province, across the Alborz mountains to the north.

Things to See
Dating from about 760 AD, the **Masjed-é Tārīkhūné** is a small four-eivān mosque with an square inner courtyard, and a towering 25m circular minaret. It is about 500m to the south-east of the main square, Emām Khomeinī Square, but is currently closed, and heavily padlocked, with no obvious signs of renovation or re-opening.

The only remaining feature of the long-vanished **Manār-é Masjed-é Jāme'** mosque is the minaret, probably dating from the mid-11th century. To get there, turn left outside the Tārīkhūné mosque and walk straight ahead for 300m, cross the road and turn into Kūché-yé Masjed.

The round **Ārāmgāh-é Pīr Alamdār** tower, 100m north of the Masjed-é Jāme', dates from 1026. It was originally domed, and is remarkable for its innovative use of brick patterns, and its inscription, visible beneath the roof level.

Places to Stay & Eat
The *Dāmghān Inn* (☎ (02233) 2070) is run by the ITTO and next to a pretty park, along Āzādī Blvd. The hotel is built to resemble a caravanserai, though the rooms are not as interesting as the exterior suggests. The rate is a ridiculous US$30 per room, and the staff couldn't care less if you stayed there, so they aren't open to negotiation.

Better value – if it is open – is the *Babak Hotel* (☎ (02233) 4164), situated on Emām Khomeinī St, for about 15,000/20,000 rials for a single/double – but bargain. The best places to eat are the hotel restaurants.

Getting There & Away
Dāmghān is an easy day trip from the nicer town of Shāhrūd on the hourly minibus, or a little further by minibus every hour from Semnān. From Shāhrūd, get off the minibus at Emām Khomeinī Square in the centre of town, rather than the distant minibus terminal. But *from* Dāmghān, you'll have to get a

private taxi to the minibus terminal. Long-distance buses often bypass Dāmghān, so you may need to get a connection in Shāhrūd or Semnān.

Dāmghān is on the Tehrān-Mashhad train line, but departures are unreliable and tickets hard to get, so take the minibus. The train station is about 2km south-east of Emām Khomeinī Square.

SHĀHRŪD شاهرود

Shāhrūd is a pleasant and manageable town which makes an ideal place to break up the *long* overland journey between Tehrān and Mashhad, or as an alternative way to or from Gorgān. Shāhrūd is also the obvious place from which to visit the pretty village of Bastām (following).

The main road through town is 22 Bahman St, which stretches from the bus terminal in the south to the turn off to Bastām and Mashhad in the north of the town.

Places to Stay & Eat

The best place to stay is the *Hotel Reza* (☎ 265 25), at the northern end of 22 Bahman St. A good room, with a large bathroom, costs 40,000 rials a double, as long as you negotiate a little. The best of the cheaper places is the friendly *New Islami Hotel*, set back a little from Jomhūrī-yé Eslāmī Square. Rooms cost 13,500 rials.

The Reza has a decent *restaurant* – open for lunch and dinner (but not until 8.30 pm). A good chelō morgh cost 6500 rials. There are also a few surprisingly good restaurants – not just the ordinary old kabābī – north along 22 Bahman St, such as the *Kohpayeh Restaurant*. There are a few decent *snack bars* and *cake shops* around Jomhūrī-yé Eslāmī and Emām squares.

Getting There & Away

Bus & Minibus There are several direct buses a day to Gorgān (3600/3900 rials for lux/super class), to Mashhad (8900/10,500 rials) and to Tehrān (4700/5000 rials). However, to places to the west, and to Gorgān, it's easier to stand at the roundabout, about 500m north of Hotel Reza, and jump on whatever is going your way. The trip to Gorgān is magnificent: one of the most interesting, short (four hours) trips in the country – barren desert and steppe turns into fertile plains, before you cross the Shāh mountains.

From the main bus terminal, about 5km south of Jomhūrī-yé Eslāmī Square, there are also hourly minibuses to Dāmghān (700 rials), and to Semnān every one to two hours (2000 rials).

Train Shāhrūd is on the line between Tehrān and Mashhad, but everyone uses the quicker and more reliable bus or minibus. The train station is about 3km south-east of Jomhūrī-yé Eslāmī Square, and like everywhere on this line, tickets are hard to get.

BASTĀM بسطام

The pretty tree-lined village of Bastām is certainly worth a look if you are in this part of the country. The beautiful **mosque** was possibly started in the 11th century, while the main part which you can see today was built during the Seljuq period of the early 13th century. It is decorated with some wonderful swirling stucco reliefs, especially in the mehrāb, and belongs to a large monastery complex, the Sōme'é-yé Bāyazīd, which has several other interesting Mongol structures, including a delightful circular **tomb-tower**.

Foreigners are welcome to look around, and enter the mosque if shoes are removed. It is open every day during daylight hours, except Friday morning. Entrance is free.

Getting There & Away

Bastām is about 7km north of Shāhrūd, just off the main road to Gorgān. By private taxi, pay about 5000 rials return, including waiting time. Alternatively, there are regular (crowded) minibuses travel between Emām Square in Shāhrūd and the mosque every hour or so. Even better is to walk at least one-way from Shāhrūd. From the square with the huge, bizarre, concrete sunflower, at the top of 22 Bahman St, follow the signs to Bastām. However, it's probably easier to find your way back on foot from Bastām to Shāhrūd.

Eastern Iran

ایران شرقی

With the qualified exception of Mashhad, you should not expect the highest standards of accommodation, restaurants or communications in this part of Iran. The east and south-east are very different from central Iran, less developed certainly but also steeped in archaeological and historical interest. If you have just arrived from the Indian subcontinent, eastern Iran will be a gentle introduction to Iranian culture; but if all your travelling has been spent in the rest of Iran, be prepared for something rather different.

The perennial civil war across the border in Afghanistan, and the smuggling of drugs and other illegal goods through Iran from Afghanistan and Pakistan, creates a certain amount of tension in many places in eastern Iran. You should be very careful when travelling overland near the Afghan border. It's wise to only cross the Pakistani border at Mīrjāvé, near Zāhedān.

Throughout this part of Iran, look for *bādgīrs*, the wind-towers designed to catch and circulate the merest breath of wind. In many places they are an essential architectural adaptation to the harsh and arid climate.

EASTERN IRAN AT A GLANCE

- **Provinces:** Khorāsān, Sīstān va Balūchestān & Kermān
- **When to Go:** Winters are cold in the north; summer is always hot and dry everywhere. April to May and late September to early November are the best times.
- **Highlights:** Old city of Bam; bazaars and mosques of Kermān; the Holy Shrine of Emām Rezā in Mashhad.

Khorāsān Province

استان خراسان

- **Capital:** Mashhad
- **Area:** 313,335 sq km
- **Population:** approx 7.2 million

Khorāsān means 'Where the Sun Rises' – and Khorāsān is as far east as you can go without leaving Iran. This immense province, the largest (at the moment) in Iran, takes in the corridor between the Caspian Sea and the salt wastes of the Dasht-é Kavīr desert. Until this century, much of the population of the south and east of the province was nomadic. Ancient Khorāsān, which once included parts of Afghanistan, Turkmenistan and Uzbekistan, was mostly destroyed by the rampaging Mongols, and earthquakes have destroyed much of what the Mongols left behind. And in mid-1997, there was another massive earthquake (see 'The Earthquake of 1997' boxed text on page 223).

Although a lot of Khorāsān is mountainous, there are many fertile valleys, and the province produces large quantities of fruit, nuts, sugar beet and cotton. Until fairly recently, opium was also an important crop. Most of the province is uninhabited, and uninhabitable, wasteland, so the highlight for most visitors, especially Shi'ite pilgrims who flock to Mashhad in their millions each year, is the magnificent Holy Shrine of Emām Rezā.

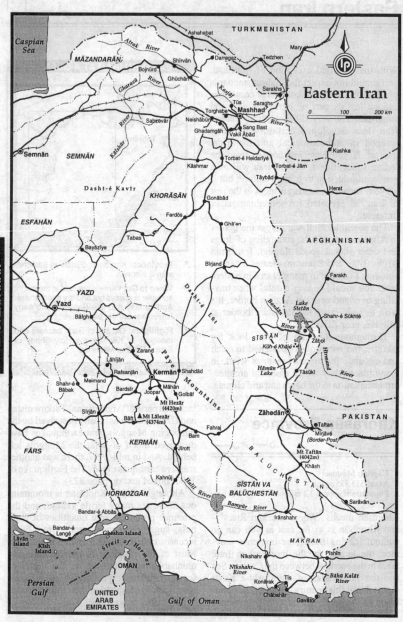

EASTERN IRAN

Khorāsān: Cut into Pieces?

At the time of research, the Majlis (parliament) approved a bill to split the huge province of Khorāsān into three or five separate provinces, because of the religious and ethnic differences among peoples in different parts of the province, and to help develop the vast area. The boundaries of the new provinces are currently unknown, but they are likely to be known as Eastern Khorāsān, Northern Khorāsān, and so on. This break-up of Khorāsān won't affect travel to this part of Iran, but take note that for a while most maps of Iran will be out of date. ∎

MASHHAD   مشهد

Mashhad literally means the Place of Martyrdom (or the Place of Burial of a Martyr). The city is extremely sacred to Shi'ites as the place where the eighth grandson of the Prophet Mohammed, Emām Rezā, died in 817. The story spread that Emām Rezā had been poisoned, so his tomb became a major Shi'ite pilgrimage site. What had been a small village by the name of Sanābād grew to become a large city, and the most important pilgrimage centre in Iran.

The population of Mashhad ballooned to more than four million during the Iran-Iraq War, simply because it was the furthest Iran city from the Iraqi border. Many remained, and the city has become huge (population: approximately 2.1 million) and unwieldy if you dare venture into the suburbs. Mashhad can get very cold in winter and there is often snow on the ground for four or five months of the year.

Around the Iranian New Year (about 21 March), and the height of the pilgrimage season (about mid-June to late July) Mashhad bursts. According to official reports, more than 12 million pilgrims visit Mashhad each year (though this seems a little hard to believe). There is little in the city to detain you longer than it takes to visit the Holy Shrine, though there are a few attractions near Mashhad, and the city is a natural staging post if you're travelling to or from Turkmenistan.

History

Mashhad grew around the legend of Emām Rezā, and the city's history is inextricably linked with that of his shrine. According to popular belief, Rezā, heir to the Abbasid caliphate and eighth of the Shi'ite emāms, died in what was then the village of Sanābād in 817 after eating some grapes. The story spread, without any apparent evidence, that he had been poisoned on the orders of the Caliph Ma'mūn after having, in some way, aroused his resentment. Whatever the truth, Ma'mūn buried him in a tower in Sanābād next to the tomb of his own father, the famous Hārūn-ar-Rashīd, and in time this burial place began to attract Shi'ite pilgrims. What had been a small village around the shrine grew into a small town, later known as Mashhad, but for many centuries it remained a pilgrimage centre of only regional importance.

In 944 the shrine was destroyed by the fervently Sunni Saboktagīn, founder of the Ghaznavid dynasty, only to be rebuilt by his son Mahmūd in 1009, but both it and the city were ransacked when the Mongols invaded in 1220. Even in the dark years of the Mongol period (1220-1380), however, Mashhad grew to become the capital of Khorāsān, in succession to the nearby town

The Earthquake of 1997

In mid-1997 (while the author was, thankfully, in another part of the country), an appalling earthquake rocked Khorāsān province, as well as nearby western Afghanistan. Figures of casualties and damage vary considerably, but the Natural Disasters Headquarters in Tehrān officially put the toll at 1568 dead; 2300 wounded; 164 villages destroyed, or partially destroyed; and more than 10,000 homes completely flattened.

Mercifully, the human toll, and damage bill – estimated at US$150 million – was far less than what can be expected for an earthquake measuring 7.1 on the Richter Scale, because the epicentre, near Bīrjand, is so remote and the province is so sparsely populated. ∎

of Tūs, and the mausoleum of Emām Rezā was restored in the early 14th century.

In the early 15th century, Shāh Rokh, son of Timur, enlarged the shrine, and his extraordinary wife, Gōhar Shād, commissioned a mosque on the site. Even under this remarkable reign, the city was troubled by Uzbek invasions, and the population fell dramatically.

Although it had always attracted pilgrims, Mashhad did not become a pilgrimage centre of the first order until the coming of the Safavid dynasty at the turn of the 16th century. Having established Shi'ism as the state creed, the most brilliant of the early Safavid rulers, Shāh Esma'īl I, Shāh Tahmāsb and Shāh Abbās I, gave the city and shrine the place they have held ever since on the Shi'ite map, frequently making pilgrimages to Mashhad themselves and generously endowing the sacred complex.

Despite its new-found importance, Mashhad's location put it at constant risk of invasion, and it was attacked on several occasions in the 16th and 17th centuries by the Uzbeks (though they respected the shrine enough to leave it unscathed), and by the Afghans in 1722. In the 18th century the shrine was again firmly established as the greatest of the Shi'ite pilgrimage centres in Iran, and Nāder Shāh, though a Sunni of missionary zeal, generously endowed the shrine and restored Mashhad to stability. Several uprisings in Mashhad during the 19th century were severely put down by the ruling Ghajars, but Mashhad returned to peace under the reign of Nasr-od-Dīn Shāh, and the city was modernised under Rezā Shāh, who built the ring road. Mashhad and the Shrine are of continuing importance to this day, shown by the current, massive reconstruction of the area around the Shrine Complex.

Orientation

As you might expect, all roads in Mashhad lead to the Holy Shrine of Emām Rezā. Almost everything of interest is within walking distance of this most unmistakable of landmarks, and all the public transport radiates from the ring road which delineates it, the Falaké-yé Haram-é Motahhar. Away from this physical and spiritual centre, the city is largely flat and characterless and there is little reason to thoroughly explore the city. Only the major streets and squares are named in English, but if you use the map in this guidebook you won't go far wrong.

Maps Maps of Mashhad are amazingly hard to find in Mashhad. Funnily enough, you can buy maps of Mashhad in most other cities where maps are sold; otherwise, try the domestic airport in Tehrān if you are flying to Mashhad from there. The red-framed map put out by the Ershad Geographic Organisation costs 1000 rials. The map provided by the tourist office is reasonably useful: streets are labelled in English, but the interesting explanations about the local attractions are all in Fārsī.

Information

Visa Extensions If you have to extend your visa, go to the back of the special visa office at Rāhnamāi'ī Square, in the north-west of the city. The staff are remarkably efficient, and some travellers have been able to get a visa extended within 40 minutes – which has to be some sort of speed record for Iranian bureaucrats.

Tourist Offices Mashhad is one of the few cities in Iran with a functioning tourist office (☎ 48 288). However, it is hard to find, extremely busy and more concerned with visiting pilgrims than foreign tourists. Staff speak some English, but they are unwilling to do more than hand out a map of Mashhad in Fārsī and English. Look for the yellow sign in English – 'Khorasan Islamic Culture and Guidance'; the office is on the 2nd floor.

Money The central branches of Bank Melli (surprisingly not signed in English), Bank Mellat, Bank Sepah and Bank Saderat all have foreign exchange counters. Also, there is a foreign exchange counter at the departure lounge (but not the arrival lounge) at the Mashhad airport.

EASTERN IRAN
The subterranean Vakīl Teahouse or *chāykhūné-yé Vakīl*, set in a restored bath house with elegant brickwork arches and vaulting in Kerman's Safavid-era Vakīl Bazaar.

DAVID ST VINCENT

DAVID ST VINCENT

DAVID ST VINCENT

SOUTHERN IRAN
Top: A buffalo about to be slaughtered in the frontier village of Kūh-é Khājé.
Left: Achaemenian royal tombs set above Sassanian-era bas-reliefs, Naghsh-é Rostam.
Right: The extraordinary mud-brick fortress and walled city of Arg-é Bam.

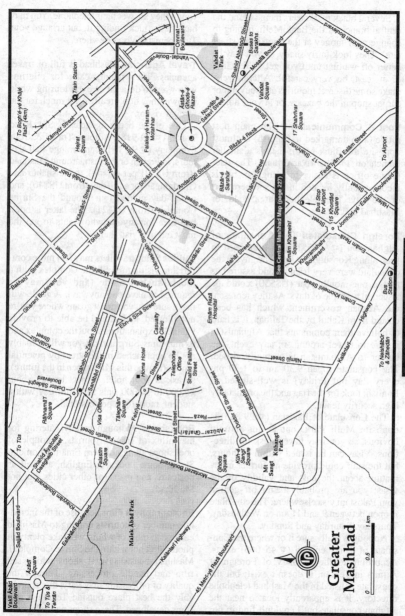

Greater Mashhad

EASTERN IRAN

Several black marketeers hang around the central branch of the Bank Melli, hoping to change your money at the unofficial 'street rate'. They look fairly shady, so you may be better off waiting until you get to Tehrān – or at least, be very careful. Alternatively, make some discreet inquiries at a souvenir or carpet shop in the bazaars, or at your hotel.

Post & Communications The main post office (also unmarked in English) is almost opposite the Bank Melli; there's a smaller branch on 17 Shahrīvar Square. The telephone office is easier to recognise, but is inconveniently located in the southern part of the city. The telephone area code for Mashhad is 051.

Foreign Consulates The Consulate of Afghanistan (☎ 97 551) is a little hard to find, along Konsūlgarī Alley. The guys at the consulate were very friendly and assured us that a one-month visa (US$30) could be issued in a couple of days. As they represent the Afghan government which has been ousted from Kabul by the Taliban, it is hard to believe their comments that Afghanistan is safe to travel around. In any event, the border to Afghanistan is currently closed. The consulate (open 9.30 am to 1.30 pm every day but Friday) is well-signed in English; look for the flag and the predictably high security fence.

The Consulate of Pakistan (☎ 29 845) is opposite Melli Park, but is not entirely obvious, so you may have to ask for directions. Visas can be issued within 24 hours, but the staff could provide no further information about the cost and validity of the visas; you are probably better off getting your Pakistani visa elsewhere. The consulate is open between 9 and 11 am on Wednesday, Thursday, Saturday and Sunday.

Nobody is really sure if or where the Consulate of Turkmenistan (☎ 45 066) exists. According to the Ministry of Foreign of Affairs in Tehrān, it doesn't exist; but the consulate is listed in the Mashhad telephone directory. It is apparently located near the Afghan consulate but I couldn't find it; nor would they answer their telephone. You may have better luck finding it, but arrange your Turkmenistan visa elsewhere.

Travel Agencies Mashhad is full of travel agencies. They mainly cater for pilgrims who want to do a bit of extra touring while in town; they don't really offer much for the foreign visitor.

One of the better agencies is Silk Road Travel (☎ 99 918). Adibian Travel & Tour Company (☎ 98 151) can arrange half-day tours, in French or English, around Mashhad (from US$21 per person); to Neishābūr and Ghadamgāh for a full day (from US$40); and a half-day guided tour around the Shrine Complex (from US$21). The latter is not a bad idea for anyone who wants to get the most out of a visit there.

Guides Some travellers may feel more comfortable visiting the Shrine Complex with a local Muslim guide (and you may be required to have one anyway). A guide will make sure that you don't go anywhere you're not allowed, and should be able to provide valuable explanations about the complex and its museums. Surprisingly, you will probably not be approached in the street by potential guides (maybe this will happen in the future), so ask at your hotel. Expect to pay about 40,000 to 50,000 rials for a full day with a student, more for a professional.

Bookshops Although mainly catering for the influx of Iranian tourists, a couple of bookshops along northern Emām Khomeinī St sell some books in English, as well as postcards and maps (of other cities, but not Mashhad).

Photography & Film Because of the incredible number of tourists coming to Mashhad each year, most of whom will take plenty of photos (but not within the Shrine Complex), Mashhad boasts several shops which sell film and handle processing. Though the quality of processing may vary, this is probably the best place outside Tehrān to get films developed. These shops naturally con-

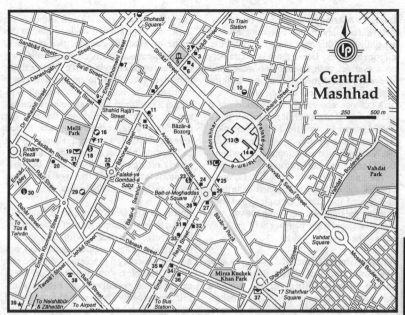

Central
Mashhad

0   250   500 m

EASTERN IRAN

PLACES TO STAY
3	Hotel Azadi
4	Amir Hotel
6	Hotel Āzarbāyjān
8	Hotel Sina
12	Iran Hotel
24	Hotel Faragi
26	Hotel Atrak & Restaurant
27	Hotel Atlas
28	Mashhad Hotel & Restaurant
31	Djavad Hotel
32	Hotel Djavaheri; Kentucky Fried Chicken; Fish Restaurant
34	Hotel Khavar
35	Hotel Sajjade
36	Hotel Nasr

PLACES TO EAT
2	Saba Chelō Kabābī
17	Chelō Kabābī-yé Ameed
21	Pars Restaurant
25	Malek Restaurant

OTHER
1	Buses to Tūs
5	Nāder Shāh Museum
7	Bookshops
9	Iran Air & Bank Mellat
10	Buses to Bogh'é-yé Khājé Rabī
11	Iran Asseman Office
13	Āstān-é Ghods-é Razavī (Holy Shrine of Emām Rezā)

14	Entrance to Shrine Complex
15	Masjed-é 72 Tan Shahīd
16	Consulate of Pakistan
18	Bank Melli (Central Branch)
19	Main Post Office
20	Abidian Travel & Tour Company
22	Gombad-é Sabz
23	Bank Sepah
29	Consulate of Afghanistan
30	Tourist Office
33	Silk Road Travel
37	Post Office (17 Shahrīvar Square)
38	Main Telephone Office
39	Police Headquarters

gregate around the bazaars, and the streets leading to the Shrine Complex.

Emergency For general emergencies, telephone the directories number (☎ 118). Of the many hospitals in Mashhad, the Emām Rezā Hospital (☎ 43 031) is probably the best and most accessible. There is also an ambulance service (☎ 197). The police headquarters (☎ 45 026) is near Emām Khomeinī Square.

Dangers & Annoyances Try to be particularly careful about not upsetting Muslim sensibilities in this most important of Iranian pilgrimage sites. Dress must be extremely conservative: men should not wear short sleeves, or roll up their sleeves, in or near the Shrine Complex; and women should wear dark colours, and cover their head as much as they can. Remember: it is a privilege for non-Muslims to visit the Shrine Complex. Any incidents involving non-Muslims are likely to make the situation much more difficult for subsequent visitors.

The fatal bombing in the Shrine Complex in 1994 significantly heightened security in and around the Shrine Complex, and even entering the train and bus terminals you may be frisked, and your baggage will probably be searched.

Āstān-é Ghods-é Razavī آستان‌قدس رضوی
The Holy Shrine of Emām Rezā, and the surrounding buildings of the *haram-é motahhar* (sacred precincts), known collectively as the Āstān-é Ghods-é Razavī, comprise one of the marvels of the Islamic world. There is so much to see in such a confined area that it is impossible to take in everything in one visit. As well as the shrine itself, this large circular walled island in the centre of Mashhad contains two mosques, three museums, 12 lofty *eivāns* or halls (two of them coated entirely with gold), six theological colleges, two main and two lesser courtyards, several libraries, a small post office, a bookshop, and many other religious and administrative buildings. Beneath the complex is a vast cemetery – to be buried near the Emām is an honour. Unlike Mecca and Medina in Saudi Arabia, which are completely off-limits to non-Muslims, the holy precincts at Mashhad (but not the shrine itself) are open to nonbelievers.

Entrance The Holy Shrine itself is strictly closed to non-Muslims (except under exceptional circumstances, with the special permission of the religious authorities), but it is not generally a problem to visit the rest of the complex. You will have to dress extremely conservatively and behave yourself impeccably, and you should avoid visiting during large religious gatherings or in the main pilgrimage season (mid-June to late July).

Due to a bombing in the complex in 1994

Āstān-é Ghods-é Razavī

Since the Revolution the foundation which manages the shrine of Emām Rezā has become one of the biggest business conglomerates in Iran, and probably Mashhad's biggest. In 1997 it managed 56 different companies and institutes, using the proceeds for its huge charity program. It may well be the only religious institution in the world to own a free trade zone, at Sarakhs on the Turkmenistan border.

One sign of the foundation's wealth and influence is the newly-built Malek Library, on the same street as the National Museum of Iran in Tehrān and almost next door to the presidential palace. The conglomerate runs numerous charities, from hospitals and pharmacies to housing for the underprivileged, building mosques and developing poorer areas of Khorāsān.

The shrine has for centuries received endowments from the wills of the pious deceased, as well as selling gravesites beneath the shrine itself. Besides pledges of money, the shrine was also given tracts of land. But since the Revolution the scale of its activities has grown enormously, with a little preferential treatment from the government. Among its larger enterprises are biscuit, bread and flour factories, a canned fruit plant, a carpet weaving company, a tile manufacturing plant, a transport company, and factories making sugar lumps, blood serum and textiles. Providing jobs is a part of its charitable works.

The result of all this business can be seen around the shrine itself. The custodians have purchased a wide swathe of property around the shrine in the heart of Mashhad's business district, which will be rebuilt with subsidised hostels for pilgrims. The extent of the shrine and related institutions will be twice that of its old territory within the Falak-yé Haram-é Motahhar. Some local businessmen aren't convinced of the benefits of this, but know that in Mashhad the Āstān-é Ghods-é Razavī is nearer to God.

Richard Plunkett

1 Manār-é Shāh Tahmāsb
   (Shāh Tahmāsb's Minaret)
2 Sahn-é Atīgh (Old Courtyard)
3 Eivān-é Shāh Abbās-é Dovvom
   (Eivān of Shāh Abbās II)
4 Madrasé-yé Mīrzā Ja'far (Theological
   College of Mīrzā Ja'far)
5 Saghghākhūné-yé Zarīn (Golden Fountain)
6 Eivān-é Telā'ī-yé Alīshīr Navā'ī
   (Golden Eivān of Alīshīr Navā'ī)
7 Madrasé-yé Bālāsar (Theological
   College of Bālāsar)
8 Madrasé-yé Parīzād (Theological
   College of Parīzād)
9 Madrasé-yé Do Dar (Theological
   College of the Two Gates)
10 Masjed-é Bālāsar (Mosque of Bālāsar)
11 Tōhīdkhūné (Place of Unification)
12 Madrasé-yé Moshtashār (Advisor's
   Theological College)
13 Mehmūnsarā-yé Āstān-é Ghods (Hotel of the
   Holy Threshold - for official guests only)

14 Haram-é Motahhar-é Emām Rezā
   (Holy Shrine of Emām Rezā)
15 Gombad-é Allāhverdī Khān (Dome of
   Allāhverdī Khān)
16 Gombad-é Hātem Khānī (Dome of
   Hātem Khān)
17 Masjed-é Azīm-é Gōhar Shād
   (Great Mosque of Gōhar Shād)
18 Eivān-é Maghsūré (Confined Eivān)
19 Eivān-é Telā'ī-yé Fath Alī Shāh
   (Golden Eivān of Fath Alī Shāh)
20 Sahn-é Jadīd (New Courtyard)
21 Mūzé-yé Ghods-é Razavī (Museum of
   His Holiness Emām Rezā)
22 Ārāmgāh-é Sheikh Bahā'ī (Tomb of
   Sheikh Bahā'ī)
23 Sahn-é Emām Khomeinī (Courtyard of
   Emām Khomeinī)
24 Madrasé-yé Pā'īn-é Pā (Permanent
   Lower Theological College)
25 Mūzé-yé Moghaddas & Mūzé-yé
   Markazī

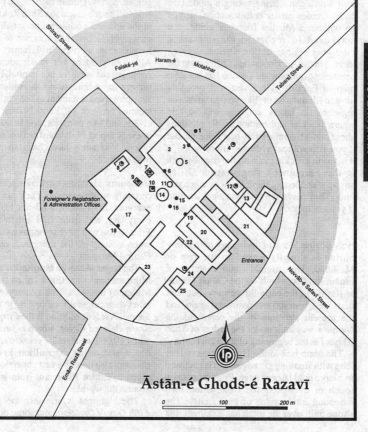

Āstān-é Ghods-é Razavī

0   100   200 m

which killed 27 people, security is very tight. No cameras are allowed inside the main gates; and you must leave all bags at the booth to the right of the main entrance. You may even need to show your passport, and you will be frisked on the way in. The entrance is near where Novvāb-é Safavī St crosses the ring road, but you can walk to the entrance along the ring road from any direction. The Shrine Complex is open from about 7 am to late in the evening; and entrance is free.

Since non-Muslims may feel a sense of guilt or embarrassment at visiting this most holy of Shi'ite pilgrimage sites in Iran, it is well worth considering taking a guide (see under Guides earlier in this section). If you go without a Muslim friend or guide, you may need to report to the unmarked Foreigner's Registration Office anyway, located in the Administration Office, near the permanent noticeboard (which has a useful map in English). Here you will probably have to fill out a form (like you do when you register in a hotel), and you will be told where you can and cannot go. Regulations about non-Muslim visitors often change, but if you visit without a Muslim friend or guide it is worth checking in with the friendly folk at the Foreigner's Registration Office anyway, and letting them know you are visiting. They may even give you a guided tour, if you are lucky.

Holy Shrine Much of the history of the Holy Shrine is directly linked to the rise of Mashhad. The original tomb chamber of Emām Rezā was built by the Caliph Hārūn-ar-Rashīd in the early 9th century, but later destroyed, restored and destroyed again, and the present structure in the centre of the complex was built under the orders of Shāh Abbās I at the beginning of the 17th century.

The tomb box in the Holy Shrine is 10m long with stunning gilt edges, and is enclosed in a large gold latticed cage. Pilgrims ritually touch or even kiss the cage, often then retreating into a pitch of near frenzy. The shrine built over the tomb has a shimmering gilded cupola and single minaret and a vast tiled eivān.

Do *not* attempt to enter the Holy Shrine unless you are a Muslim, and can prove it (probably in Fārsī) if asked.

Non-Muslims are excluded not because of their faith (or lack thereof), but because there are special cleanliness rituals and prayers to be performed before entering.

Mosque Architecturally more impressive than the Holy Shrine itself (and accessible to non-Muslim visitors) is the **Masjed-é Azīm-é Gōhar Shād** or Great Mosque of Gōhar Shād, with its 50m blue dome and cavernous golden portal. Queen of a mighty empire, wife of Timur's eldest son Shāh Rokh, patron of the arts and a powerful personality in her own right, Gōhar Shād was one of the most remarkable women in Islamic history. Although most of her major architectural commissions were at her capital Herat (in present-day Afghanistan), this mosque is the best-preserved testament to her genius. Constructed between 1405 and 1418, it has four eivāns and two minarets, and is remarkable in every aspect of its construction and decoration. Vast sums have been spent on its maintenance.

Museums The museums are excellent and certainly worth visiting. They are open to everyone from about 7.30 am to 7.30 pm every day, and from 7.30 am to noon on Friday. You will have to remove your shoes when visiting all the museums, except the Central Museum.

The larger **Mūzé-yé Moghaddas** or Holy Museum (and sometimes called the Grand Museum) houses a 16th century gold bas-relief door originally belonging to the Holy Shrine. A recent addition is the *Carpet of the Seven Beloved Cities*, which is said to have taken 10,000 weavers 14 years to make, and has a staggering 30 million knots. The museum also houses a vast collection of gifts given to Emām Khomeinī from leaders all around the world.

The highlight is arguably the gorgeous *Fifth Day of Creation*, and some other intricate masterpieces by the renowned Iranian artist Professor Farshchian. There is also a painting of Emām Rezā surrounded by adoring wildlife – the Emām was noted for his kindness to animals. A part of the museum also houses some historical photos (with captions in English) of Mashhad, the Shrine Complex, and the damage caused by the bomb blast in 1994. Most captions in the museum are in Fārsī.

Next door, the somewhat less interesting **Mūzé-yé Markazī** (Central Museum) has a collection of Islamic ornaments and writing implements, a huge 800-year-old wooden door and a one tonne stone drinking vessel made in the 12th century. Entrance costs 500 rials. Next to the entrance is a **bookshop** with postcards and a few books in Fārsī.

If you are the least bit interested in stamps or coins, then head immediately downstairs from the entrance to the Central Museum to the fascinating **Stamp and Coin Museum**. There are no explanations in English, but the display is certainly worth visiting anyway. There are stamps and coins featuring the much-hated last Shāh of Iran, and one stamp which commemorates the destruction of the US Den of Espionage (formerly known as the US embassy in Tehrān).

The ground floor of the smaller **Mūzé-yé Ghods-é Razavī**, or Holy Rezā Museum, has a display of carpets, many of them woven in Khorāsān province, examples of calligraphy in Arabic and Fārsī and a collection of valuable gifts donated by wealthy pilgrims. The glittering 1st floor houses a collection of more than 100 hand-inscribed Qurans (with some captions in English), probably the largest public display in Iran. Some are written on deerskin, paper and wood, in Arabic as well as the ancient Kufic script.

Masjed-é 72 Tan Shahīd مسجد ۷۲ تن شهید

In the Bāzār-é Bozorg only the façade of the Mosque of the 72 Martyrs (previously the Masjed-é Shāh) can be seen. The blue dome of this 15th-century mosque can be seen from the Falaké-yé Haram-é Motahhar. The building behind the façade is now occupied

by the Sepah-é Pāsdārān, and it isn't possible to go behind the barbed wire fence around it.

Gombad-é Sabz کنبد سبز

The Green Dome in the centre of its own small square is probably Mashhad's most interesting and best preserved historical building outside the Shrine Complex. It is a small quadrangular mausoleum, once used by Naghshbandī dervishes, and originally built in the Safavid period (1502-1722). The *gombad* (or dome) is almost permanently closed, but if you are lucky and can get inside, it contains the tomb of Sheikh Mohammed Hakīm Mo'men, author of a famous book on medicine.

Bogh'é-yé Khājé Rabī' بقعه خواجه ربیع

This fine octagonal 16th century mausoleum 4km north of central Mashhad is worth a visit. It contains several famous 16th century inscriptions by Alī Rezā Abbāsī, one of the greatest Persian calligraphers, and stands in the midst of a large four-walled **martyrs' cemetery** known as the Ārāmgāh-é Khājé Rabī', containing thousands of tombstones (with the usual photo displays) of martyrs killed in the Iran-Iraq War. To get there, take bus No 38 from Kūhsangī Park or north of Falaké-yé Haram-é Motahhar; or a shared taxi from outside the train station. Entrance is free.

Nāder Shāh Museum آرامگاه نادر شاه

This hideous concrete building, housing the tomb of Nāder Shāh and topped with his statue, is in a small park not far from the Shrine Complex. The Nāder museum (☎ 24 888) has a room containing a collection of guns, swords and other militaria, mostly from the time of Nāder Shāh. A smaller room to the right contains various prehistoric domestic implements from the Khorāsān region. Outside the museum there is a solitary bronze Spanish cannon, dated 1591 and later inscribed in Persian with the Persian date 1180. How it came to be here is a mystery to everyone.

The museum and park are open every day from 8 am to 7 pm. And you will only be

EASTERN IRAN

charged the Iranian price of 300 rials to enter (which is all it's probably worth anyway).

Kūhsangī Park

As an alternative to the many religious attractions, this small park is being currently developed and should be quite attractive when it's finished. There will be a fountain or two, a huge restaurant overlooking a tiny lake, and some small hills behind it to explore on foot. You can catch bus No 38 from the northern side of Falaké-yé Haram-é Motahhar, or hop on a shared taxi heading west from the city centre.

Places to Stay

There is an incredibly large range of hotels in Mashhad. All cater for pilgrims, so most are within a few minutes' walk of the Shrine Complex. Even so, for about 10 days before and after the Iranian New Year (about 21 March), and during the mid-June to late July pilgrimage season, finding a room can still be a real problem, and enough of a trial to make you identify with the origins of the name Mashhad – Place of Martyrdom. At other times, most hotels will be virtually empty, so it's easy to bargain. If you do, you may get a decent middle range place for a budget price. All places in the middle and top end range have private bathrooms.

Places to Stay – budget

Although there are plenty of mosāferkhūnés around the Shrine Complex catering for the throngs of pilgrims, getting into one as a non-Muslim is not always easy. The places listed below will take foreigners, but don't be afraid of looking around at other places nearby if you want something with a better standard or price. Remember that a sign in English does not necessarily mean the management wants foreign guests – and almost certainly doesn't mean any staff will speak English.

One good option, though often full, is the *Hotel Nasr* (☎ 97 963) – look for the word 'Nasr' in English above the door. It charges 15,000 rials per person for a clean room.

Hotel Sajjade (☎ 45 238) is in a central location, it's marked in English, and it's good value – though any place along a main road leading to the Shrine Complex will be noisy. It charges the Iranian price of 8000 rials per room. *Hotel Faragi* (☎ 54 112) costs 11,000/22,000 for a single/double, though the rooms can be noisy and most are stuffy and airless. It is signposted in English, and while not exactly fabulous, it is central.

Most places around the bus station won't take foreigners, but one that will is the *Eram Hotel* (☎ 92 656), a short walk south of the station. If you can get the 'Iranian price' of 24,680 rials for a double, or 100,000 rials for an apartment for six people, this is excellent value. However, if they start mumbling about a 'foreigner's price' of anything between US$45 and US$60, bargain long and hard – or run away.

A good cheap place recommended by a traveller after my research was completed (so I am not exactly sure where it is) is the *Doostan Alī Inn* (☎ 22 254), 'next to the Bank Ostani'. It charges a very reasonable 8000 rials for a double room; 6000 rials per person in a three-bed dorm. This is just one of several places of similar standard and price within a few minutes' walk of the Shrine Complex.

Places to Stay – middle

Mashhad Hotel (☎ 22 701) looks like something from the top-end range from the outside, but if you can bargain the manager down to 40,000 rials a double in the low season, this is the place to head for. The rooms are quiet, especially further upstairs and away from the main road, and they have air-con, a fridge and colour TV. An excellent self-service breakfast is also included. Even at the normal asking price of US$20/40 for a single/double (but payable in rials) this is worth considering.

Djavad Hotel (☎ 27 507) is not nearly as good. It charges a reasonable 40,000 rials per room, but I found the staff a little strange – perhaps they are not used to foreigners. Another popular place is the *Hotel Djavaheri*

(☎ 91 519) which charges about 40,000 rials per room – but only after a little persuasion.

Another central place to try is the *Hotel Khavar* (☎ 43 677) for about US$20/30 for a single/double room (and payment in rials is OK). Three popular places which charge around 40,000/80,000 rials for singles/doubles are: *Amir Hotel* (☎ 21 300) but it's often full; *Hotel Azadi* (☎ 51 927); and *Hotel Āzarbāyjān* (☎ 54 001), which is a little cheaper and friendlier than most in the immediate area. Because these three places are so close to each other – and the managers know it – you can negotiate. Another place which will negotiate, and which may offer a budget price of about 35,000 rials a double in the off-season if you haggle well, is the *Hotel Sina* (☎ 28 543).

Places to Stay – top end

The recognised top-class tourist hotel is the *Homa Hotel* (☎ 832 001). Prices are very high – US$75/100 for a single/double – and negotiations are frowned upon. Also in this range are the *Hotel Atrak* (☎ 22 044) and *Hotel Atlas* (☎ 45 061), both very close to the Shrine Complex. *Iran Hotel* (☎ 28 010), busy renovating at the time of research, quoted prices of US$200/300, so this may just be out of the range of most travellers.

Places to Eat

Ābgūsht is fairly popular and especially cheap in Mashhad. There are plenty of cheap eating houses around the Shrine Complex, especially along Emām Rezā St. Next door to the Hotel Djavaheri, the *Kentucky Fried Chicken & Fish Products Co Ltd* (well, that's the name in English on the front door) is likely to have lawyers working for Colonel Sanders choking on their chicken wings, but it's popular with a young crowd.

Pars Restaurant is good for tasty Iranian food at Iranian prices of about 6000 rials a plate. *Saba Chelō Kabābī*, just up from the hideous Nāder Shāh statue, has improved over the past few years, and is handy to the chain of hotels opposite. The *Chelō Kabābī-yé Ameed* is handy if you are near Melli Park, and serves a decent chelō kabāb for 3500

rials. Another excellent choice is the friendly *Malek Restaurant* – the sign is in English, but the staff only speak Fārsī. The chelō morgh, cola, tea, bread, soup and salad for 8500 rials was tasty and good value.

For something other than kebabs, it's best to see what the hotels have to offer. Most of the dozens of hotels along Emām Rezā St serve good food, in pleasant surroundings, for about 10,000 rials a dish, including soup, salad and drinks. *Mashhad Hotel* serves excellent breakfasts for guests. The lunch and dinner menu is limited but good value – a chelō kabāb, cola and soup comes to 7500 rials. The restaurant at the *Hotel Atrak* is surprisingly affordable: 4900 rials for an 'Atrak Burger', and chicken and steak dishes cost 8500 rials – plus 15% tax. You may have

---

Saffron

Saffron is a spice containing stigmas of the *crocus* plant, used for the natural flavouring and colouring of food, such as Iranian *chelō* (rice) and Spanish *paella*. Extracts from the plant can also help with digestive problems and nervous disorders. Unproven are the claims that saffron boosts energy and improves memory.

Saffron was imported from ancient Persia by many regional empires, and used for pharmaceutical purposes; as a spice; in religious ceremonies; and as a dye for the paint used in decorating holy manuscripts. Cleopatra apparently used to bathe in a mixture which included saffron. By the 18th century, seeds were successfully taken to Spain, which supplied the increasing European market.

Though Spain still dominates the international market for saffron, the plant is still grown extensively in southern regions of Khorāsān, as well as Fārs, Kermān and Yazd provinces. Saffron seeds are planted in May or August, then irrigated with care, before bright pink or violet flowers bloom for about three weeks from mid-October. These flowers must be picked during this short time, and preferably in the very early morning. The stigmas are separated, and left to dry in sheds, or hung from the roof in special containers, and then crushed into powder. About 15g of saffron powder is made from a staggering 2000 to 3000 flowers, so it's no wonder that saffron is so expensive, even in Iran. ■

EASTERN IRAN

to talk your way past the receptionist if you are not a guest, but the public are (eventually) allowed in.

Things to Buy

When they are not busy visiting the Shrine Complex, Iranian tourists love to shop, and there are several bazaars and shopping arcades to choose from. The **Bāzār-é Rezā** is 800m long, and has odd opening hours: it's generally open most mornings and evenings, except Friday. Among the usual tacky merchandise, such as the 'I wuz in Mashhad and you weren't' type of T-shirts and trinkets for pilgrims, you can buy gorgeous fabrics and rugs, as well as nuts, honey and saffron. Saffron is cheap in Mashhad: a 10g box costs about 6500 rials and makes a great souvenir. (see the 'Saffron' boxed text earlier.)

It is best not to buy turquoises in Mashhad unless you have a clear idea of their international market value and can recognise a fake. In the boom days of tourism in the 1970s, visitors to Mashhad would inevitably get a very convincing sales pitch about how much more turquoises were worth outside Iran. Needless to say, they weren't – and they still aren't. Since Mashhad has for some years been generally off the tourist trail, the turquoise racketeers in the bazaar must be having a hard time. Not much has changed over the last century since Curzon wrote:

It would be quite a mistake to suppose that by going either to Meshed (Mashhad) or to Nishapur (Neishābūr), or even to the pit mouth (of the turquoise mine), the traveller can pick up valuable stones at a moderate price. Fraser tried several years ago, and was obliged to desist from the attempt by the ruthless efforts made to cheat him. Every succeeding traveller has tried and has reported his failure. All the best stones are bought up at once by commission agents on the spot and are despatched to Europe or sold to Persian grandees. I did not see a single good specimen either in Meshed or Teheran, though I made constant inquiries...

GN Curzon
Persia and the Persian Question

Getting There & Away

Mashhad is a remote and large city, so there are regular – but often heavily-booked –

flights to most major centres in Iran. The only interesting and mildly comfortable overland trip by road or train is towards Tehrān, via Gorgān or Shāhrūd, so think about taking a relatively cheap flight to and/or from Mashhad – but book early. With the ongoing troubles in Afghanistan, and constant smuggling of drugs from Afghanistan to Iran, it is not very wise to travel overland from Mashhad to Zāhedān or Kermān. At the very least, you will be subject to endless baggage searches along the way, and it is a *very* long and hot trip through monotonous scenery.

Air Iran Air flies directly from Mashhad to:

Destination	When	Cost (rials)
Ahvāz	Tuesday and Friday	95,500
Bandar-é Abbās	Thursday and Sunday	89,500
Esfahān	Every day except Saturday and Sunday	74,500
Kermānshāh	Thursday and Sunday	94,000
Orūmīyé	Wednesday and Saturday	106,000
Rasht	Monday only	75,000
Sārī	Saturday, Tuesday and Thursday	53,000
Shīrāz	Every day except Saturday and Sunday	78,000
Tabrīz	Tuesday and Saturday	96,500
Tehrān	Several times a day (more in peak season)	66,500
Yazd	Tuesday and Saturday	61,000
Zāhedān	Monday, Tuesday and Wednesday	66,500

The Iran Air office (☎ 52 080; airport office ☎ 99 955) is open from 7.30 am to 6.30 pm every day and from 7.30 to 11.30 am on Friday and public holidays.

Most other domestic airlines also fly to Mashhad, but their schedules are erratic. Iran Asseman (☎ 58 200) flies to Tehrān every day, and to Esfahān on Wednesday, for the same prices as Iran Air. Asseman also flies to Zābol on Tuesday and Friday for 44,000 rials; Rafsanjān on Monday (62,000 rials); and sometimes to Bīrjand, about halfway between Mashhad and Zāhedān (40,000 rials).

Tiny Mahan Air links Mashhad with Kermān every Sunday for 66,500 rials; and

Saha Air and Kīsh Airlines have occasional flights between Mashhad and Tehrān. For these smaller airlines, buy your tickets at any authorised travel agency.

International Flights Mashhad is an interesting way of entering or leaving Iran. Refer to the Getting There & Away chapter at the beginning of this guidebook for more details. Trade and travel between Turkmenistan and Iran will increase in the years to come, so some airlines may put on additional flights between Mashhad and major cities in Turkmenistan.

Bus & Minibus The bus station is at the southern end of Mashhad, but easy to reach by any shared taxi (2000 rials) heading south along Emām Rezā St. The station gives the outward impression of order, with all the bus company offices arranged around one courtyard and numbered bays, but the inner reality is of general chaos, especially during peak season. No destination is signed in English, but outside the company offices there is usually someone shouting out the names of destinations for which tickets are usually immediately available.

There are buses to every major city, and regional town, but we warn you again that most trips to and from Mashhad are very long and often very boring. The train is a more comfortable option if heading towards Tehrān. If you can afford it, take a plane. If you are heading for Zābol (not a wise destination), Kermān or Zāhedān, you can expect a higher than average number of tedious checkpoints along the way.

Among other places, there are many buses and minibuses (with prices in rials for lux/super) every day to:

Destination	Distance	Time	Cost (rials)
Chālūs	877km	14 hours	9200 (lux only)
Esfahān	1338km	22 hours	14,800/17,800
(you are well-advised to break up this journey)			
Gombad-é Kāvūs	471km	8 hours	4800 (lux only)

Destination	Distance	Time	Cost (rials)
Gorgān	564km	9 hours	6800/7300
(expect a few checkpoints, with baggage searches, along the way)			
Neishābūr	114km	3 hours	3500
(several minibuses leave every morning from about 7.30 am)			
Rasht	1075km	18 hours	13,100/15,500
Sārī	695km	12 hours	12,000/13,500
Shāhrūd	517km	10 hours	8900/10,500
Tabas	521km	10 hours	11,000
(it's best to take the bus to Yazd)			
Tāybād	224km	3 hours	1600 (lux only)
(they leave every hour from about 5.30 am)			
Tehrān	924km	14 hours	9200/10,000
(they leave every few minutes)			
Tūs	23km		200
(they leave from Shohadā Square)			
Zābol	1149km	14 hours	12,650 (lux only)
Zāhedān	1001km	15 hours	10,100/13,350

Turkmenistan The border to Turkmenistan is at Sarakhs (see the Sarakhs section later in this chapter for information about crossing the border). From Mashhad to Sarakhs (185km, three hours), take a bus (3500 rials) from Vahdat Square, or ask what is heading there from the bus station. From Sarakhs, simply take whatever is going to Mashhad. Shared taxis from Sarakhs to Mashhad may want 20,000 rials per person – a rip-off, but it's the quickest way to get to Mashhad.

Train The 926km train line to Tehrān is an interesting alternative to the plane, and far more comfortable than the bus – but only if you have time and can get a ticket on a 1st class carriage. The train station (☎ 24 681) is easy to reach by shared taxi (2000 rials from the centre of town). A bus often links the train station with Beit-ol-Moghaddas Square.

Train schedules change regularly, so double-check everything. Currently, six or seven trains – some 'express', ie stopping at only a few main cities – travel between Tehrān and Mashhad every day. This is the busiest train line in the country, and there is a good chance you will get a ticket at either end. The price all the way from Mashhad to Tehrān is 9250/21,200 rials for 2nd class/1st class. It is well worth getting a 1st class ticket, as all trains travel overnight.

Turkmenistan At the time of research, the train line between Mashhad and Mary in Turkmenistan only took cargo, but there are plans to allow passengers, including foreigners, to take this train. The opening of the line was delayed in 1996 when it was realised that the trains in Iran and Turkmenistan run on different gauges, so whatever happens you will have to enjoy (or endure) watching the changing of the bogies.

When passengers are eventually allowed to cross the border by train, the trip will be known as the 'Silk Road Railway', a reference to the overblown 'Silk Road' tourist concept; and the line from Mashhad to Sarakhs has been nicknamed the 'Golden Route'. Currently, the large and modern passenger train terminal at Sarakhs stands forlorn and empty.

Details of costs and schedules were unknown at the time of writing, but the passenger train between Mashhad and Mary is likely to be up and running by the time you get there. Refer to the Getting There & Away chapter for more details, and the section on Sarakhs later in this chapter about crossing the border.

Getting Around

To/From the Airport The Mashhad Taxi Agency has the monopoly on taxis from (but not *to*) the airport, and has a counter outside the airport terminal. The official agency price to the centre of town costs from 5000 to 8000 rials, but make sure you are not charged about double this. Far cheaper, but inconvenient if you have a lot of luggage, is the public bus which travels regularly between the airport terminal and the corner of Emām Rezā and Fedā'īyān-é Eslām Sts.

Bus Most hotels are within easy walking distance of the Shrine Complex and most other attractions so buses are not normally needed – and they are usually packed anyway. One useful bus (but check the numbers and schedules when you are in

Mashhad) is No 38 which travels between Kūhsangī Park, the Shrine Complex and the Bogh'é-yé Khājé Rabī. There is also a public bus between the centre of town and the airport terminal.

Taxi Fares for shared taxis around Mashhad are reasonably low, but finding one to charter can be surprisingly hard, because they are almost always full of passengers. Shared taxis cost about 500 rials for a short ride, or 3500 to 5000 rials right across town. Be careful: some drivers do overcharge all visitors, Iranian or foreign.

Allow about 10,000 rials per hour for trips to the attractions near Mashhad by private taxi. If you can't find a private taxi on the street, ask at your hotel; some member of staff will certainly know someone who is a taxi driver.

AROUND MASHHAD

You can visit most places around Mashhad by public transport, but it's worth chartering a private taxi for about 10,000 rials per hour so you can see as much as you can in one day. Otherwise, hop on a guided tour – refer to Travel Agencies in the Mashhad section earlier.

Tūs (Ferdowsi)   طوس

Sacked in 1389 and abandoned in the 15th century, Tūs (also now known as Ferdowsi) was the regional capital before Mashhad. Parts of the walls of the citadel of the great city remain, but the present-day village is best known to most Iranians as the home town of the epic poet Ferdōsī, whose mausoleum lies over what is believed to be his exact place of death. It is a lovely place, and an easy trip from Mashhad.

Ferdōsī's Tomb Set in its own park and dominating the village of Tūs, the pale stone mausoleum of Ferdōsī was built in 1933 in preparation for the celebration of the 1000th anniversary of the poet's death a year later. It was rebuilt in 1934 because the first version was thought too plain, and partially destroyed during the earliest and most

The Great Ferdōsī

One of the most revered poets in Iranian history, Haim Abulghasim Ferdōsī was born in about 940, near Tūs. He was famous for developing the *ruba'i* (or quatrain) style of 'epic', historical poems (see Poetry under Arts in the Facts about Iran chapter for more details). His most famous work is undoubtedly the *Shahnama*, which he started when he was 40, and finished some 30 years later. This truly epic poem took quite a while to complete, because it included about 50,000 couplets.

Ferdōsī died an old, poor and grief-stricken man at Tūs, where a mausoleum to the great man has been built. His writings were deemed to be controversial during his lifetime, and for many years afterwards, but recently he has become admired for using, and keeping alive, the language of Fārsī, despite subjugation by various invaders, and for accurately detailing Persian history and culture in his poems. ■

violent throes following the Islamic Revolution because Ferdōsī was thought to be anti-Islamic. He is now revered once again.

In *The Road to Oxiana*, Robert Byron wrote of the beauty of the original, and of returning to show it to a companion:

I was saying to Christopher that ... he ought to see the Firdaussi (Ferdōsī) memorial, because it proved that a breath of architectural taste still lingered in modern Persia. The words froze on my lips: a crowd of workmen were busy demolishing it. Iron railings hid the pool. Municipal flower-beds lay ready for cannas and begonias. And at the end, instead of the pleasant unostentatious pyramid I admired in November, rose half-built copies of the bull's-head columns at Persepolis.

The best time to visit is late afternoon, when the sun is perfect for photos, but don't stay too long after dark because getting back to Mashhad by public transport can be difficult. A *café* in the gardens serves cold drinks and simple meals for lunch.

Foreigners are charged an excruciating 15,000 rials to enter the park (Iranians pay 500 rials). And you will be asked for another 15,000 rials to enter the small **Tūs Museum** (☎ 25 180) inside the park. Don't bother

forking out this extra money: all captions are in Fārsī, and it only contains a small collection of ceramics and pottery, and some items linked with Ferdōsī.

If you ask the guard at the front gate to the park, he may give you a free pamphlet in English explaining the history of the place, including a biography of Ferdōsī. The park, mausoleum and museum are open every day from 8 am to 7 pm. No cameras are allowed inside the museum or mausoleum, but they are OK in the grounds of the park.

Bogh'é-yé Hordokieh' Also known as the Gombad-é Haruniyeh, this large 14th century mausoleum, about 1km south of Ferdōsī's tomb and on the road to Mashhad, is the only remaining structure of the original city of Tūs. Although popularly associated with Hārūn-ar-Rashīd (whose remains are, however, generally accepted to have been buried near those of Emām Rezā in Mashhad), the theories about the origin of the mausoleum are varied: it is (a) the home of an unknown poet; (b) a previous place of worship for an unknown religious cult; or (c) a prison for the killer of Emām Rezā. The building is currently being renovated and a garden is being established. It should be very nice when finished.

Getting There & Away Tūs is 23km from Mashhad on a turn-off east of the road to Gorgān. Minibuses directly to the mausoleum (30-40 minutes, 200 rials) leave about every 20 to 30 minutes during the day from Shohadā Square in Mashhad. Shared taxis (about 1000 rials) leave from the same square in Mashhad, and hover outside the mausoleum in Tūs.

Neishābūr   نیشابور

Neishābūr (also known in English as Nishapur) is the earliest known capital of Khorāsān. Originally established during the Seljuq period (1051-1220), and at one time a thriving literary, artistic and academic centre, Neishābūr is now more famous as the home town of the poet, Omar Khayyām. Apart from the tomb of Omar Khayyām,

Neishābūr also has other monuments of famous men (including the 13th century mystic poet Attār-od-Dīn and the 20th century poet Kamal-ol-Molk), but these monuments are unattractive and not worth too much of your precious time.

Omar Khayyām's Tomb Omar Khayyām's very simple tombstone sits in uneasy contrast with the questionable modern structure towering above it, formed of several very tall and narrow tiled concrete lozenges linked at

Omar Khayyām
Omar Khayyām (which means Omar the Tentmaker) was born in Neishābūr in about 1047. He is probably the most well-known Iranian poet in the west because many of his poems were translated into English by Edward Fitzgerald. Omar Khayyām was famous for his *rub'ai* (quatrain) poems (there is some speculation about what he actually wrote), though many Iranians feel that his poems are too pessimistic. He is more famous in Iran as a mathematician, historian and astronomer, in particular for his studies of the Gregorian calendar and algebra. He died in 1123. ∎

the edges and redeemed only by inscriptions from the works of the great man. The gardens – **Bāgh-é Mahrūgh** – surrounding the tomb are probably more of an attraction. Also in the same grounds is the **Emāmzādé-yé Mohammad Mahrūgh**, a fine 16th century domed mausoleum. The gardens and tombs are about 1km south of Neishābūr, but if you are walking there from town, you will need to ask directions.

Caravanserai This partially restored caravanserai, dating back to the Safavid period (1502-1722) is worth a quick look. It now contains a couple of uninspiring souvenir shops, and a small **museum** (which was closed at the time of research). The caravanserai is on a roundabout, along the main road, and not hard to miss.

Places to Stay & Eat Next to the city park in the centre of town is the unmarked *Tourist Hotel*, also known as the *Neishābūr Inn* (☎ (0551) 33 445). It charges US$20/30 for a single/double, and while the manager won't negotiate, he does accept rials. The *restaurant* is excellent, and worth visiting if you are coming from Mashhad for the day. There are plenty of *hamburger joints* and *kabābīs* along the main street to choose from.

Getting There & Away Several minibuses leave every morning from Mashhad to Neishābūr (114km, 2½ hours, 3500 rials), or you can just hop on any bus heading along the main road towards Semnān, and get off at Neishābūr. You can easily combine this with a trip to Ghadamgāh (see later); hop on and off any bus heading along the Mashhad-Semnān road, or take a shared taxi (for about 2500 rials) between both places.

By private taxi from Mashhad, expect to pay about 10,000 rials per hour, but bargain hard. A taxi is a good idea because it allows you to visit several historical places between Mashhad and Neishābūr, including the ruins of the 15th century **Mosallā-yé Torāgh** (14km from Mashhad) and the Ghaznavid minaret and dome at **Sang Bast** (37km from Mashhad).

Bogh'é-yé Ghadamgāh بقعه قدمگاه

This charming octagonal 17th century mausoleum doesn't look much from the outside, but it's located in a small, pretty garden, in the otherwise dreary village of Ghadamgāh. Ghadamgāh means 'Place of the Foot', because inside the mausoleum there is a stone slab with what are believed to be the (very large) footprints of Emām Rezā. While the gardens are worth a trip, sadly the mausoleum is full of modern graffiti and badly needs renovation. Some steps inside the mausoleum lead to the source of a mountain spring, apparently created by the great Emām Rezā himself.

This place is on the busy itinerary for pilgrims who want to see everything to do with Emām Rezā. The mausoleum and village are just off the main road between Neishābūr and Mashhad. Take a shared taxi (about 2500 rials) from Neishābūr; or get off any bus heading west from Mashhad and walk south for 5km from the main road.

Vakil Ābād وکیل‌آباد

About halfway between Mashhad and Neishābūr is this lovely bit of parkland. There is plenty of clean air and scenery to enjoy, and a couple of *cafés* and *snack bars* sell cold drinks and kebabs – but avoid Fridays, when the place is crawling with Mashhadīs. If you have chartered a taxi, you could visit this park on the way to Neishābūr and/or Ghadamgāh; or get off the minibus between Mashhad and Neishābūr.

Torghabe طرقبه

This village is one of the very few in Iran which could be described as pretty – *really* pretty. It is famous for handicrafts, carpets, baskets and carvings, and it's a fantastic place to stroll around and do a bit of souvenir hunting. You can take bus No 18 from anywhere in the centre of Mashhad, or it's probably better to charter a taxi there for the short trip (about 25km) from Mashhad.

SARAKHS سرخس

The town of Sarakhs, 178km north-east of Mashhad by road (but only 120km by train), is right on the Turkmenistan border. Of course, the border did not always exist, and Sarakhs was once an important staging post along the famous Silk Road. However, there is no reason to go to Sarakhs unless you are travelling overland between Turkmenistan and Iran.

Gombad-é Sheikh Loghmān Bābā

Sheikh Loghmān Bābā was a famous 10th century teller of fables, and this vast domed monument on the outskirts of Sarakhs was constructed as his mausoleum in the 14th century. For the scale and quality of its interior and exterior decorations in brick and plaster, the remains of this mausoleum is one of the most impressive surviving structures of its period in Iran. It's not worth a lengthy detour, but make sure you visit the mausoleum if you are travelling between Iran and Turkmenistan.

Getting There & Away

Refer to Getting There & Away in the Mashhad section earlier for information about how to get to Sarakhs from Mashhad.

Crossing the Border This is the newest, and most modern, border crossing to Iran, and after decades of being closed, the border is now open to foreigners. At the time of research, foreigners had to cross the border on foot; they couldn't take a bus between Iran and Turkmenistan (currently there are no buses between the two countries), or hitch a ride on a truck. However, the train between Mashhad and Mary in Turkmenistan should have started operating by the time you get there – refer to the Mashhad section for more details.

The border crossings are at Sarakhs (Iran) and Saraghs (Turkmenistan). Crossing the border involves taking some minibuses from one control point to another, so have enough *manat* (Turkmenistan's currency) or rials to pay for the fares. If it all looks overwhelming just follow someone else – and keep asking. Both sides of the border close at 5 pm, so

The Turkmen

Of the several million Turkmen in the region, most are inhabitants of the former Soviet state of Turkmenistan, now an independent republic; but more than one million Turkmen live in eastern Iran.

Legend has it that the Turkmen are all descended from the fabled Oghuz Khan or from the warriors who rallied into tribes around his 24 grandsons. Most historians think they were displaced by nomadic horse-breeding tribes who drifted into the oases around the Central Asian Karakum desert, as well as Persia and Syria, from the foothills of the Altay mountains in the wake of the invasion by the Seljuq Turks.

Turkmen tend to be tall, and their faces show a mixture of Mongolian and Caucasian features. Males are easily recognisable (more so in Turkmenistan, than Iran) by their huge sheepskin hats *(telpek)*, either white and fleecy or black with thick ringlets like dreadlocks, worn year round, hot though the summers usually are. They usually wear baggy trousers tucked into knee-length boots, and white shirts under knee-length cotton jackets, traditionally cherry red. Females wear heavy, ankle-length, silk dresses, the favourite colours being wine reds and maroons, with colourful trousers underneath – a far more fetching sight than the ubiquitous black chādor.

Turkmen speak their own language, and have a typically nomadic liking for Sufism, which is strongly represented in Turkmenistan. The Turkmen in Iran are now largely settled as farmers. ■

make an early start; there is no public transport between Sarakhs and Mashhad after 5 pm. From Turkmenistan, you may have to wait a long time, because many Turkmen want to take bundles of cotton across, so ask for some special consideration – 'I must get to Mashhad and visit the Holy Shrine' will probably work (especially in Fārsī).

You can stay in a small, clean, unnamed *hotel* on the Iranian side of the border for 10,000 rials per person; or at the *Saraghs District Hotel* in Saraghs for the manat equivalent of about US$0.50, but it's better to get from Mary to Mashhad (or vice versa) in one day. From Saraghs you can easily get onward transport to Mary, through one or

two checkpoints where some small 'additional fees' may be requested from venal Turkmen customs officers.

TABAS   طبس

An oasis poised between the Dasht-é Lūt and the Dasht-é Kavīr deserts, Tabas is the only town of any size for hundreds of kilometres in any direction, and since you can only reach it by land, no visitor can fail to appreciate its special relationship with the desert environment. When you arrive at Tabas with its palm trees, paved roads, bazaar and public gardens, you would be forgiven for thinking you had stepped into a mirage.

The city is one of the more attractive towns in the Iranian desert, and none of its fertile land is wasted. It is easy to understand the Iranian passion for gardens if you visit the **Bāgh-é Golshan** with its lush variety of tropical trees, pools and cascades, and its utter defiance of the desolate conditions at its edge. The ruined 11th century citadel, the **Arg-é Tabas**, is also worth a look.

Places to Stay & Eat

The best place to stay and eat in town is the *Hotel Batman*, near the petrol station. A decent apartment, complete with kitchen, costs a reasonable 30,000 rials. If this is full, or more than you want to spend, ask around the bus terminal for cheaper alternatives.

Getting There & Away

Buses (with lux class only) originating in Tabas travel daily to Yazd (419km, eight hours, 7000 rials) and Mashhad (521km, 10 hours, 11,000 rials). There is a direct service to Tehrān several times a week, via Yazd. Alternatively, flag down any bus heading your way.

TĀYBĀD   تایباد

Tāybād, 224km south-east of Mashhad, is the nearest town to the border-post with Afghanistan. There is an interesting 14th century mosque, the **Masjed-é Mōlānā**, but otherwise this is definitely not a town you want to visit unless you're heading for Herat – and at the time of research, the border to Afghanistan was closed.

There are hourly buses to Mashhad (224km, three hours, 1600 rials for lux class only). If the border (11km away) reopens, you can get there from Tāybād by minibus and shared taxi. From the Afghan side of the border there should be several buses every day to Herat, about 200km to the east.

Sīstān va Balūchestān Province

استان سیستان وبلوچستان

- **Capital:** Zāhedān
- **Area:** 181,471 sq km
- **Population:** approx 1.7 million

Sīstān va Balūchestān, the second largest province in Iran, is also one of the most undeveloped and desolate. Sīstān, the northeast pocket of the province jutting into Afghanistan, was once a fertile agricultural area and the seat of many ancient kingdoms, but it's now largely barren and lawless, hampered by swamps and salt lakes and prone to fierce blizzards which bend every tree permanently southwards. Balūchestān, the main part of the province, is exceptionally arid and inhospitable country supporting little more than a few oases growing bananas, dates and limes.

Although the region of Sīstān is especially rich in ancient and prehistoric sites, this is not a province that attracts many travellers. All that most see is the dreary capital Zāhedān on the way to or from Pakistan, and few people would choose even to go there. Large patrols of customs and police officers in 4WD vehicles give a show of force along the borders with Afghanistan and Pakistan because of the rampart drug smuggling, so be especially careful if you are going off the beaten track.

ZĀHEDĀN

زاهدان

Frankly, Zāhedān is not the least bit inspiring. It is the nearest major town to the only proper crossing point between Iran and Pakistan, so most overland travellers end up there for a day or two, much to their frustration. If this is your first stop in Sīstān va Balūchestān you may want to check out the mud-brick huts with their bādgīrs in the outskirts of the city, which are typical of this region. Don't spend too much time here, however, or regard Zāhedān (population: approximately 410,000) as a typical Iranian city – there are plenty of better places to see as you head west.

Camel Races
Camel races (mosābāghé-yé shotor-é davānī) are a traditional Baluchi activity, and their audience has increased in recent years thanks to nationwide television coverage in Iran. There is usually at least one important race meeting held each year in Zāhedān, and there may be other events held elsewhere in Sīstān va Balūchestān province, but foreigners will find it difficult to get information, and you will probably have to be invited by a Baluchī. If you are lucky enough to witness a traditional camel race, please let us know. ■

EASTERN IRAN

Orientation

Zāhedān is a flat, dusty and featureless town. Though the main offices are spread all over the place, most visitors will only worry about getting from the bus, airport or bus terminals to their hotel and back, and that is easy to do. Although the whole of Zāhedān might be called one huge marketplace with no particular focus, the bazaar is probably considered the centre of town.

Maps The only map of Zāhedān which I could find in the whole country is published by the Sahab Geographic Institute and handily displayed on a wall in the main post office.

Information

Visa Extensions The oddly named 'Administration of Emigrants & Foreign Followers Affairs' (✆ 22 161) is easy to spot, just a few metres off Doktor Sharī'atī St. Some travellers have reported getting visa extensions without too much hassle, especially if you can offer the visa officer any books or magazines in English. Kermān is better, however, because you may have to wait several days in dreary Zāhedān.

Money The central branch of Bank Melli is the only bank in town which deals with foreign currency. There is a small black market for Pakistani and Afghan currency (and even for foreign passports) in the bazaar – but be *very* discreet because the Komīté are active around Zāhedān. To change US dollars into Iranian rials, try to look for an 'official' moneychanger in the bazaar (but there were none at the time of research).

Post & Communications The main post office is along Doktor Sharī'atī St; and the main telephone office is further south, along Tāleghānī St. The telephone area code for Zāhedān is 0541.

Foreign Consulates The Consulate of Pakistan (✆ 26 030) is open from 8 am to 2 pm, Saturday to Thursday. The consul claims he can issue visas 'without undue delay', and, indeed, travellers have reported getting excellent service here – much to their surprise (after dealing with Iranian bureaucracy, no doubt). The visa cost (in rials) varies according to your nationality and the type and length of visa you want.

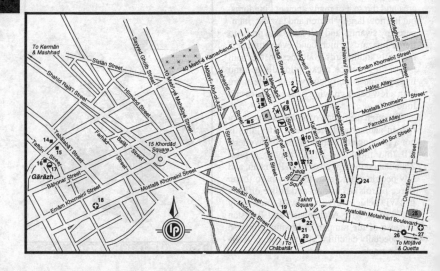

The Consulate of India (☎ 22 337) can issue visas for 15 days (30,000 rials); for three months (120,000 rials); or for six months (240,000 rials). If you get there early, you can even pick up your visa later the same day. It is open from 8.30 am to 1 pm and 1.30 to 5 pm, Saturday to Wednesday. It is a large, unsigned building; look for the fluttering Indian flag. The entrance is along a laneway at the back.

Emergency There is a general emergencies number (☎ 24 000). The main hospital (☎ 26 001) is just to the east of the train station. The police headquarters (☎ 22 092) is next to the bazaar, but hard to find, so ask directions.

Dangers & Annoyances Because there's so much drug smuggling in the area, it is a little unsafe around some parts of Zāhedān at night, and if you have a vehicle, it's a very good idea to find a safe place to leave it overnight (eg in an underground hotel car park). There is an unofficial curfew in Zāhedān; you don't see many people out on the streets after dark. Do not venture west of Zāhedān unaccompanied or on foot; gun law is in force there and the jagged hills visible

from Zāhedān are not known as the 'Black Mountains' for their colour alone.

Places to Stay
Some travellers have recently had problems finding a room in Zāhedān, and as a few places have closed in the past few years, and some cheaper places are reluctant to take foreigners, the available beds in town can fill up quickly. Arrive in the morning if possible and try not to look too scruffy. Of course, if you're coming straight from Pakistan, it might be a little difficult to achieve either aim.

Stopping at the border town of Mīrjāvé (see that section later in this chapter) is a worthy option or, if you are not completely exhausted, bypass Zāhedān altogether, and travel between the border and Bam or Kermān. Because Zāhedān is a bit grubby and not particularly safe, and you may not have much choice anyway, some travellers may have to bite the bullet and pay for a middle range place.

Places to Stay – budget
If you want to make a quick getaway by bus, there are a few places in the very grimy bus terminal area. *Abuzar Hotel* (☎ 28 692) is convenient and good value at 8000/11,000 rials for a single/double with a shared bathroom; however, it is noisy and often full. It is a large, three storey building, and easy to find. Other cheap places for about the same price (which may be reluctant to take foreigners) are the *Mosāferkhūné-yé Eslam*, which has abysmal toilets; and the grotty *Mosāferkhūné-yé Fars*. Neither are marked in English.

Hotel Momtzahirmand (☎ 22 827) is the best in this range: the staff are friendly and the place is good value at 12,500/15,000/17,500 rials for a clean single/double/triple with shared shower facilities (though don't always believe promises of hot water). It's a good place to meet other travellers who have just come from, or going to, Pakistan. The hotel is a little hard to find: head north along Doktor Sharī'atī St from the corner with Emām Khomeinī St, the hotel is along the

PLACES TO STAY	OTHER
1 Bakhtar Hotel	2 Consulate of India
3 Hotel Momtazhirmand	6 Bāzār-é Rūz
& Restaurant	7 Police Headquarters
4 Hotel Esteghlal	8 Bank Melli (Central Branch)
5 Khavar Hotel	9 Main Post Office
14 Abuzar Hotel &	10 Khaterat Zāhedān Travel &
Restaurant	Tours (Iran Asseman Agency)
15 Mosāferkhūné-yé Eslam	12 Main Telephone Office
16 Mosāferkhūné-yé Fars;	13 Visa Office
Bus Cooperative No 1	17 Bus Terminal
20 Hotel Sāleh & Restaurant	18 Hospital
21 Hotel Amin	19 Iran Handicrafts Organisation
23 Hotel Kavir	22 Iran Air Office
28 Tourist Camping	24 Consulate of Pakistan
	25 Stadium
PLACES TO EAT	26 Train Station
11 Pizza Shab	27 Hospital

Zāhedān

To Airport

Montazeri Street

Motahhari Boulevard

0   0.5   1 km

28

Forūdgāh Square

To Mīrjāvé & Quetta

EASTERN IRAN

first laneway on your left. In front of the Momtzahirmand, the *Hotel Esteghlal* (☎ 24 957) refused to accept me, but you may have better luck. Tiny rooms cost 7000/8000 rials.

Places to Stay – middle

One of the better places in this range (and one of the few that is still open) is the *Hotel Saleh* (☎ 31 797). It charges US$20/30 for a double without/with a bathroom, but they do accept rials. An extra bed costs US$7 more. The nearby *Hotel Amin* (☎ 221 954) is a last resort: the staff were particularly surly when I visited, and they wanted US$30 or 90,000 rials a room, which is too much.

One unusual option is *Tourist Camping* (☎ 20 113), also known as the *Mehmūnsarā Jahāngardī*. Run by the ITTO, this place charges an absurd US$25/50 for a single/double in an individual 'cabin' – which looks a bit like an above-ground bunker. It is convenient to the train station and airport, but to nothing else. Look for the sign in English at Forūdgāh Square: 'Room and Restaurant'.

At the time of research, the *Khavar Hotel* (☎ 28 880), *Bakhtar Hotel* (☎ 27 403) and *Hotel Kavir* (☎ 24 010) were all closed, but they could possibly reopen in the future.

Places to Eat

There are several *restaurants* in the bus terminal area; the *restaurant* in the Abuzar Hotel (marked on the window in English, 'Welcome to the Abuozar Restaurant') is the most popular and hygienic.

The best places to eat are in the hotels. *Hotel Momtazhirmand* is basic but the best in the budget range of hotels. *Hotel Saleh* also has a good restaurant. This is probably the best in the middle range: a good chelō kabāb with soup and a cola comes to little more than 10,000 rials.

A couple of decent *kabābīs* along the stretch of road between the Amin and Saleh hotels are worth trying if you are staying at either place. *Pizza Shab* was closed at the time of research – perhaps there is not a lot of demand for pizza in Zāhedān but it may reopen later. If so, check it out.

Things to Buy

Zāhedān is famous in Iran for its low prices on all manner of goods, especially cigarettes, which are imported from and often made in Pakistan (under western brand names). The grand cigarette bazaar is in the bus terminal area. If you have some time to kill, or want to pick up a last-minute souvenir before heading into Pakistan, the Iran Handicrafts Organisation shop is worth a look; otherwise wander around the **Bāzār-é Rūz**.

Getting There & Away

Air If you are sick of travelling overland, and couldn't face another boring trip of 15 or more hours across a desert, consider flying. But remember that there has been a recent reduction in the number of flights to/from Zāhedān, and these are often heavily booked by Iranians who also don't want to travel overland. While the troubles continue in Afghanistan, and drugs are being smuggled into Iran, it is unwise to travel overland between Zāhedān and Mashhad.

Iran Air (☎ 20 813) flies from Zāhedān to:

Destination	When	Cost (rials)
Chābahār	Every day but Saturday and Monday	52,000
Esfahān	Friday	78,000
Kermān	Friday	40,000
Mashhad	Monday, Wednesday and Saturday	66,500
Tehrān	Daily	91,000

Iran Asseman also has flights to Tehrān, on Tuesday, Friday and Saturday, for 91,000 rials and to Irānshahr for 45,000 rials (but there is no reason whatsoever to take this flight). Asseman did have a weekly connection between Dubai and Zāhedān, but the flight was recently abandoned. The representative for Iran Asseman is Khaterat Zāhedān Travel & Tours (☎ 25 001).

Train There is *still* talk of building a new line to complete the railway system between Kermān and Zāhedān. Of course there is a lot of talk about a lot of things in Iran without a great deal of action.

Pakistan Many travellers opt for the train between Zāhedān and Quetta, in Pakistan. While the train has plenty of character and you meet some fascinating people, it is painfully slow, and leaves only twice a week. It is much quicker to get to Mīrjāvé by bus, minibus or shared taxi, cross the border on foot (refer to the Mīrjāvé section later for details) and then take any form of transport leaving for Quetta from Taftan.

The 700km trip between the Iran-Pakistan border and Quetta ... will forever be remembered as 'The Pakistani Nightmare'. Everybody told us to take the train. It's more comfortable, everybody said. We did it and we regretted it. After twenty hours, we got about halfway ... something was broken on the rails, so we had to wait another 10 hours. How it ended up we don't know, because after those 10 hours we jumped on a bus that stopped by the train station and went to Quetta.

David Kucera, Czech Republic

In April and May, when the rains are more prevalent, delays can stretch to eight or 10 hours, making the trip unbearably long. Schedules have changed little over the years, but still check anyway. The normal passenger/cargo service leaves Zāhedān for Quetta at 7 am on Thursday, arriving at about 3 pm on Friday. The slightly better and quicker 'express' (a bit of a misnomer really) leaves Zāhedān at 8.30 am on Monday.

For both trains, tickets to the border (1000/1500 rials for 2nd class/sleeper) are available at the impressive little train station in Zāhedān from 5 pm the day before departure. (You may also be able to buy tickets in advance from a hotel in Kermān; see Travel Agencies in the Kermān city section.) Look for the sign in English – 'Divisional Railway S&B'. You can get information about train times from someone around the station or ring inquiries (☎ 24 142, extension 238). Getting a sleeper isn't that important because the train from Zāhedān to the border travels during the day (or so you hope), and you must buy onward tickets in Taftan. Getting a sleeper for a more comfortable 1st class seat is definitely worth the extra 500 rials.

From Quetta, the 'express' train leaves at 12.30 am on Saturday, arriving in Zāhedān at about 6 pm on Sunday evening. The slower, normal service leaves Quetta on Tuesday at 1 pm.

It will take three to five hours to clear both borders. If you are not travelling alone, it is easy for at least one of you to look after the luggage and the other(s) to take the passports to Iranian immigration – you do not have to personally hand over your own passport. In some cases, an immigration officer may simply come by and collect all foreign passports. From the Iranian border, the train then moves for a few minutes to the Pakistani border town of Taftan. Again, one of you can hand over your passports at the Pakistani immigration office (under the train station). The other(s) can look after your gear, and/or queue up to buy your onward ticket to Quetta (280/560 Pakistani rupees for 2nd/1st class) – on the same train, and in the same compartment if you ask.

There is no bank in Taftan, so you will have get some Pakistani rupees at the moneychangers at the train station. Change enough to buy your onward ticket and to last until you can change money in Quetta. Take plenty of food and water with you, stops and facilities are very sparse along this route. In winter take a sleeping bag or you will freeze to death (or at least be very, very cold).

One final word of warning: customs checks can be unpleasant for some (and therefore time consuming for everyone else on the train).

Border procedures on the Pakistan side were the most horrible I've ever seen. It took at least eight hours. They stop the train in the middle of the desert and check everything. Pakistani passengers (over 95% of the train) are searched completely, but we were not touched at all. It is disgusting to see, because all they (the customs officers) want is a bribe.

Zabukovac Blāz, Slovenia

Bus For those with the constitution of a camel, roads go north to Mashhad and Zābol, and south to Chābahār, but most travellers are only interested in roads east to the Pakistani border and west to Bam and Kermān. If you are headed for Zābol, Mashhad or

Chābahār, you can expect an inordinate number of checkpoints along the road.

There is no bus terminal as such: all buses leave from a grotty, sprawling area in the north-west of Zāhedān, generally known as the Gārāzh. The bus companies have offices all over the place, but if you are completely lost (and, remember, things get a whole lot easier further into Iran), look for Bus Cooperative No 1, which is located in the same building as the Mosāferkhūné-yé Fars. This bus company has a lot of buses going to most places and it's a good place to start hunting down a bus you want.

Buses leave Zāhedān several times a day (with prices for lux/super services) to:

Destination	Distance	Time	Cost (rials)
Bam	360km	6 hours	4500/6000
(alternatively, get on a bus to Kermān or Yazd, and get off at Bam)			
Bandar-é Abbās	1039km	17 hours	8800/12,300
Chābahār	691km	12 hours	8600/11,350
Esfahān	1244km	21 hours	12,900/15,300
Kermān	541km	7 hours	4500/6300
Mashhad	1001km	15 hours	10,100/13,350
Shīrāz	1088km	17 hours	11,860/14,300
Tehrān	1605km	22 hours	15,300/16,900
Yazd	928km	14 hours	7650/9900
Zābol	216km	4 hours	2450/2870

Pakistan Transport schedules and conditions at the border can change, so check the situation at the Pakistani consulate in Zāhedān or the Iranian consulate in Quetta. Currently, there are frequent buses (5000 rials), minibuses (7000 rials) or 'pik-ups' (utility-style shared taxis) for 10,000 rials between Zāhedān and Mīrjāvé (96km). Since Pakistan is 1½ hours ahead of Iran, be sure to make an early start if you're heading to Pakistan.

Remember that the Iran-Pakistan border is 15km further east of Mīrjāvé village, so clarify whether the taxi or bus is going to the village or border. In any case, it is easy enough to get something between the village and border. Once you are at the border, cross it on foot (see the Mīrjāvé section following) and then take whatever form of transport is

heading your way on the other side. From Taftan, there are regular buses – every hour at least – to Quetta for 250 Pakistani rupees.

Car & Motorcycle Drivers who are travelling between Turkey and India often describe the trip between Zāhedān and Quetta, across the vast Baluchistan desert as the worst leg of their journey. The road from Quetta to the Iranian border is barren and lonely, with virtually no facilities, and motorcyclists should consider booking their motorcycles as luggage and go by train instead. If you're travelling between Quetta and the Iranian border in your own transport, it's advisable to travel in a convoy. And remember that Zāhedān has a bad reputation for car theft, so if you are staying overnight anywhere near Zāhedān, or the Pakistani border, park your vehicle somewhere safe.

The clearly signposted road between Zāhedān and Kermān is good but short on facilities. Take plenty of water with you if you are driving, and make sure your vehicle is in good order or risk a long and unpleasant wait for repairs. Petrol is available in Mīrjāvé and in Zāhedān, but nowhere between Zāhedān and Bam.

Getting Around
To/From the Airport A private taxi between the airport and town should be no more than about 3500 rials for a single passenger, but unscrupulous drivers may demand 7500 to 10,000 rials – bargain hard. Alternatively, look for some fellow passengers to share a taxi. There is no airport bus service.

Taxis There is a shortage of official (orange) taxis and buses in Zāhedān, so vans and private cars often duplicate their services. Private taxis are reasonably priced at about 2000 rials for a trip anywhere around town; shared taxis are available along the main roads for about 250 rials a trip.

MĪRJĀVÉ   میرجاوه
Whether crossing by road or train, you'll pass through the Iranian border village of Mīrjāvé. It is a typical border town with

nothing to interest travellers, but it is marginally better than Zāhedān, so think about staying here instead.

Places to Stay & Eat
A more pleasant alternative to the limited choice of places in Zāhedān is the *Mirjaveh Inn* (☎ (05448) 4386), the only hotel in town. Large, clean doubles cost a reasonable 30,000 rials. Look for the sign in English 'Room Resturant' (sic) at the main roundabout. The attached *restaurant* is also good. It is worth staying here and avoiding Zāhedān altogether by travelling between Mīrjāvé and Bam (or Kermān) in one hit.

Getting There & Away
From the Iranian border, wait for any form of transport to fill up and leave for Mīrjāvé village, Zāhedān (where most transport goes anyway) or even Bam or Kermān, if you are lucky. However, to most places west of Zāhedān, you will probably need another connection from Zāhedān. Refer to the Getting There & Away section under Zāhedān for more information about getting to the border by train and bus from Zāhedān.

From outside the Abuzar Hotel in Zāhedān, you may approached by taxi drivers who will drive you to the border in a car (ie more comfortable than an ordinary taxi) for 40,000 rials. This is too much; you should pay about half this for a private taxi between Zāhedān and the border.

Crossing the Border
While you may want to get an early start from Kermān or Zāhedān if you are not taking the train, there is no point starting *too* early as the Pakistani border, at the time of research, was not open until 10 am – though this may change in the future. To add to the chaos, some travellers going into Iran have been put on hold while the Iranian side of the border closes between about 4 pm and 6 pm for no particular reason – maybe a late Iranian siesta. Try to time your border crossing to fit into these times, or just take pot luck and expect a bit of waiting.

Foreign travellers crossing the Iranian border are often whisked through customs and immigration, but it's very prudent for men and women crossing this border *into* Iran to dress appropriately and be polite and, for heaven's sake do not carry any drugs, or anything that even remotely looks like drugs.

Taftan is a depressing, fly-blown den of smugglers, and you can expect to spend an hour or two going through Pakistani border procedures, and waiting for onward transport. In summer this would be murder. According to Pakistani authorities, Taftan is to be developed into a township with a clean restaurant and even hotels, but, as you know, these things take a little time.

You can easily change Iranian rials or US dollars into Pakistani rupees – or vice versa – at Taftan. You won't have to look for someone; they will (quite literally) see you coming. Be careful; and try to ask someone

---

Smuggling the Hard Stuff Through Iran
Afghanistan produces more than 6000 tonnes of opium every year (and would produce more if not for the civil war), while Pakistan grows 500 tonnes a year. Almost all of this is smuggled across the provinces of Khorāsān and Sīstān va Balūchestān, and on to the lucrative European market, where heroin can fetch up to US$100,000 per kg, a mark-up of about 3000% from the time it leaves Afghanistan or Pakistan.

Iran can justifiably be proud that almost 85% of the world's drug busts (by volume) takes place in Iran, a fact recognised by the United Nations Drug Control Program. In 1996 alone, Iranian customs officials claim to have busted nearly 200 smuggling gangs, and arrested more than 4000 traffickers.

Roadblocks (which you will soon become wary of when you travel in this region) do actually recover vast amounts of drugs, sometimes as much as 500kg in any given month at any particular checkpoint. Iran takes drug smuggling very seriously, and armed battles between police and drug smugglers are not uncommon, even on the main roads – more than 200 Iranian officials have been killed in clashes with drug smugglers in the past four years. Do not carry anything remotely looking, smelling or tasting like any possible illegal drug while in Iran. ■

crossing the border the other way for the current exchange rate. You will need some Pakistani rupees to buy an onward train or bus ticket from Taftan to Quetta, but if you can wait until Quetta to change more money you will probably get a better rate. The closest place in Iran to change rials back into US dollars (if you changed money at a bank in the first place) is Kermān, though you may be able to do it with a moneychanger on either side of the border, if you have your wits about you.

There is a nice hotel in Mīrjāvé (see Places to Stay & Eat earlier), but nothing in Taftan – and who wants to stay there anyway! If you are running late, and have camping equipment, you should be able to camp, after asking nicely, at the Pakistani customs yard, but don't expect any comfort or quiet.

For more details on crossing the border by train or bus, see the Getting There & Away section under Zāhedān earlier in this chapter.

ZĀBOL زابل

This dusty overgrown village, dangerously close to the border with Afghanistan, is of no interest to travellers except as a stepping-off point for Kūh-é Khājé. Zābol has earned a name as a town where only two things matter: guns and money. Before heading to Zābol check the current situation with the visa extension-cum-foreigners' registration office in Zāhedān.

Places to Stay & Eat

Mosāferkhūné-yé Valī-yé Asr, 1km from the bus terminal, is good for a quick getaway and costs 12,500 rials per person. Close to the bazaar, there are three mosāferkhūnés, but none can be recommended.

There is no decent restaurant in Zābol. The chelō kabābī underneath the Mosāferkhūné-yé Valī-yé Asr is OK for chicken kebabs, but nothing much else stimulates the tastebuds. There are a few other places of modest gastronomic standards around the bazaar.

Getting There & Away

If you must come through here, buses link Zābol with Mashhad (1149km, 14 hours,

12,650 rials for lux only) and Zāhedān (216km, four hours, 2450/2870 rials for lux/super class). Iran Asseman also flies between Zābol and Mashhad every Tuesday and Friday for 44,000 rials.

KŪH-É KHĀJÉ كوه خواجه

Kūh-é Khājé is a small hilly island with a number of ancient remains on its peak, rising out of the seasonal Lake Hāmūn. The area is especially beautiful between early spring and early autumn when the level of the lake rises and the causeway to the island becomes impassable; in winter and late autumn it is usually possible to walk across, but at other times you will probably have to take a tūtan (a tiny wickerwork punt) at a negotiable fare.

The village, also known as Kūh-é Khājé, is 1.5km east of the island, and this is where you will be dropped off if you arrive by bus or shared taxi from Zābol. There is no accommodation or place to eat, and since you should count on at least 2½ hours to see the remains on the island and get back to the village bus stop, it is best to leave Zābol in the morning.

CHĀBAHĀR چابهار

Until very recently, the tiny Gulf of Oman port of Chābahār (the name means 'Four Springs') was extremely isolated, but since Iran Air opened a much-needed air link with the interior it is now the most accessible of all the towns of Balūchestān besides Zāhedān, though less so by road.

Chābahār is known to most Iranians as the Chābahār Free Zone (CFZ), a duty-free port along the lines of Kīsh Island. Here, thousands of Pakistanis and Baluchīs line for days and days in the searing heat to buy duty-free goods, then shift them off to cities around Iran where they are sold on for substantial profits. The entire bureaucratic nightmare seems to be a local job-creation scheme, and a way for the government to legalise (and tax) smuggling. If you can find an Iranian to show you around, it is fascinating to watch the indescribable chaos in the CFZ. (CFZ could also mean Chaotic Freaking Zoo.) Unaccompanied foreigners won't normally be allowed into the customs yard because you must have some sort of ration booklet.

Chābahār is very hot in summer and very expensive all the time. The telephone area code is 05423.

Places to Stay & Eat

Along the main street, the rather grotty *Mosāferkhūné-yé Mohammadi* (not marked in English) charges 15,000 rials for a bed with few facilities for personal hygiene, and no air-conditioning. *Mosāferkhūné-yé Azadi* is in the same class.

At the main roundabout, the *Mehmūn-sarā-yé Jahāngardī* (☎ 24 444), not marked in English or even Fārsī, is run by the ITTO, and completely unreasonable when negotiating a reduction from the US$35 per room they want from foreigners. The most bizarre hotel in Iran has to be the *Marian Hotel* (☎ 3484), a converted South Korean barge full of apartments which cost a negotiable 75,000 rials a double, with TV, fridge and air-con. It is near the main jetty. The upmarket place, along the main road, is the *Blue Star Hotel* (☎ 2566).

Fish dishes are common in this part of Iran, as you might expect. There are several *snack bars* and *chelō kabābīs* along the main road. The restaurant in the *Mehmūnsarā-yé Jahāngardī* is fairly good and inexpensive, but the best place to eat is the *Blue Star of Chābahār*, in the Blue Star Hotel, where an excellent three-course meal with drinks costs about 15,000 rials.

Getting There & Away

Air Chābahār is very isolated by land, and the most sensible way to get there is by air. Iran Air flies most days to Zāhedān (52,000 rials), with connections to Tehrān, and to Bandar-é Abbās (53,000 rials). The Iran Air office (☎ 3383) is on Sayad Blvd. Iran Asseman and Saha Air fly between Chābahār and Tehrān for the same price as Iran Air.

Bus Chābahār is only connected on a regular basis by public road transport with Zāhedān (8600/11,350 rials for lux/super) via Irān-

shahr. Roads to/from Chābahār are improving, but it is still a very long, and, in summer, very hot trip.

Pakistan There is no legal route between Iran and Pakistan except at Mīrjāvé, but this is a long way to the north of Chābahār – too far for most locals. The land crossing into Pakistan through Pīshīn is not normally possible for foreigners, and this is wild and desolate drug-smuggling territory where foreigners should not be found or seen.

Getting Around

To/From the Airport The airport is 46km away in the desolate village of Konārak, and the runway is even another 12km from the terminal. Take whatever vehicle is going from the airport to Chābahār; and ask the airline office in Chābahār about sharing transport *to* the airport.

TĪS

چابهار

Tīs is a small oasis village about 9km north of Chābahār, along the coast road. At the Tīs petrol station, turn towards the sea and you will face the remains of a **Portuguese castle** on top of a small hill. The village is well irrigated and even boasts an arboretum, known as **Bāgh-é Tīs**, with a canopy of tamarind and pine trees.

From Chābahār, you can walk the 9km to Tīs; try taking a shared taxi from the main taxi stop in town, or charter a taxi for about 12,000 rials per hour.

Kermān Province

گنبد شیخ لقمان بابا

- **Capital:** Kermān
- **Area:** 186,422 sq km
- **Population:** 2.2 million

The province of Kermān is the third largest in Iran. Its north-east takes in much of the Dasht-é Lūt desert, and most of the province is largely steppe or sandy desert, though there are some oases where dates, citrus fruits, pistachios and cereals are cultivated. In view of its barren nature, the province is very dependent on *ghanāts* (underground water channels), built many centuries ago but still used today. The climate is surprisingly varied in summer – hot and sometimes humid in the south, while considerably milder in the north.

Most foreigners travelling between Pakistan and Turkey, go through Kermān province. There is a lot to see in and around Kermān city; and don't miss the unique medieval citadel at Bam – a highlight of the province and, most would agree, one of the greatest sights in Iran. Kermānīs have quite a distinct accent, which is often hard to understand if you have managed to pick up a bit of Fārsī.

KERMĀN کرمان

If you are coming from, or going to, Pakistan you are very likely to pass through the desert city of Kermān, a pleasant place (population: approximately 330,000), set at a cool 1755m above sea level. Many travellers speed through the city or spend just enough time to arrange onward transport, which is a shame because you could easily spend a couple of days seeing the numerous sights in and around Kermān.

For many centuries the livelihood of Kermān depended on its place on the Asian trade routes, but from about the beginning of the Safavid dynasty (1502-1722) it has relied more on the production of carpets. The barren nature of the surrounding terrain has never presented much scope for agriculture, and today the main activity of the town continues to be the manufacture of carpets and other handicrafts. It has a Zoroastrian minority, though much smaller than that in Yazd.

History

Kermān has a long and turbulent history, and it has only for short spells enjoyed peace and prosperity at the same time. Believed to have been founded in the early 3rd century AD by Ardashīr I, founder of the Sassanian dynasty, it was from the 7th century ruled in turn by the Arabs, Buyids, Seljuqs, Turkmen and Mongols, and then until the Ghajar dynasty (1779-1921) by a further succession of invaders and regional despots. Kermān obtained security under the central government in Tehrān during the last century, but its relative remoteness has continued to deny it any great prosperity.

Orientation

The two main squares in Kermān are Āzādī Square to the west and Shohadā Square to the east. Most of the important offices and things to see are on or close to the road between these two squares, or in the bazaar district near Shohadā Square. Strangely, for a town which is actively promoting tourism, very few street signs are in English – but if you use the map in this guidebook, you won't get too lost (unless you wander too deep into the labyrinth of lanes in the bazaar). Be on the lookout for that Iranian traffic hazard, the bus lane along which buses hurtle down in the *opposite* direction to the rest of the traffic.

Maps Maps of Kermān are not easy to find. The tourist office has some useful maps printed by the administrative staff of the 12th International Festival of Films and Video for Children and Young Adults (now there's a snappy title) in Fārsī and English.

Information

Visa Extensions The office of the Aliens' Bureau (☎ 222 240), where you can try to get a visa extension, is currently at the police headquarters – but the visa office may move in the future. If you have any difficulties getting your visa extended or finding the relevant office, and you're staying at the Akhavan Hotel (see Places to Stay later in this section), the manager there should be able to help you out.

Tourist Office The tourist office (☎ 228 030) is trying to encourage tourists to come to the province but the staff, who were friendly and spoke a bit of English, were not much help. They could only provide a town map in English and Fārsī, and a brochure in

PLACES TO STAY
5 Amin Hotel
14 Bahar Guest House
16 Mosāferkhūné-yé Ommid
31 Akhavan Hotel
& Restaurant
32 Naz Hotel
34 Kermān Hotel & Restaurant

PLACES TO EAT
7 Second Kabob Chicken
9 Chāykhūné-yé Vakīl
26 Restōrān-é Bozorg-é
Shāhr

OTHER
1 Iran Air Office
2 Kermān National Library
3 Moayedī Ice House
4 Gombad-é Sabz
6 Masjed-é Pā Manār
8 Coin Museum
10 Masjed-é Jāme'
11 Shared taxis to Māhān
12 Masjed-é Emām
13 Hammūm-é Ganjalī Khan Museum
15 Co Services Travel Agency
17 Police Headquarters & Visa Office
18 Main Telephone Office

19 Main Post Office
20 Bank Melli (Central Branch)
21 Money Exchange Office
22 Church of St Andrew
23 Kermān Contemporary Arts Museum;
Khan-é Sayyah Kermān Restaurant
24 Cinemas
25 Tourist Office
27 Mahan Air Office
28 Iran Handicrafts Organisation
29 Kermānseir Tour Company
30 Shared taxis to Māhān,
Sīrjān & Rafsanjān
33 Bus Terminal

Kermān

0   0.5   1 km

Minor Streets Not Depicted

EASTERN IRAN

To Mashhad
To Beheshtī Hospital
(1.5km) & Gombad-é
Jabalīyé (7km)
To Airport
Jomhūrī-yé Eslāmī Boulevard
To Kermān Grand Hotel,
Train Station (8km), Sīrjān,
Yazd & Bandar-é Abbās
To Māhān
To Sarasīyāb
Square (5km)

Firūz Abādī Street
Enghelāb
Shahīd Bāhonar Street
Kārgar Street
Doktor
Chamrān
Fath Alī Shah St
Shohadā Street
Shohadā Square
Basij Square
Ganjalī Khan Courtyard
Bāzār-é Vakīl
Tohid Square
Modarres St
Kermanī Square
Fedā'īyān-é Eslām Square
Emām Khomeini Street
Shahab Street
Adālat Street
Motahharī Street
Milak-é Ashtar Street
Ghods Street
Jādde-yé Kamarbandi
Khājū-yé Kermānī Street
Esteghlāl Street
Ayatollah Sadīghī Street
Azādī Square
Bahmanyār St
Barūjī Street
Hāfez Street
Paesdārān Street
Shahīd Gharanī Street
Faleşın
Somīyé Crossroads
Vali-yé Asr Square
Sharī'atī Street
Doktor Beheshtī Street
Ferdōsī Street
Mo'allem Street
Park Motahhart

French about Māhān which looks like it was probably printed during the Safavid dynasty. However, the tourist office has produced (but does not give away or sell) some outstanding glossy brochures – good enough to take home as souvenirs – about the multitude of attractions in Kermān province. Try to look out for these.

The tourist office is in a three storey cream-brick building, on the corner of Beheshtī and Ferdōsī Sts. Look for the small sign 'Tourist Office' in English at the entrance booth. The actual office (not signed in English) is upstairs and to the left. It is open from 8 am to 2 pm every day but Friday.

Money The central branch of Bank Melli, next to the post office, will change money, but not until you've spent up to an hour shuttling from one pen-pusher to another paper-shuffler. To obtain – quickly – the unofficial 'street rate' of exchange look for the word 'exchange' on any shop window around Tohid Square. One official money exchange office which I found and used is indicated on the map.

Post & Communications The main post office is next to the Bank Melli; the main telephone office is a little further north, between Adālat and Mo'allem Sts. The Akhavan Hotel (see Places to Stay later in this section) is also useful for arranging international fax and telephone calls. Though prices will be higher than the public telephone office, service will be much quicker. The telephone area code for Kermān is 0341.

Travel Agencies For airline bookings, and to ask about local tours, try the Kermānseir Tour Company (☎ 51 551) and the Co Services Travelling Air and Turing (sic) agency (☎ 222 247), which is better at arranging tours than proof-reading its signs in English. The staff at the Akhavan Hotel (see Places to Stay later in this section) can also arrange bus, train and plane tickets (for a small fee), and claims to be able to arrange for you (for a larger fee) a ticket on the train from Zāhedān to Quetta (Pakistan).

Emergency For general emergencies, dial telephone directories (☎ 118) or for medical emergencies (☎ 115). Beheshtī Hospital (☎ 28 025), on the corner of Shohadā and Modīrīyat Sts, in the eastern part of town, is the easiest to find and deal with. The police headquarters (☎ 110 or ☎ 231 018) is along Adālat St.

Mosques
Masjed-é Jāme' The well-preserved and restored Friday Mosque, in the bazaar district, should definitely be on your itinerary. This large mosque, with its four lofty eivāns and shimmering blue tiles, was built in 1349, though much of the present structure dates from the Safavid dynasty or later. It's no problem for non-Muslims to go inside, and at the main entrance there is a useful explanation in English (well, a sort of 'Fārsglish', really). The back entrance leads directly into the bazaar.

Masjed-é Emām This quadrangular, domed mosque dates from the Seljuq period (1051-1220), and includes the remains of the original Seljuq mehrāb and minaret, though much of the building has been rebuilt since. The mosque was still being extensively renovated at the time of research, but it will be worth a look when it's finished.

Masjed-é Pā Manār This mosque dating back to the 14th century (or, according to other reports, the 12th century) is worth visiting for the fine original tilework in its portal.

Museums
Hammūm-é Ganjalī Khan This fascinating, though slightly tacky museum (☎ 25 577) contains a small collection of wax dummies showing the viewer what to do in a bath house. Originally built in the 17th century as a bathhouse by the governor of Kermān, Ganjalī Khan, the museum is worth popping in to if you are walking past.

The entrance, signposted in English, is directly opposite the Ganjalī Khan Courtyard, in the middle of the bazaar district. It is open from 9 am to 1 pm, and 4 to 7 pm every day, and costs 5000 rials. Photos are allowed, but you will need a good flash.

Coin Museum On the other side of the courtyard from the Ganjalī bath house museum is the Coin Museum, also known as the Mint Museum. It was closed at the time of research.

Kermān Contemporary Arts Museum
This interesting building contains a large collection of watercolours, mostly by local artists, including the renowned Sayyed Alī Akhbar Sanatee. There is a small entrance fee of about 500 rials. The garden surrounding the museum is picturesque, and makes a welcome respite. There is an excellent but expensive traditional Iranian restaurant in the grounds (see Places to Eat later in this section).

Gombad-é Sabz
Although the 9th century Green Dome was once one of the most important monuments in Kermān, it was irreparably damaged in the 1896 earthquake and little more remains than its small doorway with some original tilework. It is lost in the network of kūchés (alleys) east of Falastīn St and a little hard to find.

Church of St Andrew
This Anglican church is hidden in a garden behind a doorway along Doktor Sharī'atī St. It is marked with the Persian cross characteristic of all the Anglican churches in Iran. The original building founded by British missionaries was destroyed in an earthquake a few decades ago, but with a great effort the tiny congregation built a new church in stone in the 1980s.

Gombad-é Jabalīyé
Just beyond the eastern edge of Kermān, this small and unadorned octagonal double-domed structure, called the Mountain of Stone, is of unknown age or purpose. Appearing to predate the 2nd millennium AD, it may have been a Zoroastrian building.

It is remarkable because it's constructed of stone rather than the usual brick. The dome was being restored at the time of research (as was a lot of Kermān city).

It's a fair way to come just to see this dome, but the area around it is excellent for hiking (see Hiking below). To get to the dome, try to find a shared taxi from Shohadā Square, but you will probably have to charter one for about 5000 rials return.

Moayedī Ice House
This weird ice house, originally dating from the Safavid period, has been renovated so well it is impossible to regard it as old or important. Built and renovated with *khesht* (a common form of locally-made brick, dried in the sun), the ice house is now used as a library and childrens' park.

Kermān National Library
If you happen to be walking past the library, have a quick look at this interesting building, once a textile factory. The gardens are lovely and worth using for a picnic.

Hiking
If you are dying to get out into the clean air, and explore some countryside, head north or east of the city and into the forested hills which are part of the Pāye mountains. A good place to start is the Gombad-é Jabalīyé, mentioned earlier. Just strike out as far as you wish, though the hills soon give way to bone-dry desert.

Places to Stay
There isn't a great choice of places, and in summer, when there may be a few package tour groups in town, finding middle range accommodation at a decent price may be difficult. Finding *anything* in the budget range is never easy, so you may have to bargain hard with a hotel in the middle range, or stay in Bam or smaller towns near Kermān (see Around Kermān later in this chapter).

Places to Stay – budget
One of the very few cheap places that will take foreigners is the *Bahar Guest House*

(☎ 22 590). It is central and very cheap – 5000 rials per person – but, understandably, almost permanently full of Iranians. It is signposted in English, just south of Tohīd Square. One good option is the *Mosāfer-khūné-yé Ommid* (not signed in English), along northern Shahāb St. It is not easy to find, so keep asking. Reasonable rooms cost about 15,000 rials.

Kermān Hotel (☎ 224 070) is convenient to the bus station but not much else. The place is almost permanently empty, so prices are very negotiable; ask for a room for about 35,000 rials a double. The nice foyer belies the grubby rooms; you are probably better off paying a fraction more and getting somewhere cleaner and more central.

Places to Stay – middle & top end

Naz Hotel (☎ 46 786) is adequate but overpriced, and the disinterested staff speak no English. They originally wanted US$23 a room with three beds, TV, bathroom and air-con, but they easily went down to 50,000 rials. Ask for a room at the back, away from the main road.

Far better is the *Akhavan Hotel* (☎/fax 41 411). I was able to easily bargain the manager down to a reasonable 40,000 rials for a very pleasant double with TV, air-con and bathroom. (Several travellers also reported similar success at the Akhavan.) During busier times the price is normally US$20/30 for a single/double, which is still not unreasonable if you can pay in rials. The price normally includes breakfast, but may not if you get a discount. The effusive manager speaks English and understands what travellers want: a large range of postcards are for sale in the foyer; you can safely leave your vehicle (and sleep in it if you want) in their car park and use their showers for about US$1 per person per day; they can organise bus, train and airline tickets (for a fee); they can help with visa extensions; and there's an international fax and telephone service.

Another decent place is the *Amin Hotel* (☎ 221 954) for US$25/30, but try to pay in rials. The top-end place is the ITTO's

Kermān Grand Hotel, which is hopelessly overpriced at US$65/75 plus 17% tax, as well as inconveniently located about 1.5km west of Āzādī Square. You are better off paying the full price at the Akhavan.

Places to Eat

Without a doubt the most atmospheric place to eat or drink in town is the *Chāykhūné-yé Vakīl* (☎ 25 989), inside the Bāzār-é Vakīl. (It is not signposted in English, but look for the tiny letters 'ITTO' on top of the sign in Fārsī; it's also the only place leading downstairs from the bazaar.) This subterranean teahouse and restaurant with its elegant brickwork arches is known more for its elegant traditional decor than its service or meals. It offers lunch (for around 6000 rials a dish) from about noon to 2 pm, and for pots of spiced tea (500 rials) and a puff or two at the hubble-bubble throughout the day. Women are welcome.

The *Restōrān-é Bozorg-é Shahr* (marked in English 'Big Restaurant City'), a long-time favourite, was closed at the time of research but looked set to reopen soon, and should provide good food at reasonable prices. *Second Kabob Chicken* (well, that's the name in English on the window) can rustle up something other than kebabs, such as fried rice for about 5500 rials. The bazaar has dozens of snack bars, hamburger joints and cake shops.

The hotel restaurants are often your best bet. The restaurant downstairs at the *Akhavan Hotel* has a great range of tasty meals for about 10,000 rials including soup, bread, salad, tea and a soft drink. The English-speaking manager can also arrange some traditional Iranian dishes (ie not more kebabs). The 'restourant' (sic) at the *Kermān Hotel* is also not too bad.

Worth a splurge is the *Khan-é Sayyah Kermān Restaurant* in the grounds of the Kermān Contemporary Arts Museum. Set up with delightful traditional decor and furniture, they serve expensive, but tasty, food for about 10,000 rials a dish. There is a menu in English if you ask, but beware: the prices are not listed.

Entertainment

Ask your hotel, or the tourist office, about any teahouses which hold story-telling competitions or traditional music programs. If you see one, count yourself lucky – but don't be afraid to leave after a few hours if it drags on a bit. Several cinemas showing Iranian blockbusters in Fārsī are located near the corner of Ferdōsī and Doktor Sharī'atī Sts. Go there to watch the crowds rather than the films.

Things to Buy

Kermān is home to one of the most interesting and ancient bazaars in this part of the country. The **Bāzār-é Vakīl**, almost 3km long, is where you can spend hours and hours just wandering around, shopping and taking photos. It runs between Tohid Square and the Masjed-é Jāme', and houses banks, a couple of museums, a few mosques and one of the best teahouses in the country – refer to Places to Eat earlier in this section. Built in the Safavid period, the centre of the bazaar is the pretty **Ganjalī Khan courtyard** where many locals sit and relax; surrounding it is the ancient **coppersmith's bazaar**.

The Iran Handicrafts Organisation shop is worth a look, but you are likely to get better prices in the bazaar, as long as you can bargain long and hard. Kermān is renowned throughout Iran for its tapestries, and carpets and rugs made from cotton featuring bright colours. (See the special section on Persian Carpets in the Facts for the Visitor chapter for more details.)

Getting There & Away

Air To avoid some long distances by train or bus through some boring countryside, you may want to consider flying to and/or from Kermān. However, schedules, which do change between winter and summer, have been significantly reduced in recent years. Currently, Iran Air (☎ 58 871) flies (in summer) to Esfahān on Friday (52,500 rials); Tehrān every day (71,000 rials); and to Zāhedān on Friday (40,000 rials). Mahan Air (☎ 51 542) also flies to Tehrān every day for

71,000 rials; and to Mashhad on Sunday for 66,500 rials.

Bus & Minibus The bus terminal, in the south-west of Kermān, is surprisingly well set up and orderly. (If only some other stations, like the one in Zāhedān, were so easy to use.) None of the bus companies have booking offices in town – they are all represented at the bus terminal. Among other places, buses and minibuses (with prices in rials for lux/super) leave several times a day from Kermān to:

Destination	Distance	Time	Cost (rials)
Bam	194km	3 hours	2500/3000
(you may need to take the Zāhedān bus and pay the full fare instead)			
Bandar-é Abbās	498km	8 hours	5350/6850
Esfahān	703km	12 hours	6600/7200
Shahr-é Bābak (for Meimand)	238km	4 hours	4500
Shīrāz	545km	8 hours	8500/9900
Tehrān	1064km	18 hours	9500/10,700
Yazd	387km	6 hours	3800/4200
(it's easier to take the bus to Tehrān and get off at Yazd)			
Zāhedān	541km	7 hours	4500/6300

Train A 1106km rail line starts in Tehrān and ends at Kermān, so if you are heading for Pakistan you will have to continue your journey by road. To Tehrān (14,200/25,200 rials for 2nd/1st class), trains leave Kermān at 2 pm on Tuesday, Thursday and Saturday, and stop off at, among other places, Yazd, Kāshān and Ghom. It is important to note that this train does *not* go via Esfahān; to Esfahān, get off at Yazd or Kāshān and get a bus. It's far easier to take the Kermān-Esfahān bus.

Train tickets are only on sale between 6 am and 1.30 pm on the day of departure. Get the latest schedules from the tourist office in Kermān rather than from the train station (☎ 58 761), a converted warehouse (or so it seems) about 8km south-west of town. You can try getting a shared taxi (about 1200 rials) to the train station from Āzādī Square, but you will probably have to charter a taxi

EASTERN IRAN

for about 6000 rials. There will certainly be shared taxis available at the station when the train arrives.

Shared Taxi Plenty of shared taxis regularly leave Kermān for regional towns, but they all depart from different spots. From Āzādī Square, there are shared taxis to Rafsanjān, Māhān and Sīrjān. To add to the confusion, they often leave for Māhān from Fedā'īyān-é Eslām Square. To Bam (about 6000 rials), and sometimes as far as Zāhedān, they leave from Sarāsīyāb Square, about 5km east of Kermānī Square.

Getting Around

To/From the Airport There is no bus to the airport. You can try to get a shared taxi heading along Jomhūrī-yé Eslāmī Blvd from Āzādī Square, but you may have to charter a private taxi for about 5000 rials.

Bus & Minibus Many buses travel between the two main squares, Āzādī Square and Shohadā Square, but it's quicker to travel around town by shared taxi.

Taxi Taxi fares in Kermān are fairly low. You can get from Āzādī Square to Shohadā Square for about 500 rials. The main terminals for shared taxis around town are Āzādī, Valī-yé Asr and Shohadā squares.

AROUND KERMĀN

There are quite a few things to see in the vicinity of Kermān city, but with fairly infrequent public transport to these places it's worth chartering a taxi. Don't pay more than 10,000 rials per hour for a taxi with driver, and negotiate for about 35,000 rials for a half day and maybe, if you are lucky, 60,000 rials for a full day. Try to find a driver who speaks a bit of English. You may be able to tee this up with the manager of your hotel.

Māhān   ماهان
The small town of Māhān attracts visitors for its fine mausoleum, and beautiful palace and gardens.

Ārāmgāh-é Shāh Ne'matollāh Valī The dome over the tomb of Shāh Ne'matollāh Valī, a well-known Sufi dervish, dates from the early 15th century, but many of the other structures in the small enclosed complex of religious buildings around it were built in the reign of Shāh Abbās I or later. The mausoleum is renowned for its tilework, and the seven ancient wooden doors throughout the building. The doors were originally from India, but no-one knows how they got to Māhān.

You can climb up a stairway to the roof for a better view of the two slender Ghajar minarets (both being renovated at the time of research), and the vast Safavid cupola. The mausoleum is located in the middle of Māhān, and easy to find. Try to avoid Thursday afternoon and Friday, when the serenity of the place is shattered by hordes of Kermānīs. The minibuses and shared taxis from Kermān will take you straight to the mausoleum. Entrance is free.

Bāgh-é Shāhzāde Also worth a visit are these charming gardens, with a collection of pools leading to a large palace. (The palace was once the summer residence of a prince – though nobody is really sure which prince.) The palace has been partially converted into a *restaurant* which serves a decent lunch and drinks, but by late afternoon (the best time for photos) I could only buy an ice cream.

The gardens are an easy 5km walk up the main road through the village from the mausoleum, though the sign indicating the turn-off to the gardens is in Fārsī, so, if in doubt, ask. It is easy to get a private taxi between the two main attractions. Entrance is 10,000 rials.

Places to Stay & Eat A worthy alternative to Kermān is the *Māhān Inn* (☎ (03479) 2700). The six rooms are comfortable and clean, and cost US$25 per double – and rials are accepted. The *restaurant* attached is also quite good. The hotel is at a roundabout, 1.5km from the main road between Bam and Kermān. It is well signposted in English, and public transport running between Māhān and Kermān takes you past the hotel.

Getting There & Away About every hour, shared taxis (about 1500 rials) and minibuses (350 rials) travel the 35km between Kermān and Nem'atollāh Square, right in front of the mausoleum.

Joopar جوبار

If you are not 'mosqued-out' by now, and have access to a vehicle, then a visit to Joopar, 30km south of Kermān, is also worthwhile. The main attraction is the **Emāmzādé-yé Shāhzāde Hossein**, built in the Safavid period (1502-1722), and similar in design to the mausoleum in Māhān. The mirrored ceiling inside the room which contains the shrine is exquisite.

Public transport is infrequent from anywhere, including Kermān, but it's easy enough to charter a taxi from Māhān or Kermān. The mausoleum is on the main roundabout in the village.

Meimand ميمند

Meimand, 27km north-east of Shahr-é Bābak, is a beautiful, well-kept historical village perched on a hill. Though it is not a patch on Bam, it is pleasant and interesting enough to warrant a day trip if you have some time up your sleeve.

To get there, you will have to take a shared taxi from Shahr-é Bābak, accessible by bus from Kermān (4500 rials); or you can charter a taxi from Kermān or Shahr-é Bābak.

Rafsanjān رفسنجان

Rafsanjān is famous for its pistachios, which can be bought here more cheaply than anywhere else in Iran, and as the birthplace of the former president Rafsanjāni. There is nothing much else of interest to the visitor, so keep heading to Yazd, Kermān or Sīrjān.

If you do stay, the ITTO *Mehmūnsarā-yé Rafsanjān* (☎ (03431) 2050) charges US$15/25 for a single/double. The cheaper and more negotiable *Pariz Hotel* (☎ (03431) 5833), on Tāleghānī Blvd, costs about 25,000 rials a double.

Shared taxis from Kermān cost about 3500 rials, or just jump on any bus on the way to Yazd. Iran Asseman has flights between Rafsanjān and Mashhad on Monday (62,000), and to/from Tehrān three days a week (85,000 rials).

Shahdād شهداد

An interesting archaeological site has come to light about 5km east of this small town on the western border of the Dasht-é Lūt. This prehistoric mound, known as the **Tappé-yé Kohné**, has revealed many fascinating metal implements with animal motifs and clay human figurines from the 3rd millennium BC. Some are on display at the National Museum of Iran in Tehrān.

In the town of Shahdād itself there is an impressive mausoleum, the **Emāmzādé-yé Mohammad Ebn-é Zeid**, dating back to the Safavid period (though the exact period of construction is open to speculation).

There is no hotel in Shahdād, so you'll have to come from Kermān for the day. It is very difficult to get to Shahdād by public transport, so you'll probably have to charter a taxi from Kermān.

BAM بم

Bam is a pleasant town where the eucalypts down the main street are likely to make any Aussie (like me) homesick, while the plethora of date palms around the rest of Bam clearly indicate a desert oasis. But what makes Bam truly special, and probably one of the highlights of your visit to Iran, is the incredible ancient city – described by some travellers as more impressive than the ruins at Persepolis. If travelling overland to or from Pakistan, make sure you stop here for a day or two – otherwise it is worth flying especially to Kermān or Bam.

Orientation & Information

Bam is easy enough to walk around, and the ancient city is only about 3km from the centre of town, which is Emām Khomeinī Square. The Bank Melli office in the main street won't change money; they will direct you to their branch in Kermān. The main post

1 Fire Station	8 Iran Asseman Office
2 Bank Melli	9 Ali Amiri's Legal
3 Theatre	Guest House
4 Bus Cooperative No 7	10 Iran Guest House
5 Mosāferkhūné-yé Kasra	11 Main Post Office
6 Bazaar	12 Bus Cooperative No 8
7 Post & Telephone	13 Bam Inn & Restaurant
Office	14 Petrol Station

Bam

0   0.5   1 km
Approximate Scale

To Arg-é
Bam (1.5km)

Emām
Khomeinī
Square

Pāsdarān Street

Adālat
Square

To Tourist Guest
House (2km)

17 Shahrīvar
Square

2km

To Kermān

Falastin
Boulevard

To Zāhedān

office is so small you will probably walk past without knowing it. The telephone area code is 03447.

Arg-é Bam   ارگ بم

History The citadel and original city of Bam were probably founded in the Sassanian period (224-637), and some of the surviving structures must have been built before the 12th century, but the greater part of what remains dates from the Safavid period (1502-1722). Between 9000 and 13,000 people once lived in this 6 sq km ancient city until it was first abandoned following an invasion by the Afghans in 1722. Just when the inhabitants thought it was safe to return, the city was abandoned again in about 1810 when some particularly gruesome atrocities from invaders from around Shīrāz persuaded the populace to leave permanently. From then until the 1930s, the remains of the ancient city was used as an army barracks, and it is now completely deserted except for the requisite café and bookshop.

Things to See You can climb up any steep and narrow stairway to the pinnacles of the outer wall, made of clay, for the definitive

outlook over the old and new towns. This wall, which almost circles the entire city and dates to the 9th century, is about 2km long and contains nearly 30 small towers. From the wall you can see (and visit from outside the city), the curved **ice house**, which housed enormous chunks of ice during the winter, melting to become drinking water in summer.

The inner citadel dominating the town contains a fortified 17th century residence known as the **Chahār Fasl** (Four Seasons). In the **garrison**, shout something and listen to the extraordinary echo – archaeologists consider this to be a deliberate, ancient loudspeaker system. Nearby, are the 14th century **stables**, which once held 200 to 300 horses.

On the way up to the **Governor's Residence**, look into the very dark and scary dungeons, built for those who obviously displeased the governor. You'll need to take a strong torch (flashlight) to see anything. The **Residence of the Garrison's Commander** provides awesome views of the ancient town.

In the rest of the old city, the **Mirza Naeim School** is now closed to visitors, and used as a base for an archaeological research unit. Note the handles on the front door; the one on the left is only used by women, the right by men. The **bazaar square**, near the main entrance, dates backs to the Safavid period; it was once covered and the centre for hundreds of townsfolk trading in dates, cotton and spices. The main **mosque** was originally constructed in the 9th century, but has been rebuilt numerous time since.

Most of the attractions are helpfully (but discreetly) signposted and labelled in English – though you'll be glad to know that the 'toiletts' (sic) were built more recently than the 12th century. The whole complex is being restored. Hopefully, this will take a very long time to complete: full restoration would result in the whole city losing it's beauty, ambience and obvious antiquity.

Entrance The Arg-é Bam is open every day from 7 am to 6 pm. The main entrance is at the historic (southern) **gatehouse**. It costs 10,000 rials to enter – and is worth every rial.

Allow at least two hours to look around. It is worth going twice – once in the late afternoon and again in the early morning – to get the best photos, and to fully explore the city in two doses. It is easy to walk there from the centre of Bam, or get a private taxi for about 1000 rials. There is a *teahouse* above the **citadel gatehouse**, where you can relax with a hubble-bubble or a pot of tea, while soaking it all in.

Souvenir Book If you want a souvenir, pick up a copy of the excellent *Arg-e-Bam* by Abdolreza Salar-Behzadi. Though written mostly in Fārsī, the photos are superb (and have captions in English); it's a worthy memento of your visit to this majestic city. You can buy it at the entrance of the old city for a reasonable 18,000 rials.

Places to Stay
As more travellers discover Bam, more places to stay are likely to spring up. The best

place in town, and one of the nicest hotels along the route between the Pakistan border and Tehrān, is *Ali Amiri's Legal Guest House* (☎ 4481). (The 'legal' bit is a dig at the local authorities who closed down the original establishment and forced the owner to undertake a lengthy 'official tourism course' in Kermān.) The owner, who speaks good English, has a handful of clean rooms, with a spotless shared bathroom, for a negotiable 15,000 rials per person. He also knows a lot about the nearby attractions; and the guest book is jam-packed with excellent information from fellow travellers.

If Alī Amiri's is full, the *Mosāferkhūné-yé Kasra* (☎ 3700) is an alternative, though a very poor one. Tiny, grotty cubicles, in a noisy location, are overpriced, even at 10,000 rials per room. Ask for a fan to help circulate the fetid air. Not signposted in English, it is two doors east of the Bank Mellat office. As a last resort, try the *Iran Guest House* (not marked in English, but

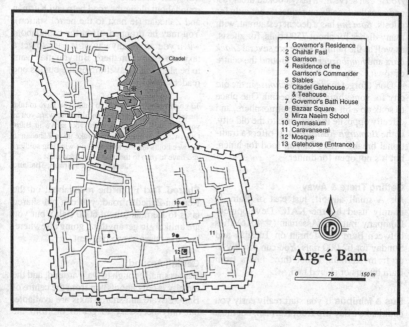

1	Governor's Residence
2	Chahār Fasl
3	Garrison
4	Residence of the Garrison's Commander
5	Stables
6	Citadel Gatehouse & Teahouse
7	Governor's Bath House
8	Bazaar Square
9	Mirza Naeim School
10	Gymnasium
11	Caravanserai
12	Mosque
13	Gatehouse (Entrance)

Arg-é Bam

0   75   150 m

known to locals) for about 10,000 rials per room.

Tourist Guest House, also known as *Serai Jahāngardī*, has been recommended by some readers, but it seemed permanently closed when I visited. Keep it in mind though if it opens again because the gardens (or what I saw through the hole in the gate) were superb, and the high fence allows female foreign guests to take off their hejāb if they wish. One traveller wrote to us to say 'if this place was anywhere else between Thailand and Greece, it would be permanently full'.

The only middle range place is the ITTO's *Bam Inn* (☎ 3323). It charges 72,000 rials a double with bathroom; 60,000 rials without. The rooms have balconies and are clean and quiet, but the prices are not open to negotiation. More rooms were being built at the time of research.

Places to Eat

Alī Amīrī's wife at *Ali Amiri's Legal Guest House* can serve up a tasty cooked breakfast and excellent meals on request – but only for guests. *Bam Inn* has a decent restaurant, with many dishes for about 7500 rials, for guests, as well as the public. There are several *snack bars* and *hamburger joints* around the centre of town.

Don't forget to visit the *teahouse* in the old city for something really special. One place to soak up a bit more of the atmosphere, and directly opposite the entrance to the old city, is the *Bamargh Restaurant*. It offers a traditional breakfast and Iranian food for lunch, but it's not open for dinner.

Getting There & Away

Air A small airport, just east of Bam, is mainly used by the KAIC Development Company, but Iran Asseman (☎ 4016) flies between Bam and Tehrān on Tuesday and Sunday for 62,000 rials. You can also fly to or from Kermān, about three hours from Bam by bus or shared taxi.

Bus & Minibus If you start really early you could take a day trip from Kermān, but most

people would travel through Bam anyway and it's worth staying in Bam to allow two visits to the old city. Buses (with prices in rials for lux/super class) leave from one of two bus company offices to:

Destination	Distance	Time	Cost (rials)
Bandar-é Abbās	449km	8 hours	6000/6600
(Co-op Bus No 7)			
Irānshahr	352km	7 hours	4500/4700
(Co-op Bus No 8)			
Kermān	194km	3 hours	2500/3000
(Co-op Bus Nos 7 and 8; or take any bus heading towards Tehrān)			
Tehrān	1258km	21 hours	12,900/14,500
(Co-op Bus Nos 7 and 8; or get a connection from Yazd or Kermān)			
Yazd	581km	9 hours	6900/7800
(you'll have to change buses in Kermān, or take the bus towards Tehrān)			
Zāhedān	360km	6 hours	4500/6000
(Co-op Bus No 8)			

Alternatively, it's not hard to catch onward transport in either direction at the main roundabout along the road between Kermān and Zāhedān (ie next to the petrol station). You may be dropped off at the roundabout when you arrive anyway; it is easy to get a taxi into town from there. But you may want to be alert when travelling on the bus, as one reader related:

To go directly from Shīrāz to Bam, you have to take the bus for Zāhedān and ask the driver to warn you as you may well be asleep when you arrive in Bam. Otherwise, you may, like me, wake up in Zāhedān in the wee hours among Kalashnikov-wielding soldiers and have to rush to the next bus backwards!

Jean-Jacques Braun, Thailand

Shared Taxi From the roundabout on the Kermān-Zāhedān road, you can get shared taxis to Kermān (about 6000 rials), but you are unlikely to get anything going elsewhere, because buses are so frequent.

Getting Around

Bam is small enough to walk around, and the old city is only about 3km from the centre of Bam. Private and shared taxis are available, but only necessary to get to or from the roundabout on the Kermān-Zāhedān road, or from the old city if you are tired after walking around there for a few hours.

SĪRJĀN سيرجان

Sīrjān is probably not worth a detour, but it's a useful place to break up a journey between Kermān and Bandar-é Abbās, or between Kermān and Shīrāz. If you do stay, there are a few attractions: the **Mir-é Zobair** contains some ancient calligraphy; the **Emāmzādé-yé Alī** is mildly interesting, but probably not worth the effort; the ancient **Firuz Fire-Temple**; and **Ghal'é-yé Sang**, the limited remains of a walled town on the northern and eastern flanks of a small hill.

Places to Stay & Eat

There is not a great choice. The only cheap hotel is the unmarked (in English) *Hotel-é Kasra*, down a laneway between the main branches of Bank Mellat and Bank Melli, in the centre of town. They charge a negotiable 8000 rials per person in basic but adequate rooms. *Hotel Suroosh*, on the main road and opposite the petrol station, is decent if you can get a room away from the highway. It charges 45,000 rials per double, with a bathroom, but won't negotiate.

Hotel Suroosh has a decent *restaurant* downstairs; otherwise you will have to make do with a hamburger or kebab from a local *snack bar*.

Getting There & Away

Sīrjān is easy to get to by shared taxi from Kermān (5500 rials), or by direct bus from Kermān, Yazd, Shīrāz or Bandar-é Abbās. There is no bus terminal, and the individual bus companies are spread all over town. It is best to take a private taxi and ask, for example, for the *termīnāl-é Yazd* (or wherever you want to go).

EASTERN IRAN

Southern Iran

ايران جنوبى

Most travellers to southern Iran understandably concentrate on Shīrāz and its nearby attractions, such as Persepolis, but there are several other, worthwhile places to visit for a glimpse of Arab life along the Persian Gulf. The Gulf hosts several islands; all of which, except Khārk (in Būshehr province), belong to the Hormozgān province.

With the exception of the duty-free islands of Kīsh and Gheshm, none of the Persian Gulf islands are equipped to entertain tourists, and few, if any, are tourist destinations in the conventional sense. Even so, they are of great interest, containing pockets of a way of life almost vanished from the mainland and in danger of disappearing from the islands too. Pearl diving was once a very important activity, but the trade has gone into decline over recent years due to the increasing popularity of cultivated pearls and a rise in the local shark population. Despite the pollution, more than 200 varieties of fish and

SOUTHERN IRAN AT A GLANCE

- **Provinces:** Boyerahmad va Kohgīlūyé, Hormozgān, Fārs, Būshehr and Khūzestān.

- **When to Go:** Avoid the Persian Gulf and islands, and around Ahvāz, during the summer from April to October; Shīrāz is OK most of the year.

- **Highlights:** Ancient ruins of Persepolis; Hormoz Island; mosques and gardens of Shīrāz; Choghā Zambīl; old Bandarī city of Būshehr.

The Bandarīs
The indigenous people of the Iranian shores of the Persian Gulf are often loosely known as Bandarīs, from the Persian word for 'port'. Descended from Arab, black African and mixed stock, the Bandarīs have darker skins than the Persians, and though they have become Persianised in many ways, they preserve their own Arabic dialect and culture. Many Bandarīs follow the Sunni sect of Islam, while most Iranians are Shi'ite Muslims.

The Bandarī women have their own style of dress, quite unlike any other in Iran: colourful embroidered or printed layers of wraps over loose trousers, leg bracelets and sandals or flip-flops, and, sometimes, owlish masks (see the boxed text 'The Masked Women of Mīnāb' later in this chapter). The men usually wear the *abā*, a long, sleeveless robe, usually white; as well as sandals, and sometimes a turban. The traditional Bandarī dress is most commonly seen in Hormozgān province, especially on the islands. ■

other marine life thrive in the Gulf (refer to 'The Persian Gulf' boxed text later in this chapter).

Illicit traffic, in goods and humans alike, does occur regularly in the Gulf, especially around the Strait of Hormoz. Keep to the main towns and roads, and don't stick your nose (or any other part of your body) anywhere it isn't wanted. Because of the Gulf region's excessive heat, the siesta is taken very seriously, even in winter, and very little, except public transport, functions between noon and late afternoon. Offices and shops close for the afternoon and reopen for a few hours at about 5 pm.

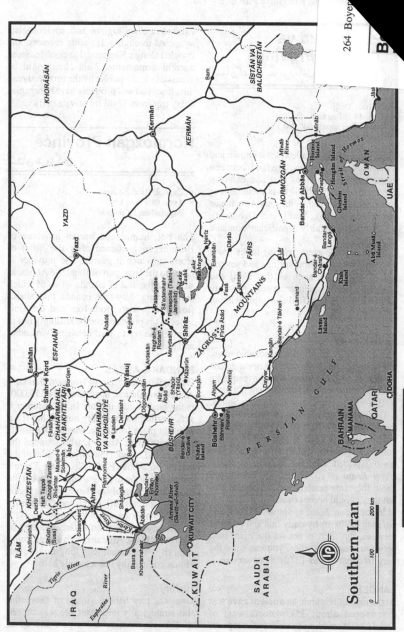

Southern Iran

oyerahmad va Kohgīlūyé Province

استان کهکلویه و بویر احمد

- **Capital:** Yāsūj
- **Area:** 14,261 sq km
- **Population:** approx 600,000

This is one of the smallest, least known and least visited provinces, wedged between larger provinces such as Fārs and Esfahān. Boyerahmad va Kohgīlūyé is mountainous and underdeveloped, with only two major towns (the capital, Yāsūj, and Dehdasht), which suits the fairly significant nomadic population.

There is some great trekking in the province, and a few natural springs and several lovely waterfalls, such as the Yāsūj and Margūn waterfalls. Unfortunately, these are almost impossible to find and enjoy without your own transport.

YĀSŪJ

یاسوج

The provincial capital is a reasonable town, but there is nothing here to justify a detour or stopover. The town has the requisite squares, mosques and bazaars, but it's more worthwhile to carry on to Esfahān or Shīrāz.

Of the limited number of places to stay, the *Jahāngardī Inn* (☎ (0741) 7616) charges about US$25/35 for a reasonable single/double, but like most places run by the ITTO it's overpriced. Another place to try is the *Hotel Eram* (☎ (0741) 3191). Rooms are about the same price as the Jahāngardī Inn, but they should accept rials.

Yāsūj is connected to Shīrāz (252km) and Esfahān (290km) by daily bus and minibus services, but as it is not on the main road between these two cities, you can't use the very frequent Shīrāz-Esfahān bus service.

LANDEH

لنده

At the time of research, an **ancient cave** was discovered about 35km north-west of Dehdasht. According to newspaper reports, excited archaeologists and speleologists squeezed through a 1m-wide entrance and crawled along a 50m tunnel to discover some ancient armaments. This cave could be accessible to the public by the time you read this. If so, you will probably have to organise a day trip from Yāsūj by private taxi.

Hormozgān Province

استان هرمزگان

- **Capital:** Bandar-é Abbās
- **Area:** 68,476 sq km
- **Population:** 1.1 million

The hot, humid and barren province of Hormozgān is named after the Strait of Hormoz, which it guards. The province is home to the large port of Bandar-é Abbās, as well as a handful of islands – two of which are thriving duty-free islands that attract flocks of tourists from Iran and the Gulf states. This province can be stiflingly hot in summer, so try to visit between November and March.

BANDAR-É ABBĀS

بندر عباس

Overlooking the Strait of Hormoz, Bandar-é Abbās (population: approximately 350,000) is the busiest port in Iran. In the summer it gets sizzling hot and very humid, but it's a pleasant place to visit in winter. Despite its links with Shāh Abbās I, who founded the town in 1622, about the only reminder of the origins of 'Abbās Port' is its name. There's not much reason to hang around here, but the city – known simply as Bandar by the locals – is a stepping-off point for the nearby islands, which are worth visiting.

The city's population is largely a mix of Arabs and black Africans, with a large Sunni minority. The small but long-established Hindu community has a temple here.

History

Once the tiny fishing village of Gāmerūn, this strategically important site was chosen as Persia's main southern port and naval dockyard after the decline of nearby Hormoz Island. The British East India Company was granted a trading concession, followed later by concessions to Dutch and French traders, all of whom established factories here. By the 17th century, Bandar-é Abbās had become the chief Persian port and main outlet for the trade in Kermānī carpets.

The port went into decline following the end of the Safavid dynasty (1502-1722). In 1759 the British East India Company moved to the new port of Būshehr, after its factory at Bandar-é Abbās was destroyed by the French. By 1793 the fortunes of Bandar-é Abbās had fallen so low that it passed into the hands of the Sultan of Oman. In 1868, the port returned to Persian control, but its role in maritime trade remained peripheral until the second half of this century. Its hour of glory came during the Iran-Iraq War, when the ports to the west – Būshehr, Bandar-é Emām Khomeinī and Khorramshahr – became too dangerous for regular shipping.

These days, Bandar-é Abbās is still the only truly active, international port on the northern shores of the Persian Gulf. The city has grown dramatically over recent years, and vast sums have been invested in expanding and improving its port facilities.

Orientation

Bandar-é Abbās stretches along an elongated, narrow coastal strip. The main east-west thoroughfare changes its name from Beheshtī Blvd (in the eastern suburbs), to Emām Khomeinī St (through the centre of town), and ends as Pāsdārān Blvd (towards the docks to the west). Around the centre of town, beware of open sewers which are neither pleasant to the nose, nor good for your well-being if you are unlucky enough to fall in one. Very few street signs are written in English, but if you use the map in this book, you shouldn't get lost.

Information

Tourist Office The tourist office (☎ 23 012) is in a tiny alley behind the police headquarters. Not marked in English, the office is impossible to find unless you ask (and ask

again) for directions to the Ershād-é Eslāmī. No-one in the office can speak English, and while pleased (or is that astounded?) that a foreigner has found the office, the staff can offer very little assistance.

Visa Extensions The visa office is on the ground floor of the police headquarters. The police are more than a little laid-back here – the sun affects everyone in Bandar – but if you give them a few days, they should be able to oblige with a visa extension. You don't want to hang around here too long though, so if you need to extend your visa, consider trying somewhere else like Kermān or Shīrāz.

Foreign Consulates The United Arab Emirates (UAE) consulate (☎ 553 063) is the only place in southern Iran where you can get a visa for the UAE. The consul is friendly and speaks English. A one month visa costs 18,000 rials, and takes two or three days to issue. You'll need three photos and a genuine sponsor in the UAE. The consulate is open from 9 am to noon, Sunday to Thursday.

Money The central branch of Bank Melli is the only bank to officially change money, but expect delays. It's best to look for an official money exchange office around the main streets, where you can quickly and easily change money at the unofficial 'street rate'. (There are three offices marked on the map.) There's a black market in UAE dirhams and other Gulf state currencies in the bazaar.

Post & Communications The main post office is 150m north of 17 Shahrīvar Square, and the main telephone office is at the intersection of Emām Khomeinī and Ghaffārī streets. You can send faxes from the post office (but no-one could tell me how much a fax to somewhere 'strange' like Australia would cost). The telephone area code for Bandar is 0761.

Travel Agencies One of the better travel agencies in this part of the country, and just about the only one in Bandar, is the *Bala*

Parvaz Travel Agency (☎ 29 881). Staff are friendly and speak enough English to be of assistance.

Emergency One of several hospitals dotted around this sprawling city is the Emergency Clinic (☎ 22 055), in the north-east of the city. The police headquarters (☎ 27 676) is easy to spot on the south-eastern side of 17 Shahrīvar Square.

Things to See & Do

Frankly, you'll be struggling to find a lot to occupy yourself. A pleasant walk heading east along Tāleghānī Blvd takes you from the daily morning **fish market** to the busy **beach** with boatmen, smugglers and seaside attractions on one side, and the bustling **bazaar** on the other. The huge **mosque**, a few metres east of the bazaar, will be something special when it's finished. If you find any beaches near Bandar which look inviting, be careful: the sharks and stinging

jellyfish are fond of foreigners. The **House of Culture** was closed at the time of research.

Places to Stay

There's often an acute shortage of accommodation in Bandar, especially in winter, when nearly everyone wants to visit. It is a good idea to take a private taxi from the bus terminal, train station or airport to help you look around, as the first couple of options may be busy.

Almost all of the cheap mosāferkhūnés, particularly along 17 Shahrīvar St, will say they are full – which is probably a blatant lie (except in winter when it may be true). The staff at the mosāferkhūnés will try to direct you to the Hotel Ghods, the overpriced tourist hotel. If you are desperate, try to get a letter of introduction (from the police headquarters) that allows you to stay at a mosāferkhūné; ask at the reception of a hotel about renting a local home; or head to Mīnāb (see later in this chapter). Make sure you

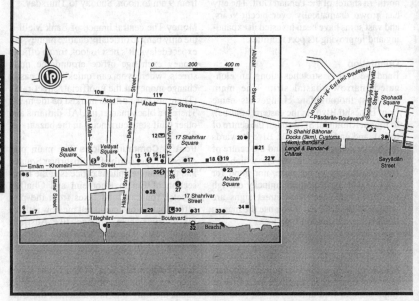

have a fan or air-conditioning in your room during the summer months.

Places to Stay – budget

Of the mosāferkhūnés that will take foreigners, the *Mosāferkhūné-yé Maharaja* (the hotel isn't signed in English) is very basic and the staff speak some English. It's in a convenient location, though the area is a bit dodgy at night. Foreigners are charged too much per room – 32,000 rials – but they do have three single beds.

Above the bazaar, there is one decent cheap place; none of the staff could decide on the name of the place, so we have called it the *Mosāferkhūné-yé Bandar*. It is noisy but clean, and certainly cheap: 5000 rials for a bed in a large dorm or 7000/10,000/12,000 rials for a single/double/triple. It is the only two storey place in the bazaar district; along the esplanade and on the corner of a laneway.

It's better to try one of the two decent places next to each other on Asad Ābādī St.

Both are central and signed in English, but they're on a main road and noisy. The *Hotel Hormozgān* (☎ 24 756) is a bit grotty: the rooms have no curtains or sheets, and the shared bathrooms are even more unappealing. But, because the hotel is poor value (25,000 rials a room), it is more likely to have rooms available.

A bit better is the *Safa Hotel* (☎ 22 651), next door. It has a couple of rooms away from the min road, so some sleep is possible. If you pay extra for air-conditioning, make sure it works before handing over your money. A doubles costs a negotiable 17,000 rials with a fan; 25,000 rials with air-con. The price is for a 24 hour period, so because I booked in at 8 am, the manager wanted an extra 5000 rials. I couldn't quite fathom his logic, but it was too hot to argue.

Places to Stay – middle & top end

The official 'tourist hotel' is the *Hotel Ghods* (☎ 22 344). It is now almost completely

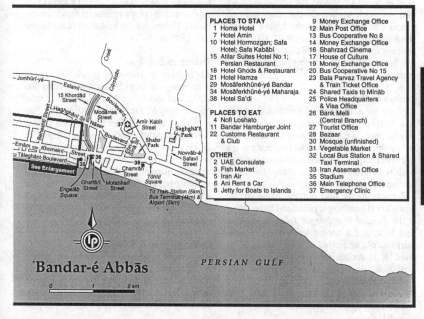

PLACES TO STAY
1 Homa Hotel
7 Hotel Amin
10 Hotel Hormozgan; Safa Hotel; Safa Kababi
15 Atilar Suites Hotel No 1; Persian Restaurant
18 Hotel Ghods & Restaurant
21 Hotel Hamze
29 Mosāferkhūné-yé Bandar
34 Mosāferkhūné-yé Maharaja
38 Hotel Sa'di

PLACES TO EAT
4 Nofi Loshato
11 Bandar Hamburger Joint
22 Customs Restaurant & Club

OTHER
2 UAE Consulate
3 Fish Market
5 Iran Air
6 Ani Rent a Car
8 Jetty for Boats to Islands
9 Money Exchange Office
12 Main Post Office
13 Bus Cooperative No 8
14 Money Exchange Office
16 Shahrzad Cinema
17 House of Culture
19 Money Exchange Office
20 Bus Cooperative No 15
23 Bala Parvaz Travel Agency & Train Ticket Office
24 Shared Taxis to Mīnāb
25 Police Headquarters & Visa Office
26 Bank Melli (Central Branch)
27 Tourist Office
28 Bazaar
30 Mosque (unfinished)
31 Vegetable Market
32 Local Bus Station & Shared Taxi Terminal
33 Iran Asseman Office
35 Stadium
36 Main Telephone Office
37 Emergency Clinic

Bandar-é Abbās

PERSIAN GULF

0   1   2 km

SOUTHERN IRAN

taken over by Russian traders, so all signs are in Russian, and no-one speaks English. It is often full, and the staff are unfriendly. The rooms are quite pleasant but overpriced at 62,000/110,000 rials for a single/double.

The best in this range is the *Hotel Hamze* (☎ 22 303). Try to book ahead because it's also often full. The hotel is also a little inconvenient (and about 30m down an alley), but the staff are friendly. Doubles cost US$15 and they reluctantly accept rials.

Other middle-range places to consider are the *Hotel Sa'dī*, in the eastern part of the city; and the *Hotel Amin* (☎ 20 541). Not to be confused with the overpriced Amir Inn, the Hotel Amin has decent views, pleasant rooms and is popular with Iranian tourists, who obviously don't have to fork out the US$30 (or 90,000 rials) per room that foreigners are charged.

With its tennis courts and swimming pool, the *Homa Hotel* (☎ 554 080) must have been a good hotel once, but it has been going slowly downhill for several years. Prices start at about US$45/65 for singles/doubles and go much higher. Of the other top-end places catering for the winter tourist crowd, the *Atilar Suites Hotel No 1* (☎ 27 420) is the best option, though they do charge foreigners a silly US$50/65/75 for single/double/triple rooms.

Places to Eat

Despite the abundance of seafood, there are few really good restaurants in Bandar, and it would only take a day or two for eating out to become monotonous. The best thing to try is chelō meigū – battered prawns or shrimps with boiled rice – which is cheap, fresh and served almost everywhere.

I could never find out the name of the town's best hamburger place, so I have called it the *Bandar Hamburger Joint*. It is clean and new, and a decent western-style hamburger, cola and salad is a bargain at 3500 rials. It is recognisable by the bright red entrance. Another favourite is the *Safa Kabābī*, directly under the Safa Hotel. For 6000 rials, you can get a plate of tasty beef kebabs, bread and tomatoes, as well as a cold

drink. Also try *Nofl Loshato*, a popular place with locals who enjoy the tasty, western-style hamburgers (about 3500 rials).

Some of Bandar's hotels serve decent fare. The *Persian Restaurant*, in Atilar Suites Hotel No 1, is worth a splurge; the service is excellent and some staff speak English. The service at the restaurant on the ground floor of *Hotel Ghods* is also good and the staff can find a menu in English, but 12,000 rials for a so-so chelō kabāb is too much. There are also several other good *restaurants* near the Hotel Ghods; head along the eastern part of Emām Khomeinī St and find a place that takes your fancy.

One of the more bizarre places must be the *Customs Restaurant & Club*. It was closed at the time of research, but is likely to reopen later. Check it out for something which is bound to be a little unusual.

Entertainment

Bandar is one of the few cities in Iran with a decent, functioning cinema. The *Shahrzad Cinema* – signed in English and a local landmark – usually plays violent Iranian films (in Fārsī). Tickets for the best seats in the house cost 1200 rials.

Things to Buy

All manner of imported goods are traded here, many of them brought over from the UAE, and mostly sold at prices lower than on the rest of the Iranian mainland. You won't buy as cheaply here as on Kīsh Island, but the range of goods is wider. If you're looking for some local souvenirs – traditional Arab clothes, coarse rugs and carpets, woollen blankets, and various implements woven from the fibres of the date palm leaf – visit the bazaar in Bandar, and don't forget the market in Mīnāb (see later in this chapter).

Getting There & Away

Air Bandar is well-connected by air, which is just as well, because overland travel to and from Bandar is tiresome; flying is a good option. Iran Air (☎ 39 595) is normally open Saturday to Thursday, from 7 am to 7.30 pm;

Friday, from 7 am to noon. The office has a complicated numbering system for waiting customers, which I could never work out. Try to get there early and look helpless; someone will probably help you.

Iran Air flies from Bandar-é Abbās to:

Destination	When	Cost (rials)
Chābahār	Monday, Wednesday and Saturday	53,000
Esfahān	Monday, Thursday and Saturday	70,000
Mashhad	Thursday and Sunday	89,500
Rasht	Thursday and Sunday	109,000
(however, this flight will probably be cancelled in the future)		
Shīrāz	Daily	45,500
Tehrān	Twice a day	92,000

As a worthy alternative to Iran Air, Iran Asseman (☎ 29 096) now operates in and out of Bandar. It flies to Tehrān and Shīrāz several times a week for the same price as Iran Air, and to Kīsh Island on Monday and Tuesday for 96,000 rials. Kīsh Airlines also flies between Kīsh Island and Bandar for 24,500 rials, which beats the hell out of taking the squalid boat. However schedules for Kīsh Airlines are a mess; and you will have to book tickets through a travel agency.

International Services One interesting way out of Iran is a hop across the Persian Gulf to the UAE, on Iran Air or Iran Asseman, to Dubai (US$62/124 one way/return) on Tuesday and Sunday; or to Sharjah (for the same price) on Thursday and Saturday.

If you fly out of Bandar-é Abbās on any international flight, you will be slugged an outrageous 70,000 rials for departure tax (which is the cost of a domestic flight from Bandar to Esfahān!).

Bus Bandar enjoys better road communications with central Iran than any other place along the southern shores. However, heavy truck traffic, poor facilities along the road, endless expanses of desert and punishing temperatures for most of the year, mean that few people willingly take the long and dusty bus trip.

The bus terminal is not far from the airport, in the far east of town. You may need to take two shared taxis: one to the turn-off to the bus terminal (ie on the corner of Emām Khomeinī and Gholāmī Sts), and another to the bus terminal itself. The terminal is a surprisingly dreary place (not that bus terminals in Iran are ever particularly cheerful) and is full of locals who wish they could afford to fly. A couple of the bus companies have booking offices in town.

There are several buses each day, from Bandar to the following places (prices listed are for lux/super class):

Destination	Distance	Time	Cost (rials)
Ahvāz	1169km	19 hours	16,500/18,000
Bam	445km	8 hours	6000/6600
Bandar-é Lengé	253km	4 hours	3500 (lux only)
(leaving about every hour)			
Būshehr	921km	16 hours	11,500 (super only)
Esfahān	1082km	18 hours	8900/11,600
Kermān	498km	8 hours	5350/6850
Mīnāb			2100 (lux only)
(better to take a minibus (2500 rials) from near 17 Shahrīvar Square)			
Shīrāz	601km	10 hours	6650/8950
Tehrān	1313km	20 hours	13,700/14,500
Yazd	671km	11 hours	6950/10,750
Zāhedān	1039km	17 hours	8800/12,300

Train Don't bother too much about the train. The services and the station itself are all a bit of a shambles at the moment. The train along the 1483km track to Tehrān, via Sīrjān and Yazd, among other places, leaves every Monday, Wednesday and Friday. Tickets to Tehrān cost 33,250 rials in 1st class.

The train station is being rebuilt. It will be quite impressive when completed, though it's unclear whether this will improve the current services. The station is in the far north of the town and as it's not on the way to anywhere else, you'll probably have to charter a private taxi to get there. There is a handy ticket office in town (no sign in English though) which is one door east of the Bala Parvaz Travel Agency (which is signed in English).

SOUTHERN IRAN

Shared Taxi Shared taxis leave from the terminal on the esplanade, and from around the main streets. The most likely place you'll need one for is Mīnāb.

Boat If you want to visit Kīsh Island, and you don't plan to buy anything large, like a 68cm colour TV with remote control, while you're there, it's far easier and quicker to go via Bandar-é Chārak, a small village west of Bandar-é Lengé (see Getting There & Away – Sea in the Kīsh Island section later in this chapter). The direct boat from Bandar-é Abbās is scruffy, and the ticket place looks, well, like a refugee camp – it is a dreadful place, behind a large fence in the Shahīd Bāhonar docks district. Tickets cost 7000 rials one way. Refer to the Kīsh Island section of this chapter for more details.

Boats from Bandar to the nearby islands of Hormoz and Gheshm leave from the main jetty, near the bazaar. You must pay a 1000 rial port tax before you enter the jetty, then you pay the full fare for the trip on the boat – 2500 rials to Hormoz and 4000 rials to Gheshm. (The fare when you return will include the 1000 rial tax.) Ask locals which boats leave from where, and triple-check that you are on the right boat. The boat trips are fast and frantic, and you may be constantly splashed, so cover anything important. You may want to postpone a trip if the weather is rough – the seas can be choppy even on fine days. Refer to the Getting There & Away section of Hormoz Island and Gheshm Island later in this chapter for more details about how to get to these islands.

You can take a ferry between Bandar-é Abbās and Sharjah (UAE). It leaves Bandar every Monday, Wednesday and Saturday, and returns from Sharjah the next day. The cost for passengers is US$49/46/38 for 1st/2nd/ 3rd class – it is worth paying a little extra for 1st class. Taking a car will cost an extra US$300. Passenger ferries (ie no cars) also leave Dubai for Bandar on Wednesday, and return to Dubai from Bandar on Thursday. Fares are US$55/52/45 for 1st/2nd/3rd class. These ferries are quiet and only take about 3½ hours.

You can buy tickets for all international ferry services at travel agencies around the town, or from the Valfajre-8 office (☎ 553 856). If you have any hassles, ask to speak to a manager, most of whom can speak English and are helpful. International ferries leave from the Shahīd Bāhonar docks in the far western part of town. The Valfajre-8 office is on the way to the docks; you'll have to charter a taxi to get there.

Getting Around
To/From the Airport The airport is about 8km east of the bazaar. It is easy enough to charter a taxi, to or from the airport, for about 5000 rials. A shared taxi (which is harder to find *to* the airport) will cost about 1000 rials.

Taxi Shared taxis are easy to find and cost a reasonable 500 rials around town. To places like the bus terminal, train station and airport, you'll probably need to change taxis, so consider your comfort and charter something. Plenty of taxis hang around the terminal on the esplanade, otherwise you can catch one from around the main streets.

Car There aren't too many places to see around Bandar, but renting a car is worth considering. Ani Rent a Car (%y555 539), where staff speak good English, charges an all-inclusive 10,000 rials for the first hour, and 8000 rials for every subsequent hour. The hourly rate is slightly more if you are going into the countryside. If you want air-conditioning, the charge is double the normal rate. Save money, and open the window of a cheaper car.

MĪNĀB　　　　　　　　　　　　　ميناب
Although Mīnāb was one of the earliest and largest settlements in the area, it's better known for the luxuriant date plantations which dominate the area and, more recently, (and incredibly) the cultivation of mangoes. A visit to the pleasant town of Mīnāb is worth considering, as a day trip from Bandar-é Abbās or as an alternative place to stay.

On the left, on a hilltop as you approach Mīnāb from Bandar-é Abbās, there is an

The Masked Women of Mīnāb

If you travel around southern Iran, particularly near Mīnāb, you may come across Bandarī women wearing a *borqa*. This is an inflexible mask, covering all of the face not hidden by the chādor, with the exception for two tiny slits for the eyes. Interestingly, ethnologists do not believe these masks have any religious links, but rather they are a fashion accessory dating back to the period when the Portuguese ruled the region. ∎

historic tower with houses perched all the way up to it. It's the custom that couples from the town must walk once around this fortress, in the company of their families, before taking their marriage vows.

Places to Stay & Eat

Mīnāb is a charming, quiet and cheap alternative to Bandar-é Abbās. The *Mīnāb Inn* (☎ (07623) 2263) is pleasantly located inside a park, 3km past the main bridge as you come from Bandar. A single/double with balcony, air-con and private bathroom costs a reasonable 25,000/35,000 rials. The nice *restaurant* is open to guests and the public.

The only other place to stay is the *Sadaf Hotel* (☎ (07623) 8999), about 800m before the main bridge as you come from Bandar, and 100m before the bus terminal. Clean rooms with bath cost 22,000/32,000 rials.

Things to Buy

Try to visit Mīnāb on market day, held each Thursday (check if the market is on before leaving Bandar-é Abbās, if you can). The makeshift stalls are set up around the main bridge and roundabout as you enter from Bandar. You can buy heaps of handicrafts made from palm trees, known as *zaribafī* weaving; *kilim* carpets; pottery; and some tacky shell products.

Getting There & Away

About every hour, a minibus (2500 rials) or bus (2000 rials) from Bandar-é Abbās will drop you off at the bus terminal not far from the Sadaf Hotel. A taxi for a half-day trip from Bandar, from a recognised taxi or car rental agency, will cost about 60,000 rials. You may be able to negotiate this down to 40,000 rials for an ordinary private taxi.

BANDAR-É LENGÉ   بندر لنگه

The population of Bandar-é Lengé (or Lengé to the locals) is half Sunni and half Shi'ite, and Arabic and Fārsī are spoken. Lengé is an infectiously lethargic place, and although there isn't a great deal to do here, even outside the rigidly observed five or six hour siesta. It's a pleasant overnight stop before or after visiting Kīsh Island, or a day trip from Bandar-é Abbās. Sadly, there are beggars, often aggressive, who ply the streets of Lengé.

Things to see around town include several colourful, **pale stone mosques**, with single minarets decorated in the Arab style, and a few old and largely derelict **Bandarī buildings** made of mud brick.

Orientation & Information

The main streets are Emām Khomeinī Blvd (the coastal road and esplanade in the town) and Enghelāb St, which heads to Bandar-é Abbās. This is not a town where foreigners are expected: not one street, shop or hotel is signed in English, but it would be hard to become lost. The Bank Melli branch may change money, but don't count on it. For

SOUTHERN IRAN

some reason, bottles of Damarvand mineral spring water are easier to buy here than in Tehrān. The telephone area code is 07622.

Places to Stay & Eat

Although some staff at the *Hotel Amid* (☎ 2311) speak English, it is not great value: 21,000 rials for a three-bed room with shared bath. For some reason, the manager gave me 3500 rials back as I was about to check out – maybe he felt guilty about charging so much initially. There is a small but decent *restaurant* downstairs. Another unnamed *restaurant*, in the same building as the Amid, does a decent BBQ chicken and rice for 8000 rials.

The *Hotel Babu* is slightly better, 18,800 rials for a double with a shared bathroom. The hotel is an unmistakable four storey white building with a 'resturant' (sic) downstairs. Beware of overcharging, I had to pay an exorbitant 14,000 rials for a chicken kebab, rice and salad. The best of the limited range is the *Hotel Villa*, closed for extensive renovations at the time of research, which also boasts the best *restaurant* in town. A new hotel should be open by the time you visit, and hopefully will provide a good middle-range option.

The *Restōran-é Shafa'igh* is also worth a try. There are a few *teahouses* in the bazaar, where the hubble-bubble comes without a pipe – the mouthpiece leads directly into the water jug. There are several *food stalls* along the main road, and the coastal road east of the harbour. Sadly, chicken is more widely available than fish. Finish off your meal with a visit to the excellent little *bakery*, which is north of the bazaar.

Getting There & Away

Air The huge, incongruous Iran Air office (☎ 2799) is one of the most impressive in the country, yet it has only one flight: the daily special to Tehrān (27,800 rials) via Shīrāz (13,800 rials).

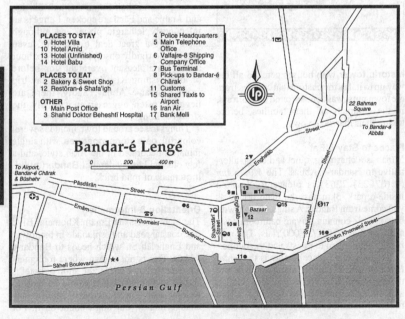

PLACES TO STAY
9 Hotel Villa
10 Hotel Amid
13 Hotel (Unfinished)
14 Hotel Babu

PLACES TO EAT
2 Bakery & Sweet Shop
12 Restōran-é Shafa'igh

OTHER
1 Main Post Office
3 Shahid Doktor Beheshtī Hospital
4 Police Headquarters
5 Main Telephone Office
6 Valfajre-8 Shipping Company Office
7 Bus Terminal
8 Pick-ups to Bandar-é Chārak
11 Customs
15 Shared Taxis to Airport
16 Iran Air
17 Bank Melli

Bandar-é Lengé

0   200   400 m

To Airport,
Bandar-é Chārak
& Būshehr

Pāsdārān Street

Emām Khomeinī

Sāhelī Boulevard

Enghelāb Street

Bazaar

Shahrdārī Street

Emām Khomeinī Street

22 Bahman Square

To Bandar-é Abbās

Persian Gulf

SOUTHERN IRAN

Bus The bus terminal is convenient and easy to deal with. For long-distance destinations, you will need to get a connection from Bandar-é Abbās. Buses to Bandar-é Abbās (253km, four hours, 3500 rials for lux class only) leave about every hour, from early morning to evening. Several buses to Būshehr (656km, nine hours, 7000 rials for lux class only) leave daily. There is also at least one bus every day to Shīrāz (654km, 12 hours, 7500/8200 for lux/super).

Boat Lengé's main claim to fame (perhaps its only claim) is its daily ferry to Kīsh Island, the duty-free hot spot in the Persian Gulf. Ferries from Lengé suit locals because they are large, allowing them to carry bundles of duty-free goods. The fare is cheap (4000 rials) – but conditions are poor and the trip is long. You are better off taking the speed-boat from Bandar-é Chārak (see Getting Around – following).

Tickets for the ferry, available at the Valfajre-8 Shipping Company office, are in short supply, but foreigners are sometimes given priority. The office is often closed (like everything else) during the heat of the day, from noon to 5 pm. By about 4 pm, hot and angry passengers start to huddle around the front door of the office waiting to buy tickets for the ferry leaving that evening. You may be able to buy a ferry ticket from an agency around town for a small extra fee.

Getting Around
To/From the Airport From the airport, just jump in a shared taxi (1000 rials) – which is normally an unusual type of open-air utility truck, known locally as a *pik-up* – to the bus terminal or bazaar, from where it is easy to walk to a hotel.

Taxi There are very few of the shared or private taxis you see around the rest of the country here, as the town is small enough to walk (or saunter) around. Any long distances can be covered in pik-ups which leave from the unofficial stops around the bus terminal. Pik-ups to Bandar-é Chārak (for the speed-boats to Kīsh Island) leave Lengé at about 6 am, so passengers can get to Kīsh before the heat becomes unbearable.

HORMOZ ISLAND   جزيره هرمز
The 42 sq km Hormoz Island is definitely worth a visit, and is easily accessible from Bandar-é Abbās. There's one small town,

---

The Persian Gulf

The mighty Persian Gulf *(Khalīj-é Fārs)* is 965km long, stretching from the Shatt al-Arab River, which is part of the border between southern Iraq and Iran, and the Strait of Hormoz, which becomes the Sea of Oman to the east. The Gulf is between 50km and 370km wide; is 233,100 sq km in area; and is quite shallow – no more than 90m deep. It is bordered by Iran, Iraq and the Gulf states of Kuwait, the United Arab Emirates, Qatar, Oman and Saudi Arabia, while the island nation of Bahrain is in the south.

As the world's major oil-producing region, it is not surprising that pollution in the Gulf is rife. In the early 1980s, dozens of catastrophic oil spills resulted from the Iran-Iraq War; 200,000 tonnes of crude oil from one oil rig (near Khārk Island) destroyed by Iraqi bombers spilled into the Gulf. Again, during the Gulf War, an estimated one million tonnes of crude oil poured into the Gulf. Leakages from oil tankers continue unabated today.

The increasingly industrialised and populated shores of the Gulf, including the unrestrained development on the Iranian islands of Kīsh and Gheshm, have caused extensive damage to the Gulf's fragile ecosystem; for example, the dumping of rubbish and untreated sewage; industrial and agricultural chemicals finding their way into rivers, and then the Gulf; and the effects of dredging used to create and maintain deep channels for shipping.

Hopefully, the new Regional Organisation for the Protection of Marine Environment, created by the countries bordering the Gulf, will find some way of tackling these serious problems. ■

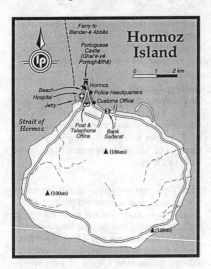

Ferry to
Bandar-é Abbās

Hormoz Island

Portuguese
Castle
(Ghal'é-yé
Portoghālīhā)

0   1   2 km

Hormoz
★ Police Headquarters
Customs Office

Beach
Hospital
Jetty

Strait of
Hormoz

Post &
Telephone
Office

Bank
Saderat

▲ (186m)

▲ (100m)

▲ (100m)

called (naturally) Hormoz, on the northern promontory and the rest of the island is virtually uninhabited. Its interior is hilly and infertile, and worth hiking around if you have an inkling, although it does get very hot when the breeze stops. The island is famous for the red tones of its soil and some of its stone, both of which are used as building materials in Hormoz.

History

The island was, until the 14th century, known as Jarūn Island, while Hormoz was the name of a famous and long-established commercial town on the mainland, probably on the Mīnāb River. Around 1300, the damage caused by repeated Mongol raids made the 15th Amīr of Hormoz shut up shop and move. He took many of his subjects with him and together they briefly stopped on Kīsh Island before finally settling on Jarūn Island.

This new Hormoz soon became the main emporium of the Persian Gulf, attracting immigrants from the mainland, and traders from as far away as India. Visitors to Hormoz described it as heavily fortified, bustling and opulent. It naturally attracted some Euro-

pean traders, mainly Portuguese who built a castle there (see 'The Portuguese on Hormoz' boxed text in this chapter). After the Portuguese left Hormoz in the early 17th century, Shāh Abbās I selected the small mainland fishing town of Gāmerūn to be the new outlet for Persian trade, changing its name to Bandar-é Abbās after himself. Hormoz quickly fell into a period of decline, from which it has never recovered, with most of its former splendour reduced to ruins within a few years.

Today, the town of Hormoz is still an impoverished outpost where foraging goats and barefoot children are rarely disturbed by motorised traffic, though some of the traditional mat huts have been replaced by low-roofed stone dwellings.

Registration

One traveller wrote to say that following her arrival on the island in early 1996, she was asked to register with the police in Hormoz village. When I visited later, however, I walked past the police headquarters and the officers gave me a friendly wave, but said nothing. If you do have to register, it should be painless.

Portuguese Castle

Some 750m to the north of Hormoz beach, and easily reached by foot, is the famous Portuguese castle (ghal'é-yé Portoghālīhā) of Hormoz Island. It is without doubt the most impressive colonial fortress in Iran, but it's neglected, badly in need of renovations, and used by locals as a rubbish tip. Yet it is still hauntingly beautiful and well worth a visit.

Constructed of reddish stone on a rocky promontory, the castle was originally cut off from the rest of the island by a moat, traces of which remain. Although most of the roofing caved in long ago, much of the lower part of the very substantial outer walls are intact, with the remains lying on different levels of the site. A few cannons and cannonballs lay scattered. There is no gate or entrance fee.

SOUTHERN IRAN

The Portuguese on Hormoz

In 1507, the talented Portuguese admiral and empire builder, Afonso de Albuquerque (also known as Afonso the Great), besieged and, after a battle, conquered Hormoz, in an attempt to establish a network of Portuguese bases, including Goa, Aden and Malacca (present-day Melaka in Malaysia). The castle of Hormoz, which he started the same year, was completed in 1515; in the meantime he took Goa in 1510 and Malacca in 1511. In 1515 he left Hormoz to return to Goa, only to be informed by the ungrateful Portuguese authorities that he was out of a job – he died in Goa later the same year.

With Hormoz Island as their fortified base, the Portuguese quickly extended their gains and came to hold sway over all shipping in the Persian Gulf. Virtually all trade with India, the Far East, Muscat (Oman) and the Gulf ports was funnelled through Hormoz, to which the Portuguese, under an administration known for its justice and religious tolerance, brought great prosperity for over a century.

But Portugal's stranglehold over vital international trading routes could hardly fail to arouse the resentment of Persia and the other rising imperial powers of the day. In 1550, Ottoman forces besieged the fortress of Hormoz for a month but failed to take the island.

Early the next century, Shāh Abbās I granted the British East India Company trading rights with Persia through the port of Jāsk, thus enraging the Portuguese. Abbās cajoled the English into sending a force to assist him, and in 1622 the joint expedition, despite a brave defence by the Portuguese, succeeded in gaining control of Hormoz Island. ■

Hormoz Village   هرمز

This pleasant little village is interesting, though there's nothing much to do except ramble through the small maze of kūchés (alleys). In the northern-most part of Hormoz village is the **Masjed-é Jāme'-yé Emām Shāfe'ī**, a small Sunni mosque, with a fine single minaret of pale stone.

Sadly, little of the great medieval settlement remains around present-day Hormoz village: the Islamic palace of the former rulers of Hormoz was demolished by the Portuguese, and a fine 15th century mosque, which stood until the 19th century, has also become unidentifiable rubble.

Places to Stay & Eat

There are no places to stay or eat on Hormoz Island. There are a couple of poorly-stocked shops but it's advisable to bring food and water from the mainland. A picnic at the castle, overlooking the sea, is wonderfully relaxing.

Getting There & Away

People from Bandar-é Abbās prefer to go to Gheshm because Hormoz is so sparsely populated – which is reason enough to go there rather than Gheshm. Speedboats tear along the stretch of water between Bandar-é Abbās

and Hormoz whenever they have their full complement of about 10 passengers – about every 40 to 50 minutes. Start early if you want to make sure of catching a boat back to Bandar-é Abbās. The 30 minute journey costs 2500 rials, plus a 1000 rials 'tax'. Beware of some possible shenanigans on the boat (see the 'Piracy on the Persian Gulf?' boxed text later in this chapter).

Getting Around

The best option is to walk.

GHESHM ISLAND   جزیره قشم

Gheshm is by far the largest island (1335 sq km) in the Persian Gulf, more than twice the size of Bahrain but with less than 15% of its population. The island is mountainous, with a largely rocky coastline, dotted with villages and small towns and few settlements of any size in the interior. The main town and administrative centre is Gheshm. The best time to visit is between October and March.

From the island's first post-Revolutionary five year plan, launched on 31 January 1990, grandiose schemes emerged for Gheshm Island to become a duty-free area and tourist attraction, along the lines of Kīsh Island. These plans have not gone down well with the islanders, who have become justifiably worried that development will lead to the demolition of their houses and mass resettlement. (Just look at what has happened to Kīsh.) Still, unlike Kīsh, Gheshm Island doesn't (yet) resemble a construction site, and it manages to retain some charm. Things are bound to change quickly, however.

History

Gheshm Island has been referred to briefly in documents from the Achaemenian period (559-330 BC), and has for many centuries been a trading centre between the continents and subcontinents. However, Gheshm lacks the historical status of the smaller Hormoz Island, and very little is known of its early development. The island was mentioned by Marco Polo, and later marked out for potential colonisation by Vasco da Gama. The Portuguese built a castle on the eastern side of Gheshm Island, during their occupation of Hormoz, and the island came under the sway of the Dutch, French, Germans and British until it was brought back firmly under the control of Iran shortly after WWI.

Orientation & Information

Gheshm is the largest town (officially, a city) on the island, with wide roads and a main square, but it's tiny by mainland standards. There are plans to build a bridge at Laft-é Kohneh, linking the island to the mainland at Bandar-é Pol, but this is many years from completion. For foreign travellers without a car, the ferry between Bandar-é Abbās and Gheshm town will always be easier. The telephone area code for the island is 07629.

Things to See & Do

Conical **water reservoirs** are scattered all over the island, with the highest concentration around Gheshm town. They have small holes at the top of the dome which let rain in, two narrow doors, and pools from which the islanders once gathered water for washing.

There are a few Arab-style mosques around the island, both Sunni and Shi'ite. There are remains of a **Portuguese fortress** *(ghal'é-yé Portoghālīhā)* in Gheshm town, but they are not nearly as impressive as those on Hormoz Island. The village of **Lāft** is

---

Piracy on the Persian Gulf?

Suddenly the speedboat, on the trip from Hormoz Island to Bandar-é Abbās, stopped in the middle of the Persian Gulf, the waves going up and down, up and down ... all the passengers, including a slightly green foreigner (me), were told to transfer to another speedboat which had mysteriously pulled up alongside. With plenty of trepidation, everyone, including the boatman, stepped from one boat to another – everyone, except for four local women who refused to change boats, obviously knowing something I didn't. After some heated, but unsuccessful, demands from the owner of the new speedboat, the four women were set adrift without the boatman.

The owner of the new boat stopped the engine. He looked at me, and asked to see my passport; I told him that I had left it at the hotel (not true). In reply to my hostile (but green) expression, a few passengers whispered the word 'police' to me. The policeman then asked for money; I showed him the few thousand rials I had in my pocket (but he didn't take them), claiming that the rest was at my hotel too (also not true). To stop this line of questioning, I feigned serious seasickness (which was certainly becoming a reality) – the boat was going up and down, up and down ...

After about 30 minutes, the policeman started the engine, and found the four women in the other boat. The passengers were allowed to delicately transfer to the original boat, but after another 15 minute argument with the policeman, the four women, by now cursing heavily in a local dialect, reluctantly gave him a bundle of lovely, handmade scarves. The policeman then sped off, while we restarted our journey back to terra firma, through the increasingly high waves, going up and down, up and down ...

No-one bothered asking for any identification from the policeman and his assistant, but it seems likely that this was evidence of some sort of modern piracy. I did not suffer anything but seasickness, though passengers travelling between Bandar-é Abbās and the nearby islands should take care (leave your valuables at your hotel, if you can) – particularly if you have chartered a boat.

Paul Greenway

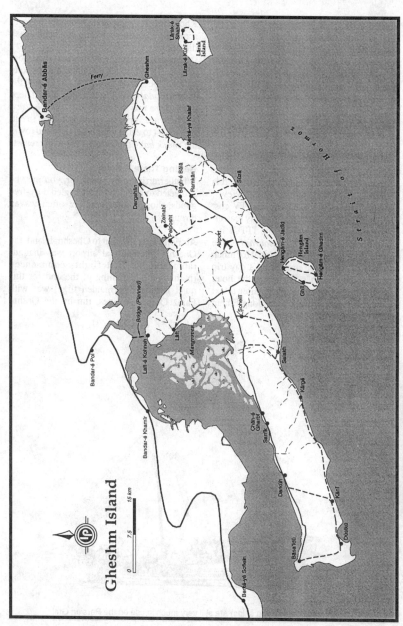

Gheshm Island

worth a visit. It's a pretty place, with a real Persian Gulf atmosphere: there are wind-towers, wells and an empty beach. Ask about minibuses, or charter a taxi from Gheshm town. Thankfully, the island is not set up with theme parks and shopping centres like Kīsh, but sadly it is only a matter of time.

Places to Stay & Eat
More and more places will be built over the coming years, as Gheshm Island attempts to rival Kīsh as an upmarket duty-free port. Currently, the best place to stay is the *Gheshm Inn* (☎ 2001) in Gheshm town. It is pleasant, friendly and has great views. Doubles with a fridge, air-con and TV cost foreigners 40,000 rials – surprisingly reasonable if you are taking a day trip from Bandar-é Abbās. To reach the hotel from the port, you can either charter a taxi for the short ride, or walk west along Emām Khomeinī St – you will probably have to scramble up some rocks and will need to ask directions.

Upmarket places near Gheshm town, from around US$35/45 for a single/double room, include the *Sarah Hotel* (☎ 4571) and the *International Gheshm* (☎ 5305). You'll need to charter a taxi to find them.

There are very few exciting places to eat. so it's best to eat at your hotel. Around town, the *snack bars* and *kabābīs* are a last resort.

Getting There & Away
Whether arriving by sea or air, you may be subjected to a search for smuggled duty-free goods, though foreigners are often waved through.

Air Following my visit to Gheshm Island, the Gheshm international airport was inaugu-rated and the first flights commenced (perhaps the beginning of the end for this quiet island). The maiden flight was with Faraz Qeshm Airlines, run by the Qeshm

Dhows (traditional sailing ships) are still very much in use on the Persian Gulf.

Free Trade Zone, which plans to fly between Gheshm and Tehrān on Tuesday, Thursday and Sunday. Further details about flights, costs and schedules were unavailable at the time of research, but any travel agency in Gheshm or Tehrān will be able to help.

Boat The main jetty is at the northern end of Gheshm town. There are regular speedboats between Bandar-é Abbās (45 minutes, 4000 rials, plus 1000 rials for 'port tax') and Gheshm, but they will wait until they have their full seaworthy capacity of about eight to 10 passengers before sailing. It is an exhilarating ride and you may get a little wet, so take care of your money belt and camera, and watch out for sunburn.

There are also very occasional services between Bandar-é Abbās and Dargahān, about 20km west of Gheshm town. Boats to and from other destinations, such as Hormoz or Lārak islands, are arranged as required, according to the number, and wealth, of passengers. You could also inquire about hiring a boat to Hengām Island from one of the villages on the southern coast of Gheshm Island, but as there is a military base on Hengām, this may not be a wise idea.

Getting Around

There's no organised public transport, but things are likely to change as the island becomes more developed. Currently, shared taxis, vans and pik-ups take passengers along the coastal road: the fare between Gheshm and Dargahān is about 500 rials per person. You might also be able to hire a private van or taxi in Gheshm town for a tour of the island (about 8000 rials per hour; or 50,000 rials per day), but you won't be able to circle the island along any paved roads.

KĪSH ISLAND
جزیره کیش

Kīsh Island is a bizarre place: a little bit of Singapore with highways and towering apartment blocks and hotels; a quasi-Disneyland with theme parks; and a poor man's California with beaches and bicycle paths – all with a unique Iranian style. The main attraction for Iranians, however, is the availability of duty-free electrical goods.

First impressions are that the 90 sq km island resembles a huge construction site – which it does – but among the chaos there is order. All public transport is air-conditioned, all drivers wear seat belts, and, believe it or not, most (but not all) vehicles stop at pedestrian crossings!

But be warned: Kīsh is *very* expensive, and anything more than an overnight stop will be too much for many travellers. The theory is that if you can afford to come to Kīsh, you can also afford to be overcharged – for everything. If the idea of paying about 80,000 rials for a simple room, and 20,000 rials for a sit-down meal makes you choke on your kebab, don't bother staying here. Day trips are possible if you get an early start.

History

In the Middle Ages, Kīsh Island became an important trading centre under its own powerful Arab dynasty, and at one time it supported a population of 40,000. The island was known for the quality of its pearls; when Marco Polo was visiting the imperial court in China, he remarked on the beauty of the pearls worn by one of the emperor's wives – he was told that they had come from Kīsh.

The island fell into decline in the 14th century. It remained obscure until just before the Islamic Revolution (in 1979), when it was developed as an almost private retreat for the Shāh and his privileged guests, with its own international airport, palaces, luxury hotels and restaurants, and even a grand casino. Shortly after the Revolution, the new

The duty-free port of Kīsh sports its own logo.

SOUTHERN IRAN

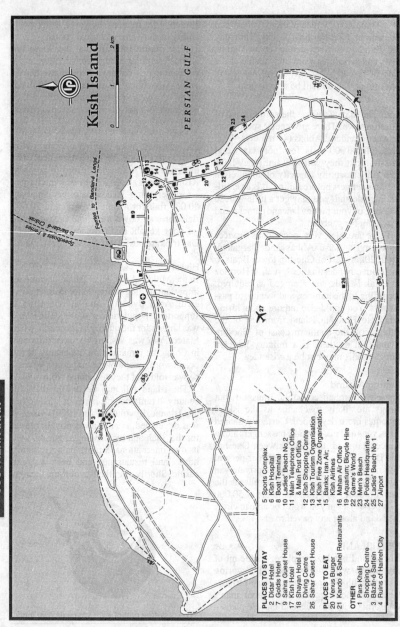

Kīsh Island

PERSIAN GULF

Ferries to Bandar-é Langé

Speedboats & ferries to Bandar-é Chārak

PLACES TO STAY
2 Didar Hotel
7 Goldis Hotel
9 Sahra Guest House
17 Kish Hotel
18 Shayan Hotel & Diving Centre
26 Sahar Guest House

PLACES TO EAT
20 Venus Burger
21 Kando & Sahel Restaurants

OTHER
1 Pars Khalij Shopping Centre
3 Bāzār-é Saffein
4 Ruins of Harirein City
5 Sports Complex
6 Kish Hospital
8 Boat Terminal
10 Ladies' Beach No 2
11 Main Telephone Office & Main Post Office
12 Kish Shopping Centre
13 Kish Tourism Organisation
14 Kish Free Zone Organisation
15 Banks; Iran Air; Kish Airlines
16 Mahan Air Office
19 Aquarium; Bicycle Hire
22 Game's World
23 Men's Beach
24 Police Headquarters
25 Ladies' Beach No 1
27 Airport

SOUTHERN IRAN

government established Kīsh as a duty-free port, taking advantage of the facilities already in place and its proximity to the wealthy Gulf states.

Orientation & Information

There's no real centre to Kīsh Island, despite signs in English indicating a 'City Centre', and there are no addresses as such. The Arab settlements are the town of Saffein, on the north coast, and the small oasis village of Bāghū, in the south-west of the island. Most people live near the main roads along the northern and eastern coasts, and many of the offices, shops and hotels are along a small section of road in the north-east. The telephone area code for the island is 07653.

Tourist Offices The best place to get any information, as wells as maps (in English, French and Spanish), is the Kīsh Tourism Organisation. Staff are friendly, and some speak English. It is open from about 8 am to 5 pm, Saturday to Thursday. Next door, the Kīsh Free Zone Organisation (KFZO) (☎ 2141) is more involved in attracting businesses to construct lots and lots of concrete buildings, but staff speak some English and they are willing to help if the tourist office can't. The KFZO also has an office in northern Tehrān (☎ (21) 8797 380).

Money There are three branches of the main banks in the business heart of the island, including Bank Melli, where you can change money.

Emergency Hopefully, you won't need to call the police headquarters (☎ 2143) or the Kīsh Hospital (☎ 2111).

Harireh & Saffein   حريره وصفين

Among all this unrestrained development, there is actually something old on the island: the ruins of the ancient cities of Harireh and Saffein. Little is known about the origins of Harireh – about 800 years ago, the city, which was home to up to 40,000 people, was completely pillaged, so almost nothing remains. The ruins of an 11th or 12th century

palace, and other historical structures of the old city of Saffein, are nearby, but again very little remains. No attention is given to the ruins; there are plenty of ancient sites on mainland Iran, and Iranians come to Kīsh for the beaches and shops.

Beaches

Kīsh is one of the very few places in Iran where swimming is actively encouraged. There are sandy, uncrowded beaches around most of the coast, but the authorities request that female swimmers use either **Ladies Beach No 1** or **Ladies Beach No 2**, while men have to use the **Men's Beach**. Foreign men and women should not flaunt segregation rules unless they are able to find a very, *very* discreet beach away from apartments and hotels, or bulldozers and cement mixers – which is not easy.

Theme Parks

Efforts have been made to green the island, and there are already several small parks of tropical trees. Theme parks, such as the **Family Park** and **Deers Park** (sic), are being completed, meanwhile tourists can currently visit the **Aquarium** and **Game's World**.

Diving

Most development has been on land, so some of the underwater beauty has been spared (so far). There's a wide range of decorative fish around the coral reefs off Kīsh, including the rare emperor fish. Kīsh is the only place in Iran which has a diving centre, though it's certainly in its infancy. Make inquiries at the Diving Centre (☎ 2771) at the Shayan Hotel. No further details were available at the time of research, but it's a fair guess that prices will be high, while standards may be low.

For those with heaps and *heaps* of money, you could also jump on the helicopter shuttle service to the tiny **Hendourabi Island**, 24km away, where there is a promise of more pristine coral reefs. A slightly cheaper option is to hire a boat from the boat terminal to see the **turtle colony** (*dasté-yé lāk-é poshté ābī*), off the southern coast.

Places to Stay

An initial warning: you may be horrified by the prices of hotels on Kīsh, and the cheapest places are often full of itinerant traders and construction workers.

The guesthouses are the best places to try. The *Sahra Guest House* (☎ 2110) and *Sahar Guest House* (☎ 2067) – just a little confusing – charge from 60,000 rials for a double, but they are almost permanently full. Ask around for the locations, and prices, of other guesthouses and villa complexes.

One idea is to look for an apartment to rent. Depending on the demand, you could get away with a room in an apartment for as 'little' as 40,000 rials per person. Make some inquiries at the tourist office, or at the boat terminal where touts sometimes hang about when business is slow.

One place which is reasonably priced – for Kīsh, that is – is the *Didar Hotel* (☎ 2706), which charges a negotiable 100,000 rials for a huge air-con room with TV and fridge. Breakfast is extra.

There are many other top-end hotels and resorts along the northern and eastern coasts, and many more to come if the number of cranes and bulldozers are any indication. If you have a heap of money, try the *Goldis Hotel* (☎ 2237) or *Kīsh Hotel* (☎ 2771) which charges about US$45/55 for singles/doubles, plus taxes. One excellent, central place is the *Shayan Hotel* (☎ 2771) which charges foreigners the odd figure of 221,130 rials for a luxurious double room. If you've changed your money unofficially at the 'street rate', and fancy a splurge somewhere on your trip, this is a good place to do it.

Places to Eat

Kīsh is the sort of place where you can buy 15 different types of 'steam/dry/spray irons (with detachable water tank)', but you could spend three days looking for somewhere to buy a cup of tea. And when you do find one, you will be charged the earth, and sometimes a mysterious tax of 10%.

One place with decent prices is the *Venus Burger*, a western-style hamburger joint where burgers, including a drink, cost from 6500 rials, plus tax. For something tasty, from about 15,000 rials a plate, try the *Kando Restaurant* or the *Sahel Restaurant* nearby.

The only places to get food at a reasonable price are at the handful of *cafés* and *restaurants* in Saffein village, about five minutes' walk north of the Didar Hotel. Here you can get a burger and cola for a bargain 4000 rials. Avoid the restaurant at the *Didar Hotel* which charged me a jaw-dropping 25,000 rials for an ordinary chelō kabāb with no drinks or bread.

Things to Buy

The glossy brochures extol the attractions of the 12 or more 'bazaars' on Kīsh Island. Don't be fooled, these are little more than concrete malls – but it is fascinating to watch busloads of Iranians go on a shopping frenzy. **Bāzār-é Saffein**, a mud brick tunnel, is one of the more interesting malls-cum-bazaars. Its authenticity is somewhat tarnished by the flashing neon signs advertising electronic goods from Japan. Handy to most visitors are the **Kīsh Shopping Centre**, in the busiest part of town, and the **Pars Khalij Shopping Centre**.

Customs Regulations Customs regulations seem to change as often as the wind. At the time of research no-one is able to take out any duty-free goods bought on Kīsh worth more than US$22. So, you *can* pick-up that 'steam/dry/spray iron (with detachable water tank)' without declaring it, as long as you have your receipt. If you buy anything worth more than US$22 in total, you will have to line up in the chaos of the customs office at the boat terminal or airport, and wait to be processed. You will soon wish you had bought it somewhere else.

Before you commit yourself to buying anything and taking it out of Kīsh, you are strongly advised to ring local customs (☎ 2577) or the KFZO (☎ 2141) and find out what you have to do to be able to take it off the island.

Getting There & Away

If the cost of staying on Kīsh will put a huge

hole in your budget, don't ignore the possibility of taking a day trip. This is quite possible by boat from Bandar-é Lengé, as long as you start very early . As silly as it may sound, flying in and out of Kīsh in one day from somewhere close, or even from Tehrān, is worth considering if the schedules work in your favour.

Customs Checks Whichever way you arrive and depart, you will be subject to lengthy customs searches, so allow plenty of time – and these searches may not always be pleasant, as I found out:

My clothes were sprawled across the dirt floor of the customs yard by grumpy customs officers at the boat terminal on Kīsh, much to the disgust of local onlookers who graciously helped me to stuff the dusty clothes back into my backpack. With an undeniable smirk of satisfaction, I later read a newspaper article which reported an outbreak of fisticuffs between customs officers and fed-up passengers at the boat terminal on Kīsh, with about 10 officers – but no passengers – taken to hospital with minor injuries.

Air Most of the domestic airlines have daily charter flights to and from Kīsh, but the schedules vary according to demand and the season. Tickets to Kīsh on any airline are difficult to get, because they are usually sold only two weeks before departure, demand is heavy, and travel agencies are more interested in selling you a package deal that includes accommodation, tours etc.

Iran Air has charter flights from Tehrān and sometimes, according to demand, from Shīrāz, Esfahān and Mashhad. The main airline is Kīsh Airlines, part of the KFZO, which links Kīsh with Tehrān and, depending on demand, other major cities. Staff at the Kīsh Airlines office (on Kīsh) were unable to provide any departure times and prices – while the airline is reliable, its schedules certainly are not.

Mahan Air (☎ 2844) also flies between Kīsh and Tehrān, more so in winter and during public and school holidays. Iran Asseman is more reliable and flies almost every day between Kīsh and Tehrān (69,000 rials). Book your tickets for these smaller airlines at a reputable travel agency and book a return ticket before you arrive in Kīsh.

Boat Valfajre-8 sails to Kīsh from three ports. In Bandar-é Abbās, hundreds of Iranians wait for the next boat in a compound, which looks and smells like a refugee camp. Boats are irregular (maybe twice a week, maybe not) and unreliable, but very cheap (7000 rials one way). Overcrowded boats leave Bandar-é Lengé (4000 rials) every night at 9 pm. From Būshehr, boats are irregular and the trip is very long. Buy your tickets for boats operated by Valfajre-8 at the boat terminal in Kīsh.

Easily the best way for travellers to visit Kīsh is to take the speedboat from Bandar-é Chārak – an easy ride from Bandar-é Lengé in a pik-up (90 minutes, 9000 rials). The pik-up will take you to the beach at Chārak, where most of your fellow passengers will pile into an 8 to 10 person speedboat (18,000 rials), after luggage and passports have gone through a perfunctory check. To visit Kīsh in one day, start from Lengé at about 6 am, and allow enough time to get back.

Getting Around
To/From the Airport You will probably have to charter a taxi from the airport for about 5000 rials, and negotiation isn't usually possible. Watch out for the overcharging of overspending visitors.

To/From the Port From the boat terminal, you can crowd onto a local minibus or, if you have some luggage, a private taxi is better. Be careful before taking any taxi as they charge like the proverbial bull: up to 30,000 rials per hour, but mercifully the vehicles are air-conditioned.

Minibus One highlight are the excellent minibuses (500 rials) which travel along the northern and eastern road, known as the World Road. These modern vehicles are air-conditioned and very comfortable. Standing is not allowed, so you may have to wait a while before a minibus with empty seats stops.

SOUTHERN IRAN

Bicycle One welcome innovation is the well-marked Special Bicycle Route which circles the island. This would be great if it wasn't so damn hot most of the year, and bikes were easy to hire. I did find some bikes for hire near the aquarium, but the manager was nowhere to be found. Taking a siesta, no doubt.

OTHER ISLANDS

Foreigners are free to visit any of the other islands around the Persian Gulf without special permission, except for Abū Mūsā, where there is an important naval station. However, it's wise not to go to any of these other islands without written authority from the *ostāndārī* (provincial government office) or tourist office in Bandar-é Abbās. Abū Mūsā was previously claimed by the UAE, but it's now firmly under Iranian control, though very difficult to get to from the mainland. None of the other islands are on any regular passenger transport route, though some can be reached by chartering a fishing boat from the major islands.

If you really want to go, don't be put off by the difficulty of touring the islands, as they're undoubtedly a source of vast and largely undocumented ethnological and zoological interest, and as far off the tourist trail as one can get. You would probably have to charter a boat for several days from Bandar-é Abbās and be completely self-sufficient. Good luck!

Fārs Province   استان فارس

- **Capital:** Shīrāz
- **Area:** 126,489 sq km
- **Population:** 4.2 million

Historically, Fārs extends far beyond its present boundaries and covers much of the southern region of Iran. This is where the Persians or Fārsīs first settled, and where the great empires of the Achaemenians (559-330 BC) and Sassanians (224-637 AD) were centred. Persepolis, once the greatest city of

the region, is the principal attraction today, but it's far from the only reminder of Persia at its peak.

Shīrāz, the provincial centre since the 7th century AD, claims its own glory as a capital of several Islamic dynasties and, perhaps more importantly, as a major artistic centre. The people of Fārs are mostly Persian, though there are still some nomadic tribes which even Chinggis Khaan (Genghis Khan) and Timur could never pacify.

Fārs province has a varied topography, and includes most of the mighty Zāgros mountain range. These mountains are home to some recently introduced yellow deer and up to 80,000 nomads from the Mamassanī, Khamsé and Ghashghā'ī tribes, who speak Turkish dialects and Lorī, the Lor language.

SHĪRĀZ   شیراز

To the three weeks which I spent in Shīrāz I look back with unmixed pleasure. The associations connected with it are familiar to every student of Persian; its natural beauties I have already feebly attempted to depict; its inhabitants are, amongst all the Persians, the most subtle, the most ingenious, the most vivacious, even as their speech is to this day the purest and most melodious.

Edward Browne
A Year Amongst the Persians (1893)

Shīrāz was one of the most important cities in the medieval Islamic world and was the Iranian capital during the Zand dynasty (1747-79), when many of its most beautiful buildings were built or restored. Through its many artists and scholars, Shīrāz has been synonymous with learning, nightingales, poetry, roses and, at one time, wine. It's now an important university town with lots of students eager to speak English, and the medical faculty is the most prestigious in Iran. In many ways Shīrāz continues to justify its former epithet of Dār-ol-Elm (House of Learning). The two most famous Persian poets – Hāfez and Sa'dī – were also born in Shīrāz, and both are honoured with mausoleums.

Shīrāz (population: approximately 1.1 million) lies at an altitude of 1491m, in a fertile valley once famed for its vineyards

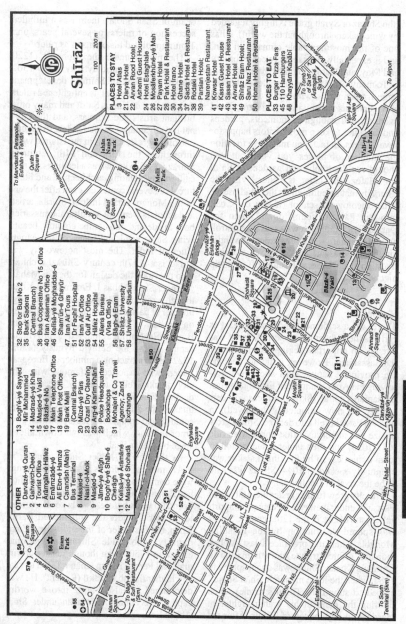

Shīrāz

0   100   200 m

To Marvdasht, Persepolis,
Esfahan & Tehrān

Qurān Square

To Tomb
of Sa'dī
(Ārāmgāh-é
Sa'dī)

To Airport

Jahān Namā
Park

Qurān Square

Eram Square

Namāzi Square

To Bāgh-é Aft Ābād
(5km)
To South
Terminal (5km)

SOUTHERN IRAN

PLACES TO STAY
3   Hotel Atlas
21   Darya Hotel
22   Arvan Rood Hotel;
     Ashemi Guest House
24   Hotel Estaghlale
26   Mosāferkhūné-yé Mah
27   Payam Hotel
28   Park Hotel & Restaurant
30   Hotel Irano
34   Ghane Hotel
37   Sadra Hotel & Restaurant
38   Rodaki Hotel
39   Parsian Hotel;
     Narenjestan Restaurant
41   Kowsar Hotel
42   Kasra Guest House
43   Sasan Hotel & Restaurant
44   Anvari Hotel
49   Shīrāz Eram Hotel;
     Saru Naz Restaurant
50   Homa Hotel & Restaurant

PLACES TO EAT
33   Burger Pizza Fars
45   110 Hamburgers
48   Khayyām Kabābi

OTHER
1   Darvāzé-yé Quran
2   Gahvarch-Deed
4   Tourist Office
5   Ārāmgāh-é Hāfez
6   Emāmzādé-yé Nō
7   Alī Ebn-é Hamzé
     Bus Terminal
8   Masjed-é
     Nasīr-ol-Molk
9   Masjed-é
10   Jāmé-yé Atīgh
11   Kelīsā-yé Ārāmané
     Cherāgh
12   Masjed-é Shohadā
13   Boghʻé-yé Sayyed
     Mir Mohammed
14   Madrasé-yé Khān
15   Masjed-é Vakīl
16   Bāzār-é Nō
17   Main Telephone Office
18   Main Post Office
19   Bank Melli
     (Central Branch)
20   Mūzé-yé Pārs
23   Ozari Dry Cleaning
25   Arg-é Karīm Khānī
29   Police Headquarters;
     Bookshops
31   Mohajeri & Co Travel
     Agency; Zand
     Exchange
32   Stop for Bus No 2
35   Bank Saderat
     (Central Branch)
36   Bus Cooperative No 15 Office
40   Iran Asseman Office
46   Kelīsā-yé Moghaddas-é
     Shamʻūn-é Ghayūr
47   Iran Air Tours
51   Dr Faqhi Hospital
52   Iran Air Office
53   Gulf Air Office
54   Hāfez Hospital
55   Aliens Bureau
     (Visa Office)
56   Bāgh-é Eram
57   Shīrāz University
58   University Stadium

(the Shiraz or Syrah grape is highly regarded by winemakers throughout the world). It has one of the most agreeable climates in Iran, and is especially pleasant between February and May, and October and November.

To many, Shīrāz is the most pleasant of the large Iranian cities, with relaxed, cultivated and generous inhabitants, wide tree-lined avenues, and enough monuments, gardens and mosques to keep most visitors happy for several days. In fact, you may have to ration the number of places you visit, but you should see the tombs and gardens of Sa'dī and Hāfez (the latter is better), visit the Cherāgh mausoleum, enter the Madrasé-yé Khān theological school (if you can), call into the Pārs Museum, climb up to the Darvazé-yé Quran gateway, and take a stroll around the charming Eram garden. A wander around the bazaar, and a pot of tea in a tradition al teahouse, will round off your trip nicely.

History

There was a settlement at Shīrāz at least as early as the Achaemenian period, and it was already an important regional centre under the Sassanians. However, it did not become the provincial capital until about 693, following the Arab conquest of Estakhr, the last Sassanian capital (8km north-east of Persepolis, but now completely destroyed), in 684. As Estakhr fell into decline, Shīrāz grew in size and importance first under Arab rule (637-1050) and then under a succession of local dynasties, so by the time Estakhr was eventually sacked in 1044, Shīrāz was said to be the rival of Baghdad.

The city grew further under the Atābaks of Fārs and, under their rule, became an important artistic centre in the 12th century. Shīrāz was spared destruction by the invading Mongols when the province's last Atābak monarch offered tribute and submission to Chinggis Khaan. Shīrāz was again spared in 1382, when the local monarch, Shāh Shojā', agreed to submit to Timur's armies, even offering the hand of his granddaughter in marriage to a grandson of Timur. After the death of Shāh Shojā', there was a turbulent succession of rulers for several years, until Timur appointed his own son as ruler.

The period under the Mongols (1220-1380) and the Timurid dynasty (1380-1502) marked the peak of Shīrāz's development. The encouragement of its enlightened rulers, the presence of Hāfez, Sa'dī and many other brilliant artists and scholars, and the city's natural advantages, helped Shīrāz to become one of the greatest cities in the Islamic world throughout the 13th and 14th centuries. Shīrāz was also known as a leading centre of calligraphy, painting, architecture and literature. For several centuries, even after the end of the Mongol period in Iran. Shīrāz' artists and scholars went out as cultural emissaries, both inside and outside the country, beautifying Samarkand and many of the Mogul cities of India. The most noteworthy was Ostād Īsā, a 17th century Shīrāzī architect who provided the design for the Taj Mahal.

Under Shāh Abbās I, Emām Gholī Khān, the governor of Fārs, constructed a large number of palaces and other ornate buildings on the lines of the royal capital at Esfahān. But while Shīrāz remained a provincial capital during the Safavid dynasty (1502-1722), even attracting a number of European traders who exported its famous wine, the city quickly fell into nearly a century of decline. This was worsened by several earthquakes, the Afghan raids of the early 18th century, and an uprising led by Shīrāz' governor in 1744, which was put down after a siege by Nāder Shāh.

At the time of Nāder Shāh's murder in 1747, most of Shīrāz's historical buildings were damaged or ruined, and its population had fallen to 50,000, a quarter of what it had been 200 years before. Shīrāz soon returned to prosperity under the enlightened Karīm Khān, the first ruler of the short-lived Zand dynasty, who made Shīrāz the national capital in 1750. Even though master of virtually all Persia, Karīm Khān refused to take any higher title than Vakīl (Regent). He was determined to raise Shīrāz into a worthy capital, the equal of Esfahān under Shāh Abbās I.

Karīm Khān was a benevolent and wise ruler, and one of the greatest patrons of the arts in Persian history. Employing more than 12,000 workers, he founded a royal district in the area of the Arg-é Karīm Khānī and commissioned many fine buildings, including the finest bazaar in Iran. However Karīm Khān's heirs failed to secure his gains, and when Agha Muhammed Khān, the cruel founder of the Ghajar dynasty, came to power, he wreaked his revenge on Shīrāz by destroying the city's fortifications and, in 1789, moving the national capital to Tehrān, taking with him the remains of Karīm Khān. Although lowered to the rank of provincial capital, Shīrāz maintained a level of prosperity due to the continuing importance of the trade route to Būshehr, and its governorship was a prerogative of the royals throughout the Ghajar period (1779-1921).

The city's role in transit trade greatly diminished with the opening of the trans-Iranian railway in the 1930s, when the bulk of its business passed to the ports in Khūzestān. Much of the architectural inheritance of Shīrāz, and especially the royal district of the Zands, was either neglected or destroyed as a result of irresponsible town planning under the Pahlavī dynasty (1921-79). Lacking any great industrial, religious or strategic importance, Shīrāz is now largely an administrative centre, although its population has grown considerably since the Islamic Revolution of 1979.

Orientation

The main street of Shīrāz is the wide, tree-lined Karīm Khān-é Zand Blvd. No-one has ever dared to change the name, but it is often shortened to Zand. This boulevard runs about as far east and west as you would want to go without actually leaving Shīrāz. Most of the things to see, and nearly all the hotels, are along Zand or within walking distance of it, so this is a street you'll keep coming back to again and again.

The old city and the commercial centre of Shīrāz are south of the Khoshk River, while the smarter residential areas are to the north. The modern university buildings and dormitories are on a steep hill in the north-west of Shīrāz. The city centre is Shohadā Square (still widely known as Shahrdārī Square), on Zand. The Khoshk, which is almost permanently dry, is crossed by seven bridges. None of these are of any great historical interest, and are a disappointment after the majesty of the river and bridges in Esfahān.

Maps If you want to explore a bit further in depth there are three decent maps to choose from. The *Guide Map of Shīrāz*, published by the Ershad Geographic Organisation, has a red cover and costs 1000 rials. The roads, parks, squares and hotels are listed in English, but the index for other places is in Fārsī. The *Guide Map of Shīrāz City & Fārs Province*, given out for free by the tourist office, was published in 1989. It is a little dated, but everything is listed in English, and the map of Fārs is very useful for exploring the countryside. The best of the three is the *Tourist Map of Shīrāz City* (6000 rials), published by Gita Shenasi.

Information

Visa Extensions Shīrāz is probably the best place in the country to extend your visa. Staff at the office are used to foreigners, making it easy to organise a visa extension. Shīrāz is also a great place to hang around if it takes a day or two to process. The courtyard of the Aliens Bureau is well set up with a Bank Melli branch to buy your stamp, a shop with a photocopy machine and booth for passport photos, and a little café to wait at. If he's still there, ask for Colonel Rasty, who is friendly and speaks very good English.

The Aliens Bureau is a little hard to find, so you may need to ask for directions. Take a shared taxi to the Hāfez Hospital; get off at the unnamed street before the hospital, walk uphill for about 400m, veer right at the end of the street, and turn immediately right again. Then follow the dozens of Iranians clutching their passports.

Tourist Office The tourist office (☎ 20 791) can hand out some brochures (in German and English) and a useful, free map. But like most of its compatriots in other cities, this tourist office is not particularly useful: staff are more interested in implementing policy than helping tourists. The office is on the ground floor of a building (not marked in English), opposite Melli Park. It is open Saturday to Thursday, from 7.30 am to 2.30 pm.

Foreign Consulate The Consulate of India (☎ 331 615) is at 233, Lane No 21, Bāgh-é Eram St, in the outer suburbs. It can issue visas on the same day, if you get there early enough. Visa charges depend on your nationality. Opening hours are from 8 am to 1 pm, and 1.30 to 5 pm, Saturday to Wednesday.

Money There are three ways to change your money. The central branches of the major banks have foreign exchange facilities, but the immense Bank Melli office, being built at the time of research, just east of the Kowsar Hotel, will be the main place to head for. The Bank Melli branch at the airport will also change money.

The best way to change money at the unofficial 'street rate' is at the official money exchange offices along Zand. They change US dollars (which is what they really want), deutschmarks, Swiss francs and Canadian dollars. The appropriately named Zand Exchange is a good place to stock up on rials.

The black marketeers hang around the Arg. They offer about the same 'street rate' (but sometimes a little less) as the official money exchange offices, but you will have to change money illegally on the street, rather than in the safety of a legal exchange office.

Post & Communications The main post office is behind the central branch of the Bank Melli, the entrance to the post office is along a side alley. The main telephone office is just a little further up at 22 Bahman St. Though unmarked from the outside, the main telephone office has signs in English inside and the staff are helpful. The telephone area code for Shīrāz is 071.

Travel Agencies There are several decent travel agencies along Zand. One of the best is the Mojaheri & Co Travel Agency (☎ 26 366) and one traveller has reported excellent service from the Galbang Travel Agency, along Keshenastī St, in the outer suburbs. For tours of Shīrāz and other attractions such as Persepolis, talk to the friendly guys at Iran Air Tours.

Bookshops A couple of shops, at the eastern end of Zand, sell books in English and other languages, including some about Persepolis, as well as maps of Shīrāz and other cities in Iran. The International Bookshop is probably the best of the bunch. An excellent range of books (with a few in English) and postcards are available at the bookshop at the Shāh-é Cherāgh mausoleum.

Laundry Shīrāz is one place where you can relax and get some washing done professionally. There are many laundries along Anvarī St; and my large and very dirty load was lovingly washed and ironed within 24 hours at Ozari Dry Cleaning for 8000 rials.

Emergency Shīrāz is famous for the standard of its medical training, so this is probably the best place to fall ill outside of Tehrān. Of the numerous hospitals around the city, the most central is Dr Faqihī Hospital (☎ 23 211). Just a little south of Namari Square is a cluster of other hospitals that can cater for most ailments. There is also a medical emergency number (☎ 49 111) or you can ring general inquiries (☎ 115). The police headquarters (☎ 22 576) is on Shohadā Square.

Dangers & Annoyances Sadly, the influx of comparatively wealthy tourists has increased the temptation and opportunity for low-level crimes against foreign travellers. Although very rare, robberies have recently taken place in Shīrāz, as one traveller attested:

I was robbed in a shared taxi in Shīrāz. It was the old trick of one passenger creating a distraction (pretending to poke me) while the other empties the victim's pockets. Shīrāz police advised that this is common here. There was another incident of a rucksack snatched by a motorcyclist.

J Gallantry, England

Museums & Castles
Arg-é Karīm Khānī The imposing structure of the Citadel of Karīm Khān dominates the city centre. This well-preserved fortress with four circular towers was, in the time of the Zand dynasty, part of a royal courtyard which Karīm Khān planned to rival that of Esfahān.

Currently, there is little to see inside the fortress, but restoration is continuing (which should include the correction of the disturbing slope of the tower on the south-eastern side). The 10,000 rial entrance fee is not worth it at the moment, but it may be when the restoration is complete. The entrance is on the eastern side of the Arg. It is open daily from about 8 am to 6 pm.

Mūzé-yé Pārs Opposite his Arg, Karīm Khāni built a small octagonal pavilion in the Nazar Garden. Originally used for official receptions, the building later became his tomb, until the vengeful Agha Muhammed Khān moved the royal remains to his new capital of Tehrān, out of spite for the dynasty he had overthrown. Earlier this century, the building was converted into the Pārs Museum, and now contains a small exhibition of items relating to the life of Karīm Khān, along with other historic artefacts displayed in cases set among four alcoves.

The museum (☎ 24 151) is officially open Saturday to Thursday, from about 7 am to 7 pm (but don't count on it being open that early or late). Entry costs 5000 rials.

Mosques & Mausoleums
Masjed-é Vakīl The Regent's Mosque, built in 1773 by Karīm Khān at one of the entrances to his bazaar, is certainly worth visiting – if you can get in. The mosque has two vast *eivāns* (open rectangular halls) to the north and south, a magnificent inner courtyard surrounded by beautifully tiled alcoves and porches, a vaulted *mehrāb* (a niche facing Mecca) with 48 impressive columns and a remarkable 14-step marble *membar* (pulpit). Although the structure of the mosque dates from 1773, most of the tiling, with its predominantly floral motifs, was added in the early Ghajar era.

When my Iranian friend and I tried to get in, the scruffy old caretaker told us, in no uncertain terms, that we were not welcome inside, despite the letters of introduction we showed him, from people we thought were important. (The caretaker said a letter from the President may have persuaded him, but my contacts don't quite reach that high!) Other travellers have had luck getting in for a quick look around the time of noon prayers (ie from about noon to 1.30 pm).

Masjed-é Shohadā The Martyrs' Mosque, at the end of a short lane leading north-west from Ahmadī Square, is one of the largest ancient mosques in Iran. Although its rectangular courtyard covers more than 11,000 sq metres, this mosque attracts nowhere near as many visitors as the Shāh-é Cherāgh mausoleum (see below).

Founded at the start of the 13th century, the mosque has been partially rebuilt many times, and now has very little in the way of tiling or other decorations, though it does boast some impressive barrel vaulting. Sadly, it seems to be permanently closed, but you may be lucky if you ask around.

Bogh'é-yé Shāh-é Cherāgh The famous tomb of the King of the Lamp houses the remains of Sayyed Mīr Ahmad (brother of Emām Rezā of Mashhad fame) who died, or was killed, in Shīrāz in 835. A mausoleum was first erected over the grave in the mid-14th century, and it's been an important Shi'ite place of pilgrimage ever since.

The shoe repository outside the doorway to the shrine is as hectic as that of any mosque in Iran, and it's fascinating to see the hordes of supplicants and the piles of money and gold they give every day. Non-Muslims should ask for permission before entering –

SOUTHERN IRAN

if you are well presented and ask nicely, you should be allowed in. One traveller wrote to say that his socks were smelled before he was given permission to enter! The multi-coloured reflections from the vast numbers of minute mirror tiles inside the shrine are quite dazzling.

Past the shrine is the small, unmarked **Shāh-é Cherāgh Museum** (☎ 22 158). It contains a display of fine china and glassware, exquisitely inscribed old and modern Qurans, and some old coins – all helpfully captioned in English. Entrance to the museum costs 200 rials. The **bookshop** near the entrance of the mosque has a good range of postcards and some books in English.

Entry to the mausoleum complex is free, and it's open daily from about 7 am to 10 pm. All visitors should dress very respectfully – foreign women will be more welcome if they wear a chādor rather than just a coat and headscarf. Photos are allowed in the grounds of the mausoleum, but certainly not in the shrine itself.

Masjed-é Jāme'-yé Atīgh This ancient mosque, first built in 894, is in an alley south-east of the Shāh-é Cherāgh mausoleum. Virtually all the original structure has disappeared, as a result of various earthquakes, and most of the building dates from the Safavid period (1502-1722) onwards.

It is mainly of interest for the very unusual turreted rectangular building in the centre of the courtyard. Known as the Khodākhūné (House of God), it was built in the mid-14th century as a repository for valuable Qurans, and is believed to be modelled on the Kaaba at Mecca. Although most of it was very skilfully rebuilt in the early 20th century, the House of God still bears an original and unique inscription in raised stone characters on a tiled background.

Madrasé-yé Khān The *khān* (feudal lord) in question was Emām Gholī Khān, governor of Fārs, who founded this serene theological college for about 100 students in 1615. The original building has been extensively damaged by earthquakes and only a small part remains. The mullahs' training college (still in use today) has a fine stone-walled inner courtyard set around a small garden. The building can be reached from a laneway through a very impressive portal which has an unusual type of stalactite moulding inside the outer arch and some very intricate mosaic tiling in the inner doorway.

Sadly, this place is also often closed, but if you find the caretaker and slip him an inducement of about 1000 rials (the locals also pay to get the door open), he will happily open it up for you. The building, in the bazaar district, is not startlingly easy to find so you may need to ask for directions.

Masjed-é Nasīr-ol-Molk Further down the bazaar from the Madrasé-yé Khān, this relatively 'modern' mosque was built around 1888. It has some fine stalactite moulding in the smallish outer portal and on the tilework throughout the mosque, but it's not as intricate or stunning as those of the religious buildings mentioned above. If you are all 'mosqued-out', you can give this one a miss.

Emāmzādé-yé Alī Ebn-é Hamzé Virtually all of the original 10th century structure has disappeared, after several earthquakes and successive repairs and extensions, but there are some interesting tombstones in the forecourt, and the tiled dome is of some appeal.

Bogh'é-yé Sayyed Mīr Mohammed This mausoleum was built for the brother of Mīr Ahmad, who also died in Shīrāz. The shrine has intricate mirror tiling and some inscriptions in the dome, but it's of less interest – yet more welcoming for foreigners – than the Shāh-é Cherāgh mausoleum.

Churches
Kelīsā-yé Moghaddas-é Sham'ūn-é Ghayūr The Church of St Simon the Zealot is Anglican, though the old building itself is very Iranian in character and is known for its very valuable stained glass windows. According to local tradition, St Simon was martyred in Persia together with St Thaddeus, another of the 12 Apostles. The great

metal door bearing a Persian cross is usually closed, but if you come at the right time, and knock hard enough, someone will let you in. The building behind the church used to be the Anglican Hospital.

Kelīsā-yé Ārāmāné The Armenian Church, built in the 17th century, lies in an alley off Ghā'ānī St, but is not as interesting as other attractions in Shīrāz.

Parks, Gardens & Tombs

Ārāmgāh-é Hāfez The tomb of the celebrated poet Hāfez is north of the river, and easy to spot along Golestān Blvd. The garden with its two pools is very pleasant and restful, especially in the warmer months when the flowers are in full bloom. The mausoleum itself is simpler and more attractive than that of Sa'dī (see following entry).

The marble tombstone, engraved with a long verse from the poet's works, was placed here, inside a small shrine, by Karīm Khān in 1773. In 1935, an octagonal pavilion was put up over it, supported by eight stone columns, beneath a tiled dome. Karīm Khān also built an eivān close to the shrine, which was enlarged at the same time as the pavilion was erected.

The grounds are open daily from about 8 am to 9 pm and foreigners are charged 10,000 rials. Cameras are OK and the best time for photos is later in the afternoon. There's a wonderfully atmospheric teahouse in a private, walled garden inside the grounds (see Places to Eat later in this section) where tea and cakes are served and tour groups try out the hubble-bubble, much to the amusement of onlooking locals. There is also a small **library**, full of books (some in English) about Iranian culture; and a very good **bookshop** (open from about 10 am) which sells postcards, a few books in English (including some about Hāfez) and some handicrafts.

You can hop in a shared taxi from Shohadā Square, or, if you fancy a bit of adventure, bus No 2 from Sa'dī St takes you straight there.

Ārāmgāh-é Sa'dī While not as impressive as the gardens at the Tomb of Hāfez, the garden at the Tomb of Sa'dī is tranquil, with a natural spring in a valley at the foot of a hill. Now part of a rather grandiose complex,

---

Hāfez, the Great Shīrāzī Poet

Khājé Shams-ed-Dīn Mohammad, or Hāfez (One Who Can Recite the Quran from Memory), as he became known, was born in about 1324. His father died while he was still young, so the boy was educated by some of the leading scholars in Shīrāz, and apart from learning the Quran by heart at an early age, he became deeply interested in literature. He wrote many verses which are still used in everyday speech today. Much of his poetry, known as the *Dīvān-é Hāfez*, has a strong mystical and untranslatable quality which has always appealed to the Persian mind, though on another level, much of it was about wine, nightingales and courtship.

Although he lived in turbulent times, Hāfez refused many generous invitations to some of the great courts of the day, both inside and outside of Iran because of his love for his birthplace of Shīrāz. Hāfez' poetry helped to make Shīrāz famous well beyond his lifetime, and it's fitting that his tomb is still one of the city's most popular attractions. Hāfez died in 1389.

Here are a few lines from *Last Night I Dreamed*:

*Last night I dreamed that angels stood without
The Tavern door, and knocked in vain and wept;
They took the clay of Adam, and slept.
Oh dwellers in the halls of Chastity!
You brought Love's passionate red wine to me,*

If you want more information about Hāfez – and Sa'dī – contact the Hāfez and Sa'dī Study Centers (☎/fax (071) 21 071) at PO Box 71455-414, Shīrāz, Fārs, Iran . ∎

Sa'dī, Another Great Shīrāzī Poet

Sheikh Mohammad Shams-ed-Dīn, known by his pen name of Sa'dī, lived from about 1207 to 1291. Like Hāfez, he lost his father at a tender age and his education was entrusted to some of the leading teachers of Shīrāz. However, unlike Hāfez, Sa'dī spent a large part of his life travelling to many countries, even becoming involved in the Crusades, before he settled down to writing in his home town of Shīrāz.

Many of his elegantly phrased verses reflect the philosophy of humility and compassion which he developed during his travels, and they are still commonly used in conversation. His most famous work is the *Golestān* (Rose Garden), which has been translated into many languages. Before he died Sa'dī moved to this retreat which was then well beyond the edge of Shīrāz, and his tomb has become an important pilgrimage site. ■

the fairly unattractive marble tomb, which dates from the 1860s, is in an octagonal stone colonnade, inscribed with various verses from Sa'dī, supporting a tiled dome, from where a metal chandelier hangs.

The entrance fee is the usual 10,000 rials. The useful bus No 2 leaves from the city centre, and stops at a terminal about 50m from the entrance to Sa'dī's tomb and gardens. Alternatively, a shared taxi is possible, though not many will want to go all the way to the tomb. There are plenty of places to buy food and drink near the entrance, so you can enjoy an impromptu picnic in the gardens. There's no teahouse inside these gardens.

Bāgh-é Eram Famous for its cypress trees, the delightful and extensive Garden of Paradise is the place where any 'budding' botanist should head. Most plants and trees are labelled in English and there's a special rock garden. Moreover, it's far better arranged than other gardens in Shīrāz and the entrance fee is a very reasonable 1000 rials. The best time for photos is early in the morning. Alongside a pretty pool is the charming 19th century Ghajar palace, the

Kākh-é Eram, though at the time of research visitors could not enter the palace.

The gardens are easy enough to reach by taking any shared taxi going along Zand and heading towards the university.

Bāgh-é Afīf Ābād These pretty gardens once belonged to the Shāh (but didn't everything?) and contain the **Afīf Ābād Palace**. Built in 1863, and influenced by the Ghajar style of architecture, the lower floor of the palace is now a **military museum** (☎ 667 343). Also in the grounds are the remains of a Turkish bath house and a small teahouse. The gardens have odd opening hours – 4.30 to 7.30 pm every day – and foreigners are charged 10,000 rials to get in. Cameras are allowed.

The gardens are a fair way from the city centre so you'll probably have to charter a private taxi. It is worth combining a visit to the gardens with a (late) lunch or dinner at the excellent, but pricey, Sufi Restaurant, a few hundred metres away (see Places to Eat later in this section). Look out for the occasional exhibition at the gardens during summer.

Darvazé-yé Quran On the outskirts of Shīrāz is the Quran Gateway, the burial tomb for Mir Alī, grandson of Emām Musā Kazem. The exact dates of construction are conflicting, but it is known that the great Karīm Khān added a room at the top of the gateway to house a holy Quran.

In the general complex, you can visit the **Tomb of Kharjū-yé Kermānī**, another famous poet and a contemporary of Sa'dī. A bust of Kermānī is also on display. Those with good leg muscles may want to look for some **bas-reliefs** further up the hill, from where the views of Shīrāz are breathtaking.

The teahouse is a perfect spot for a break. Look for the sign in English, 'Welcomo to Taehouse' (sic), but the steps up to it are quite steep. Next to the 'taehouse', is an underground **waterfall**, which is complete with a mechanical lion that is programmed to roar when you enter the room. The 'taehouse' is probably a better place to spend your time.

If you have chartered your own vehicle to Persepolis or beyond, stop here on the way. Getting a shared taxi to the gateway is not easy, but you could combine it with a visit to the tomb of Hāfez, which is within walking distance – just head up Hāfez St. Entrance is free. This is a popular place for locals, so avoid it on Friday. The immense set of rusting girders on the hill is the framework of a hotel, abandoned through lack of money.

Gahvarch-Deed Directly opposite from the Quran Gateway is a lookout, right at the top of a very steep, but inviting, trail. The lookout was used to spot invading armies; a fire would be lit to warn the next lookout of the impending doom. If you follow the main trail for about 6km beyond the lookout, you'll find the source for the renowned **Chahé-Morteza Alī** spring water.

Places to Stay

There are plenty of hotels to suit all budgets in Shīrāz, and the best place to base yourself is near Zand – but not too near, because it's a very noisy area. If you are a bit fussy, and you're travelling in a couple or group, one of you can look around for a decent room, while the other(s) looks after the gear. Almost without exception, every place is signposted in English and easy to find, and just about everywhere in Shīrāz will accept foreigners, often for the normal 'Iranian price'. If only other cities in Iran were as welcoming.

Places to Stay – budget

One place to check around, to find something at the standard and price you want, is Pīrūzī St. Of the dozen or more similar places along that street the *Ashemi Guest House* (☎ 25 270) has good doubles for 13,000 rials, the *Darya Hotel* (☎ 20 858) is priced at 10,000/ 12,000/15,000 rials for a single/double/triple and the *Arvan Rood Hotel* is not too bad, for about the same price as the Darya.

The *Hotel Estaghlale* (☎ 28 827) is excellent value: 10,000/15,000 rials for a single/ double with private shower (with hot water) and a shared toilet. It is just off the main road, so is quieter than most places, and the

manager speaks some English. Last resorts along Zand include the noisy *Hotel Irano* (☎ 40 219), which has basic rooms with a strange aroma for 10,000 rials for a double. Look for the 'Hotel' sign on the 3rd floor. There are many other grubby places nearby.

Along the quieter 22 Bahman St there are two good places, slightly better than most in this range. The *Payam Hotel* (☎ 28 994) is friendly and costs 20,000 rials for a double room with a shared bathroom. The upper floors have views, while the lower floors overlook an uninspiring courtyard. Nearby, the *Mosāferkhūné-yé Mah* (☎ 25 607) is unmarked in English, but is easy to spot and costs about the same as the Payam.

Three reasonable and popular places are next to each other along Anvarī St. The *Kasra Guest House* (☎ 34 957) is not particularly friendly to foreigners but it's good value at 13,000 rials for a double with shared facilities. The *Sasan Hotel* (☎ 337 830) is popular among travellers, so it's often full, but I thought the manager was a bit surly. Prices are also a little steep: doubles with bathrooms range from 25,000 to 40,000 rials.

The *Anvarī Hotel* (☎ 337 591), also called the *Madaen Hotel*, is better value and also deservedly popular. Staff are friendly, but the rooms, with a private bathroom, can be a bit dingy. Singles cost from 15,000 to 18,000 rials, and doubles cost from 18,000 to 22,000 rials; an extra person costs 10,000 rials. Travellers with their own transport can leave their vehicles in the car park opposite.

Places to Stay – middle

Three recommended places in this price range are along the quieter Rūdaki St. The *Sadra Hotel* (☎ 24 740) has clean, large rooms with a fridge and lovely bathroom. It is friendly and a very good choice at US$15/30 for a single/double, especially if you can persuade them to accept rials. The lovely *Parsian Hotel* (☎ 331 000) is overpriced at US$62 a double, but this is one of the few top-end places where you can negotiate a middle-range price – try for US$40 a double, all-inclusive, and pay in rials. Lastly, the *Rodaki Hotel* (☎ 26 909) is pretty good value for US$30 a double, and costs a reasonable US$40 if you feel like pampering yourself in a suite. Staff are also open to negotiation and should accept rials.

The *Kowsar Hotel* (☎ 335 724), along the very noisy Zand, is overpriced (US$20/30 for a single/double), and several travellers have written to us to complain about the way they deal with credit cards. The price is not open to negotiation, so you can do better elsewhere. One of the best in this range is the *Shīrāz Eram Hotel* (☎ 337 201). It was being renovated at the time of research, so may increase its prices later on, but at US$20/30 for a large single/double with a huge fridge, sunny bathroom and enormous beds, it's very good value. The manager is happy to negotiate, and he accepts rials. The *Hotel Atlas* (☎ 47 748) is a little inconvenient and on a noisy corner. The manager wants US$20/30 for singles/doubles, but try for a lower price in rials.

Finally, one place definitely worth checking out is the *Ghane Hotel* (☎ 25 374). Set back from the main road, and quieter than most other places, it offers doubles with a bathroom for 50,000 rials. This may seem a lot compared to other places in Shīrāz, but it's worth a splurge.

Places to Stay – top end

The expensive and expansive *Park Hotel* (☎ 21 426), along an alley north of Shohadā Square, is very popular with upmarket tour groups and has a nice outdoor garden (with an empty pool). Rooms cost US$45/65/81 for a single/double/triple, but this is far too high considering the bargains elsewhere in town. Part of the national chain, the *Homa Hotel* (☎ 28 000) costs the same, but it is not convenient because most restaurants and attractions are not within walking distance. It has a 'Down With USA' sign inside, above the main entrance, in beautifully polished brass letters as befits a hotel in its class.

Places to Eat

For those on a budget, Zand is lined with plenty of cheap *kabābīs* and *hamburger*

joints, but Shīrāz is one place where you may want to fork out a few more rials and enjoy some decent meals.

Shīrāzīs take the art of liquid refreshment very seriously. Although, in Iran, the world-famous Shiraz (Syrah) grape is no longer made into the wine that inspired Omar Khayyām to poetry, there are several substitutes that won't leave you with a hangover, such as tea, ice cream and fruit juice. Places along Zand serve these refreshing answers to a hot summer's day.

Teahouses The most atmospheric *teahouse* in Shīrāz is the small outdoor one, set around a rectangular pool, in the grounds of the tomb of Hāfez. You can sit on cushions, in one of the niches in each of its four walls, and drink pots of tea for 500 rials, or puff at the hubble-bubble to your heart's (dis)content. It also serves ice cream and cakes. You may stumble across a few other *teahouses* around the Vakīl Bazaar and the one at the Quran Gateway is worth trying, even if the owner can't spell in English (see Darvazé-yé Quran earlier in this section). There are also several makeshift *tea stalls* along the pavements on or around Zand.

Fast Food Maybe I was just hungry after travelling in the far south for a while, but the western-style hamburgers in Shīrāz seemed bigger and tastier than those in most other cities in Iran. One of the best places serving these burgers is *110 Hamburgers*, handy to the hotels along Anvarī St. You can get a large burger, chips (French fries) and cola for about 5000 rials. Not quite as good, but still worth a visit, is the *Burger Pizza Fars* which is popular with the local youth. Individual pizzas (5000 rials) weren't half bad, and the western-style burgers were also fairly good.

Restaurants Of the dozen or so *kabābīs* along Zand, one of the best is the *Khayyām Kababī*, unmarked in English. Excellent beef kebabs, with tomato, bread and a cola, cost 5500 rials.

The *Sufi Restaurant* is a long way out from the city centre and hopeless for public transport, but it's worth visiting for good food and atmosphere. Menus are in English, but they don't list the prices – so be careful before you order. A plate of Iranian food, with fresh bread, cheese, drinks and a visit to one of Iran's very few self-serve salad bars, costs about 14,000 rials. But you will be charged for everything you eat, such as the bread and bowl of olives. Scruffily dressed people may be unwelcome.

Hotel Restaurants The best among the hotels around Rūdaki is the elegant restaurant in the *Sadra Hotel*. Expect to pay about 12,500 rials for a decent three course meal. Even if you're not staying in the area, it's worth the short walk to the restaurant at the *Sasan Hotel*. Dishes cost about 9500 rials each, and the service is good, but nothing gets going until after 8 pm.

One of my favourites is the *Sarv Naz Restaurant*, on the 1st floor of the Shīrāz Eram Hotel. It has a menu in English and serves tasty chicken kebabs (7500 rials) and other dishes for about 10,000 rials. But there is an annoying 15% tax, and be wary of a bit of overcharging as well.

If you want to splash out, but still get good value for money, the ground-floor restaurant in the *Homa Hotel* is excellent. More central, and equally expensive, are the restaurants at the *Park Hotel* and the *Narenjestan Restaurant* in the Parsian Hotel.

Things to Buy
Most of the items you can buy in Tehrān and Esfahān are also available in Shīrāz, though not in the same quantity or variety. On the other hand, you are less likely to be overcharged. Good buys in the bazaar include metalwork and printed cottons, especially tablecloths and rugs woven by Fārs nomads. Along the streets off Zand, there are plenty of places to stock up on dates and pistachios.

The **Bāzār-é Vakīl** was constructed by Karīm Khān as part of a plan to make Shīrāz into a great trading centre. The vaulted brick ceilings ensure that the interior is cool in the summer and warm in the winter, and it has often been described as the finest bazaar in

Iran. Like many Iranian bazaars, a lot of interest lies in the architecture and the whole atmosphere, rather than the goods themselves. This bazaar has its own bath house, the **Hammūm-é Vakīl**, dating from Karīm Khān's time. The **Bāzār-é Nō** (New Bazaar) is also worth a stroll around. A few more modern arcades can be found along Zand.

Getting There & Away
Air The Iran Air office (☎ 330 041) is the most unimpressive in the country which is amazing considering the size and importance of Shīrāz. The office is about 20m on the left down Faghīhī St, look for the small Iran Air sticker and head up the stairs. Despite appearances, the office is computerised and the staff are friendly.

The airport was undergoing some extensive renovation at the time of research, and should be quite spiffing when finished.

Iran Air flies from Shīrāz to:

Destination	When	Cost (rials)
Bandar-é Abbās	Daily	45,500
Bandar-é Lengé	Daily	13,800
(this flight is a bargain, and worth using)		
Būshehr	Wednesday	41,000
Esfahān	Daily	40,000
Mashhad	Five times a week	78,000
Tehrān	Several daily	61,500

Funnily enough, some staff at the Iran Asseman office (☎ 336 556) speak better French than English, though a notice board in the office lists all flight details in English. Asseman flies to the following places:

Destination	When	Cost (rials)
Bandar-é Abbās	Monday, Tuesday, Wednesday and Sunday	45,500
Lāmard (Fārs province)	Monday, Wednesday, Friday and Saturday	37,500
Lār (Fārs)	Daily	37,500
Tehrān	Monday, Saturday and Sunday	67,500
Yazd	Wednesday	40,000

Tiny Caspian Air has some flights, but schedules were unavailable at research time. Make inquiries at travel agencies in Shīrāz.

International Services Shīrāz is a great place to start or finish your trip to Iran. For details of all international flights to and from Shīrāz, refer to the Getting There & Away chapter. The Gulf Air office (☎ 301 962) is along the western part of Zand. For all international flights from Shīrāz, you will be slugged 70,000 rials for the departure tax.

Bus & Minibus The main bus terminal is the Carandish bus terminal, also known as the Termīnāl-é Bozorg. There is a smaller terminal in the southern outskirts for a few places to the south, such as Būshehr, but buses going to just about everywhere, including Būshehr, will leave from the Carandish terminal. Some of the bus companies have offices along, or just off, Zand, which is a handy way of booking a ticket in advance.

The Carandish bus terminal is orderly and getting a ticket is easy enough. Buses and the occasional minibus (with prices shown for lux/super) leave regularly for:

Destination	Distance	Time	Cost (rials)
Ābādān	615km	10 hours	6600/8700
Ahvāz	568km	10 hours	6100/8600
Arāk	772km	12 hours	10,000/11,000
Bandar-é Abbās	601km	10 hours	6650/8950
Bandar-é Lengé	654km	12 hours	7500/8200
Būshehr	320km	5 hours	3600/3800
Esfahān	481km	8 hours	5500/6000
Hamadān	918km	15 hours	9300/2500
Kermān	548km	8 hours	8500/9900
Kermānshāh	1077km	18 hours	14,000/15,200
Sīrjān	381km	6 hours	3800/5200
Tabrīz	1519km	24 hours	18,800/19,800
Tehrān	895km	16 hours	8800/9700
Yazd	440km	7 hours	5300/5800
Zāhedān	1088km	17 hours	11,860/14,300

Shared Taxi From the Carandish bus terminal, shared taxis leave for regional towns such as Kāzerūn, Fīrūz Ābād and Marvdasht (for Persepolis) as often as there is enough demand. It may take a while to find enough passengers, but there are occasional shared taxis all the way to Esfahān. Because distances from Shīrāz to most other cities are vast, buses are the normal form of transport.

Train Shīrāz is the only major city in Iran without a train line. For several decades, Shīrāzīs have been promised a train line 'in about 10 years' by the authorities (probably the same ones who promised Tehrānīs an underground railway about 30 years ago). It's safe to assume that the bus will be the only form of overland transport for a while.

Getting Around

To/From the Airport A ticket for the airport bus service costs 1500 rials from the office in the arrivals lounge. The buses have several destinations, probably not all going your way. The local bus No 10 also leaves from the airport and will drop you off behind the Arg. A private taxi between the airport and the city centre should cost about 5000 rials while a shared taxi from Valī-yé Asr Square to the airport costs about 1000 rials.

Bus & Minibus There are terminals for local buses and minibuses outside the Arg, on Ahmadī Square and in front of Sa'dī's tomb. One very handy bus worth using is bus No 2 (with 'English' numerals, and sometimes marked 'Sa'adi' in English). It leaves from outside the Burger Pizza Fars and passes the tourist office; the corner of Golestān and Salmān-Fārsī Blvds, from where you can walk to the Carandish bus terminal; Hāfez' tomb; and finishes outside Sa'dī's tomb. Bus tickets cost 50 rials for a short trip; 100 rials is the longest trip around the city. Buy your tickets from the booths along Zand.

Taxi You can take a shared taxi around the city for 300 to 500 rials. They travel along the main streets, but you may need to take more than one. Chartering a taxi around the city will cost from 3000 to 5000 rials. Watch out for the occasional 'tourist price' charged by taxi drivers; ask someone what the current fare is, or just pay what the locals pay.

AROUND SHĪRĀZ

Besides Persepolis and Naghsh-é Rostam, which are described in detail in a special section later in this chapter, there are a few
continued on page 302

Top: The legendary
Achaemenian imperial
centre of Persepolis.

Bottom: Carvings of the
subject peoples of the
Achaemenian Empire
climb one of the grand
stairways at Persepolis.

RICHARD EVERIST

RICHARD EVERIST

DAVID ST VINCENT

ANDREW HUMPHREYS

Artists from across the Persian Empire worked together at Persepolis to create a uniquely uniform style.

Persepolis (Takht-é Jamshīd)

One of the highlights of your trip to Iran will be a visit to Persepolis, known locally as Takht-é Jamshīd or Throne of Jamshīd, after one of the mythical kings of Persia. While most of the city has been destroyed and ransacked over the centuries, you will still get a great idea of its majesty – especially if you carry a map and use a bit of imagination. Most of the limited captions and explanations around the site are in Fārsī. Hopefully, this will change in the future. Photography is allowed everywhere except inside the museum.

The lotus flower, an ancient Persian creation symbol (photograph by Andrew Humphreys).

History

The earlier capital of the Achaemenian empire (559-330 BC) was at Pasargadae, further north, but in about 512 BC, Darius I (the Great) started constructing this massive and magnificent palace complex to serve as the summer capital. It was completed by a host of subsequent kings, including Xerxes I and II, and Artaxerxes I, II and III, over a period of 150 years.

The city sits on a shelf on the slopes of Mt Rahmat and at one time it was surrounded by a 18m-high wall. The original name was Pārsā; the first known reference to it by its Greek name of Persepolis – meaning both 'city of Pārsā' and 'Persian city' and also 'destroyer of cities' – dates from after its sacking.

Persepolis was burnt to the ground, during Alexander the Great's time, in 331 BC, although historians are divided about whether it was accidental or in retaliation for the destruction of Athens by Xerxes. The ruins you see today are a mere shadow of Persepolis' former glory, even though

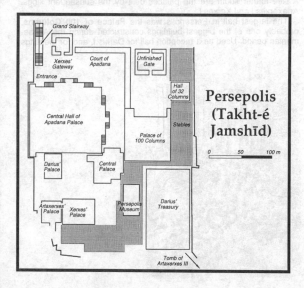

Grand Stairway

Xerxes' Gateway

Entrance

Court of Apadana

Unfinished Gate

Hall of 32 Columns

Central Hall of Apadana Palace

Stables

Palace of 100 Columns

Darius' Palace

Central Palace

Artaxerxes' Palace

Xerxes' Palace

Persepolis Museum

Darius' Treasury

Tomb of Artaxerxes III

Persepolis (Takht-é Jamshīd)

0   50   100 m

they are much more revealing than the few surviving traces of the less-preserved Achaemenian administrative capital at Sh-sh. As you survey the land around the ruins, remember that this area was once far more fertile than it is today. Incredibly the whole site was covered with dust, earth and the sands of time before it was rediscovered, and excavations commenced, in the early 1930s.

Things to See

The original city was spread over an area of 125,000 sq metres. One of the first things you'll see is **Xerxes' Gateway**, with three separate doors and a hallway, which once covered an area of more than 600 sq metres. The remaining doors are still covered with inscriptions and carvings in ancient Elamite, as well as many other ancient languages. To the east, near the **Unfinished Gate**, look for the double-headed eagles.

The southern door of Xerxes' Gateway leads through to the immense **Apadana Palace** complex, where the kings received visitors, and Nō R-z (Iranian New Year) celebrations were held in earnest. Inside the complex is the **Court of Apadana,** built from materials somehow taken from the nearby mountains. The roof of the **Central Hall** was supported by 36 stone columns, each 20m high. Look for the double-headed bulls and the superb reliefs that decorate the stairways, each representing ancient nationalities. Altogether the stairways are more than 300m long; in Persepolis' heyday they were brightly coloured and must have been an amazing spectacle. Plenty of gold and silver was discovered in the palace, but it was predictably looted by Alexander the not-so-Great, and what he forgot to take is in the National Museum of Iran in Tehrān.

Behind the Central Hall, and connected by another stairway, is the smaller **Darius' Palace**, also known as the Tachara. Used as the private residence of Darius I, it was filled with statues covered with jewels and doors made of gold. All that remains are the carvings along the staircase. A little further south are the palaces built by the subsequent kings, Artaxerxes I and Xerxes I.

The largest hall in Persepolis was the **Palace of 100 Columns**, probably one of the biggest buildings constructed during the Achaemenian period. Used as a reception hall for Darius I, and for meetings

The bas-reliefs of Persepolis are a blend of styles from all over the Achaemenian Empire – from Egypt and Greece to India.

Left: The image of the lion devouring a bull appears many times at Persepolis.

Right: Vassals present gifts to honour the ancient rulers of Persia.

with his army commanders, it contained 100 columns, each about 14m high, with reliefs showing Darius struggling with evil spirits. **Darius' Treasury** was a large collection of rooms housing the wealth of the city, predictably looted by Alexander's mob.

A short distance to the east of the centre of Persepolis is the **Tomb of Artaxerxes II**, carved in the mountain like the tombs at Naghsh-é Rostam (see later in this section).

Museum

The small **Persepolis Museum** has been created from the ruins of the building which contained the harem of Xerxes I. (Some historians claim the building was the Queen's palace.) The museum contains some ceramics, carvings, cloths and coins discovered in Persepolis, and in nearby Eshktar city. Thankfully, all captions are in English, though some of the better exhibits are predictably in the National Museum of Iran in Tehrān. The entrance fee to the museum will set you back 10,000 rials (Iranians pay 1000 rials), and no photography is allowed. The museum is open every day from 7 am to 7 pm, but closes for lunch from about 12.30 to 1.30 pm.

Entrance

Persepolis is open daily from about 7 am to 7 pm, but try to avoid Friday and public holidays when it can be *really* packed. In summer, it's wise to visit the area early in the morning or late in the afternoon to avoid the intense midday heat, to get better photos and to elude the busloads of tourists that swarm the site. Entrance to the complex (excluding the museum) costs a hefty 15,000 rials (Iranians pay 2000 rials).

There were signs around the place advertising a sound and light show which was abandoned a few years ago. If it restarts, the cost should be an extra 15,000 rials, but it promises to be quite spectacular.

Bookshop

Next to the museum, a well-stocked shop sells postcards and books. Though prices are a little high, this shop has one of the best ranges of books in English (and other European languages) in or around Shīrāz. If you want further information about Persepolis, pick up the useful – but tourist-priced (6000 rials) – pamphlet and map called *Persepolis, The*

Fabulous Art of Ancient Persia. Written in English, it contains more details, about what is – or used to be – in Persepolis, than we are able to provide in this guidebook.

Places to Stay & Eat

There are a couple of places inside the complex, and more outside, which sell drinks, but there is nowhere to buy food – thankfully the place is not full (yet) of kabābīs and hamburger stalls. From the highest points of Persepolis, you can see the remnants of a tent city which was assembled in 1971 for the 2500th anniversary of the Persian Empire, a swansong of the Shāh, attended by a glittering array of ambassadors and international royalty, that outstripped even the parades of supplicants depicted in the Achaemenian bas-reliefs. It now houses an expensive *restaurant*, set up mainly for package-tour groups.

The only place to stay and eat is the imaginatively named *Hotel & Restaurant Persepolis* (☎ (07283) 2499), on the corner of the car park outside the main entrance to Persepolis. It charges a reasonable US$14/22 for a clean and comfy single/double. Staying at the hotel allows you to explore Persepolis early and/or late in the day, and would be perfect if the sound and light show ever gets going again. The hotel is an excellent place for a meal; it offers a limited menu of Iranian dishes for about 7500 rials each.

Getting There & Away

Since Persepolis, Naghsh-é Rostam and Pasargadae (see under Around Shīrāz later in this chapter) can be visited in one trip, the following information applies to all three.

Persepolis is 57km from Shīrāz, just off the Esfahān road. Naghsh-é Rostam is about 6km north of Persepolis, and Pasargadae is 130km from Shīrāz, in the same direction as the other two sites but further off the main road. Getting to these sites and back again isn't straightforward; allow a whole day for the round trip for all three from Shīrāz.

Minibus & Bus To cover all three sites by public transport, you will have to catch a minibus from Shīrāz to Marvdasht and from there take a shared taxi to Persepolis. From Persepolis you can either walk or take a shared taxi the 6km to Naghsh-é Rostam. To get to Pasargadae you will need to catch a shared taxi to Sā'adatshahr and then another to Pasargadae. When returning to Shīrāz from Pasargadae you might be lucky and get a direct minibus, bus or taxi; otherwise you will have to take a succession of shared taxis via Sā'adatshahr or Marvdasht, or both. It's difficult to find any transport out of Pasargadae after dark.

Alternatively, you could visit the sites in the chronological order they were built in by taking a bus from Esfahān to Shīrāz, stopping off at Pasargadae, and from there go to Persepolis and Naghsh-é Rostam via Marvdasht.

Minibuses for Marvdasht (40 minutes, 750 rials) leave Shīrāz about every hour, from a special terminal at the back of the main Carandish bus terminal. Marvdasht is a large industrial centre of no interest in itself. Surprisingly there is nowhere to stay in the town, but there are a few places to eat along the main road.

Alternatively, take a bus between Shīrāz and Esfahān and get off at the turn-offs to Persepolis or Pasargadae, from where you can walk or hitch a ride to either site. You will probably have to pay the full Shīrāz to Esfahān fare though.

Taxi To save a lot of time, but not money, you could charter a taxi from Shīrāz for a complete tour of Persepolis and Pasargadae. Ask other travellers about sharing a private taxi; every visitor to Shīrāz will, at least, want to go to Persepolis, and will be wondering how they are going to do it. Taxi drivers are getting used to the idea of big-spending tourists, which makes it hard to bargain them down to a reasonable price. Allow about 35,000 rials per car for a half-day trip to Persepolis, and about 65,000 rials for a full day to all three places.

Using shared taxis is not easy. You probably won't find one from Shīrāz to Persepolis, but you might from Persepolis to Naghsh-é Rostam – but not to anywhere further. If you can get to Persepolis under your own steam, it's not too hard to get a shared taxi directly back to Shīrāz, from the main entrance to Persepolis.

Organised Tours Naturally, all travel agencies in Shīrāz (see those listed under Travel Agencies in the Shīrāz section earlier in this chapter) and some hotels, such as the Shīrāz Eram Hotel, organise tours to Persepolis. These are expensive, of course, and quite unnecessary for Persepolis on its own, but useful if you wish to visit all three sites in one day.

Naghsh-é Rostam

Hewn out of a cliff, at a lofty height from the ground, the four tombs of Naghsh-é Rostam are believed to be those of Darius I, Artaxerxes, Xerxes I and Darius II (from left to right as you look at the cliff), though this is subject to intense debate among historians. There are also eight **reliefs** from later in the Sassanian dynasty, cut into the stone below the façades of the Achaemenian tombs, depicting various scenes of imperial conquests and royal investitures. There is also what is probably a **fire-temple** from Achaemenian times. It is believed the reliefs were created to celebrate the victory of the Sassanian king, Shāp-r, over the Roman invader, Valerian, in the 3rd century.

Visitors used to be able to climb a ladder and clamber inside the tombs, but this is no longer the case. The entrance fee will set you back 10,000 rials, but if you are feeling a little stingy, or annoyed by the constant demands for high entrance fees, you can admire the tombs from outside the main gate. It is open every day during daylight hours. A large sign just inside the entrance explains the history of the tombs – in Fārsī. For more speculation about the tombs and the fire-temples, take along Robert Byron's *The Road to Oxiana*.

Getting There & Away

Naghsh-é Rostam is about 6km along the road leading north from Persepolis towards Pasargadae. If you are walking, the road is fairly obvious when you start from Persepolis, but it gets a bit confusing near the bridge – hopefully some signs (in English) will be erected soon. While the tombs at Naghsh-é Rostam are fascinating, don't rush around Persepolis just to see them. If you want to take some photos, get there before mid-afternoon or the tombs will be covered in shadows. See under the Persepolis Getting There & Away section above for details of how to get here from Shīrāz, Persepolis and Pasargadae.

continued from page 296

lesser-known archaeological sites, including Pasargadae, to visit near Shīrāz. Getting public transport to these spots isn't easy, so chartering a taxi for about 10,000 rials per hour is worthwhile, particularly if you want to visit a few places in one day.

Estehbān استهبان

Once famous for its grapes, Estehbān is now renowned for the manufacture of carpets. Though it only contains a couple of unimportant shrines and the **Masjed-é Jāme'**, exploration of the town is still worthwhile. If you have a vehicle, head for the **Bakhtegān National Park**, a quasi-protected area for cranes, bustards and flamingos, based around the Bakhtegān and Tashk lakes.

There is nowhere to stay in Estehbān, so you'll have to make a day trip from Shīrāz. Take a bus between Shīrāz and Kermān and just hop off at Estehbān; or charter a taxi.

Fīrūz Ābād فیروزآباد

One place often missed by those who rush off to Persepolis is the remains of the old cities of Fīrūz and Gūr, dating back to the Sassanian period. If you are there around April or May, you will see plenty of nomads crossing the Zāgros mountains.

About 6km before Fīrūz, along the road from Shīrāz, you'll see a **chair lift**, with cables stretching across the road, leading to the **Ghal'é Doktar** or Maiden's Palace. This is a three storey fort with a courtyard, built by Shāpūr I. Sadly, the chair lift doesn't work, so you'll have to scramble up the rocky hill to see the remains of the palace. The views from the top are worth the effort.

About 2km further on, towards Fīrūz, an unsigned rocky trail leads to the **Āteshkadé-yé Ardeshir** fire-temple, the best of the ruins of ancient Fīrūz. If your taxi driver is reluctant to drive across the low Tang-Ab River, you'll have to take a lengthy 20km detour. If you don't mind getting your feet wet, stride across the river, then walk about 800m along the rocky trail. The limited remains of the Sassanian **Artaxerxes Palace** are also not far away; ask for directions.

Places to Stay & Eat The only place to stay in Fīrūz is the overpriced *Jahāngardī Inn*, (☎ (07242) 2105), run by the ITTO, where a single/double costs US$25/35. It's better to take a day trip from Shīrāz.

There are plenty of *hamburger joints* and *kabābīs* in town, but taking food and drink from Shīrāz, and having a picnic by the tiny lake at the fire-temple, is a great idea. Fīrūz is famous for the quality of its dūgh. Maybe here you will develop a taste for this sour milk drink – but then again, maybe not.

Getting There & Away There is at least one bus every day between Shīrāz and Fīrūz, but make sure you find out when it returns, otherwise you may be forced to stay the night in the expensive Jahāngardī Inn. To see most of the remains of both ancient cities, it's best to charter a taxi, which you can do either from Shīrāz or Fīrūz.

Kāzerūn & Shāpūr شاپور کازرون

Just off the main road between Shīrāz and Būshehr are the small but fascinating ruins of another two ancient cities: Kāzerūn and, about 25km to the west, Shāpūr. At Kāzerūn (the name comes from the ancient word for 'people who wash cotton clothes'), there are some mildly interesting **bas reliefs** from the Sassanian period, though they are more interesting to archaeologists for their unique inscriptions.

Shāpūr is larger and more fascinating. The remains of this Sassanian city include the **Palace of Shāpūr** and a nearby **fire-temple**. The **Tand-é Chogan** (or Shāpūr Cave) contains the mighty **Statue of Shāpūr I**, which stands 7m high. Along both sides of the river there are some excellent **bas reliefs**, which commemorate, among other historical moments, the victory of Shāpūr citizens over Roman invaders.

The trip to this part of Fārs province is pretty, and it is worth dedicating a day to. You could get off the bus along the road between Būshehr and Shīrāz, but you'll still need a vehicle to find the ruins. It's best to charter a vehicle from Shīrāz or Būshehr.

Pasargadae پاسارگاد

Begun under Cyrus (Kouroush) the Great in about 546 BC, the city of Pasargadae was superceded soon after Cyrus' death by Darius I's magnificent palace at Persepolis; some historians suggest that the construction of Persepolis may actually have started under Cyrus. It's nowhere near as visually stimulating as Persepolis, and what remains is fairly widely scattered, so you'll need your own transport.

The first structure you'll come across is the six tiered **Tomb of Cyrus**. Constructed on a stone platform, Cyrus' impressive stone cenotaph was originally much taller than its present height, but even so this now empty tomb is the best preserved of the remains of Pasargadae. Within walking distance of the tomb (you'll need to ask directions) are the insubstantial remains of three **Achaemenian Palaces**; the ruins of a tower on a plinth, known as the Zendān-é Soleimān or **Prison of Solomon**; a large stone platform on a hill known as the Takht-é Mādar-é Soleimān or **Throne of the Mother of Solomon**; and two **stone plinths** which originally formed part of a pair of altars within a sacred precinct.

Pasargadae is open from about 7.30 am to 6 pm every day, but it's better not to arrive later than about 3 pm if you are relying on public transport. Unless you arrive by private transport, you'll have to walk between the remains. For details about getting to this site from Persepolis, Shīrāz and Naghsh-é Rostam, see under Getting There & Away in the special Persepolis section above.

Būshehr Province
استان بوشهر

- **Capital:** Būshehr
- **Area:** 25,357 sq km
- **Population:** approx 850,000

Occupying a narrow corridor between the coast and the extensive Zāgros mountain range, Būshehr province is a modern and largely artificial creation. The province has

nothing going for it except the fascinating and lethargic capital of Būshehr and the island of Khārk, which is of little interest to most visitors.

BŪSHEHR بوشهر

Būshehr is the most pleasant of the larger towns along the Iranian shores of the Persian Gulf. It lacks the frantic bustle of Bandar-é Abbās (even before the Iran-Iraq War, the shipping trade was in decline here) and is mostly free of the complete and utter lethargy of Bandar-é Lengé. The Būshehrīs have time to talk to foreigners, the pace of life is relaxed, the food is good, and the old part of town stands more or less untouched by developers. Its indigenous population is predominantly Arab in origin.

Būshehr is very hot and humid in summer (April to October), though sea breezes give some relief near the coast. A few mosquitos somehow find the energy to annoy anyone with an inch of exposed skin during the summer.

History

The original settlement at Rīshahr, 12km south of modern Būshehr, may have been founded in the time of Ardashīr, or even as early as the Elamite era. From the early Arab period (637-1050) until at least the 16th century, Rīshahr was one of the chief trading centres of the Persian Gulf, but it lost its importance after Bandar-é Abbās was established in the early 17th century.

In 1734, the site of Būshehr, then only a small fishing village, was chosen by Nāder Shāh to be the principal port and naval station of Persia. Its prosperity was assured when, in 1759, the British East India Company, then the dominant power in the Persian Gulf, moved its base to Būshehr after the destruction of its factory at Bandar-é Abbās by the French. By the end of the 18th century Būshehr had become not only the main outlet of Fārs but the chief port of Persia.

Under the rule of Karīm Khān Zand, Būshehr, together with the surrounding area and even Bahrain, remained peaceful and prosperous within the domain of their hereditary Arab ruler, Sheikh Nasr, who maintained trading relations with Muscat and India. However, Sheikh Nasr's son was on bad terms with Loftallāh Khān, and after a long period of tension and misrule, the area returned to central Persian control in the mid-19th century. At about the same time, Būshehr became the seat of the British Political Residency on the Persian Gulf, and the town was occupied by the British from 1856 to 1857, and again during WWI.

With the completion in the 1930s of the trans-Iranian railway, which bypassed

Būshehr in favour of the ports in Khūzestān province, Būshehr began to decline. The British moved their Political Residency to Bahrain in 1946, and the British consulate closed in 1951, following the nationalisation of the Anglo-Iranian Oil Company. The town was of some importance to the navy during the Iran-Iraq War, but most of its commercial activities collapsed, much to the benefit of the less exposed Bandar-é Abbās to the east.

Orientation

The old town is in the northern tip of Būshehr; while the town centre is Shohadā

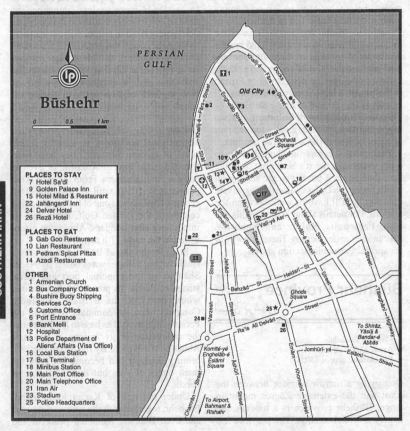

Būshehr

0   0.5   1 km

PLACES TO STAY
7 Hotel Sa'dī
9 Golden Palace Inn
15 Hotel Milad & Restaurant
22 Jahāngardī Inn
24 Delvar Hotel
26 Rezā Hotel

PLACES TO EAT
3 Gab Goo Restaurant
10 Lian Restaurant
11 Pedram Spical Pittza
14 Azadi Restaurant

OTHER
1 Armenian Church
2 Bus Company Offices
4 Bushire Buoy Shipping
   Services Co
5 Customs Office
6 Port Entrance
8 Bank Melli
12 Hospital
13 Police Department of
   Aliens' Affairs (Visa Office)
16 Local Bus Station
17 Bus Terminal
18 Minibus Station
19 Main Post Office
20 Main Telephone Office
21 Iran Air
23 Stadium
25 Police Headquarters

WESTERN IRAN
Top: The ruins of Ecbatana, the 'Place of Assembly' and one-time summer capital of
Achaemenian Persia, now surrounded by the modern city of Hamadān.
Bottom: The vast and austere Masjed-é Jame' in Hamadān, built during the Ghajar dynasty.

DAVID ST VINCENT

DAVID ST VINCENT

PAUL GREENWAY

WESTERN IRAN & CASPIAN PROVINCES
Top Left: The Armenian-built Ghara Kelīsā or Church of St Thaddeus, near Mākū.
Top Right: Distinctive Caspian coast architecture exemplified by this tomb in Sārī.
Bottom: The charming village of Māsūlé, 1050m above sea level in the forests of Gīlān.

Square. Būshehr is of a manageable size to explore on foot, unlike some Iranian ports which stretch for kilometres along the coast. Most of the attractions and the hotels, restaurants and bus terminal are in the northern part of Būshehr. Even the airport is as close as it could be to the centre. Watch out for large empty spaces along the footpaths, leading to the sewers – just the perfect size for unsuspecting travellers.

No maps of the town are available anywhere in Iran, but if you are curious, the Bank Mellat, near the Bank Melli, has a map of Būshehr town, in English, on its wall.

Information

Visa Extensions You could try to get your visa extended at the 'Police Department of Aliens' Affairs' (it is signposted in English as such); one traveller did report that her visa was extended easily and without fuss. However, you are better off trying in Shīrāz, not far away. The staff at the department were so bored, they stopped me simply to check my passport. No malice was intended; it was just that they hadn't seen a foreigner for so long.

Money Only the Bank Melli will change money, despite the 'Foreign Exchange' sign in the window of the Bank Tejarat building on Shohadā Square. The teller at the Bank Melli surprised me by asking how much I wanted for my US$100 bill. He made some telephone calls and then gave me a wad of rials at the official rate, but without a receipt – all a bit dodgy. It's probably a better idea to change your greenbacks elsewhere, eg Shīrāz.

Post & Communications The post and telephone offices are easy to spot, along Valī-yé Asr St. The telephone area code for Būshehr is 0771.

Emergency For general emergencies, dial telephone inquiries (☎ 115); for medical problems, contact the main hospital (☎ 23 564). The police headquarters (☎ 23 035) is on Ghods Square.

Old City

The old city is one of the largest living museums of traditional Bandarī architecture. Unlike so many other ports in the Persian Gulf, the old city has been spared the destructive effects of development. You will undoubtedly meet some locals, but watch out for the open sewers.

Most of the old houses in the narrow winding kūchés and blind alleys are still inhabited by families and many women are dressed in the traditional, brightly coloured layers of clothing unique to the Persian Gulf. The houses are made of mud brick covered with a thin layer of sand-coloured plaster, with tall façades; latticed windows without glass; and arched balconies. There are four **mosques** in the historical quarter.

The best time to visit is at sunset or later in the evening, as one traveller described:

Walk in the old city after 9 pm, while dusk takes over the squalid decay, and wander, and wander and wander, as if you were without a compass ... You will begin to walk through Moroccan squares, stare at Mexican courtyards and pass by Peruvian mud-walls ... And without knowing how, you are back in front of your mosāferkhūné.

Massimo Giannini, Italy

Armenian Church

This small, typically English, stone building, concealed from the street by a high wall, was built in 1819 by members of the then substantial British community. It has since been taken over by Armenians and is presently marked in English as the 'Armenian Church (Apostolic)'. Although the congregation only numbers about a dozen, they have gone to great efforts to renovate and redecorate the small stone church, and the results are impressive. There's a small graveyard (entered through the church) with tombs of a cosmopolitan mixture of parishioners, spanning the history of British missionary activity, including one who rejoiced in the name of Mackertich Goolzad (RIP 18 May 1915). Some of the tombs are still in good condition, but a number are missing their headstones.

SOUTHERN IRAN

Beaches

A lot of money is being spent on extending and renovating the esplanade, with the aim of making Būshehr a 'beach resort'. There's a small beach, the **Pelāzh-é Shahrdārī**, not far south of Komīté-yé Enghelāb-é Eslāmī Square (but not near the Shahrdārī at all). Men (but sadly not women) can swim a short distance out to sea, if they don't mind sharing that bit of the ocean with a few sharks and jellyfish. The better beaches are further south of town. (See the Around Būshehr section later in this chapter.)

Places to Stay

There is not a great choice; and some cheaper places will look the other way if you ask for a room. In winter, you may be struggling to find somewhere and prices are fairly high year-round. If you are on a really tight budget, you may wish to avoid Būshehr altogether, or just take an overnight trip from the cheaper Shīrāz. If none of the cheaper places in Būshehr will take you, get a letter from the police headquarters allowing you to stay at the mosāferkhūnés – this has worked well for several travellers.

The best place in town is the *Hotel Milad* (☎ 22 017). The grand foyer belies the rooms, which are a little grubby. With a fan, shared bathroom and a hole in the bedroom wall (indicating that air-con may be available in the future), twin rooms cost 30,000 rials. The hotel is along the end of a lane leading west from near Shohadā Square; it is signposted in English.

The *Hotel Sa'dī* (☎ 22 605) was not overly keen about foreign guests, but you could always beg for a room. The budget-priced *Golden Palace Inn* may reopen sometime in the future, but it looked permanently closed at the time of research, which is a shame. The *Rezā Hotel* (☎ 27 171) is way overpriced these days: 90,000 rials for a double with a bathroom, fridge, air-con and telephone. The prices are not open to negotiation, and it's a bit too far from the town centre.

The rooms at the quiet *Jahāngardī Inn* (☎ 22 346) used to have good views, until a café was built across the road. Doubles cost US$30, and like most places run by the ITTO, the staff won't negotiate down from the 'foreigners' price'. The only upmarket place in town is the luxurious *Delvar Hotel* (☎ 26 276) which costs US$65 for a single or double.

Places to Eat

A few *kabābīs* along Enghelāb and Leyān Sts serve a cheap meal of kebabs and rice for about 4000 rials, but you should try the fish while you're here – even if fish is hard to find. *Gab Goo* may have a weird name, but it serves reasonable Iranian-style hamburgers (2500 rials), fried chicken and kebabs (of course) – but don't get excited about the adverts on the windows for pizzas. For these, try the *Pedram Spical Pittza* joint (Who makes the signs in Būshehr anyway?). It was closed when I visited, but should be a good place for 'pittza'.

For some fresh air and great views go to the unnamed *café*, on the esplanade and directly opposite the Jahāngardī Inn. It serves Iranian-style hamburgers, cold drinks and ice creams. One of the cosiest places in town, with friendly staff and meals for about 6000 rials, is the *Azadi Restaurant*. Also very good, and worth a splurge, is the *Lian Restaurant*, complete with an aquarium (though none of the occupants are on the menu). Fish cutlets, rice, salad and a drink costs a reasonable 8000 rials.

The *restaurant* belonging (and next door) to the Hotel Milad is the best in town, though the plastic chairs and glass tables do not enhance the ambience. Excellent fish kebabs with rice and trimmings costs 10,000 rials, and the manager speaks English.

Getting There & Away

Air At the time of research, Iran Air (☎ 22 041) flies from Būshehr to Shīrāz (41,000 rials) and on to Esfahān (51,500 rials) on Wednesday; and to Tehrān every afternoon (73,500 rials). Tiny Caspian Air has a nice little office at Shohadā Square, but it seemed to be closed; flights between Būshehr and Tehrān on Caspian Air have been cancelled, but they may restart later.

SOUTHERN IRAN

Though there are few internal flights, Būshehr has two international links: Iran Air flies to/from Doha (Qatar) on Sunday for US$103/206 one way/return; and to/from Dubai (UAE) for US$116/232 on Thursday.

Bus & Minibus A few bus companies have booking offices along the esplanade, in the old city, though the bus terminal is easy to reach on foot from most hotels. Minibuses for regional towns, which you are unlikely to want to visit, leave from another special terminal. Among other destinations, buses leave the bus terminal at least every day to:

Destination	Distance	Time	Cost (rials)
Ābādān	691km	11 hours	5000
			(lux class only)
Ahvāz	626km	10 hours	5500
			(lux class only)
Bandar-é Abbās	921km	16 hours	11,500
			(super class only)
Bandar-é Lengé	656km	9 hours	7000
			(lux class only)
Shīrāz	320km	5 hours	3600/3800
			(lux/super class)
(this is a very popular trip, so book as soon as you can)			
Tehrān	1185km	19 hours	11,200/12,900

Boat From Būshehr, a few ferries and boats sail across the Persian Gulf, and occasionally to Kīsh Island, but at the time of research these seemed to have ceased because there are more frequent boats from Bandar-é Abbās and flights from Būshehr and Shīrāz. To find out what may be going from Būshehr, talk to the staff at the Bushire Buoy Shipping Service Co (☎ 24 941) – if you can find anyone there or if they are awake.

Getting Around

To/From the Airport A private taxi from the Būshehr airport into town costs an 'official' 5000 rials. There is no airport bus service. To get to the airport, you could try taking a shared taxi from Komīté-yé Enghelāb-é Eslāmī Square for around 750 rials, but you may have to take a private taxi anyway.

Bus Local buses can be found at the main terminal near the Hotel Milad. From here, you can catch a bus to Bāhmanī and Rīshahr (see following entries), or to look for a decent beach along the coast heading south.

Taxi Būshehr is a small enough place to walk around, but there are shared taxis, for about 500 rials, for any trip around town.

AROUND BŪSHEHR
Bāhmanī   بهمنی

Bāhmanī is 7km south of Būshehr. The **British Cemetery** (*Ghabrestān-é Engelīsīhā*), in what appears to be a temporarily abandoned building site, has been vandalised since the Islamic Revolution to such a degree that almost none of the tombstones are intact. The only undamaged tomb is that of a Sri Lankan sailor buried in 1981, with the inscription etched by finger in wet cement. Buses and shared taxis go to Bāhmanī from the bus terminal in Būshehr.

Rīshahr   ریشهر

Despite its historical importance, very little remains of the ancient city of Rīshahr, built during the Elamite and Sassanian eras. In any case the ruins currently stand within sight of no fewer than three top-security military installations and is not very easy to explore.

Along the 12km stretch of road between Būshehr and Rīshahr, especially south of Bāhmanī, there are quite a few carved **tombstones** from the early Arab period. Excavations along the same road have revealed a more or less continuous line of buried earthenware vases, believed to contain the remains of Zoroastrians after the vultures had done their work.

Rīshahr can be reached on foot or by shared taxi from Bāhmanī, or by bus from the bus terminal in Būshehr.

KANGĀN & BANDAR-É TĀKHERĪ
کنگان و بندر تخری

Kangān is a pretty little fishing village further along the south-eastern coast of Būshehr province. There are some excellent **beaches** and **coral** if you wish to try some snorkelling and diving (if you've brought your own gear). About 40km further south, another picturesque fishing village, Bandar-é Tākherī, boasts the **ruins** of a fascinating 18th century colonial building, and the **views** from the wind-tower over the Gulf are superb. To get to both places, you may wish to charter a taxi. To get to one or the other, jump on any bus or minibus travelling along the coastal road, then wave down any public transport between the two, if required.

KHĀRK ISLAND جزیره خارک

Thirty-one nautical miles north-west of Būshehr, this small coral island is the only island of any size in this part of the Persian Gulf. Khārk is best known today as one of the world's most important crude oil pumping stations, and for the devastation wreaked on it during the Iran-Iraq War. Although there are historical remains to see, the island is difficult and expensive to reach, and it is not set up for tourists.

Technically part of Būshehr province, Khārk is for most purposes under the control of the National Iranian Oil Company. There are occasional passenger flights from Tehrān, and sometimes boats from Būshehr. There's a couple of middle-range guesthouses on the island set up for oil workers.

Khūzestān Province
استان خوزستان

- **Capital:** Ahvāz
- **Area:** 67,132 sq km
- **Population:** 3.8 million

The province of Khūzestān, in the southwest of Iran, is probably best known for its oil, but the vast swampy Khūzestān plain is also an important agricultural area where dates, wheat, tomatoes and citrus fruits somehow flourish. The province was once part of the large kingdom of Elam, and contained cities built during the dynasties of the Parthians (190 BC-224 AD) and Sassanians (224-637). While there is now plenty of re-

development in the cities, following the devastating Iran-Iraq War, excited archaeologists continue to sift through the sand and swamps, especially at places like the Elamite ziggurat at Choghā Zambīl.

Although the indigenous population is largely Arab in origin and language, Arab culture only predominates in the smaller towns outside of Ahvāz.

AHVĀZ اهواز

This sprawling industrial city (population: approximately 950,000) on the banks of the Kārūn River owes its prosperity to the discovery of oil nearby at Masjed-é Soleimān in 1908. Much of Ahvāz was devastated by unremitting Iraqi bombardments throughout the Iran-Iraq War, and has since been ruined by uncontrolled redevelopment. The only aspect of Ahvāz worthy of making into a postcard is the modern suspension bridge, and that is only pretty at night.

Ahvāz is very pleasant in winter, but hideous in summer (April to October) when the heat, regularly more than 40°C, makes it all but impossible to leave your hotel room between 10 am and 5 pm. There is no need to spend too long here: Andīmeshk is a better base for visiting Shūsh or Choghā Zambīl, though Ahvāz is a useful staging post between western Iran and the southern cities such as Būshehr and Shīrāz.

Orientation

Ahvāz is sprawling and featureless. The main square is Shohadā Square just to the east of the suspension bridge – Pol-é Mo'allagh – and the main shopping district and new bazaar is south-east of this square. Tourists are not expected, nor are they catered for – or perhaps all the signs in English were destroyed during the Iran-Iraq War. The muddy Kārūn River is the only navigable river in Iran, but it's not worth exploring, nor is there any long-distance transport along it.

Information

Visa Extensions For visa extensions, try the police headquarters, but don't get your hopes up too high. If you're feeling lucky, ask for the visa extension to be done quickly, otherwise you may have to hang around this dreary city for a few days.

Money You can change money at the central branch of the Bank Melli. There are no official moneychangers, nor, surprisingly, any black marketeers in town.

Post & Communications The main post office is inconveniently on the western side of the river; the main telephone office is not far from Shohadā Square. The telephone area code for Ahvāz is 061.

Emergency The police headquarters (☎ 110 or ☎ 22 231) is in a nice position, alongside the river. There is a medical emergencies number (☎ 335 999) or you can ring the Jondishapur Hospital (☎ 28 075).

Things to See & Do
There's very little to do in Ahvāz. It's possible to take a short **cruise** along the river in a small motorboat, from a tiny jetty near the Restōrān-é Rudkenar. It's quite pleasant to walk along the river side at night when the bridges are illuminated – and the fierce sun has disappeared for a while.

Places to Stay
A few of the cheap places around the new bazaar district refuse to take foreigners. The best value place in the budget range is the *Hotel Star* (☎ 218 125). Perfectly adequate singles/doubles, with a fan and shared bathroom, cost a very reasonable 13,000/18,000 rials. It's a white, three storey building on the corner of an unmarked lane and Emām Khomeinī St; the door has a small sign in English above it.

The best place in the middle range for standards, but at a budget price, is the excellent *Hotel Iran* (☎ 218 200). Staff can speak

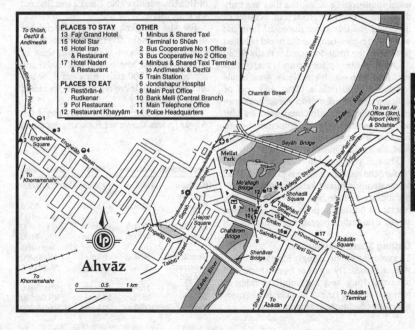

PLACES TO STAY
13 Fajr Grand Hotel
15 Hotel Star
16 Hotel Iran
   & Restaurant
17 Hotel Naderi
   & Restaurant

PLACES TO EAT
7 Restōrān-é
   Rudkenar
9 Pol Restaurant
12 Restaurant Khayyām

OTHER
1 Minibus & Shared Taxi
   Terminal to Shūsh
2 Bus Cooperative No 1 Office
3 Bus Cooperative No 2 Office
4 Minibus & Shared Taxi Terminal
   to Andīmeshk & Dezfūl
5 Train Station
6 Jondishapur Hospital
8 Main Post Office
10 Bank Melli (Central Branch)
11 Main Telephone Office
14 Police Headquarters

To Shūsh, Dezfūl & Andīmeshk

Andīmeshk – Road

Enghelāb Square
Enghelāb Street

To Khorramshahr

To Khorramshahr

Ahvāz

0   0.5   1 km

Chamrān Street

Chamran Street

Kārūn River

Seyāh Bridge

Mellat Park

Mo'allagh Bridge

Shohadā Square

Tāleqhāni Street

Emām Street

Khomeinī St

Ābādān Square

Behbahānī Street

Sābeh St

Hejrat Square

Chahārom Bridge

Salmān St

Engelāb St

Takhti Street

Shenāvar Bridge

Fārsi St

Kārūn River

Sharī'ati St

To Ābādān

To Ābādān Terminal

To Iran Air Office (3km), Airport (4km) & Shūshtar

Āzādegān Street

Sharī'ati St

Highway

SOUTHERN IRAN

some English and a comfy single/double room with a bathroom, a fan and a TV costs 25,000/35,000 rials. Normally recommended, but now a place to avoid until they can get their act together, is the *Hotel Naderi* (☎ 229 000). I was charged the ridiculous price of 60,000/90,000 rials for a tiny room, mercifully with air-con. The receptionist then had the gall to charge me 8000 rials for breakfast (which was free for Iranian guests).

The top-end place to stay is the four-star *Fajr Grand Hotel* (☎ 220 091). Most of the luxurious rooms have views of the river, and it's in a quiet location. The highlight is unquestionably the swimming pool (which is not open to the public, sadly). The cheapest rooms are US$35/50/66 for a single/double/triple.

Places to Eat

The river fish here are among the best in Iran, but surprisingly hard to find. Ahvāz is also one of the best places in the country for fruit shakes; they are more expensive than the usual tooth-rotting colas, but they are truly delicious. Around the Hotel Iran, a couple of unnamed *kabābīs* serve the usual fare, but with a difference because the bread is baked just inside the front door, and is really fresh.

One of the best places to eat is the *Restaurant Khayyām* which has views, great meals for about 7500 rials a plate, and pots of delicious tea. The *Restōrān-é Rudkenar* is an old favourite, but getting there involves a bit of a walk across the bridge from most hotels. For fish, it's hard to go past the *Pol Restaurant*, under the Chahārom bridge.

Though you shouldn't stay at the *Hotel Naderi*, the restaurant there is excellent. I had an outstanding mixed kebab, which incredibly did not include fish, for 9500 rials. The restaurant on the 1st floor of the *Hotel Iran* serves a fantastic khōresh for 7500 rials.

Getting There & Away

To avoid any excruciatingly long and hot bus ride, it's worth flying to or from Ahvāz; and to avoid long and hot minibus rides to regional towns, take a quicker (and sometimes air-conditioned) shared taxi.

Air Iran Air flies from Ahvāz to Tehrān two or sometimes three times a day for 51,500 rials; to Mashhad on Tuesday and Friday for 95,500 rials; and to Esfahān every day for 40,000 rials. Iran Asseman sometimes flies to/from Ahvāz, but the schedules and prices were unclear at the time of research.

Iran Air has two offices, both hopelessly inconvenient. One is along Pāsdārān Blvd, on the way to the airport, and accessible by shared taxi. The other office (☎ 42 094) is larger and very busy, and is in the Kiyan Pars district in the far northern suburbs – you'll have to charter a taxi out there.

The airport is a bit chaotic, and the check-in process can be painfully slow, so allow plenty of time.

Bus & Minibus There is no specific bus or minibus terminal, so they all leave from different places. It's best to charter a taxi to the terminal you want, to ensure that you get to the right one. Alternatively, go to the offices of Bus Cooperatives No 1 and 2 and find out what they have.

For Ābādān, take a minibus (2000 rials) or shared taxi (4000 rials) from the new terminal, which is about 800m south-west of Ābādān Square. Minibuses (2000 rials) and shared taxis (4000 rials) for Dezfūl, Shūsh and Andīmeshk leave regularly from places along Enghelāb St.

There are buses at least every day from Ahvāz (prices shown are for lux/super class) to:

Destination	Distance	Time	Cost (rials)
Bandar-é Abbās	1169km	19 hours	16,500/18,000
Būshehr	626km	10 hours	5500 (lux class only)
Esfahān	765km	14 hours	12,500/15,000
Hamadān	465km	7 hours	8600 (lux class only)
Kermānshāh	509km	9 hours	7400/8200
Khorram Ābād	390km	6 hours	5000/5500
Shīrāz	568km	10 hours	6100/8600
Tehrān	881km	14 hours	8500/9500
Yazd	1008km	20 hours	11,500/16,700

Train Although the line from the Ahvāz station runs in two directions, there are no passenger services south to Khorramshahr; the train will only take you as far as Tehrān (816km north). Two overnight trains leave Ahvāz every day for Tehrān (8300/19,150 rials for 2nd/1st class). There is also one train per day as far as Ghom (11,200/17,300 rials). Among other places, these trains stop at Andīmeshk and Shūsh.

Shared Taxi All shared taxis leave from the bus and minibus terminals, which are all over town. Refer to the Bus & Minibus earlier in this section for details.

Getting Around

To/From the Airport There's no airport bus service, but you can take a private taxi to the city centre for a reasonable 4000 rials. From the airport, you should be able to share a taxi for about 1000 rials. Allow plenty of time to check in.

Taxi Ahvāz is a complicated place to catch shared taxis. They cost about 1000 rials for most trips, but this is one city where you should save your sanity and energy by paying extra for a private taxi.

ANDĪMESHK & DEZFŪL   اندیمشک، دزفول

Andīmeshk is a pleasant village, though it's hot in summer and there are always lots of flies. It is a far better place to base yourself for trips to Shūsh and/or Choghā Zambīl than Ahvāz, or to break up a journey between southern and western Iran. Andīmeshk is mainly inhabited by the Lors people, who are actively engaged in vegetable farming, courtesy of the incredible Dez Dam about 30km north of Dezfūl. The Lors are generally not well-liked by the central government, so Andīmeshk has (thankfully) been spared the unabashed redevelopment of other nearby cities – nor does it seem to have suffered much from the Iran-Iraq War.

In contrast, Dezfūl, a few kilometres away, and once a glorious Sassanian city, has been significantly rebuilt following exten-sive bombing during the Iran-Iraq War. Dezfūl could easily be renamed 'Dreadful', and the only reason to go there is to watch the spectacular sunset over the mud brick buildings along the Dez River.

Just about everything in both towns sensibly closes between 1 and 5 pm, when Andīmeshk looks like a ghost town. Both places liven up once the sun has set.

Places to Stay

I was in Andīmeshk in May, during one of those unpredictable times when the village is completely overrun by vegetable traders from places as far afield as Russia. I visited every hotel and fleapit in both towns, but not one room was available. I eventually shared a room with two huge, affable Āzarī traders. However, finding a room shouldn't normally be too much of a problem. There is nowhere decent to stay in Dreadful, er, Dezfūl.

The best hotels in Andīmeshk are along the main road heading north from the highway. They all have signs in English, and charge foreigners about 40,000 rials for a reasonable double room with a bathroom and, usually, air-con. The *Hotel Apadana* is a bit dated; the *Hotel Rostam*, opposite, is better but the staff are unfriendly; the best is *Hotel Eghbal*, right on the square in the middle of town.

Places to Eat

Most hotels have *restaurants* which serve decent food, but not much more than kebabs are on offer – though the locally-grown tomatoes are large and delicious. Things start late in Andīmeshk and if you get to your hotel restaurant before 8.30 pm there may be a panic and a rush to find the cook. There are also a few *snack bars* selling hamburgers and cakes around the main square.

Getting There & Away

Bus & Minibus Though there are some bus companies in Andīmeshk with direct services to Tehrān, most buses leave from Dezfūl. To save you going to Dezfūl, just stand along the side of the highway, next to the major roundabout, and hail down a bus which is going your way. When arriving in Andīmeshk, ask to be dropped off at the roundabout on the highway, otherwise you may end up in Dezfūl.

From the minibus terminal – 200m towards Ahvāz from the roundabout on the highway – minibuses go to Khorram Ābād (3500 rials), Ahvāz and Shūsh (both cost 2000 rials each), Dezfūl (1000 rials) and Shūshtar (1500 rials). From outside the minibus terminal, there are also shared taxis to Khorram Ābād (6000 rials), Ahvāz (4000 rials) and Dezfūl (2500 rials).

Train From Andīmeshk there are trains to Ahvāz, Tehrān and Ghom three times a day. The station is the most convenient in the country; it's only 150m west of the town square in Andīmeshk and close to all hotels.

SHŪSHTAR   شوشتر
About 90km north of Ahvāz, along the old road between Ahvāz and Dezfūl, the pretty town of Shūshtar was mostly spared from the effects of the Iran-Iraq War, so retains some quaintness. The town was built on the Kārūn River and is famous for the ancient **Shadorvan Bridge** and **Band-é Ghaisar Bridge**, both constructed during the Sassanian period (224-637), and the **water mills**. The 9th century **Masjed-é Jāme'**, renowned for its minarets and inscriptions, is also worth a look.

There is nowhere to stay in Shūshtar, but it is possible to take a day trip from Andīmeshk (1500 rials) or from Ahvāz (2000 rials), either by minibus (1500 and 2000 rials respectively) or by using the occasional shared taxi.

SHŪSH (SUSA)   شوش
Although Shūsh was one of the great ancient cities of Iran, and is one of the earliest to have been explored by archaeologists, there's no longer very much to see compared with the better preserved and more extensive site of Persepolis. Many visitors are disappointed by how little is left of Shūsh, and, ironically, the castle built by the French to defend the

archaeologists is easily the best thing to see – and that is closed to the public.

History
Though best known as an Achaemenian capital, Shūsh was in fact a prehistoric settlement from at least the 4th millennium BC, and an important Elamite city from about the middle of the 3rd millennium. Around 640 BC, Shūsh was burnt by the Assyrian King Ashurbanipal, but it regained prominence in 521 BC when Darius I set it up as his winter capital. Darius fortified Shūsh and built palaces and other buildings, so at one time Shūsh must have been similar in grandeur to Persepolis.

In 331 BC Shūsh fell to Alexander the Great, and its days of splendour were over. It later became the Sassanian capital, and, during Shāpūr I's reign in the 4th century AD, an important centre of Christianity. Shūsh faded away after about 1200 and didn't come back to attention until 1852 when WK Loftus, a British archaeologist, was the first to survey the site. His work was continued by the French Archaeological Service from 1891, more or less continuously until the Islamic Revolution in 1979.

Ancient City
Many fine examples of pottery, from various periods, showing the development of the typically Persian, highly stylised animal motif, as well as bronzes, have been found here. Most are now on display at the National Museum of Iran in Tehrān, while a famous 4th century BC bulls' head capital is now in the Louvre, Paris.

If you enter through the gate from the street, ie the only official entrance, you cannot fail to notice the **Acropolis**. This castle, quite unlike any other archaeological camp, was built by the French Archaeological Service at the end of the 19th century, as a necessary defence against the unpacified Arab tribes of the region. It is now the most imposing structure at Shūsh, but sadly the public is not welcome inside.

The city was built on four small mounds. Next to the Acropolis, the largest mound contains the remains of the **Royal Town**, once the quarter of the court officials. North-west of this was the **Apadana**, where Darius I built his residence and two other palaces. Two well-preserved foundation tablets found beneath the site of **Darius' Palace** record the noble ancestry of its founder; they are now in the National Museum of Iran in Tehrān. The mound labelled as the **Artisans' Town** dates from the Seleucid (331-190 BC) and Parthian (190 BC-224 AD) eras. Traces of an Arab mosque were found here, but little else of substance remains.

At the time of research the **museum** was closed to the public, and no-one could say if, or when, it would reopen. (It did look permanently closed.)

The entrance to the site is along the main street in the village. Foreigners are charged 5000 rials, and it is open from 8 am to 6 pm every day. You may need to show your passport to the guard at the entrance (and sometimes even have to leave it with him) because the site is used by the military. Near the entrance is a board with some interesting explanations in English about the ancient city.

Ārāmgāh-é Dānyāl

Also dominating the village of Shūsh is the unusual Tomb of Daniel, a short walk west of the entrance to the ancient city. Though not particularly old (it was built in 1870), the tomb is quite interesting, not least because it's dedicated to a Jewish prophet.

Places to Stay & Eat

Shūsh is a mildly interesting place to stroll around. There are plenty of *snack bars* and *kabābīs*, but nothing to get excited about gastronomically – though the tomatoes, which somehow flourish in this most arid region, are huge, cheap and delicious. There is nowhere to stay in the town.

Getting There & Away

Shūsh is 116km north-west of Ahvāz and 38km south of Andīmeshk. Minibuses travel when full – ie about every hour – between Shūsh and Andīmeshk. From Ahvāz, there are also regular minibuses, or just get off the bus along the road heading north.

A chartered taxi from Andīmeshk is a good option because you can combine it with a detour to Choghā Zambīl for about 20,000 rials return, including waiting time. Shūsh is also on the train line between Ahvāz and Tehrān. Trains only pass through Shūsh three times a day, so a minibus or shared taxi is far quicker.

CHOGHĀ ZAMBĪL   چفا زنبیل

Alongside the Dez River, the remarkably well-preserved ziggurat of Choghā Zambīl is the best surviving example of Elamite archi-tecture anywhere, and it has now been recognised and registered with UNESCO. Originally it had five concentric storeys but only three remain reaching a total height of some 25m. It's hard to believe that such an imposing landmark could have been lost to the world for more than 2500 years, which was the case until it was accidentally discov-ered in 1935 during an Anglo-Iranian Oil Company aerial survey.

History

In ancient times the inhabitants of Iran attached great religious importance to moun-tains, and where they had no mountains, they made their own imitations, thereby creating the distinctive pyramidal style of building known as *ziggurat*. This ziggurat was the *raison d'être* of the town of Dur Untash, founded by King Untash Gal in the middle of the 13th century BC. It reached its peak towards the start of the 12th century BC, when it had a large number of temples and priests, but was later sacked by the Assyrian King Ashurbanipal around 640 BC.

The ziggurat, which is now the most imposing structure of Dur Untash, was ded-icated to Inshushinak, the chief god of the Elamites and patron of Shūsh; there was originally a quadrangular temple to him on the summit of the ziggurat, accessible only to the elite of Elamite society. The ziggurat was built on a square plan, with its sides measuring 105m, and its storeys were erected vertically from the foundation level,

SOUTHERN IRAN

as a series of concentric towers, rather than one on top of another like a wedding cake.

Things to See

You can still climb the surviving three storeys of the ziggurat by a steep staircase on the north-west side. The **ziggurat** was built on a low base as a precaution against flooding, as this was once a fertile and forested area, though nowadays the setting is bleak, barren, windswept, and hot, even in winter.

You can still clearly see the cuneiform **inscriptions** on many of the bricks, bearing the name of Untash Gal, though the original blue and green mosaic tiles are no longer in place. There was originally a complex of chambers, tombs, tunnels and water channels on the lowest level, as well as two temples to Inshushinak on the south-east side. The ziggurat was surrounded by a paved courtyard protected behind a wall, outside of which were the living quarters of the town, as well as 11 temples dedicated to various Elamite gods and goddesses.

The rest of the city is not well-preserved, but there are still the remains of three simple, but well-constructed **royal palaces**. One of these was the king's residence, one was probably the harem, and the other was a royal gate. There are also traces of an ingeniously designed water and drainage system; and a **sundial** which still works. Many of the artefacts found here are now on display in the National Museum of Iran in Tehrān.

One guide makes a living, albeit not a busy one, showing visitors around the site. It is not worth using him unless you understand Fārsī, though he can still show you the inscriptions, footprints and stairs which are hard to find otherwise. He will expect a tip of around 2000 rials.

Entrance

Even in this most remote place, a man will come out of nowhere, sit on a chair under a makeshift tin roof, blow the dust off the book of entrance tickets and charge a foreigner 10,000 rials to get in. There is no fence at all, so there are no opening times. In summer, get there before 10 am or after 5 pm; the midday

sun will surely weaken any enthusiasm about exploring the site. Look for the helpful sign which has some explanations in English. Photography is allowed.

Getting There & Away

Choghā Zambīl is 45km from Shūsh, and 65km from Andīmeshk. Because it's off the beaten track, you should consider chartering a taxi from Andīmeshk for about 20,000 rials return, including waiting time, which can include a stop in Shūsh (see the previous section on Shūsh).

Alternatively, you can get dropped off from any minibus or bus heading along the highway. The sign to the Choghā Zambīl is not signposted in English; the road leading there is the first main road south of the turn-off to Haft Tappé (which is signposted in English). You will then need to hitch a lift – it shouldn't take more than about two hours to get there – via two roadblocks.

HAFT TAPPÉ   هفت تپه

To the left of the road as you leave Choghā Zambīl for Shūsh, look out for the remains of this 2nd millennium BC Elamite town. Haft once had several ziggurats as well as various royal buildings, tombs and temples. There's less to see than at Choghā Zambīl or Shūsh, because the site here is much more spread out than the other two, but the **museum**, closed since 1979, should reopen soon.

ĀBĀDĀN   آبادان

Ābādān is unusual because it is actually on a 270 sq km island, between the Bahmanshir and Arvand rivers. It was a tiny village until 1910, when thousands of westerners came here to exploit its new-found oil wealth. The town grew and grew, and boasted such places as the Bostan Club, the Watersports Club and the Jockey Club. Times have changed.

When the Iran-Iraq War started, the remaining foreigners packed up and left, and waves of locals also sought to escape the incessant Iraqi bombardments. The War largely destroyed Ābādān, and there is still plenty of redevelopment needed.

Ābādān is actually a little cooler that Ahvāz (most places are), and is probably a better place to stay than Ahvāz.

Places to Stay

There isn't much to choose from: most budget establishments won't take foreigners, and the others were mostly bombed into oblivion. The only place currently available is the *Keivan Hotel* (☎ 23 651), opposite the park and near the port. They seemed reluctant to bother with foreigners, but they will if you smile nicely and look confident. A

single/double room, with air-con, costs 20,200/29,050 rials.

Getting There & Away

Iran Air flies between Ābādān and Tehrān two or three times a day for 58,500 rials; and Iran Asseman flies to Tehrān for the same price on Sunday. Shared taxis between Ābādān and Ahvāz leave regularly, about every 20 minutes, for 4000 rials. Ābādān can also be reached from Ahvāz by minibus (2000 rials).

SOUTHERN IRAN

Western Iran

ایران غربی

There is evidence of settlement in western Iran as early as the 6th millennium BC, and many of the earliest empires and kingdoms of Persia had their capitals here. Standing at the frontiers with Mesopotamia and Turkey, much of the region has been vulnerable to incursions from the west throughout its long history.

During the Iran-Iraq War the region was thrown into turmoil; its towns were bombed and, in some cases, were occupied by Iraqi forces. Refugees from Iraq fled to western Iran throughout the Iran-Iraq War and, to an even greater extent, following the Gulf War and the widespread oppression of the Kurds in Iraq. You will come across a lot of road-blocks in this part of Iran, intended to dissuade Kurdish refugees and separatists rather than anything to do with the region's proximity to Iraq.

Little of the population of western Iran is Persian, so the national language is seldom heard. Kurds are predominant in the Kordestān and Kermānshāh provinces; Lors in Īlām and Lorestān; and Āzarīs in Āzarbāyjān-é Sharghī, Āzarbāyjān-é Gharbī and Ardabīl.

Tribal dress is still very much in everyday use, and nomadism is still widely practised in the remoter regions. Anyone interested in travelling extensively in the region should read Dame Freya Stark's *The Valleys of the Assassins*, which she had originally intended to call *A Treasure Hunt in Luristan*. Also recommended is *Journeys in Persia and Kurdistan*, written in 1889, by the adventurous Isabella Bird.

There are few facilities for visitors outside the main towns. Only a few places are connected by air to the rest of Iran, and the railway system will not get you far. The ancient royal highways connecting the central plateau with Mesopotamia and Turkey are still very much in use, and you can see the remains of many ancient caravanserais along the roads.

WESTERN IRAN AT A GLANCE

- **Provinces:** Lorestān, Īlām, Kermānshāh, Hamadān, Kordestān, Zanjān, Āzarbāyjān-é Gharbī, Āzarbāyjān-é Sharghī and Ardabīl.
- **When to Go:** Summer and spring (May to September) are ideal; winters can be long and harsh; around Ardabīl province, be prepared for rain at any time.
- **Highlights:** Alī Sadr caves, near Hamadān city; Gombad-é Soltānīyé, near Zanjān city; Ghara Kelīsā, near Mākū; Tāgh-é Bostān, near the city of Kermānshāh; and Takht-é Soleimān.

Lorestān Province

استان لرستان

- **Capital:** Khorram Ābād
- **Area:** 28,803 sq km
- **Population:** approx 1.8 million

This province is often omitted from the official tourist handouts, suggesting that foreign tourists neither visit, nor are expected to do so. The Lors, who are not well-regarded by the authorities in Tehrān, have attracted a

WESTERN IRAN

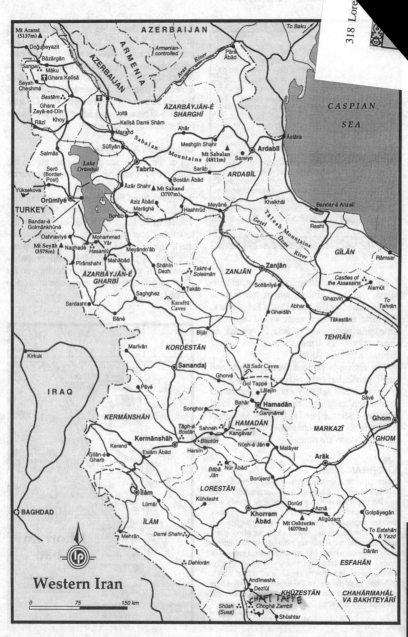

Western Iran

The Lors

The Lors either speak their own dialect of Arabic known as *Avesta*, or their own language known as *Lorī*. They are renowned for their horsemanship, sheep farming, metalwork and, especially, production of carpets and rugs. The Lors do not obligingly toe the government line, so they are not well-regarded by Tehrān, nor is this region the subject of much development – which seems to suit the Lors just fine.

The Lors mainly inhabit villages in the province of Lorestān, while Lor nomads live in several other mountainous regions of western Iran. Some dissidents were exiled from Lorestān during the Pahlavī dynasty and sent to the Zanjān and Khorāsān provinces, where they still live. The most famous Lor was the benevolent Karīm Khān Zand, who ruled Persia for a few years in the 18th century. ■

small number of distinguished, intrepid travellers, foremost among whom are women such as Isabella Bird and Dame Freya Stark. Exploration of the province would take some time, and your own vehicle is needed, so most travellers limit themselves to the capital, Khorram Ābād.

The region is famous for its carpets and rugs, particularly the striped *gabbeh*. The authorities are actively encouraging carpet production as a tourist attraction and local industry. (See the Persian Carpets section in the Facts about Iran chapter.) About 10 % of the population are nomads.

KHORRAM ĀBĀD

خرم آباد

Picturesque at a distance beyond any Persian town that I have seen ... Khorram Ābād successfully rivals any Persian town in its squalor, dirt, evil odours, and ruinous condition. Two-thirds of what was 'the once famous capital of the Atabegs' are now 'ruinous heaps'. The bazars are small, badly supplied, dark, and rude; and the roads are nothing but foul alleys, possibly once paved, but now full of ridges, holes, ruins, rubbish, lean and mangy dogs, beggarly-looking men, and broken channels of water, which, dribbling over the soil in the bazars and everywhere else in green and black slime, gives forth pestiferous odours in the hot sun.

Isabella Bird
Journeys in Persia and Kurdistan (1889)

While the redoubtable Ms Bird described accurately what she saw in the late 19th century, Khorram Ābād is now quite a pleasant town. Boasting a magnificent fortress in the middle of the city, Khorram Ābād makes a decent stopover between Hamadān and Kermānshāh, or between Ahvāz and Esfahān. There are also some fine places for rock-climbing in the area.

Orientation & Information

All of the hotels are along Sharī'atī St, the main road heading north-east towards Hamadān and south towards Ahvāz. The tree-lined Alavī St is the main shopping district, one block downhill from Sharī'atī St. The fortress, Falak-ol-Aflak, dominates the town and acts as the most important landmark; the bazaar is immediately to the west. The staff at the Bank Melli will probably have a fit if you ask to change money, so do it before you arrive. The telephone area code is 0661.

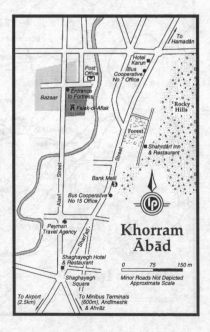

Khorram Ābād

Falak-ol-Aflak

This strong and impressive fortress, with its 12 towers, stands on a rocky prominence, dominating the city. It was the citadel of the Atābaks, the powerful rulers of the Lorestān Province from the 12th century until about 1600, when the last Atābak king was defeated and killed by Shāh Abbās I.

The fortress stands about 40m high, and is more than 5000 sq metres in area. It was undergoing massive renovations at the time of research, so only a small section was open to the public. Once fully restored, you will be able to explore the four halls and two courtyards, in the meantime you can admire the **views** of the city from the top of the fortress. There is an ancient **well** inside the fortress which still draws fresh water from a spring 40m below the ground. A **museum** (☎ 4090) should be open by the time you visit.

The fortress is open daily from about 7 am to 4.15 pm. I strolled around and no-one asked for any money – but don't expect that to last very long as there will be an entrance fee (probably 10,000 rials).

Rock Climbing

For anyone who likes to scramble up rocky hills, those in Khorram Ābād, east of the road towards Hamadān, are superb – just pick a spot and start scrambling. This is one of the best and, importantly, most accessible areas for rock climbing in the whole country, so enjoy.

Places to Stay

One of the better places to stay, as long as you can get a room away from the main road, is the *Hotel Karun* (☎ 25 408). The large, clean rooms, with or without a bathroom, cost 12,000/20,000 rials. In contrast, the *Shaghayegh Hotel* (☎ 22 648), on the square of the same name, is not good value at US$20/30 for a single/double, but the manager is certainly open to negotiation and will accept rials.

The *Shahrdarī Inn*, run by the ITTO, is behind a small forest, with some awesome views of the city and fortress. The rooms are pleasant, and some have balconies and views, but it's overpriced; they charge foreigners a ridiculous and non-negotiable US$23/34 for a single/double – try to pay with rials.

Places to Eat

There is nothing but *kabābīs* along the two main streets, so eating at a hotel is the best idea. The *Shaghayegh Hotel* has a good restaurant, with meals for about 7500 rials. The best place is the *Shahrdarī Inn*, though the views are far better than the meals or the service.

Things to Buy

Khorram Ābād is famous for its handicrafts, including bronzes, painted glass and china items, miniatures, charming cordless hubble-bubbles and decorative smoking pipes. These can be bought from the bazaar, or from a couple of decent souvenir shops along Alavī St.

Getting There & Away

Air Iran Asseman is the only airline that flies in and out of Khorram Ābād, on Tuesday, Thursday and Saturday for 65,000 rials. Book at the airport (about 3km south of the bazaar); or at Peyman Travel Agency, the local agent for Iran Air and Iran Asseman.

Bus There is no bus terminal. You can catch a direct bus, to the places listed below, from outside the appropriate bus company office along Sharī'atī St. You can also hail down a passing bus, at the roundabout near the Hotel Karun, to anywhere immediately east, such as Hamadān and Arāk, or to places to the south. To get to some places, like Īlām, you may need to catch a connecting bus to somewhere like Kermānshāh.

The road between Borūjerd and Khorram Ābād is winding and steep, and full of suicidal truck drivers. If you are driving, take care; if you are in a bus, close your eyes. Buses leave several times a day (with prices for lux/super class) to:

WESTERN IRAN

Destination	Distance	Time	Cost (rials)
Andīmeshk	241km	4 hours	3000
		(lux class only; or take a minibus)	
Ahvāz	390km	6 hours	5000/5500
Esfahān	368km	6 hours	5700/6200
Hamadān	252km	4 hours	9000
		(the pricey 'special' class only)	
Shīrāz	852km	12 hours	10,500/12,500
Tehrān	491km	8 hours	6000/6700

Minibus Minibuses are a common form of transport in this part of Iran. From special terminals, 600m south of Shaghayegh Square, minibuses go to Andīmeshk (3500 rials) and Kermānshāh (4500 rials) when they have enough passengers.

Getting Around
Khorram Ābād is small enough to walk around, and you can reach the transport terminals on foot. Shared taxis speed along the two main streets and are available for about 250 rials a trip.

AROUND KHORRAM ĀBĀD
Borūjerd   بروجرد
The town of Borūjerd, on the main road between Hamadān and Khorram Ābād, is of interest for its 11th century **Masjed-é Jāme'**, which has a Seljuq-era dome and mehrāb containing an inscription from the same period. The Ghajar **Masjed-é Soltānī** and the 12th century **Emāmzādé-yé Ja'far** are also worth visiting. To get to Borūjerd, simply get off any bus travelling between Khorram Ābād and Hamadān.

Bābā Jān   بابا جان
Among the many pre-Islamic mounds uncovered in the province, the most interesting is Bābā Jān. Occupied from at least the 3rd millennium BC, this large mound shows the indistinct remains of a town, partly burnt in the 7th century BC and abandoned 200 years later. Its fortifications have excited archaeologists, though there is not much to see.

The ruins are accessible from the village of Nūr Ābād, about 90km north-west of Khorram Ābād. You will have to charter a vehicle from Khorram Ābād, Hamadān or Kermānshāh.

Īlām Province   استان ایلام

- **Capital:** Īlām
- **Area:** 19,086 sq km
- **Population:** approx 530,000

Īlām is the least populated province in Iran and one of the most remote. There is almost nothing to be seen of the ancient Elamite empire that flourished in this region in ancient times, though there are limited remains at Darré Shahr and Dehlorān. Given its proximity to Iraq (Īlām is only a grenade-throw from Baghdad), you are advised to stay away from remote areas of the province and limit your trip to Īlām city.

ĪLĀM   ایلام
Until just before WWII this city was the seat of the Vālī Khāns, the Lor chieftains of the region. The remains of their palaces can still be seen in the north of Īlām province, but otherwise the town is drab.

The main street is Heydarī St, which changes its name to Ferdōsī St as it heads west. Most of the offices and restaurants are around 22 Bahman Square.

Places to Stay & Eat
The best hotel in town is the *Jahāngardī Inn* (☎ (08495) 2470), which charges foreigners US$15/25 for a pleasant single/double. It is run by the ITTO and is on Jonūbī Blvd, at the southern end of the city. Other cheaper places for around 40,000 rials a double include the *Hotel Ferdōsī*, on Ferdōsī St, and the *Hotel Dalaho* (☎ (08495) 6898) which is on Vaasetī St. You are advised to eat at one of the hotels.

Getting There & Away
Currently, there is no legal crossing into Iraq from Īlām province for independent travellers. Iran Asseman flies between Īlām and Tehrān (75,000 rials) four days a week, but flights are not reliable. Tiny Saha Air also links Tehrān with Īlām, but don't rely on these flights. Book tickets for either airline at the airport or at a travel agency in Tehrān.

WESTERN IRAN

There are direct buses every day from Īlām to Ahvāz, Khorram Ābād, Sanandaj and Tehrān, but most public transport goes to Kermānshāh (6500 rials by minibus), from where you must take a connecting bus.

Kermānshāh Province
استان باختران

- **Capital:** Kermānshāh
- **Area:** 23,667 sq km
- **Population:** approx 1.95 million

Kermānshāh province (previously known as Bākhtārān) has some of the most interesting and famous archaeological sites in this part of Iran, dating from before recorded history through the Achaemenian (559-330 BC), Parthian (190 BC-224 AD) and Sassanian (224-637) dynasties to the Arab period (637-1050). The climate is pleasant for most of the year, the largely mountainous scenery is stunning and the soil is fertile.

KERMĀNSHĀH کرمانشاه
An important station on the ancient trading route to Baghdad, Kermānshāh is by far the largest and busiest city in this part of Iran. While there is little to see in the city itself, Kermānshāh is the perfect place to base yourself while exploring the mid-western region of the country. At an altitude of 1322m, the city has a beautiful setting, framed by permanently snow-clad mountains. Kermānshāh should be avoided in winter, but the climate is very pleasant for the rest of the year.

History
First built on a site a few kilometres from the present town, Kermānshāh probably dates from the 4th century AD. Its vulnerable position has always rendered it liable to incursions – it was captured by the Arabs in 649, invaded by the Seljuqs in the 11th century, and then sacked by the Mongols in the early 13th century. After several centu-

ries of relative peace and prosperity, Kermānshāh's strategic position on the road to Baghdad attracted very heavy Iraqi missile and bomb attacks during the Iran-Iraq War, and the rubble is still plain to see.

Orientation
Kermānshāh is one of the very few major towns in Iran without any street signs in English. Still, it's easy enough to get around: most of what you want is along Modarres St, between the mammoth Āzādī Square and the junction with Motahharī St.

Information
The 'Tourism Information Office' at the airport was closed at the time of research. The old Bank Melli branch, along Modarres St, will doubtless be supplanted by the enormous new Bank Melli building, currently under construction on Āzādī Square. Bank Mellat and Bank Sepah won't change money, but they act as good landmarks, as

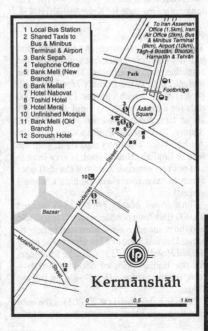

1 Local Bus Station
2 Shared Taxis to Bus & Minibus Terminal & Airport
3 Bank Sepah
4 Telephone Office
5 Bank Melli (New Branch)
6 Bank Mellat
7 Hotel Nabovat
8 Toshid Hotel
9 Hotel Meraj
10 Unfinished Mosque
11 Bank Melli (Old Branch)
12 Soroush Hotel

Kermānshāh or Bākhtarān?

The city has, throughout its history, usually been known as Kermānshāh or Kermānshāhān – City of the King (or Kings) of Kermān – because its founder had formerly been the governor of Kermān province. After the Islamic Revolution of 1979 the name was dropped from official use, because of the new regime's distaste for the word 'shāh' and all of its connotations, following the overthrow of the last shāh of the Pahlavī dynasty.

However, former president Rafsanjānī conceded that since the ancient name had no connection with the ousted Pahlavī shāh, there was no reason why the name Kermānshāh should not replace Bākhtarān. Older maps and some street signs may still show Bākhtarān, though you will mostly come across the correct name of Kermānshāh these days. ∎

does the unfinished mosque on Modarres St. There is a number for medical emergencies (☎ 20 050); and for the police (☎ 110). The telephone area code for Kermānshāh is 0431.

Places to Stay

There isn't a great range, and most cheapies will not take foreigners, but you should find something that's suitable. The best of the budget range is the friendly *Hotel Nabovat* (☎ 831 018) which charges 12,000/18,000 rials for a clean but noisy single/double. It's about 10m down a laneway, just off Āzādī Square; look for the English sign: 'A Hotel An Inn' (sic). The hotel next door, with the sign in English 'Hottel' (sic), is very strange and not recommended, even if the staff does agree to take foreigners (it didn't when I visited).

The *Hotel Meraj* (☎ 26 288) wanted 30,000 rials for a double, which is too much, and the manager wasn't interested in negotiating. Use this hotel as a last resort. The noisy *Toshid Hotel* (☎ 22 713) will take foreigners for the Iranian price of 6800/9000 rials – look for the broken 'Hotel' sign on the top floor.

The *Soroush Hotel* (☎ 27 001) is the only middle-range place in town, but it's a little

inconvenient. The rooms with bathrooms are small but cosy; and the management will easily negotiate down from US$25 to 50,000 rials for a double, which includes a decent breakfast.

Places to Eat

There are plenty of *kabābīs*, as well as cake and sweet shops, around the southern parts of Āzādī Square and along Motahharī St. None of the hotels have restaurants, except the *Soroush Hotel* which only serves breakfast for guests.

Opposite the Iran Air office, the shop with the sign in English, *Kentucky Fri* (sic), is likely to have Colonel Sanders' lawyers choking on their finger lickin' chicken, but it beats another plate of kebabs. Take a shared taxi from Āzādī Square.

Easily the best places for lunch and a relaxing pot of tea are the restaurants at Tāgh-é Bostān (see Around Kermānshāh later in this section).

Things to Buy

The large bazaar is either side of Modarres St. Here you can pick up a few items unique to the province: a kind of woven shoe known as a *giveh*, sweets called *nān-é berenjī* (rice bread) and a type of guitar known as a *tar*.

Getting There & Away

Air Iran Air (☎ 56 010) has daily flights to Tehrān for 42,000 rials, and to Mashhad (94,000 rials) every Thursday and Sunday. Iran Asseman (☎ 831 255) also flies to Tehrān (42,000 rials) on Tuesday, Friday, Saturday and Sunday; and very occasionally to other cities in western Iran – but don't count on it. The airport is small, chaotic and hopelessly inadequate, so allow plenty of time to check in.

Bus & Minibus The main bus and minibus terminal is quite a long way from Āzādī Square – take a shared taxi from the junction near the walkway, or bus No 2 from the local bus terminal. The locals in the terminal are very helpful, and if you look lost or helpless, someone – probably a bus tout – will show you where to go. If you haven't pre-booked a ticket and just turn up at the terminal, you will probably find something going your way in less than 30 minutes.

Among other places, buses (with prices for lux/super class) go, at least several times a day, to:

Destination	Distance	Time	Cost (rials)
Ahvāz	509km	9 hours	7400/8200
Esfahān	665km	9 hours	7800/8500
Hamadān	189km	3 hours	4000/4500
Īlām	208km	4 hours	6500
			(minibus only)
Khorram Ābād	197km	3 hours	4500
			(minibus only)
Orūmīyé	596km	11 hours	9200/10,000
Sanandaj	136km	2 hours	1500
			(minibus only)
Shīrāz	1077km	18 hours	14,000/15,200
Tabrīz	578km	11 hours	10,700/11,600
Tehrān	525km	9 hours	6300/6900

Shared Taxi To get to the major regional centres, such as Hamadān, Īlām, Khorram Ābād and Sanandaj, take one of the shared taxis which leave from the main bus/minibus terminal.

Getting Around
To/From the Airport You may be lucky enough to find a local bus going between the airport and the local bus terminal on Āzādī Square, but you'll probably end up having to take a shared taxi to/from the taxi junction at Āzādī Square for about 1000 rials. A private taxi between your hotel and the airport should cost no more than 5000 rials.

Bus The local bus terminal is next to the walkway on Āzādī Square. Bus No 2 is the best one to use: it links Āzādī Square with the Iran Air office and the bus terminal.

Taxi You will probably only need to use a shared taxi along Modarres St (which is a one-way street, heading south), for about

250 rials, or as far as the bus/minibus terminal or airport, for about 1000 rials. Naturally, Āzādī Square is the terminal for shared taxis, and there are thousands of them heading in all directions. If in doubt, ask – and ask again – to make sure you are going the right way.

AROUND KERMĀNSHĀH
Hiking
The area around Kermānshāh is begging to be explored by foot. The best spots are along the road to Bīsotūn; just get off anywhere you fancy and start hiking. However, when hiking anywhere in Iran you should always be careful if you come across anything that looks like a military area.

Bīsotūn
بیستون

Overlooking the main road to Hamadān, and a few kilometres east of Bīsotūn village, are famous bas-reliefs carved out of a dramatic mountain imbued with religious significance in pre-Islamic times. The fact that the rock was also on the ancient royal road between Iran and Iraq made it an ideal location for these tablets.

Things to See Opposite a bridge and a pretty pool are two heavily eroded **Parthian bas-reliefs**. The one on the left shows King Mithradites standing before four suppliants. The one on the right depicts several scenes relating to Gotarzes II: one of him on horseback spearing an enemy, another of him at his investiture, and a third is a religious ritual. A much later Safavid inscription in Arabic has defaced this.

About 50m to the north (towards the village and Hamadān), the unimpressive mid-2nd century BC **sculpture of Hercules** (Heracles) lies under a tacky tin shelter.

About 100m south of Hercules (back towards Kermānshāh), and 50m up the cliff, is the **tablet of Darius I**. This relief represents Darius' hard-won victory over several rebel princes, including the pretender Gaumata, who had passed himself off as Cyrus the Great's second son Bardiya. The figure of the king is taller than any other mortal presence, and is only overshadowed by the symbol of the deity Ahura Mazda hovering above the whole group. At the time of research, scaffolding had completely blocked off the Darius tablet, so it was a bit disappointing. If you want a better look at the tablet, go to the restaurant across the road, and have a look at the photo of it on the wall.

In the cliffs, another 200m towards Kermānshāh, there is a vast unfinished **stone panel** which is exceptionally smooth. Probably started in about the early 7th century BC under the orders of Khosrō II, its intended purpose remains a mystery.

Most of the area (except the stone panel) is surrounded by barbed wire. No-one asked for an entrance fee; and in any case, you can see everything from the main road.

If you are near Bīsotūn village, look out for the 115m **bridge** built during the Safavid period (1502-1722), which was partly built from stones taken from structures dating back to the Sassanian era.

Places to Stay & Eat There is nowhere to stay in the village, so take a day trip from Kermānshāh or Hamadān. The *restaurant* opposite the Darius tablet has simple but tasty Iranian food and cold drinks for sale. Better still, bring some food and drink and enjoy a picnic in the pretty forest, or next to the pool, opposite the bas-reliefs.

Getting There & Away The Darius tablet, and statue of Hercules, are about 2km west of Bīsotūn village, and the stone panel another 200m further on. You can easily combine this with a trip to Kangāvar (see later in this chapter).

If you are coming from Kermānshāh, don't get off at the terminal in Bīsotūn village. Disembark about 2km beforehand, as soon as you see what is obviously a stone panel carved out of a cliff, and walk about 300m across the fields. If you are travelling by bus from Hamadān, you will have to walk from the village to the carvings.

You can take any bus going between Kermānshāh and Hamadān. Alternatively, from Kermānshāh minibuses (350 rials) leave every 10 to 15 minutes for Bīsotūn village. The best time for photos is in the morning. After here you can move on to Kangāvar, if you want.

Tāgh-é Bostān   طاق بستان

One of the highlights of western Iran, the bas-reliefs and carved alcoves at Tāgh-é Bostān date back to the Sassanian dynasty and overlook a large pool and pleasant garden. The carvings are easy to see close up, are more accessible than the ones at Bīsotūn and you can enjoy a meal or pot of tea nearby.

Things to See As you enter from the main gate you will see a large grotto, with a lower panel depicting an armoured figure seated on a horse and holding a lance, and an upper panel showing a royal investiture. Both are believed to represent Khosrō II, a contemporary of the Prophet Mohammed, and a famous hunter. The inner walls of this monument are decorated with reliefs of royal hunting scenes. Next to it, a small arched recess, carved out of the cliff in the 4th century AD, shows Shāpūr II and his grandson, Shāpūr III, created by the latter as a testament to his own dynastic credentials.

Further along the carvings depict the investiture of Ardeshīr II, at the same time celebrating a victory over the Romans, by the deities Ahura Mazda to the right and Mithras to the left (holding a symbolic sacred bunch of twigs). On the symmetrical façade are two winged angels, representing victory, above some simple floral reliefs. Originally decorated in bright colours, the figures are rather more formal and stylised than those on the Darius relief at Bīsotūn.

The gardens are open every day, from 8 am to sunset. Entrance costs 5000 rials. The man at the gate will want another 500 rials if you take a still camera with you (it's worth paying for some great photos) and another 1000 rials for a video camera. Try to avoid visiting on a Friday or any other public holiday, when the place is wall-to-wall with Iranian picnickers.

Places to Eat Around the entrance and along the main roads to the gardens, there are dozens of pleasant *restaurants*. For lunch, fried chicken, kebabs (of course), and sometimes fish are available. You should at least stay for a pot of tea and a puff on the hubble-bubble.

Getting There & Away Lazy people (and Lonely Planet authors in a hurry) can charter a return taxi from Kermānshāh for about 4000 rials, including about 30 minutes waiting time. It is easy to take a shared taxi from the huge square next to the bus terminal – there are actually signs to the gardens in English. Afterwards, perhaps stroll back to the square next to the bus terminal (4km), and take a shared taxi back to the city.

Kangāvar
كنگاور

Built during the Parthian period (190 BC-224 AD), with a temple dedicated to Anahita, the water goddess, the original city of Kangāvar showed some influence from Persepolis. But don't be fooled: this is a disappointing collection of rocks and half-demolished columns, allowing no real idea of what the city may have looked like. None of the remains have been identified or restored. Only fervent archaeologists would get much out of this. Entrance costs 5000 rials and the site is open every day from about 8.30 am to 6 pm.

Kangāvar is about half way between Kermānshāh and Hamadān, and accessible by public transport travelling between these two cities. From Kermānshāh, the ruins can be combined with a trip to Bīsotūn by taking a minibus from Bīsotūn village to the pretty village of Sahneh (where there are a few great kabābīs on the main square), and then another minibus or shared taxi to Kangāvar.

Coming from Kermānshāh the ruins are on the left, about 2km before the town centre. There's a sign along the main road in English.

Hamadān Province
استان همدان

- **Capital:** Hamadān
- **Area:** 19,445 sq km
- **Population:** approx 1.9 million

A fertile province in the middle of western Iran, Hamadān is cold from September to May, with a lot of snow in the higher regions. Hamadān province is multicultural, populated with more Kurds, Lors and Turks than Persians. The province is famous for its raisins, with more than 1500 hectares of vineyards producing more than 4800 million rials' worth every year. There is not that much to see in the province, except the various monuments in Hamadān city and the awesome Alī Sadr caves nearby.

HAMADĀN
همدان

The tourist brochures trot out silly phrases such as 'Older Than History' to describe Hamadān. The city has always been a major stop on the ancient royal road to Baghdad, and it remains an important trading and transit centre. The population (approximately 400,000) is largely Persian, with a significant Āzarī minority. A sizeable Jewish community has been here at least since the 5th century AD, and possibly as early as the time of Xerxes I.

Hamadān, sitting on a high plain dominated by Mt Alvand (3580m), is a popular retreat for Iranians during the autumn and spring months when the climate is one of the most pleasant in the country. The city boasts numerous things to see and do, but some are simply not worth the 5000 or 10,000 rials constantly demanded of foreigners, so you may want to ration your time and money accordingly. But don't miss out on the Alī Sadr caves (see Around Hamadān later in this section).

History

According to one legend, Hamadān was founded by the mythical King Jamshīd. The

PLACES TO STAY
9   Hamadān Guest House
12 Hotel Yass & Restaurant
16 Mosāferkhūné-yé Fārsī
17 Ekbatan Hotel
27 Bouali Hotel & Restaurant

PLACES TO EAT
20 Shilan Restaurant

OTHER
1   Emām Khomeinī Hospital
2   Ārāmgāh-é Bāhā Tāher
3   Bus Terminal
4   Minibus Terminal
5   Tappé-yé Hekmatāné
6   Gombad-é Alavīyān

7   Emāmzādé-yé Abdollah
8   Masjed-é Jāme'
10 TBT Bus Cooperative No 15 Office
11 Iran Peyma Bus Office
13 Bank Melli (Central Branch)
14 Ārāmgāh-é Ester va Mördekhāy
15 Cinema
18 Tappé-yé Mosallā
19 Bookstall (Maps)
21 Air Bouali Travel Agency
22 Avicenna (Bū Alī Sīnā) Mausoleum
23 Borj-é Ghorbān
24 Sang-é Shīr
25 Main Post Office
26 Tourist Office
28 Police Headquarters
29 Main Telephone Office

Hamadān

0   250   500 m
Minor Streets Not Depicted

city has been inhabited since at least the 2nd millennium BC. Under Cyrus the Great, it became the Median capital in the 6th century BC, when the city was known as Ecbatana or Hagmatāné ('meeting place'). When it reached the height of its glory as the summer capital of the Achaemenian empire (559-330 BC), Hamadān was described as one of the most opulent cities, with splendid palaces, buildings plated with precious metals, and seven layers of town walls, the inner two of which were coated in gold and silver.

These glorious riches naturally attracted hordes of invading armies. Hamadān faded in importance after the Arab Conquest in the mid-7th century, but became the regional capital under the Seljuqs for some 60 years in the late 12th century. The city was devastated by the Mongols in 1220 and again by Timur in 1386, but soon returned to relative prosperity and remained so until the 18th century. Hamadān then fell into a serious decline and suffered from an invasion by the Turks, from which the city did not recover until the mid-19th century.

Some valuable finds from the ancient town have come to light this century, but the lower layers of settlement remain unexplored – and will remain so unless the present city is uprooted.

Orientation

Despite its history, Hamadān is a rather drab town. In this century, the city was rebuilt and designed around a main square, now predictably called Emām Khomeinī Square. From the square, six straight avenues radiate outwards, along which the main offices and hotels are located, while some of the attractions are a little further out. Unlike some cities in western Iran, the streets and squares are signed in English.

Maps One of the better maps of an Iranian city is the *Guide Map of Hamadān City & Road Map of Alisadr Cave* (2500 rials). Though there are certainly no roads in the Alī Sadr cave, the map is worth picking up for greater detail of Hamadān city, and additional information about the caves. You can

buy the map at the Avicenna (Bū Alī Sīnā) mausoleum, or from a bookstall along Bū Alī Sīnā St.

Information

Visa Extensions Travellers have not had much luck extending their visas at the police headquarters in Hamadān. You are likely to have more of a chance in Kermānshāh, Tabrīz or Esfahān.

Tourist Office There is a tourist office (☎ 20 093), but I had no luck at all finding anyone either inside the building or willing to answer the telephone. Perhaps you will be more fortunate.

Money The central branch of Bank Melli dominates the northern side of Emām Khomeinī Square, and is the only place to change money, though the process is so slow and inefficient that you are better off trying another city.

Post & Communications The main post office is about 150m south of Bū Alī Sīnā Square. You will need to take a shared taxi to get to the main telephone office, but there are telephone booths for local and interstate calls outside the main post office. The telephone area code for Hamadān is 0261.

Bookshops Hamadān is not somewhere you would expect a surfeit of books, but the tiny bookshop at the Bouali Hotel has an outstanding range of titles about Iran – probably the best in the country. They are mostly in English, with some in French and German. Many of the books were published before the Islamic Revolution in 1979, though they are still relevant. You will be able to pick up some gems: travel guides extolling the virtues of discos and nightclubs in Tehrān, and new and old books about Iranian carpets, cooking, history, culture and language. There are also some phrasebooks and dictionaries as well as postcards and stamps.

Emergency For medical emergencies, go to the Emām Khomeinī Hospital (☎ 33 014), or

WESTERN IRAN

ring the general emergencies number (☎ 2888). The police headquarters (☎ 30 111) is in the southern stretch of town.

Mosques & Muslim Shrines

In the bazaar district, the requisite **Masjed-é Jāme'** is vast, with some 55 columns. It was built during the Ghajar dynasty (1779-1921), and is worth a visit, not least because it's free to get in. Also worth a (free) look is the **Emāmzādé-yé Abdollah**, in the middle of the roundabout of the same name. The 12-sided, 13th century, tomb tower **Borj-é Ghorbān** is fairly uninspiring, and not worth trying to find.

Ārāmgāh-é Ester va Mōrdekhāy

The most important Jewish pilgrimage site in Iran, this is believed to contain the bodies of Esther, the Jewish wife of Xerxes I, who is credited with organising the first Jewish emigration to Persia in the 5th century, and her uncle Mordecai. In fact, it more probably covers the grave of a much later Jewish queen, Shūshān, who is said to have persuaded her husband, Yazdgerd I, to allow a Jewish colony at Hamadān in the early 5th century AD.

The tomb is often closed, but if you ask around you might find the gatekeeper, who may be inclined to open it up for you.

Gombad-é Alavīyān

This well-preserved 12th century mausoleum of the Alavī family – the pre-eminent family in the town during most of the Seljuq period (1051-1220) – is probably the most noteworthy monument in Hamadān. It is interesting for the outstanding quality of its stucco ornamentation, with whirling floral motifs on the exterior walls and intricate geometric designs on its mehrāb. The tombs are in the crypt, reached by a spiral staircase. The shrine stands in a small square at the end of a small laneway, which leads east from Alavīyān Blvd.

The mausoleum was closed at the time of research, but should have reopened by the time you visit.

Sang-é Shīr

This famous 14th century stone lion in the square of the same name in south-east Hamadān, is the only distinct, visible monument of the ancient city, Ecbatana. It originally guarded a city gate and may have been carved at the behest of Alexander the Great. The statue is now seriously eroded, and hardly worth the walk out there.

Avicenna Memorial

Obviously modelled on the magnificent Gombad-é Kāvūs tower near Gorgān, this dominating structure was built as recently as 1954, in memory of Bū Alī Sīnā (see the 'Bū Alī Sīnā' boxed text). Inside, there's a **library** with more than 5000 books, and a **museum** (☎ 95 360) relating to the life and works of Bū Alī Sīnā. In the gardens, there is also the **tomb** of a 20th century poet, Abolghasseim Aref.

Bū Alī Sīnā

The great Bū Alī Sīnā was born in the village of Khormassin in 980, and revered during his lifetime as a philosopher and physician. He is more commonly known in the west as Avicenna, the name under which his widely respected medical encyclopaedia was published in Europe. He died in Hamadān in 1037. ∎

Entrance to the museum for foreigners is 10,000 rials, and it's not worth it; you can see the outside of the building for nothing. The museum is open daily from 8 am to 1 pm and from 2 to 4 pm – but opening times do have a habit of changing regularly. At the entrance, there is a good selection of postcards, maps of Hamadān and books for sale.

Ārāmgāh-é Bābā Tāher

This rather ugly mausoleum is dedicated to the poet Bābā Tāher. You can see the tower for nothing from the park surrounding it, but if you want to get inside, you'll need to fork out 5000 rials.

The Great Bābā Tāher

Bābā Tāher lived in the 11th century, but little is known about the great poet's life. The grandson of Omar Khayyām (see the boxed text 'Omar Khayyām' in the Eastern Iran chapter), Bābā Tāher developed the 'mystic' form of poetry, still loved by the Kurds and Lors of western Iran, and influenced by the Ahl-é Hagh sect of Islam which he followed.

Here is a famous, dramatic poem:

> Beneath the tyranny of eyes and heart
> I cry
> For all that the eyes see, the heart
> stores up
> I'll make myself a pointed sword of
> steel
> Take out my own eyes, so set my
> heart free. ■

Museum of Natural History

Easily the most interesting and best-value attraction in Hamadān is this museum at the Bū Alī Sīnā University. It boasts the best collection of stuffed animals in the country, as well as (live) fish in tanks and unfortunate insects pinned to boards. This is the closest you will ever get (or want to get) to the huge, horned Alborz red sheep or the creepy black vulture. It has captions in English, and is highly recommended.

The museum is open most days from 8 am to whenever the gatekeeper feels like closing the door. It only costs 1000 rials, but no cameras are allowed . The museum is poorly signed (in any language), and located behind a green fence at the end of Azadegan Blvd, about 5km from the city centre. You will probably have to charter a taxi there and back for about 3000 rials, including waiting time.

Tappé-yé Hekmatāné

Some ruins of the ancient city can be seen around this extensive plot of land. Some small items found here, and elsewhere in Hamadān, have been put on display in the **museum** in the centre of the site, but most are in the National Museum of Iran in Tehrān. Currently undergoing extensive excavations and renovations, the complex is not particularly exciting at the moment, but it – and the **Tappé-yé Mosallā** nearby – should be more interesting in the future. Tappé-yé Hekmatāné is open every day from about 9 am to 1 pm and from 3 to 6 pm, and is way overpriced at 10,000 rials. Save your money until it improves.

Places to Stay

Many of the mosāferkhūnés won't take foreigners, so don't bother trying anywhere not listed below – you will be wasting your time. Most of the other places are overpriced, grubby, noisy or closed. Hamadān is not a great place for hotels.

One of the very few to accept foreigners is the *Mosāferkhūné-yé Fārsī* (☎ 224 895) – directly opposite the Hotel Yass and up some stairs on the 1st floor. It costs 10,000 rials per twin (or less per person in a four-bed dorm), but the shared bathrooms have no showers. Another place, more welcoming than others, is the *Ekbatan Hotel* (☎ 224 024) which offers a twin room for 7000 rials, but like other places along Shohadā St, it is noisy.

The most popular place for travellers, and deservedly so, is the friendly *Hamadān Guest House* (☎ 227 577), a two storey building with a blue sign in English. The management charges foreigners a reasonable 15,000 rials per twin room, with shared bathroom. Try to get a room away from the main road if you want any sleep (or if you haven't brought industrial-strength earplugs).

Once popular, but now overpriced and unfriendly, is the *Hotel Yass* (☎ 22 464) (also known as the *Kakh Hotel*). It is worth maybe 30,000 rials a room, but the manager would not budge from a silly 60,000 rials per room, and it's in a noisy location.

One of the nicest places to stay in this part of Iran is the *Bouali Hotel* (☎ 33 070). The rooms are excellent, and there's a swimming pool (which presumably doubles as an iceskating rink for much of the year), but it's overpriced for foreigners: US$46 per double room. If that is too much, still check out the wonderful restaurant and bookshop inside the hotel.

Places to Eat

All the best *kabābīs* are based around Emām Khomeinī Square, but none distinguish themselves. One of the best restaurants in town is the *Shilan Restaurant*. Signposted in English, it offers a decent selection of Iranian food for about 5500 rials per dish.

Of the hotel restaurants, the *Hotel Yass* is OK, but the best restaurant in town, and one of the best in western Iran, is at the *Bouali Hotel*. Treat yourself to some excellent service and decor, and dig into your wallet for a reasonably priced meal – from 9000 to 12,000 rials, plus 15% tax, for excellent schnitzels and steaks. The *Italian Ice Cream Stall*, right outside the entrance to the Bouali Hotel, is very popular, and worth a visit.

If you visit the Alī Sadr caves (and you should), you can enjoy lunch or a drink inside or outside the caves. There are also a few *kabābīs* and drink stalls at Ganjnāmé (see the Around Hamadān section).

Things to Buy

Hamadān is justly famous for its carpets, as well as the ceramics, leather and copper products made in the region. You can buy these in nearby village markets, or at the bazaar in Hamadān. The nearby village of Lālejīn is the place for pottery and ceramics, and is worth a day trip for some souvenir hunting (see the Around Hamadān section following). You can also stock up on ceramics from a few shops near the Bāhā Tāher mausoleum, and don't forget to check out the bookshop at the Bouali Hotel.

Getting There & Away

Air Hamadān is close to Tehrān, so no airlines bother flying here on a regular basis. Iran Asseman does have some flights, but these are infrequent – so much so that their staff couldn't even provide any details. Book tickets at the Air Bouali Travel Agency.

Bus Hamadān is only about five hours by bus from Tehrān by either the expressway via Tākestān or the more direct road via Sāvé.

A few bus companies have offices in the bazaar. The main bus terminal is within walking distance of the bazaar and most hotels, though a shared taxi will save your legs if you have heavy luggage. If you take the bus to Hamadān from anywhere between Tehrān and Kermānshāh, you will often be dropped off at the corner of Pāsdārān and Abbās Ābād Blvds. From here you can get a shared taxi to your hotel. This is also a good place to catch a passing bus going in either direction.

Buses leave at least several times a day (with prices for lux/super class) to:

Destination	Distance	Time	Cost (rials)
Ahvāz	465km	7 hours	8600
			(lux class only)
Esfahān	492km	7 hours	5700/7200
Ghazvīn	234km	4 hours	3500
			(lux class only)
Kermānshāh	189km	3 hours	4000/4500
Khorram Ābād	252km	4 hours	9000
			(special class only)
Shīrāz	918km	15 hours	9300/2500
Tehrān	336km	5 hours	4100/4400

Minibus From the minibus terminal, not far from the main bus terminal, there are minibuses to Arāk, Sanandaj, Alī Sadr and Lālejīn. For minibuses to Khorram Ābād, there is a special minibus terminal in the eastern part of town; take a shared taxi from Emām Khomeinī Square.

Getting Around

Hamadān is easy enough to walk around. Otherwise, take a shared taxi along any of the main streets, and to the bus or minibus terminals, for about 400 rials a trip.

AROUND HAMADĀN

Also see to the Around Kermānshāh section earlier in this chapter for other ideas of places to go for a day trip from Hamadān.

Ganjnāmé   گنجنامه

This charming little piece of greenery, with a waterfall, rock carvings and opportunities for hiking, is easy to reach and free to enjoy. The morning is the best time to visit for photos.

Things to See The misleadingly named Treasure Book is actually a pair of famous **Achaemenian rock carvings** of Darius I (on the left) and his son Xerxes I. Inscribed in the Old Persian, Elamite and Neo-Babylonian languages, these tablets list the kings' titles and hence the extent of their empires at the time. Nearby, there is a translation of the writings in English.

More enticing is the pretty **waterfall**: climb to the top for some charming views of the surrounding countryside of the Abbās Ābād valley. The area is also a popular place with Hamadānīs – for **skiing** in winter, and picnicking and **hiking** in summer. Just head up into the hills and enjoy a few hours in the fresh air.

The area is crowded with *kababīs* and *snack bars* where you can buy food and drinks, or even better, bring some food from Hamadān and enjoy a picnic.

Getting There & Away Ganjnāmé is only about 8km from Hamadān. You can charter a taxi from the city centre for about 5000 rials return, which includes about 20 to 30 minutes waiting time. It's best to spend a few hours hiking around, however, so charter a taxi for 3000 rials one way and, maybe, walk back – downhill – to Hamadān. Shared taxis are not easy to find to Ganjnāmé; try at either Ghaem and/or Abbās Ābād Squares in the south-west of the city.

Nūsh-é Jān نوش جان

This mound, about 50km south of Hamadān, in the district of Malāyer, contains the remains of a **Median fire-temple**. It dates from the 8th century BC and is one of the earliest discovered in Iran. It is between the tiny villages of Nakmīl Ābād and Shūshāb, 20km north-east of Malāyer, and is most easily reached by chartering a taxi from Hamadān.

Lālejīn لالجين

This village, 32km north of Hamadān, is famous for its **pottery** and boasts several dozen workshops producing all kinds of ceramics, particularly with the turquoise glaze for which the region is known. You can simply walk around and admire (or buy) the goods, or ask to visit a small factory to watch the experts at work. But this is like walking into a carpet showroom in Esfahān; the hard sell will make it difficult to leave without some large, expensive item which perhaps you didn't really want.

Minibuses to Lālejīn leave from the minibus terminal in Hamadān about every hour; a one-way trip costs 1500 rials.

Alī Sadr Caves

If you don't think you can be bothered seeing another mosque, archaeological site or museum, take a detour to these remarkable caves, about 100km north of Hamadān. The caves, discovered only 40 years ago by a local shepherd looking for a lost goat, are up to 40m high, and contain several huge lakes with clear water up to 8m deep. Nothing lives in the water – surprisingly bats don't even find it worth hanging around here – and there are no signs of any inhabitants from past centuries. You can take a day trip from Hamadān, or stay overnight so you can visit the caves more than once.

Things to See The local tourist authorities have tried to create something to see by labelling (in English) some of the stalactites, with names such as the 'Statue of Liberty' (named by someone who obviously hasn't seen the grand lady). But it's the majesty and eeriness of the caves themselves which is the main attraction.

The entrance fee includes a tour in a boat – you sit in a small rowboat, attached to a paddle boat, which the guide steers. The tour is in Fārsī, but there's little to explain anyway. The guide paddles away, while towing your boat, for about 20 to 30 minutes, then you walk around the middle of the cave for another 20 to 30 minutes – there is nearly 1km of walkways, and plenty more under construction. Then it's another 20 to 30 minute paddle, along a different route, back to the cave entrance.

A ticket into the caves costs 10,000 rials, and is worth every single one. It can be cool inside the cave, so a light jumper (sweater) is a good idea. The caves are well lit in some areas, but if you have a really strong torch (flashlight), bring it. Very few camera flashes will be good enough to take any decent photos. The *Guide Map of Hamadan City & Road Map of Alisadr Cave* (2500 rials), available in Hamadan, gives some useful information about the caves (in English) – though you will glad to know there are no roads (yet) in the caves.

If at all humanly possible, avoid visiting on a Friday and on public holidays when this place is usually crawling with Iranian families and hundreds of screaming school kids.

Places to Stay & Eat Staying near the caves, or at the village close by, allows you to see the caves in the afternoon and again in the following morning. Outside the caves there is a real carnival atmosphere, with playgrounds and souvenir shops, though it's not too tacky (yet).

The only hotel is the *Ali Sadr Hotel* (☎ (08262) 2099), run by the ITTO. It charges 35,000/45,000 rials, plus 17% tax, for a clean single/double with a bathroom. It is worthwhile booking ahead, and doublechecking the price, before carrying your luggage out there (or leave it in Hamadan). Expect a few cheap places to pop up in the village in the future. Near the caves, there are some wooden *huts* (they are called 'villas' in the brochure, which is stretching the truth somewhat) for Iranian tourists. No information about prices was available.

Several *stalls* around the cave entrance sell cold drinks and pots of tea, and some *kababis*, and a decent *restaurant*, serve the usual sort of Iranian food. There is even a *café* inside the cave, just by the entrance.

Getting There & Away Minibuses travel to Ali Sadr village, from the minibus terminal in Hamadan when there are enough passengers – perhaps every hour (more frequently on holidays). Alternatively, if you want to visit (and stay at) the caves, and have little luggage, you can always take a bus between Hamadan and Bijar, and get off at Gol Tappé, from where you can hike (14km) or hitch a ride to the caves.

If you are in a hurry, or have some spare cash, chartering a taxi from Hamadan will cost about 20,000 rials return, plus about 8000 rials an hour waiting time – but only after some hard bargaining.

Kordestan Province
استان کردستان

- **Capital:** Sanandaj
- **Area:** 27,885 sq km
- **Population:** approx 1.5 million

Although the name translates as Kurdistan, the border of this province does not mark the limits of Kurdish settlement in Iran; there are many Kurds throughout the two Azarbayjan provinces and as far south as Ilam province. Kordestan is mountainous and home to thousands of nomads, constantly seeking new

---

The Kurds

There are about 4.5 million Kurds in Iran, mainly living in the provinces of Kordestan, Zanjan and Kermanshah. Many Kurds are nomadic, and most follow ancient traditions, particularly at times of birth, death and marriage.

They are divided into various tribes, such as the Sanjabi and Kalhor, and speak different dialects of Kurdish, a language quite different to Farsi. Kurds predominantly follow the Sunni sect of Islam (while most Iranians are Shi'ite Muslims), often with a few embellishments. A minority of Kurds are Yezidis, a sect that combines elements of Islam with paganism. The men often wear traditional clothes, while the Kurdish women in the villages, and on the plains, make acclaimed carpets and rugs – all made of hardy wool from local sheep. ■

pastures for their stock and avoiding the obnoxious weather during the long winter. The mighty Gezel Ūzan River originates in the northern parts of the province, and flows all the way to the Caspian Sea.

SANANDAJ سنندج

Although Sanandaj dates back to at least the Middle Ages, it is not of any great architectural or historical interest. Many travellers come here for a glimpse of the Kurdish way of life. The city has gradually emerged as the chief market town for the Kurds. In recent years many of the pastoralists and nomads who used to drive their flocks and bring their wares to Sanandaj have settled in the city, ensuring that Sanandaj remains the most Kurdish city in Iran.

Orientation
The two main squares are the northern Enghelāb Square (the one lined with bricks, and no doubt symbolising something or other), and Āzādī Square (with the white arches) to the south. They are connected by the main shopping thoroughfare, Ferdōsī St. The bazaar district is east of Enghelāb Square.

Information
The central branch of the Bank Melli is just north of Shohadā Square; the main post office is 150m north-west of Āzādī Square; and the main telephone office is 250m east of the same square. The telephone area code is 04321.

Things to See
The **Sanandaj Museum** (☎ 5455) is on the south side of Emām Khomeinī St, about 400m north-west of Enghelāb Square. The building itself, built in the early 16th century, is quite interesting, while the museum contains some rather unexciting archaeological exhibits, and some more interesting displays about the Kurds. The museum is open Saturday to Thursday between 8 am and noon and 4 and 7 pm.

Nearby, the large **Masjed-é Jāme'** dates from 1813 and has some attractive Ghajar tilework, a dome and two pretty minarets. About 6km east of Sanandaj is the impressive **Gheshlakh Bridge**, reminiscent of the Sī o Sé bridge in Esfahān but not nearly as grand. Approximately 10km north of the city is the enormous **Vahdat Dam**, which is great for **fishing**, and you can go **hiking** in the area.

Places to Stay & Eat
Most of the mosāferkhūnés around the bazaar are very reluctant to take foreigners, so you are really forced to stay at one of three places. Two are central (along Ferdōsī St), signed in English and offer clean doubles with private bathrooms. The *Hedayat Hotel* (☎ 24 117), nearer to Enghelāb Square, has doubles for 15,000 rials. It has a useful map of Sanandaj in the foyer.

The friendly *Abidor Hotel* (☎ 41 645) has a manager who speaks some English and it charges 17,000 rials for a double. The other alternative is the ITTO's *Jahāngardī Inn* (☎ 63 525) which is overpriced (US$20/30 for a single/double room), non-negotiable and inconvenient (2km from Āzādī Square), so you'll need to charter a taxi.

There are a few *snack bars* and *kabābīs* huddled around the two main squares, but you are better off eating at one of the hotels.

Getting There & Away
Air Iran Asseman has scheduled flights between Sanandaj and Tehrān, but like most of Asseman's flights to western Iran, it is unclear whether the route will continue in the future. If they are running, book at a travel agent.

Bus & Minibus Some bus companies have booking offices around Enghelāb Square. For some destinations, such as Īlām and Ahvāz, you'll have to get a connecting bus in Kermānshāh. The main bus and minibus terminal is in the south of the town (charter a taxi to get there); the smaller terminal in the north has buses and minibuses to regional villages only.

There are minibuses and buses several times a day (with prices for lux/super class) to:

Destination	Distance	Time	Cost (rials)
Esfahān	672km	10 hours	9400/10,300
Hamadān	176km	3 hours	1600 (minibus only)
Kermānshāh	136km	2 hours	1500 (minibus only)
Orūmīyé	460km	9 hours	8100/8800
Shīrāz	1133km	19 hours	15,000/16,500
Tabrīz	442km	8 hours	8100/8800
Tehrān	512km	9 hours	6800/7600
Yazd	968km	16 hours	14,270/15,590

Shared Taxi Shared taxis to Kermānshāh (5000 rials) and Hamadān (5500 rials) leave from the southern bus/minibus terminal.

Getting Around
Everything you want in the city, except the bus terminals, is within walking distance of the town centre. Shared and private taxis are available for longer trips. The airport is about 6km south of the city; charter a taxi to get there.

BĪJĀR
بیجار
On the road between Takāb and Hamadān, this pleasant town is one of the highest in the country, so it's appallingly cold in winter. There is nowhere to stay, but if you are camping, or want to take a day trip from Takāb or Hamadān, there is some wonderful **hiking** and **rock climbing** in the area. If you have a vehicle, and a local guide, you can explore some of the remains of nearby ancient cities, such as **Ghom Choga**, which has a few walls of a castle dating back about 3000 years.

KARAFTŪ CAVES
غار کرفتو
If you take a powerful torch (flashlight) you can explore the labyrinthine grottoes of Karaftū, about 115km north of Sanandaj. Among other traces, of what once must have been a sanctuary carved out of the cliff, there is a Greek inscription mentioning the name of Heracles (Hercules), who had a cult following in this region during the Parthian

period (190 BC-224 AD), as well as several chambers and passageways. You will need to charter a taxi to get there, and to find it, from Sanandaj.

Zanjān Province
استان زنجان

- **Capital:** Zanjān
- **Area:** 25,495 sq km
- **Population:** approx 1.2 million

Nestled between the Āzarbāyjān provinces and the Caspian region, Zanjān province is home to a dozen or more hot and cold mineral springs, caves (though you will need a vehicle and guide to find them), as well as the southern parts of the mighty Mt Alam (see Trekking in Iran in Facts for the Visitor). The majority of the people in Zanjān province are Kurds, and there are also a few thousand nomads called Shahsovans. The province is famous for its seedless grapes, which, not so long ago, were made into wine.

ZANJĀN
زنجان
The provincial capital is not nearly as interesting or pleasant as the larger city of Ghazvīn (see later in this section), but it's not a bad place to break up the journey between Tehrān and Tabrīz, and to use as a starting point for the magnificent ruins at Takht-é Soleimān (see Takht-é Soleimān under Āzarbāyjān-é Gharbī Province later in this chapter) and the impressive Soltānīyé mausoleum (see later in this section). There is a large and busy **bazaar**, built during the Ghajar period (1779-1921), and a few **mosques** of little note. For some reason, Zanjān is the centre for making knives, and literally hundreds of shops sell all sorts of household and ornamental knives.

Orientation & Information
The centre of town is Enghelāb Square, about 1km south of the train station. In the south of the city, along the main road between Tabrīz and Ghazvīn, there is a bus

and minibus junction, and shared taxis also gather at the corner of this road and Ferdōsī St. The telephone area code is 0241.

Places to Stay & Eat

There is not a great choice of places to stay or eat. The *Khay Hotel* costs 5000/8000 rials for a single/double, and is very basic, but friendly enough. It is along Ferdōsī St and has a sign in English. You could try the *Amīr Kabīr Hotel*, close to Enghelāb Square, but the manager was not interested in showing me a room or, later, serving me a meal.

The *Hotel Sepid* (☎ 26 882), on Enghelāb Square, is overpriced at US$20/30/37 for a single/double/triple, but the restaurant is very good. It doesn't open until 8.30 pm for dinner. On Khorramshahr Blvd, on the way to the bus terminal, the *Jahāngardī Inn* (☎ 26 062) is expensive – US$15/25 – and inconveniently situated.

It's best to eat at a hotel restaurant, or you could try one of the ubiquitous *kabābīs* along the main streets. Several shops around Enghelāb Square sell milkshakes and cakes.

Getting There & Away

There are daily buses to Takāb (3200 rials), as well several every day to Tehrān, Tabrīz, Ghazvīn, Rasht and Hamadān. Most leave from the main bus terminal, about 2km east of the city centre. You can also hop on any bus, minibus or shared taxi heading your way along the Ghazvīn-Tabrīz road, particularly at the junction of this road with Ferdōsī St.

Zanjān is also on the train line between Tehrān and Tabrīz, but the departure times are lousy and tickets are hard to get.

Getting Around

Zanjān is small enough to walk around. Plenty of shared taxis ply the main streets.

SOLTĀNĪYÉ سلطانيه

This once great Mongol city (meaning Town of the Sultans), built in the early 14th century, is now no more than a large village with only one important building of the period remaining intact, but this alone warrants a visit.

Gombad-é Soltānīyé

The building for which Soltānīyé is deservedly famous is the great mausoleum of the Mongol Soltān Oljeitū Khodābandé, with one of the largest domes in the world, up there with the Blue Mosque in Istanbul and St Pauls in London. The mausoleum was originally built as the final resting place of Alī, the son-in-law of the Prophet Mohammed, but this never eventuated. The Mongol sultan was left with a vast mausoleum and no-one to occupy it. The building was converted to become the sultan's own tomb, and he was buried here in about 1317.

Visible from far across the surrounding plain, the mausoleum's very striking dome is 48m high, and nearly 25m in diameter. Little remains of the eight minarets or the vast portals, but through the main entrance on the east side is a chamber decorated with exquisite, recently restored plaster mouldings, brickwork, inscriptions and mosaic tilework dating from the early 14th century. The intricate, raised inscriptions on its stucco mehrāb are among the finest in Iran.

Entrance costs a whopping 15,000 rials (three times more than the cost of my room for the night in Zanjān), but it's probably worth it. If you don't want to pay this, you can still admire the building from the outside, and wander around the village for nothing. The entrance fee does, however, include a guided tour in hesitant, but comprehensible, English by an enthusiastic local student, and the views of the countryside from the top of the dome are stupendous.

Getting There & Away

The mausoleum is just off the main road between Zanjān and Ghazvīn – and is very easy to spot. Catch an irregular minibus from Zanjān to the village of Soltānīyé, or, better, take any bus, minibus or shared taxi between Ghazvīn and Zanjān. You can get off at the junction (signed in English), and catch another shared taxi (which can be chartered) to the village. If you want to walk from the main road (a pleasant 5km), don't get off at the junction: get off at the point where the mausoleum looks closest to the road, and walk across the fields from there. It may be a little hard to get a taxi to take you there from Zanjān; the lowest price I could get was 25,000 rials return, including 40 minutes waiting time.

GHAZVĪN قزوین

Famous for its carpets and seedless grapes, the large town of Ghazvīn has always been an important transit centre. Today, the town is a useful and pleasant stop between places in the west, such as Tabrīz and Hamadān, and the Caspian region. It is far more interesting than the provincial capital, Zanjān, and you

could even take a day trip from Tehrān, if you start early.

History

Founded by the Sassanian King Shāpūr I in the 3rd century BC, Ghazvīn was prosperous under the Seljuq rulers (1051-1220) who erected many fine buildings. It briefly rose to prominence much later, when the Safavid Shāh Tahmāsb I, a great patron of the arts, transferred the Persian capital here from Tabrīz. He embarked on an ambitious architectural plan for Ghazvīn, but the fine buildings founded here were only a dress

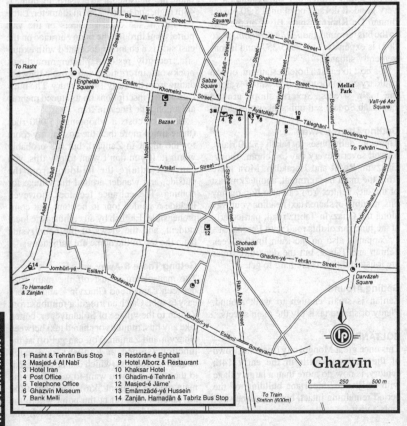

1 Rasht & Tehrān Bus Stop	8 Restōrān-é Eghbalī
2 Masjed-é Al Nabī	9 Hotel Alborz & Restaurant
3 Hotel Iran	10 Khaksar Hotel
4 Post Office	11 Ghadim-é Tehrān
5 Telephone Office	12 Masjed-é Jāme'
6 Ghazvīn Museum	13 Emāmzādé-yé Hussein
7 Bank Melli	14 Zanjān, Hamadān & Tabrīz Bus Stop

Ghazvīn

0   250   500 m

To Train
Station (600m)

rehearsal for Esfahān, where his successor, Shāh Abbās I, set up court in 1598. Ghazvīn has been devastated by earthquakes more than once, and what remains is only a shadow of its former splendour, though there are still some fine Safavid and Seljuq structures to admire.

Orientation & Information

The recommended hotels and restaurants are all within a few hundred metres of the town centre, Sabze Square. Most of the town's many attractions are also an easy stroll from the square and your hotel. No street or square is signed in English, which makes getting around a little difficult. The telephone area code is 0281.

Masjed-é Jāme'

This ancient mosque with four *eivāns* (a rectangular hall opening into a courtyard) has some features dating back to the early Arab period (637-1050). The dome dates from the 11th century, as does the main prayer hall beneath with its fine marble mehrāb, beautiful inscriptions and geometric plaster mouldings. The two minarets and the imposing southern eivān were added in the Safavid period (1502-1722). There is also a pretty courtyard, very busy on Friday and religious holidays.

Emāmzādé-yé Hussein

This large mausoleum was built in the 16th century, then renovated during the Ghajar period (1779-1921). It is particularly beautiful, and revered by locals and other Iranians. You must take your shoes off, of course, to enter the shrine, and try to avoid Friday and religious holidays when it's very busy and foreigners are not so welcome.

Masjed-é Al Nabī

The Mosque of the Prophet, in the middle of the bazaar district, is certainly worth a visit. Built mainly during the Safavid period, it was extended under the Ghajar rulers. It is heavily guarded, so you must leave your bag

at the entrance, and no cameras are allowed inside. The left-hand side of the laneway leads to the entrance for ladies; the right-hand side is for men.

Ghazvīn Museum

This museum, set in a lovely park, was closed at the time of research, but should be worth visiting when it reopens.

Ghadim-é Tehrān

The Gateway to Tehrān is in fact 140km from Tehrān, but it's an impressive sight, with its extensive tilework dating back to the Ghajar period. It has been repaired many times over the centuries. You can walk there, or take a shared taxi from Sabze Square (you will have to change taxis at Shohadā Square).

Places to Stay

There are very few hotels in Ghazvīn, which doesn't matter because the city does have one of the best-value places to stay in the region. The *Hotel Iran* is central, and has clean singles/doubles, with a private shower (but shared toilet), for the 'Iranian price' of 9000/18,000 rials. It is friendly, and, above all, the staff does not discriminate against foreigners.

The *Khaksar Hotel* (☎ 4229) has rooms for about 15,000/25,000 rials; look for the small sign in English on a light-blue building along Tāleghānī Blvd. The *Hotel Alborz* (☎ 26 631) is the upmarket place in town. Rooms have a TV, fridge and air-con and it's not bad value at 54,000/81,000 rials (especially if you can negotiate a reduction, to say 40,000/60,000).

Places to Eat

The best place to eat is the *Restōrān-é Eghbalī*: one reader wrote to us to claim that the 'khōresht was the culinary highlight' of his entire trip. There is no menu as such, so to avoid the customary kebabs, try the tasty and filling beef khōresht and rice for 5500 rials. It is upstairs, along Tāleghānī St, and signposted in English.

The only other alternatives are the *kabābīs* at places along Tāleghānī Blvd or Shohadā Sts. The restaurant on the 1st floor of the *Hotel Alborz* caters mainly for guests, but if you ask nicely they will probably let you in.

Getting There & Away

Bus & Shared Taxi Every day there are several buses and shared taxis to Zanjān, Tehrān, Hamadān, Rasht and Tabrīz. Like most junction towns, there is no terminal for buses, minibuses or shared taxis. All public transport, either originating in Ghazvīn or passing through, departs from one of the main squares in the suburbs. For transport to Zanjān, Hamadān and Tabrīz, go to the junction of Asad Ābādī and Jomhūrī-yé Eslāmī Blvds; and for Rasht and Tehrān, go to Enghelāb Square.

Train Ghazvīn is on the train line between Tabrīz and Tehrān, but arrival and departure times are anti-social and not conducive to a restful night – use road transport instead. The train station is directly south of Sabze Square.

Getting Around

Everything you want to use or see is within walking distance, except the roundabouts for road transport. These are well connected by shared taxis (about 250 rials a trip) from Sabze and Shohadā squares.

CASTLES OF THE ASSASSINS

دژهای حشیشیون

In the remote valleys north-east of Ghazvīn, in the southern foothills of the Alborz Mountains, are the historic fortresses known as the *Dezhā-yé Hashīshīyun* (Castles of the Assassins). They were first brought into European literature by the returning Crusaders, and were made famous this century in Dame Freya Stark's classic *Valleys of the Assassins*.

The castles were the heavily fortified lairs of the adherents of a bizarre religious cult, based loosely on the precepts of the Ismaili sect. The word 'assassin' originates from the name of this sect (See 'The Assassins' boxed

---

The Assassins

The Assassins cult was founded in the 11th century by Hasan Sabah (1040-1124), known in western folklore as the 'Old Man of the Mountains'. At its height, the cult extended from Syria to Khorāsān province until the Mongols captured its castles in 1256. However, some scholars claim that the reputation of the Assassins for widespread carnage – and the extent of their reach – were exaggerated.

This heretical and widely feared sect despatched killers throughout the region to murder leading political and religious figures. Its followers, the Hashīshīyun (assassins), were so called because of the cunning ruse, by their leaders, of taking them into beautiful secret gardens (filled with equally enticing young maidens), sometimes getting them stoned on hashish, and then sending them out on their homicidal assignments under the illusion that Hasan Sabah had the power to transport them to paradise. ■

---

text). As one might expect, the outlaws' mountain hideaways were designed to be impregnable and inaccessible. Sadly, these days all that remains is little more than rubble, but the views and the countryside are attractions in their own rights.

All but one of the castles are accessible only to experienced and well-equipped trekkers. Alternatively, you can hire a guide and donkeys in a nearby village, but be warned, this is no stroll in the countryside – the saddles will be uncomfortable, the donkeys stubborn, the trails tough, and the weather changeable. A complete tour of all the castles in this mountainous region would take about six days.

Alamūt

The only accessible castle (though there is little left to see) is Alamūt. It is still known in the local dialect as The Old Man of the Mountains, dedicated to the founder of the Assassins. It was originally built in about 860, and captured in 1090 by the Assassins, who occupied it until 1256.

Alamūt castle is reached by a paved road heading north-east from the outskirts of

Ghazvīn to the village of Alamūt, also known as Mo'allem Kalāyé (73km from Ghazvīn). From Alamūt, head north along a rough road (a 4WD or sturdy car is needed) to the village of Gāzor Khān (another 21km). Look out for the white-domed house on the left (northern) side of the road in the village, and turn left along the next trail. Take sturdy shoes because the climb to the castle from Gāzor Khān (20 to 30 minutes) is slippery, though not that difficult. Allow at least six hours for the return trip from Ghazvīn.

One of the easiest ways to get there and back for a quick look at Alamūt is with a tour from Ghazvīn. The Hotel Iran in Ghazvīn can organise a tour for about US$25 per car, including everything, as well as a picnic. But bargain hard.

Āzarbāyjān-é Gharbī Province

استان آذربایجان غربی

- **Capital:** Orūmīyé
- **Area:** 37,588 sq km
- **Population:** approx 2.7 million

Western Āzarbāyjān, the province on the border of Turkey and the independent republic of Azerbaijan, is, as you would expect, a curious mixture of Turkish and Āzarī language and culture. The province is famous for the huge Orūmīyé Lake, and the seedless grapes, fruits and tobacco grown in the more fertile regions.

ORŪMĪYÉ
ارومیه

Orūmīyé lies at an altitude of 1312m, on a large and fertile plain, to the west of the lake of the same name. Despite its relatively remote position, cut off from the interior by the vast salt lake, it does lie on a trade route with Turkey that is increasing in importance. The city is more Turkish and Āzarī than Persian, so many locals do not understand Fārsī.

History of the Āzarbāyjān Provinces

The region in Iran known as Āzarbāyjān (the two Āzarbāyjān provinces and Ardabīl province) has always been an important staging post between Asia and Europe, the gateway taken by a succession of invaders and settlers. Part of the Urartian Empire and later the Median Empire, it was the centre of some of the earliest civilisations in Persia. In 330 BC it was taken by Alexander the Great, who appointed his general, Atropates, as governor.

Atropates soon established his own autonomous dynasty, and the land was given the name Atropatene, from which the present name of Āzarbāyjān is derived. This kingdom lasted until about the time of the Sassanian era, when it returned to the control of the central Persian government, and became an important centre of Zoroastrianism. Later it fell to Arabs, Turks and then Mongols, until the Safavid dynasty, with its own roots firmly entrenched in Āzarbāyjān, recovered it.

Āzarī influences became very important in Persian life under the shāhs of the Ghajar dynasty, themselves of Āzarī origin, and Tabrīz was established as the seat of the crown prince. At the same time Āzarbāyjān began to come under Russian influence. In WWI, this part of Persia was invaded by the Turks, who attempted to launch an attack on the Russians through Persian territory. Until the Bolshevik Revolution, Russians had also occupied much of northern Persia, building a railway line from Tabrīz to the border at Julfa.

During WWII, the Soviet army occupied Āzarbāyjān and much of northern Iran in an attempt to secure the supply route through to the Persian Gulf. They proved reluctant to leave in 1945 and tried to set up a puppet government in Āzarbāyjān, provoking the Tehrān government to send a force to expel them in December 1946. ∎

Orūmīyé is more pleasant than Tabrīz, though Orūmīyé doesn't boast many attractions (but neither does Tabrīz). The hills up the Shahr Chāy River from Shahr Park look inviting for some short, day **hikes**.

History
Orūmīyé may date back to the middle of the 2nd millennium BC. It is one of the many places claimed to have been the birthplace of Zoroaster, but evidence of its early history is very scant. It fell to the conquering Arabs in

the mid-7th century, and subsequently came under the control of the Seljuqs (1051-1220) and the Mongols (1220-1380). From then on, its history has been less eventful and more peaceful than that of Tabrīz.

Also known as Ūrmīyé (and sometimes Urmia, among other transliterations), and from 1930 to 1975 known as Rezā'īyé, the city is of interest as the centre of a large and long-established Christian community. Christians comprise something like one-third of the population of Orūmīyé, probably the highest proportion of any town in Iran. In the 19th century and the first half of the

20th century, foreign missionaries were particularly active in Orūmīyé, and many of the locals were converted to Protestantism or Catholicism, but the largest churches belong to the Chaldeans, Armenians, Assyrians and Nestorians.

In 1918, most of the Christian population fled Orūmīyé in the face of an Ottoman invasion, mindful of the appalling massacres of Armenians in Turkey, still remembered with anger and horror by Iranians today. Most of those who remained were brutally slaughtered, but the Christian community soon re-established itself, free of the Turkish threat.

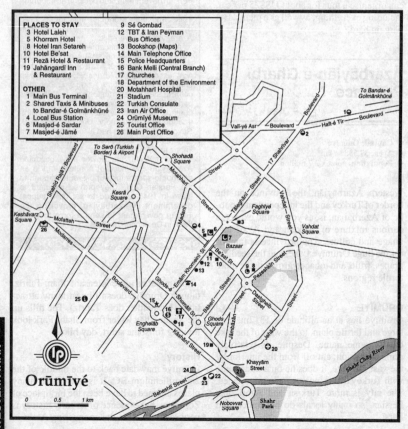

PLACES TO STAY
3 Hotel Laleh
5 Khorram Hotel
8 Hotel Iran Setareh
10 Hotel Be'sat
11 Rezā Hotel & Restaurant
19 Jahāngardī Inn
    & Restaurant

OTHER
1 Main Bus Terminal
2 Shared Taxis & Minibuses
    to Bandar-é Golmānkhūné
4 Local Bus Station
6 Masjed-é Sardar
7 Masjed-é Jāmé

9 Sé Gombad
12 TBT & Iran Peyman
    Bus Offices
13 Bookshop (Maps)
14 Main Telephone Office
15 Police Headquarters
16 Bank Melli (Central Branch)
17 Churches
18 Department of the Environment
20 Motahharī Hospital
21 Stadium
22 Turkish Consulate
23 Iran Air Office
24 Orūmīyé Museum
25 Tourist Office
26 Main Post Office

Orūmīyé

0   0.5   1 km

WESTERN IRAN

Orientation

Orūmīyé is flat and easy to get around on foot. Most streets are signposted in English, though, unusually, none of the squares are. Most of the shops, restaurants and hotels are along Emām Khomeinī St, or near Faghīyé and Enghelāb squares.

Maps

The new *Tourist Map of Province Āzarbāyjān-é Gharbī* (3500 rials) is of limited interest: the streets on the maps for Orūmīyé and Mākū are in English, but the provincial map is in Fārsī. The map is available at the city museum, tourist office and the bookshop near the main telephone office.

Information

Visa Extensions You may have little or no success extending your visa in Orūmīyé, but you can always try at the police headquarters. It is probably better to go to Tabrīz, where visa extensions are particularly painless and quick.

Permits To visit Kabūdī Island in Orūmīyé Lake (see the Orūmīyé Lake section later in this section), you will need to visit the Department of the Environment *(Edāré-yé Koll-é Hefāzat-é Mohīt-é Zīst;* ☎ 40 620). You must speak Fārsī (or have a guide), and have a good reason to go to the island. If successful, allow a few days for the permit to come through.

Tourist Office The tourist office (☎ 45 018), in the Ministry of Culture & Islamic Guidance building, is one of the few in Iran to have its act together. Open from 8 am to 4 pm Saturday to Thursday, the staff can supply information (in English) about visiting the lake, and, if you ask, provide a map of the province (see Maps above).

Foreign Consulates The Turkish consulate *(Konsūlgarī-yé Torkīyé;* ☎ 28 970) is easy to find – look for the telltale, red Turkish flag

waving in the breeze, and the friendly machine-gun toting guards outside. The consulate is open Saturday to Wednesday from 8 am to 1 pm. Give them a visit if you want to cross the border into Turkey at Serō.

Money Turkish lira can be bought and sold at the official rate, at the central branch of Bank Melli using rials, or at the more favourable and unofficial 'street rate', in the bazaar with rials or US dollars. If you hang around the Turkish consulate, someone will probably make you an offer, but you should know the current rate before making any transaction. (One man ordered the driver of his shared taxi to make a U-turn so he could ask me if I wanted any Turkish lira.)

Bank Melli will also change US dollars cash into rials, and one surprised traveller reported that he was even able to get a cash advance, in US dollars, on his Visa card at this bank. There are no money exchange offices, but you may be able to change US dollars at the 'street rate' from a black marketeer near the Bank Melli building.

Post & Communications The main post office is a little inconvenient for walking, so take a shared taxi from Enghelāb Square. The main telephone office is far closer. The telephone area code for Orūmīyé is 0441.

Emergency The Motahharī Hospital (☎ 37 077) is quite close to the centre of town. The police headquarters (☎ 110) is on the north side of Enghelāb Square.

Masjed-é Jāme'

This large quadrangular Seljuq mosque, in the bazaar district, has some very fine plaster mouldings in its original 13th century mehrāb, and a dome of very generous proportions. Much of the present structure dates from later than the Seljuq dynasty, but this sand-coloured mosque is still an impressive sight.

Masjed-é Sardar

This mosque may not look much from the outside, but if you ask nicely you can go inside and admire the delightful interior (but not on Friday).

Sé Gombad

This late 12th century, circular tomb tower is notable for its stucco and stalactite decorations. According to local historians, the tower was either a Sassanian fire-temple, an early type of lookout, or a replica of one of the towers in Marāghé.

The tower is currently fenced off, so you can't get too close, which is disappointing. A helpful notice board on the western side of the tower gives a useful history in English. Take the second lane on your left along Jāmbāzān St, north of the intersection with Dastgeheib St; the tower is at the end of the laneway.

Orūmīyé Museum

The city museum (☎ 27 722) has a small display of cultural costumes, some boring rocks, a few bits and pieces of ancient pottery, and a huge brick tablet, moved from an important archaeological site near the Iraqi border to escape destruction during the Iran-Iraq War. All captions in the museum are in Fārsī. Foreigners are charged 5000 rials. It is open daily from 8 am to 1 pm and 3 to 8 pm. Look for the sign in English along Beheshtī St: 'Ormia Museum' (just one of the variety of spellings of Orūmīyé).

Churches

The various communities here – Assyrian, Armenian, Nestorian, Protestant, Orthodox and Roman Catholic (Chaldean Rite) – all have their own places of worship, and Orūmīyé is the seat of a Chaldean archbishopric. Several of these churches are huddled together and accessible from Ghods-é Shomālī St.

The most noteworthy church is that of St Mary, the **Kelīsā-yé Maryam-é Moghaddas**. This low-roofed, old building of white stone stands on the site of a much older church and has some interesting tombs inside, one of them inscribed in Russian and Persian. Next to St Mary's is a large modern church built in the 1960s and used by the Orthodox community, most of whom are remnants of a White Russian influx earlier this century.

Places to Stay

The really cheap places appear to be under instructions not to accept foreigners. There are no places to stay close to the bus terminal, but buses and long-distance shared taxis, especially ones arriving after dark, often drop passengers off at Faghīyé Square, within easy walking distance of most places.

One of the few cheap hotels to take foreigners is the *Hotel Iran Setareh* (☎ 54 454), which is not signed in English. Clean and comfortable rooms, with a separate sitting room and private bathroom, cost 15,000/ 18,000/25,000 rials for a single/double/ triple. Nearby, the best value in town is at *Khorram Hotel* (☎ 25 444) (look for the sign in English along Emām Khomeinī St). It is behind the Masjed-é Sardar, so potentially noisy at times, but it's away from the busy main road. The manager is friendly, speaks English and charges a reasonable 14,800/ 22,000 rials for a single/double.

If you are able to get the 'Iranian price' (not that hard), the *Rezā Hotel* (☎ 26 580) is a bargain. Though often full, and not over-friendly, a large single/double with private facilities costs 15,000/30,000 rials. In a good spot, but a little noisy, is the *Hotel Be'sat* (☎ 36 128), with a large sign in English. Rooms with a private bathroom cost a negotiable 20,000 rials. The *Hotel Laleh* (☎ 52 740) costs a negotiable US$10 (but payment in rials is OK). The rooms are small, but it's in a quieter spot than most others.

The upmarket place in town, the ITTO-run *Jahāngardī Inn* (☎ 23 080) is quite comfortable, though heavily indebted to Soviet architecture. It charges foreigners US$32 which is hopelessly bad value compared with what else is on offer.

Places to Eat

Orūmīyé is western Iran's centre for citrus fruits, and many bottles and cartons of fruit juice are produced around here. If in season, try some grapes, watermelons, oranges or peaches. One tasty change from yet more kebabs are potatoes – roasted in their skin and wrapped in crumbly bread. This snack is unique to Orūmīyé, and sold from stalls in the middle of the city.

For a decent meal it is best to visit a hotel restaurant. The large restaurant on the 1st floor of the *Rezā Hotel* is worth a visit; a tasty chelō morgh, with bread and a cola, cost me 7500 rials. The restaurant in the *Jahāngardī Inn* is huge, but if the service at the hotel is any indication, you may want to try somewhere else.

Things to Buy

Various goods, many of them cheap clothes and trinkets imported from Turkey, can be picked up in the bazaar. Local souvenirs include excellent wood carvings, rugs and other handicrafts, and miniatures and picture frames. There are several good souvenir shops along Emām Khomeinī St. Orūmīyé is a good place to buy some last-minute mementos before you head to Turkey.

Getting There & Away

Air The Iran Air office (☎ 40 530) is upstairs next to the Turkish consulate. Iran Air flies to Tehrān twice a day for 54,000 rials and to Mashhad on Wednesday and Saturday for 106,000 rials. There are no flights to anywhere in western Iran.

Bus A couple of bus companies, such as Iran Peyman and TBT (Bus Cooperative No 15), have handy booking offices along Emām Khomeinī St. The main bus terminal is on the eastern approach to the city; catch a shared taxi (400 rials) heading north from Faghīyé Square or from anywhere along Emām Khomeinī St.

For some destinations further afield, for example to the far east or far south of Iran, you will have to change buses at Tabrīz, Kermānshāh or Sanandaj. From Orūmīyé, there are several buses (with prices listed for lux/super class) which depart to:

Destination	Distance	Time	Cost (rials)
Kermānshāh	596km	11 hours	9200/10,000
Mākū	286km	5 hours	3200
		(on Iran Peyman; lux class only)	
Marāghé	224km	4 hours	3600
		(lux class only)	
Sanandaj	460km	9 hours	8100/8800
Tabrīz	322km	5 hours	4300/4800
	(buses take the long way around the lake)		
Tehrān	894km	15 hours	9800/10,700
	(the super-duper 'special deluxe' costs 20,300 rials)		

Minibus For some reason, there are four minibus terminals in Orūmīyé. If you are in doubt, just charter a taxi to the terminal you need. The only minibuses you are likely to want are to Tabrīz, which leave from the main bus terminal; to Serō, from Tōhīd Square; and to Bandar-é Golmānkhūné, from the junction marked on the map.

Shared Taxi From outside the main bus terminal, plenty of shared taxis go to Tabrīz for 8000 rials. Taxis and minibuses (but not heavier buses) can use the bridge and ferry across Orūmīyé Lake, a quicker and more interesting way between the two cities. Shared taxis also make the journey to Bandar-é Golmānkhūné and depart from the same place as the minibuses.

Getting Around

To/From the Airport There is no airport bus service, so you'll have to take a taxi. But beware, prices are high. From the airport (about 20 minutes from town), the taxi agency will ask 10,000 rials per passenger in a shared taxi. To the airport, chartering a taxi should cost no more than 7000 rials per *vehicle*, but bargain hard. Shared taxis to the airport leave infrequently from Tōhīd Square.

Bus There is not a lot of point taking local buses, but if you want to ask what is going where, someone at the local bus terminal, north-west of the underpass beneath Emām Khomeinī St, will be able to help you.

Taxi Shared taxis run along all the main roads around Orūmīyé, with the greatest concentration along Emām Khomeinī St, and around Enghelāb and Faghīyé squares. Taxis can be chartered for trips to regional towns, and to the border at Serō.

SERŌ

The nondescript little village of Serō is mainly used by Iranians and Turks to cross the Iranian-Turkish border, but it's open to (but rarely used by) foreigners. However, before heading to the border, check whether it is open, and inquire about the current safety aspects, with the Turkish consulate in Orūmīyé. There is nowhere to stay, eat or change money at the village or border, so it is not nearly as useful as the Gürbulak-Bāzārgān border further to the north. But the drive between Orūmīyé and Serō is gorgeous – it's worth chartering a taxi to the border just for the scenery.

Getting There & Away

Roads east of the Turkish side of the border head into potentially dangerous regions of Kurdish insurgency, so get some current

information about the situation in this part of Turkey before you cross this border. This information is available from the Turkish consulate in Orūmīyé (see Foreign Consulates in the Orūmīyé section earlier in this section); the tourist office in Van, Turkey (☎ (432) 2163 675); or the Iranian consulate in Erzurum, Turkey (☎ (442) 218 3876).

From the Turkish side of the border, there may be buses and shared taxis direct to the regional centre of Van, but you will more probably have to hitch or take a shared taxi to Yüksekova (40km from the border). If you are desperate for somewhere to stay for the night, you could risk staying in Hakkari, 124km from the border, where there are a couple of hotels, but it is better to head north as soon as you can, and avoid this part of eastern Turkey.

From the Iranian side of the border, a few shared taxis patiently wait for passengers going to Orūmīyé. If you don't want to wait for an hour or two for the taxi to fill up, charter one for 15,000 rials. Minibuses also travel between a special minibus terminal in Orūmīyé and the border-cum-village of Serō. If you leave Orūmīyé early in the morning, you should be able to get to Van the same day, or vice versa.

ORŪMĪYÉ LAKE   درياچه اروميه

This huge (6000 sq km) lake has an average depth of between 6m and 16m, according to the season. The lake is far too salty for anything but the most primitive creatures, such as the Artimasalenya worm, but it does attract plenty of migratory waterbirds, including about 50,000 flamingos, each year.

With its jagged, rocky islands and barren shores, the lake is not the most enticing of places, nor is it easy to explore and most travellers will only see the lake while on a minibus or shared taxi between Tabrīz and Orūmīyé. There are a few ports, several hotels and some low-key resorts along the shore, but you will need your own transport to find these; the lakeshore is surprisingly undeveloped. The waters are believed to have therapeutic benefits and to be excellent for relieving rheumatism.

The Āzarīs

The Āzarīs are related to the Turks, but they are divided by religion. The Iranian Āzarīs are almost entirely Shi'ite, whereas the Turks are predominantly Sunni. But all Āzarīs, whether in Iran, Turkey or the independent republic of Azerbaijan to the north, are united by the language of Āzarī, a tongue descended many centuries ago from Anatolian Turkish, but now a language in its own right.

Older Āzarī men traditionally wear brimmed felt hats, and Tabrīz, the main town of the region, is one of the few places in Iran where it is not uncommon to see men wearing ties, still branded un-Islamic and un-Iranian by the central authorities.

After a few years of bad relations, following the Islamic Revolution in Iran, there is now more contact with the republic of Azerbaijan, though private visits by Āzarīs in either direction are still limited, and have been restricted by border closures in the past. ■

Kabūdī Island جزیره کبودی

The second largest of the hundred or so islands in the lake, Kabūdī is 32 sq km in area, has a highest point of almost 1600m, and is almost completely covered in trees. Also known as Jazīré-yé Ghoyūn Dāghī or Sheep Mountain Island, it has a spring which supports a small village and, naturally, a few wild sheep. The island also hosts a wide variety of migratory birds, including flamingo, wild duck and pelican.

On this island, Hulagu Khan, grandson of Chinggis Khaan (Genghis Khan), sacker of Baghdad and founder of the Mongol dynasty (1220-1380), set up his treasury. In 1265 he was buried on the island accompanied by –

as was demanded by the Mongol custom of the time – the ritual slaughter of virgins.

Kabūdī Island is now a conservation area of considerable interest to local naturalists and UNESCO. Foreigners can only visit the island with the permission of the Department of the Environment in Orūmīyé (see Permits under Information in the Orūmīyé section earlier in this chapter); ordinary tourists are not welcome. When you get a permit, the Department will let you know when the ferry to the island leaves Bandar-é Golmānkhūné.

Bandar-é Golmānkhūné بندرگلمانخانه

The main port for the western side of the lake is unsigned, but it, well, looks like a port. There is a jetty, used by ferries, but there's no regular transport to Kabūdī Island. The port is a reasonable spot to have a look at the lake, and as a base for some **hiking** in the area. The port is 17km from Orūmīyé; take a minibus or shared taxi from the special terminal in Orūmīyé.

Getting Around

The construction of a causeway across the narrowest part of the lake commenced in the 1970s, but stopped for a while, and though construction has recommenced, it is still not finished. The causeway reaches about three-quarters across the lake starting from the western shore, so you must continue the journey by ferry. The ferry costs 2500 rials per car, and another 2500 rials per person; this should be included in the fare for any minibus or shared taxi between Orūmīyé and Tabrīz. The ferries travel between 7 am and 8 pm every day, and leave when there are enough passengers and/or vehicles on board – about every 30 to 40 minutes.

TAKĀB تکاب

Takāb is a delightful mid-sized town, and the best place to base yourself while you explore the impressive ruins of Takht-é Soleimān (see the following entry).

Places to Stay & Eat

The only hotel in town is *Hotel Randji* (☎ (04837) 3179), so bargaining is not easy,

Flamingos are one of the bird species most commonly seen in the conservation area on Kabūdī Island.

WESTERN IRAN

but the manager responded to some haggling, and dropped the 'foreigners price' from US$20 to 40,000 rials for a double. The rooms are large, comfortable and have a private bathroom. Some even have a fridge. If this hotel is not suitable, or the manager won't lower his price, the only other option is the *Hotel Esteghlal* in Shāhīn Dezh, further up the road towards Meyāndo'āb.

There are a few *kabābīs* along the road down from the Randji, and around the market, but the Randji has a decent *restaurant* for guests and the public.

Getting There & Away

Takāb is awkward to reach from Tabrīz, but easier from Zanjān. From Tabrīz, take the half-hourly bus (2100 rials) to Meyāndo'āb, then take a regular, but often crowded, minibus to Shāhīn Dezh, and then take another crowded minibus to Takāb. To find the exact departure points for the minibuses in Meyāndo'āb and Shāhīn Dezh, you will have to ask for directions. Allow the best part of a day to get from Tabrīz to Takāb.

From Takāb, daily buses (leaving early in the morning) travel to Tehrān, via Bījār (from where you can carry on to Hamadān), and Zanjān. From Zanjān, a bus passes Takāb at least once a day – no transfers are needed.

TAKHT-É SOLEIMĀN تخت سلیمان

Takht-é Soleimān (Throne of Solomon) is one of the more interesting archaeological sites in this part of Iran. Though not as expansive as Bam or as spectacular as Persepolis, the setting is superb. Anyone interested in the ruins of an ancient city and some gorgeous scenery should detour to this part of the country. This area is so remote that you are likely to be wandering around the Throne of Solomon all on your own.

Ruins

The remains of this large, fortified settlement (12 sq km) are built around a small lake on a hilltop. The original 38 towers along the wall – which probably dates from the 3rd century AD – have worn away to the same height as the wall, which is largely intact.

There are remains of buildings from the Achaemenian (559-330 BC), Parthian (190 BC-224 AD), Sassanian (224-637) and Arab (637-1050) periods, many of them rebuilt or enlarged several times following invasions by the Romans and Arabs, among others. The city was again expanded during the Mongol period (1220-1380), but the whole place was later abandoned for reasons unknown. The oldest remaining structures are the ruins of a **Sassanian palace** and the substantial **fire-temples** which once formed part of a temple complex, now largely in ruins.

The only entrance is remarkable in itself; a stone gate, with Kufric inscriptions, and a tiny creek running through it. Even in this remote part of the country, there is a ticket booth and an employee demanding that foreigners fork out 10,000 rials to enter – but it is worth it, and you have come a long way.

A very helpful map (2500 rials), published by the West Āzarbāyjān Cultural Heritage Organisation, is available from the ticket booth and provides an interesting history of the city and explanations of the sights, in English. The complex is open daily from 7 am to 7 pm – try to get there early or late for the best photos.

You can eat at the *Tesulaimen Restaurant* at the far end of the village, a short walk down from the ruins.

Zendan-é Soleimān

This conical mountain, known as Solomon's Prison, dominates the area, and is about 2.5km west of the ruins. Inside some caves, ancient implements dating back more than 1000 years ago have been found. It is easy to walk up and you are rewarded with stunning views of the countryside, village and ancient city.

Getting There & Away

See the Takāb section earlier in this chapter for details of transport to Takāb. From Takāb, you can take a minibus to the tiny village of Nosratabad, 42km from Takāb. Taking the minibus allows you plenty of time to explore the ruins and have a look around the village. You could also climb the nearby mountain.

The easiest – but most expensive – way is to charter a taxi from Takāb. Just hail down any empty taxi, but don't pay more than about 20,000 rials for the return trip, including about one hour's waiting time – this doesn't really allow you enough time to fully explore the area. If you have a vehicle, use the second (northern) entrance leading to the car park.

HASANLŪ حسنلو

Hasanlū was an important Iron Age settlement and later a citadel, first settled as early as the 6th millennium BC. At the beginning of the 1st millennium BC the centre of the site became a hefty citadel with walls of great thickness and height. Despite Hasanlū's impressive fortifications, the skeletons of people who died here under violent circumstances suggest that the town was destroyed by the Urartians in the 9th century BC. It is perhaps best known for a priceless 11th century BC golden chalice uncovered during excavations here.

You can still see the outer walls of the citadel and the outline of the original town, with its alleys, mud-brick houses, storerooms and various administrative and other buildings, dating back over four distinct periods.

Getting There & Away

Hasanlū is about 5km west of the village of Mohammad Yār, just south of the southernmost tip of Orūmīyé Lake, along the main road between Marāghé and Orūmīyé. You can get off any bus heading that way and walk to the site, or charter a taxi from Orūmīyé. There are no set opening hours and entrance is free.

BASTĀM بسطام

Bastām is probably the most important of the many Urartian archaeological sites found in Iran. A mighty Urartian citadel, larger than any other discovered in Iran, with great stone walls, two large gateways and the remains of a hall, has been unearthed, together with a number of interesting ceramics and other finds. The settlement is believed to have lasted until a Median attack in about the 5th century BC and, much later, to have been the site of an Armenian village.

You can get there by taking the first turn to the left after leaving Ghara Zeyā'-ed-Dīn, on the road west to Seyah Cheshmé, and driving straight ahead for 6km along a badly constructed road until you come to the tall hill on which Bastām stands.

GHARA KELĪSĀ قره کلیسا (کلیسای تادی مقدس)

The Church of St Thaddaeus is probably the most remarkable Christian monument in Iran. It is often called Ghara Kelīsā (Āzarī for 'Black Church'), but the church is more accurately known as the Kelīsā-yé Tādī – the Church of St Thaddaeus. This famous church is clearly visible from afar, at the edge of a promontory, behind a fortified wall with buttresses.

The period of construction is unknown, and very little remains of the original church. It was largely rebuilt after extensive earthquake damage in the 13th century, but there are some older parts, perhaps from the 10th century, around the altar. The original building was constructed of black and white stone, giving it the name Ghara Kelīsā. The present structure, most of which dates from the 17th century, is the colour of sand. It is roughly divided into two sections: most of the eastern part was built with black stone, and includes a dome, altar and courtyard; the western section was built with white stone, and has distinctive columns and arches.

The church has one service a year, on the feast day of St Thaddaeus (around 19 June), when Armenian pilgrims from all over Iran camp for three days to attend the ceremonies. This pilgrimage is an incredible sight, and worth being a part of, if you happen to be in Iran at this time. Accommodation in the region is likely to be very scarce, but if you have a tent, you can camp nearby like the pilgrims. The church is open every day, during daylight hours. Sadly it is now on the tourist trail, and foreigners have to fork out 10,000 rials to get in.

Getting There & Away

Reaching Ghara Kelīsā is not easy, but is worth the effort if you are in this neck of the woods. You can charter a taxi for about 10,000 rials per hour from Mākū, Orūmīyé, or even Tabrīz (with an early start and a fistful of rials). Taxi drivers are becoming familiar with big-spending tourists these days, so negotiating a decent price is not easy.

It is best to base yourself in Mākū. From there, catch any bus or shared taxi towards Bāzārgān, get off at a junction with the sign (in English) to 'Kandi Kelisa'. There are usually one or two hopeful shared taxis waiting at the junction, which you can charter for about 10,000 rials per hour. Alternatively, try waving down a lift on anything going along the road.

MĀKŪ

The quaint town of Mākū, 22km from the Turkish border, is of little interest, though many travellers spend some time here because it's a good place to stop just before, or after, you cross the border.

Orientation & Information

Everything in Mākū is along one very long street, part of the road between Tabrīz and the Turkish border. You can change US dollars, Turkish lira and Iranian rials into any of the other two currencies in town; you will hear many whispers of 'Change money?' in the streets. Changing money in Mākū seems to be a rather furtive business compared with the Bāzārgān border-post, which is probably a better place to change your money. In any case, be careful. The new Bank Melli branch will also change money.

The one and only travel agency, in the upper part of town, is good for confirming or booking flights as soon as you arrive from Turkey, but don't expect anything to be done with too much speed – it is probably quicker to go directly to Tabrīz or Orūmīyé to book

tickets than to hang around Mākū for a day or two. The telephone area code is 04634.

Things to See

There are a few Urartian sites around Mākū, and on either side of the road between here and Orūmīyé to the south, but none of significance are easily reached from Mākū. If you are interested, you could charter a taxi to the small Urartian citadel of **Sangar**, about 10km to the west of Mākū, just off the road to Bāzārgān. From Mākū, you can also visit Ghara Kelīsā (see earlier in this section).

The **Mākū Palace** (☎ 36 455), also known as the Baghch-jugh Palace, is an impressive building from the Ghajar period (1779-1921). It was the private residence of the local governor until 1974, and is now a museum with some carpets and local handicrafts. Open daily from about 8 am to noon and from 5 to 6 pm, it costs 5000 rials to enter, and is probably not worth worrying too much about. It is about 6km from Mākū, so you will have to charter a taxi there.

Hiking

Mākū is spectacularly located in a mountain gorge at an altitude of 1634m. If you have time, try hiking up the rocky hills around Mākū, but be extremely careful and stay within eyesight of the town. This area is very close to the border and trigger-happy guards may not understand your intentions. Mākū has a few mosquitoes in the summer – they presumably crossed illegally from Turkey.

Places to Stay & Eat

Beware of unscrupulous hoteliers and restaurant owners who may assume you have just arrived from Turkey (as many have) and do not know the proper price for food and rooms. I was charged an outrageous 13,000 rials for a 'special' chelō kabāb and cold drink – nearly three times the normal price.

There is some surprisingly good value among the hotels in Mākū – alas, not typical of the rest of the region. On the town's main square , the *Hotel Alvand* (☎ 23 491) has nice singles/doubles, with a shared bathroom, for

10,000/18,000 rials. Directly opposite, the rooms at the *Hotel Laleh* (☎ 3441) are not quite as good, but they are larger and some are quieter than the rooms at the Alvand. They cost 9000/12,000 rials for singles/doubles.

Another cheap one, easy to spot along the noisy main road, is the very basic *Iran Tourist Hotel*. The *Āzādī Inn*, in the upper part of town, was closed at the time of research, but the *kabābī* in the same building is quite decent.

More upmarket is the ITTO's *Mākū Inn* (☎ 23 212), in the upper end of town, and just off the main road (so it's quiet). They charge 70,380/105,570 rials, though the manager couldn't really make up his mind about the exact price for foreigners. In any case, the price won't be cheap nor negotiable.

None of the hotels have restaurants – except for the Mākū Inn, which is really only for guests. You will have to make do with a motley bunch of *kabābīs* around the main square. Watch out for overcharging.

Getting There & Away
Buses to Tabrīz (3200 rials) usually leave about every two hours until about 2 pm, but when I was there only one or two left early every morning, and they were fully booked (though I did squeeze on after some begging). If the buses are full, and you don't want to hang around Mākū, take a shared taxi to Tabrīz (12,500 rials). To Orūmīyé, the buses are often also heavily booked; the alternative is a minibus to Khoy, and then another minibus on to Orūmīyé. If you are staying in Mākū, pre-book a ticket as soon as you can from any bus company office along the main street.

The terminal for buses, minibuses and shared taxis is about 3km from the town centre, in the western end of town (towards Tabrīz), so take a shared taxi. There are plenty of shared taxis from the main road in Mākū to Bāzārgān (1000 rials), right on the Turkish border. Refer to the Bāzārgān section following for information about crossing the border.

BĀZĀRGĀN   بازرگان
This is a typical border town, existing solely to service people crossing the frontier – but it does have a superb setting under the twin peaks of Mt Ararat (5137m and 3895m) in Turkey. If your one and only purpose is to cross the Iran-Turkey border, and you need to stay somewhere, then stay at Bāzārgān, though Mākū does have more atmosphere and things to do. English is spoken by many locals in Bāzārgān. The telephone area code is 04638.

Places to Stay & Eat
The main road from Mākū, which goes through Bāzārgān and stops at the border, is lined with dozens of cheap hotels. There is no need to stay too far from the border; one within walking distance will suffice. One of the best is the *Hotel Jafapour* (☎ 2058) right next to the border. The manager, who speaks English and can organise money changing, charges a bargain 5000 rials per person. Also within a camel's spit of the border is the *Hotel Sahar* (☎ 2761) which charges 10,000 rials per double, with a private bathroom. If neither of these suit, just walk a few metres down the road and find one that does.

There are also dozens of uninspiring places for a hamburger or a kebab along the main road.

Getting There & Away
Minibus & Shared Taxi To get to Mākū, you can take a shared taxi from right outside the border for 1000 rials (but watch for overcharging); or walk about 1km down the road to the Bāzārgān terminal for a minibus (300 rials). A shared taxi is quicker and easier.

If you want to bypass Bāzārgān and Mākū, there are often shared taxis all the way from the border to Tabrīz (15,000 rials per passenger). This fare is definitely a 'foreigner just crossed the border and they don't know any better' price, but it's a quick and easy way to make some distance.

Crossing the Border This is the major border between Iran and Turkey. It is apparently open 24 hours, but some travellers have reported being stranded for a couple of hours, while the infamous Iranian siesta takes place between about 1 and 3 pm. It is best to start early from either side anyway. Both sides are well set up with transport, money changers and hotels.

You can take a direct bus between a Turkish town and an Iranian town, such as between Erzurum and Tabrīz, but this will end up being slower because you have to wait for a few dozen Turks or Iranians to suffer laborious customs and immigration checks – while you may breeze through both borders in an hour or so. It is far better to cross the border yourself, and in stages.

From the Iranian side (or in reverse from Turkey), take any sort of regular transport from Mākū, or walk from Bāzārgān, cross the border, and from the Turkish border town of Gürbulak catch anything heading to Doğubeyazit – sometimes referred to as Doğ Biscuit by weary travellers – or straight on to the best place to stay in the region, Erzurum.

Some travellers have reported being asked for a bribe on the Iranian side, but this is unusual – just ignore it. Expect a few checkpoints along the road into Iran, which are normally painless for foreigners.

As recently as 1996, travellers had to declare their cash and travellers cheques at the Bank Melli branch at the Iranian border. The amount of money you wanted to declare was written in your passport, but not checked when you left Iran in any case. Thankfully this regulation has ceased, and we have heard of no traveller needing to declare or change money at the border. Therefore, you are able to change money at the favourable 'street rate' in Bāzārgān or Mākū – try to find out the current 'street rate', otherwise you will certainly be ripped off (though probably not by much). The Bank Melli branch at the Iranian border will change Iranian rials into Turkish lira, and vice versa, and offers Iranian rials in exchange for US dollars, UK pounds or deutschmarks in cash – but all at the unfavourable official rate.

Crossing both borders can take up to five hours, but foreigners are very often whisked through in less than two hours, especially if you go out of your way to look 'helpless', as one reader reported:

We crossed the border from Turkey and were immediately whisked right to the front of the huge queue of Iranians. I noticed their luggage being overhauled; ours was barely glanced at. We were asked a few cursory questions about our baggage, then were free to proceed.

KHOY خوی

The junction town of Khoy has nothing startling to justify a stop, but if buses between Mākū and Orūmīyé are full, you can take a connecting minibus bus to either town from here.

If you do stay, have a look at the **Masjed-é Motalieb Khan**, dating from the Mongol period. The local **museum**, open from 8 am to 2 pm every day but Friday, contains a small collection of archaeological and ethnological items. Probably the most fascinating thing in town is the statue of two huge flamingos, joined at the side like Siamese twins, in the town square.

For places to stay, there's the cheap *Hotel Amir*, opposite the Bank Melli, on the main road; or try the central *Jahāngardī Inn* (☎ (0461) 40 351), which costs US$15/25 for a single/double.

Āzarbāyjān-é Sharghī Province

استان آذربیجان شرقی

- **Capital:** Tabrīz
- **Area:** 49,287 sq km
- **Population:** approx 3.9 million

TABRĪZ تبریز

Tabrīz has had a spell as the Persian capital, and was until quite recently the second city of Iran. It is an oasis city (population approximately 1.3 million) in an enclosed valley, but after the beauty of the mountains, Tabrīz is an anticlimax and most travellers regard it as just another unexciting Iranian city. It does, however, have the best pizza joint in Iran, and it's a good place to extend your visa – two important selling points.

It is possible to **ski** near Tabrīz in winter. Ask the tourist office for details, and see under Skiing in the Activities section of the Facts for the Visitor chapter.

History

Although the early history of Tabrīz is shrouded in legend and mystery, the town's origins are believed to date back to distant antiquity, perhaps even before the Sassanian period (224-637). Tabrīz was the capital of Āzarbāyjān in the 3rd century AD and again under the Mongol dynasty (1220-1380), though for some time Marāghé supplanted it.

In 1392, after the end of the Mongol rule, the town was sacked by Timur. It was soon restored under the Turkmen tribe of the Ghara Ghoyūnlū, who established a short-lived local dynasty. Under the Safavids (1502-1722) it rose from regional to national capital for a short period, but the second of the Safavid kings, Shāh Tahmāsb, moved the capital to Ghazvīn because of the vulnerability of Tabrīz to Ottoman attacks. The town

then went into a period of decline, and was fought over by Persians, Ottomans and Russians and stricken by earthquakes and disease.

Tabrīz was the residence of the crown prince during the early Ghajar dynasty (1779-1921), but the town did not return to prosperity until the second half of the 19th century. In 1908, it was the centre of a revolt against Mohammed Alī Shāh, which was only put down with the brutal intervention of the Russians. The city was occupied by Russians several times in the first half of this century, including most of both world wars. Their main legacy was the train line to the Azerbaijani border (not currently used as a passenger service).

Orientation

The main street is predictably called Emām Khomeinī St – and this is the best place to base yourself. The business centre is around Shahrdārī Square, though a few government departments and transport terminals are spread around town.

Maps Be careful before you buy any locally produced maps of Tabrīz. The map called the

---

Tabrīzīs: Awful or Awfully Nice?
In *A Year Amongst the Persians*, published in 1893, Edward Browne said this about the Tabrīzīs:

The natives of Adharbāyjān ... with their scowling faces and furtive gray eyes, are not popular among the Persians, whose opinions about the inhabitants of their metropolis, Tabrīz, is expressed in the following rhyme: ... *From a Tabrīzī thou wilt see naught but rascality: Even this is best, that thou shouldst not see a Tabrīzī.*

The author of the first edition of this guidebook agreed with Mr Browne. Since then, some travellers have written to us to dispute this perception:

This Tabrīzī doctor was speaking excellent English, and did his best to help me during the train trip. He was really interested in the previous Lonely Planet guidebook on Iran, and eventually came to read the comment: 'Tabrīzī people are not known for their hospitality'. He then denied this fact, and the whole train learned about the story. Fortunately, they kept smiling and joking about it during the whole journey and everybody was nice with us. Our new friend wished we could go back to Tabrīz to enjoy his house, and other travellers we met had the same good experiences with Tabrīzī people.

Raphäel Clerici, Switzerland

You can make up your own mind about the Tabrīzīs. ■

PLACES TO STAY
2 Hotel Darya
3 Hotel Iran &
   Restaurant
6 Hotel Passargade &
   Hotel Ghods
13 Hotel Golshan
19 Ark Hotel
21 Azarbaidjan Hotel
23 Park Hotel
24 Hotel Sepid
26 Morvarid Hotel;
   Hotel Sina &
   Restaurant
29 Tabrīz International
   Hotel

PLACES TO EAT
16 Afsahe Pizza Place
22 Ahmadpour Chelō Kabābī
25 Modern Turkish Restaurant

OTHER
1 Train Station
4 Shafa Hospital
5 Minibus Station
7 Kelīsa-yé Maryam-é
   Moghaddas
8 Bank Melli (Central
   Branch)
9 Main Telephone
   Office
10 Main Post Office

11 Āzarbāyjān Museum
12 Masjed-é Kabūd
14 Tourist Office
15 Iran Air Office
17 Bookshops
18 Arg-é Tabrīz
20 Shared Taxis to Bus
   Terminal
27 Kelīsa-yé Sarkīs-é
   Moghaddas
28 Stadium
30 Turkish Consulate
31 Department of Foreign
   Affairs (Visa Office);
   Police Headquarters
32 Main Bus Terminal

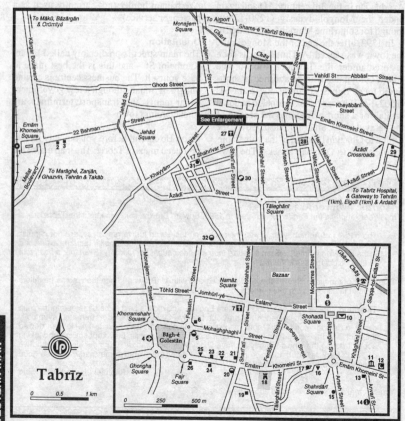

Tabrīz

WESTERN IRAN

Guide Map of Tabrīz City is out of date – the bus terminal has recently moved into the outer suburbs. The best map is the *Tourist Map of Province Āzarbāyjān-é Sharghī*, published by the Ministry of Culture & Islamic Guidance, and available for free from the tourist office. Other maps of Tabrīz are not easy to find in Tabrīz, which is no problem as the map in this guidebook is really all you need.

Information

Visa Extensions Tabrīz is one of the best places in the country to get a visa extension. With bated breath, I was able to get a 15-day extension, with no fuss, in about 10 minutes (I had given up in Tehrān after four days of begging). Other travellers report similar outstanding success.

Go to the police headquarters (unsigned in English) on 17 Shahrīvar St; take a shared taxi heading south along Sharī'atī St. The visa office is part of the Department of Foreign Affairs (☎ 498 234), also unsigned in English, on the top floor of the building to the right as you enter the main gate of the police headquarters compound. If in doubt, ask at the information booth in the grounds.

Tourist Office Tabrīz has one of the best tourist offices in the country – even though there is so little to see in the city. Staff speak English, and, if they can drag themselves away from tending the courtyard garden, can offer decent advice and a free map of Āzarbāyjān-é Sharghī province.

The tourist office (☎ 68 491) is about 150m down the laneway next to the Hotel Golshan – look for the new, green sign in English along Emām Khomeinī St. It is open from 8 am to 2 pm, Saturday to Thursday.

Turkish Consulate The consulate (☎ 477 590) is not easy to find, so look for the fluttering Turkish flag on the roof. It is open between 10 am and 1 pm, from Wednesday to Saturday.

Money The central branch of the Bank Melli is not a great place to change money; some

travellers have reported waiting hours and hours, and sometimes even giving up. Given the proximity to the Turkish border, it's surprising that changing money unofficially at the 'street rate' is so difficult. If you are desperate, you can always make discreet inquiries in the bazaar or at your hotel. It's best to stock up on rials at the border if you have come from there.

Post & Communications The main post office is on the eastern side of Shohadā Square, and the main telephone office is just next to the bridge, along Saqqa-tol-Eslām St. The telephone area code for Tabrīz is 041.

Travel Agencies One of the few travel agencies in town is ALP Tours (☎ 310 340), which organises occasional day trips to nearby attractions, such as Takht-é Soleimān and the Kelīsā Darré Shām (Church of St Stephanos; see later in this chapter). The agency is on Bozorg Square, way out in the suburbs, but they regularly advertise their tours on posters along Emām Khomeinī St.

Bookshops Along the eastern part of Emām Khomeinī St, there are a handful of bookshops worth popping into for a browse. They sell maps of regional cities in western Iran (but rarely Tabrīz), and neighbouring countries such as Armenia and Azerbaijan; as well as current editions of *Time* and some German magazines.

Emergency There is a general emergency number (☎ 118). The most central hospital is Shafa Hospital (☎ 807 168); the main Tabrīz Hospital (☎ 35 053) is near the Gateway to Tehrān building in the south-eastern part of the city. The police headquarters (☎ 58 035) is along 17 Shahrīvar St. (See Visa Extensions earlier in this section for directions.)

Masjed-é Kabūd

The Blue Mosque (built in 1465) has been badly damaged by earthquakes over the centuries, but it's still notable for the extremely intricate tilework. The mosque is in a rather sorry state, with the blue mosaics in its portal either heavily damaged or missing. The mosque is now almost permanently closed due to extensive renovation work. It will eventually reopen, but probably not for several years.

Arg-é Tabrīz

This huge and crumbling brick citadel was built in the early 14th century, on the site of a massive mosque which collapsed more than 500 years ago. In earlier times criminals were hurled from the peak of the citadel into a ditch below, but, according to local legend, one woman was saved from death by the parachute-like effect of her chādor. Well, it makes a good story.

While this remarkable building serves as an ideal landmark, it is permanently fenced off while restoration continues. It is unlikely to be open to the public for years, but you can take a peek through a hole in the fence.

Āzarbāyjān Museum

This museum (☎ 66 343) contains a mildly interesting ethnological display, including much about the Āzarīs; archaeological items taken from regional excavations, such as Hasanlū; and some boring stuff about modern Iranian history. The entrance price of 10,000 rials (ten times more than Iranians pay) – plus an extra 5000 rials for a still camera – is way too much, so some travellers may want to give this a miss.

The museum (not signed in English) is a two storey building about 50m west of the Blue Mosque – look for the wooden door and the two stone sheep outside. The museum is officially open every day from 9 am to 8 pm, though I walked past it twice during what was deemed to be opening hours, and it was closed.

Churches

From the earliest days of Christianity there has been a sizeable Armenian community in Tabrīz, and the city boasts a number of churches, including one mentioned by Marco Polo on his travels. Probably the most interesting is the old but substantially rebuilt **Kelīsā-yé Maryam-é Moghaddas** (Church

of St Mary) near the bazaar. Three other churches, such as the **Kelīsā-yé Sarkīs-é Moghaddas** (Cathedral), are close to each other, in the southern part of town.

Elgolī

This pleasant and large park is promoted as a major attraction, and rightly so because there is so little else to see in Tabrīz. It's a lovely spot to escape the city, and is often full of young couples discreetly courting. If you are keen, you can hire paddleboats for a splash about the **Shahgolī Shāh lake** inside the grounds. Entrance is free, but try to avoid it on Friday and public holidays.

The ITTO used to have some tents at the park for hire, but they seemed to have been pulled down. The park would be a pleasant place to stay, but you would be surrounded by dozens of large, noisy Iranian families. There are a few decent *kabābīs* inside the gardens, or you can try the elegant *restaurant* in the middle of the lake.

The gardens are a few kilometres south-east of the city, so take a shared taxi from Shahrdārī Square.

Places to Stay – budget

The really cheap places will not generally accept foreigners. Some travellers have managed to stay at the *Hotel Passargade* (☎ 57 571), but the manager wouldn't even show me a room. There are a few other mosāferkhūnés, such as the *Hotel Sepid*, along Emām Khomeinī St, but don't expect to be welcomed with open arms.

However, do not despair. Two clean and central places accept foreigners, charge the 'Iranian price', and have single rooms. The *Park Hotel* (☎ 51 852) is good value for 15,000/25,000 rials for a single/double with a shower (but shared toilet) and fridge, though the nicely painted hallway belies the musty rooms. Also good value is the friendly *Morvarid Hotel* (☎ 65 398) which charges 15,000/20,000/25,000 rials for a clean single/ double/triple. The rooms have private facilities, a fridge and a B&W TV – but get a room away from the main road, otherwise you may never get any sleep.

Near the train station, but inconvenient to the rest of the city, is the friendly *Hotel Iran* (☎ 459 515) which charges a reasonable 30,000 rials for a double. The *Ark Hotel* (☎ 51 277) – named after the castle nearby, not Noah – is also recommended charging 24,000 rials a double. As a last resort, try the *Hotel Golshan* (☎ 69 273) with doubles for 40,000 rials, if you bargain; or the *Hotel Ghods* (☎ 68 098), which charges the same price, but it's a noisy spot.

Places to Stay – middle & top end
All places in this range have private bathrooms. Next to the Morvarid Hotel, the *Hotel Sina* (☎ 66 211) is overpriced with doubles for 60,000 rials, but it is off the main road, so many of the rooms are quiet. The new *Azarbaidjan Hotel* (☎ 59 051), recognisable by the red and white columns on the outside, is the best in this range. The rooms cost 40,000/80,000 rials, and worth a splurge. Close to the train station, but to nothing else, the *Hotel Darya* (☎ 459 501) costs US$20/30 for singles/doubles, but the staff are not very friendly, and it's no better than the cheaper Hotel Iran nearby.

The top-end place is the four-star *Tabrīz International Hotel* (☎ 341 082) which charges like the proverbial wounded bull: US$65/75, plus taxes.

Places to Eat
There are plenty of *kababīs, hamburger joints, teahouses* and *ābgūsht places* along Emām Khomeinī St, mainly within about 50m either side of the Park Hotel. One of the special little treats around the city are the *stalls*, just off Emām Khomeinī St, which sell tea, boiled eggs and delicious baked potatoes in their jackets.

The large *Modern Turkish Restaurant*, downstairs and signed in English, is worth a try. This is one of those places where the waiter plonks a salad, soup, bread and cola on your table (all of which you pay for) almost before you've sat down. If you don't want it, say so quickly. A reasonable chelō morgh, with the trimmings, costs 8000 rials. Close by is the *Ahmadpour Chelō Kabābī*;

Ābgūsht
Tabrīz is the best place in Iran for *ābgūsht* (also known as *dīzī*), a stew made of fatty meat, usually beef or mutton, and thick chunks of potato and lentils, traditionally served in a *pipkin* (small bowl) and eaten with a spoon.

A pestle is provided for grinding up the meat and potatoes, and there is a great art to pouring the ābgūsht from the pipkin and then pounding the ingredients into just the right consistency, without using up all the gravy too soon. If possible, it is a good idea to take a local with you the first time you try this triumph of Iranian cuisine. ■

it's not signed in English, so look for the English words 'Chicken Kebab' on the window. A chelō morgh, with soup, salad, bread and a cola costs 9000 rials.

Arguably the greatest attraction in Tabrīz (and, I reckon, the best pizza joint in Iran) is the *Afsahe Pizza Place*. The words, in English, on the window say 'Agreeable food in proper enviroment (sic) is more desirable' – hear hear! Pizzas for one cost 7000 rials, and while the 'meat' is actually Iranian sausage, the rest of it, especially the crust and the cheesy topping, is worth a flight from Tehrān. Well, almost. But watch out for the low ceilings in the restaurant.

Of the hotels, the small restaurant in the *Hotel Sina* is decent; meals cost about 8500 rials, with soup and salad. The restaurant in the *Hotel Iran* is worth the short shared taxi ride out of town.

Things to Buy
The pedestrian-cum-shopping **mall**, along Tarbeyat St, is so unusual for Iran that it's worth walking up and down a few times to window shop and enjoy the lack of traffic – except for the inevitable motorcyclists, of course.

The large and labyrinthine **bazaar** is about 3km long. It was probably built more than 1000 years ago, but most of what remains today dates back to the 15th century. It's a great place for getting hopelessly lost amid the dusty architectural splendours. Carpet making is still the main trade, but Tabrīz is also renowned for its silverware, jewellery and delicate products woven from local silk. The **spice bazaar**, one of the most pungent and impressive in Iran, is an excellent place for picking up henna. Look out also for the traditional Āzarī hats resembling those worn by the gypsies of Eastern Europe.

Getting There & Away

Air There are surprisingly few flights to or from Tabrīz. Iran Air (☎ 52 000), which has an unimpressive little office about 300m down Artesh St, flies to Mashhad three times a week (but schedules change regularly) for 96,500 rials; Rasht on Saturday (40,000 rials); and Tehrān, four times a day (49,500 rials). Iran Asseman did apparently fly between Tabrīz and Tehrān at one time, but as there is no office in town, flights have probably been discontinued.

International Services Every Friday morning, Iran Air flies to Baku, in the republic of Azerbaijan, for a huge US$210/420 one way/return. (The bus only costs 26,200 rials one way!) At the time of research, the quirky little airline, Bon Air, planned to link Tabrīz with Damascus (Syria) every week. No other details were available, and given Bon Air's reputation, don't expect this flight to still be operating by the time you get to Tabrīz.

Bus The huge, modern bus terminal (☎ 57 134) is in the far southern stretches of the city. If you get the opportunity when coming to Tabrīz by bus, get off somewhere in the city, probably near the train station, from where you can take a shared or private taxi to your hotel. However, going to the terminal when you arrive allows you to pre-book a ticket to your next destination.

Between the bus offices and the bus lanes, there is an information office (no telephone number) in a squat, brick building. It is currently staffed by a helpful, English-speaking guy who will point you to the right direction. Go to this office rather than rely on the annoying touts working for the buses and shared taxis.

To get to the terminal, take a private taxi (3000 rials) or a shared taxi (1000 rials) from the southern corner of Emām Khomeinī and Sharī'atī Sts. At the terminal, try to avoid the overpriced Terminal Taxi Service, though you can share these taxis with other passengers.

Every hour or so, there are buses (with prices listed below for lux/super class) to:

Destination	Distance	Time	Cost (rials)
Ardabīl	216km	4 hours	4000/5000
Bandar-é Anzalī	416km	7 hours	6100/6750
Esfahān	1038km	16 hours	12,000/12,800
Jolfā	137km	3 hours	2250 (lux only)
Kermānshāh	578km	11 hours	10,700/11,600
Mākū	242km	4 hours	3200 (lux only)
Marāghé	143km	3 hours	2100 (lux only)
Orūmīyé	322km	5 hours	4300/4800
(this takes the long way around the lake, so shared taxis are better)			
Rasht	481km	8 hours	6100/6750
Sanandaj	452km	8 hours	8100/8800
Shīrāz	1519km	24 hours	18,800/19,800
Tehrān	624km	9 hours	7700/8500

International Services There are also bus services to and from the following cities in neighbouring countries: Baku (Azerbaijan) on Thursday and Sunday (26,200 rials); Istanbul via Ankara (Turkey), on Wednesday and Sunday (both fares are 72,800 rials); and Damascus (Syria) for 200,000 rials, several days a week. The days of departures change regularly, so check with the bus companies at the main terminal, and book ahead.

Minibus The minibuses that leave from the special terminal in town are handy for transport to regional towns (sometimes they leave from the main bus terminal). Ask around for the one that you want.

Train Tabrīz is on the 736km line from Tehrān, via places such as Marāghé, Zanjān and Ghazvīn. The line continues to Jolfā, on the Azerbaijani border, but currently there are no passenger trains on this line. There is also no train to Turkey.

Tabrīz is one of the few places in Iran where it is worth using the train, particularly to go to Tehrān. The scenery is often picturesque, departures are regular and reliable, tickets are not too hard to obtain in Tabrīz (while nothing is easy in Tehrān), the 1st class sleeper carriage is comfortable and has a restaurant car, and the station is easy to reach. If only travelling by train was as easy elsewhere in Iran.

To Tehrān, two 'express' trains and one 'regular' train leave every evening, and a ticket costs 17,150/12,650 rials (1st/2nd class). The ticket office at the station opens at about 4 pm for bookings for trains leaving that evening. The station (☎ 47 666) is at the far western end of town, and very easy to reach by shared taxis heading along Emām Khomeinī St.

Shared Taxi Tabrīz is well connected to many places in western Iran by shared taxi, so they are ideal for quick and painless travel. They all leave from a special section within the main bus terminal. Shared taxis between Tabrīz and Orūmīyé (8000 rials) use the bridge and ferry across the lake (it's a fascinating trip). There are also regular shared taxis from the main bus terminal to Mākū and Bāzārgān (for the Turkish border).

Getting Around

To/From the Airport If you only have a little luggage, you can catch a public bus between the airport and the local bus terminal in front of the bazaar. Private taxis from the airport are very reasonably priced – about 5000 rials – but it should cost less *to* the airport. The drivers who work for the Terminal Taxi Service at the airport will naturally want more, so look for an ordinary taxi or ask about sharing. A shared taxi to the airport is hard to find, but you can look around Khorramshahr Square.

Bus & Minibus There are plenty of buses and minibuses which run along Emām

Khomeinī St, but you are better off taking a shared taxi.

Taxi Getting around is mostly a matter of saying *mostaghīm* (straight ahead) to shared taxi drivers, and covering small distances on foot. From the centre of town you will have no problem getting a shared taxi in any direction, and as far as the train station, bus terminal or Elgolī.

AROUND TABRĪZ

Mt Sahand   کوه سهند

This majestic mountain is 3707m high, and dominates the area between Tabrīz and Marāghé. See the special Trekking in Iran section in the Facts for the Visitor chapter for information about climbing the mountain.

Marāghé   مراغه

The best day trip from Tabrīz is to the pleasant town of Marāghé, a former capital of the Mongol dynasty (1220-1380). The name Marāghé means 'wallowing place for a beast', probably because the Mongols favoured this site as pasture for their horses. The centre of town stretches a few hundred metres between Mosallā Square (with something that looks like two huge tuning forks in the middle) and Fajr Square (the one without the tuning forks).

Things to See Although almost nothing remains of the famous **observatory** that Hulagu Khan established in a cave outside Marāghé in the 13th century, four interesting brick **tomb towers** have survived. The Gombad-é Kabūd, Borj-é Mādar-é Hulagu Khan and Gombad-é Sorkh tombs are from the 12th century, and the Gombad-é Ghaffārīyé dates from the early 14th century, and is notable for the glazed tiling used to decorate its exterior walls.

The sights around the town are difficult to find, so it's worth hiring a taxi, and using the driver as a guide. This should cost about 8000 rials per hour.

Places to Stay & Eat About 300m west of the bus terminal, the *Darya Hotel* (☎ (0422)

250 305) is overpriced at US$30/50 for a single/double; the management is under the misapprehension that all foreigners have more money than sense. Far better value can be found at the *Aria Hotel* (☎ (0422) 2294), which is halfway between the train station and Mosallā Square.

The Darya does have the best *restaurant* in town; it's an ideal place for anyone taking a day trip from Tabrīz.

Getting There & Away From Tabrīz, buses leave every 30 minutes (2100 rials), and there are also regular buses from Orūmīyé (3600 rials). The bus terminal in Marāghé is on the Tabrīz side of town, about 1.5km from Mosallā Square.

Marāghé is on the train line between Tabrīz and Tehrān. The impressive train station is about 300m south of Mosallā Square. (See Getting There & Away in the Tabrīz section for details.)

JOLFĀ جلفا

At one time, Jolfā was the major settlement of Armenians in Persia, until Shāh Abbās I moved them to 'New Jolfā', now part of Esfahān. Jolfā is now a border-post, and the best place to base yourself to visit Kelīsā Darré Shām (see the following section). At the time of research, it was not entirely clear whether foreigners were allowed to cross the Iran-Azerbaijan border at Jolfā. Until the tension between Azerbaijan and Armenia abates, travellers should cross the border at Āstārā anyway (see the Caspian Provinces chapter for details).

There are a few nondescript hotels in Jolfā, but nothing to get excited about; the best is probably the grubby *Jolfā Hotel*, along the western end of the main road. Jolfā is linked with regular buses from Tabrīz (2250 rials) and minibuses from the nearby junction town of Marand.

KELĪSĀ DARRÉ SHĀM کلیسا دره شام

The Church of St Stephanos is a spectacular and very remote Armenian monastery in the hills, but a little close to the Azerbaijan border for comfort. The earliest surviving part of the building dates from the 14th century. A church is said to been founded on the site by St Bartholomew (one of the earliest Christian apostles in Armenia) around 62 AD. The well-preserved but hauntingly isolated stone building is remarkable for very fine exterior reliefs, with Armenian crosses, angels and other Christian motifs. The scenery on the way there, and the landscapes surrounding the church, are superb.

The monastery is right where the Aras and Āgh Chāy rivers meet, 16km west of Jolfā. Organised trips are sometimes run by ALP Tours in Tabrīz (see Travel Agencies in the Tabrīz section earlier in this chapter), which is probably the best idea considering the remoteness and proximity to the Azerbaijan border. If you wish to visit the church independently, check with the Kōmité in Jolfā first; they will write you a letter allowing you to pass the numerous checkpoints, or someone may even accompany you.

Ardabīl Province استان اردبیل

- **Capital:** Ardabīl
- **Area:** 17,814 sq km
- **Population:** approx 1.4 million

Ardabīl is one of the newest provinces in the country, recently separated from its larger neighbour, Āzarbāyjān-é Sharghī. Most of the attractions are in or around Ardabīl city, but if you have your own vehicle, and a guide (if you don't speak Fārsī), there is plenty more to explore. The province is mountainous, and often beautifully (and unusually) carpeted with forests. The highest peak is the volcano, Mt Sabalān (4811m). There are numerous rivers, such as the Aras (after which the locally-made cola is named) and many lakes, which are home to a number of migratory waterbirds.

The province is understandably more Āzarī than Persian, and most locals speak Āzarī. The region is also home to the El-Sevans nomads, who are mainly based around Meshgīn Shahr.

The 1997 Earthquake
In February 1997, an earthquake measuring 5.5 on the Richter scale struck near the city of Ardabīl. In the following three months, 32 tremors over 4 on the Richter scale, and more than 1800 aftershocks, rocked the new province of Ardabīl.

Like so many things in Iran, it is difficult to get consistent figures about the amount of damage, but it seems that the earthquake and aftershocks killed over 550 people, injured over 3000, destroyed over 16,000 homes in 126 villages, and left over 50,000 people homeless.

The damage was exacerbated, and the rescue attempts hindered, by the harsh winter of north-western Iran. A rescue helicopter crashed in a blizzard and villagers died of exposure while waiting to be rescued, meanwhile others burnt wood from the walls of their own homes to keep warm. Resources were severely limited at the time because many tents, medical supplies and so on had been used to assist a particularly large influx of Kurdish refugees from Turkey and Iraq. ∎

ARDABĪL اردبیل
Ardabīl city is really a long way from any-where, and only useful for people travelling to or from Azerbaijan, via Āstārā, or as a stopover between the Caspian region and the north-west. The city is not a dull place, but there is nothing much to see except the **Sheikh Safī-od-Dīn mausoleum** and the **bazaar**, which is one of the best in the region.

Orientation & Information
The main part of the city is the triangle between Emām Hussein, Emām Khomeinī and Alī Ghāpū squares. Modarres St heads south-east from Emām Khomeinī Square to the river, which has pleasant parkland along its banks. The whole town can be reached on foot. The labyrinthine bazaar is south of Emām Hussein Square. The telephone area code is 0451.

Sheikh Safī-od-Dīn Mausoleum
Dedicated to Sheikh Safī-od-Dīn, forefather of the Safavid dynasty (1502-1722), this is an exquisite and fascinating collection of various bits and pieces. It includes the tomb of Safī-od-Dīn, with its charming octagonal dome; the Khan-é Chini or **House of Porcelain** with its striking interior; the Khan-é Chelleh or **House of Lamps**; a mosque; the tombs of other less notables; and a garden.

According to the notice outside the entrance, photos are not permitted inside the complex (☎ 23 665); neither are any 'edible amusements'. Shoes must be taken off inside the buildings. The entrance is on Alī Ghāpū Square, in the middle of town and not hard to miss. The entrance fee for foreigners is the usual 10,000 rials.

Places to Stay
Unfortunately, most cheap places won't accept foreigners. One place that will is the *Ojahan Inn* (☎ 22 481), right on Emām Khomeinī Square (there is a small sign above the door in English). It is very noisy, but cheap at 10,000 rials a room. The best in the middle range is the *Hotel Sheikh Safī* (☎ 24 111), on Sharī'atī St, which charges 25,000/35,000 rials for a single/double.

The recognised 'tourist hotel', which many mosāferkhūnés may direct you to, is the *Hotel Sabalān* (☎ 49 991) on Sheik Safī St. Though convenient to the mausoleum complex, it is overpriced for foreigners – 60,000/70,000 rials – and the manager flatly refused to negotiate when I was there.

Places to Eat
There are a few *kabābīs* along Emām Khomeinī St, and around the entrance to the mausoleum complex. A couple of places near Emām Khomeinī Square sell yummy ice cream in crunchy cones.

The huge restaurant on the 1st floor of the *Hotel Sabalān* is easily the best place to eat. The menu is limited, but they can rustle up a decent chelō morgh, including soup, salad, bread and a drink for 7500 rials. You can finish off the meal with a pot of tea in the foyer.

Things to Buy
The region is famous for its Sabalān honey, so if you have a sweet tooth, buy some at the bazaar in Ardabīl.

Getting There & Away

Air Saha Air and Iran Asseman apparently fly between Ardabīl and Tehrān, but no information about their schedules was available at the time of research. It is better to stick with Iran Air, which flies between Ardabīl and Tehrān once a day for 44,500 rials.

Bus The regular buses (4000/5000 rials for lux/super class), minibuses and shared taxis from the main bus terminal in Tabrīz take the road to Ardabīl via Bostān Ābād. There are also daily buses to Rasht, Zanjān or Tabrīz, from where you will probably have to get connections to places further afield. The road to Āstārā goes through some rare forest and is worth a trip just for the scenery. You will need to charter a taxi to and from the distant bus/minibus terminal in Ardabīl.

AROUND ARDABĪL

There are quite a few things to see within a short trip from Ardabīl, but for most places you will need your own transport.

Meshgīn Shahr   مشکین‌شهر

This handsome village (about 60km from Ardabīl) is famous for its hot springs (though those at Sareiyn are more accessible), its nomadic population and the 9th century **Arshoq castle**.

Khalkhōrān   خالکوران

Sheikh Safī-od-Dīn's father, Sheikh Jebrā'īl, is buried in a 16th century **mausoleum** in the village of Khalkhōrān, 3km north-east of Ardabīl. The mausoleum contains two porches, a pretty tiled dome and many tombs of Safavid-era generals. The village is surrounded by forest and is worth exploring on foot. Charter a taxi there for about 2000 rials.

Sareiyn   سرعین

For a long soak and bath it is hard to beat the hot mineral springs at Sareiyn. The springs contain sulphur and other minerals reportedly able to cure anything from baldness to syphilis. The village also gained unwanted fame as the virtual epicentre of a devastating earthquake in early 1997 (see 'The 1997 Earthquake' boxed text on the previous page). Extensive damage is still evident, and will be for some time, but the villagers are slowly recovering. The village is nestled under the majestic Mt Sabalān, and is worth a visit if only for the ride out there, the **hiking** and the scenery in the region.

Hot Springs If you take a chartered taxi, the driver will take you to one of nine hot springs around the village; otherwise, you will have to ask directions to find one. The cheaper, communal baths are often grubby and you may pick up a few nasty bacteria. You are far better off paying a marginally higher fee to use the cleaner and more modern 'Hydrotherapy Complex', the main baths in the village. Naturally, the baths are segregated, but foreigners are charged 'Iranian prices' – which depend on the length of your visit.

Places to Stay & Eat While it's easy to take a day trip from Ardabīl, you can stay at the *Roz Hotel* (☎ (045441) 4411) in Sareiyn, which also has a 'restyrent' (sic). The manager had to dust off a piece of paper listing the prices he was allowed to charge foreigners (US$20/30 for a single/double), but was open to negotiation. There are a couple of mosāferkhūnés in town, but none were interested in telling me their prices.

There had been plans to build several more upmarket hotels in the village, but these were thwarted by the earthquake.

Getting There & Away It is a little difficult to charter a normal taxi from Ardabīl to Sareiyn – most drivers claim you need to hire an (expensive) agency taxi, but I found one eventually. Count on 10,000 rials return, including a short 20 minute soak. If you need longer to soak off the dirt you've collected on your trip, or want to explore the village or countryside for longer, minibuses leave Ardabīl for Sareiyn about every hour or so.

Caspian Provinces

The provinces of Gīlān and Māzandarān occupy the coastal belt between the Alborz Mountains and the southernmost shores of the Daryā-yé Khazar (Caspian Sea). The Caspian region, known as the Shomāl (the North), is a tourist area favoured by many Iranians, especially Tehrānīs, but is often ignored by travellers.

The two provinces have a varied terrain, with thick forests, mountains and a coastal plain up to 100km wide. The towering Alborz mountains block moisture from the Caspian from reaching the central plateau. On the northern slopes the forest, especially that of southern Māzandarān, is rich in wildlife. Much of it is all but impenetrable and gives cover to a wide range of animals, including wild boar, jackal, leopard and tiger. This shouldn't put you off the excellent hiking in the region (see the Trekking in Iran section in the Facts for the Visitor chapter). Afterwards, you may wish to wallow in the hot and cold mineral springs which are within a short taxi ride of Rāmsar and Āmol.

The Caspian coastline is one of the most densely populated regions in Iran, but it hasn't always been so. Small settlements have existed in both provinces from the earliest times, but until this century the area was too unhealthy, because of its malarial swamps, and too forested to permit settlement on a large scale. Although much of the land has been cleared and drained over the centuries, the southern parts of the provinces are still thinly populated.

The rainy Caspian littoral (which receives about 2000mm of rain a year) is ideal for growing rice and tea, the main agricultural crops of the region. Cotton is also harvested in both provinces, and oranges and other citrus fruits are becoming increasingly important crops in Māzandarān. Many varieties of sea and river fish are found here, most notably sturgeon, salmon, perch and pike; and caviar processing is very lucrative. The Caspian Sea itself is surprisingly

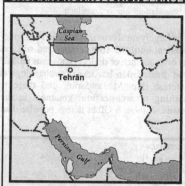

CASPIAN PROVINCES AT A GLANCE

- **Provinces:** Gīlān and Māzandarān
- **When to Go:** A bit of rain and cloud can be expected all year; mumidity can be high in summer; spring and autumn are the best times.
- **Highlights:** Māsulé, near Rasht; Nahar Khorān, near Gorgān; Rāmsar; Gombad-é Kāvūs

peripheral to the activities of most of the coastal inhabitants, and doesn't even get much use by the domestic tourists and holidaymakers who come here in droves. There are few beaches or other seaside attractions, and tourism, though important, is very much a do-it-yourself affair. There's remarkably little in the way of organised activities for visitors, and most Iranian visitors make their own fun.

Except during the peak holiday season and on public holidays, accommodation is rarely a problem; there are hotels, motels and mosāferkhūnés along all the main roads, especially in the main tourist areas on the coast. Accommodation prices are higher than elsewhere on mainland Iran, but the standard is above average.

Gīlān Province استان گیلان

- **Capital:** Rasht
- **Area:** 14,811 sq km
- **Population:** approx 2.6 million

The largely rural province of Gīlān was independent until the 16th century and still has its own distinctive dialect (known as Gīlākī) and dress. Gīlān has less of archaeological interest than Māzandarān, and there is nothing of architectural greatness in the towns. Although Gīlān is less popular than Māzandarān, there are many scenic attractions, particularly around Āstārā where some of Iran's few forests remain. There are swamps around Lāhījūn, some of which, near Bandar-é Anzalī, have been protected (though to what extent is debatable) to safeguard the bird life.

Gīlān's capital is Rasht, the most important city in the region. Its main port is Bandar-é Anzalī, at the mouth of the Mordāb-é Anzalī (Anzalī Lagoon). The largest river is the Sefīd, stretching from the Sadd-é Sefīd Rūd (Sefīd Dam), on the border with Zanjān province, to the Caspian Sea.

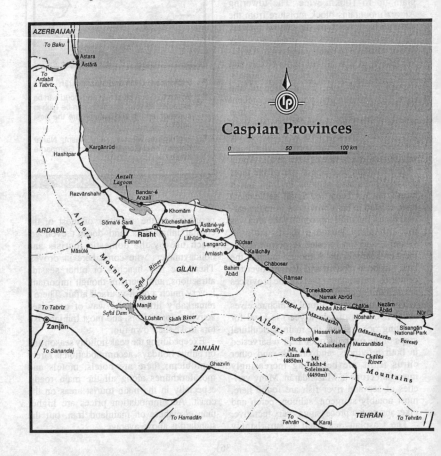

Caspian Provinces

The province produces silk, tobacco and tea (which is now the major agricultural speciality of Gīlān). Fishing and the production of caviar are also vital industries.

RASHT رشت

Some 7m below sea level and 15km inland from the Anzalī Lagoon, Rasht is the largest city in the Caspian provinces (population approximately 390,000) and the industrial centre of the region. Only 324km north-west of Tehrān along a good motorway, Rasht is a very popular weekend and holiday destination for Tehrānīs, for whom the change in climate and scenery is enough in itself. The city has little to offer travellers, but it's a good place to unwind while you explore the region. Be prepared: Rasht is one of the wettest places in Iran, and can be uncomfortably humid in summer.

History

Rasht grew into a town around the 14th century, and soon became the major settlement in Gīlān province. The city has been occupied by Russians several times in its history, most ruinously in 1668 when almost the whole population was massacred by the

The Mighty Caspian Sea

The Caspian Sea (*Daryā-yé Khazar*) is the world's largest lake. Covering an area of 370,000 sq km and measuring 1210km from north to south and between 210km and 436km from east to west, the Caspian is five times bigger than the next largest lake (Lake Superior, on the border of the US and Canada) and contains 44% of all the water in the world's lakes. The Caspian has many large tributaries, such as the Volga, Zhem and Ural rivers, but has no outlet to the ocean.

A salt lake, about one-third as salty as sea water, the Caspian's surface is about 30m below sea level, but the water level is rising at the alarming rate of 15cm to 20cm per year, for reasons that are not entirely known. One theory is that the clearing of land for agriculture around the Caspian has led to increased water run-off. The Caspian has an average depth of 170m, which is nearly twice as deep as the Persian Gulf.

Slowly but surely the countries bordering the Caspian Sea – Iran, Russia, Turkmenistan, Azerbaijan and Kazakhstan – are starting to realise the potential benefit of a joint regional economic zone, boosted by transport across the Caspian, and have formed the nascent Caspian Cooperation Organisation (CASCO).

The Caspian is home to vast numbers of fish, including the sturgeon that produces caviar; migratory birds; tortoises; and the unique Caspian seal. However, the Caspian's ecology is under threat from shipping, the development of ports, industrial chemical waste, oil and gas exploration, and broken oil and gas pipelines. One million tonnes of crude oil leaked in to the Caspian Sea during the 1960s (the most recent figure available). We can only hope that the littoral states also expend some time and energy to form an organisation to deal with the continuing ecological damage. ■

forces of the Cossack brigand Stenka Razin. Razin had already destroyed the Persian navy in the Caspian Sea, and his sole aim in life appears to have been to rape and pillage.

During WWI the city was again occupied by Russians, and in 1920 the Bolsheviks destroyed much of the bazaar, driving many of the townpeople into temporary exile.

Orientation

The three main thoroughfares, Sharī'atī St, Sa'dī St and Emām Khomeinī Blvd, converge at the vast Shohadā Square, which, during summer, is reminiscent of the worst pedestrian and traffic chaos that Tehrān has to offer. If you stay somewhere close to this square you will find it easy enough to get around Rasht.

Maps Gita Shenasi publishes a map of Rasht (1500 rials) with a familiar red cover. Like other city maps, it lists street names in English, but the index is in Fārsī. Moreover, the map is hard to find in Rasht.

Information

Visa Extensions For visa extensions inquire at the police headquarters. Rasht is

one of the best places in the region to get your visa renewed, and is a reasonable place to stay while you're waiting.

Money The three major banks will change money. A great place to stock up on rials at the unofficial 'street rate', but in a safe and legal money exchange office, is the Mehra Pooya Currency Exchange. The office is signed in English, and at the end of the lane, off Emām Khomeinī Blvd where the Hotel Golestān is located.

Rashtīs – the Butt of Many a Joke

The people of Rasht are popularly believed to be the kindest and most hospitable in Iran, but also the most slow-witted. Rashtī jokes are as much part of the national culture of Iran as Irish jokes are in England. Much fun is made of the curiously lisping Rashtī accent, which can sound a little comical to the outsider. Some jokes run along the lines of: 'There is this Rashtī, and an Esfahānī ...', poking fun at the meanness and cleverness of the Esfahānī and the naivety and unquestioning generosity of the Rashtī. ■

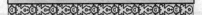

Post & Communications The most convenient post office for visitors is in the large building on the north side of Shohadā Square. You can also make telephone calls from there. The telephone area code for Rasht is 0131.

Laundry There are several laundries huddled around Shohadā and Sabze squares, so Rasht may be a good place to get some washing done.

Emergency There is an official emergency number (☎ 60 825). Alternatively, try directory inquiries (☎ 118). There are several hospitals: the best and most central is the Razi Hospital (☎ 23 963) on Sardār Jangal St. The police headquarters (☎ 27 777) is on the north-east side of Shohadā Square.

Rasht Museum

The Rasht Museum (☎ 27 979) is worth a look, if only to enjoy the wonderful air-con inside the building during summer. The museum contains a small collection of ceramics, pottery, traditional clothes and implements, but everything is labelled in Fārsī. Open from 9 am to 6 pm Tuesday to

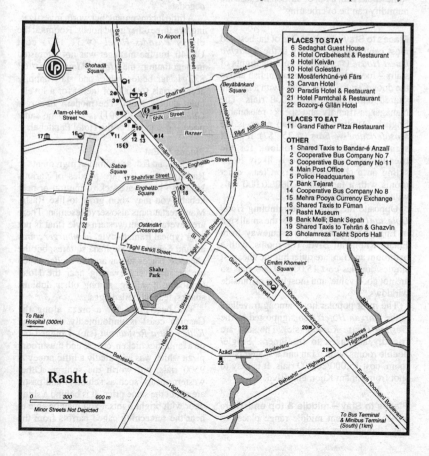

PLACES TO STAY
6 Sedaghat Guest House
8 Hotel Ordibehesht & Restaurant
9 Hotel Keivān
10 Hotel Golestān
12 Mosāferkhūné-yé Fārs
13 Carvan Hotel
20 Paradis Hotel & Restaurant
21 Hotel Pamtchal & Restaurant
22 Bozorg-é Gīlān Hotel

PLACES TO EAT
11 Grand Father Pitza Restaurant

OTHER
1 Shared Taxis to Bandar-é Anzalī
2 Cooperative Bus Company No 7
3 Cooperative Bus Company No 11
4 Main Post Office
5 Police Headquarters
7 Bank Tejarat
14 Cooperative Bus Company No 8
15 Mehra Pooya Currency Exchange
16 Shared Taxis to Fūman
17 Rasht Museum
18 Bank Melli; Bank Sepah
19 Shared Taxis to Tehrān & Ghazvīn
23 Gholamreza Takht Sports Hall

Rasht

0   300   600 m

Minor Streets Not Depicted

Sunday, the museum is not signed in English, but it, well, looks like a museum anyway – look for the largish building behind an iron fence. The entrance fee is 10,000 rials.

Places to Stay

The greatest concentration of budget accommodation is around the bazaar district, which is the most convenient – but noisiest – place to stay. However, some places will not take foreigners, and you may have a little trouble finding somewhere cheap in the peak season (May-September). In summer you must find somewhere with a fan or air-con because the humidity can be overbearing.

Places to Stay – budget One of the best and most central places to stay is the *Sedaghat Guest House* (☎ 46 088), up four flights of stairs – look for a tiny sign in English above the door. Clean double rooms with a fan and shared bathroom cost 15,000 rials. The manager is friendly and speaks reasonable English. Another good cheap place is the *Mosāferkhūné-yé Fārs* (☎ 25 257). It is not signposted in English, so look for the friendly old manager who is likely to be sitting on a chair downstairs. Clean, quiet rooms with a fan cost 15,000/20,000 rials without/with a bathroom.

Opposite the Fārs is the rambling *Hotel Golestān* (☎ 29 131) – look for the small sign in English pointing down a laneway from Emām Khomeinī Blvd. The rooms, with a bathroom and fan, are quiet but the cheapest singles/doubles cost 15,000/20,000 rials so are not good value, and most have no outside windows.

The most popular hotel among travellers is the *Carvan Hotel*, also signposted as the *Gesting House Karvan* (sic). The staff are friendly and used to foreigners. Single/double rooms, with a fan and a shared bathroom, cost 15,000/20,000 rials. It is easy to spot from Emām Khomeinī Blvd.

Places to Stay – middle & top end There are several decent middle range places to stay, though the 'foreigners' prices' they charge are less negotiable in the busier summer period.

Many foreigners end up at the *Hotel Ordibehesht* (☎ 22 210), on Shahrdārī Square immediately to the west of Shohadā Square. Very convenient if you arrive in town by shared taxi and only too visible from the main square, this monstrous tower block isn't half bad. Large and clean air-con singles/doubles with, of all things, a bidet, cost 60,000/90,000 rials. A similar standard is available at the *Hotel Keivān*, but the rooms are noisier and the staff are not quite so friendly, though the prices are easier to negotiate.

A little inconvenient, but worth investigating, are three other good hotels. Rooms at the classy *Paradis Hotel* (☎ 31 177) cost US$40, but the manager was not interested in negotiating; the *Hotel Pamtchal* (☎ 63 822) is far better value, and staff happily accepts rials (60,000 of them) for a lovely, quiet double room. The modern *Bozorg-é Gīlān Hotel* (☎ 30 991) is about the same price and standard as the Hotel Pamtchal.

Places to Eat

Chicken and fish are common ingredients in Rashtī cooking, as are pickles of various kinds, so if you are sick of mutton or beef kebabs you may soon grow to like Rasht. Many restaurants also serve fesenjān. There are several decent western-style (that is not your typical Iranian-style) *hamburger joints* around Sabze and Shohadā squares, but the cheapest places to eat are the *stalls*, which are set up every evening near the Hotel Ordibehesht selling, among other dubious snacks, tea and boiled eggs.

The best place for a pizza along the Caspian coast is undoubtedly the *Grand Father Pitza Restaurant* (sic). I pigged out on a fantastic chicken, cheese and mushroom pizza which was admittedly a little pricey at 9500 rials, but worth the splurge. Other western meals, such as schnitzel and pasta, are about the same price. It is behind a shiny door with bright lights. (You may be able to hear the screeching caged parrots from the street.)

Of the hotels, the *Paradis Hotel* has an elegant restaurant, and the *Hotel Pamtchal* is worth the short shared taxi ride from the town centre. The best place in town is in the *Hotel Ordibehesht*; open for lunch, and dinner (from 8 pm). Schnitzels cost 10,300 rials and chicken kebabs are very good value at 7800 rials. You pay an extra 15% for service, but it's worth it. You get mayonnaise for your salad, a bucket of ice for your soft drink and – heaven! – crispy, fresh French-style bread.

Getting There & Away

Air Iran Air (☎ 22 444) currently flies from Rasht to Tehrān every day (40,000 rials), which is a worthy alternative to the bus; to Mashhad (75,000 rials) on Tuesday and Saturday; to Bandar-é Abbās on the same days (109,000 rials; but this flight is likely to be cancelled soon); and to Tabrīz on Saturday for a bargain 40,000 rials.

The Iran Air office is in the suburb of Shahrak-é Golsār, a little north of the city centre. Take a shared taxi from Shohadā Square to 'Golsār' (250 rials), and look for the well-signed building on the left-hand side of the main road. The airport is a short distance north of Rasht on the road to Bandar-é Anzalī.

Bus The bus terminal is a little way out of town, so take a shared taxi from outside the Hotel Keivān, heading south along Emām Khomeinī Blvd. You can buy tickets at one of several bus companies in the centre of town; one of the best to check out is the Cooperative Bus Company No 7 (☎ 22 599).

Among other places, there are several buses (with prices for lux/super class) every day to:

Destination	Distance	Time	Cost (rials)
Esfahān	737km	12 hours	7900/9500
Ghazvīn – take the Tehrān bus and pay the full fare
Gorgān	511km	9 hours	6200/7300
Mashhad	1075km	18 hours	13,100/15,500
Sārī	380km	7 hours	5100/5600
Tabrīz	481km	9 hours	6100/6750
Tehrān	324km	6 hours	4900/5600

To get to places east of Rāmsar, take a bus to Sārī, Gorgān or Mashhad and ask to be dropped off along on the way.

Minibus The two minibus terminals are in the outer suburbs. Minibuses leave from near the main bus terminal, every 15 to 20 minutes to places as far east as Chālūs (2500 rials). Minibuses to Bandar-é Anzalī (about 1200 rials) and Āstārā (about 2800 rials) leave from the small Īstgāh-é Anzalī – to get there take a shared taxi from Shohadā Square.

Shared Taxi The location of the terminals for the shared taxis is confusing. Those going to Rāmsar (5000 rials) have no particular departure point, but generally leave from around Shohadā Square; those to Fūman (for a connection to Māsūlé) from Sabze Square; and those to Bandar-é Anzalī (2000 rials) leave from around the post office at Shohadā Square. Shared taxis to Tehrān (about 15,000 rials) and Ghazvīn (6000 rials) depart from outside the Hotel Ordibehesht and a spot along Emām Khomeinī Blvd (indicated on the map). To get to other destinations, try the Īstgāh-é Anzalī.

Getting Around

To/From the Airport There's no airport bus service. Count on around 3000 rials for a chartered taxi or ask around for a shared taxi at Shohadā Square.

Taxi Hundreds of shared and private taxis congregate around Shohadā Square and go up and down the main roads for 250 to 500 rials per trip.

AROUND RASHT

If the hustle and bustle and the heat and humidity of Rasht is getting you down, then head into the countryside and up to the hills for some cooler weather and fantastic hikes.

Māsūlé ماسوله

There are many traditional and unspoilt mountain villages throughout Gīlan province, but one of the most breathtakingly beautiful is Māsūlé, which is a cool 1050m above sea level. This perfectly preserved village appears to have grown out of its surroundings, like a limpet clinging to a rock. It's formed by several irregular levels of terraced, pale cream houses with grey slate roofs, interspersed with evergreen trees. So steep is the slope that the familiar Iranian network of narrow alleys is entirely absent, and instead the flat roofs of many houses form a pathway for the level above.

Māsūlé has few facilities to offer the visitor, but its inspiring setting makes it a perfect antidote to travel in the dry and dusty central plateau, and it's well worth a day trip from Rasht. It's bitterly cold in winter, with snow sometimes 3m deep, but the climate in summer is extremely pleasant and bracing. There are no established **hiking trails**, so just head up the valley or anywhere else you want. A local guide may want to show you around for a negotiable fee, but it's not necessary; just wander around at your leisure.

Places to Stay & Eat Currently the only place to stay is the *Monfared Masooleh Hotel* (☎ (01864) 3250), easy to spot, next to the main bus and taxi stop. Though overpriced at 50,000 rials for a double, the setting in this gorgeous little village is worth a splurge. It boasts a stupendous rooftop *restaurant*, with some of the best views in the country. A cooked breakfast costs 2500 rials.

If you ask around the village, you may be able to get a *room* in a local home, with your own kitchen and bathroom, for as little as 15,000 rials for a double. Prices are likely to go up in the future, but a room in a local home should be less than the hotel, and certainly more cosy.

This area is probably one of the nicest places to *camp* in the country, and there is nothing to stop you pitching a tent anywhere you want near the village. At the time of research some *cabins* were being built, about 5km before the end of the road to Māsūlé. Other hotels (probably upmarket ones) and restaurants are likely to be built in Māsūlé in the future, which may spoil the tranquillity of the village.

Getting There & Away Getting to Māsūlé from Rasht (56km away) is a little complicated, but well worth the effort. Allow most of the day for a trip there and back. Firstly, take a shared taxi (1500 rials) to Fūman, a surprisingly large and pleasant junction town worth exploring. (According to a large sign in the town centre, Fūman is famous for the 'Fouman Traditional Cookie'. Let us know if you taste one.) From Fūman, take another shared taxi (about 1000 rials) or minibus (800 rials) past stunning rice paddies, tea plantations and dense forest to Māsūlé. You will need to ask in Fūman where the transport to Māsūlé or Rasht departs.

Alternatively, it is worth chartering a taxi between Rasht and Māsūlé to allow a leisurely drive and stops for photos. The trip should cost about 15,000 rials return, plus waiting time.

Bandar-é Anzalī   بندرانزلی

This town came into prominence in the early 19th century as a result of the increasing Russian dominance over trade in the Caspian Sea. When traders from western Europe were most active in the region, the river port of Langarūd, 96km to the east, was the main outlet to northern Persia. Around 1800 the Russians established their trading post at Bandar-é Anzalī, taking advantage of its unrivalled natural harbour. Since then it has been the only major port along the southern Caspian coast, and today is the only one actively trading with the former Soviet states. The Russian influence over Anzalī has been strong, and the city bears a remarkable physical likeness to the Azerbaijani port of Baku, its main trading partner in the northern Caspian Sea.

Orientation & Information Bandar-é Anzalī is divided in two by the outlet of the Anzalī Lagoon; two bridges connect the town to the small and undeveloped Beheshtī Island, just inside the mouth of the lagoon. The docks and Customs House are on Gomrok Square, but the main commercial centre is around Emām Khomeinī Square, past the second bridge as you approach from Rasht.

A wide and often windswept promenade lies along the west bank, facing the harbour; from there you can organise boat trips into the lagoon. Bank Melli and Bank Sepah, both on Emām Khomeinī Square, will change money.

Things to See Anzalī has a major **caviar-processing factory** (though it's difficult to buy the stuff in town), managed by the state-run Iranian Fishing Company. The public is not currently allowed to visit the factory. (The secret process of caviar production is a serious and very competitive business, earning the country millions of dollars.)

There are some crumbling old **ruins** from the 19th century, very Russian in character, around Emām Khomeinī Square, and the daily **Shanbeh bazaar** is particularly busy on Saturday. Anzalī is the only Iranian Caspian port with a real promenade, and it's worth spending a few hours wandering around and soaking up a bit of Iranian seaside *joie de vivre*.

Anzalī Lagoon If you have your own vehicle, and are a keen bird-watcher, you may wish to head south to the 450 sq km Anzalī Lagoon. You will need to ask directions, or hire a guide in Anzalī or Rasht, to find the road to the lagoon and the best places to spot migratory waterbirds, such as the glossy ibis. A better option is to hire a boat from the promenade in Anzalī.

Places to Stay & Eat The only budget place to stay is the *Tehrān Hotel*, a charming place upstairs on Emām Khomeinī Square. However, the manager refused to offer me a room – maybe you will have better luck.

The *Hotel Iran* (☎ (0181) 22 524), just east of Emām Khomeinī Square, is comfortable but overpriced for foreigners at 90,000 rials per room. It is often full of Iranians paying a fraction of this. It boasts a very good restaurant.

Around Emām Khomeinī Square there are several quality *snack bars* and upmarket *restaurants* serving western-style food, but fish is a surprisingly rare item on menus.

Getting There & Away Shared taxis leave for Rasht (2000 rials, about one hour) from Emām Khomeinī Square. Regular minibuses and shared taxis to Āstārā depart from the junction heading north from near the second bridge as you come from Rasht. To get to most other places you are better off going to Rasht and getting a connection there. There are a couple of bus companies, which have offices on Emām Khomeinī Square, with services to Āstārā, Tehrān, Ardabīl and Tabrīz.

Sea The Sea section in the Getting There & Away chapter has information about occasional passenger-cum-cargo boats between Anzalī and Baku, the capital of the republic of Azerbaijan.

Lāhījūn لاهيجان

Lāhījūn, on the road between Rāmsar and Rasht, is a small town which tends to be a bottleneck for traffic. There are plenty of old **traditional Caspian houses** with sloping, channelled brick roofs and walls of pastel shades such as violet. Most of these old houses are being superceded by modern houses of metal, plastic and cement.

Lāhījūn was once the only settlement of any size in Gīlān, but it fell into decline after the 14th century, when Rasht grew into a town and eclipsed it. It does attract some tourists, but its main claim to fame is the tea grown in the region.

Masjed-é Chahār Ōleyā' The Mosque of the Four Guardians is on Sardār Jangal Square, in the west of Lāhījūn. This mausoleum, probably dating from the 13th century, is dedicated to four members of the Sādāt-é Keyā family, though there are only tombs visible for the first three. You can see some excellent examples of wood carving inside the mausoleum. One of its carved wooden doors, among the finest surviving examples of its kind, is in the National Museum of Iran in Tehrān.

Bogh'é-yé Sheikh Zāhed A short distance east of Lāhījūn, along the road to Langarūd, is this historic and typically Caspian mausoleum. The square building has a tiled roof surmounted by a sculpted pyramid-shaped, painted roof, supported by white pillars on three sides. The inner vault is covered with colourfully tiled plaster mouldings and contains the tombs of Sheikh Zāhed and two other religious figures, Sayyed Rezā Keyā and Gholām Sheikh. The date on the carved wooden tomb of Sheikh Zāhed corresponds to 1419, though part of the original structure may have been built before this date.

Sheitān Kūh Sheitān Kūh – literally Devil Mountain – is a tree-covered hill south of the eastern approach to Lāhījūn, with a natural pool and large park on its slopes. If you have the urge, there are plenty of forested hills for **hiking** in, around the eastern part of town.

Places to Stay & Eat There is no need to stay because it's a fairly unexciting town, and it's an easy day trip from Rasht. The only hotel is the pleasant *Chaharfasi Guest House*, named in English and on Shohadā Square – the main square with the unimpressive, oversized pot plant in the middle. Rooms cost a negotiable 15,000 rials, and are clean and comfortable, but noisy. There are quite a few *hamburger joints* and *kabābīs* along the main streets.

Getting There & Away Several bus companies have offices around Shohadā Square. Buses from other towns, such as Rasht, Sārī and Gorgān, also stop for passengers at Lāhījūn. Alternatively, you can easily catch a shared taxi to regional towns east or west along the main coast road, from the same square.

ĀSTĀRĀ آستارا

This small town, in the far north of Gīlān, is on the border, which divides it from the town of Astara in the republic of Azerbaijan. This is currently the only reliable and safe road crossing between Iran and its northern neighbour. Although devoid of any great historical interest, Āstārā is not unattractive, and there are worse places to spend the night; however,

if you've come into Iran from Azerbaijan, it's better to keep heading towards Rasht or Ardabīl. If you have some time to kill, you can visit the nearby **Abbās Ābād** gardens.

Places to Stay & Eat

There are a few mosāferkhūnés around Shahrdārī Square, but some may not take foreigners; if they do, they charge about 15,000 rials for a basic room. The best of the lot is the *Hotel Aras*. The recognised 'tourist hotel' is the lovely, two star *Āstārā Guest House* (☎ (01854) 6063), which is set in a pretty garden, only a few metres from the Azerbaijan border. It charges US$40 for a double, and like most ITTO places you won't have much luck negotiating a reasonable price. There are a few *kabābīs* around Shahrdārī Sq, but the best place to eat in town is the *restaurant* at the Āstārā Guest House.

Getting There & Away

Every hour, shared taxis and minibuses head towards Rasht, Bandar-é Anzalī and Ardabīl, from where you can get onward connections – but you will have to charter a private taxi to take you to the right taxi/minibus terminal in Āstārā. An alternative way to get to Rasht, Bandar-é Anzalī or Ardabīl is take a private taxi to the main road (3km from the town) and wave down any transport going your way.

See the Getting There & Away chapter for information about crossing the border into Azerbaijan.

Māzandarān Province
استان مازندران

- **Capital:** Sārī
- **Area:** 46,456 sq km
- **Population:** approx 4.5 million

The largely rural province of Māzandarān stretches from the eastern border of Gīlān to the frontiers of Khorāsān province and the republic of Turkmenistan in the north-west,

The New Gorgān Province
At the time of research, the *Majlis* (parliament) seemed likely to approve the formation of the Gorgān province out of the existing province of Māzandarān. The new province will cover the cities of Gombad-é Kāvūs and Bandar-é Torkamān, among others, and the capital will, naturally, be Gorgān. No other details are available. The creation of this province will not affect travel to this part of Iran in any way, but most maps will be slightly out of date for a while. ■

and is flanked to the south by the provinces of Zanjān, Semnān and Tehrān.

The coastal strip, from the western border with Gīlān to the Bay of Gorgān, at the far east of the southern Caspian littoral, is fairly similar to Gīlān in its climate and terrain, though slightly drier. At its narrowest and most attractive point, roughly between Rāmsar and Sīsangān, the thickly forested northern slopes of the Alborz Mountains roll almost to the sea. In the north-east, the forest is less dense and the peaks are lower than further west.

To the north, the province is largely inhospitable steppe and marshland. The Torkaman Sahrā – the harsh Turkmen desert – occupies the strip south of the Atrak River, which forms a section of the border with Turkmenistan. The more fertile Dasht-é Gorgān (Gorgān plain), between the desert and the mountains, formed, until recently, the boundary between the settled and nomadic populations. The population is largely Turkmen, and the threat posed to the settled communities by this previously wild and nomadic tribe only receded at the end of the last century. Māzandarān was settled earlier than Gīlān, and the Gorgān plain in particular is believed to contain some of the most important archaeological sites in west Asia.

The main tourist area in Māzandarān is the coastal strip between Rāmsar and Bābolsar, where facilities are well developed by Iranian standards. While development remains unmitigated in the western part of

the province, there are pockets of lovely forest in the east with places to stay and go hiking.

SĀRĪ
ساری

Sārī is not an unattractive city – it has a few *emāmzādés* (mausoleums) and some typical Māzandarānī houses with sloping timber roofs to admire. Sārī is much smaller and less developed than Rasht and attracts far fewer Iranian holidaymakers, but it does retain a certain charm that is fast disappearing with the development of the Caspian coast. It makes a reasonable stopover between Gorgān and Chālūs or Rāmsar, or a good base to explore some nearby towns (see Around Sārī later in this section), but the main disincentive is the lack of decent accommodation.

History
The origins of Sārī are lost in the mists of antiquity, but it is known to have been the first capital of the province (then known as Tabarestān) perhaps from as early as the Sassanian period (224-637) until the 8th or 9th century. This was the last part of Iran to yield to Islam following the Arab Conquest (637-1050). Some centuries after the capital was moved to Āmol, Sārī was sacked, first by the Mongols and later by Timur. In 1937, Sārī once again became the provincial capital.

Orientation
The main square is the small Haft-é Tīr Square, commonly known as Meidūn-é Sā'at (Clock Square) because of the public clock in the centre – a rare landmark in Iran (even if the clock has no hands). The bazaar, the old part of Sārī and most other points of interest are within walking distance of this square. Sārī is one of the few places in Iran where streets are not signed in English so getting around can be a little confusing.

Maps The red Gita Shenasi map of Sārī (1500 rials) is reasonably detailed but has very little practical information in English; it's also very difficult to find, especially in Sārī. The bookshops and magazine stalls along Enghelāb and Jomhūrī-yé Eslāmī Sts may have a copy gathering dust somewhere.

Information

Visa Extensions I tried to renew my visa at the visa office in Sārī, but after the officer looked at me and my passport for 45 minutes he decided it was all too hard, and suggested I go elsewhere. Try in Tehrān.

Money The central branch of the Bank Melli is also unexcited about dealing with nuisance foreigners. It's best to change your money elsewhere.

Post & Communications The main post office is 500m north-west of Shohadā Square, and the main telephone office is 400m south of Clock Square. The telephone area code for Sārī is 02431.

Emergency For emergencies, dial the general directories number (☎ 118) or try the special emergencies number (☎ 2031). The main hospital (☎ 3456) is near the train station. The police headquarters (☎ 3020) is just past Emām Khomeinī Square.

Emāmzādé-yé Yahyā

Yahyā's mausoleum, which was built in the 15th century, is inside the bazaar district in a small square. This simple circular building with its tiled pyramid-shaped roof is highly regarded for its original wooden doors and tomb box. You can go inside normally only on Thursday afternoon and Friday, but if you ask around on other days someone may let you in. The laneway leading to this and the Borj-é (see following entry) is directly opposite the Hotel Nader.

Borj-é Soltãn Zein-ol-Ābedīn

A few metres west of Yahyā's mausoleum, this early 15th century small, square brick tomb tower has a lower roof leading up to a tiled octagonal dome. Apart from some

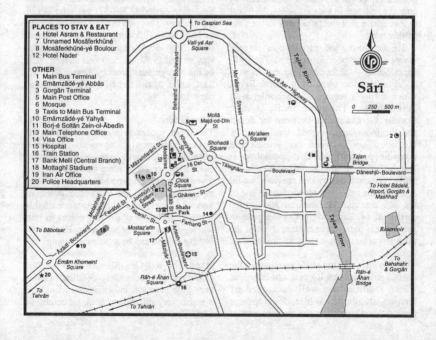

PLACES TO STAY & EAT
4 Hotel Asram & Restaurant
7 Unnamed Mosāferkhūné
8 Mosāferkhūné-yé Boulour
12 Hotel Nader

OTHER
1 Main Bus Terminal
2 Emāmzādé-yé Abbās
3 Gorgān Terminal
5 Main Post Office
6 Mosque
9 Taxis to Main Bus Terminal
10 Emāmzādé-yé Yahyā
11 Borj-é Soltān Zein-ol-Ābedīn
13 Main Telephone Office
14 Visa Office
15 Hospital
16 Train Station
17 Bank Melli (Central Branch)
18 Mottaghī Stadium
19 Iran Air Office
20 Police Headquarters

Sārī

plain, arched brick friezes below the lower and upper roof levels, the exterior is unadorned. The main interest lies inside the building, but unfortunately the heavy wooden door is almost permanently locked. If you have luck getting into Yahyā's mausoleum, ask to have a look inside this tower too.

Emāmzādé-yé Abbās

The largest of the historical mausoleums in Sārī, the Emāmzādé-yé Abbās is about 300m east of the Tajan River – take a shared taxi from Clock Square. This brick tower features a conical dome and has only simple exterior decorations. It is attached to a low rectangular modern annexe. According to the date on the tomb, which Abbās shares with two others, the wooden box was carved in 1491.

Places to Stay

If you have a vehicle, or despair of the choice in Sārī itself, the best place to stay is *Hotel Bādelé* (☎ 3128), 10km from Sārī on the road to Gorgān. More of a motel than a hotel, this place is very busy in the holiday season. It costs US$25/35 for a single/double, but staff will take rials if business is slow. Getting from the hotel into town by shared taxi is easy enough: just stand opposite the hotel and flag one down.

In Sārī, there are a handful of cheap hotels in the centre of town, all of them far from luxurious but adequate for one night. The *Hotel Nader* (☎ 2357) is 200m south-west of Clock Square; look for the four storey place with the word 'Nader' on top. They charge a negotiable 10,000/15,000 rials for a noisy but reasonably clean single/double room. The best value place in town is the *unnamed mosāferkhūné* (well, it doesn't have a name). Dorm beds cost 4000 rials per person; a quiet triple with a fan costs a very reasonable 12,000 rials. It isn't signposted in any language; it's on the corner of a laneway off Khayyām St.

The *Mosāferkhūné-yé Boulour* is a very noisy option, right on Clock Square. The rooms are clean but overpriced at 15,000 rials, and the fans may not always work. The place is not signed in English, but is not hard

to find – it's upstairs at the beginning of Modarres St.

The only top-end place is the *Hotel Asram*, convenient to the bus terminal but nothing else. It is large, modern and has a good restaurant, but the rooms are expensive at the 'foreigners' price' of US$35/45 for singles/ doubles.

Places to Eat

If you think the choice of hotels is poor, good luck trying to find somewhere decent to eat. The *Hotel Bādelé* has a reasonable restaurant and is worth a shared taxi ride out there if you are staying in Sārī. There are no decent restaurants in Sārī, so you will have to make do with the *snack bars* and *kabābīs* around Clock Square.

Getting There & Away

Air Sārī is a stopover on the Saturday, Tuesday and Thursday flights between Tehrān (40,000 rials) and Mashhad (53,000 rials). But if you are going to or from Mashhad, and have the time, the scenery is good enough to justify a long bus ride. The Iran Air office (☎ 90 921) is on the way to Emām Khomeinī Square from the town centre.

Bus & Minibus The main bus terminal is on the ring road, near the west bank of the river. Shared taxis out there are easy to find from Clock Square. Touts will show you where to buy your ticket.

Among other places, several buses (with prices for lux/super class) leave Sārī every day to: Ardabīl (645km, 11 hours, 8900/9900 rials); Mashhad (695km, 12 hours, 12,000/ 13,500 rials); Rasht (380km, seven hours, 5100/5600 rials); and Tehrān (250km, five hours, 3800/4200 rials).

There are also minibuses, from the special Gorgān terminal, to Gorgān (2100 rials), Bābol (1200 rials) and other local destinations. The Gorgān terminal can be reached by shared taxi from Clock Square. To get to Rasht, take a minibus to Rāmsar and change there; to Chālūs, take a minibus to Bābol first.

Train Trains to Tehrān leave on Thursday, Friday and Sunday at 9.30 pm (3950/11,500 rials for 2nd/1st class). A train to Gorgān (three hours), via Behshahr and Bandar-é Torkamān, leaves Sārī every day at 2.30 pm, only 2nd-class tickets (1000 rials) are available – and the train is often very full. Try getting a 1st class ticket on the direct Tehrān-Gorgān train.

The train station (☎ 21 082) is about 1km south of Clock Square. It is easy to reach on foot or by shared taxi.

Shared Taxi The quickest way from Sārī to Gorgān, and any place in between, is by shared taxi (5000 rials). They leave about every 15 minutes or so from outside the Gorgān terminal. Shared taxis from the stand in the Eastern bus terminal in Tehrān go all the way to Sārī (about 15,000 rials), or you can get a connection in Āmol.

Chartered Taxi If you are sick of the unrelenting urban sprawl along the main Caspian road, you will be pleased to know that the Sārī to Gorgān road is still pretty, flanked by sunflower plantations, rice paddies and stunning mountains. It is worth chartering a taxi to properly enjoy the scenery. Expect to pay about 25,000 rials between Sārī and Gorgān if you bargain hard.

Getting Around
Shared taxis around Sārī are some of the cheapest in the country; it currently costs 100 rials between Clock Square and the train station. But Sārī is small enough to walk around anyway.

To/From the Airport The airport is 15km from Sārī, off the main road to Gorgān. You will probably have to charter a taxi there for about 5000 rials. From the airport, jump on anything heading into town.

AROUND SĀRĪ
Āmol   آمل
Āmol succeeded Sārī as the capital of the former region of Tabarestān in the 9th century, and became renowned for a distinc-

tive style of glazed earthenware pottery which reached its peak between the 10th and 13th centuries. After the devastation of the Mongol invasions (1220-1380), Āmol reverted to relative obscurity. In 1888, Edward Browne described it as 'one of the chief cities of Māzandarān, a picturesque straggling town divided into two parts by a large river, which is spanned by a long narrow bridge built of bricks'. Sadly, the town is no longer of any great beauty.

You will normally bypass Āmol when travelling between Chālūs and Sārī, but Āmol is the best place to look for transport to mighty **Mt Damāvand** if you are keen to climb it from the northern side. (See Trekking in Iran in Facts for the Visitor for details.) There is no place to stay in Āmol, so you must take a day trip from Sārī.

Mashhad-é Mīr Bozorg This mausoleum, built during the reign of Shāh Abbās I, is the most interesting sight in Āmol. With its huge dome and brick construction, tiles dating from the Safavid period (1502-1722) and restored tomb box (dated 1623), this sanctuary of the martyred Mīr Bozorg lies a short distance north of Āmol on the west bank of the river.

Getting There & Away There are four main roads out of Āmol, all served by regular shared taxis; and Āmol is a junction for regional transport to and from Tehrān. The north road takes you to the small coastal town of Mahmūd Ābād (20km); the east to Bābol (29km); the south to Tehrān (174km); and the west to Nūr (45km), where you can get connections to Nōshahr and Chālūs. From Tehrān, shared taxis (about 15,000 rials) and minibuses (3000 rials) leave from the Eastern bus terminal.

Bābolsar   بابلسر
The port of Bābolsar was at one time the province's main international trading outlet, and more recently it was established as a fashionable resort town with a luxury seaside hotel complex. Nowadays the dock is dry, tourism is virtually nonexistent and Bābolsar

is no longer an inspiring place, though Iranian tourists still go there. If you can't get enough of mausoleums, ask for directions to the **Emāmzādé-yé Ibrahim**, dating back to at least the early 15th century. The telephone area code is 01291.

Beach The main part of the town is 4km inland, and the walk between it and the coast is lonely and disappointing. The beach area isn't inspiring, consisting of a dead-end road looking out over a short and usually deserted stretch of sand, with a small children's playground at the junction of the road back into the centre. To experience the excitement of the beach, you can take a shared taxi northeast from the main square in Bābolsar.

Places to Stay & Eat There's a good modern hotel, *Hotel Michka* (☎ 24 656), along the dead-end road opposite the beach, unusually built in the style of a Mediterranean villa. It charges about 40,000 rials a room, but you'll need to bargain hard. The *restaurant* in the Hotel Michka is good but quite expensive. Otherwise try a few of the *fish restaurants* along the beach, or, as a last resort, the *kabābīs* in town.

Getting There & Away Bābolsar is linked by frequent shared taxis to Bābol (1000 rials), from where you can get onward connections.

Bābol بابل
Founded in the early 16th century, on the main east-west route through the Caspian provinces, Bābol was once a busy and pleasant river port with its harbour at Bābolsar. Nowadays it's a sprawling, drab commercial centre and transport junction, with only a few isolated ancient buildings. If you have some time up your sleeve, a walk along the **river** is a pleasant diversion, and boats are available for hire at very negotiable prices (if you're lucky enough to find the owners).

Maghbaré-yé Soltān Mohammad Tāher
This late 15th century tomb tower stands in an old cemetery in the village of Soltān

---

Iranian Tea
Arguably Iran's best and most famous *chāy* (tea) comes from around Lāhijūn, in Gīlān province. More than 90% of the tea grown in Iran comes from Gīlān province, for a total output of about 60,000 tonnes per year. Even so, this is not enough to meet the demands of tea-loving Iranians.

The Indians and Chinese were busy cultivating and enjoying the tea leaf centuries ago, but tea did not reach Persia until the 17th century, and then it was only available among the Persian elite, through the limited influence of the Russians.

During the Ghajar period, initial attempts to grow tea in Persia failed through a lack of expertise. In about 1900, an Iranian consul living in India somehow learnt the secret art of tea manufacturing and brought home 4000 saplings of the tea plant. (A mausoleum for the consul has been built near Lāhijūn.)

The climate of the Gīlān and Māzandarān provinces, squeezed between the Caspian Sea and the mountains, is ideal for growing tea. You will see plenty of plantations along the main road between Rasht and Gorgān. ■

Mohammad Tāher, 4km from Bābol on a road to the east (but not on the main road to Ghā'emshahr). The exterior features a simple arched frieze beneath its polygonal tiled dome, shallow arched recesses on each outer wall and a tall narrow portal over the original carved wooden door. The carved wooden tomb box (from 1470) remains inside the mausoleum.

Getting There & Away Shared taxis and minibuses for Chālūs (128km, two hours, 1200 rials) and Ghā'emshahr (20km, 15 minutes, 900 rials) leave from the Chālūs terminal in the far western part of Bābol. From that terminal, you can also get immediate connections by shared taxi and bus to Sārī. To Rasht and Tehrān, you are better off going to Āmol and finding a connection.

RĀMSAR رامسر
Since the mountains stop only a few hundred metres short of the coast at this point, Rāmsar is squeezed into little more than a couple of

main streets, which has helped to make this one of the more attractive seaside resorts. The last shāh built a palace in the thickly wooded hills overlooking Rāmsar; and who could blame him, for the setting is one of best anywhere along the Caspian coast.

There isn't much in the way of activities here, nor is there much of historical or architectural interest, but the scenery is enough for most visitors – even if unrestrained development has spoilt a lot of the area. The people here are very friendly and like to see foreigners, bringing back memories of the boom years before the Islamic Revolution.

Orientation & Information

Rāmsar stretches many kilometres along the coast and a few blocks either side of the coast road. The main street through Rāmsar is Motahharī St, but a lot of traffic bypasses the town and travels along the main road closer to the beach. The telephone area code for Rāmsar is 01942.

Beach

If you have spent some time in the hot and barren deserts of Iran and Pakistan, this beach will do nothing but disappoint. The main road from near the Iran Asseman office leads to a dirty gravel beach with a few empty cafés, and some horses for hire nearby. Some cabins were being built at the time of research, presumably waiting for a tourist rush. The official, and slightly better, beach – with separate swimming spots for men and women – is a little further east, down the road heading north from the Rāmsar Grand Hotel.

Mūzé-yé Kākh-é Shāh

The front gate of the Shāh's Palace Museum, next to the Rāmsar Grand Hotel, was heavily locked at the time of research, and no-one could say if, or when, the museum or gardens would reopen. It is worth asking because the grounds, and views from them, look very inviting.

Places to Stay

Accommodation isn't terribly cheap, but you do have the option of staying at a 'suite', a furnished apartment; or a 'homestay' (both words are part of the local vernacular) – a room at the home of a friendly local. For the latter, either ask at the snack bars near the Iran Asseman office, or just look lost for a

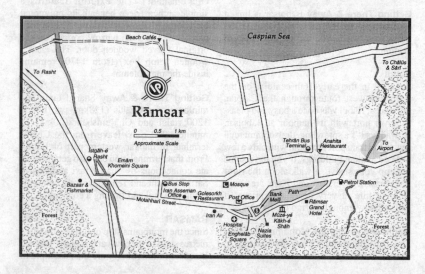

few minutes – someone will offer you something soon enough. I paid 20,000 rials (of which the tout who led me there pocketed 5000 rials commission) for a double room in a home a few minutes from the beach. Other offers came later for as little as 10,000 rials for a double, but the quality will vary, and be careful you don't end up in a remote part of town.

The best place to head for is the huddle of 'suites' known collectively as *Nazia Suites*, not far from the Grand Hotel. The first place (☎ 6600) you see as you enter from the road costs a reasonable 30,000 rials for an apartment with two beds, kitchen, fridge, TV, sitting room and bathroom. Next door, another place (☎ 4588) has sumptuous apartments, with everything but a bar, for 50,000 rials a night; the price is cheaper per night for longer stays.

The grand four-star *Rāmsar Grand Hotel* (☎ 3592) is set on a splendid hillside, overlooking the whole town. Although not in the same class as the Caspian Enghelāb Hotel near Chālūs, it's very comfortable and probably had the best view of any hotel in the Caspian provinces until construction of some huge concrete apartments started nearby. Comfortable rooms in the new annexe cost US$40/55/65 for a single/double/triple, while a single/double in the more atmospheric older wing costs US$40/60. Add 17% tax; prices are not negotiable.

Places to Eat
There are several very reasonable *kabābīs* and *hamburger joints* along Motahharī St, mainly catering for passing traffic. The *Golesorkh Restaurant* is about the best; it can even manage a menu in English (but without prices, so check before you order). Prices can reach 11,000 rials per dish, which is too high; try the tasty chelō morgh for 7700 rials. The Anahita Restaurant is also worth trying.

The menu in the *Shaghayegh Restaurant* in the Rāmsar Grand Hotel is also in English (well, sort of). Prices are high, as you would expect – mostly from about 14,000 to 19,500 rials a dish, plus 15% tax. But they do serve

a 'spaketi with bolonez sauce' (I think I know what they mean) for 8000 rials. If that is still too much, try a tea or coffee in the sumptuous lounge area just for the experience.

Getting There & Away
Air Although Iran Air (☎ 2788) doesn't fly to or from Rāmsar, it does have a small office along the main street in town. Staff are helpful, perhaps because they don't have many customers. The nearest Iran Air flights are from Sārī and Rasht.

Iran Asseman (☎ 4525) also has an office on the main street, and it has flights between Tehrān and Rāmsar (40,000 rials) on Tuesday and Friday.

Bus & Minibus About 200m north of the bazaar, on the east side of the road, the Īstgāh-é Rasht (Rasht terminal) has frequent minibuses and shared taxis to Rasht and Chālūs; and less frequent services to Lāhījūn.

To get to Chālūs, Sārī and Gorgān, you can also catch any bus going through Rāmsar – it is important to note that most public transport does not go along Motahharī St, but detours at the western entrance to Rāmsar and hurtles along the main street closer to the beach. Just stand at the unofficial bus stop, indicated on the map, and flag down something going your way.

To add to the confusion, direct buses to Tehrān (5700/6100 rials for lux/super class) leave from a small terminal a few hundred metres below (north) the Grand Hotel.

Shared Taxi As with most of the region, the shared taxi is the quickest but not the cheapest way to travel. To get to Rasht (5000 rials), take a shared taxi from the Rasht terminal. To get to Chālūs, ask around at the Bank Melli in the centre of town or flag something going along the northern main road – but not along Motahharī St.

Getting Around
Getting around town is easy: just hail a taxi and say *mostaghīm* (straight ahead). They all travel between the Rasht terminal and Bank

Melli, and down the two main roads to the beach, for 250 rials a trip. Or just walk.

To/From the Airport The airport is about 2km from Rāmsar, on the way to Chālūs. You should be able to get into town from the airport in a shared taxi for not much more than 500 rials, but you'll probably need to charter one to get to the airport from Rāmsar (about 1500 rials).

AROUND RĀMSAR
Bahim Ābād   بهیم‌آباد
There isn't a whole lot to do in the region around Rāmsar, but a visit to Bahim Ābād is a good idea. Though actually in Gīlān province, it's only 5km south of Kalāchāy, which is 33km west of Rāmsar and along the main road to Rasht. This friendly little village is made popular by Rāmsarīs who flock here for the **mineral hot springs**. You will probably need to charter a taxi from Rāmsar, or ask to be dropped off by a shared taxi at Kalāchāy, and then walk to Bahim Ābād.

NŌSHAHR & CHĀLŪS   نوشهر وچالوس
Nōshahr is a far nicer place to wander around and stay than Chālūs, a sprawling industrial and junction town only 5km west of Nōshahr. Since transport is no problem, even late at night, you can pick and choose between the hotels, restaurants and other facilities in either town. There are more trees in Nōshahr than Chālūs, and there's an impressive, recently built mosque, the **Masjed-é Jāme'**. The port of Nōshahr has been enlarged in the last two years to engulf what used to be a popular beach for paddling, but there's little shipping business as yet, so the town must rely on domestic tourism for its livelihood.

Once two of the quaintest villages along the Caspian road, they are now part of the horrid urban sprawl between Rasht and Sārī, and the only reason to stay in either town is to explore the nearby attractions (see Around Nōshahr and Chālūs later in this section). The telephone area code is 0191.

Places to Stay & Eat
The only place to stay in Nōshahr, and the best option in either town, is the *Shalizar Restaurant & Hotel* (☎ 34 264). The rooms, with air-con, fridge, bathroom and views, officially cost US$25/30 for a single/double. The manager eventually offered me a 'tourist price' (I never heard of this term elsewhere in Iran!) for a very reasonable 35,000/45,000 rials.

Two comfortable, middle range places are opposite each other at the official, western entrance to Nōshahr: the *Hotel Malek* (☎ 2627) wanted US$25 for a double, but accepted 40,000 rials instead; and the *Hotel Kourosh* (☎ 2396) which is about the same price but less negotiable. In Chālūs, the *Hotel Gamshid* – look for the broken sign 'Hotel G' along the main road – is the cheapest option. The staff will reluctantly accept foreigners for 25,000 rials a double.

The best, and most expensive (of course), place to stay is the five star *Caspian Enghelāb Hotel*, in the village of Namak Abrūd (see Around Nōshahr & Chālūs later in this section). Unfortunately, this temple to western hedonism is largely a preserve of the well-to-do Iranian and the upmarket tourist. Prices are about US$95/120 for singles/doubles. There are several other motels along the road between Rāmsar and Chālūs catering for Iranian families on holidays. Foreigners are welcome but the motels are more convenient for those with their own transport.

A few decent *pizzerias* and western-style *hamburger joints* are spread along the main road, and are easy enough to find using a shared taxi. One of the best is *Toranj Pizza* in Chālūs. The *Malek* and *Kouroush* hotels have good restaurants, though they don't open until 8 pm for dinner. The *Shalizar Restaurant* in Nōshahr is very large and classy with, as the manager promised, dancing! A huge plate of fish kebabs costs 15,000 rials.

Getting There & Away
Air Iran Asseman flies to Nōshahr from Tehrān (40,000 rials) about once a week, and

usually more often in summer,. Their office, which is rarely open, is on the main road into Nōshahr from Chālūs. The airport is north of the main road between the two towns; take a private taxi.

Bus & Minibus The main terminal for buses, minibuses and shared taxis, serving both towns, to points east, west and south is the Tonekābon terminal, in the western end of Chālūs, and a few hundred metres from the road heading south to Tehrān. There are all sorts of vehicles heading towards Rasht and Rāmsar (minibuses to Rasht leave about every 15 minutes in summer); east to Sārī and Gorgān (about every hour); and every 30 minutes or so to Tehrān (205km, five hours). There are also a couple of buses every day to Mashhad (877km, 14 hours, 9200 rials), Sārī (180km, three hours, 3800 rials) and Tabrīz (679km, 11 hours, 11,800 rials).

The fairly long and windy road between Tehrān and Chālūs will be improved considerably (and decreased to 121km or about two hours) with the planned construction of a new freeway. The road will contain an amazing 40 tunnels, with a combined length of 54km, so about 45 per cent of the whole road will be underground. When this will be finished is anyone's guess.

To get to anywhere between Nōshahr and Nūr, take a minibus from the main square in Nōshahr.

Shared Taxi There are shared taxis to Tehrān (about 12,000 rials) which depart from outside the main bus terminal in Chālūs, and the nearby Tehrān turn-off, when they have enough passengers. Shared taxis also regularly run to Rāmsar and Āmol from the main bus terminal.

Getting Around
There are minibuses (200 rials), every few minutes throughout the day until about 6 pm, between Nōshahr and the main square of Chālūs. It is easier to take one of the many shared taxis (400 to 600 rials) which speed along the main road.

AROUND NŌSHAHR & CHĀLŪS
There are actually some half-decent beaches along the road between Nōshahr and Nūr. It is not quite the Caribbean or the French Riveria but there is some sand, and a surprising lack of development (so far). If you want a plunge, just get on and off the shared taxis and minibuses which regularly scream along the road.

Namak Abrūd   نامک‌آبرود
This village, about 10km west of Chālūs, is where an up-market European-style resort will be built some time in the future. At the moment, the village boasts some upmarket holiday and retirement homes, the incredible Caspian Enghelāb Hotel (see Places to Stay & Eat in the Nōshahr & Chālūs section) and the remarkable telecabin.

This **telecabin**, or chair lift, cruises up to the top of the 1050m-high **Mt Medovin**; you can see the thin line bisecting the densely forested hill from the main road. It is a magnificent ride, but very cold even in summer, and if you are unlucky the hill will be covered in low cloud and the magnificent views will be spoilt – so get an early start, before the clouds set in. There are plans to build a second telecabin in the region, and even to extend the original one all the way to Tehrān. Perhaps this is a little ambitious.

A return trip on the telecabin costs 8000 rials, and it is open Wednesday to Monday, from 10 am to 4 pm. The entrance is on the main Rāmsar-Chālūs road, but the chair lift itself is a couple of kilometres further back; you could probably hitch a ride from the entrance gate to the chair lift, or just walk – it is easy enough to spot.

Kalardasht   کلاردشت
Kalardasht is a fertile depression more than 1250m above sea level. It is an historical place where recent archaeological discoveries (now in the National Museum of Iran in Tehrān) show habitation dating back to the 10th century AD. The main town in the region is Hasan Keif, on the road between Abbās Ābād and Marzanābād.

Kalardasht is also the place to head for if you are hankering after some outdoor activities. There is nothing established but if you ask around, or just explore the region yourself, you will find some great **hiking trails**, especially around the tiny and peculiarly-shaped Velesht lake; **fishing spots** (for trout) in nearby streams; and in winter, **cross-country skiing**. See the Trekking in Iran section in the Facts for the Visitor chapter for information about **climbing** the nearby mountains of Alam and Takht-é Soleimān.

Nūr نور

The town of Nūr retains some semblance of quaintness, and is worth a stop or an overnight stay to allow you to explore the nearby attractions which include the tiny pocket of jungle known as the **Kajvil Forest**.

The only place to stay in Nūr is the two-star *Nūr Hotel* which costs about US$25/35 for a single/double. Nūr is easy enough to reach by minibus (500 rials) or shared taxi (1000 rials) from Nōshahr, or you can just jump off (but wait until it stops) any transport travelling along the Chālūs-Āmol road.

Sīsangān National Park پارک ملی سی سنگ

This small national park, 31km east of Nōshahr, is a lovely pocket of very precious and rare forest, a sad indication of how nice this part of Iran must have once been. In the park, there are a few paved roads and unmarked **trails** leading to nowhere in particular, but hikers should find enough to keep them satisfied for a few hours. You can even hire **horses** for short trots around the park.

There is nowhere to eat, but you can cook something, if you have cooking equipment, on the open (concrete) fireplaces; and there are also tables and toilets around the place. No camping is allowed; Iranian families put up tents just for the day. Avoid Friday, or public holidays in summer, when this park is bumper to bumper Paykans and picnic hampers.

Getting There & Away From Nōshahr, take a minibus (45 minutes, 500 rials) or shared taxi (1000 rials) towards Nūr and get off when you see the sign in English 'Jangali Park' (Jungle Park). Entrance is free.

BEHSHAHR بهشهر

Behshahr is a small sleepy town on the main road between Sārī and Gorgān, and is one of the more pleasant places along the main Caspian road. The Bay of Gorgān lies 12km to the north and immediately south are hills and woodland which you can **hike** around (but be careful about military posts in the area).

You can easily spend an hour or two in the delightful **Shahr Park**, on the main road just south of Emām Khomeinī Square. You can also hire a taxi to see the small **Abbāsābād Lake**, built by Shāh Abbās I, with a small fort in the middle. It is quite an odd place.

Kākh-é Safī Ābād

On Mt Kākh, a tall hill thick with trees south-west of Behshahr, are the remains of a Safavid palace. In about 1612, Shāh Abbās I set about building a palace complex in a royal water garden, the Bāgh-é Shāh, on this idyllic woodland perch. Many palaces and other buildings for the king and his court grew up on the same site, which gradually expanded to become the town of Ashraf (present-day Behshahr), but over the centuries they fell into ruin and today the only remaining structure is the Safī Ābād Palace.

While the palace stands majestically on the hill as you approach from Sārī, the area is currently part of a military complex and strictly off-limits to foreigners. If you go hiking in the area, be very careful about stumbling into military property.

Prehistoric Caves

There are two rather interesting caves near Behshahr which have revealed prehistoric pottery perhaps dating back to the 10th millennium BC, as well as evidence of some unusual ancient burial rites. To get to the caves, take a shared taxi from Behshahr and ask to be dropped off at the Serāh-é Torūjan-é Bālā, about 3km west of Behshahr on the main road to Sārī. From there walk south for

Māzandarān Province – Gorgān 381

CASPIAN PROVINCES

about 300m until you come to a small village, Torūjān-é Bālā, where you will see the Hōtū Cave overlooking the road. The Kamarband Cave is a very short distance south of here.

Places to Stay & Eat
The best place to stay and eat if you want to break up the journey between Sārī and Gorgān, or if you want to have a good look around the area, is the *Miankaleh Hotel* (☎ (01572) 29 161), a few metres north of the main square named (of course) Emām Khomeinī Square. The charge of US$25 for a double is too much, but negotiations are possible.

Getting There & Away
You can take a shared taxi, minibus or bus to Gorgān or Sārī from anywhere along the main road. Alternatively you could catch any transport going to nearby towns from the bus terminal, on the south side of the main road, near the western edge of Behshahr. Behshahr is on the main Tehrān-Gorgān train line. The train station is about 1.5km north of Emām Khomeinī Square.

GORGĀN گرگان
On the northern edge of the Alborz, and at the southern frontier of the north-eastern steppe, Gorgān (formerly known as Aster Ābād) has, for much of its long history, been the last secure outpost of Persian civilisation. Settled since ancient times, it has, with the exception of a series of incursions in the last century, been geographically positioned to resist the threat of Turkmen raids, unlike Gombad-é Kāvūs and other Māzandarānī towns to the north and east. The Turkmen started to give up their nomadic and pillaging ways at the turn of the 20th century, and it's one of the twists of history that they eventually conquered Gorgān not by violence, but by peaceful settlement.

Gorgān became the new railhead of the Caspian provinces after a branch line was constructed from Bandar-é Torkamān in the 1970s, but it's still little more than a provin-

cial market town (population approximately 200,000). Some of its individuality has been replaced over recent years by Persian uniformity, and very few people now wear the distinctive Turkmen dress. Gorgān is still a pleasant base for exploring the region, and contains a couple of interesting buildings.

Orientation & Information
Most of the main thoroughfare, Emām Khomeinī St, is flanked to the west by the bazaar, a network of narrow winding kūchés along which there are many fine examples of traditional Māzandarānī houses, with tiled

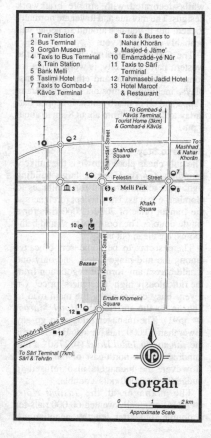

1 Train Station
2 Bus Terminal
3 Gorgān Museum
4 Taxis to Bus Terminal & Train Station
5 Bank Melli
6 Taslimi Hotel
7 Taxis to Gombad-é Kāvūs Terminal
8 Taxis & Buses to Nahar Khorān
9 Masjed-é Jāme'
10 Emāmzādé-yé Nūr
11 Taxis to Sārī Terminal
12 Tahmasebi Jadid Hotel
13 Hotel Maroof & Restaurant

Gorgān

Approximate Scale
0   1   2 km

sloping roofs and charming wooden balconies. The centre of town is Shahrdārī Square. The telephone area code is 0371.

Things to See

Built around a quadrangle in the bazaar, the **Masjed-é Jāme'** is a single storey mosque with a traditional sloping tiled roof and an unusual minaret. It dates from the 15th century, though it's been repaired numerous times because of the many devastating earthquakes that have struck this area.

The **Emāmzādé-yé Nūr**, about 200m west of the mosque, is a small 14th or 15th century polygonal tomb tower, its outer walls decorated with simple brickwork designs. The mosque and tower are normally locked, but if you ask around someone will probably open it for you.

The **Gorgān Museum** (☎ 2453), in the western part of the city, is worth a visit for some archaeological and ethnological displays, including tombstones, from Tūrang Tappé and other nearby sites. It is open Saturday to Thursday from about 8 am to about 6 pm.

Places to Stay

The only cheap place in town is the unlikely sounding *Tourist Home*, a large building right next to the terminal for minibuses to Gombad-é Kāvūs. They accept foreigners at the Iranian price of 7000/11,000 rials for a single/double. The rooms, with shared bathrooms, are clean but noisy.

There seems to be some sort of cartel among the mid-range hotels, and only one would accept any form of negotiation from the ridiculously high 'foreigners' price'. On a very busy corner along the main road to Tehrān is the unfriendly *Hotel Maroof* (☎ 5591). The manager refused to go any lower than 60,000 rials for a double. Nicer is the *Tahmasebi Jadid Hotel* (☎ 2780), a few hundred metres north-east of the Maroof. However, the managers also refused to budge from 60,000 rials a double.

The manager at the *Taslimi Hotel* (☎ 4814) originally wanted 60,000 rials for a double, but after lengthy negotiations,

which included shameless begging and bursts of anger (from me), he agreed to a more reasonable 40,000 rials. Though the rooms were good, the bedbugs were not welcome and the hot water was sporadic.

Places to Eat

The range of restaurants in Gorgān is as disappointing as the range of hotels, though not as overpriced. Only the *Hotel Maroof* has a restaurant, so you will probably have to make do with a hamburger or another kebab at the dozens of places around the main squares. There aren't even any decent cake shops to satisfy the sweet tooth.

Getting There & Away

The road east to Mashhad is a spectacular drive, passing through dramatic forest scenery, but expect a few thorough baggage checks because of drug trafficking from Turkmenistan. Gorgān airport doesn't currently have any passenger services.

Bus & Minibus The main bus terminal is north-west of Shahrdārī Square. It is easy enough to reach by shared taxi (250 rials). Among other more remote destinations, buses and minibuses (with prices for lux/super class) go to:

Destination	Distance	Time	Cost (rials)
Mashhad	564km	9 hours	6800/7300
(sometimes via Gombad-é Kāvūs)			
Rasht	511km	9 hours	6200/7300
Sārī	37km	2 hours	2100
(minibus only)			
Shāhrūd	124km	4 hours	3600/3900
(this trip offers fantastic scenery, and is a good way to travel between Gorgān and Tehrān)			
Tehrān	387km	7 hours	4700/5000

The smaller Sārī terminal, on the main road to Tehrān, is about 3km south-west of the town centre. From there, minibuses (departing about every hour) and, less frequently, shared taxis, go to Sārī (137km, 2½ hours) via Behshahr. The tiny minibus terminal for Gombad-é Kāvūs is north of the town, and easily reached by shared taxi.

Train The 497km train trip between Tehrān and Gorgān is one of the best journeys in the country. From Gorgān, there is a daily train to Sārī (1000 rials for 2nd class; there is no 1st class) which travels on to the junction of Pol-é Sefīd, from where you can get a connection to Tehrān. However, the train to Sārī leaves from Gorgān at the ungodly hour of 4.30 am.

It's better to try to get a seat (not always easy) on the Gorgān-Tehrān train which leaves on Tuesday, Friday and Sunday (the departure times were unclear at the time of research). You miss a lot of scenery on the overnight trip to Tehrān, but it does arrive in Tehrān at 6.40 am. Tickets to Tehrān cost 4900/12,150 rials for 2nd/1st class.

The train station (☎ 27 911) is a few hundred metres west of the bus terminal, and is easily reached by shared taxi from the centre of town.

Shared Taxi There are frequent shared taxis to Sārī (5000 rials) from the Sārī terminal.

Getting Around
You can easily walk around the centre of town and there are plenty of shared taxis to the bus and train terminals.

AROUND GORGĀN
While Gorgān may not be the most exciting or inexpensive place in Iran, there are plenty of great day trips from Gorgān to justify a detour to this part of the country.

Nahar Khorān   ناهارخوران
One of the nicest spots in the country is the pocket of forest known as Nahar Khorān, only about 6km south of Gorgān. Though there are some holidays cabins and the requisite ugly children's playground nearby, the concrete mixers and bulldozers that have ploughed through the rest of the Caspian region have (so far) left this part of Iran almost pristine. There are plenty of **hiking trails** through dense forest which are easy to find and just begging to be explored.

Though Nahar Khorān can be a bit crowded in summer, especially on Friday and public holidays, you may have the whole area to yourself the rest of the time.

Places to Stay & Eat At the end of the road from Gorgān is the *Hotel Shahrdārī Gorgān* (☎ (0271) 8077), a grand old place which has probably seen better days. It is understandably busy at peak times (June to August). The staff member on duty was unwilling to provide a price to a foreigner, but it shouldn't be more than 50,000 rials for a double, and is worth it if only for the gorgeous setting.

Nearby, the only alternative is the hotel and brightly coloured cabins collectively called the *Nahar Khorān Inn* (☎ (0271) 21 278). The manager quoted the 'foreigners' price' of US$10 per room, which seemed unusually reasonable for somewhere run by the ITTO. It's best to double-check the price. There is nothing and no-one stopping you discreetly *camping* anywhere in the area.

Both places serve meals and hot drinks to the public. The cooked breakfast at the Nahar Khorān Inn is superb for 3500 rials.

Getting There & Away You could easily charter a taxi (about 2500 rials) from Gorgān, but the nicest way to get here is to catch the half-hourly bus from Khakh Square (100 rials) in Gorgān. Nahar Khorān is at the top of a steepish road, so if you want to walk one way, get a bus (or taxi) there, and if you still have the energy, walk back – it is easy to follow the main road back into Gorgān.

Bandar-é Torkamān   بندرترکمن
A coastal town just south of the narrow inlet to the Bay of Gorgān, Bandar-é Torkamān is, as the name suggests, the Turkmen port of Iran. For a long time it was a major channel of trade with Russia, despite the attentions of Turkmen pirates who were a scourge to shipping on these shores until the 19th century. With the establishment of the trans-Iranian railway in the 1930s Bandar-é Torkamān also became the sole railhead of Iran's Caspian coast. The decline in the shipping trade has left Bandar-é Torkamān a small and

Caviar Anyone?

Caviar is such an important and lucrative commodity that the fishing, production and export of caviar is controlled through the government-owned Shilat Trading Company. Shilat often seems to be as busy arguing with other Caspian littoral states about fishing rights in the Caspian Sea and stopping smuggling from Russia, as it is making money from exporting caviar.

Caviar is fished at more than 50 areas along the Iranian part of the Caspian coast, but most of it is caught near Bandar-é Torkamān, in Māzandarān province. Normally dozens of large wooden boats, with huge mesh nets, catch the sturgeon, though in recent times Shilat has established hatcheries to ensure continuing supplies. In 1996, about 150 tonnes of caviar was exported from Iran, fetching up to US$250 per kg.

However, overfishing encouraged by such high prices, pollution (see 'The Mighty Caspian Sea' boxed text earlier in this chapter) and the construction of dams on the Volga River have reduced the numbers of sturgeon fished from the Caspian in recent years, from 30,000 tonnes in 1985 to 2100 tonnes in 1994. ∎

largely Turkmen settlement with the air of a frontier town. There is nowhere to stay but it is an easy day trip from Gorgān.

The region is more famous as the caviar production centre of Iran. In 1997, almost 50% of the country's caviar was caught from Bandar-é Torkamān. About 150 ships are based at the port, trailing up and down the 160km coastline looking for those precious sturgeon and their valuable little fish eggs.

The most striking thing about this town is that the Turkmen women wear gorgeous bright shawls and gowns, which are quite a contrast to the ubiquitous black chādors worn elsewhere.

If you happen to be around on a Monday morning, it's definitely worth visiting the traditional **weekly market** where you can buy local produce and handicrafts, such as the bright shawls and Turkmen rugs which are often a maroon colour. Foreign women can wear these bright shawls in the region, but they may raise the interest of the Kōmité

elsewhere in the country where darker colours are the norm.

Getting There & Away Bandar-é Torkamān is on the train route between Gorgān and Tehrān. Most road transport will drop you off at the main square at the nearby junction of Kordkūy. From there, you can walk about 8km along an interesting road (flanked by many small Turkmen farms), or take a shared taxi to Bandar-é Torkamān.

Tūrang Tappé

Tūrang Tappé, destroyed in the Mongol period (1220-1380), was a major regional caravan station and town. Excavations early this century revealed five distinct layers, the earliest dating back to the 6th millennium BC and the latest to the early Arab period (637-1050). Lapis lazuli beads and ceramic pieces indicate that this was a major pottery-producing centre, with its peak in the 2nd and 3rd millennia. The more important items of pottery are now on display in Tehrān at the National Museum of Iran.

Getting There & Away Tūrang Tappé is north-east of Gorgān, 22km by road and dirt track. It is impossible to reach by public transport, and even by private car it's almost inaccessible in bad weather. You can hire a taxi from Gorgān for around 20,000 rials including waiting time.

Sadd-é Eskandar

The remains of a historical wall called Alexander's Wall stretch more than 160km from just west of Gombad-é Kāvūs to within about 5km of the sea. Probably built in the 6th century (and therefore not by Alexander the Great) as a bulwark against warring tribes to the north, this equivalent of Hadrian's Wall has crumbled or been cannibalised for building materials along most of its length. The foundations at least are still clearly visible, and in places its original purpose can still be imagined.

Getting There & Away The wall is difficult to get to and, since it's near the Turkmenistan border, it isn't advisable to go there without permission in writing from the *farmāndārī* (district administrative headquarters) in Gorgān. After getting this permit, you can charter a taxi for not more than 10,000 rials an hour. It isn't at all safe to walk there.

Gombad-é Kāvūs   گنبدکاوس

This otherwise featureless, but pleasant, Turkmen town, known locally as Gombad, is famous for, and named after, one thing; but for this alone it repays a day trip from Gorgān. The Gombad-é Kāvūs is a spectacular **tomb tower** built by Ghābūs ebn-é Vashmgīr – the name Kāvūs is a corruption of Ghābūs. It's a remarkable memorial to a remarkable man. Famous as a poet, scholar, general and patron of the arts, Ghābūs was prince of the local Ziyarid dynasty. He ruled the surrounding region of Tabarestān at the turn of the 11th century and decided to build a monument to last forever. The monument was completed in 1006, six years before Ghābūs was slain by an assassin.

This earliest of skyscrapers is 55m tall (though surprisingly the statistics do vary). The tower rests on a large earth mound formed around its substantial foundations, which are at least 12m deep. Built of brick, the circular structure has 10 buttresses rising from the base to the pointed dome, which itself measures 18m in height. There are two rings of inscriptions around the tower, one on a moulded cornice below the dome and the other a metre above the doorway. Originally the glass coffin of Ghābūs hung from the dome of the tower, but it vanished long ago (nobody knows how), and there's no longer anything to see inside. In any case, the arched doorway on its east side is permanently locked, and it has never been possible to climb to the top of the tower. Robert Byron's *The Road to Oxiana* (see Books in the Facts for the Visitor chapter) gives more details about the history of the tower.

Remarkably, entrance to the park surrounding the tower is free. (It would be pointless charging people anyway: you can't go inside the tower, and you can see it up to 30km away on a clear day.)

Places to Stay & Eat The *Hotel Ferdosy*, on the main road from Gorgān, refused to accept me as a guest, but you may have better luck. Alternatively, you can stay at *Hotel Āstārā* at Mīnudasht, about 20km away; or the *Park Hotel* at Āzād Shahr, the junction town 18km south of Gombad. But it's better to take a day trip from Gorgān.

There are a few *hamburger places* and *ice cream parlours* in Gombad but nothing to get excited about. You may want to bring a picnic from Gorgān and sit in the tiny park which surrounds the tower.

Getting There & Away From Gorgān, minibuses (93km, 1000 rials) leave about every hour from the special Gombad terminal. There are also daily buses from Gombad to Mashhad and Tehrān. Some buses also pass through Gombad on their way between Mashhad and Gorgān, or you can go to the junction of Āzād Shahr, and easily get onward transport from there.

This is one of the few stretches of road in the country where chartering a taxi, with a driver, for a half or full-day is worth considering (for about 10,000 rials per hour). The urban sprawl along the Caspian seems to stop east of Gorgān, and the Gorgān-Gombad road passes through lovely scenery.

Along the way, in Alī Ābād, there are two **waterfalls** which can only be reached by private transport – they are signposted on the road with paintings of the falls. Also along this stretch of road are two small forest parks, **Gologh Park** and **Park Deland** – both are ideal for short walks.

Getting Around To get to the tower itself, take a shared taxi (300 rials, about 1km) from where the bus from Gorgān drops you off. Ask for the Mīl-é Gombad, as the tower is known locally – Gombad is the unofficial name of the town, not the tower.

Glossary

Generally, the Persian words in this book are transliterations of colloquial usage. Other words are also given in the Language chapter, particularly in the Food and Menu Guide on page 398.

ābambār – water storage tank
āghā – sir; gentleman
āghā-yé – the equivalent of Mr, but commonly used with the forename only
Allāh – Muslim name for God
Allāho Akbar – 'God is Most Great': a Muslim declaration of faith
ārāmgāh – resting-place; burial-place; tomb
arg, ark – citadel
āstān-é – sanctuary; threshold
āteshkadé – a Zoroastrian fire-temple
āyatollāh – literally a 'sign or miracle of God': Shi'ite cleric of the highest rank; used as a title before the name
āzād – free; liberated
āzādī – freedom

bādgīr – wind-tower or ventilation shaft used to catch any breeze and funnel it down into a building for cooling
bāgh – garden
bandar – port; harbour
Bandarī – pertaining to a port; person native to a port; indigenous inhabitant of the Persian Gulf coast and islands
basīj – mobilisation; Mobilisation Corps: an organisation set up in 1980 to dispatch volunteers of all ages to fight at the front in the war against Iraq
bāstān – ancient; ancient history; antiquity
bāzār – bazaar; market; market place
bāzār-é āzād – 'free' market; black market
behesht – paradise
bogh'é – mausoleum
bolvār – boulevard
borj – tower
borqa – a mask worn by some Bandarī women with two tiny slits for the eyes
bozorg – big; large; great

bozorgrāh – urban motorway; expressway

Caliphate – the dynasty of the successors of the Prophet Mohammed as rulers of the Islamic world
CFZ – Chābahār Free Zone; the duty-free port of Chābahār
chādor – literally 'tent'; a cloak, usually black, covering all parts of a woman's body except the hands, feet and face
chahārrāh – intersection; crossroads
chāy – tea
chāykhūné – teahouse
chelō – boiled rice
chelō kabāb – lamb kebab served with rice: a staple at Iranian restaurants
chelō kabābī – place serving *chelō kabāb*; restaurant in general

daftar – office
daftar-é seir va seyāhat – tourist office
darvāzé – gate; gateway, especially a city gate
daryā – sea
daryāché – lake
dasht – plain; plateau; desert, specifically one of sand or gravel

edāré – department; administration; office
eivān – rectangular hall opening onto a courtyard
Emām – leader; title of one of the 12 descendants of Mohammed who, according to Shi'ite belief, succeeded him as religious and temporal leader of the Muslims
emāmzādé – descendant of an *emām*; shrine or mausoleum of an *emāmzādé*
enghelāb – revolution
enghelāb-é Eslāmī – Islamic Revolution
enshāllāh – 'God willing'
ershād – guidance; an abbreviation for the Ministry of Culture & Islamic Guidance
eskelé – jetty; dock; harbour
eslām – Islam: literally 'submission' (ie to the will of God)
eslāmī – Islamic

falaké – round open space; roundabout
farhang – culture
farsh – carpet
Fārsī – Persian language or people
forūshgāh – shop

ghal'é – fortress; fortified walled village
ghalyān – water pipe; hubble-bubble
ghanāt – underground water channel
ghar – cave
ghollé – summit; peak
golestān – rose garden; name of poem by Sa'dī
gombad – dome; domed monument; tomb-tower

hajj – pilgrimage to Mecca
Hajjī – one who has performed the *hajj*, used as a title before the forename; polite form of address for an old man
halāl – permitted by Islamic law; lawful to eat or drink
hammūm – bath; bath house; bathroom
hāmūn – plain; desert; salt waste; marsh
harām – forbidden by Islamic law; unlawful to eat or drink
Hazrat-é – title used before the name of Mohammed, any other apostle of Islam, or a Christian saint
hegira – see *hejrat*
hejāb – veil; the 'modest dress' required of Muslim women and girls
hejrat – the flight of the Prophet Mohammed from Mecca on 16 July 622 AD; the starting-point of the Muslim lunar calendar and the Persian solar calendar
Hezbollāh – 'Party of God': a loose grouping of hardline fundamentalist Muslims

IRISL – Islamic Republic of Iran Shipping Line
īstgāh – station (especially railway station)
ITTO – Iranian Touring & Tourism Organisation; a government-run travel and hotel agency

jāddé – road
jāddé-yé kamarbandī – ring-road
jahāngard – tourist

jangal – forest; jungle (name used for the Māzandarān forest)
jazīré – island
jihad – holy war; crusade
jom'é – Friday, the Muslim day of rest and worship

kabāb – kebab(s): meat, fish, poultry or seafood grilled on a skewer
kabābī – anywhere that sells kebabs; a general term for a snack bar
kabīr – great
kākh – palace
kavīr – salt desert
kelīsā – church (sometimes cathedral)
khalīj – gulf; bay
khān – feudal lord
kheyābūn – street; avenue
khūné – house; home
Komīté – committee, in particular a local 'committee' of the Islamic Revolutionary Guards Corps, or religious police
konsūlgarī – consulate
kūché – lane; alley
kūh – mountain
kūhha – mountain range
KFZO – Kīsh Free Zone Organisation; the organisation which runs the duty-free island of Kīsh

lux – regular class of bus

madrasé – school; also Muslim theological college
maghbaré – tomb; burial ground
Majlis – Iranian Parliament
manār – minaret: tower of a mosque
markaz – centre; headquarters
markazī telefon – main telephone office
masjed – mosque: Muslim place of worship
masjed-é jāme' – congregational mosque, literally 'Friday mosque'
mehmūn – guest
mehmūnkhūné – hotel
mehmūnpazīr – a simple hotel
mehmūnsarā – government-owned rest house or hotel
mehrāb – chevron-shaped niche inside a mosque indicating the direction of Mecca,

often ornately decorated with tiling and calligraphy

meidūn – town square; open space

membar – pulpit of a mosque

MFA – Iranian Ministry of Foreign Affairs

Moharram – first month of the Muslim lunar calendar, Shi'ite month of mourning

mojihad – soldier of the *jihad*

mosāfer – traveller; passenger

mosāferkhūné – lodging-house or hotel of the cheapest and simplest kind, sometimes offering only dormitory accommodation

mostaghīm – 'straight ahead': the usual answer to any request for directions

Muezzin – functionary at a mosque who calls Muslims to prayer

Mullah – Islamic cleric; sometimes used as a title

mūzé – museum

Nō Rūz – Iranian New Year's Day, celebrated on the vernal equinox (usually falls around 21 March)

ostān – province: Iran is divided into 26 *ostānhā*

ostāndārī – office of the provincial government

otōbān – motorway

pā'īn – down; downwards; low; of low status

Pārs – Fārsī for Persia or Iran

pāsāzh – passage; shopping arcade

Persia – the previous name for Iran

Persian – adjective and noun frequently used to describe the Iranian language, people and culture

pik-up – utility vehicle used for passenger services

pol – bridge

polō – rice cooked together with other ingredients

Quran – the holy book of the Muslims

Ramazān – ninth month in the Muslim lunar calendar; month of fasting

rial – currency of Iran; equal to one-tenth of a *tōmān*

rūd, **rūdkhūné** – river; stream

rūz – day

sahn – court; courtyard

sahrā – desert

salām – 'peace'; a greeting

sālon-é ghezā – food-hall; simple restaurant

savārī – private car; local word for a *shared taxi*

Seyed – male descendant of Mohammed, used as a title before the forename

Sepah-é Pāsdārān – 'Army of Guards': paramilitary unit of the Islamic Revolutionary Guards, mainly active in rural areas

serāh – 'three roads': Y-junction or T-junction

shāh – king; the usual title of the Persian monarch

shahīd – martyr; used as a title before the forename of a fighter killed during the Islamic Revolution or the Iran-Iraq War

shahr – town or city

shahrbānī – the police; provincial police headquarters

shahrdārī – administrative headquarters of a *shahr*; municipal office; town hall

shared taxi – five or so passengers squeezed into a private car or taxi for a local or inter-provincial trip

shomāl – north; the Caspian provinces of Gīlān and Māzandarān

super – the superior class of bus

takht – throne

tappé – hill; mound

tar – traditional stringed instrument, not unlike a lute

termīnāl – terminal; bus station

tōmān – unit of currency equal to 10 *rials*

UAE – United Arab Emirates

ziggurat – pyramidal temple with a series of tiers on a square or rectangular plan

zurkhané – traditional wrestling venue

Persian Language Guide

Persian grammar is refreshingly simple, and what few rules there are have few exceptions. For most people the greatest barrier to learning Persian is the script, but even this is relatively easy to decipher, at least in the printed form.

In the transliterations, proper nouns which would otherwise look odd in English have been capitalised, with no change in the pronunciation. Where an apostrophe occurs at the beginning of a Persian word, it has not been included since it makes no difference to pronunciation. Hyphens have been used before the *ezāfé* (see below), between compound words which are pronounced as one word but written as two, and where a combination of consonants would otherwise be mispronounced.

In most cases the colloquial pronunciation or word is used. Colloquial Persian, as spoken most of the time by most Iranians, is not the equivalent of slang, although many slang expressions are used. Classical Persian is not the language of everyday speech; it is oratorical or written Persian, which would be used for reading a speech or writing a book.

PRONUNCIATION
In general, the last syllable of a multisyllable word is stressed, unless it is a short vowel at the end of a word eg *emĀm* but *bAlé* (with the stress on the capital letter).

Vowels & Diphthongs
A macron over a vowel (ā, ī, ō and ū) indicates a longer vowel sound. This is very important in Persian as the wrong vowel length can completely change the meaning of a word, or make it incomprehensible. For example, *māst* (rhyming with 'passed') means 'yoghurt', while *mast* (rhyming with 'gassed') means 'drunk'. Fortunately no sounds in Persian are completely alien to the English-speaker, and it should not take very long to pick up a workable pronunciation.

a	as in *map*, but slightly more rounded
ā	between the *a* in *class* and the *a* in *what*
e	similar to *e* in *beg*
é	*e* with a slight rising tone, as in *café*, often a mere glide or even inaudible
ī	similar to *i* in *Fiji*
o	between the *o* in *god* and the *oo* in *good*
ō	similar to the *o* in *bone*
ū	similar to the *u* in *ruse*; never as in *use*
ei	similar to *ei* in *rein*
oi	similar to *oy* in *boy*

Consonants
The letters **b, d, f, j, m, n, p, sh, t** and **z** are pronounced as in English.

ch	as in *rich*
g	hard *g* as in *bag*, never as in *age*; at the end of a word or before *ā, e, é, ei* or *ī* the *g* is palatised, rather like the *gg* in *egg yolk* read quickly
gh	soft gargling sound, sometimes pronounced as a *g* from the back of the throat
h	never silent; always unvoiced as in *harm*, not *hit*

k	as in English; at the end of a word or before *ā*, *e*, *é*, *ei* or *ī* the *k* is palatised, rather like the *ck* in *backyard* read quickly
kh	as *ch* in Scottish *loch* or German *achtung*
l	as in *leg* not *roll*, even when doubled (but see note below)
r	trilled *r* as in Italian or Russian, never silent or diphthongised
s	always as in *sad*, never as in *rise*
v	as in English, but tending towards *w*
y	always consonantal *y* as in *yak*
zh	as *zh* in *Zhivago* or *g* in *mirage*
'	very weak glottal stop, as in Cockney *bo'l* for *bottle* or in *go away*

Note that doubled consonants are always pronounced distinctly as in *hat trick* not *battle*; the sole exception is the word for God, *Allāh*, in which the *l*s are swallowed as in English *doll*.

GRAMMAR

The verb usually comes at the end of the sentence or clause. Punctuation is not always used, or at least not as often as in English. For most purposes, it is only necessary to learn two tenses of each verb, the present (also generally used for the future) and the past, and verb endings are regular in all verbs.

To ask a question it is usually enough merely to alter the intonation, as in English: in writing a question mark is usually used. To be certain, you can use the question word *āyā* at the beginning of the sentence.

There is no gender (he and she are the same word in Persian), although inanimates and lower animals are treated differently in some cases from rational beings.

I	*man*	من
you (singular)*	*to*	تو
he/she	*ū*	او
it	*ān*	آن
we	*mā*	ما
you (plural)*	*shomā*	شما
they (of people and higher animals)	*īshān*	ایشان
they (of things and lower animals)	*ānhā*	آنها

*In Persian *shomā* is the formal, polite form of the second person singular pronoun; *to* is only generally used when talking to close friends and relatives of the same generation or later, and to children and animals.

Ezāfé

This is a grammatical device which links a noun to a following word which describes or qualifies it in some way. It is equivalent to 'of' in English. The ezāfé takes the form of the suffix *-é* after nouns which end with a consonant or diphthong. If the noun ends with a vowel, the ezāfé is the suffix *-yé*. For example:

ketāb (book)	*ketāb-é Rezā* (Rezā's book)
tangé (strait)	*Tangé-yé Hormoz* (the Strait of Hormoz)
kheyābūn (street)	*Kheyābūn-é Zand* (Zand Street)
otāgh (room)	*otāgh-é arzūntar* (a cheaper room)

The ezāfé is not normally indicated in written Persian (except after $\bar{a}$, $\bar{o}$ or $\bar{u}$), which is a problem for students of the language.

Plurals

Nouns remain in the singular when preceded by a numeral or qualified by a noun of quantity, so plural forms are less common than in English. In common usage, names of foods and drinks do not normally take the plural suffix.

Plural forms depend on whether the noun is for a rational being (ie a person), which takes the suffix -*an*, or an inanimate object or non-rational being, which takes the suffix -*ha*. There are also different plural forms if the noun ends in a vowel.

In everyday speech it is acceptable to use the suffix -*hā* as the plural for almost any noun, although a few animates ending in -*é* or -*ā* never take the inanimate plural. Where the plural -*hā* follows a word ending *g*, *k*, *s* or *z*, a hyphen has been inserted between the two for ease of pronunciation.

Useful Words & Phrases

Polite Forms of Address

When addressing a stranger, especially one older than you, it is polite to drop in one of the words for 'sir' or 'madam' at the beginning of the first sentence or after one of the standard greetings. The standard words for sir and madam are *āghā* and *khānom* respectively. *Āghā-yé* and *Khānom-é* are the equivalents of Mr, and Mrs/Miss/Ms. *Āghā* can be used before or after the first name as a title of respect, eg *Mohammad Āghā* or more likely *Āghā Mohammad*. For a list of some of the other common titles and forms of address (eg, *hajjī*, *sayyed*, and *āyatollāh*) see the Glossary.

Greetings & Civilities

The all-purpose greeting in Iran is *salām aleikom*, which does duty for good morning, good afternoon and good evening. The same expression is used throughout the Muslim world, so if you can learn only one phrase in Iran, this is the one. The Iranians are very courteous people and there are many polite or informal greetings and replies, but the following are some of the commonest:

welcome	*khōsh āmadīd*	خوش آمدید
thank you: you are very kind	*motashakkeram, shomā kheilī mehrabūn hastīd*	متشکرم ، شما خیلا مهربان هسیتد
hello	*salām*	سلام
peace be upon you	*salām aleikom*	سلام علیکم
good morning	*sobh bekheir*	صبح بخیر
good night, good evening	*shab bekheir*	شب بخیر
goodbye	*khodāfez* or more formally *khodā hāfez*	خدا حافظ
How do you do?	*hāl-é shomā chetōr ast?*	حال شما چطور است ؟
How are you?	*hāl-é shomā khūb é?*	حال شما خوب است ؟
How are you doing?	*chetōr é?*	چطور است
praise be to God! (ie I'm fine, thank you)	*alhamdolellāh*	الحمد لله
not bad, thanks	*mersī, bad nīstam*	مرسی، بد نیستم

What is your name?	esmetān chī st?	اسمتان چیست ؟
My name is...	esmam...é	اسم ... است .
Bon voyage!	safar bekheir!	سفر بخیر !
yes	balé	بله
yes (answering a negative question)	cherā?	چرا؟
no	nakheir, na (less polite although not rude)	نخیر یا نه
No, you must be joking.	na bābā	نه‌بابا
God willing	enshāllāh or more correctly enshā'allāh	انشا ءالله
please (requesting something, literally 'kindly')	lotfān	لطفاً
please (offering something)	befarmed or more correctly befarmā īd	بفرمائید
thank you	mersī/tashakkor/motashakkeram	مرسی یا تشکر یا متشکرم
thank you very much	kheilī mamnūnam	خیلی ممنونم
Don't mention it.	ghābel nabūd	قابل نبود
It's nothing	chīzī nīst	چیزی نیست
excuse me/I'm sorry	bebakhshīd	ببخشید

Small Talk

Where do you come from?	shomā ahl-é kojā hastīd?	شمااهل کجا هستید ؟
I'm from...	man ahl-é...hastam	من...هستم .
America	Āmrīkā	آمریکا
Australia	Osterālyā	استرالیا
Canada	Kānādā	کانادا
Iran	Īrān	ایران
New Zealand	Zelānd-é Nō	زلاند نو
the UK (or England)	Engelestān	انگلستان
What's your occupation? (or What are you doing (here)?)	shoma chekār mīkonīd?	شما چکار میکنید؟
I'm a...	...hastam	...هستم
I'm not a...	...nīstam	...نیستم
businessman/businesswoman	ādam-é kāseb	آدم‌کاسب
diplomat	dīplomāt	دیپلمات
foreigner	khārejī	خارجی
friend of...	dūst-é...	دوست...
guest (of...)	mehmūn (-é...)	مهمان (...)
journalist	khabarnegār	خبرنگار
pilgrim	zovvār	زوار
spy	jāsūs	جاسوس
student	dāneshjū	دانشجو
tourist	jahāngard	جهانگرد
traveller/passenger	mosāfer	مسافر
Are you a Muslim?	shoma mosalmān hastīd?	شما مسلمان هستید ؟
No, I'm a Christian/Jew/Zoroastrian	nakheir, masīhī/yahūdī/zartoshtī hastam	

نخیر ، مسیحی / یهودی/ زرتشتی هستم

Useful Phrases

Do you know...?	*shomā...baladīd?*	شما...بلدید ؟
Persian	*Fārsī*	فارسی
English	*Engelīsī*	انگلیسی
French	*Ferānsé*	فرانسه
German	*Ālmānī*	آلمانی
a little/very little	*kamī/kheilī kam*	کمی/خیلی کم
I'm sorry: I don't speak Persian.	*bebakhshīd: Fārsī balad nīstam*	
		ببخشید ، فارسی بلد نیستم .
What is this/that?	*īn/ān chīst?*	این/آن چیست ؟
Do(n't) you have...?	*shomā...(na)dārīd?*	شما...(ذ) دارید ؟
How many...?	*chand...?*	چند...؟
persons	*nafar*	نفر
How many? (of things)	*chand tā?*	چند تا ؟
How much is it? (of money)	*chand é?*	چند است ؟
How much is this/that (one)? (of money)	*īn/ān (yekī) chand é?*	این/آن (یکی) چند است ؟
There is...	*...hast*	...هست
It is...	*...é*	...است
There/it isn't...	*...nīst*	...نیست
too much	*kheilī zeyād*	خیلی زیاد
too little	*kheilī kam*	خیلی کم
very/too...	*kheilī...*	خیلی
important	*mohemm*	مهم
cheap/expensive	*arzūn/gerūn*	ارزان/گران
big/small	*bozorg/kūchek*	بزرگ/کوچک
hot (*or* warm)/cold	*garm/sard*	گرم/ سرد
new	*jadīd or nō*	جدید یانو
old (of things)	*ghadīm*	قدیم
beautiful/ugly	*ghashang/zesht*	قشنگ/زشت
good/bad	*khūb/bad*	خوب /بد
far/near (from/to...)	*dūraz/nazdīk (-é...)*	دور (از...)/نزدیگ (...)
easy/difficult	*āsān/moshkel (or sakht)*	آسان/مشکل (یاسخت)
dangerous/safe	*khatarnāk/bī khatar*	خطرناگ/بی خطر
open/closed	*bāz/taˀīl*	باز/تعطیل
OK	*dorost*	درست
Where?	*kojā?*	کجا ؟
Where is...?	*...kojāst?*	...کجاست ؟
Why?	*cherā?*	چرا ؟
When?	*kei?*	کی؟
Who?	*kī?*	کی؟
What?	*chī?*	چه؟
Which...?	*kodām...?*	کدام...؟
and...	*va... (in compound numerals and certain expressions pronounced o)*	و...
but...	*valī...*	ولی...
in...	*dar/tū...*	در/تو...

restaurant	*restōrān* or *chelō kabābī* or *sālon-é ghezā*	رستوران یا چلو کبابی یا سالن غذا
teahouse	*chāykhūné*	چایخانه
food	*ghezā*	غذا
drink	*nūshābé*	نوشابه
hotel	*hotel* or *mehmūnkhūné*	هتل یا مهمانخانه
cheap hotel, lodging-house	*mosāferkhūné*	مسافرخانه
lavatory	*dast shū ī*	دست شوئی

Accommodation

Do you have a...for tonight?	*emshab...dārīd?*	امشب ...دارید؟
room	*otāgh*	اطاق
single room	*otāgh-é ye nafarī*	اطاق یگ نفری
double room	*otāgh-é do nafarī*	اطاق دو نفری
triple room	*otāgh-é sé nafarī*	اطاق سه نفری
suite	*sū īt*	سوئیت
better room	*otāgh-é behtar*	اطاق بهتر
cheaper room	*otāgh-é arzūntar*	اطاق ارزانتر
with bathroom	*bā hammūm*	باحمام
without bathroom	*bī hammūm*	بی حمام
for how many nights?	*chand shab?*	چند شب ؟
just for one night	*faghat yek shab*	فقط یگ شب
How much is a room for one night?	*otāgh shabī chand é?*	اطاق شبی چند است؟

Getting Around

bus/train station	*termīnāl/īstgāh*	ترمینال/ایستگاه
Where is the...to Tabrīz?	*...betabrīz kojāst?*	...بتبریز کجاست ؟
The...has gone	*...raft*	...رفت
What time does the...leave?	*...chī vaght harakat mīkonad?*	...چه وقت حرکت میکند ؟

train	*ghetār*	قطار
bus	*otōbūs*	اتوبوس
first bus	*otōbūs-é avval*	اتوبوس اول
last bus	*otōbūs-é ākherīn*	اتوبوس آخرین
ship	*kashtī*	کشتی
motor-launch	*lenj*	لنج
boat, skiff, caïque	*ghāyegh*	قایق
taxi (any kind)	*tāksī*	تاکسی
minibus	*mīnībūs*	مینیبوس
savārī	*savārī*	سواری
aeroplane	*havāpeimā*	هواپیما
car (*or* taxi)	*māshīn*	ماشین
motorcycle	*mōtōrsīklet*	موتورسیکلت

airport	*forūdgāh*	فرودگاه
jetty, dock, harbour	*eskelé*	اسکله
ticket office	*daftar-é belīt forūshī*	دفتر بلیط فروشی

I would like to go to...	*mīkhāham bé...beravam*	میخواهم به...بروم .
Are you going to...?	*shomā bé...mīrīd?*	شما به...میروید ؟
It's full.	*jā nīst*	جا نیست
It's urgent.	*fōrī é*	فوری است
How many km is it to...?	*az īnjā be...chand kīlōmeter é?*	از اینجا به...چند کیلومتر است ؟
How many hours is the journey?	*safar chand sā'at é?*	سفر چند ساعت است ؟
I would like a..., please.	*lotfān...mīkhāham*	لطفاً...میخواهم .
ticket	*belīt*	بلیط
...seat	*sandalī-yé...*	صندلی
good	*khūb*	خوب ـ
1st class	*darajé-yé yek*	درجه ١
2nd class	*darajé-yé do*	درجه ٢
3rd class	*darajé-yé sé*	درجه ٣
sleeper	*sandalī dar vāgon-é takht-é khāb dār*	
		صندلی در واگن تخت خواب دار

Around Town

Note that in Iran, at least outside Tehrān, street numbers are not used very much and addresses are often given as opposite, near, behind etc. Never ask 'Is it this way?', especially in rural areas, as the almost inevitable answer will be *mostaghīm* (straight ahead). Never take the directions given too seriously; Iranians do not like to appear unhelpful and would rather give you the temporary satisfaction of thinking you know where you're going.

Excuse me, where is the...?	*bebakhshīd,...kojāst?*	ببخشید ،...کجاست ؟
house	*khūné* or *manzel*	خانه یا منزل
street, avenue	*kheyābūn*	خیابان
square	*meidūn*	میدان
lane, alley	*kūché*	کوچه
cul-de-sac, blind alley	*bombast*	بن بست
route, road	*rāh*	راه
road to...	*rāh-é...*	راه/...
town centre	*markaz-é shahr*	مرکز شهر
mosque	*masjed*	مسجد
church	*kelīsā*	کلیسا
embassy	*safārat*	سفارت
consulate	*konsūlgarī*	کنسولگری
museum	*mūzé*	موزه
post office	*postkhūné*	پستخانه
telegraph office	*telegrāfkhūné*	تلگرافخانه
here	*īnjā*	اینجا
there	*ānjā*	آنجا
this way	*īn taraf*	این طرف
that way	*ān taraf*	آن طرف
straight ahead	*mostaghīm*	مستقیم
left	*dast-é chap*	دست چپ
right	*dast-é rāst*	دست راست

Times & Dates

Time on the hour is given as *sā'at-é* (the hour of) followed by the number of hours. Time after the hour is given as the hour followed by *o* (and) followed by the number of minutes (or *yek rob'* for a quarter past, or *nīm* for half past). Time before the hour is given as the number of minutes (or *yek rob'* for a quarter to) followed by *bé* (to) followed by the hour. The 24 hour clock is widely used in written Persian.

2 pm	*sā'at-é do ba'd az zohr*	ساعت ۲ بعد از ظهر
2.10	*sā'at-é do o dah daghīghé*	۲/۱۰
8.30	*sā'at-é hasht o nīm*	۸/۳۰
10.45	*yek rob'bé sā'at-é dah*	۱۰/٤٥
11.23 Thursday evening	*panjshambé shab sā'at-é yāzdah o bīst o sé daghīghé*	پنجشنبه شب ساعت ۱۱/۲۳
What's the time?	*sā'at chand é?*	ساعت چند است ؟

today	*emrūz*	امروز
tomorrow	*fardā*	فردا
yesterday	*dīrūz*	دیروز
tonight	*emshab*	امشب
tomorrow night	*fardā shab*	فرداشب
last night	*dīshab*	دیشب
this morning	*emrūz sobh*	امروزصبح
morning, am	*sobh*	صبح
noon	*zohr*	ظهر
afternoon, pm	*ba'd az zohr*	بعد از ظهر
night, evening	*shab*	شب
minute	*daghīghé*	دقیقه
half an hour	*nīm sā'at*	نیم‌ساعت
quarter of an hour	*rob'sā'at*	ربع‌ساعت
hour	*sā'at*	ساعت
day	*rūz*	روز
week	*hafté*	هفته
month	*māh*	ماه
year	*sāl*	سال
this year	*emsāl*	امسال
next year	*sāl-é āyandé*	سال آینده
last year	*pārsāl*	پارسال
date	*tārīkh*	تاریخ
in 20 minutes' time	*bīst daghīghé-yé dīgar*	۲ دقیقه دیگر

Sunday	*yekshambé*	یکشنبه
Monday	*doshambé*	دوشنبه
Tuesday	*seshambé*	سه شنبه
Wednesday	*chahārshambé*	چهار شنبه
Thursday	*panjshambé*	پنجشنبه
Friday	*jom'é*	جمعه
Saturday	*shambé*	شنبه

Numbers

0	*sefr*	٠
1	*yek*	١
2	*do*	٢
3	*sé*	٣
4	*chahār*	٤ or ۴
5	*panj*	٥ or ۵
6	*shesh*	٦ or ۶
7	*haft*	٧
8	*hasht*	٨
9	*noh*	٩
10	*dah*	١٠
11	*yāzdah*	١١
12	*davāzdah*	١٢
13	*sīzdah*	١٣
14	*chahārdah*	١٤
15	*pūnzdah*	١٥
16	*shānzdah*	١٦
17	*hefdah*	١٧
18	*hejdah*	١٨
19	*nūzdah*	١٩
20	*bīst*	٢٠
21	*bīst o yek*	٢١
22	*bīst o do*	٢٢
25	*bīst o panj*	٢٥
30	*sī*	٣٠
40	*chehel*	٤٠
50	*panjāh*	٥٠
60	*shast*	٦٠
70	*haftād*	٧٠
80	*hashtād*	٨٠
90	*navad*	٩٠
100	*sad*	١٠٠
110	*sad o dah*	١١٠
169	*sad o shast o noh*	١٦٩
200	*devīst*	٢٠٠
300	*sīsad*	٣٠٠
400	*chahārsad*	٤٠٠
500	*pūnsad*	٥٠٠
600	*sheshsad*	٦٠٠
700	*haftsad*	٧٠٠
800	*hashtsad*	٨٠٠
900	*nohsad*	٩٠٠
1000	*hezār*	١٠٠٠
1371	*hezār o sīsad o haftād o yek*	١٣٧١
2000	*do hezār*	٢٠٠٠
10,000	*dah hezār*	١٠,٠٠٠
100,000	*sad hezār*	١٠٠,٠٠٠
(one) million	*(yek) mīleyūn*	ميليون (يگ)
1000 million	*(yek) mīleyārd*	ميليارد (يگ)

¼	*(yek) rob'*	١/٤
½	*nesf (nīm* with hours)	١/٢
¾	*sé rob'*	٣/٤

Colloquial Expressions

Here is a list of some common colloquial expressions in Persian, with their idiomatic equivalents in English. Because they are normally used only in speech, Persian script has not been used in this section. These phrases will lose their effect if pronounced with an atrocious accent.

It's OK; it's cool.	*bāsh é*
I'm fed up; I've had enough.	*kaf kardam*
Pigs might fly! (literally, the ceiling has cracked)	*saghf tarak khõrd*
None of your business!	*torā sannanā!*
Don't spill the beans.	*sé nakon*
You put me to shame. (ie with your generosity)	*chūb kārī nakon*
What's the damage? How many bucks does it cost?	*chand chūb é?*
Don't talk rubbish.	*chart o part nagū*

Persian Food & Menu Guide

The following menu translator is written with the optimist in mind. Few of these dishes are regular items on the menu, and many of them are far more often seen in cookery books than on the Iranian dinner table. However, if you make a point of asking for a menu at every restaurant you go to, and, if you can't read Persian, ask for all available dishes to be read out to you, you should get to appreciate that Iranian cooking is far more than *chelō kabāb*.

Breakfast

Breakfast is usually *lavāsh* bread with goat's milk cheese, yoghurt, jam or honey, sometimes a fried egg or two, and always washed down with tea. Cornflakes and the like are available, but very expensive and a luxury or an irrelevance for most Iranians. Many hotels serve breakfast, but this is not usually included in the room charge.

bread	*nūn* (in classical Persian, *nān*)	نان
cheese (many varieties, mostly of goats' milk, similar to Greek *feta*	*panīr*	پنیر
egg	*tokhm-é morgh*	تخم مرغ
honey	*angabīn*	انگبین
jam	*morabbā*	مربا
yoghurt	*māst*	ماست
dish of sheep's trotters	*gālé pāché*	گاله پاچه

Soups

soup	*sūp*	سوپ
soup or light stew	*āsh*	آش

lentil soup	*sūp-é jō*	سوپ جو
onion soup	*sūp-é peyāz*	سوپ پیاز
yoghurt soup	*sūp-é māst*	سوپ ماست
thick vermicelli and vegetable soup	*āsh-é reshté*	آش رشته
eggplant and meat soup	*ābgūsht-é bādenjūn*	آبگوشت بادنجان

Salads, Side-Dishes & Vegetables

salad	*sālād*	سالاد
yoghurt	*māst*	ماست
with chopped spinach	*...va esfenāj*	... و اسفناج
with diced cucumber	*...va kheyār*	... و خیار
with chopped mint	*...va na'nā'*	... و نعناع
pickle	*torshī*	ترشی
pickled dates	*torshī-yé khormā*	ترشی خرما
vegetables	*sabzī*	سبزی
onion	*peyāz*	پیاز
cucumber	*kheyār*	خیار
gherkins	*kheyār-é torshī*	خیار ترشی
olive	*zeitūn*	زیتون
tomato	*gōjé-yé farangī*	گوجه فرنگی
lettuce	*kāhū*	کاهو
spinach	*esfenāj*	اسفناج
eggplant	*bādenjūn* (in classical Persian, *bādenjān*)	بادنجان
green beans	*lūbyā*	لوبیا
beetroot	*choghondar*	چغندر
potato	*sīb-é zamīnī*	سیب زمینی
peas	*nokhōd*	نخود

Vegetable Dishes

rice cooked together with vegetables	*sabzī polō*	سبزی پلو
very thick omelette	*kūkū*	کوکو
vegetable *kūkū*	*kūkū-yé sabzī*	کوکوی سبزی
green bean *kūkū*	*kūkū-yé lūbyā*	کوکوی لوبیا
potato *kūkū*	*kūkū-yé sīb-é zamīnī*	کوکوی سیب زمینی
eggplant *kūkū*	*kūkū-yé bādenjūn*	کوکوی بادنجان
stuffed vine-leaf, or almost any stuffable vegetable or fruit	*dolmé*	دلمه

Fish & Seafood

fish	*māhī*	ماهی
Iranian whitefish	*shīrmāhī*	شیرماهی
whitefish, whiting	*māhī-yé sefīd*	ماهی سفید
sturgeon	*sag māhī*	سگ ماهی
salmon-trout	*māhī-yé āzād*	ماهی آزاد
trout	*ghezel ālā*	قزل آلا
perch	*māhī-yé khārdār*	ماهی خاردار
carp	*māhī-yé gūl*	ماهی گول

pike	*ordak māhī*	اردک ماهی
fish and vegetable stew	*ghormé-yé sabzī bā māhī*	قرمه سبزی با ماهی
fish kebab	*māhī kabāb*	ماهی کباب
fish with boiled rice	*chelō māhī*	چلو ماهی
prawns, shrimps	*meigū*	میگو
grilled prawns or shrimps with boiled rice	*chelō meigū*	چلو میگو
crab, lobster or crayfish	*kharachang*	خرچنگ
caviar	*khāveyār*	خاویار

Poultry & Game

(half a) chicken	*(nesf-é) jūjé*	(نصف) جوجه
hen, chicken	*morgh*	مرغ
duck	*ordak*	اردک
goose	*ghāz*	غاز
pigeon	*kabūtar*	کبوتر
pheasant	*gharghāvol*	قرقاول
quail	*belderchīn*	بلدرچین
turkey	*būghalamūn*	بوقلمون
duck, goose, chicken or quail in pomegranate and walnut sauce	*fesenjūn* (in classical Persian, *fesenjān*)	فسنجان
chicken with boiled rice	*chelō morgh*	چلو مرغ
chicken and tangerine stew	*khōresh-é nārangī*	خورش نارنگی
chicken kebabs	*jūjé kabāb*	جوجه کباب

Meat & Meat Dishes

meat	*gūsht*	گوشت
lamb	*gūsht-é barré*	گوشت بره
mutton	*gūsht-é gūsfand*	گوشت گوسفند
veal	*gūsht-é gūsālé*	گوشت گوساله
beef	*gūsht-é gāv*	گوشت گاو
goat meat	*gūsht-é boz*	گوشت بز
buffalo meat	*gūsht-é gāvmīsh*	گوشت گاومیش
camel meat	*gūsht-é shotor*	گوشت شتر
kebab, usually of lamb or mutton, with boiled rice	*chelō kabāb*	چلو کباب
made with inferior ground meat	*(chelō kabāb-é) kūbīdé*	(چلو کباب) کوبیده
made with thin, average quality meat	*(chelō kabāb-é) barg*	(چلو کباب) برگ
'special' *chelō kabāb*, thicker and of good quality meat	*(chelō kabāb-é) makhsūs*	(چلو کباب) مخصوص
lamb fillet kebab	*fīllé kabāb*	فیله کباب
small spicy meat kebabs like Turkish shish kebab, served with bread)	*shīshlīk* (or *shesh kabāb*)	شیشلیگ (یا شش کباب)
meat (or chicken) in thick sauce with vegetables and chopped nuts	*khōresh* (or *khōresht*)	خورش (یا خورشت)
with boiled rice	*chelō khōresh*	چلو خورش
meat and sour cherry stew	*khōresh-é ālūbālū*	خورش آلوبالو

meat and eggplant stew	khōresh-é bādenjūn	خورش بادنجان
meat and spinach stew with dried lime	ghormé-yé sabzī	قرمه سبزی
stew with thick chunks of potato, fatty meat and lentils	ābgūsht (or dīzī)	آبگوشت (یا دیزی)
meat and dried fruit stew	ābgūsht-é mīvé	آبگوشت میوه
meatballs	kofté	کفته
kofté à la Tabrīz – spicy meatballs stuffed with eggs and dried fruit in tomato sauce	kofté-yé Tabrīzī	کفته تبریزی
apple stuffed with rice and minced meat	dolmé-yé sīb	دلمه سیب
quince stuffed with rice and minced meat	dolmé-yé beh	دلمه به
stew of lamb, spinach, yoghurt and lentils	būrānī-yé gūsht	بورانی گوشت
steak	esteik	استیگ

Desserts & Sweets

ice-cream	bastanī	بستنی
pistachio ice-cream	bastanī-yé pesté	بستنی پسته
halva – sweet pastry with rosewater, saffron and chopped nuts	halvā	حلوا
vermicelli sorbet with rosewater, ground pistachios and sultanas	pālūdé (or fālūdé)	پالوده (یا فالوده)
flaky pastry filled with nuts and soaked in syrup	bāghlavā	باقلوا [*
rice-pudding with cinnamon and rosewater	shīr berenj	شیر برنج
finely-shredded pastry filled with nuts and soaked in syrup	konāfé	کنافه
compote or fruit salad	khōshāb	خوشاب
nougat (speciality of Esfahān)	gaz	گز
pistachio brittle	sōhūn (in classical Persian sōhān)	سوهان
sweets in general	shīrīnī	شیرینی

Fruit

fruit	mīvé	میوه
apple	sīb	سیب
apricot	zardālū	زردآلو
banana/plantain	mōz	موز
cherries	gīlās	گیلاس
dates	khormā	خرما
figs	anjīr	انجیر
grapes	angūr	انگور
grapefruit	gereipfrūt	گریپفروت
(sour) lemon	līmū	لیمو
sweet lemon	līmū-yé shīrīn	لیموی شیرین
lime	līmū-yé Ommānī (or līmū-yé sabz)	لیموی عمانی (یا لیموی سبز)

melon	*kharbūzé*	خربوزه
orange	*portoghāl*	پرتقال
peach	*holū*	هلو
pear	*golābī*	گلابی
persimmon	*khormālū*	خرمالو
pineapple	*ānānās*	آناناس
plum	*ālū*	آلو
pomegranate	*anār*	انار
prune	*ālū-yé Bokhārā*	آلوی بخارا
quince	*beh*	به
raisins	*keshmesh*	کشمش
strawberries	*tūt-é farangī*	توت فرنگی
tangerine	*nārangī*	نارنگی
watermelon	*hendevāné*	هندوا

Nuts

almond	*bādām*	بادام
hazelnut	*fondogh*	فندق
walnut	*gerdū*	گردو
pistachio	*pesté*	پسته
salted pistachio	*pesté-yé namakīn*	پسته نمکین
unsalted pistachio	*pesté bī namak*	پسته بی نمک

Drinks

drink	*nūshābé*	نوشابه
tea	*chāy*	چای
coffee	*ghahvé*	قهوه
Turkish coffee	*ghahvé-yé Tork*	قهوه ترک
instant coffee (generic term)	*neskāfé*	نسکافه
water	*āb*	آب
boiled drinking water	*ābjūsh*	آبجوش
desalinated water	*āb-é shīrīn*	آب شیرین
fruit juice	*āb-é mīvé*	آب میوه
orange juice	*āb-é portoghāl*	آب پرتقال
cherry juice	*āb-é gīlās*	آب گیلاس
grape juice	*āb-é angūr*	آب انگور
pomegranate juice	*āb-é anār*	آب انار
cola	*kōkā*	کوکا
churned sour milk or yoghurt with salt, mint and other herbs	*dūgh*	دوغ
ice	*yakh*	یخ
lemonade	*līmōnād*	لیموناد
orangeade	*sharbat-é nāranj*	شربت نارنج
non-alcoholic beer ('Islamic beer' or 'Iranian beer')	*mā'-osh-sha'īr*	ماء الشعیر
hot chocolate	*shīr-é kākā'ō-yé garm*	شیر کاکائوی گرم
iced coffee	*kāfé gelāsé*	کافه گلاسه
with...	*bā...*	با ...

without...	*bī...*	بی...
lump sugar	*ghand*	قند
granulated sugar	*shekar*	شکر
bottle	*shīshé*	شیشه
milk	*shīr*	شیر
lemon	*līmū*	لیمو
salt	*namak*	نمک
alcohol	*alkol*	الکل
beer	*ābjō*	آبجو
wine	*sharāb*	شراب
vodka	*vodkā*	ودکا

Condiments & Accompaniments

salt	*namak*	نمک
pepper	*felfel*	فلفل
sumac – a reddish seasoning made from ground berries of the sumac tree (generally served only with chelō kabāb)	*somāgh*	سماق
rice	*berenj*	برنج
...of the day (as in 'soup of the day')	*...-é/-yé rūz*	... روز
rice cooked together with...	*...polō*	... پلو
boiled rice with...	*chelō...*	چلو
garlic	*sīr*	سیر
sauce	*sōs*	سوس
omelette	*omlet*	املت
bread	*nūn* (in classical Persian *nān*)	نان
butter	*karé*	کره
sandwich (*or* snack-bar)	*sāndvīch*	ساندویچ
sausage	*sōsīs*	سوسیس
cream	*sarshīr*	سرشیر
cake	*keik*	کیک
vegetarian food	*ghezā-yé geyāh khār*	غذای گیاه خوار
lemon juice	*āblīmū*	آبلیمو

Miscellaneous

knife	*kārd*	کارد
fork	*changāl*	چنگال
spoon	*ghāshogh*	قاشق
paper tissue	*kelīnīks*	کلینیکس
breakfast	*sobhāné*	صبحانه
lunch	*nāhār*	ناهار
dinner	*shām*	شام
Do you have...?	*shomā...dārīd?*	شما...دارید
What's on the menu today?	*emrūz ghezā chī é?*	امروز غذا چیست ؟
I'd like the..., please	*lotfān...mīkhāham*	لطفاً...میخواهم
menu	*sūrat-é ghezā*	صورت غذا
bill	*sūrat-é hesāb*	صورت حساب
This is for you, waiter.	*āghā, īn māl-é shomāst*	آقا، این مال شماست

Thank you, it was delicious.   *mersī, khōsh mazé būd*   مرسی ، خوش مزه بود
This isn't good.   *īn khūb nīst*   این خوب نیست

Index

TEXT

Ābādān 314-15
Abbās Ābād 120, 379
Abbās Ābād Valley 331
abgūsht 355
Abū Mūsā Island 284
Abyaneh 209-10
Ābyek 120
accommodation 105-8
  budget 107-8
  middle 108
  top end 108
Achaemenians 13
activities, *see* individual
  activities
Afghanistan 92, 214, 247
Afghans 30
Agha Muhammed 155
Agha Muhammed Khān 15
agriculture 26
Ahvāz 308-11, **309**
  getting around 311
  getting there & away 310-11
  information 308-9
  places to eat 310
  places to stay 309-10
air travel 124-31, 140-2
  glossary 126-7
  to/from Asia 131
  to/from Australia & New
    Zealand 129
  to/from Europe 129-30
  to/from UK 129
  to/from USA & Canada 128-9
  travellers with special needs
    126-7
  within Iran 140-2
Alamūt 338
alcohol 115
Alexander the Great 13, 213, 339
Ali 45
Alī Ābād 385
Alī Ghāpū Palace 196-7
Alī ibn Mohammed Bagar 209
Alī Sadr 332
Alī Sadr Caves 331-2
Amīr Kabīr 207
Āmol 374
Andīmeshk 311-12
Anzalī Lagoon 369

Arabs 14, 30
Arāk 188-9
architecture 47-51
Ardabīl 359
Ardabīl Province 358-60
Ardakān 217
Ardehal 209
Ardestān 205
Arg-é Bam 258-9
Armenians 31, 45, 169, 198, 347
arts & crafts 31-41
Arvand Rūd (Shatt al-Arab) 273
Aryans 13
Assādābād National Park 25
Assassins, the 338
Assembly of Experts 18
Āstān-é Ghods-é Razavi 43,
  228-31, **229**
Āstārā 370
Atropates 339
Avicenna 328
Āzād Shahr 120, 385
Āzādī Monument 167
Āzarbāyjān 339
Āzarbāyjān-é Gharbī Province
  339-50
Āzarbāyjān-é Sharghī Province
  350-8
Āzarīs 30, 344
Azerbaijan 344
Aziz Ābād 122
Aznā 122

Bābā Jān 320
Bābā Tāher 329
Bābol 375
Bābolsar 374-5
Bāgh-é Tārīkhī-yé Fīn 207-8
Bāghū 281
Baha'is 43
Bahim Ābād 378
Bāhmanī 307
Bākhtarān, *see* Kermānshāh
Bakhtegān 24
Bakhtegān National Park 297
Bākhtiarīs 31
Baluchis 31, 241
Bam 259-61, **258**
  Arg-é Bam 258-59, **259**

Bandar-é Abbās 264-70, **266**
  getting around 270
  getting there & away 268-70
  information 265
  places to eat 268
  places to stay 266-8
Bandar-é Anzalī 368-9
Bandar-é Golmānkhūné 345
Bandar-é Lengé 271-3, **272**
Bandar-é Pol 276
Bandar-é Tākherī 307
Bandar-é Torkamān 383-4
Bandarīs 262, 271
bargaining 69
Bastām (Āzārbāyjān-é Gharbī
  Province) 347
Bastām (Semnān Province) 220
Bayāzīye 120
Bāzārgān 349-50
Behesht-é Zahrā 187
Beheshtī Island 368
Behshahr 380-81
bicycle travel 104, 149-50, 284
Bījār 120, 334
birds, *see* fauna
Bīrjand 223
Bīsotūn 120, 323
black market 68
boat travel 135-6, 150
books 71-4, 81, 149
  driving 149
  general 74
  guidebooks 72
  handicrafts 73
  history & politics 73
  language 74
  Lonely Planet 72
  poetry 73
  travel 72-3
  health 81
Borūjerd 320
Boyerahmad va Kohgīlūyé
  Province 264
British 15, 265, 275
Bū Alī Sīnā 328
bus travel 133-5, 142-4
  to/from Azerbaijan 134
  to/from Pakistan 246
  to/from Turkey 133-4

LONELY PLANET PHRASEBOOKS

Building bridges,
Breaking barriers,
Beyond babble-on

Listen for the gems

Speak your own words

Ask your own
questions

Master of
your
own
image

- handy pocket-sized books
- easy to understand Pronunciation chapter
- clear and comprehensive Grammar chapter
- romanisation alongside script to allow ease of pronunciation
- script throughout so users can point to phrases
- extensive vocabulary sections, words and phrases for every situation
- full of cultural information and tips for the traveller

'...vital for a real DIY spirit and attitude in language learning' – Backpacker

'the phrasebooks have good cultural backgrounders and offer solid advice for challenging situations in remote locations' – San Francisco Examiner

'...they are unbeatable for their coverage of the world's more obscure languages' – The Geographical Magazine

---

Arabic (Egyptian)
Arabic (Moroccan)
Australia
  Australian English, Aboriginal and Torres Strait languages
Baltic States
  Estonian, Latvian, Lithuanian
Bengali
Brazilian
Burmese
Cantonese
Central Asia
Central Europe
  Czech, French, German, Hungarian, Italian and Slovak
Eastern Europe
  Bulgarian, Czech, Hungarian, Polish, Romanian and Slovak
Ethiopian (Amharic)
Fijian
French
German
Greek

Hindi/Urdu
Indonesian
Italian
Japanese
Korean
Lao
Latin American Spanish
Malay
Mandarin
Mediterranean Europe
  Albanian, Croatian, Greek, Italian, Macedonian, Maltese, Serbian and Slovene
Mongolian
Nepali
Papua New Guinea
Pilipino (Tagalog)
Quechua
Russian
Scandinavian Europe
  Danish, Finnish, Icelandic, Norwegian and Swedish

South-East Asia
  Burmese, Indonesian, Khmer, Lao, Malay, Tagalog (Pilipino), Thai and Vietnamese
Spanish (Castilian)
  Basque, Catalan and Galician
Sri Lanka
Swahili
Thai
Thai Hill Tribes
Tibetan
Turkish
Ukrainian
USA
  US English, Vernacular, Native American languages and Hawaiian
Vietnamese
Western Europe
  Basque, Catalan, Dutch, French, German, Irish, Italian, Portuguese, Scottish Gaelic, Spanish (Castilian) and Welsh

---

LONELY PLANET TRAVEL ATLASES

Lonely Planet has long been famous for the number and quality of its guidebook maps. Now we've gone one step further and produced a handy companion series: Lonely Planet travel atlases – maps of a country produced in book form.

Unlike other maps, which look good but lead travellers astray, our travel atlases have been researched on the road by Lonely Planet's experienced team of writers. All details are carefully checked to ensure the atlas corresponds with the equivalent Lonely Planet guidebook.

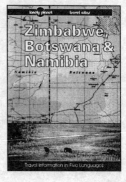

The handy atlas format means no holes, wrinkles, torn sections or constant folding and unfolding. These atlases can survive long periods on the road, unlike cumbersome fold-out maps. The comprehensive index ensures easy reference.

- full-colour throughout
- maps researched and checked by Lonely Planet authors
- place names correspond with Lonely Planet guidebooks
  – no confusing spelling differences
- legend and travelling information in English, French, German, Japanese and Spanish
- size: 230 x 160 mm

Available now:
Chile & Easter Island • Egypt • India & Bangladesh • Israel & the Palestinian Territories •Jordan, Syria & Lebanon • Kenya • Laos • Portugal • South Africa, Lesotho & Swaziland • Thailand • Turkey • Vietnam • Zimbabwe, Botswana & Namibia

LONELY PLANET TV SERIES & VIDEOS

Lonely Planet travel guides have been brought to life on television screens around the world. Like our guides, the programmes are based on the joy of independent travel, and look honestly at some of the most exciting, picturesque and frustrating places in the world. Each show is presented by one of three travellers from Australia, England or the USA and combines an innovative mixture of video, Super-8 film, atmospheric soundscapes and original music.

Videos of each episode – containing additional footage not shown on television – are available from good book and video shops, but the availability of individual videos varies with regional screening schedules.

Video destinations include: Alaska • American Rockies • Australia – The South-East • Baja California & the Copper Canyon • Brazil • Central Asia • Chile & Easter Island • Corsica, Sicily & Sardinia – The Mediterranean Islands • East Africa (Tanzania & Zanzibar) • Ecuador & the Galapagos Islands • Greenland & Iceland • Indonesia • Israel & the Sinai Desert • Jamaica • Japan • La Ruta Maya • Morocco • New York • North India • Pacific Islands (Fiji, Solomon Islands & Vanuatu) • South India • South West China • Turkey • Vietnam • West Africa • Zimbabwe, Botswana & Namibia

The Lonely Planet TV series is produced by:
Pilot Productions
The Old Studio
18 Middle Row
London W10 5AT UK

For video availability and ordering information contact your nearest Lonely Planet office.

Music from the TV series is available on CD & cassette.

PLANET TALK

Lonely Planet's FREE quarterly newsletter

We love hearing from you and think you'd like to hear from us.

*When...*is the right time to see reindeer in Finland?
*Where...*can you hear the best palm-wine music in Ghana?
*How...*do you get from Asunción to Areguá by steam train?
*What...*is the best way to see India?

For the answer to these and many other questions read PLANET TALK.

Every issue is packed with up-to-date travel news and advice including:

* a letter from Lonely Planet co-founders Tony and Maureen Wheeler
* go behind the scenes on the road with a Lonely Planet author
* feature article on an important and topical travel issue
* a selection of recent letters from travellers
* details on forthcoming Lonely Planet promotions
* complete list of Lonely Planet products

To join our mailing list contact any Lonely Planet office.

Also available: Lonely Planet T-shirts. 100% heavyweight cotton.

LONELY PLANET ONLINE

Get the latest travel information before you leave or while you're on the road

Whether you've just begun planning your next trip, or you're chasing down specific info on currency regulations or visa requirements, check out Lonely Planet Online for up-to-the minute travel information.

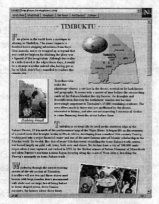

As well as travel profiles of your favourite destinations (including maps and photos), you'll find current reports from our researchers and other travellers, updates on health and visas, travel advisories, and discussion of the ecological and political issues you need to be aware of as you travel.

There's also an online travellers' forum where you can share your experience of life on the road, meet travel companions and ask other travellers for their recommendations and advice. We also have plenty of links to other online sites useful to independent travellers.

And of course we have a complete and up-to-date list of all Lonely Planet travel products including guides, phrasebooks, atlases, Journeys and videos and a simple online ordering facility if you can't find the book you want elsewhere.

www.lonelyplanet.com
or
AOL keyword: lp

LONELY PLANET PRODUCTS

Lonely Planet is known worldwide for publishing practical, reliable and no-nonsense travel information in our guides and on our web site. The Lonely Planet list covers just about every accessible part of the world. Currently there are nine series: *travel guides, shoestring guides, walking guides, city guides, phrasebooks, audio packs, travel atlases, Journeys – a unique collection of travel writing and Pisces Books - diving and snorkeling guides.*

EUROPE

Amsterdam • Andalucia • Austria • Baltic States phrasebook • Berlin • Britain • Canary Islands • Central Europe on a shoestring • Central Europe phrasebook • Czech & Slovak Republics • Denmark • Dublin • Eastern Europe on a shoestring • Eastern Europe phrasebook • Estonia, Latvia & Lithuania • Europe • Finland • France • French phrasebook • Germany • German phrasebook • Greece • Greek phrasebook • Hungary • Iceland, Greenland & the Faroe Islands • Ireland • Italian phrasebook • Italy • Lisbon • London • Mediterranean Europe on a shoestring • Mediterranean Europe phrasebook • Paris • Poland • Portugal • Portugal travel atlas • Prague • Romania & Moldova • Russia, Ukraine & Belarus • Russian phrasebook • Scandinavian & Baltic Europe on a shoestring • Scandinavian Europe phrasebook • Slovenia • Spain • Spanish phrasebook • St Petersburg • Switzerland • Trekking in Spain • Ukrainian phrasebook • Vienna • Walking in Britain • Walking in Italy • Walking in Switzerland • Western Europe on a shoestring • Western Europe phrasebook

Travel Literature: The Olive Grove: Travels in Greece

NORTH AMERICA

Alaska • Backpacking in Alaska • Baja California • California & Nevada • Canada • Chicago • Deep South • Florida • Hawaii • Honolulu • Los Angeles • Mexico • Mexico City • Miami • New England • New Orleans • New York City • New York, New Jersey & Pennsylvania • Pacific Northwest USA • Rocky Mountain States • San Francisco • Seattle • Southwest USA • USA phrasebook • Washington, DC & the Capital Region

Travel Literature: Drive thru America

CENTRAL AMERICA & THE CARIBBEAN

• Bahamas and Turks & Caicos • Bermuda • Central America on a shoestring • Costa Rica • Cuba • Eastern Caribbean • Guatemala, Belize & Yucatán: La Ruta Maya • Jamaica • Panama

Travel Literature Green Dreams: Travels in Central America

SOUTH AMERICA

Argentina, Uruguay & Paraguay • Bolivia • Brazil • Brazilian phrasebook • Buenos Aires • Chile & Easter Island • Chile & Easter Island travel atlas • Colombia Ecuador & the Galápagos Islands • Latin American Spanish phrasebook • Peru • Quechua phrasebook • Rio de Janeiro • South America on a shoestring • Trekking in the Patagonian Andes • Venezuela

Travel Literature: Full Circle: A South American Journey

ISLANDS OF THE INDIAN OCEAN

Madagascar & Comoros • Maldives • Mauritius, Réunion & Seychelles

AFRICA

Africa - the South • Africa on a shoestring • Arabic (Moroccan) phrasebook • Cairo • Cape Town • Central Africa • East Africa • Egypt • Egypt travel atlas • Ethiopian (Amharic) phrasebook • The Gambia & Senegal • Kenya • Kenya travel atlas • Malawi, Mozambique & Zambia • Morocco • North Africa • South Africa, Lesotho & Swaziland • South Africa, Lesotho & Swaziland travel atlas • Swahili phrasebook • Tunisia • Trekking in East Africa • West Africa • Zimbabwe, Botswana & Namibia • Zimbabwe, Botswana & Namibia travel atlas

Travel Literature: Mali Blues • The Rainbird: A Central African Journey • Songs to an African Sunset: A Zimbabwean Story

MAIL ORDER

Lonely Planet products are distributed worldwide.They are also available by mail order from Lonely Planet, so if you have difficulty finding a title please write to us. North American and South American residents should write to 150 Linden St, Oakland CA 94607, USA; European and African residents should write to 10a Spring Place, London NW5 3BH; and residents of other countries to PO Box 617, Hawthorn, Victoria 3122, Australia.

NORTH-EAST ASIA

Beijing • Bhutan • Cantonese phrasebook • China • Hong Kong • Hong Kong, Macau & Guangzhou • Japan • Japanese phrasebook • Japanese audio pack • Korea • Korean phrasebook • Kyoto • Mandarin phrasebook • Mongolia • Mongolian phrasebook • North-East Asia on a shoestring • Seoul • South-West China • Taiwan • Tibet • Tibet phrasebook • Tokyo

Travel Literature: Lost Japan

MIDDLE EAST & CENTRAL ASIA

Arab Gulf States • Arabic (Egyptian) phrasebook • Central Asia • Central Asia phrasebook • Iran • Israel & the Palestinian Territories • Israel & the Palestinian Territories travel atlas • Istanbul • Jerusalem • Jordan & Syria • Jordan, Syria & Lebanon travel atlas • Lebanon • Middle East • Turkey • Turkish phrasebook • Turkey travel atlas • Yemen

Travel Literature: The Gates of Damascus • Kingdom of the Film Stars: Journey into Jordan

ALSO AVAILABLE:

Brief Encounters • Travel with Children • Traveller's Tales• Not the Only Planet

INDIAN SUBCONTINENT

Bangladesh • Bengali phrasebook • Bhutan • Delhi • Goa • Hindi/Urdu phrasebook • India • India & Bangladesh travel atlas • Indian Himalaya • Karakoram Highway • Nepal • Nepali phrasebook • Pakistan • Rajasthan • South India • Sri Lanka • Sri Lanka phrasebook • Trekking in the Indian Himalaya • Trekking in the Karakoram & Hindukush • Trekking in the Nepal Himalaya

Travel Literature: In Rajasthan • Shopping for Buddhas

SOUTH-EAST ASIA

Bali & Lombok • Bangkok • Burmese phrasebook • Cambodia • Ho Chi Minh City • Indonesia • Indonesian phrasebook • Indonesian audio pack • Indonesia's Eastern Islands • Jakarta • Java • Laos • Lao phrasebook • Laos travel atlas • Malay phrasebook • Malaysia, Singapore & Brunei • Myanmar (Burma) • Philippines • Pilipino phrasebook • Singapore • South-East Asia on a shoestring • South-East Asia phrasebook • South-West China • Thailand • Thailand's Islands & Beaches • Thailand travel atlas • Thai phrasebook • Thai audio pack • Thai Hill Tribes phrasebook • Vietnam • Vietnamese phrasebook • Vietnam travel atlas

AUSTRALIA & THE PACIFIC

Australia • Australian phrasebook • Bushwalking in Australia • Bushwalking in Papua New Guinea • Fiji • Fijian phrasebook • Islands of Australia's Great Barrier Reef • Melbourne • Micronesia • New Caledonia • New South Wales • New Zealand • Northern Territory • Outback Australia • Papua New Guinea • Papua New Guinea phrasebook • Queensland • Rarotonga & the Cook Islands • Samoa • Solomon Islands • South Australia • Sydney • Tahiti & French Polynesia • Tasmania • Tonga • Tramping in New Zealand • Vanuatu • Victoria • Western Australia

Travel Literature: Islands in the Clouds • Sean & David's Long Drive

ANTARCTICA

Antarctica

THE LONELY PLANET STORY

Lonely Planet published its first book in 1973 in response to the numerous 'How did you do it?' questions Maureen and Tony Wheeler were asked after driving, busing, hitching, sailing and railing their way from England to Australia.

Written at a kitchen table and hand collated, trimmed and stapled, *Across Asia on the Cheap* became an instant local bestseller, inspiring thoughts of another book.

Eighteen months in South-East Asia resulted in their second guide, *South-East Asia on a shoestring*, which they put together in a backstreet Chinese hotel in Singapore in 1975. The 'yellow bible', as it quickly became known to backpackers around the world, soon became *the* guide to the region. It has sold well over half a million copies and is now in its 9th edition, still retaining its familiar yellow cover.

Today there are over 350 titles, including travel guides, walking guides, language kits & phrasebooks, travel atlases and travel literature. The company is the largest independent travel publisher in the world. Although Lonely Planet initially specialised in guides to Asia, today there are few corners of the globe that have not been covered.

The emphasis continues to be on travel for independent travellers. Tony and Maureen still travel for several months of each year and play an active part in the writing, updating and quality control of Lonely Planet's guides.

They have been joined by over 80 authors and 200 staff at our offices in Melbourne (Australia), Oakland (USA), London (UK) and Paris (France). Travellers themselves also make a valuable contribution to the guides through the feedback we receive in thousands of letters each year and on our web site.

The people at Lonely Planet strongly believe that travellers can make a positive contribution to the countries they visit, both through their appreciation of the countries' culture, wildlife and natural features, and through the money they spend. In addition, the company makes a direct contribution to the countries and regions it covers. Since 1986 a percentage of the income from each book has been donated to ventures such as famine relief in Africa; aid projects in India; agricultural projects in Central America; Greenpeace's efforts to halt French nuclear testing in the Pacific; and Amnesty International.

'I hope we send people out with the right attitude about travel. You realise when you travel that there are so many different perspectives about the world, so we hope these books will make people more interested in what they see. Guidebooks can't really guide people. All you can do is point them in the right direction.'

– Tony Wheeler

LONELY PLANET PUBLICATIONS

Australia
PO Box 617, Hawthorn 3122, Victoria
tel: (03) 9819 1877 fax: (03) 9819 6459
e-mail: talk2us@lonelyplanet.com.au

USA
150 Linden St
Oakland, CA 94607
tel: (510) 893 8555 TOLL FREE: 800 275-8555
fax: (510) 893 8572
e-mail: info@lonelyplanet.com

UK
10a Spring Place,
London NW5 3BH
tel: (0171) 428 4800 fax: (0171) 428 4828
e-mail: go@lonelyplanet.co.uk

France:
1 rue du Dahomey, 75011 Paris
tel: 01 55 25 33 00 fax: 01 55 25 33 01
e-mail: bip@lonelyplanet.fr

World Wide Web: http://www.lonelyplanet.com
or *AOL* keyword: lp